THE BEST OF PARIS

6th Revised Edition

Translation and Adaption
Sheila Mooney

Coordination
Sophie Gayot
Assisted by
Stéphanie Masson

Publisher
Alain Gayot

Editorial Staff, French-Language Guide

Directed by
Monique Pivot

Contributing Editors
V. Boissarie, P. Crisol, J. Dupont, M. Fort, J-L. Galesne, M-M. Giraud, M. de Kesling, C. Le Got, M-P. Mouly, P. Mozdzan, C. Nerson, I. de Peufeilhoux, F. Pigelet-Lambert, L. Sanchez, M. Soyer, G. Vincent-Rejet, S. Wolf

Editorial
Camille Chaplain, Bernard Crayssac, Florence Saint-Martin

AGP GAYOT PUBLICATIONS

Paris ▪ Los Angeles ▪ New York ▪ London ▪ Munich ▪ San Francisco

AGP GAYOT PUBLICATIONS

Bring You

The Best of Chicago
The Best of Florida
The Best of France
The Best of Germany
The Best of Hawaii
The Best of Hong Kong
The Best of Italy
The Best of London
The Best of Los Angeles
The Best of New England
The Best of New Orleans
The Best of New York
The Best of Paris
The Best of San Francisco
The Best of Thailand
The Best of Toronto
The Best of Washington, D.C.
The Best Wineries of North America

The Food Paper - Los Angeles
The Food Paper - New York
The Food Paper - San Francisco
Tastes Newsletter

Published by Gault Millau, Inc.
5900 Wilshire Blvd.
Los Angeles, CA 90036

Advertising Sales:
Pascal Meiers Communication
5 bis, avenue Foch, 94160 Saint-Mandé, France
tel. (1) 43 28 20 20, fax (1) 43 28 27 27

Please address all comments regarding
The Best of Paris to:
Gault Millau, Inc.
P.O. Box 361144
Los Angeles, CA 90036
Fax (213) 936-2883

Library of Congress Cataloging-in-Publication Data

Guide Gault Millau Paris. English
The Best of Paris / translation and adaptation, Sheila Mooney;
coordination, Sophie Gayot; publisher, Alain Gayot. — 6th rev. ed.
p. cm.
"AGP Gayot publications".
Cover title: Gayot's the best of Paris.
Includes index.
ISBN 1-881066-17-7
1. Paris (France)—Guidebooks. I. Mooney, Sheila. II. Gayot,
Sophie. III. Gayot, Alain. IV. Gault Millau (Firm) V. Title.
VI. Title: Gayot's the best of Paris.
DC708.G3313 1995
914.4'36104839—dc20 94-49149
CIP

Printed in the United States of America

CONTENTS

INTRODUCTION 5

RESTAURANTS 9

Gault Millau's penchant for observing everything that's good (and bad) about food and the dining experience is what made these guides so popular in the first place. Here you'll find candid, penetrating, and often amusing reviews of the very, very best, the undiscovered, and the undeserving. Listed by arrondissements of the city, with a section on the suburbs. Includes the Toque Tally.

HOTELS 107

A hotel guide to suit every taste. Where to spend a few days treated like royalty. Where to get the most for your money. Where to find the finest service, the most charm, the best location.

CAFES & QUICK BITES 145

Paris's palate may be found in its restaurants, but its heart and soul are found in its many cafés, wine bars, and *salons de thé*. Where to hang out with a coffee and a copy of *Libération*, where to refresh yourself with a snack or a glass of wine.

NIGHTLIFE 169

A tour of some of the city's most amusing and exciting bars and nightspots, with discerning commentary on what goes on in Paris after dark. Where to go and where to avoid.

A disclaimer

Readers are advised that prices and conditions change over the course of time. The restaurants, hotels, shops, and other establishments reviewed in this book have been reviewed over a period of time, and the reviews reflect the personal experiences and opinions of the reviewers. The reviewers and publishers cannot be held responsible for the experiences of the reader related to establishments reviewed. Readers are invited to write to the publisher with ideas, comments, and suggestions for future editions.

PARIS

A CITY ABOIL

City of Light, Stupefying Spectacle, or Moveable Feast—call it what you will, Paris is as alive in the collective fantasies of the Western world as its streets are crawling with humanity of every imaginable origin, shape, shade, size, and social station. From the crêpe-stand–studded Rue Saint-André-des-Arts, which snakes through the Latin Quarter, to the silk-wrapped glamour and classic chic of the Avenue Montaigne, to the Marché d'Aligre, which looks like it was lifted from downtown Algiers, Paris is one of those throbbing capitals that churns out legends like they were going out of style. As we dash to press, Paris is aboil: clubs, restaurants, and museums are popping up as fast as others are closing down. More than 11 million inhabitants (2.2 million within the old city walls) are this minute tearing along underground freeways, winging into busy airports, and commuting to ultramodern, futuristic satellite business centers, making Paris shine among the world's most up-to-date cities. Yet nothing *seems* to have changed in decades, perhaps centuries. The familiar face of central Paris changes slowly indeed, almost imperceptibly. The bustling *grands boulevards* are still lined with giant sycamores that spread over crowded cafés. *Bouquinistes* go on hawking their books along the Seine's noisy *quais*. The open-air markets and specialty food shops in practically every *quartier* disgorge their wares on teeming sidewalks. And gardens lifted from Impressionist paintings, like the Luxembourg or Parc Monceau, continue to fill daily with armies of au pairs pushing luxurious baby carriages down carefully raked gravel lanes. No wonder droves of urban trekkers, travel enthusiasts, and pilgrims to the mecca of existentialism spend their days seeking the Paris of yore. Well, Paris is the quintessential Old World city, groaning under the weight of artistic wonders that are the envy of much of the civilized world. And it is old, old, old.

Since Day One, about 5,000 years ago, Parisian life has flowed along the Seine. Paris's twenty arrondissements spiral outward clockwise from the Ile de la Cité, its geographical and historical hub. The Cité, where Notre-Dame rears its Gothic bell towers, was the fortified capital of the Parisii, a Gallic tribe that Julius Caesar trounced circa 52 B.C. Thus began the Gallo-Roman era, which lasted several centuries. Although this period left practically no monuments (save the baths at Cluny and the Arena, both in the Latin Quarter), the city was laid out once and for all. Fast forward: Clovis makes Paris the capital of his empire in 508. Fast forward again: Hugues Capet, the founding father of the Capetian dynasty, makes Paris (i.e., the Ile de la Cité) his capital. And here we are, 1,000 years later, and the Cité is still an island, detached in every sense from the life of the Left and Right Banks and from the nearby Ile Saint-Louis, famous nowadays as much for its ice cream as for its seventeenth-century architecture. Only Place Dauphine, with its lovely triangular garden, antique shops, and brasseries, affords a backward glance at old Paris.

Far back in 1208, the cathedral schools of Paris were united into a single university on the Left Bank. As you might expect, students flooded into the neighborhood. And there they have remained. Since Latin was the scholars' *lingua franca* until the Revolution, their turf (from Jussieu in the fifth arrondissement to Saint-Germain-de-Prés in the sixth) has always been known as the *Quartier Latin*. These narrow, twisting streets are still thronged by a decidedly young, casual crowd, who frequent the district's late-night cafés, clubs, art galleries, and bistros. To many, the Latin Quarter is synonymous with The Real Paris: Saint-Michel, Saint-Germain, Odéon.

The Latin Quarter's slightly snooty neighbor—still part of the Left Bank but altogether a different world—is the fashionable seventh arrondissement. The key words here are: Eiffel Tower, Invalides, École Militaire, and Palais Bourbon, plus at least a dozen ministries (don't get flustered when cabinet officials and visiting dignitaries descend with their bullet-proof retinues). Some of Paris's finest restaurants, shops, and hotels line the seventh's wide, handsome avenues.

At about the time the Latin Quarter was sprouting around the *civitas philosophorum*, the less-than-humble *Ville* on the Right Bank was lifting its patrician nose. Starting in the Middle Ages, merchants and the middle class settled into the *bourgs* around the villas and palaces of the nobility. Over time, the Louvre, the Tuileries, the Palais-Royal, Place Louis-XV (now Place de la Concorde), Place Vendôme, and Place des Victoires became the landmarks that set the tone of the Right Bank. In the eighteenth and nineteenth centuries the well-bred and better-heeled citizenry built major theaters there: the Opéra-Comique and Comédie-Française, the Palais Garnier Opéra, and many others. They were soon flanked by the Grand Palais and Petit Palais. Napoléon's Arc de Triomphe crowns this upscale ensemble. Now, as then, the Champs-Élysées and surrounding grand avenues and boulevards of the first, eighth, and sixteenth arrondissements are the best place to take a mink for a stroll or shop for diamonds before dining at Taillevent or Lucas-Carton, to name two of the most famous. But tennis shoes are equally at home: the Champs-Élysées—on every tourist itinerary—has also become the haunt of the *banlieusards.* These youngsters from the suburbs take the RER express subway to Étoile and spend hours at the Virgin Megastore, or at the dozens of fast-food *restos* and multiscreen movie theaters strung along the drag.

But many a Right Bank devotee will steer you off the thoroughfares and into the maze of nineteenth-century *passages*—Passage des Panoramas or Galerie Vivienne, for example—scattered around the second, ninth, and tenth arrondissements. Chockablock with boutiques, restaurants, food and wine shops, and even hotels, these covered emporium-passageways are animated year-round, not just during a rainstorm. The soulful, industrious *faubourgs*—former working-class neighborhoods that lie beyond central Paris—whose higgledy-piggledy buildings snake out from the grand boulevards, are all too often overlooked. Likewise the garment district in the second and third arrondissements. A cross between Bangkok and lower Manhattan, it is a colorful hive of incessant activity and a great place to buy ready-to-wear clothing direct from the manufacturer.

The Marais district, which stretches from the Centre Pompidou to the Musée Picasso and east to the Place de la Bastille, used to be up and coming. Now it's up, up, and away, a Parisian showcase of gentrification with a sky-high boutique-per-block ratio. The Musée Carnavalet and Hôtel de Sully have been scrubbed and buttressed. The elegant Place des Vosges (1605) has been trimmed and returfed, its newly plumbed fountains splashing to the great delight of locals and tourists alike. The Marais is also home to France's ancient and distinguished Jewish population. Take a walk down the Rue des Rosiers and discover any number of delicatessens and kosher food markets.

On the other side of the Place de la Bastille, big bucks and revolutionary zeal have worked their magic on the neighborhood. The recent Opéra de la Bastille is the turbo-charged motor that has transformed the Faubourg Saint-Antoine, Rue de la Roquette, Rue de Lappe, and Rue de Charonne into the latest haven for hipsters, artists, and restaurateurs with a flair for the profitably offbeat. High rents are now the rule in this former working-class neighborhood.

Above all, Paris is a city for walking, and this may be your best way to see Montmartre, although the refurbished funicular will carry those with sore feet to the top. Nowadays young night hawks haunt the notoriously naughty Place Pigalle, where strip joints and porno shops are daily giving way to trendy late-night bars and clubs. Speaking of dancing, the old Moulin Rouge still stands at the foot of Montmartre, a beacon for nostalgia buffs for whom the cancan remains the essence of gay Paree. But just a little farther up the hill, the steep steps and winding byways of Montmartre keep a village atmosphere alive in this most sophisticated of cities. Don't despise the droves of sightseers and would-be Picassos packed onto Place du Tertre, a traditional stronghold of artists. Instead, duck into that wedding cake of a church, Sacré-Cœur, and admire the stupendous view of Paris laid out at your feet.

Guidebooks invariably refer to unassailable authorities when serving up Paris in introductions like this one. We think that's fine, except for one small problem: what does *unassailable* mean? Ernest Hemingway, child of the tipsy Twenties and a dubious authority on Paris-beyond-La-Coupole, correctly called this sprawling metropolis "a moveable feast." Food—both spiritual and material—is indeed paramount here, from snails and scallops served with a cool Sancerre to duck breast in a green-peppercorn sauce washed down with a brawny Bordeaux. While she doubtless enjoyed the feast, writer Katherine Anne Porter called Hemingway's Paris "shallow, trivial, and silly." George Orwell was down and out in Paris, dreaming of a rare *steack frites,* while Henry Miller was discovering the tropics in brasseries around the seamy Place Clichy. A gourmand at heart, Lawrence Durrell loved Paris because here he felt "on a par with a good cheese or a bad one."

Since selection is the rod by which guidebooks are measured, we will spare you the wisdom of Henry James, F. Scott Fitzgerald, Victor Hugo, and all the rest. In short, you can find anything in Paris: the great, the mediocre, the mundane, the sublime, and the overrated. We hope the pages that follow will inspire you to seek—and help you to find—the very best that Paris has to offer.

André Gayot

RESTAURANTS

INTRODUCTION

A MANY-SPLENDORED EXPERIENCE

For food-lovers, the lure of Paris's *haute cuisine* is at least as powerful as the temptations of *haute couture* for followers of fashion, or *haute culture* for the high-minded. In fact, we know of one American lady who planned her entire trip abroad around a dinner reservation (made months in advance, of course) *chez* mega-chef Joël Robuchon, so compelling was her craving for his langoustines aux morilles. Nor is it rare for people who have never even set foot in the French capital to know the names and specialties of all the city's fashionable chefs. Dining out in Paris is a many-splendored experience. Elegance reigns here to a degree not often attained in the restaurants of other cities; Le Grand Véfour, Maxim's, and Lucas-Carton, for instance, are classified historical landmarks, with interiors of unparalleled beauty. These and the city's other top establishments also offer distinguished service: from the maître d'hôtel and the sommelier to the humblest busboy, the staffs are stylish and professional, a real *corps d'élite*. And the food, on a night when a chef like Claude Peyrot of Vivarois is particularly inspired, can be memorable, even thrilling, a joy to the eye and a feast for the palate.

If your tastes (or finances!) lead you to prefer less exalted eating houses, we urge you to peruse our reviews for Paris's many marvelous bistros, brasseries, and homestyle restaurants, where prices are—usually—far lower than in *grands restaurants* and where the atmosphere veers more toward relaxed informality. Parisians are fiercely loyal to their neighborhood bistros where they regularly tuck into familiar, traditional dishes with pronounced regional accents (Gascon, Alsatian, Provençal)—if you go in for local color, those are the places to try. Brasseries are perfect when you want to eat just a single dish rather than a multicourse meal (but don't try ordering only a salad *chez* Lipp). And they offer sustenance at odd hours—that's important if you're jet-lagged; brasseries also tend to stay open late, and generally do not require reservations.

RESTAURANT SAVVY

• At top Parisian restaurants, you must **reserve a table** far in advance—at least three weeks, sometimes two or three months for such places as Robuchon and Taillevent. Reservation requests from abroad are taken much more seriously if they are accompanied by a deposit of, say, 300 F (about $60). Tables at less celebrated spots can be reserved one or two days ahead, or even on the morning of the day you wish to dine. If you cannot honor your reservation, don't forget to call the restaurant and cancel.

• **Men should wear** a jacket and tie in any Parisian restaurant of some standing. **Women are well advised to dress up**, wearing pantsuits only if they are impeccably tailored. Luxury restaurants do not take the question of dress lightly, so be forewarned. At modest eateries, of course, more casual wear is perfectly acceptable (but jogging suits or running shorts and tank tops are looked at askance).

• When you go to a top restaurant, let the **headwaiter** suggest some possibilities from the menu (you'll find that they quite often speak English, though they always appreciate an attempt on the diner's part to speak French). Likewise, the **sommelier**'s job is to give diners expert advice on the choice of a suitable wine—regardless of price. Don't be afraid to seek his opinion, or to tell him your budget.

• **Dinner service** begins around 8pm in most Paris restaurants. People start appearing in the finer restaurants about 9pm. **Luncheon is served** between 12:30pm and 2pm. In addition to the standard **carte**, or à la carte menu, you will frequently be offered a choice of all-inclusive fixed-price meals called **menus**, which are generally a very good value. Also common in finer restaurants is the many-course sampling menu, or **menu dégustation**, a good (though not always economical) way to get an overview of a restaurant's specialties. Daily specials, or **plats du jour**, are usually reliable, inexpensive, and prepared with fresh ingredients that the chef found at the market that morning.

• French law mandates that the **service charge**, usually 15 percent, always be included in the menu prices. You are not obliged to leave an additional tip, but it is good form to leave a little more if the service was satisfactory.

• The **opening** and **closing times** we've quoted are always subject to change, particularly holiday closings, so be sure to call ahead.

• Many chefs have the bad habit of **changing restaurants frequently**, which means a restaurant can turn mediocre or even bad in just a few days. Chef-owned restaurants tend to be more stable, but even they can decline. A successful owner may be tempted to accept too many diners, which can result in a drop in quality. Should this be your experience, please don't hold us responsible!

ABOUT THE REVIEWS

RATINGS & TOQUES

Gault Millau ranks restaurants in the same manner that French students are graded: on a scale of zero to twenty, twenty being unattainable perfection. The rankings reflect *only* the quality of the cooking; décor, service, reception, and atmosphere do not influence the rating, though they are explicitly commented on within the reviews. Restaurants ranked thirteen and above are distinguished with toques (chef's hats), according to the following table:

Exceptional 4 toques, for 19/20 and 19.5/20

Excellent 3 toques, for 17/20 and 18/20

Very good 2 toques, for 15/20 and 16/20

Good 1 toque, for 13/20 and 14/20

Toques in red denote restaurants serving modern, inventive cuisine; toques in white denote restaurants serving classic or traditional food.

Keep in mind that these ranks are *relative*. One toque for 13/20 is not a very good rating for a highly reputed (and very expensive) temple of fine dining, but it is quite complimentary for a small place without much pretension.

PRICES

At the end of each restaurant review, prices are given—either **C** *(A la carte)* or **M** *(Menu(s))* (fixed-price meals) or both. A la carte prices are those of an average meal (an appetizer, main course, dessert, and coffee) for one person, including service and a half-bottle of a relatively modest wine. Lovers of the great Bordeaux, Burgundies, and Champagnes will, of course, face stiffer tabs. The menu prices quoted are for a complete multicourse meal for one person, including service but excluding wine, unless otherwise noted. These fixed-price menus often give diners on a budget a chance to sample the cuisine of an otherwise expensive restaurant.

OTHER INFORMATION & ABBREVIATIONS

A restaurant name in red indicates that its à la carte and/or set menu prices offer particularly good value for money. Look for the prices printed in red at the end of the review.

A laurel wreath indicates restaurants serving outstanding traditional or regional recipes.

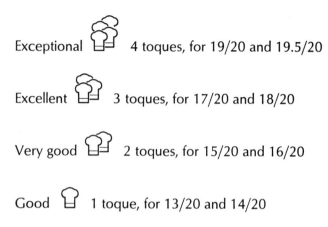

TOQUE TALLY

Red toques: Modern cuisine

White toques: Traditional cuisine

The numbers following each restaurant refer to its arrondissement or suburban town.

Four Toques (19.5/20)

19.5

Robuchon, *Paris 16th*

Four Toques (19/20)

L'Ambroisie, *Paris 4th*
Arpège (Alain Passard), *Paris 7th*
Carré des Feuillants, *Paris 1st*
Lucas-Carton (Senderens), *Paris 8th*
Guy Savoy, *Paris 17th*
Vivarois, *Paris 16th*

Four Toques (19/20)

Taillevent, *Paris 8th*

Three Toques (18/20)

Amphyclès, *Paris 17th*
Apicius, *Paris 17th*
Le Bourdonnais, *Paris 7th*
Jacques Cagna, *Paris 6th*
Le Divellec, *Paris 7th*
Faugeron, *Paris 16th*
Ledoyen, *Paris 8th*
Paul Minchelli, *Paris 7th*
Michel Rostang, *Paris 17th*
Les Trois Marches, *Versailles*

Three Toques (18/20)

Le Grand Véfour, *Paris 1st*
La Tour d'Argent, *Paris 5th*

Three Toques (17/20)

Les Ambassadeurs, *Paris 8th*
Chiberta, *Paris 8th*
Clos Longchamp, *Paris 17th*
Jean-Claude Ferrero, *Paris 16th*
Le Jardin du Royal Monceau, *Paris 8th*
Jules-Verne, *Paris 7th*
Laurent, *Paris 8th*
Montparnasse 25, *Paris 14th*
Au Petit Montmorency, *Paris 8th*
Le Pré Catelan, *Paris 16th*
Sormani, *Paris 17th*
La Table d'Anvers, *Paris 9th*

Three Toques (17/20)

Gérard Besson, *Paris 1st*
Drouant, *Paris 2nd*
Goumard-Prunier, *Paris 1st*
La Marée, *Paris 8th*
Morot-Gaudry, *Paris 15th*

1st arrondissement

10/20 Joe Allen

30, rue P.-Lescot
42 36 70 13,
fax 40 28 06 94

Open daily until 1am. Bar: until 2am. Terrace dining. Air cond. V, AE, MC.

Relaxed and casual: American, in short. Come to Joe's when you feel the urge to sink a few beers or dig into a chef's salad, chili burger, barbecued spare ribs, or apple pie. **C** 170-250 F.

17 Gérard Besson

5, rue Coq-Héron
42 33 14 74,
fax 42 33 85 71

Closed Sun. Open until 10:30pm. Priv rm: 40. Air cond. Garage pkg. V, AE, DC, MC.

Behind an understated exterior, Gérard Besson's restaurant conceals a dining room of well-bred elegance that incorporates rosy-beige fabrics, bleached-wood furnishings, and gleaming *bibelots*. The initial impression of comfort and refined taste is abetted by the menu, a repertoire of noble foodstuffs prepared with polished classicism.

Besson divines with unerring precision the exact time each dish must spend on the fire. His baked John Dory, his pan-roasted sweetbreads, his poached sea bass, and Riesling-braised turbot are all finished to perfection. Seduced by such apparently effortless grace, the dazzled diner falls to with abandon.

Some critics find fault with the occasional superfluous garnish or achingly rich sauce. They should remember that for a classically trained chef, such "virtuoso" touches are second nature. And when it suits him, Besson throws the rule book out the window to produce bold marriages, like his sardine fillets with English mustard and caviar.

Hard choices must be made at dessert time: will it be the confoundedly good iced raspberry biscuit or the novel and delectable lentil confit in vanilla syrup? A competent young sommelière simplifies the task of choosing from the lengthy (costly!) wine list. Martine Besson oversees the relaxed yet efficient service. **C** 450-550 F. **M** 260 F (weekday lunch), 400 F & 650 F (weekdays).

12/20 Brasserie Munichoise

5, rue D.-Casanova
42 61 47 16

Closed Sat lunch, Sun, Aug. Open until 12:30am. Priv rm: 20. V, MC.

A cozy little brasserie that serves good grilled veal sausages and one of the best choucroutes in Paris. Excellent Hacker-Pschorr beer on tap. **C** 250 F.

11/20 Café Marly

93, rue de Rivoli
49 26 06 60

Open daily until 1:30am. Priv rm: 300. Air cond. No pets. Garage pkg. V, AE, DC, MC.

Here in the Louvre's new Richelieu wing, you may order the most expensive club sandwich in Paris or a humbler *plat du jour*, served in magnificent surroundings. A very dressy crowd of fashion and literary notables has staked out its turf here—you may find yourself sitting next to Karl Lagerfeld! **C** 200 F.

13 Carpaccio des Halles

6, rue P.-Lescot
45 08 44 80,
fax 40 26 84 73

Open daily until 12:30am. No pets. V, AE, DC, MC.

This engaging little Italian eatery will satisfy your cravings for carpaccio: beef and duck versions are offered, both served with a deliciously tangy sauce. Pasta features prominently on the menu too, in the form of tender ravioli or pappardelle topped with shellfish or bits of prosciutto. Uncomplicated fare at unpretentious prices. **C** 150 F. **M** 71 F, 89 F, 92 F.

19 Carré des Feuillants

14, rue de Castiglione - 42868282,
fax 42 86 07 71

Closed Sat lunch, Sun, Aug. Open until 10:30pm. Priv rm: 14. Air cond. V, AE, DC, MC.

Alain Dutournier carries off toque number four this year! Mind you, he's made no radical changes in his now-familiar repertoire. But lately his technique has acquired a brillant sheen that compels us to revise our (already high) opinion of his skills. The regularity with which Dutournier produces dishes with layer upon layer of deep, resonant flavors convinces us that he has moved up into the very top rank of French chefs.

His success is based on a firm foundation of authentic ingredients from first-rate producers. He regularly nips down to his birthplace in southwest France, a gastronomic paradise bounded by the Adour River and the countryside of Béarn, to visit his suppliers, sniff the cèpes, and stimulate his appetite. Paris? His restaurant's sophisticated setting of stone, blond wood, and hyper-real vegetable paintings might as well be in Gascony!

Here Dutournier works with the foods he's loved since childhood, enhancing them with fresh, personal ideas. Crisp-fried eel atop a salad of tarragon and other herbs with a startlingly good nougatine of peppery caramelized garlic; a frothy pheasant consommé dotted with chestnuts; foie gras spread on warm cornbread; savory Pauillac lamb in a tight, sapid jus; a robust garbure (cabbage soup) with duck confit; slow-simmered veal shank that is lacquered on the outside and meltingly tender within—all these dishes brim over with vigorous, exhilarating flavors.

The exciting cellar harbors a mother lode of Southwestern wines, many of them eminently affordable. Indeed, for a table of this caliber Le Carré des Feuillants is surely one of the best values in Paris. **C** 550-800 F. **M** 260 F (weekday lunch), 740 F (4 wines incl), 560 F.

15 Les Cartes Postales

7, rue Gomboust
42 61 02 93

Closed Sat lunch, Sun. Open until 10:30pm. Air cond. V, MC.

Scores of postcards adorn the beige-and-white walls of this small, pretty, flower-filled restaurant. Yoshimasa Watanabe, disciple of the great Robuchon, creates outstanding cuisine with just the right pinch of the exotic. His dual culinary heritage yields a menu that offers scallops in papaya sauce or mackerel with white radishes and shizo as well as oxtail braised in Médoc wine and a very *grande cuisine* macaronnade of sweetbreads and foie gras. Though varied, the options are relatively few, and desserts are a tone below the rest. Take note of the set lunch: it's a remarkable value. **C** 350-400 F. **M** 135 F (weekday lunch), 285 F, 350 F.

12/20 Le Caveau du Palais

17-19, pl. Dauphine
43 26 04 28,
fax 43 26 81 84

Closed Sun (& Sat: Oct 1-Apr 30), 10 days at Christmas. Open until 10:30pm. Priv rm: 20. Terrace dining. Air cond. Pkg. V, AE, MC.

The deft, honest cooking (croustillant de chèvre chaud, grilled grouper with basil butter, veal grenadin in a creamy chive sauce) is served in a charming Place Dauphine cellar divided down the center by a wine bar. **C** 230-360 F. **M** 160 F.

11/20 Le Comptoir

14, rue Vauvilliers
40 26 26 66,
fax 42 21 44 24

Open daily until 1am. Terrace dining. Air cond. V.

Reasonable prices for decent tapas (Spanish-style chicken, cold grilled vegetables, raw tuna) served in a lively bistro atmosphere. **C** 130-168 F. **M** 100 F (Sun lunch), 69 F, 89 F.

12/20 Chez Elle

7, rue des Prouvaires
45 08 04 10

Closed Sat, Sun, hols. Open until 11pm. Priv rm: 20. Terrace dining. V, AE, MC.

"Elle" is a cheeky sort, judging by the collection of naughty photos that warm up the pale-yellow dining room. The frill-free bistro cooking is as nice as can be: warm lentil salad with bacon, veal kidney with bone marrow, and good crème brûlée. **C** 200-250 F. **M** 95 F (weekday dinner).

16 L'Espadon

Hôtel Ritz,
15, pl. Vendôme
42 60 38 30,
fax 42 61 63 08

Closed Aug. Open until 11pm. Garden dining. Air cond. Heated pool. Valet pkg. V, AE, DC, MC.

At lunchtime, business executives join the hotel's elegant clientele to partake of chef Guy Legay's graceful cuisine. Classic but not conventional, his menu presents a lush charlotte de foie gras aux navets, foie gras once again (this *is* the Ritz) as a filling for ravioli afloat in a truffled chicken bouillon, turbot with fava beans in an admirably light jus, and a colossal, exquisitely tender chop of milk-fed veal. Splendid desserts (don't miss the apricot bergère with chocolate sorbet); sumptuous cellar. The service, need we add, is sheer perfection. **C** 500-800 F. **M** 350 F (lunch), 550 F (dinner).

13 La Fermette du Sud-Ouest

31, rue Coquillière
42 36 73 55

Closed Sun. Open until 10:30pm. V, MC.

Tables are cramped together, but the rustic interior is warm and welcoming. The Fermette boasts an able chef who avoids the clichés of Southwestern cuisine. Snails with bacon and eggs make an interesting dish, and the duck breast with cèpes is nicely handled. For dessert, we like the tasty tarte Tatin. **C** 220-320 F.

13 Gaya

17, rue Duphot
42 60 43 03,
fax 42 60 04 54

Closed Sun. Open until 10:30pm. Priv rm: 35. Air cond. Garage pkg. AE.

Each day the tide pulls sparkling fresh seafood into this bright and elegant bistro, the lower-priced annex of Goumard-Prunier (see below). The catch of the day sometimes features marinated fresh anchovies, goujonnettes de sole au basilic, or sea bream anointed with virgin olive oil and expertly grilled. **C** 260-360 F.

17 Goumard-Prunier

9, rue Duphot
42 60 36 07,
fax 42 60 04 54

Closed Sun (summer), Mon. Open until 10:30pm. Priv rm: 25. Air cond. Garage pkg. V, AE, DC.

Jean-Claude Goumard regularly treks out at 3am to the Rungis market to net the very best sole and turbot, the fattest lobsters and prawns, for his chef Georges Lardiot—fish and crustaceans so perfect that no flambé or croûte is ever allowed to mar them. A pinch of turmeric to enliven the shellfish fricassée; a drop of veal juices with soy sauce to accompany the braised sole; precious little butter all around: in short, nothing to interfere with the fresh taste of the sea. Other possibilities include enormous Brittany prawns baked in their shells, crab with Sherry aspic and a delicate parsley sauce, truffled coquilles Saint-Jacques, or a sumptuous and authentic bouillabaisse. Dessert brings excellent chocolate fondant with coffee sauce. Fine cellar; and the service is truly excellent. Little remains, alas, of the restaurant's original décor, designed by Majorelle—the only vestiges, it so happens, are in the restrooms! **C** 400-700 F.

12/20 Restaurant du Grand Louvre

Museum entrance, under the pyramid
40 20 53 41,
fax 42 86 04 63

Closed Tue. Open until 10pm. Priv rm: 80. Air cond. No pets. Garage pkg. V, AE, DC.

Something is cooking under I.M. Pei's glass pyramid. In contrast with the chilly décor, the Louvre's restaurant serves warming, reasonably priced fare: try the meaty headcheese, the grilled salmon with sauce béarnaise, and the fruit gratin laced with Grand Marnier. Non-stop service. **C** 250-380 F. **M** 170 F.

18 Le Grand Véfour

17, rue de Beaujolais
42 96 56 27,
fax 42 86 80 71

Closed Sat, Sun, Aug. Open until 10:15pm. Priv rm: 25. Air cond. No pets. Valet pkg. V, AE, DC.

Guy Martin got off to a rough start here. Nearly every food critic in town greeted Martin's arrival at Le Grand Véfour with a cutting review. Well, we've been following his career for years, and we know that the very worst one could say of Martin's cooking was that some dishes verged on the baroque, with too many discordant flavors vying for attention. Martin's current, more mature style has outgrown these excesses of exuberant youth. The truth is, one dines splendidly at Le Grand Véfour. Surely, the sophisticated gourmands who flock to this exquisite eating house have not been dragged in by force! Martin chooses prime foodstuffs for his classically balanced, robustly flavorful bill of fare. A fanciful touch emerges here and there (there's a delicious braised eel in Port sauce with rutabagas and preserved lemons, for example); yet overall a measured harmony prevails, as in the ravioles de foie gras à la crème truffée, or plump prawns seared in fragrant olive oil, in the baked whole turbot with anchovy purée, or a masterly roast Bresse chicken Miéral, its breast coated with a creamy cèpe sauce and toasted hazelnuts. For our money, this is food worth a solid triple toque.

Of course, much of the

magic of the Grand Véfour resides in the sublime surroundings: carved boiserie ceilings, graceful painted allegories under glass, plush carpeting, snowy napery, and fragile Directoire chairs. The service is as elegant as the cosmopolitan clientele. And the bill? Astronomical. **C** 650-1,000 F. **M** 305 F (weekday lunch).

15 A la Grille Saint-Honoré

15, pl. du Marché-St-Honoré
42 61 00 93,
fax 47 03 31 64

Closed Sun, Mon (exc dinner in hunting seas), Aug 1-21. Open until 10:30pm. Priv rm: 30. Terrace dining. Air cond. Pkg. V, AE, DC, MC.

The Place du Marché Saint-Honoré is currently a mess, owing to the construction of a glass gallery designed by Riccardo Bofill. But don't let that discourage you from visiting the glossy pink-and-gray restaurant where Jean Speyer serves tasty, imaginative "market cuisine": sautéed escargots with fennel fondue, lobster fricassée sparked with paprika, roast veal kidneys with anchovies, and wonderful game dishes (partridge with wild mushrooms...) in season. The set meals and affordable wines are Speyer's strongest suit. **C** 310-380 F. **M** 180 F.

11/20 Lescure

7, rue de Mondovi
42 60 18 91

Closed Sat dinner, Sun, Aug. Open until 10:15pm. Terrace dining. Air cond. V, MC.

Tried-and-trusted French fare served in a feverish bistro atmosphere. Sample the hearty veal sauté or duck confit. Game dishes are highlighted in the autumn and winter hunting season. **C** 150-180 F. **M** 100 F (lunch, wine incl).

11/20 Le Louchebem

31, rue Berger
42 33 12 99

Open daily until 11:30pm. No pets.

Carnivores can count on satisfaction here: huge portions of grilled or roasted beef, lamb, and pork, tripe, pigs' trotters and the like, accompanied by wonderful pommes frites, are served in a butcher's-shop décor (rather cold with all those tiles). Modest, well-chosen wine list. **C** 200-250 F. **M** 90 F (dinner), 105 F.

15 Mercure Galant

15, rue des Petits-Champs
42 96 98 89,
fax 42 96 08 89

Closed Sat, Sun. Open until 10:30pm. No pets. V, MC.

The service in this grand old restaurant is charming, the décor elegant, and the cuisine better than ever. These days, chef Pierre Ferranti is cooking in a lighter, more imaginative vein, producing such delectable dishes as warm oysters with perfectly cooked cabbage and Belgian endive, scallops with basmati rice and a generous garnish of fresh morels, and lamb fillet seasoned with spiced olive oil. Interesting cellar with a wide range of Bordeaux. **C** 400-550 F. **M** 210 F (lunch exc Sun), 280 F & 400 F (dinner exc Sun).

16 Le Meurice

Hôtel Meurice,
228, rue de Rivoli
44 58 10 50,
fax 44 58 10 15

Open daily until 11pm. Priv rm: 180. Air cond. No pets. V, AE, DC, MC.

Rosy nymphs cavort across a ceiling further adorned with gilt and crystal chandeliers, in what is surely one of the city's most sumptuous restaurants. Le Meurice is not all show, however: the food served in this royal setting is truly superb. Marc Marchand eschews the pompous cuisine one might expect to find here, for full-bodied dishes with plenty of rustic flavor, like a salad of crisp-cooked cauliflower with langoustines and smoked eel, a delicate crab cake partnered with wee stuffed squid, red mullet accompanied by wild-mushroom risotto, or veal stewed to tenderness with morels and artichokes. Marchand also knows his way around desserts: just taste his nougat soufflé embellished with a scoop of almond ice cream. Faultless service, and a cellar administered by Antoine Zocchetto, an expert sommelier. **C** 450-550 F. **M** 380 F (dinner, wine incl), 300 F (lunch).

14 La Passion

41, rue des Petits-Champs
42 97 53 41

Closed Sat lunch, Sun. Open until 10:30pm. Priv rm: 10. Air cond. No pets. V, MC.

Gourmet abandon is what the restaurant's name suggests, but in fact Gilles Zellenwarger's cooking is of the earnest, serious sort. Yet a passionate devotion to culinary craft is evident in his meticulous attention to detail. The classic bill of fare features a rich cassolette of chicken and sweetbreads, skate perfumed with tarragon, and an elegantly herbal sole sautée. Judicious cellar; too bad the setting lacks charm. **C** 320-400 F. **M** 150 F, 200 F, 360 F.

15 **Chez Pauline**
5, rue Villedo
42 96 20 70,
fax 49 27 99 89

Closed Sat lunch, Sun. Open until 10:30pm. Priv rm: 35. Air cond. V, AE, MC.

By now this wonderful old bistro has earned the rank of institution, for it perfectly represents a certain ideal of French cuisine. Robust and full of frank flavors, the neo-bourgeois dishes are based on uniformly fine ingredients prepared by a veteran chef. Subtlety is not the strong suit here: braises, sautés, and long-simmered stews are André Genin's stock in trade. A recent meal brought a fine calf's-head salad, a rosy escalope of foie gras surrounded by plump grapes, savory baked veal shanks, and a fabulous strawberry soup. The cellar holds memorable Burgundies, and there is an excellent selection of coffees. **C** 350-500 F. M 250 F (weekday lunch, wine incl), 220 F, 320 F.

15 **Paolo Petrini**
9, rue d'Argenteuil
42 60 56 22,
fax 42 36 55 50

Closed Sat lunch, Sun, Aug. Open until 11pm. Air cond. V, AE.

Paolo Petrini hails from Pisa, he's a genuine Italian chef (Paris has so few)! His cooking is as spare and stylized as his small (25 seats) austerely decorated dining room. Yet the full spectrum of Italy's distinctive savors are present in his warm, basil-scented salad of squid, clams, and cannellini beans; a delectable risotto ai porcini; a grilled beef fillet, sliced thin and dressed with balsamic vinegar; pappardelle sauced with a rich, winy hare napped; or tagliarini swathed in melted Fontina. Desserts are well above the ordinary, too, along with a superb selection of Italian wines. **C** 280-340 F.

12/20 **Au Pied de Cochon**
6, rue Coquillière
42 36 11 75,
fax 45 08 48 90

Open daily 24 hours. Priv rm: 40. Terrace dining. Air cond. V, AE, DC, MC.

The atmosphere is at once frantic and euphoric in this Les Halles landmark, renowned for serving thundering herds of pigs' trotters (85,000 annually) and a ton of shellfish every day of the year. **C** 220-350 F.

15 **Restaurant Pierre**
10, rue de Richelieu
42 96 09 17,
fax 42 96 09 62

Closed Sat, Sun, hols, Aug. Open until 10pm. V, AE, DC, MC.

Country delights from the four corners of France fill the lovely handwritten menu of this traditional bistro. The cuisine is in the reliable hands of Roger Leplu, who uses top-quality ingredients to produce such pillars of French cooking as boudin with onions, mackerel in cider, and bœuf à la ficelle, as well as stuffed cabbage bourguignonne or sheep's tripe and trotters à la marseillaise. Superb desserts. **C** 300-400 F. **M** 210 F.

14 **Le Poquelin** ✪
17, rue Molière
42 96 22 19,
fax 42 96 05 72

Closed Sat lunch, Sun, Aug 1-20. Open until 10:30pm. Priv rm: 8. Air cond. Garage pkg. V, AE, DC.

In the red-and-gold dining room where portraits of Molière look down from the walls, chef Michel Guillaumin wins the applause of his regular patrons (many from the Comédie-Française across the street) for his renditions of popular favorites: there's a rustic salad of pig's trotters and white beans, pikeperch poached in Saint-Pourçain wine, spice-coated duck breast, veal kidney in balsamic vinegar sauce, and canard Duchambais. Good notices too for his warm pear tart, and a standing ovation for Maggy Guillaumin's smiling welcome. **C** 330-450 F. **M** 185 F.

13 **Velloni**
22, rue des Halles
42 21 12 50

Closed Sun, hols, Aug 15-25. Open until 11pm. No pets. V, AE, DC, MC.

A bright, comfortable establishment run by a genial Italian host. The chef acquits himself like a born Tuscan in his preparation of tagliarini with fresh crab sauce, beef jowls braised in vino di Montalcino, and ravioli stuffed with spinach and ricotta. Uneven cellar. **C** 230-330 F. **M** 130 F.

12/20 Chez la Vieille

"Adrienne," 37, rue de l'Arbre-Sec
42 60 15 78

Lunch only (dinner by reserv for 8 or more). Closed Sat, Sun. Priv rm: 25. Garage pkg. V, MC.

Adrienne Biasin has put away her pots and pans, but her generous homestyle cuisine lives on: the kitchen is now supervised by the excellent Gérard Besson (see above). So the regulars—bankers, press barons, and show-business personalities—still come around for the tasty terrines, quenelles, braised veal, pot-au-feu, and such comforting desserts as baba au rhum and floating island. Comforting is not how we'd describe the prices. **C** 350-380 F.

12/20 Willi's Wine Bar

13, rue des Petits-Champs
42 61 05 09,
fax 47 03 36 93

Closed Sun. Open until 11pm. V, MC.

Mark Williamson and Tim Johnston are a witty, wise pair of wine experts. Their cellar holds treasures from all over France and the world, including a peerless collection of Côtes-du-Rhônes. Enjoy them (by the glass, or better, the bottle) along with a good quail salad, tarragon-scented rabbit, or a nice bit of Stilton—a glass of cream Sherry would be good with the latter. If you can't nab a table in the smallish dining room, join the customers sitting elbow-to-elbow at the polished wood bar. **C** 260-320 F. **M** 155 F (wine incl).

2nd arrondissement

12/20 Bistrot du Louvre

48, rue d'Argout
45 08 47 46

Closed Sat lunch, Sun. Open until 10:30pm. Terrace dining. V, AE.

Outside, this likeable bistro looks awfully like a Swiss chalet. But inside you'll find the regulation wood bar, mirrors, banquettes, and yellowed posters on the wall. Journalists from *Le Figaro*, among others, appreciate the fresh, generous cooking: deep-fried baby soles, tuna steak au pistou, and thick-sliced calf's liver with shallot confit. **C** 250-300 F.

13 Café Runtz

16, rue Favart
42 96 69 86

Closed Sat, Sun, hols, May 14-23, Aug 7-29. Open until 11:15pm. Priv rm: 40. Air cond. V, AE, MC.

This is an 1880s Alsatian *winstub* whose classic fare ranges from foie gras to excellent choucroute or potato salad with pork knuckle. Good French Rhine wines; cheeky service. **C** 200-300 F.

12/20 Canard'Avril

5, rue Paul-Lelong
42 36 26 08

Closed Sat, Sun. Open until 10pm. Priv rm: 35. V.

The menu's just ducky: gizzard salad, confit, and magret de canard feature prominently, alongside a handful of similarly hearty Southwestern dishes. The cheap and cheerful prix-fixe meals are sure to quack you up. **C** 200-250 F. **M** 85 F, 125 F.

16 Le Céladon

Hôtel Westminster,
15, rue Daunou
47 03 40 42,
fax 42 60 30 66

Closed Sat, Sun, hols, Aug. Open until 10pm. Priv rm: 60. Air cond. Valet pkg. AE, DC, MC.

Three tastefully lit, flower-filled, and impeccably elegant dining rooms in what is possibly the city's loveliest *restaurant de palace* form the perfect setting for a romantic dinner. Le Céladon's able chef, Emmanuel Hodencq, creates resolutely refined dishes such as a lush timbale of cèpes, macaroni, and tender snails, a superlative beignet of foie gras sparked with caramel vinegar in a Port sauce hinting of truffles, and an appetizing combination of tender lamb chops and lamb sausage abetted by a savory jus. Only the lobster steamed in a (tough!) cabbage leaf fails to inspire praise. Desserts are divine—try the sautéed pears with licorice ice cream or the lime gratin studded with candied grapefruit peel and laced with rum. Interesting, eclectic cellar. **C** 350-500 F. **M** 220-290 F.

12/20 Coup de Cœur

19, rue St-Augustin
47 03 45 70

Closed Sat lunch, Sun. Open until 10:30pm. Priv rm: 60. Air cond. V, AE, MC.

The appealing set meals served in this intimate *salle* (designed by Philippe Starck) win our hearts: the gingery lamb's sweetbreads layered with airy puff pastry, finnan haddie escorted by buttery cabbage, earthy oxtail terrine, red mullet with artichokes, and upside-down mango tart are all delicious and deftly rendered. On the wine list you'll find a wealth of half-bottles. **M** 170 F (dinner exc Sun, wine incl), 185 F (weekday lunch, wine incl), 160 F (weekday lunch).

14 Delmonico

Hôtel Édouard-VII
39, av. de l'Opéra
42 61 44 26

Closed Sat, Sun, Aug. Open until 9:45pm. Priv rm: 20. Air cond. Pkg. V, AE, DC, MC.

With its lightened décor and livelier atmosphere, this old standby has stepped briskly into the age of the business lunch. Chef Alain Soltys prepares a classic *carte* and laudably generous set meals. We like his curried brill (it deserves better vegetables), roast squab au jus with a wholesome accompaniment of cabbage and wheat berries, and the dainty melon gratin glazed with brown sugar. The service is uniformly charming and there's a fine cellar. **C** 280-360 F. **M** 128 F, 168 F.

17 Drouant

18, rue Gaillon
42 65 15 16,
fax 49 24 02 15

Open daily until 10:30pm (midnight at Le Café). Priv rm: 30. Air cond. Valet pkg. AE, DC, MC.

The cream of the city's biz and show-biz sets meet and greet in the Drouant's grand Art Deco staircase. The house repertoire is fairly classic, but Louis Grondard's consummate skill keeps the menu fresh and appealing. First-rate foodstuffs, robust flavors, and perfectly balanced seasonings result in a memorable charlotte de langoustines aux aubergines confites (molded prawns with slow-roasted eggplants), John Dory with tiny squid in a saffron-tinged jus, a succulent fillet of Pauillac lamb in an herbal crust, or roast beef served with rich and mellow bone marrow. Few palates would fail to appreciate desserts like the tarte au café with walnut custard sauce or chestnut croquant and honey-gentian ice cream. The Café Drouant is the haunt of business lunchers (at noon) and theater-goers (at night) in search of reasonably priced bourgeois cooking. **C** 600-750 F. **M** 250 F (at Le Café; exc weekday lunch), 290 F (coffee incl), 600 F.

12/20 Gallopin

40, rue N.-D.-des-Victoires
42 36 45 38,
fax 42 36 10 32

Closed Sat, Sun. Open until 11pm. Terrace dining. V, AE, DC.

The brassy Victorian décor is a feast for the eyes. The food at Gallopin isn't bad either. Try the house specialties: sole meunière and hot apple tart. Jolly service. **C** 200-300 F. **M** 150 F (dinner, wine incl).

12/20 Le Grand Colbert

2, rue Vivienne
42 86 87 88,
fax 42 86 82 65

Closed Jul 29-Aug 28. Open until 1am. Air cond. V, AE, MC.

Classic brasserie cuisine (oysters and shellfish, andouillette ficelle, bœuf gros sel, and poached chicken) served in a sprucely restored historic monument complete with frescoes and ornate plasterwork, brass railings and painted glass panels. Expect a warm welcome and swift, smiling service. **C** 160-250 F. **M** 155 F (wine incl).

13 Pierre

"A la Fontaine Gaillon," pl. Gaillon
42 65 87 04,
fax 47 42 82 84

Closed Sat lunch, Sun, Aug. Open until 12:30am. Priv rm: 40. Terrace dining. Air cond. Garage pkg. V, AE, DC, MC.

The young chef's personality and well-honed technique shine through the resolutely classic menu, which features an excellent duo of raw salmon and sculpin, duck confit with sautéed potatoes, and praline croustillant. The dining room of this delightful old *hôtel particulier* was recently restored, and the grand terrace's fountain is spectacular when illuminated at night. If only the staff would crack an occasional smile... **C** 250-400 F. **M** 165 F (dinner), 210 F.

14 Pile ou Face

52 bis, rue N.-D.-des-Victoires
42 33 64 33,
fax 42 36 61 09

Closed Sat, Sun, Dec 24-Jan 1, Aug. Open until 10pm. Priv rm: 20. Air cond. Garage pkg. V, MC.

Why fiddle with a winning formula? That seems to be the philosophy of the three partners who run Pile ou Face. This year, like last

Market culture

A stroll round a Parisian *street market* is one of the best ways to see, smell, and sample French food. Start out early to admire the carefully constructed stacks of fruits and vegetables—and stick around for bargains when stallholders close up shop at about 1pm. The speed with which they dismantle their stalls and pack up their produce is a spectacle in itself. Most markets are held twice a week, some three times a week, and there are 57 sites to choose from. For contrasting views of Parisian shopping and eating habits, visit the resolutely upscale Saint-Didier market in the sixteenth arrondissement (go down the Rue Mesnil from Place Victor-Hugo) held on Tuesday, Thursday, and Saturday, and the funky, multiracial market on the Place de la Réunion in the twentieth arrondissement on Thursday or Sunday.

year, we'll tick off the same specialties that showcase the restaurant's fresh farm produce: scrambled eggs with morels, marmelade de lapin au romarin, and free-range chicken sautéed with garlic. New dishes do occasionally make an appearance, and an appealing single-price menu is now served at lunch. The red-and-gold décor with *fin de siècle* touches perfectly complements chef Claude Udron's cuisine. Very fine wine cellar. **C** 310-470 F. **M** 235 F (lunch), 280 F & 320 F (dinner).

Le Saint-Amour

8, rue de Port-Mahon - 47 42 63 82

Closed Sat lunch, Sun, hols. Open until 10:30pm. Air cond. V, AE, DC, MC.

Impeccable service and a simple, fresh, generous cuisine distinguish Le Saint-Amour. The new chef offers a 155 F set lunch that delivers a creamy crab and lobster soup brightened with basil, cod pot-au-feu, an ample portion of nicely matured Brie, and decent chocolate cake. Concise but interesting wine list. **C** 300-400 F. **M** 155 F.

3rd arrondissement

L'Alisier

26, rue de Montmorency - 42 72 31 04, fax 42 72 74 83

Closed Sat, Sun, Aug. Open until 10pm. Priv rm: 35. Air cond. No pets. V, AE, MC.

An inviting, old-fashioned bistro (ask for a table upstairs) where you can enjoy Jean-Luc Dodeman's personalized versions of hearty French favorites. Eggs poached in tarragon-scented veal gravy, beef jowls braised in red wine, and brown-sugar tart with yogurt ice cream are representative of the house style. **C** 230-300 F. **M** 149 F.

Ambassade d'Auvergne

22, rue du Grenier-St-Lazare
42 72 31 22, fax 42 78 85 47

Closed Aug 1-16. Open until 10:30pm. Priv rm: 35. Air cond. Garage pkg. V, AE, MC.

Each visit to this embassy brings the same heart-warming experience. The Petrucci tribe's hospitality knows no bounds. The décor, featuring timbers hung with hams, is worn but authentic; the atmosphere is genuinely convivial.

Authenticity is equally present in the house specialties: aged country ham, cabbage and Roquefort soup, boudin with chestnuts, cassoulet of lentils from Le Puy, legendary sausages served with slabs of delicious bread, duck daube with fresh pasta and smoky bacon, and so forth. Good desserts (try the aumonière à l'orange, or the mousseline glacée à la verveine du Velay). The cellar is vast and boasts some little-known Auvergnat wines (Chanturgue, Saint-Pourçain) in a wide range of prices. **C** 215-300 F.

L'Ami Louis

32, rue du Vertbois
48 87 77 48

Closed Mon, Tue, Jul 15-Aug 25. Open until 11pm. V, AE, MC.

Despite its improbably shabby décor (note the

peeling, brownish walls), L'Ami Louis jealously claims the title of "the world's costliest bistro." It is certainly dear to the hearts of the tourists, suicidal overeaters, and skinny fashion models who battle to book a table at this famous *lieu de mémoire*. The heirs of old Père Magnin carry on the house tradition of huge portions, but the ingredients are not so choice as they once were. And nowadays the sauces are sometimes thick or sticky, and the fries a shade too oily. Yet you can still count on gargantuan servings of foie gras fresh from the Landes, giant escargots de Bourgogne, whole roast chicken, or an incomparable gigot of baby Pyrenees lamb. The desserts are ho-hum, the cellar respectable. **C** 600-800 F.

11/20 Le Bar à Huîtres

33, bd Beaumarchais - 48 87 98 92

See *14th arrondissement.*

12/20 Au Bascou

38, rue Réaumur
42 72 69 25

Closed Sat, Sun, 3 wks in Aug, 1 wk at Christmas. Open until midnight. No pets. V, AE, DC, MC.

Basque-country native Jean-Guy Loustau (formerly the sommelier of Le Carré des Feuillants) runs this smart address. We made a fine meal here of shirred eggs with foie gras, lamb kidney with eggplant caviar, and caramel mousse with crunchy bits of walnut brittle. The wines are top-notch, but why aren't there more half-bottles? **C** 200-240 F. **M** 85 F (lunch).

12/20 Chez Janou

Corner of 56, rue des Tournelles and 2, rue R.-Verlomme
42 72 28 41

Closed Sat, Sun, hols. Open until 11pm. Terrace dining. V, AE, DC, MC.

An honest little old-fashioned bistro with turn-of-the-century décor and a pleasant terrace. The neighborhood (Place des Vosges/Bastille) has gone up-market and so have Janou's prices, but the country cooking (poached eggs with chanterelles, Jerusalem artichokes tossed in hazelnut oil, duck confit) still tastes authentic. Improved wine list. **C** 200-300 F. **M** 180 F (wine incl), 200 F.

11/20 Chez Jenny

39, bd du Temple
42 74 75 75,
fax 42 74 38 69

Open daily until 1am. Priv rm: 150. Terrace dining. Pkg. V, AE, DC, MC.

This grand, historic monument of a brasserie, with lovely marquetry upstairs, is still going strong. Many good "world-famous" choucroutes and superb Alsatian charcuteries. **C** 180-300 F. **M** 99 F & 160 F (wine incl).

12/20 Chez Nénesse

17, rue de Saintonge
42 78 46 49

Closed Sat, Sun, last wk of Feb, Aug. Open until 10pm. V, MC.

Nénesse puts on the dog for dinner: he covers the Formica tables of his old neighborhood bistro with spotless white napery. Though prices are low, portions (of lobster and prawn salad with asparagus, roast pigeon, and pineapple-strawberry gratin) are on the small side. **C** 180-250 F.

11/20 Chez Omar

47, rue de Bretagne
42 72 36 26

Information not available.

Mysteries of *la mode...* Fashion plates (and the designers who dress them) simply adore this cramped, graceless bistro. Omar oversees the efficient, good-humored waiters who serve forth mediocre couscous and excellent méchoui (roast lamb). No reservations accepted. **C** 100-200 F.

4th arrondissement

19 L'Ambroisie

9, pl. des Vosges
42 78 51 45

Closed Sun, Mon, Feb school hols, 1st 3 wks of Aug. Open until 10:30pm. Priv rm: 14. Air cond. No pets. Valet pkg. V, MC.

Bernard and Danièle Pacaud transformed this former goldsmith's shop under the arcades of the Place des Vosges into the Marais's most gracious and elegant dining room. The setting is worthy of a château, with high ceilings, inlaid stone and parquet floors, book-lined shelves, and a sumptuous seventeenth-century tapestry adorning the honey-hued walls. L'Ambroisie has the lived-in feel of a beautifully maintained private home, of which Danièle is the charming hostess. Don't expect to see much of

Bernard, though. He prefers the sizzling sounds of his kitchen to the applause of an appreciative public. Vivid flavors and masterly technique are the hallmarks of a concise *carte* that comprises seven starters, six fish, and seven meat options, as well as a few *surprises du jour* announced at the table. Creamy lobster soup with scallops and a truffle turnover; red mullet napped with a delicate sauce hinting of orange, honey, and carrot; turbot braised with celery and celery root; saddle of Pauillac lamb in a truffled persillade; a majestic poularde en demi-deuil—all are flawlessly finished: no superfluous detail, no obtrusive spice disturbs their balanced harmony. Come time for dessert, a caramel millefeuille with tart apples, a bitter-cocoa soufflé, or a croquant de riz à l'impératrice prolongs the pleasure of a perfect meal. The wines, too, are faultless, selected by Pierre Le Moullac, an exemplary maître d'hôtel-sommelier. **C** 650-1,000 F.

11/20 **Auberge de Jarente**

7, rue de Jarente
42 77 49 35

Closed Sun, Mon, wk of Aug 15. Open until 10:30pm. Priv rm: 20. Terrace dining. Air cond. V, AE, MC.

Here you'll find unpretentious Basque dishes served in a charming old Marais atmosphere. The fixed-price menu, which includes pipérade de Saint-Jean, cassoulet, cheese, and gâteau basque, is above reproach. **C** 200 F. **M** 75 F (weekday lunch, wine incl), 115 F, 130 F & 185 F (wine incl).

13 **Baracane**

38, rue des Tournelles - 42 71 43 33

Closed Sat lunch, Sun. Open until midnight. V, MC.

Tables fill quickly in this popular little Southwestern enclave, because the cooking is full-flavored and generous to boot. Lentil salad with slices of dried goose breast or cassoulet with duck confit precede truly delectable desserts (the apple croustillant laced with plum brandy is our favorite). Low-priced regional wines wash it all down. Affable service. **C** 220-300 F. **M** 120 F (wine incl), 75 F.

14 **Benoit**

20, rue St-Martin
42 72 25 76

Closed Sat, Sun, Aug. Open until 10pm. No pets. No cards.

The more things change, the more Benoit's solid, bourgeois cooking stays the same. This is the archetypal Parisian bistro (and surely one of the priciest): velvet banquettes, brass fixtures, lace curtains, and a polished zinc bar compose a seductive décor. Owner Michel Petit (who is anything but!) continues the lusty tradition begun before the Great War by his grandfather. His chef turns out a delicious bœuf à la parisienne, good cassoulet, and a creditable codfish with potatoes and cream. Tasty but unexciting desserts. The excellent cellar is stocked with reasonably priced bottles from Mâcon, Sancerre, Beaujolais, and Saumur. **C** 450-600 F.

13 **Coconnas**

2 bis, pl. des Vosges
42 78 58 16

Closed Mon (exc summer), Tue (Oct-Mar), Dec 15-Jan 15. Open until 10pm. Priv rm: 65. Air cond. V, AE, DC, MC.

Claude Terrail (La Tour d'Argent) comes around regularly to keep an eye on his little bistro on the lovely Place des Vosges. The menu is short, the atmosphere lively: sample generously served favorites such as poule au pot with a "garden of vegetables" or merlan (whiting) Coconnas. The fixed-price meal offers good value. **C** 300-450 F. **M** 160 F.

14 **L'Excuse**

14, rue Charles-V
42 77 98 97

Closed Sun, wk of Aug 15. Open until 11pm. No pets. V, AE, MC.

For an elegant dinner in the Marais, why not reserve a table at this dainty little candybox of a restaurant, decorated with mirrors, engravings, and posters. A new chef has raised the kitchen's standards, witness the well-defined flavors of his vegetable feuilleté with fresh herb sauce, turbot fillet, and white-and-dark chocolate fondant. Long, eclectic wine list; efficient service. **C** 260-400 F. **M** 145 F.

13 **Le Fond de Cour**

3, rue Ste-Croix-Bretonnerie
42 74 71 52,
fax 48 87 30 97

Closed Sat lunch, Sun. Open until 11pm. Priv rm: 15. Terrace dining. Pkg. V, AE, MC.

At the back of the courtyard, as the name suggests,

you'll find this amusingly decorated restaurant. The chef prepares a classic but never boring menu that proposes house-made foie gras de canard, a pleasing duo of roasted scallops and langoustines, and a commendable chocolate cake. The cellar is still quite young. **M** 119 F & 149 F (lunch), 159 F & 179 F (dinner).

10/20 Jo Goldenberg

7, rue des Rosiers
48 87 20 16

Open daily until midnight. Priv rm: 60. Terrace dining. Air cond. V, AE, DC.

This is the archetypal, and most picturesque, of the Goldenberg restaurants in Paris (see seventeenth arrondissement). The Central European Yiddish cuisine is served in the heart of the Marais's Jewish district. Prepared foods are sold in the take-out shop. **C** 150-200 F.

11/20 Au Gourmet de l'Isle

42, rue St-Louis-en-l'Ile - 43 26 79 27

Closed Mon, Tue. Open until 10pm. V, MC.

The reception is charming, the crowd young and cheerful, the stone-and-beams décor appealingly rustic. Au Gourmet de l'Isle has enjoyed over 40 years of deserved success for one of the city's surest-value set menus priced at 125 F. Lots of à la carte choices too: artichoke "Saint Louis", beef stewed in Marcillac wine, andouillette with kidney beans. **C** 190 F. **M** 130 F.

13 Le Grizzli

7, rue Saint-Martin
48 87 77 56

Closed Sun. Open until 11pm. Terrace dining. Garage pkg. V, AE, MC.

At age 95 this Grizzli is still going strong, serving lusty specialties rooted in the Southwest: white-bean salad with duck confit, rabbit with raisins, and veal stewed with dried cèpes. **C** 200-250 F. **M** 120 F (lunch), 155 F.

14 Le Maraîcher

5, rue Beautreillis
42 71 42 49

Closed Mon lunch, Sun, Aug. Open until 11pm. V, MC.

Lured by the appetizing 120 F set lunch, hungry hordes descend upon this attractive little spot at noon. But even the stiffer à la carte tariffs don't discourage Le Maraîcher's many fans from indulging in the delicate scallop ravioli showered with zucchini curls and sesame seeds, the calf's liver meunière deglazed with Sherry vinegar, and warm orange soup with caramel ice cream. Attentive service. **C** 250-300 F. **M** 120 F (lunch, wine incl).

15 Miravile

72, quai de l'Hôtel-de-Ville
42 74 72 22,
fax 42 74 67 55

Closed Sat lunch, Sun. Open until 10:30pm. Priv rm: 45. Terrace dining. Air cond. Garage pkg. V, AE, MC.

Gilles Épié made a shrewd move when he decided to throw out the Miravile's expensive *carte* in favor of a 220 F single-price menu. Instead of costly ingredients, Épié relies on his considerable talent to create imaginative dishes packed with robust flavors. Pimientoes with codfish and crushed potatoes or rémoulade of duck liver and celeriac are appetizing preludes to skate with sea urchins and spinach, or Provençal-inspired rabbit with olives, or chicken and onion tagine. These, in turn, can be followed by a tarte au café laced with single-malt whisky or bitter-chocolate and caramel ice cream. To drink, there are some 40 wines priced between 115 F and 250 F. Little wonder, then, that customers are flocking back into the Miravile's sunny, Italianate dining room. **M** 220 F.

13 Le Monde des Chimères

69, rue Saint-Louis-en-l'Ile
43 54 45 27

Closed Sun, Mon, Feb school hols. Open until 10:20pm. Pkg. V, MC.

A delightful old "island bistro" run by former TV personality Cécile Ibane. The cuisine is reminiscent of Sunday dinner *en famille*—if, that is, your family included a French granny who was also a marvelous cook! We recommend the eggs scrambled with fennel, grilled fillet of pollack dressed with olive oil and lemon, oxtail terrine garnished with sweet-and-sour quince and cherries, or chicken sautéed with 40 cloves of garlic. Yummy homemade desserts. **C** 280-380 F. **M** 155 F.

Red toques signify modern cuisine; white toques signify traditional cuisine.

13

Palais de Fès

41, rue du Roi-de-Sicile
42 72 03 68

Open daily until 11:30pm. No pets. V, AE, DC, MC.

This may be the only Moroccan hotel-restaurant in the city, but a palace it's not. The glittery décor isn't exactly palatial, either, but it's tidy and inviting. Good food is the drawing card here: order the assiette marocaine (spicy sausage, bits of lamb, cold peppers and eggplant), followed by one of a half-dozen delicious couscous variations, or a tagine (the lamb with onions would be our choice), or the more-than-decent pigeon pastilla. Excellent value. **C** 150 F. **M** 70 F.

5th arrondissement

13

L'Atlas

12, bd St-Germain
46 33 86 98

Open daily until 11pm. Priv rm: 30. Air cond. Pkg. V, AE.

Here's a first toque, which we bet will be followed by more, for Monsieur Eljaziri's surprising, slightly cerebral, determinedly modern version of Moroccan cuisine. The range of options extends well beyond couscous and tagines (though a dozen excellent varieties are offered) to such uncommon dishes as lamb with mallow, monkfish with thyme blossoms, and kidneys with sea-urchin butter. Desserts are more traditional. Decorated with mosaics and ornamental plasterwork, the dining room is perfectly lovely, and so is the service. **C** 190-230 F.

15

Auberge des Deux Signes

46, rue Galande
43 25 46 56,
fax 46 33 20 49

Closed Sat lunch, Sun, May 1, Aug. Open until 10:30pm. Pkg. V, AE, DC, MC.

If there is one restaurant in Paris that must be seen to be believed, it is this medieval hostelry lovingly restored and run by Georges Dhulster. Solid oak beams, Gothic vaults, and windows that frame Notre-Dame: the setting is nothing short of spectacular (despite some heavy-handed neo-Louis XIII touches). The food, consistently generous and well prepared, deserves two solid toques: try the salade périgourdine, boiled-beef ravioli with ginger-scented cabbage, or turbot with buttery leeks. The 140 F set lunch offers relief from the high prices à la carte. Courteous service. **C** 400-650 F. **M** 140 F (weekday lunch), 230 F.

10/20 Le Balzar

49, rue des Écoles
43 54 13 67

Closed Dec 24-Jan 1, Aug. Open until 1am. Air cond. V, AE.

This Left-Bank/Sorbonne haunt, with its Art Deco woodwork and mirrors, offers decent renditions of traditional brasserie fare (calf's liver, choucroute). **C** 200-300 F.

13

Le Bistrot d'à Côté

16, bd St-Germain
43 54 59 10

Closed Sat lunch, Sun. Open until 11pm. Terrace dining. Air cond. V, AE, MC.

Michel Rostang has set up another of his popular bistro annexes at this Left-Bank location. He spruced up the 1950s-style interior and put two trusted assistants in charge of the kitchen. Lively house specialties include lentil soup with garlic sausage, codfish fricassée à la lyonnaise, and veal kidney in red-wine sauce. To drink, there are regional wines sold by the half-liter for around 60 F. **C** 135-200 F. **M** 98 F (lunch), 178 F.

Le Bistrot du Port

13, quai Montebello
40 51 73 19

Closed Tue lunch, Mon. Open until 10:30pm. Terrace dining. Air cond. No pets. Garage pkg. V.

The comfortable dining room and quayside terrace boast a magnificent view of Notre-Dame. Owner Iza Guyot has decided to take over the cooking duties herself, proposing the likes of profiteroles stuffed with goat cheese in a fresh tomato sauce, lamb noisettes with braised carrots, and old-fashioned coconut custard. Sounds good, but we'll hold back on the rating until Iza gets used to her new post. **C** 240-330 F. **M** 138-168 F.

15

La Bûcherie

41, rue
de la Bûcherie
43 54 78 06,
fax 46 34 54 02

Open daily until midnight. Priv rm: 40. Terrace dining. Air cond. Garage pkg. V, AE, DC, MC.

Bernard Bosque is built like a Breton buccaneer and has been running his "Hôtel du Bon Dieu" (the Bûcherie's name at the turn of the century) for over 30 years with great success. Handsome woodwork and contemporary engravings adorn the walls, and there are views of Notre-Dame through the windows of the covered terrace. The cuisine, classic and understated, reflects the seasons. There's game in autumn, a salad of truffled lamb's lettuce, scallops, and foie gras in winter, newly hatched eels from January to March, baby lamb or asparagus and morels in spring. Prices are not of the giveaway variety, but the 230 F lunch menu is quite attractive. The wine list is rich with vintage Bordeaux. **C** 300-470 F. **M** 230 F (wine incl).

13 Campagne et Provence

25, quai de la Tournelle - 43 54 05 17,
fax 42 74 67 55

Closed Sun, lunch Sat & Mon. Open until 11pm (w-e 1am). Air cond. V, MC.

Gilles Épié had a bright idea when he turned his ex-Miravile into a Provençal annex. The food is sunny, unhackneyed, and pleasingly priced. We find it hard to resist the mussel soup enriched with fragrant pistou, the meaty grilled peppers with anchovies, a vivid pumpkin risotto studded with bits of bacon, sea whelks accented by spicy chorizo, or rosemary-scented lamb tian. Every wine in the astutely assembled cellar costs under 100 F. A short but sweet 99 F lunch menu is on offer, too. **C** 220-250 F. **M** 99 F (lunch).

12/20 Chieng-Mai

12, rue F.-Sauton
43 25 45 45

Closed Sun, Aug 1-15, Dec 16-31. Open until 11:20pm. No pets. V, AE.

Its cool, stylized atmosphere, efficient service, and interesting Thai menu have won Chieng Mai a growing corps of admirers (it is wise to reserve your table). The repertoire features shrimp soup perfumed with lemongrass, baked crab claws with angel-hair pasta, steamed spicy seafood served in a crab shell, duck breast with basil and young peppercorns, and a remarkable coconut-milk flan. Service is courteous and competent, but the tables are set too close together. **C** 220 F. **M** 122 F, 136 F, 159 & 173 F (exc Sun).

14 Les Colonies

10, rue St-Julien-le-Pauvre
43 54 31 33

Dinner only. Closed Sun, Aug. Open until 1am (Mon until 10:30pm). Air cond. V, AE.

The decorator of L'Ambroisie took this old building, which faces the church of Saint-Julien-le-Pauvre, and transformed it with subtle refinements such as painted woodwork, luxurious fabrics, and fine china. A warm breeze from some imaginary Spice Island stirs many of chef Spyros Vakanas's creations, witness his salad of chayote squash dressed with tangy Japanese vinegar, a juicy duck enhanced with the warm flavor of nutmeg, rib steak coated with crushed spices, or the chocolate "shell" with sweet saffron cream sauce. Charming service and a fashionable clientele. Book ahead for late dining. **C** 300-400 F. **M** 170 F, 250 F.

13 Dodin-Bouffant

25, rue F.-Sauton
43 25 25 14,
fax 43 29 52 61

Closed Sat lunch, Sun, Dec 24-26. Open until 11pm. Terrace dining. Air cond. Garage pkg. V, AE, DC, MC.

Economic hard times have hit even this popular spot, where high and not-so-high-society diners once jostled for tables. Franco-American chef Mark Singer prepares the 215 F single-price menu, which we found to be something of a minefield on a recent day. Neither the ho-hum vegetable salad with its stingy garnish of foie gras, nor the overcooked lamb in a gluey tarragon sauce piqued our appetite. Only the delicious hot banana soufflé kept the meal from being a total rout. Just one toque left, and it's looking mighty wobbly... Good-natured service. **M** 215 F.

13 Les Fontaines

9, rue Soufflot
43 26 42 80

Closed Sun, Aug. Open until 10:30pm. V.

Roger Lacipière was right to set aside the back room of his otherwise charmless corner café and turn it into a delightful restaurant. Jolly waiters bring on generously robust and reasonably priced dishes like salmon-stuffed crêpes, Bresse chicken fricassée, and strawberry gratin with ice cream. Wonderful game in season. The wine list includes a fine selection of Loire and Bordeaux wines, and Beaujolais by the carafe. Be sure to book your table. **C** 160-260 F.

14 Inagiku

1, rue de Pontoise
43 54 70 07

Closed Sun. Open until 11pm. Air cond. V, AE.

Armed with our experience of Japanese restaurants, which we often leave as hungry as we'd come, it seemed a good idea to order a side of sashimi in addition to the Matsu, or big menu. Well, after putting away the assortment of delectably fresh raw fish, the sushi with avocado, the ineffably crisp fried hors d'œuvres, a pile of fat shrimp, some succulently tender beef fillet, and a duo of yummy ginger and chestnut sorbets, we waddled out, happy and absolutely stuffed! **C** 260-360 F. **M** 138 F, 168 F, 188 F, 248 F, 348 F.

12/20 Léna et Mimile

32, rue Tournefort
47 07 72 47

Closed Sat lunch, Sun. Open until 11pm. Terrace dining. V.

The terrace of this cozy bistro stretches out onto a charming square. From an appealing single-price menu (apéritif, wine, and coffee are all included) one can choose a basil-scented tourte of fresh sardines, braised pork shanks with lentils, and a satisfying pear feuilleté. **M** 185 F (wine incl), 98 F (lunch).

13 Mavrommatis

42, rue Daubenton
43 31 17 17

Closed Sun. Open until 11:30pm. Priv rm: 25. Terrace dining. No pets. Pkg. V.

The Mavrommatis brothers have raised the level of Greek cuisine served in Paris by several notches! Settle down into an Aegean-blue chair and order one—or several—of the 30 delicious hot and cold starters (octopus salad, tuna carpaccio with sesame seeds, stuffed eggplant, lamb meatballs, etc.). If you can resist making a meal of these mezes, there are worthwhile main dishes too, like red mullet grilled in vine leaves, smothered leg of lamb with herbs, or veal with oaten pasta. The selection of Greek wines is slowly improving. **C** 200-300 F. **M** 120 F ("business" lunch).

13 Moissonnier ✪

28, rue des Fossés-St-Bernard
43 29 87 65

Closed Sun dinner, Mon, Jul 28-Aug. Open until 10pm. V.

Reserve your table on the ground floor, where Jeannine trots to and fro serving regulars from the university nearby, her arms laden with rib-sticking Lyonnais specialties (tablier de sapeur, quenelles, andouillette au vin blanc) and *pots* of Morgon, Brouilly, and other Beaujolais wines drawn from the barrel. A delightful bistro run by the Moissonnier family for the last 34 years. **C** 200-300 F.

15 Au Pactole

44, bd St-Germain
46 33 31 31,
fax 46 33 07 60

Closed Sat lunch. Open until 11:45pm. No pets. V, AE, MC.

Roland Magne's lightened traditional dishes offer exceptional value, and his wife, Noëlle, is a perfectly charming hostess. What a shame that the restaurant is not fuller at lunchtime! Dinner is another matter, altogether: even François Mitterrand has been spotted here of an evening (he once brought along his food-loving friend Helmut Kohl). Connoisseurs appreciate Magne's delicious ravioli d'escargots à la crème d'ail, his succulent steak of flash-smoked cod, and one of the best ribs of beef in Paris (it's roasted in a salt crust), which can be followed by a tasty apple tart with sabayon sauce. Sharp-eyed wine buffs can unearth the occasional bargain in Le Pactole's fine cellar. **C** 250-320 F. **M** 149 F, 279 F.

11/20 Perraudin

157, rue St-Jacques
46 33 15 75

Closed lunch Sat & Mon, Sun, Aug 15-31. Open until 10:15pm. Terrace dining. Garage pkg. No cards.

This establishment is run by one of the city's specialists in homey, country-style cooking. Heartwarming Vouvray andouillette, bœuf bourguignon, and duck confit are served in a modest but charming early 1900s décor. **C** 170 F. **M** 60 F (lunch).

12/20 Le Petit Navire

14, rue des Fossés-St-Bernard
43 54 22 52

Closed Sun, Mon, 2nd wk of Feb, Aug 1-15. Open until 10:15pm. Priv rm: 30. Terrace dining. Pkg. V, AE, DC, MC.

Anchored not far from the Seine for the past twenty-odd years, Le Petit Navire regales its many regular customers with tapenade, garlicky shellfish soup, grilled sardines, and delightful growers' wines. **C** 250-350 F. **M** 150 F.

12/20 Rôtisserie du Beaujolais

19, quai de la Tournelle - 43 54 17 47, fax 44 07 12 04

Closed Mon. Open until 11:30pm. Terrace dining. Pkg. V.

Claude Terrail of the Tour d'Argent (across the road) owns this facsimile of a traditional Lyonnais bistro, a nice little place to spend a lively evening with friends. The spit-roasted Challans duck is a delight, the saucisson pistaché and the salad of boiled beef and lentils are equally delicious. Splendid cheeses, and exemplary Beaujolais (all ten *crus*) from Dubœuf. **C** 185-230 F.

16 La Timonerie

35, quai de la Tournelle - 43 25 44 42

Closed Mon lunch, Sun. Open until 10:30pm. Air cond. Pkg. V, MC.

Philippe de Givenchy continues to surprise us with his contemporary, streamlined cuisine. A trifle too trendy in its presentations (lots of clever little heaps and "bushes", now that vertical arrangements are all the rage), his cooking is saved from affectation by its use of simple, unpretentious ingredients: mackerel, pollack, inexpensive cuts of lamb and beef, offal, and pork. Another chef would make bistro chow out of foods like these, but Givenchy turns them into great modern dishes. Anyone who does what he does with hogs' jowls and a little red wine, or with a mackerel fillet and a handful of herbs, deserves our attention. Not to mention his sea bream roasted with tarragon and chilis in a tight red-wine sauce. Desserts follow the same vein: a homey repertoire glorified by virtuoso technique. The cellar is not vast, but it is perfectly à propos, with a fine selection of growers' wines. **C** 350-420 F. **M** 220 F (lunch).

18 La Tour d'Argent

15-17, quai de la Tournelle
43 54 23 31,
fax 44 07 12 04

Closed Mon. Open until 10:30pm. Priv rm: 60. Air cond. No pets. Valet pkg. V, AE, DC.

We hope the sight of those sweet little ducks and drakes bobbing on the Seine between the Ile Saint-Louis and your panoramic table doesn't take away your appetite for the best canard à l'orange you'll ever taste—a pressed duck paddling in a deeply flavorful sauce which has been a house specialty for 100 years. Chef Manuel Martinez, now a Tour d'Argent veteran, knows better than anyone how to work wonders with the web-footed fowl.

Don't expect any audacious novelties or revolutionary changes in the Tour d'Argent tradition. Owner Claude Terrail, eternally charming and diplomatic, has chosen his field of honor once and for all. And what better aide-de-camp than Martinez, battle-tested at the Relais Louis-XIII? Within the limits of a "noble"—but not boring—repertoire, he imbues his creations with such flavor and harmony that you might be too delightedly dazed to notice the astronomical bill. But then, who notices the bill when it's time to buy the Rolls and the diamonds?

You can easily waste 600 F on a ghastly meal elsewhere, and though it might seem galling to spend twice that here, you'll never question the quality of this cuisine: ravioli de foie gras et homard, ragoût de truffes, tantalizing truffled brouillade (scrambled eggs) sauce Périgourdine, crab-stuffed turbot, or a voluptuously tender double veal chop. And what of the *nec plus ultra* of ice creams, the Tour d'Argent's vanilla or pistachio? A year from now you won't have forgotten it! Nor will you forget the sight of dusk's golden light on Notre-Dame or the impressive cityscape spread out before you.

The fabled cellar harbors bottles with prices in four and even five digits—but it also holds unsung marvels costing less than 250 F. And do remember: the lunch menu is only 375 F—put aside a franc and a centime each day for a year and there you are! **C** 1,200 F and up. **M** 375 F (lunch).

14 Restaurant Toutoune

5, rue de Pontoise
43 26 56 81

Closed Mon lunch, Sun. Open until 10:45pm. V, AE.

The arrival of a new chef with a Provençal repertoire has infused fresh life into this popular spot. The 150 F single-price menu features fragrant soups, tasty terrines, snails in a garlicky tomato sauce, sea bream with zucchini, and grapefruit gratin with sabayon sauce. Lively atmosphere. **M** 150 F.

6th arrondissement

13 Chez Albert

41, rue Mazarine
46 33 22 57

Closed Aug. Open until 11pm. No pets. V, MC.

Most of the patrons don't even realize that Albert's is a Portuguese restaurant. The menu, indeed, is largely French but the tasty pork with clams, rabbit à la Ranhado, and half-dozen dishes featuring salt cod (our favorite is the one with eggs and onions) point clearly to the owner's Lusitanian origins. So does the wine list, with its Dãos and Douros. **C** 180 F. **M** 95 F.

13 Allard

41, rue St-André-des-Arts - 43 26 48 23

Closed Sun, Dec 23-Jan 3, Aug. Open until 10pm. Priv rm: 25. Air cond. V, AE, DC, MC.

Prices are starting to cool down a bit, but otherwise little has changed at Allard, from the mellow décor to the handwritten daily menu of saucisson chaud lyonnais, bœuf braisé aux carottes, turbot au beurre blanc, duck with olives, and tarte Tatin. The nostalgic ambience continues to charm the cosmopolitan patrons. **C** 300-400 F. **M** 150 F (lunch), 200 F (exc Sat lunch).

11/20 L'Arbuci

25, rue de Buci
44 41 14 14,
fax 44 41 14 10

Open daily until dawn. Priv rm: 90. Terrace dining. Air cond. V, AE, MC.

Here's a huge, often crowded brasserie specializing in fresh shellfish, decent spit-roasted poultry and meats, and banane flambée au Grand Marnier. **C** 200-270 F. **M** 72 F & 99 F (lunch, exc Sun).

13 La Bastide Odéon

7, rue Corneille
43 26 03 65

Closed 3 wks in Aug. Open until 11pm. No pets. V, MC.

New and noteworthy. Gilles Ajuelos's fresh, clever take on Provençal cooking has us salivating over every dish on the menu. Vigorous flavors distinguish his oven-roasted peppers and tomatoes served forth with crusty country bread, the thick steak of roasted cod with saffron-tinged vegetables and tangy capers, sardine roulade stuffed with herbed chèvre, and snail gnocchi with Swiss chard and garlic confit. For dessert, we like the lemon-berry feuillantine. A warmer touch would improve the rudimentary décor, but the welcome and service are charming. **C** 230 F.

13 La Bauta

129, bd du Montparnasse
43 22 52 35

Open daily until 11pm. Priv rm: 45. Terrace dining. Air cond. Garage pkg. V, MC.

A *bauta*, or carnival mask, is the emblem of this pretty restaurant that proposes a short, appealing list of Venetian specialties. Among the well-executed offerings you'll find marinated sardines, whole-wheat spaghetti topped with tiny squid, gnocchi enriched with sage butter, and crisp-fried seafood tidbits. You can finish up with an authentic tiramisù. While the food is priced within reason, the Italian wines are not. **M** 105 F & 195 F (lunch, wine incl), 200 F (wine incl).

13 Le Bélier

L'Hôtel, 13, rue des Beaux-Arts
43 25 27 22,
fax 43 25 64 81

Open daily until 1am. Priv rm: 90. Air cond. V, AE, DC, MC.

The theatrical setting, complete with a flower-decked fountain, attracts an elegant, cosmopolitan crowd. Chef Christian Schuliar's classic cuisine is occasionally inconsistent, but his salmon and sculpin in saffron aspic and the succulent sweet-and-sour duck with mushrooms are reliable bets. Prices have been scaled back considerably. **M** 120 F (lunch), 180 F (dinner).

13 Le Bistrot d'Alex

"La Foux", 2, rue Clément
43 25 77 66

Closed Sun, Dec 24-Jan 2. Open until 10pm. Priv rm: 14. Air cond. V, AE, MC.

Stéphane Guini has stepped up to the stove, to replace Alexandre, his late, lamented father. Lyon and Provence continue to inspire the bistro's zestful menu of pistachio-studded saucisson, fragrant daube de bœuf, and tasty orange flan. You can count on a delightful welcome. **C** 250-350 F. **M** 140 F, 190 F.

Les Bookinistes

53, quai des Grands-Augustins
43 25 45 94,
fax 43 25 23 07

Closed Sat lunch, Sun. Open until midnight. Priv rm: 30. Terrace dining. Air cond. Pkg. V, AE, MC.

The latest addition to Guy Savoy's successful string of bistros sports an avant-garde look that obviously suits the young, Left Bank crowd. Crowded is how you might feel in this elbow-to-elbow eatery, but don't let that diminish your enjoyment of the sweet-sour marinated duck breast flanked by yummy fig and onion marmalade, or pan-roasted cod set atop red-cabbage compote, or full-flavored steak of Angus beef. Tasty desserts, too, and brisk, professional service. **C** 220-240 F. **M** 160 F (lunch).

12/20 Brasserie Lutétia

Hôtel Lutétia,
23, rue de Sèvres
49 54 46 76

Open daily until midnight. Priv rm: 400. Air cond. Valet pkg. V, AE, DC, MC.

The no-nonsense cooking is prepared with considerable finesse in the same kitchens as Le Paris (see below). The superb seafood is attractively priced, and the satisfying bourgeois dishes (veal chop with macaroni gratin, poulet au thym) always hit the spot. **C** 200-250 F. **M** 295 F (wine incl).

Jacques Cagna

14, rue des Grands-Augustins
43 26 49 39,
fax 43 54 54 48

Closed Sat lunch, Sun, 3 wks in Aug, 1 wk at Christmas. Open until 10:30pm. Priv rm: 10. Air cond. V, AE, DC, MC.

The roaring success of his bistro annexes has not distracted Jacques Cagna from the business of pleasing the moneyed, cosmopolitan gourmets who prefer to dine at the "old original," with its ancient oak beams and woodwork, Flemish still lifes, and subdued lighting. Elegant? Yes, but this is no museum: food, drink, and—measured—merriment are perfectly at home here.

Lately Cagna has brought his essentially classic *carte* up to date with some rousing, rustic offerings and others that exhale a discreet but seductive Southern perfume. Choosing among them is a delicious dilemma: it's not easy to overlook the lush lobster with beurre blanc sauce, but neither can we resist the daube of suckling pig embellished with tomato ravioli, nor the crisp-crusted sturgeon partnered with herbed pasta in a classic sauce Choron. Dazed by all this deliciousness, we decided to try two exciting, very modern creations that recently appeared on the menu: a divine carpaccio of pearly sea bream with an invigorating garnish of caviar-strewn céleri rémoulade; and superb langoustine fritters served with vegetable "chips" and gazpacho sauce, a dish full of beguiling nuances.

Dessert? Of course! No one needs prodding to sample such superlative sweets as a fragile vacherin piled high with candied chestnuts or apple clafoutis with gingerbread ice cream.

Jacques Cagna's adorable sister, Anny, who glides among the tables dispensing smiles and good counsel, also oversees a cellar brimming with Hermitages, Côte-Rôties, and vintage Burgundies. **C** 600-900 F. **M** 260 F (lunch), 480 F.

12/20 Le Caméléon

6, rue de Chevreuse
43 20 63 43

Closed Sun, Mon, Feb, Aug. Open until 10:30pm. V, MC.

An exemplary bistro that dates from the golden age of Montparnasse, Le Caméléon serves uncomplicated, homey dishes (braised veal with fresh pasta, cod Provençal, pear clafoutis). Charming service and an excellent list of growers' wines. **C** 200-250 F.

12/20 Casa Bini

36, rue Grégoire-de-Tours - 46 34 05 60,
fax 43 25 59 62

Closed Sat lunch, Sun. Open until 11pm. V, AE, DC, MC.

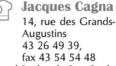

Anna Bini is uncompromising when it comes to quality. She travels all the way to Tuscany to seek out the best ingredients. Her little restaurant could easily become one of the top Italian spots in town, but Anna chooses to keep things simple, offering a limited menu of carpaccio, crostoni, and pasta. Her trendy Saint-Germain patrons are perfectly content with this tasty, uncomplicated (and rather too expensive) fare. Anna recently opened two branches of an Italian-style snack bar, Lo Spuntino (94, rue des Saints-Pères, seventh arrondissement; and 17, rue de la Banque, second arrondissement). **C** 220-245 F.

13 **Aux Charpentiers**

10, rue Mabillon
43 26 30 05

Open daily until 11:30pm. Terrace dining. V, AE, DC.

Although he is occupied by his seafood restaurant across the street (L'Écaille de PCB), Pierre Bardèche continues to serve honest home-style cooking in this former carpenters' guild hall. The menu revolves around *plats du jour* such as cod aïoli, stuffed cabbage, and veal sauté, prepared by a capable new chef. Cheerful atmosphere. **C** 180-250 F. **M** 150 F (dinner, wine incl), 100 F (lunch).

14 **Le Chat Grippé**

87, rue d'Assas
43 54 70 00

Closed Sat lunch, Mon, Aug. Open until 10:30pm. Air cond. V.

Robert Bernacchia is the owner and Michel Gallichon the new chef of Le Chat Grippé. Conservative but not fusty, the menu offers lots of delicious options, notably an oxtail salad with a zesty dressing, codfish set atop a smooth brandade (interesting contrast of textures), and tender lamb cooked to pink perfection, accented by a bright chive jus. The 160 F set lunch is most attractive, and there's a well-constructed wine list. **C** 350-450 F. **M** 160 F (weekday lunch), 235 F, 320 F.

12/20 **Dominique**

19, rue Bréa
43 27 08 80

Closed Jul 15-Aug 15. Open until 10:30pm. Priv rm: 42. Air cond. V, AE, DC, MC.

This famed Montparnasse Russian troika—takeout shop/bar/ restaurant—steadfastly refuses perestroika when it comes to cuisine and décor: purple-and-gold walls, steaming samovars, and goulash Tolstoy. Rostropovitch and Solzhenitsyn have been spotted here, sampling the delicious smoked salmon, borscht, and blinis. And there's vodka, of course, both Russian and Polish. **C** 230-340 F. **M** 80 F (lunch, exc Sun), 155 F.

14 **L'Écaille de PCB**

"Pierre et Colette Bardèche," 5, rue Mabillon
43 26 73 70,
fax 46 33 07 98

Closed Sat lunch, Sun. Open until 11pm. Priv rm: 8. Terrace dining. Air cond. V, AE.

Pierre and Colette Bardèche welcome the literary lights of this intellectual neighborhood into their warm, mahogany-lined seafood restaurant. Marinated sardines with fennel or a salad of finnan haddie and bacon are lively preludes to the popular osso buco de lotte à l'orientale, John Dory enlivened with coarse-grain mustard, or superb scallops in a creamy garlic sauce. The cellar is of only middling interest, with the exception of a fine, bone-dry Jurançon from Charles Hours. **C** 250-350 F. **M** 125 F, 190 F, 210 F.

12/20 **Chez Henri**

16, rue Princesse
46 33 51 12

Closed Sun. Open until 11:30pm. No pets. No cards.

There's no sign outside, since the trendy denizens of the Rue Princesse know just where to find Henri Poulat and his bistro specialties. The cooking can be uneven, but calf's liver with creamed onions, farm chicken in vinegar, roast lamb, and apple clafoutis are usually good bets. Nervous service. **C** 220-250 F. **M** 160 F (dinner).

12/20 **Joséphine**

"Chez Dumonet,"
117, rue du Cherche-Midi
45 48 52 40,
fax 42 84 06 83

Closed Sat, Sun, Jul. Open until 10:30pm. Terrace dining. V, MC.

Joséphine is an early-1900s bistro frequented by prominent jurists, journalists, and an intellectual theater crowd. The food isn't bad, but it used to be better: the current menu lists warm scallop salad, noisettes of lamb with a coffee-flavored sauce, roasted rabbit with sage jus, and pear millefeuille spiced with star anise. Chummy atmosphere, animated by owner Jean Dumonet, a former yachting champ. **C** 300-500 F. **M** 235 F.

Lapérouse

51, quai des Grands-Augustins
43 26 68 04,
fax 43 26 99 39

Closed Mon lunch, Sun. Open until 11pm. Priv

rm: 50. Air cond. Valet pkg. V, AE, DC.

Lapérouse, a ravishing Belle Époque landmark, has yet another new owner, still another new chef. As for the menu, it's ultraclassic, inspired by the cooking of Escoffier and Dumaine. As soon as we've sampled the timbale Augustin, tournedos Rossini, and omelette soufflée, we'll turn in our rating—stay tuned! **C** 400-800 F. **M** 200 F (lunch), 290 F, 495 F, 680 F.

11/20 Lipp

151, bd St-Germain
45 48 53 91,
fax 45 44 33 20

Open daily until 1am. Air cond. V, AE, DC, MC.

Despite the often disappointing food (choucroute, bœuf gros sel) and the cruel whims of fashion, this glossy turn-of-the-century brasserie still manages to serve some 400 to 500 customers a day. And one often catches sight of a powerful politician or a beauty queen ensconced at a ground-floor table, admiring the gorgeous décor. **C** 270-320 F.

11/20 La Lozère

4, rue Hautefeuille
43 54 26 64,
fax 44 07 00 43

Closed Sun, Mon, Jul 23-Aug 22, Dec 23-31. Open until 10:15pm. Air cond. V.

You can smell the bracing air of the rural Lozère region in the warm winter soups, herbed sausages, and pâtés served in this charming old-Paris establishment, a regional tourist office, crafts shop, and restaurant combined. **C** 180 F. **M** 91 F (weekday lunch & Sat, wine incl), 122 F & 149 F (exc Sun).

13 La Marlotte

55, rue du Cherche-Midi - 45 48 86 79

Closed Sat, Sun, Aug. Open until 11pm. Priv rm: 8. Terrace dining. Air cond. Garage pkg. V, AE, DC, MC.

The rustic, timbered setting is softened by madras upholstery and candlelight in the evening. A traditional repertoire is meticulously prepared by chef Patrick Duclos. Try his sprightly vegetable terrine, rabbit with sautéed apples, or braised veal kidney with fresh pasta, then round things off with the delectable chocolate gâteau. Crowded both at lunch and dinner, often with the smart set. **C** 250-330 F.

12/20 La Méditerranée

Place de l'Odéon
43 26 46 75,
fax 44 07 00 57

Closed May 1. Open until 11pm. Priv rm: 30. Valet pkg. V, AE, DC, MC.

Thanks to Marc Richard's deft and spirited seafood cuisine, this handsome restaurant on the Place de l'Odéon is once again afloat. The sparkling-fresh fish tartare, grilled sea bass, and bouillabaisse are all absolutely shipshape. Wide-ranging cellar. **C** 300-500 F. **M** 195 F.

13 Le Muniche

7, rue St-Benoît
42 61 12 70

Open daily until 1am. Terrace dining. Air cond. V, AE, DC, MC.

In a new location (just around the corner from its former site) the Muniche remains the liveliest, most frenetically crowded of Parisian brasseries. The Layrac brothers and their attentive, smiling staff will regale you with oysters, choucroute, thick-sliced calf's liver, and grilled pigs' ears, washed down with decent *pots* of red, white, and rosé. **C** 250-300 F. **M** 165 F.

16 Le Paris

Hôtel Lutétia,
45, bd Raspail
49 54 46 90,
fax 49 54 46 64

Closed Sat, Sun, Aug. Open until 10pm. Priv rm: 400. Air cond. Valet pkg. V, AE, DC, MC.

Philippe Renard captains the kitchens of Le Paris, a restaurant that looks for all the world like the dining room of a cruise ship. Again this year, Renard confirmed our high opinion of his inventive cuisine. Subtle, well-defined flavors distinguish his bright sorrel soup dotted with Basque country ham and grilled duck liver, his charlotte of crisp-cooked asparagus and plump crayfish, the briny duo of red mullet and lobster with truffled leeks, and braised veal shanks with mushroom-studded pasta. Note the light and luscious desserts, and the excellent 250 F prix-fixe meal. **C** 380-540 F. **M** 250 F (lunch), 495 F (wine incl), 350 F.

10/20 Le Petit Mabillon

6, rue Mabillon
43 54 08 41

Closed Sun, Mon lunch. Open until 11pm. Terrace dining. V, AE, MC.

The home-style Italian menu features two pasta choices daily (fusilli,

UNE HEURE ET DEMIE PASSEE DANS VOTRE ETABLISSEMENT EST LE PREMIER DES PRIVILEGES. LE SECOND EST D'Y BOIRE DE L'EAU D'EVIAN.

PARIS • NEW-YORK • SYDNEY • HONG-KONG • LOS ANGELES • MONTREAL • MILAN • LONDRES • STOCKHOLM • BERLIN • SINGAPOUR • TOKYO • GENEVE • SHANGHAI • BUENOS AIRES • AMSTERDAM • MEXICO • TEL-AVIV • SAINT PETERSBOURG • VIENNE • BRUXELLES • COPENHAGUE • LUXEMBOURG • SAN FRANCISCO • PEKIN • ATHENES • PRAGUE • VARSOVIE • BUDAPEST • PORT-AU-PRINCE • HELSINKI • DUBLIN • LISBONNE • SOFIA • BEYROUTH • MADRID • ROME • MOSCOU • BONN • ABIDJAN • JOHANNESBURG • LE CAP • CASABLANCA • DAKAR • DUBAI • BARCELONE • JERUSALEM • BERNE • MANILLE • BANGKOK •

EURO RSCG / HENOCQ, BENITAH & JULIEN

EVIAN. L'EAU MINERALE DES MEILLEURES TABLES DU MONDE.

Ooooh. Je t'aime!
MOËT
IMPÉRIAL
MOËT & CHANDON
CHAMPAGNE
ÉPERNAY FRANCE
WHERE CELEBRATION IS BORN™
© 1994 Schieffelin & Somerset Co., NY, NY.

lasagne), as well as carpaccio and comforting osso buco. Picturesque décor, leafy garden courtyard. **C** 160-200 F. **M** 75 F.

10/20 Le Petit Saint-Benoît

4, rue St-Benoît
42 60 27 92

Closed Sat, Sun. Open until 10pm. Terrace dining. No pets. No cards.

The crowded sidewalk terrace is a refuge for fashionable fast-food haters in search of cheap eats: hachis parmentier, bacon with lentils, bœuf bourguignon, lamb sauté. **C** 130 F.

13 Le Petit Zinc

"Les Frères Layrac,"
11, rue Saint-Benoît
42 61 20 60,
fax 45 66 47 64

Open daily until 1am. Terrace dining. Air cond. V, AE, DC, MC.

Le Petit Zinc shares the same kitchen and country cooking as the equally popular Le Muniche (see above), but with an emphasis on Southwestern specialties: oysters, shellfish, poule au pot, thick-sliced calf's liver, savory leg of lamb. In summer the terrace spreads its fluttering tablecloths across the pavement. **C** 250-300 F. **M** 165 F.

13 La Petite Cour

8, rue Mabillon
43 26 52 26,
fax 44 07 11 53

Open daily until 11:30pm (winter 11pm). Garden dining. V, MC.

Owners and chefs may come and go, but the discreet charm of this comfortable restaurant endures. Patrick Guyader is the man in the kitchen these days, and his repertoire runs to satisfying home-style dishes: sardines gratinées, turnip "choucroute" with smoked fish, and duck tucked under a blanket of mashed potatoes. **C** 300-350 F.

11/20 Polidor

41, rue Monsieur-le-Prince - 43 26 95 34

Open daily until 12:30am (Sun 11pm). No cards.

Familiar and soothing blanquettes, bourguignons, and rabbit in mustard sauce are served in a dining room that time has barely touched in more than a century. **C** 130 F. **M** 55 F (weekday lunch), 100 F.

10/20 Le Procope

13, rue de l'Ancienne-Comédie
43 26 99 20,
fax 43 54 16 86

Open daily until 1am. Priv rm: 80. Pkg. V, AE, DC, MC.

The capital's oldest café, restored to its original seventeenth-century splendor, is perhaps not your best bet for a meal. A clientele made up mainly of tourists feeds on unremarkable brasserie fare (shellfish, coq au vin) and uninspired desserts. **C** 200-350 F. **M** 99 F (lunch & until 8pm), 119 F (dinner, wine incl, from 11pm), 185 F (summer), 289 F (winter).

15 Relais Louis-XIII

8, rue des Grands-Augustins
43 26 75 96,
fax 44 07 07 80

Closed Mon lunch, Sun, Jul 25-Aug 23. Open until 10:15pm. Priv rm: 22. Air cond. V, AE, DC, MC.

Louis XIII was proclaimed King of France in this luxurious seventeenth-century tavern with its beams and polished paneling. Fresh, scrupulously classic offerings include a warm salad of truffled scallops and mushrooms, a flawless turbot enhanced with sea-urchin roe, and a rich, chocolatey palais d'or with pistachio sauce. In addition to many stupendous and shockingly expensive bottlings (1934 Latour, 1921 Quarts de Chaume), the cellar boasts a few accessibly priced wines. Note that a (nearly) affordable set meal is offered at lunch. **C** 420-560 F. **M** 190 F & 240 F (lunch), 250 F & 350 F (dinner).

13 Le Rond de Serviette

97, rue du Cherche-Midi - 45 44 01 02,
fax 42 22 50 10

Closed 1st 3 wks of Aug. Open until 11pm. Priv rm: 40. Terrace dining. V, AE, DC, MC.

You don't need a fat bank account to enjoy the 128 F prix-fixe meal (it includes coffee and a glass of wine) served in this pretty pink dining room. But even the à la carte offerings are reasonably priced: a mere 98 F buys a perfectly roasted turbotin garnished with whipped potatoes. Cheerful, professional service. **C** 220 F. **M** 128 F (wine incl), 158 F.

Remember to call ahead to reserve your table, and please, if you cannot honor your reservation, be courteous and let the restaurant know.

13 La Rôtisserie d'en Face

2, rue Christine
43 26 40 98,
fax 43 54 54 48

Closed Sat lunch, Sun. Open until 11pm. Priv rm: 20. Air cond. V, AE, DC, MC.

Jacques Cagna's smart rotisserie with its single-price menu (195 F) continues to attract Parisians hungry for rousing bistro food at reasonable prices. Start off a satisfying meal with crisp, deep-fried smelts or ravioli stuffed with escargots, then follow with thyme-showered lamb chops or spit-roasted farm chicken with mashed potatoes, and finish with an Alsatian apple tart. Whatever you choose, you'll find a frisky, inexpensive wine to accompany it from among the twenty or so on offer. There is another Rôtisserie in the seventeenth arrondissement, at 6, rue Armaillé, tel.: 42 27 19 20. **M** 195 F.

11/20 Chez Claude Sainlouis

"Le Golfe Juan,"
27, rue du Dragon
45 48 29 68

Closed Sat dinner, Sun, 2 wks at Easter, Aug. Open until 11pm. Air cond. No cards.

Reliable salads and steaks are served here in an amusing, theatrical setting. **C** 150-200 F.

15 Yugaraj

14, rue Dauphine
43 26 44 91,
fax 46 33 50 77

Closed Mon lunch. Open until 11pm. Priv rm: 18. Air cond. No pets. V, AE, DC, MC.

The best Indian restaurant in the city, hands down. We love the refined surroundings, the smiles of the formally suited waiters, and—especially—the rare delicacies culled from every province of the subcontinent. We unreservedly recommend the herbed chicken sausages redolent of mint, cumin-spiced crab balls, tender lamb that is first roasted in a tandoori oven then sautéed with herbs, or cod suavely spiced with turmeric and fenugreek: the beautifully harmonized flavors bloom subtly on the palate. To finish, try one of the refreshing ices perfumed with cardamom, pistachios, or mango pulp. **C** 230-330 F. **M** 130 F (lunch), 180 F, 220 F.

7th arrondissement

19 Arpège

"Alain Passard,"
84, rue de Varenne
45 51 47 33,
fax 44 18 98 39

Closed Sun lunch, Sat. Open until 10:30pm. Priv rm: 12. Air cond. V, AE, DC, MC.

Some call it cold, some say it's stark. But we admire Alain Passard's sleekly elegant dining room from which pictures and *bibelots* have been banished, the better to highlight honey-hued walls of warm wood and etched glass. It is true, though, that the space is small and at certain tables diners may feel hemmed in.

But Passard and his *brigade* now have plenty of elbowroom in the spacious kitchens, where they prepare some of the finest food to be had in Paris. Passard cooks in the *grand bourgeois* register, but with a jeweler's precision and the imagination of a poet. Even his more familiar creations seem new at each tasting: we're thinking of the lobster with sweet-and-sour turnips, a tuna fillet in melted butter fired with chili, rack of lamb enhanced by a truffle fondue, or rosemary-scented sweetbreads flanked by a zingy lemon purée. In season, game dishes like juniper-spiced pheasant or grilled baby boar are not to be missed. Passard's desserts (chocolate gratin perfumed with star anise, tomate confite with a dozen different spices) are as ingenious as they are seductive. Less seductive, surely, are the prices, which rocketed skyward this year. **C** 850-1,000 F. **M** 390 F (lunch), 890 F.

13 L'Auberge Bressane

16, av. La Motte-Picquet - 47 05 98 37

Closed wk of Aug 15. Open until 10:45pm. Terrace dining. Air cond. Valet pkg. V, MC.

The menu is not half so old-fashioned as the medieval décor may incline you to expect. We made a fine meal here not long ago of crispy snail fritters, a tender, beautifully cooked farm chicken with morels, and chocolate fondant with a flavorsome vanilla custard sauce. Too bad the cellar's half-bottles are so inclemently priced. **C** 230-340 F. **M** 99 F & 119 F (lunch, exc Sat).

Red toques signify modern cuisine; white toques signify traditional cuisine.

Beato

14

8, rue Malar
47 05 94 27

Closed Sun, Mon, 1 wk at Christmas, Aug. Open until 11:30pm. V, AE.

Sure, the setting and service are still starchy, but Beato's menu has visibly loosened up. Alongside the incomparable scampi fritti, shellfish soup, and noble chop of milk-fed veal, you'll now find terrific zuppa di fagioli, warming bollito misto, and tasty gnocchi with hare. It all adds up to a diverse and highly appetizing Italian repertoire. **C** 230-380 F. **M** 145 F (lunch, exc Sat).

Le Bellecour

15

22, rue Surcouf
45 51 46 93,
fax 45 50 30 11

Closed Sat lunch, Sun, Aug. Open until 10:30pm. Priv rm: 40. V, AE, DC.

Denis Croset presides over the preparation of gastronomic classics that have made this establishment—a vintage bistro with a vaguely colonial setting—a perennial favorite with the well-heeled locals. We can vouch for the langoustines perfumed with thyme blossoms, plump mushroom-stuffed ravioli, spicy poached skate, lobster risotto, and veal fillet garnished with a lively julienne of pickled lemons. The weekday set lunch is a fine value. Exciting cellar, particularly rich in Burgundies. **C** 300-400 F. **M** 160 F (weekday lunch), 250 F (weekdays), 380 F.

11/20 Le Bistrot de Breteuil

3, pl. de Breteuil
45 67 07 27,
fax 42 73 11 08

Open daily until 10:30pm. Priv rm: 50. Terrace dining. Air cond. Garage pkg. V, AE, DC, MC.

An old corner café converted into an up-to-date bistro, the Breteuil's claim to fame is an all-inclusive menu (your apéritif, coffee, and wine incur no extra charge). On a given day, it might feature salmon tartare, calf's liver in Marsala, or skate in cider-vinegar deglazing sauce. Pleasant terrace. **M** 172 F (wine incl).

Le Bourdonnais

18

113, av. de La Bourdonnais
47 05 47 96,
fax 45 51 09 29

Open daily until 11pm. Priv rm: 30. Air cond. Garage pkg. V, AE, MC.

Philippe Bardau's inspiration never flags. His current menu is a tour de force, just brimming with flavorful innovations. If you dine à la carte, why not order the creamy lobster soup underscored by a touch of tarragon and finished with a crisp cabbage beignet, then plump for a tender poached squab served with a bouquet of baby vegetables? Or try the juicy grilled salmon made more interesting still with crisp, smoky bacon. For dessert, the stuffed tangerines en chaud froid are gorgeous, light, and refreshing. At lunchtime, the 240 F menu (it even includes wine) is a paragon of generosity, featuring (for example) curried skate soup, garlicky roast lamb, and a short-crusted bitter-chocolate tart with caramel ice cream. Owner Micheline Coat, a peach of a hostess, greets newcomers as warmly as the politicos and financiers who number among her faithful customers. **C** 350-600 F. **M** 240 F (lunch, wine incl), 320 F (dinner), 420 F (tasting menu).

Clémentine

13

62, av. Bosquet
45 51 41 16

Closed Sat lunch, Sun, Aug 15-30. Open until 10:30pm. Priv rm: 25. Terrace dining. Air cond. No pets. V, MC.

Michèle and Bernard Przybyl (you're right, that's Polish) pay homage to the cuisine of their respective/adopted homes: Languedoc (duck cassoulet) and Brittany (skate with capers, lobster à la nage). The rosy décor is dandy, but the tables are still a bit too close for real comfort. **C** 250-300 F. **M** 189 F.

Duquesnoy

16

6, av. Bosquet
47 05 96 78,
fax 44 18 90 57

Closed Sat lunch, Sun, 2 wks in Aug. Open until 10:30pm. Air cond. V, AE, MC.

The top drawer of business and TV flocks to Jean-Paul Duquesnoy's comfortable little restaurant, filling both lunch and dinner sittings year round. The light touch extends from the décor and service (directed with discreet charm by Françoise Duquesnoy) to the cooking. Jean-Paul steers a skillful course between classicism and novelty, pleasing his elegant patrons with crab-stuffed zucchini blossoms, roasted sweetbreads with a peppery caramelized coating and a garnish of sautéed artichokes, and dainty babas au rhum enhanced with candied pineapple and a scoop of coconut ice cream. Exquisite wines from the Loire, Burgundy, and Côtes-du-Rhône swell the rather stiff à la carte prices. **C** 500-700 F. **M** 450 F & 550 F (weekdays, Sat dinner), 250 F (weekday lunch).

Écaille et Plume

25, rue Duvivier
45 55 06 72

Closed Feb school hols, Jul 30-Aug 28. Open until 10:30pm (hunting seas 11:30pm). Priv rm: 10. Air cond. V, MC.

Seasonal game specialties and seafood are Marie Naël's strong points: try the briny salade océane, hake with citrus fruits, foie gras en terrine with potatoes or, in its short season, Scottish grouse flambéed with single-malt whisky. The décor is cozy, the Loire wines well chosen but oh-so-expensive. **C** 250-330 F.

La Ferme Saint-Simon

6, rue Saint-Simon
45 48 35 74,
fax 40 49 07 31

Closed Sat lunch, Sun, Aug 7-16. Open until 10:15pm. Priv rm: 20. Air cond. V, AE, DC, MC.

Parliamentarians, publishing magnates, and food-loving executives savor succulent specialties in the intimate dining rooms of "the farm" (rustic only in name). The cooking is generous and traditional, but with a modern touch: lasagne d'escargots, brill with veal jus, sautéed scallops in puff pastry, fillet of roast spiced duck, and caramelized almond pastry or bitter-chocolate tart. Large and small appetites—and thick and thin wallets—will be equally satisfied. **C** 300-470 F. **M** 170 F (lunch).

La Flamberge

12, av. Rapp
47 05 91 37,
fax 47 23 60 98

Closed Aug 12-20. Open until 10:30pm. Priv rm: 25. Air cond. No pets. Valet pkg. V, AE, DC, MC.

Roger Lamazère (a professional magician before he bought into the food biz) disappeared from the Rue de Ponthieu only to pop up—hey, presto!—here on the Left Bank. He brought along the jars of truffles, foie gras en terrine, and handcrafted duck confit that won him renown in his former restaurant. Here too, costly Southwestern dishes account for the best picks on the menu (the cassoulet is memorable). The finishing touches need attention, though: the mediocre garnishes, appetizers, and petits-fours need an extra touch of magic to come level with the rest. **C** 300-500 F. **M** 160 F (weekdays, Sat dinner).

11/20 La Fontaine de Mars

129, rue St-Dominique - 47 05 46 44,
fax 45 50 31 92

Closed Sun. Open until 11pm. Priv rm: 16. Terrace dining. V.

Checked tablecloths, low prices, and hearty country food are the perennial attractions of this modest establishment (duck breast salad, chicken with morels, Southwestern-style apple pie...). To drink, try the good, inexpensive Cahors. **C** 220 F. **M** 85 F (lunch).

Le Florence

22, rue du Champ-de-Mars
45 51 52 69

Closed Sun, Aug. Open until 10:30pm. Priv rm: 10. Air cond. V, AE, DC, MC.

Charm and elegance combine to make this Italian restaurant an alluring place to dine. Frédéric Giraudeau cooks *con brio*, preparing handcrafted pasta (try the savory duck ravioli), superb sardines marinated in oil and balsamic vinegar, and tender lamb piccata flanked by a gardenful of vegetables (fava beans, artichokes, broccoli, eggplant...). Only the heavy batter coating our scampi fritti marred an excellent repast. Owner Claude Étienne oversees the superb cellar and attentive service. **C** 250-350 F. **M** 89 F (lunch), 180 F (wine incl).

Chez Françoise

Aérogare des Invalides - 47 05 49 03,
fax 45 51 96 20

Open daily until midnight. Priv rm: 45. Terrace dining. Air cond. Valet pkg. V, AE, DC, MC.

Chez Françoise is an immense subterranean restaurant, a perennial favorite with hungry parliamentarians from the neighboring Assemblée Générale. They blithely ignore the prix-fixe specials and opt instead for the pricier à la carte offerings, like duck terrine with onion compote, roast rack of lamb, poule au pot, and crème brûlée. We, on the other hand, usually choose one of the set meals, which are really a very good deal! **C** 250-400 F. **M** 148 F (exc weekday lunch, Sat dinner, wine incl), 168 F (weekday lunch), 200 F (exc weekday lunch, wine incl), 250 F (weekday dinner, Sat, wine incl).

13

Gaya Rive Gauche

44, rue du Bac
45 44 73 73,
fax 42 60 53 03

Closed Sun. Open until 11pm. No pets. V, AE, MC.

A new branch of the successful Goumard-Prunier seafood empire. Here you'll find the same ultra-fresh fish and unfussy preparations: we recommend the bracing tartare of tuna and John Dory, the pan-roast of tiny red mullet, and the suavely spiced tagine à l'orientale. **C** 250-300 F.

14

Les Glénan

54, rue de Bourgogne - 45 51 61 09

Closed Sat, Sun, 1 wk in winter, Aug. Open until 10pm. Priv rm: 20. Air cond. V, AE, MC.

The fame of Alain Passard's Arpège ought not to obscure the merits of this intimate seafood spot, situated just a few doors away. Christine Guillard manages Les Glénan with energy and charm, while the kitchen is in the capable hands of Thierry Bourbonnais. His sensitive touch brings out all the delicate nuances of his fine ingredients. The 195 F set meal, which includes a half-bottle of Loire Valley wine, features creamy scallop soup, crisp tuna fillet with herbed Belgian endive, and semolina pudding with caramelized pears. **C** 300-350 F. **M** 195 F (wine incl).

17

Jules-Verne

Tour Eiffel, second floor - 45 55 61 44,
fax 47 05 29 41

Open daily until 10:30pm. Air cond. No pets. Valet pkg. V, AE, DC, MC.

Chef Alain Reix has succeeded in putting his personal stamp on the repertoire of the high-flying Jules Verne. His is a virile, self-assured style that makes no concessions to prevailing culinary mannerisms or to the current fashion for old-fashioned fare. Each dish has a distinct personality, a "signature" purely its own. His latest menu features a rousing sauté of baby eels with garlicky dandelion greens, as well as fat grilled scallops to which olives and a fennel tart give an extra dose of sunny flavor, and a thick veal chop astutely enhanced with mellow figs and an exotic touch of coriander. The superb ingredients express all their intrinsic savors in a harmony that never falters. For a fitting finale to your feast, you can choose an outstanding apple strudel with spice ice cream, or a warm chocolate-cherry cake. **C** 600-850 F. **M** 300 F (weekday lunch), 660 F (dinner).

18

Le Divellec

107, rue de l'Université - 45 51 91 96,
fax 45 51 31 75

Closed Sun. Open until 10pm. Air cond. No pets. Valet pkg. V, AE, DC.

France's Présidents de la République—past and present—honor Jacques Le Divellec with their presence, as do press moguls, TV idols, and other high-toned patrons who fill this "yacht-club" dining room noon and night.
But let's be frank: it's not the bigwigs that make this establishment great, it's the fish! The ocean's choicest denizens show up in Jacques Le Divellec's kitchen, where he enhances their pristine flavors with skill and restraint. His scallops steamed to pearly opacity over oyster liquor, and his house-smoked sea bass roasted to moist perfection are both simple and sublime. And nowhere will you find more magnificent raw oysters and sea urchins than at Le Divellec. Of course, if your appetite craves richer fare you could plump for frogs' legs and crayfish in a classic sauce poulette, or braised John Dory with a winy ragoût of sea snails, or the wildly extravagant pressed lobster—the sauces are delicate, the seasonings admirably precise. Desserts, we're pleased to note, have improved of late, and the wine list is better than ever. **C** 700-900 F. **M** 270 F & 370 F (lunch).

13

Maison de l'Amérique Latine

217, bd St-Germain
45 49 33 23,
fax 40 49 03 94

Closed dinner Sat & Sun, Nov 16-Apr 30, Jul 29-Aug 22. Open until 10:30pm. Priv rm: 80. Terrace dining. No pets. V, AE, DC, MC.

This gorgeous town house on the Boulevard Saint-Germain boasts a terrace, a flower-filled garden, and—finally!—a chef worthy of the name. To dine here in summer, amid birdsong and fluttering leaves, on Yasuo Nanaumi's delicate prawn tempura, soy chicken, and tangerine custard soufflé, is a rare treat. To enjoy it, be sure to book your table in advance! True to its cultural vocation, the Maison features a South American wine list. **C** 300-350 F. **M** 215 F (lunch).

13 Chez Marius

5, rue de Bourgogne
45 51 79 42,
fax 47 53 79 56

Closed Aug. Open until 10:30pm. Priv rm: 55. Air cond. Pkg. V, AE, DC, MC.

Dominating the newly refitted décor of this elegant dining room is a scale model of the Palais-Bourbon—that's where the MPs who patronize Marius spend their working hours. We were surprised to find (small) scale models on our plates as well! Though ungenerously apportioned, the seafood à l'américaine, pan-roasted sea bream, and chocolate cake are full of authentic flavor. Costly cellar, heavy on Bordeaux. **C** 300-500 F. **M** 250 F (wine incl), 180 F.

18 Paul Minchelli

54, bd Latour-Maubourg - 47 05 89 86,
fax 45 56 03 84

Closed Aug. Open until 10:30pm. Air cond. V, MC.

Everyone knows Paul Minchelli: he's the man who "reinvented seafood" by stripping away meretricious sauces to reveal pure, virginal flavors. Minchelli recently shipped out of Le Duc, the celebrated restaurant he ran with his late brother, and fetched up here, in premises once occupied by Chez Les Anges. Slavik redesigned the space in a spare Art Deco style, featuring Norwegian birch, frosted glass, framed seascapes, and a huge black bar with a dozen stools for casual dining. Minchelli's culinary minimalism requires fish of optimal quality and freshness. He has few equals when it comes to choosing, for example, a sea bass that is perfectly delicious even in its raw state, merely sliced into strips and drizzled with olive oil; or tuna served en tartare with just a bit of crunchy sea fennel for garnish; or sea whelks poached for a brief moment in court-bouillon (they bear no relation to the rubbery mouthfuls encountered elsewhere); or salmon adorned only with a sprinkling of sea salt. Depending on what the tide brings in, Minchelli might choose to pay tribute to a special creature from the deep: lobster, for instance, could be offered in six or seven different guises. In one memorable version, the crustacean is flavored with a touch of honey and chili, and presented with its caramelized juices mixed into al dente bow-tie pasta. Prices here are more moderate than they were at Le Duc, including the tariffs posted on the fine wine list. **C** 350-550 F.

13 Montalembert

3, rue de Montalembert - 45 48 68 11,
fax 42 22 58 19

Open daily until 10:30pm. Priv rm: 20. Terrace dining. Air cond. No pets. Valet pkg. V, AE, DC, MC.

Publishers, writers, and antique dealers frequent this hushed, stylish dining room, where a young chef trained by Alain Passard provides an attractive prix-fixe lunch. The à la carte choices are reasonable too; especially good are the herbally fragrant ravioles de langoustine, pikeperch roasted with bone marrow, and the juicy veal chop showered with wild mushrooms. **C** 260-320 F. **M** 175 F (weekday lunch, Sat).

12/20 L'Œillade

10, rue St-Simon
42 22 01 60

Closed Sat lunch, Sun, hols. Open until 11pm. Priv rm: 70. Air cond. Pkg. V, MC.

The single-price menu looks reasonable enough, and the salmon-stuffed crêpes with avocado mousse, spareribs with lentils, and rum-raisin pudding are perfectly decent; but beware of the expensive wine list, which could send your bill right through the roof! **M** 160 F, 195 F.

15 Le Petit Laurent

38, rue de Varenne
45 48 79 64,
fax 42 66 68 59

Closed Sat lunch, Sun, Aug. Open until 10:15pm. V, AE, DC, MC.

Robust cooking is served here in an ultraclassic, comfortable Louis XVI décor. Try the terrine of sweetbreads, the pikeperch with onions in Bourgueil wine, or the roast sea bream with lemon and mango: you'll appreciate, as we do, their precise, clearly defined flavors. Cheerful Sylvain Pommier is making an admirable effort to keep prices down. In fact, his appetizing 175 F menu is one of the best deals on the Left Bank. **C** 300-400 F. **M** 175 F, 240 F.

11/20 La Petite Chaise

36, rue de Grenelle
42 22 13 35

Open daily until 11pm. Priv rm: 50. Terrace dining. Garage pkg. V.

This charming little restaurant has been serving since the days of Louis XIV (1680). Sit elbow-to-elbow with university students and publishing people and tuck into the fixed-price menu: onion pizza with a flaky crust, steak with Roquefort butter, saumon au beurre blanc are typical offerings. **M** 170 F (wine incl).

15 Le Récamier

4, rue Récamier
45 48 86 58,
fax 42 22 84 76

Closed Sun. Open until 10:30pm. Priv rm: 14. Garden dining. Air cond. Garage pkg. V, AE, DC, MC.

Courtly Martin Cantegrit, owner of this elegant Empire-style establishment, has worked with chef Robert Chassat for more than fifteen years, a most felicitous union. Burgundian classics (game pâtés, jambon persillé, beef bourguignon with fresh tagliatelle) flank subtly lightened dishes (tiny scallops with mushrooms, pan-roasted tuna with pesto sauce), and a top-notch apple tart. Cantegrit's farm supplies the fresh produce. Le Récamier's clientele—politicians, publishers, and media moguls—also enjoy tapping the 100,000-bottle cellar, surely one of the city's best. In summer the restaurant's lovely terrace spills across a sheltered pedestrian zone for fume-free outdoor dining. **C** 400-600 F.

13 Chez Ribe

15, av. de Suffren
45 66 53 79,
fax 47 83 79 63

Closed Sat lunch, Sun. Open until 10:30pm. Priv rm: 30. Terrace dining. Garage pkg. V, AE, DC, MC.

You can still eat here for not much more than 200 F, including a Bordeaux *primeur* or a tasty little white Saumur. Granted, a 168 F prix-fixe meal is not—yet—hard to find, even in Paris, but the frequently changing menu is reliably delicious and well prepared. Recent options have included a tasty terrine de canard, plaice with fresh pasta, and rack of lamb with mild garlic, all graciously served in turn-of-the-century surroundings. **M** 168 F.

14 Tan Dinh

60, rue de Verneuil
45 44 04 84,
fax 45 44 36 93

Closed Sun, Aug. Open until 11pm. No cards.

Tan Dinh's huge wine list has few equals, even among the city's top restaurants—some say it outclasses the food. But Robert and Freddy Vifian are justly proud of their innovative Vietnamese repertoire, which spotlights light and refined dishes like smoked-goose dumplings, lobster toast, shrimp rolls, chicken with Asian herbs, or veal with betel nuts. If you can resist the cellar's pricier temptations, a dinner here amid the select and stylish Left-Bank crowd need not lead to financial disaster. **C** 300-500 F.

11/20 Thoumieux

79, rue St-Dominique - 47 05 49 75

Open daily until midnight. Priv rm: 110. Air cond. No pets. V.

A busy, popular bistro where you can tuck into the hearty classics of Auvergne and the Southwest: terrines, cassoulets, duck breast with blackcurrants, etc. Don't overlook the fine boudin noir, or the cheap-and-cheerful wine list. The dinner crowd is surprisingly glossy. **C** 230 F. **M** 67 F.

13 Vin sur Vin

20, rue de Montessuy - 47 05 14 20

Closed Sun, lunch Sat & Mon, Dec 23-Jan 3, Aug 7-21. Open until 10pm. V.

Former sommelier Patrice Vidal has assembled a first-rate cellar made up exclusively of growers' wines, from which he selects a few each week to sell by the glass. They accompany such sturdy bistro standbys as escargots en croûte, veal and vegetable stew, and a tasty pear and chocolate tart. Prices are high and climbing, however, with no prix-fixe relief in sight. **C** 330-430 F.

Restaurant names in red draw attention to restaurants that offer a particularly good value.

8th arrondissement

12/20 Al Ajami

58, rue François-Ier
42 25 38 44,
fax 42 56 60 08

Open daily until midnight. Terrace dining. Air cond. V, AE, DC, MC.

Fortunately the menu's perfunctory French offerings are outnumbered by authentic dishes from the Lebanese highlands—assorted mezes, chawarma, keftedes, and deliciously sticky pastries. The wines contribute a dash of local color to the refined, gray-and-blue dining room. **M** 99 F (weekday lunch), 119 F (weekdays), 149 F.

12/20 L'Alsace

39, av. des Champs-Élysées
43 59 44 24,
fax 42 89 06 62

Open daily 24 hours. Terrace dining. Air cond. Garage pkg. V, AE, DC, MC.

Since this lively brasserie never closes, you can go there any time at all to enjoy perfect oysters, delicious sauerkraut, and the fresh white wines of Alsace. Expect a hospitable welcome, whatever the hour. **C** 200-400 F. **M** 185 F.

17 Les Ambassadeurs

Hôtel de Crillon,
10, pl. de la Concorde - 44 71 16 16,
fax 44 71 15 02

Open daily until 10:30pm. Priv rm: 72. Terrace dining. Air cond. No pets. Valet pkg. V, AE, DC, MC.

The magnificent and intimidating dining room, rich with gilt and marble, seems more fitting for an ambassadors' banquet than an intimate dinner or convivial feast. Diners keep their voices low and their elbows off the table; looks of terror accompany the accidental fall of a fork. Happily, Christian Constant's vivid cuisine goes far to warm up the formal setting. His velouté of Jerusalem artichokes topped with calf's-foot jelly, peppered whiting on polenta with crushed black olives, and sautéed pollack with puréed white beans share an earthy directness that whets the appetite. In a more modern register, he turns out an admirable confit de foie gras with fig purée, a superb sea bream with lemon and fennel, and a truly marvelous double veal chop tenderly simmered in its juices, escorted by braised baby vegetables. The excellent wine list can make an already stiff bill harder to swallow, but sommelier Jean-Claude Maître can usually recommend some more affordable selections. **C** 550-700 F. **M** 340 F (business menu, weekday lunch), 610 F (tasting menu, exc weekday lunch).

11/20 Aux Amis du Beaujolais

28, rue d'Artois
45 63 92 21,
fax 45 62 70 01

Closed Sat (summer), Sun, 1 wk in Aug, Christmas-New Year's day. Open until 9pm. Priv rm: 90. Air cond. Garage pkg. V.

The full gamut of French bistro food is represented here—poule au riz, rabbit in mustard sauce, calf's head, or catch of the day—washed down with one of the ten tasty *crus* of Beaujolais, which the jolly owner bottles himself. Friendly prices, full plates, forgettable décor. **C** 150-200 F.

The milk of Sacré-Cœur

An evergreen favorite with amateur artists and the most popular subject of Parisian postcards, the Sacré-Cœur owes its dazzling whiteness to a stone that secretes a milky substance when it rains. Whether you love or loathe its striking Byzantine architecture, it's hard to escape the basilica, which stands atop the highest point of Montmartre. It took more than 40 years to build and since its consecration in 1919 a continuous succession of faithful volunteers have been praying round the clock to atone for the sins of humanity. Climb up to the dome for a sweeping view that takes in Montmartre cemetery and a patchwork of private walled gardens.

14 **L'Avenue**
41, av. Montaigne
40 70 14 91,
fax 49 52 08 27
Open daily until midnight. Priv rm: 75. Air cond. Pkg. V, AE.

If you book a table in the elegant upstairs dining room, you can mingle with the chic couture and media crowd that flocks into L'Avenue for Christian Hennin's stylish specialties: sea bream with tomato chutney, spicy grilled scampi, lamb noisettes with pistou ravioli, and robust *plats du jour.* Desserts are vastly improved, and the cellar holds lots of unpretentious but tasty little wines. Indeed, considering the classy location at the corner of Avenue Montaigne and Rue François-Ier (the heart of the Golden Triangle), prices are downright reasonable. **C** 220-320 F.

12/20 **Bice**
Hôtel Balzac,
6, rue Balzac
42 89 86 34,
fax 42 25 24 82
Closed Sat lunch, Sun, Dec 22-Jan 2, Aug 4-Sep 1. Open until 11:30pm. Priv rm: 40. Air cond. Pkg. V, AE, DC, MC.

Amiable Italian (or Italian-style) waiters leap and dash among the young, moneyed clientele (Saint-Tropez, *prêt-à-porter,* the Levant) that forgathers in this refined, blond-wood version of Harry's Bar. If you choose carefully—trofie (house-made pasta), osso buco with risotto alla milanese—you won't be disappointed. Other options tend to be bland and/or overcooked, with the exception of the nicely handled desserts. In any case it's a pricey *pasto,* friends, and the Italian wines are expensive too. **C** 350-450 F.

13 **Le Bistrot du Sommelier**
97, bd Haussmann
42 65 24 85,
fax 53 75 23 23
Closed Sat, Sun, Dec 25-Jan 2, Aug. Open until 11pm. Priv rm: 25. Air cond. V, AE, MC.

Crowned "World's Best Sommelier" in 1992, owner Philippe Faure-Brac naturally encourages his chef to cook with wine. Thus, the menu features Bresse chicken au vin du Jura, ris de veau au maury, and rabbit with tiny onions in Chablis. But it's the cellar that captures the true wine buff's interest, with bottles from all over France—and the world. At dinner, a special prix-fixe meal brings six dishes paired with compatible wines. **C** 300-400 F. **M** 370 F (dinner, wine incl).

12/20 **Le Bœuf sur le Toit**
34, rue du Colisée
43 59 83 80,
fax 45 63 45 40
Open daily until 2am. Air cond. V, AE, DC, MC.

From a seat on the mezzanine watch the dazzling swirl of diners and waiters reflected a hundredfold in this mirrored, Art Deco dining room. But don't get so distracted that you can't enjoy the plentiful shellfish platters, the juicy steak with shallots, or the fruity young wines served in *pichets.* **C** 200-300 F. **M** 109 F (lunch, wine incl), 185 F (after 10pm, wine incl).

15 **Le Bristol**
Hôtel Bristol,
112, rue du Fg-St-Honoré
42 66 91 45,
fax 42 66 68 68
Open daily until 10:30pm. Priv rm: 60. Air cond. No pets. Valet pkg. V, AE, DC, MC.

The atmosphere and prices are about what you'd expect in this heavily guarded hotel near the French President's residence. Seated in the sumptuous wood-paneled dining room or on the garden patio, you'll be served predictably luxurious food (lobster salad, médaillons de Saint-Pierre, tropical fruit laced with Kirsch). The idyll, alas, is sometimes marred by an inattentive waiter or an occasional culinary lapse. The cellar, as you doubtless have guessed, boasts a breathtaking array of expensive vintages. **C** 600-850 F. **M** 330 F, 450 F, 620 F.

12/20 **Cap Vernet**
82, av. Marceau
47 20 95 36
Closed Dec 24-25. Open until midnight. Air cond. V, AE, MC.

The 100 F set meal, revised every day, brings such appetizing dishes as a deliciously minty sardine tabbouleh followed by whiting fillet with gnocchi and floating island with green-apple coulis. Fish and shellfish assortments dominate the à la carte offerings. **C** 250-370 F. **M** 158 F (exc Mon lunch, wine incl), 100 F.

15 Le Carpaccio
Hôtel
Royal Monceau,
35-39, av. Hoche
42 99 98 90,
fax 42 99 89 94

Closed Aug. Open until 10:30pm. Air cond. No pets. Valet pkg. V, AE, DC, MC.

Executives in expensive suits are the backbone of Le Carpaccio's sleek clientele. Here, in a spectacular winter-garden setting, they feed on scallops wreathed in smoked ham with fava-bean purée, shellfish and assorted fresh vegetables encased in the lightest imaginable tempura batter, dusky cuttlefish tagliatelle topped with spears of crisp asparagus, and an improbably good raspberry-vinegar gelato. Outrageously priced, these fine dishes (and excellent wines) are served by a rather haughty staff. **C** 450-550 F. **M** 270 F (lunch).

13 Casa Sansa
45, rue des Mathurins - 42 65 81 62,
fax 44 94 00 44

Open daily until 1am. Priv rm: 35. Terrace dining. Air cond. Garage pkg. V, AE, MC.

Jean-Marie Pujades is the jovial host of this Catalan outpost, an exuberantly decorated dining room where the fiesta never stops. Suitably vibrant specialties include escalivada (a salad of oven-roasted vegetables), suquet de peix (a lusty seafood stew), squid presented either roasted (a la planxa) or stewed in their ink, escargots à la catalane, and boles de picolat (meatballs in a zesty sauce). The region's heady wines make ideal partners for the food. **C** 170-250 F. **M** 78 F (weekday lunch), 250 F.

12/20 Caviar Kaspia
17, pl.
de la Madeleine
42 65 33 32,
fax 42 66 60 11

Closed Sun. Open until 12:30am. Priv rm: 25. Air cond. V, AE, DC.

The fine-feathered folk who frequent this dark but charming upper room opposite the Madeleine come to nibble (caviars, salmon roe, smoked sturgeon) rather than feast (smoked fish assortments, borscht, etc.). But all the offerings, large and small, are quite good and are courteously served. Vodka, naturally, is the tipple of choice. **C** 300-500 F.

17 Chiberta
3, rue A.-Houssaye
45 63 77 90,
fax 45 62 85 08

Closed Sat, Sun, Aug. Open until 11pm. Air cond. No pets. V, AE, DC, MC.

Along with Fouquet's, Chiberta is the only haunt of *le Tout-Paris* left on the Champs Élysées. Nabobs from the worlds of finance and television gather here for lunch, relayed by the *beau monde* in the evening. The dining room is discreet, the modern décor is aging gracefully, the floral displays are as sumptuous as ever, and the food has never been better. Chef Philippe Da Silva executes a menu that highlights sublime sauces and sophisticated herbs and seasonings. Among his recent successes are a salad of red mullet with a coriander jus, pan-seared tuna given a lively touch of chive, turbot braised with bay leaves in a Riesling-based sauce, and stuffed poussin roasted with chanterelles. Along with desserts like the bright grapefruit soup with forest honey and pineapple sorbet, these dishes attest to Da Silva's finesse and polished technique. Proprietor Louis-Noël Richard's passion for red Burgundies is infectious—and fatal for one's bank account! **C** 500-800 F. **M** 290 F.

14 Clovis
Hôtel Sofitel, 4, av.
Bertie-Albrecht
45 61 15 32,
fax 42 25 36 81

Closed Sat, Sun, hols, Dec 22-Jan 2, Jul 28-Aug 28. Open until 10:30pm. Priv rm: 70. Air cond. Valet pkg. V, AE, DC, MC.

The understated salmon-pink setting is particularly suited to business lunches, a fact that has not escaped the city's executives. Chef Dominique Roué has revved up the house repertoire with a perfectly cooked sole fillet abetted by spiced olives and basmati rice, lake char in a sour-cream sauce with Belgian endive, and an array of delicate desserts (try the macaron malaga). Extensive cellar; attentive service. **C** 350-480 F. **M** 190 F (dinner), 210 F.

14 La Couronne
Hôtel Warwick,
5, rue de Berri
45 63 14 11,
fax 45 63 75 81

Closed Sat lunch, Sun, hols, Aug. Open until 10:30pm. Priv rm: 100. Air cond. Valet pkg. V, AE, DC, MC.

Winner of international cooking awards, Paul Van Gessel is in top form these days. A bright Southern touch marked a recent meal here, composed of succulently tender lamb with Niçois vegetables and cracked-wheat salad, a langoustine ragoût with crisp little artichokes and asparagus, and a rich bitter-chocolate cake. The dining room, unfortunately, is stuck into a corner of the Hotel Warwick lobby; that's a shame, because Van Gessel's fine work deserves a larger audience than hotel guests and the business-lunch crowd. **C** 350-480 F. **M** 220 F, 270 F.

13 Diep

55, rue P.-Charron
45 63 52 76,
fax 42 56 46 56

Open daily until midnight. Air cond. No pets. Valet pkg. V, AE, DC, MC.

This is the flagship of the Diep family's restaurant fleet. The décor is Bangkok swank and the food Asian eclectic, but your best bets are the vibrantly spiced and herbed Thai dishes. You'll make a memorable feast if you order the steamed stuffed crab with plum sauce, pork satay dressed with a sweet vinaigrette, giant shrimp sautéed with basil and onions, and the lipsmacking Thai rice dotted with bits of chicken and shellfish. Desserts are not Diep's strong suit: enough said. **C** 250-310 F. **M** 420 F (for 2), 780 F (for 4).

Gault Millau's ratings are based solely on the restaurants' cuisine. We do not take into account the atmosphere, décor, service and so on; these are commented upon within the review.

11/20 Drugstore des Champs-Élysées

133, av. des Champs-Élysées
47 23 54 34,
fax 47 23 00 96

Open daily until 2am. Priv rm: 300. Terrace dining. Air cond. No pets. V, AE, MC.

Believe it or not, the food at this landmark of 1960s chic is not bad at all. The main-course salads, grills, and crisp pommes frites go very well with the noisy, bustling atmosphere. **C** 150-300 F.

14 Chez Edgard

4, rue Marbeuf
47 20 51 15,
fax 47 23 94 29

Closed Sun, Aug 1-16. Open until 12:30am. Priv rm: 38. Terrace dining. Valet pkg. V, AE, DC.

Just because it has often been said that the *gratin* of French politics eats here, don't expect to see Édouard Balladur or Jacques Chirac seated across from you. "Monsieur Paul" serves up to 500 meals here each day, and in any case the Parisian powers-that-be are always whisked off to the quiet private rooms upstairs. Downstairs, amid the typically Gallic brouhaha, the rest of us can choose from a wide range of dishes, from fresh thon à la basquaise to onglet à l'échalote, all prepared with care and skill. **C** 250-350 F. **M** 250 F, 295 F & 355 F (wine incl).

16 Les Élysées du Vernet

Hôtel Vernet,
25, rue Vernet
44 31 98 00,
fax 44 31 85 69

Closed Sat, Sun, hols, Dec 25-31, Jul 31-Aug 31. Open until 10pm. Priv rm: 22. Air cond. No pets. Valet pkg. V, AE, DC, MC.

Which way to the Riviera please? We'd suggest this elegant address just off the Champs-Élysées. Although you won't have a view of the Mediterranean, chef Alain Solivérès brings the fragrances and flavors of Provence into the glass-roofed dining room. Why not whet your appetite with a dish of brandade-stuffed red peppers before you move on to a magnificent dish of fresh crab with pumpkin gnocchi perfumed by pungent pistou, or a pinkly roasted pigeon flanked by a hachis of its giblets and black olives. To wind things up, try the bitter-chocolate ravioli, a clever and delicious conceit. Competent, attentive service; reasonably priced cellar. **C** 360-580 F. **M** 290 F (weekday lunch), 420 F (weekday dinner).

13 L'Étage Baumann

15, rue Marbeuf
47 20 11 11,
fax 47 23 69 65

Closed wk of Aug 15. Open until 12:30am. Priv rm: 22. Air cond. Valet pkg. V, AE, DC.

The name is new and so is the freshly refurbished décor, but the menu still features glossy fresh shellfish, colossal choucroutes (topped with fish, or ham shanks, or confit de canard...), and expertly aged meats from Scotland and Southwest France. We like the chocolate cake, too, and the thirst-quenching Alsatian wines. **C** 180-300 F. **M** 118 F, 150 F.

13

Fakhr el Dine

3, rue Q.-Bauchart
47 23 74 24,
fax 47 27 11 39

Open daily until midnight. Air cond. V, AE, DC, MC.

Delicious Lebanese mezes dazzle the eye as they delight the palate: bone-marrow salad, brains in lemon sauce, spinach fritters, fried lamb's sweetbreads, etc. These tidbits are offered in batches of 8, 10, 15, or 20, depending on the size of the company and your appetite. **C** 300-400 F. **M** 250 F (Sun, lunch weekday & Sat, wine incl), 190 F (exc Sat dinner), 335 F & 385 F (wine incl), 150 F (lunch).

14

La Fermette Marbeuf 1900

5, rue Marbeuf
47 20 63 53,
fax 40 70 02 11

Open daily until 11:30pm. Terrace dining. Air cond. V, AE, DC, MC.

Owner Jean Laurent now pours wines from his personal vineyard in Ramatuelle for his celebrity pals (and the rest of us), who flock to the Fermette for honest, unpretentious fare: andouillette sausage, sole beurre blanc, fillet steak, and so on. Moderate prices, quality foodstuffs, and affable service are the rule in the stunning Salle 1900, an Art Nouveau masterpiece. The fine 160 F set menu is now served both noon and night. **C** 280-320 F. **M** 160 F.

14

Finzi

182, bd Haussmann
45 62 88 68

Closed Sun lunch, hols. Open until 11pm. Air cond. V.

Finzi is a sleek Italian eatery that owes its enviable success to a diverse and appealing menu. Some fifteen excellent pastas top the list, ranging from an odd lamb-stuffed variety which also involves pineapple and curry, to spaghetti topped with cockles. But there are also seven kinds of tasty carpaccio, an array of Italian hams and salamis, and lemony veal scalloppine with spinach. For dessert, try the apricot ravioli with custard sauce. Swift, smiling service; pricey wines. **C** 180-280 F.

13

Flora Danica

142, av. des Champs-Élysées
44 13 86 26

Closed Christmas eve, May 1. Open until 11pm. Priv rm: 60. Terrace dining. Air cond. V, AE, DC, MC.

Salmon—smoked, pickled, marinated, or grilled—and delicious tender herring prepared in every imaginable way are the stars of this limited menu. Upstairs, more elaborate (and costly) dishes are served (there's an interesting terrine of foie gras and reindeer). If the weather is fine, ask to be seated on the patio behind the Flora Danica. **C** 220-400 F. **M** 200 F (beer incl), 270 F.

13

Fouquet's

99, av. des Champs-Élysées
47 23 70 60,
fax 47 20 08 69

Open daily until 1am. Priv rm: 160. Terrace dining. Valet pkg. V, AE, DC.

After a bout of bad publicity, Fouquet's seems poised for a fresh departure. This listed landmark on the Champs-Élysées (in whose recent revamp Fouquet's played an important part) has acquired the services of Philippe Dorange, one of Jacques Maximin's star pupils. He supervises an attractive menu (roast cod served with white-bean purée, marinated scallops rémoulade...) executed by Laurent Broussier. Fouquet's owners now hope to lure back the fashionable lunchers who have gravitated down the Champs to the Cercle Ledoyen. Here's wishing them luck... **C** 350-450 F. **M** 330 F, 350 F, 400 F, 450 F.

10/20 Chez Francis

7, pl. de l'Alma
47 20 86 83,
fax 47 20 43 26

Open daily until 1am. Priv rm: 60. Terrace dining. Air cond. Valet pkg. V, AE, DC, MC.

The smart patrons are reflected and multiplied by rows of engraved mirrors—so much the better for them, since they obviously take more pleasure in whom they're seeing than in what they're eating (though the canard en daube au gratin de macaroni is quite good, as are the shellfish). **C** 200-350 F. **M** 180 F.

11/20 Germain

19, rue J.-Mermoz
43 59 29 24

Closed Sat, Sun. Open until 9:30pm. No pets.

One of the last bastions of French home cooking anywhere near the Champs-Élysées, this 30-seat restaurant offers beef bourguignon, coq au vin, etc. at popular prices. **C** 180 F.

16

Le Grenadin

44-46, rue de Naples
45 63 28 92,
fax 45 61 24 76

Closed Sat (exc dinner Sep-Apr), Sun. Open until 10:30pm. Priv rm: 14. Air cond. Pkg. V, AE, DC, MC.

Patrick Cirotte's newly refurbished dining room is more in tune with his intrepid, good-humored cuisine. Pungent herbs and bold harmonies are the hallmarks of his current repertoire. Cirotte's affinity for keen, acidulous flavors is evident in his crab rillettes with leeks in a sprightly vinaigrette, a salad of cabbage and sea urchins, or veal fillet flanked by asparagus and kumquats. But he can also strike a suave note, as in a saddle of rabbit cloaked with a mild, creamy garlic sauce. Desserts don't get short shrift either: his rich chocolate cake with pumpkin coulis, thin sugar tart with tea ice cream, and flawless millefeuille tempt even flagging appetites. Mireille Cirotte offers reliable advice on wine (note that Sancerres are the pride of her cellar). Just next door is Berry's, Cirotte's successful, value-priced bistro annex. **C** 380-430 F. **M** 188 F, 238 F, 298 F, 320 F.

15

Le Jardin des Cygnes

Hôtel
Prince de Galles,
33, av. George-V
47 23 55 11,
fax 47 20 96 92

Open daily until 10:30pm. Priv rm: 180. Garden dining. Air cond. No pets. Valet pkg. V, AE, DC, MC.

Four months of extensive redecorating have resulted in a newly spacious yet cozy dining room that opens onto a charming patio. It's an alluring stage for Dominique Cécillon's sunny, flavorful cuisine. Recent offerings have included ravioles of foie gras with peppery goat cheese, a subtly spiced pigeon pastilla, pan-roasted red mullet with Provençal vegetables, and white-bean cassoulet enriched with red mullet, lobster, and scallops. All are very nearly as delicious as they are expensive, and are delivered to your table by a high-class staff. If economy is your aim, head over instead to the hotel's Regency Bar, for a good, light little meal. **C** 350-600 F. **M** 260 F (exc Sun lunch), 240 F (Sun lunch).

17

Le Jardin du Royal Monceau

Hôtel
Royal Monceau,
35, av. Hoche
42 99 98 70,
fax 42 99 89 94

Open daily until 10:30pm. Garden dining. Air cond. No pets. Heated pool. Valet pkg. V, AE, DC, MC.

You step into another world when you enter the candy-pink dining room, its french windows opening onto manicured lawns and immaculate flower beds. Surrounded by buildings, this garden seems to have been brought to central Paris by the wave of a magic wand. The same spell operates in the kitchen, where Bruno Cirino, a Southern chef of considerable gifts, conjures up radiantly flavorful Provençal fare.

Cirino is no recent convert to this now familiar repertoire. Provençal cooking is his birthright, and he has a native's knack for finding the foodstuffs that make his cuisine unimpeachably authentic. Like the asparagus (thick as tree trunks!) that compose, along with tiny artichokes and haricots verts, a sumptuous vegetable starter dressed with truffled vinaigrette. Or the chapon de mer and galinette, Mediterranean fishes that he respectively braises in a saffron-stained broth or pan-roasts with squid, green garlic, tomatoes, and picholine olives.

Luscious fruit desserts display the same sunny spirit: braised burlat cherries, verbena-scented baked peaches, pineapple perfumed with lemongrass and swirled with lime sabayon... Service is impeccable, and a youthful sommelier provides sound advice on a wine list studded with such rarities as an amazing late-harvested Sancerre. **C** 490-700 F. **M** 290 F (weekday lunch), 390 F (weekday dinner).

15

Lasserre

17, av. F.-Roosevelt
43 59 53 43,
fax 45 63 72 23

Closed Mon lunch, Sun, Jul 30-Aug 28. Open until 10:30pm. Priv rm: 56. Air cond. No pets. Valet pkg. V, AE, MC.

One of the few surviving examples of *le grand restaurant à la française*, this grandiose establishment merits your attention for the ethnological interest it presents. Nowhere else is the service so minutely choreographed, the atmosphere so festive yet well-bred (piano music, soft lights, glowing silver, silken carpets...). Don't forget to look up as Lasserre's retractable roof brings you (weather and visibility permitting) the stars. As you look back down you'll notice that the menu is a compendium of costly culinary clichés: duck à l'orange, tournedos béarnaise, and crêpes flambées (too often marred, lately, by heavy sauces and overcooking). But no matter how hard you look at the wine list, you won't find a bottle priced under 300 F! **C** 700-1,000 F.

17

Laurent

41, av. Gabriel
42 25 00 39,
fax 45 62 45 21

Closed Sat lunch, Sun, hols. Open until 11pm. Priv rm: 84. Terrace dining. No pets. Valet pkg. V, AE, DC, MC.

The economic climate is warming up! At Laurent this welcome change in the weather has brought smiles back to the waiters' faces, and the *carte*, too, reflects the sunnier trend, with lighter dishes and sprightlier sauces. Philippe Braun executes a menu designed by his mentor, Joël Robuchon, which includes fresh anchovies on a bed of fresh-tasting vegetable brunoise, duck liver set atop black beans fired up with hot chilis, and a superb veal chop escorted by tender hearts of lettuce in a savory jus. Now, you may have to sell off a few T-bonds to pay the bill—or else you can do as many of the other high-powered patrons do, and order the excellent 380 F prix-fixe menu. Whatever course you choose, sommelier Patrick Lair will advise you on the appropriate wine. **C** 800-1,000 F. **M** 380 F.

13

Cercle Ledoyen

Carré
des Champs-Élysées
47 42 23 23,
fax 47 42 55 01

Closed Sat, Sun, Aug. Open until 10:30pm. Air cond. Garage pkg. Valet pkg. V, MC.

Jacques Grange is the man behind the elegantly spare interior of this spacious restaurant, now a favorite haunt of the city's chic and famous. Jean-Paul Arabian oversees the impeccable service, while Ghislaine Arabian does the same for the concise menu. Zesty starters like mackerel in white wine or salmon with horseradish segue into baked bass with roasted apples or rabbit chasseur, and such toothsome sweets as tiramisù or dôme au chocolat. Irrigated by modest but tasty little wines, these offerings add up to perfectly modern meals at a perfectly moderate price. **C** 250-300 F.

18

Ledoyen

Carré des Champs-Élysées
47 42 23 23,
fax 47 42 55 01

Closed Sat, Sun, Aug. Open until 10:30pm. Priv rm: 150. Air cond. Valet pkg. V, AE, DC, MC.

Lille's Ghislaine Arabian, whom we once dubbed "the best *cuisinière* in the North," has proved her mettle at the luxurious and eminently Parisian Ledoyen. After introducing the locals to Flemish flavors—sauces laced with beer and gin, smoked mussels, gingerbread, and pungent North-country cheeses—she has shown that she can also work wonders outside of her regional register. Thus, while Ghislaine's signature dishes (crispy hops fritters, crayfish with toasted barley, waffles topped with ice cream redolent of cherry-flavored kriek beer) hold their own on the menu, she balances them with, for example, a tarragon-scented Breton lobster with marinated lettuce, warm calf's head sausage with firm little potatoes, sweet-and-sour duck with rhubarb, and a startlingly good chaud-froid of lightly smoked chicken. Desserts are dazzlingly original. Where else could one find gingerbread and caramelized pears gratinéed with fromage blanc, or a sweet potato simmered to melting tenderness in gueuze beer, or a crème brûlée of incomparable suavity, perfumed with cinnamon and orange? Such marvels have their price, of course, but we say they're worth it! **C** 550-950 F. **M** 290 F (weekday lunch), 520 F (weekdays), 590 F, 750 F.

Lucas-Carton

9, pl. de la Madeleine - 42 65 22 90,
fax 42 65 06 23

Closed Sat lunch, Sun, Dec 22-Jan 4, Jul 29-Aug 25. Open until 10:30pm. Priv rm: 14. Air cond. No pets. Valet pkg. V, MC.

Two camps—one violently pro, the other determinedly con—have turned the Gault Millau office into a battlefield! The bone of contention? The famous half-point that is our highest accolade, our recognition of a chef's supremecy over all but a handful of his peers. One camp avers that Alain Senderens deserves the honor; the adverse camp just as adamantly refuses to bestow it. And since unanimity is our rule for awarding the coveted 19.5, we've arrived at an unprecedented compromise: we're giving Senderens four toques—but no numerical rating. For the record, here's the gist of the opposing arguments.

Not even the naysayers question Senderens's prodigious talent and imagination. Yet, they maintain, nowadays he is more restaurateur than chef. The stoves at Lucas-Carton are manned by the talented Bernard Guéneron, who interprets his mentor's style and ideas. But even the most brilliant disciple (so goes the objectors' argument) cannot replace the master. For proof, they advance Exhibits A, B, and C: breaded turbot à la Kiev; langoustines encased in fried vermicelli and garnished with asparagus and a truffled egg; and croustillant of veal sweetbreads with a novel accompaniment of spiced crayfish and...popcorn! All these dishes are interesting, ingenious, delicious even: but where (they ask) is the heart? The emotion?

In reply, Senderens supporters evoke the thrill of sampling his now classic foie gras de canard steamed in a cabbage leaf—a pure marvel of harmonious flavors. They also point to a fabulous starter based on lobster: first poached, then briefly baked and dressed with cask-aged vinegar, the crustacean is presented with its claw wrapped in paper-thin pastry. Finally, his fans triumphantly cite Senderens's extraordinary saddle of rabbit: stuffed with foie gras, glazed with sugar, cinnamon, and other spices, then enveloped in a crackling phyllo crust—a miraculous dish, made more marvelous still by a glass of vintage Hermitage. You want art? You want emotion? It's all right there!

As you can see, we had reached an impasse. So we'll leave it to you to decide if Alain Senderens merits 19 or 19.5. All you need is a reservation—and sufficient cash to pay one of the world's brawniest tabs! **C** 800-1,500 F and up. **M** 375 F (lunch), 780 F, 880 F, 1,200 F.

15 La Luna

69, rue du Rocher
42 93 77 61,
fax 40 08 02 44

Closed Sun. Open until 11pm. Air cond. V, AE, MC.

La Luna lost some of its luster when it moved from the Left Bank to its present location near Villiers, but the tides still deposit first-quality seafood right at the door. The retro décor doesn't give a clue to the kitchen's resolutely modern manner of preparing fish: the chef highlights its natural flavors with short cooking times and a light hand. The menu changes from day to day, but you could start out with a trio of tartares (raw salmon, tuna, and sea bream), or a heap of tiny flash-fried squid, then proceed to langoustines baked with rosemary blossoms, sautéed baby soles, or a perfect charcoal-grilled sea bass. Each day, owner Jean-Pierre Durand offers two wine "specials" priced under 100 F. **C** 280-350 F.

16 Maison Blanche

15, av. Montaigne
47 23 55 99,
fax 47 20 09 56

Closed Sat lunch, Sun. Open until 11pm. Priv rm: 60. Terrace dining. Air cond. Valet pkg. V, AE.

Here in La Maison Blanche atop the Théâtre des Champs-Élysées, diners look out on the glittering dome of the Invalides, the shimmering Seine, and the magnificent buildings that line the quais. In contrast, the dining room sports a spare, avant-garde look that is vaguely Californian. The service, we're pleased to report, is now trouble-free, and the wide-ranging cellar is run by a competent sommelier. So far so good, you say, but what about the food? It's terrific: José Martinez's talent shines brighter every day, in dishes that deftly combine simplicity and sophistication. Don't miss his sun-dried-tomato ravioli, or succulent pan-roasted veal chop with walnuts and chanterelles, or his lush almond cake with apricots. In a word, we've got a winner! **C** 500-600 F.

12/20 Le Manoir Normand

77, bd de Courcelles
42 27 38 97

Closed Sat lunch, Sun, wk of Aug 15. Open until

10:30pm. Terrace dining. Garage pkg. V, AE, MC.

In France, a restaurateur named Pommerai (roughly equivalent to "apple orchard"), can hardly do otherwise than give his restaurant a Norman accent. But apart from some fish in cream-based sauces and a fine apple tart, the menu is agreeably free from regional chauvinism. Featured are good *plats du jour*, and meats grilled in the big fireplace. Glass-enclosed terrace. **C** 280-350 F. **M** 100 F, 145 F, 200 F.

Le Marcande

52, rue de Miromesnil - 42 65 19 14,
fax 40 76 03 27

Closed Aug 5-21. Open until 10:30pm. Terrace dining. V, AE.

A new lease on life for this warm, spacious restaurant which boasts a lovely garden patio. The chef takes the trouble to seek out fine foodstuffs for his lively, attractively presented cuisine. We like the cold potato soup dotted with scampi, the pinkly tender rack of Pyrenees lamb, and the richly flavorful coffee délice. The cellar holds an enviable store of Champagnes and premium vintages, all inclemently priced. Obtrusive service. **C** 300-420 F. **M** 220 F (weekdays).

La Marée

1, rue Daru
43 80 20 00,
fax 48 88 04 04

Closed Sat, Sun, Aug. Open until 10:30pm. Priv rm: 36. Air cond. Valet pkg. V, AE, DC.

For the last few years Éric Trompier has worked hard to bring the family's restaurant up to snuff; we're gratified to see him succeed. Forgoing routine, Trompier's chef has composed a menu of seductive, modern dishes that display unerring technique and imaginative flavors. We're thinking of the lobster salad with beet chips, a mile-high millefeuille brimming with fresh vegetables, brill encased in potato "scales" and embellished with a rosemary cream sauce, and la petite marmite tropézienne, a seafood extravaganza that brings all the perfumes of the Riviera to your table. These and other dishes are served, as always, in splendidly comfortable surroundings by a courteous, even benevolent staff. Take your time over the wine list, which features some exceptional bargains. **C** 500-900 F.

Maxim's

3, rue Royale
42 65 27 94,
fax 40 17 02 91

Closed Sun. Open until 10:30pm (Sat 11:30pm). Priv rm: 90. Air cond. No pets. Valet pkg. V, AE, DC, MC.

Rumors were rife a few months back that Pierre Cardin was looking to divest himself of Maxim's; the sorry state of the restaurant's façade lent credence to those whispers. Though nothing has occurred to date to confirm—or belie—the gossip, the heart seems to have gone out of this once-glamorous Belle Époque monument. Meanwhile, the stylish staff soldiers on in the half-empty dining room, as if nothing were amiss; and Maxim's most faithful patrons still come in for Michel Menant's coquilles Saint-Jacques à la nage, sole Albert, poularde truffée, and other proficient but vaguely fusty offerings. Perhaps the fun-loving, free-spending Parisians who kept Maxim's legend alive are just waiting for a signal to fill the place with sophisticated chatter and start the Champagne corks popping once again—but who will give that signal? And when? Here's hoping it comes soon! **C** 600-1,000 F.

Daniel Metery

4, rue de l'Arcade
42 65 53 13,
fax 42 66 53 82

Closed Sat lunch, Sun, 1st wk of Aug. Open until 10:15pm. Priv rm: 24. Pkg. V, AE.

Daniel Metery has declared war on indigestible prices. He's concocted a trio of judicious single-price menus that let you savor any dish you like from his intelligent, subtle repertoire, with no worries about the cost. We recently composed a commendable meal from such options as artichoke croustillant with plump escargots in a parsley jus, lamb enhanced by a pleasingly sharp vinegar sauce with a faint hint of coconut, and warm madeleines with honey-walnut ice cream. The eclectic wine list has an interesting Bordeaux section. **M** 250 F (dinner), 175 F, 235 F.

Gault Millau's ratings are based solely on the restaurants' cuisine. We do not take into account the atmosphere, décor, service and so on; these are commented upon within the review.

11/20 **Mollard**
Hôtel Garnier,
113, rue St-Lazare
43 87 50 22
Open daily until 1am. Garage pkg. V, AE, DC, MC.

An extraordinary turn-of-the-century ceramic mural depicts destinations of the trains that depart from the Gare Saint-Lazare across the street. The food is not quite so enchanting. Safe bets include the very good shellfish platter, skate with browned butter, and refreshing crab and salmon tartare. Courteous welcome, discreet service. **C** 220-500 F. **M** 185 F (wine incl).

12/20 **L'Obélisque**
Hôtel de Crillon,
10, pl. de la Concorde - 44 71 15 15
Closed hols, Aug. Open until 10:30pm. Priv rm: 72. Terrace dining. Air cond. Valet pkg. V, AE, DC, MC.

To eat at the Hôtel de Crillon without breaking the bank, try its other, less formal restaurant. You'll still benefit from top-notch service and a menu supervised by Christian Constant, chef of Les Ambassadeurs (see above). The food is classic bistro fare: pig's trotter sausage with potato purée, pot-au-feu, calf's head, tongue, and brains in sauce gribiche. Sixteen wines are offered by the glass or half-liter jug. **C** 300-420 F. **M** 270 F.

17 **Au Petit Montmorency**
5, rue Rabelais
42 25 11 19
Closed Sat, Sun, Aug. Open until 10:30pm. Priv rm: 10. Air cond. No pets. V, MC.

Gun-toting soldiers assigned to the nearby Israeli embassy made Au Petit Montmorency the best-guarded restaurant in Paris! Chef-owner Daniel Bouché, however, found the military presence a trifle overwhelming. So he jumped at the chance to acquire a shop next door to his restaurant, which gave him a new address and an unimpeded entrance. Architect Pierre Parat transformed the space into an elegant, distinctive dining room with red-lacquer walls and midnight-blue seating—a bold scheme that stands out from the all the pink, beige, and gray one sees nowadays.
In short, there's never been a better time to discover Bouché's splendid repertoire, with its soupe aux cèpes, oysters in a fragrant chervil broth, an exquisite rabbit pâté enlivened with chutney, rich duck liver accented by a peppery caramelized sauce, or a sumptuous truffled potato tourte. And by all means save room for the splendid croquembouche, a tower of cream puffs with a quartet of different fillings, or for the airy and delicate hazelnut soufflé. Note too that if your fancy runs to game, you should make a point of dining *chez* Bouché in the hunting season. And in every season, Nicole Bouché will help you choose the perfect wine to partner your meal. Lulled by this deliciousness, your shock may be all the greater when the waiter presents the bill. **C** 450-800 F. **M** 250 F (weekdays).

13 **Le Pichet**
68, rue P.-Charron
43 59 50 34,
fax 45 63 07 82
Closed Sat, Sun, Dec 20-Jan 2, Aug 9-31. Open until midnight. Air cond. V, AE, DC.

This old Pichet enjoys considerable success with its fresh shellfish assortments, *plats du jour*, and some creditable fish dishes (skate in warm vinaigrette; cod à l'unilatérale). These and other simple dishes please a sporty but urbane crowd, which sometimes includes François Mitterrand. **C** 300-450 F.

14 **Les Princes**
Hôtel George-V,
31, av. George-V
47 23 54 00,
fax 47 20 40 00
Open daily until 10:30pm. Priv rm: 460. Terrace dining. Air cond. Valet pkg. V, AE, DC, MC.

In fine weather, book a table on the beautiful flower-covered patio, far more inviting than the cavernous 1930s-style dining room. Wherever you sit, you're sure to savor Jacky Joyeux's attractive menu, filled with piquant, exotic touches. We especially like his cocktail of scallops and lobster with sesame-papaya dressing and the tournedos of sea bream and red mullet in a sauce hinting of coconut. For dessert, try the delectable crêpes soufflées with apple compote. The cellar has improved too, in our estimation, and the service, as always, is impeccable. **C** 450-750 F. **M** 240 F, 450 F.

15

Le Régence

Hôtel Plaza Athénée, 25, av. Montaigne - 47 23 78 33, fax 47 20 20 70

Open daily until 10:15pm. Priv rm: 100. Garden dining. Air cond. Valet pkg. V, AE, DC, MC.

Chef Gérard Sallé's light, spare style has transformed what used to be a pretty stuffy menu. Lobster soufflé and mixed grill have given way to the likes of salmon and bass tartare dressed with fragrant olive oil, braised sea bream with shallots and a zest of coriander, moist charcoal-grilled sea bass, and Bresse chicken simmered en cocotte with tender apples. Flavors are fresh and precisely defined; the ingredients are absolutely prime. The cellar, filled exclusively with mature bottles, is ruinously expensive, but that doesn't seem to bother the wealthy diners who frequent this opulently luxurious room. Perfect service. **C** 550-700 F. **M** 330 F (w-e).

14

Régine's Montaigne

14, rue de Marignan 40 76 34 44, fax 40 76 34 34

Closed Aug 1-15. Open until 10:30pm. Priv rm: 70. Air cond. Garage pkg. V, AE, DC, MC.

This pleasantly cozy and intimate restaurant, attached to the Marignan theater, is concealed behind an extremely discreet façade that is easy to miss. Once inside, you'll be warmly welcomed and invited to partake of Antoine Anclin's delicious Provençal cooking: tender baby squid, for example, with a zingy eggplant garnish, or rack of lamb enhanced by a savory jus, and a colorful dessert composed of mandarin oranges and tangy tomato jam. The cellar is small but select. **C** 260-330 F. **M** 180 F, 250 F.

13

Le Relais Vermeer

Hôtel Golden Tulip, 218, rue du Faubourg-St-Honoré 49 53 03 03, fax 40 75 02 00

Closed Sun, hols, Aug. Open until 10pm. Priv rm: 195. Air cond. Pkg. V, AE, DC, MC.

A luxurious restaurant for a luxurious hotel, owned by the Dutch Golden Tulip chain. In a restful gray-blue-and-pink dining room, sample tasty rabbit terrine with figs, John Dory with Belgian endive, delicate sweetbreads, and gratin de fruits au champagne prepared by the aptly named chef, Frédéric Lecuisinier. **C** 270-430 F. **M** 195 F.

14

Richemond Trémoille

7, rue La Trémoille 47 23 88 18

Closed Sat, Sun, Aug. Open until 10:30pm. Priv rm: 20. Terrace dining. V, AE, DC, MC.

Gilles Poyac is the fresh face in the kitchen, now in charge of revving up the classic house repertoire. He's succeeded admirably, for the menu now lists such appealing options as ravioli stuffed with sweetbreads and artichokes vigorously spiced with coriander, excellent aiguillettes of duck breast in a gingerbread jus, and lushly flavorful roast pears flanked by a crisp almond craquelin. These sprightly savors contrast oddly with the solemn, wood-paneled *salle*. Admirable cellar. **C** 320-400 F. **M** 190 F.

13

Le Saint-Moritz

33, av. de Friedland 45 61 02 74, fax 53 75 03 18

Closed Sat, Sun. Open until 10:15pm. No pets. V, AE, DC, MC.

Chef Alain Raichon hails from the Jura, and his cooking too is rooted in that mountain region. Sample his scallops with foie gras beignets, tasty sweetbreads with fresh, tender morels, or sole fillets cooked in white Arbois wine. The cellar holds bottles for every budget. **C** 340-400 F. **M** 185 F.

14

Les Saveurs

8, rue J.-Goujon 45 63 17 44, fax 42 25 06 59

Closed Sat, Sun, Aug. Open until 10:30pm. Priv rm. Terrace dining. Air cond. Valet pkg. V, AE, DC, MC.

Chef Didier Lanfray works hard to strike a balance between creative cooking and updated traditional food. We think he's done the job, with dishes like asparagus and crayfish in a shellfish coulis, rabbit accented with ginger and red radishes, or pig's cheeks and trotters braised with lemon and rosemary, or turbotin perfumed with verbena. Remarkable desserts (yummy warm madeleines with Bourbon-vanilla ice cream); worthy cellar. The house annex, La Maison des Centraliens at 5, impasse d'Antin, serves tasty, moderately priced bistro chow. **C** 300-380 F.

M 150 F & 280 F (wine incl), 160 F, 220 F.

12/20 Sébillon Élysées

66, rue P.-Charron
43 59 28 15,
fax 43 59 30 00

Open daily until midnight. Priv rm: 60. Air cond. Valet pkg. V, AE, DC, MC.

As in the sister establishment in Neuilly (see The Suburbs), excellent but expensive shellfish platters are followed here by Sébillon's famous leg of lamb, cooked to rosy tenderness and carved before your eyes. Elegant décor, energetic service. **C** 200-400 F.

14 Shing-Jung

7, rue Clapeyron
45 22 21 06

Open daily until midnight. No pets. V, AE, DC, MC.

The smiling and cooperative owner of this unprepossessing establishment will try to convince you that Koreans are far more generous than their Japanese neighbors. Indeed, a colossal assortment of raw fish, listed on the menu as "medium", comprised sea bream, salmon, tuna, brill, and mackerel. For the same money (120 F) most Japanese places would serve about one-quarter the quantity. Other unusual and tasty offerings are jellyfish salad, barbecued beef strips, a hotpot of vegetables and beef, and stuffed lentil-flour crêpes. Everything is delicious and incredibly inexpensive. **C** 120 F. **M** 65 F (weekdays).

13 Stresa

7, rue de Chambiges
47 23 51 62

Closed Sat dinner, Sun, Dec 20-Jan 3, Aug. Open until 10:30pm. Priv rm: 12. Terrace dining. Air cond. Pkg. AE, DC.

This shabby but somehow soothing dining room is always full of press, fashion, and theater people who love the antipasti drizzled with fruity Tuscan olive oil, the toothsome osso buco, and the smooth tiramisù prepared by Marco Faiola. Claudio and Toni Faiola seat their guests with a sure social sense of who's up, who's down, who's in, who's out. **C** 270-370 F.

19 Taillevent

15, rue Lamennais
44 95 15 01,
fax 42 25 95 18

Closed Sat, Sun, Jul 23-Aug 22. Open until 10:30pm. Priv rm: 32. Air cond. No pets. Valet pkg. V, AE, DC.

Though he keeps one eye on his newest project, the resuscitated Prunier-Traktir restaurant (see sixteenth arrondissement), and another on the grandiose Château Français that he opened in Tokyo with his pal, Joël Robuchon, Jean-Claude Vrinat always knows exactly what's cooking at his cherished Taillevent. In the kitchen Philippe Legendre, formerly number two here, is fully in charge and obviously at ease in his job. He delivers a refined, brilliantly realized repertoire that perfectly suits Taillevent's conservative yet sophisticated clientele. So attuned is Legendre to the tastes of his public that he can even risk offering a few rustic *plats*, like pig's foot sausage—though it's truffled, of course—and still garner applause. But most of the menu is more classically inclined: creamy crab soup with panisses (chickpea-flour crêpes), vivid sea-urchin mousse with asparagus tips, red mullet stuffed with black olives, sweetly spiced sea bass with carrots, and a rabbit and spinach pie redolent of wild thyme. Among the wonderful desserts, a luscious caramel and gingerbread "fantasy" stands out in our memory. Some Taillevent habitués may be startled to observe that the dining room has been—discreetly!—remodeled: the bay window is larger, the decoration has a spruce, youthful look. But one thing that will never change here is the incomparable quality of the cellar, brimful of rare and glorious (occasionally affordable) wines selected by Vrinat and his daughter, Sabine. And as always at Taillevent, the service functions at the highest level of unobtrusive efficiency. **C** 700-900 F.

13 Chez Tante Louise

41, rue Boissy-d'Anglas
42 65 06 85,
fax 42 65 28 19

Closed Aug. Open until 10:30pm. Priv rm: 12. Air cond. Pkg. V, AE, DC, MC.

The regulars love being pampered in this snug little restaurant. Chef Michel Lerouet cooks up lightened, up-to-date versions of traditional French favorites. So rev up your appetite and come in for his mouthwatering cannelloni stuffed with salmon and cod, braised quail with green grapes, potatoes, and onions, and a delicious pineapple gratin. **C** 300-420 F. **M** 168 F.

14 Le Trente

Fauchon, 30, pl. de la Madeleine
47 42 56 58,
fax 42 66 38 95

Closed Sun. Open until 10:30pm. Priv rm: 20. Garden dining. Air cond. Valet pkg. V, AE, DC, MC.

Whoever dreamed up the name (Le Trente—30—is the building's address) of Fauchon's restaurant won't win any prizes for creativity, but the decorator might, for his "Roman fantasy" interior complete with atrium, columns, and *trompe-l'œil* paintings. More patrons show up at lunch than at dinner to feed on Bruno Deligne's attractive offerings: a bracing tartare of salmon and John Dory, grilled sea bass with sauce vierge, and poached Bresse chicken with vegetables. These low-fat options leave plenty of leeway to indulge in the stupendous pastries crafted by Pierre Hermé. **C** 350-500 F. **M** 240 F (dinner).

12/20 Le Val d'Or

28, av. F.-Roosevelt
43 59 95 81

Lunch only. Closed Sat, Sun. V.

Madame Rongier holds firmly to the traditions of French home cooking, pleasing her patrons with beef in bone-marrow sauce and lapin à la moutarde, escorted by well-chosen wines at reasonable "bistro" prices. The ground-floor bar stays open at night, serving wine by the glass, charcuterie, and sandwiches. **C** 250-300 F.

16 Vancouver

4, rue A.-Houssaye
42 56 77 77,
fax 42 56 50 52

Closed Sat, Sun, hols, Aug. Open until 10pm. Air cond. Valet pkg. V, AE.

He shouts, he moans, he never admits he's wrong—but we can't stay mad long at Jean-Louis Decout. Heck, a man who cooks as well as he does can't be all bad! Decout has an instinctive, limpid way of handling fish and shellfish. His style delivers all of the seafood's natural goodness along with a discreet but brilliant touch that puts the briny flavors into even sharper focus. After a plate of perfectly delicious little rock lobsters roasted with the merest hint of herbs and spice, we greedily devoured a smooth red-mullet brandade served with a fillet of the same fish and an anise-scented tomate confite. Nor did we leave a speck of the sweet-and-sour sea bream, its crisp skin "lacquered" with apple cider. Dessert? Of course! How could we resist the feather-light fruit tartlets or the lush chocolate éclairs? Chantal Decout welcomes guests with warm hospitality into a lovely bilevel dining room done in tones of ivory with Art Deco stained glass. **C** 320-420 F. **M** 190 F, 380 F.

Restaurant names in red draw attention to restaurants that offer a particularly good value.

13 Chez Vong

27, rue du Colisée
43 59 77 12,
fax 43 59 59 27

Closed Sun. Open until midnight. Priv rm: 60. Air cond. Valet pkg. V, AE, DC.

Here's everyone's dream of a Chinese restaurant: embroidered silk, furniture inlaid with mother-of-pearl, lots of little nooks, an air of mystery, and dishes named "quail in a nest of happiness" or "merry shrimps." The cooking is quite well done. Oddly enough, the cellar is rich in fine (and costly) claret. **C** 280-360 F. **M** 250 F (for 10 pers min).

15 Yvan

1 bis, rue J.-Mermoz
43 59 18 40,
fax 45 63 78 69

Closed Sat lunch, Sun. Open until midnight. Air cond. Valet pkg. V, AE, DC.

Yvan Zaplatilek is café society's darling, but he is also a hard-working chef who gives his customers very good food at moderate prices in a most elegant setting. The menu is primarily French, with an occasional Belgian touch here and there (mussels and fries, rabbit ravioli in a beer-based sauce, cod waterzoï). Yvan also has a penchant for exotic seasonings, and turns out an excellent lotte with ginger, foie gras showered with sesame seeds, and veal kidneys spiced with cumin. Note that his newest venture, Le Petit Yvan, just next door, offers an unbeatable all-in menu for 138 F (tel. 42 89 49 65). **C** 250-400 F. **M** 168 F, 188 F, 238 F, 278 F, 298 F.

9th arrondissement

12/20 L'Alsaco

10, rue Condorcet
45 26 44 31

Closed Sat lunch, Sun, Dec 24-Jan 4, Aug. Open until 11pm. Priv rm: 40. V.

Look beyond the unremarkable façade and discover an authentic Alsatian *winstub*, decked out in traditional painted wood paneling. Invariably crammed with regulars, L'Alsaco serves a generous rendition of choucroute garnie, a crisp-crusted cream and onion tart (flammekueche), and potatoes blanketed with savory melted Munster cheese and crunchy bits of bacon. To drink, there are Rieslings and Pinot Blancs galore, as well as a huge selection of clear fruit brandies. **C** 150-230 F. **M** 78 F (weekday lunch), 85 F (dinner), 168 F.

13 Auberge Landaise

23, rue Clauzel
48 78 74 40

Closed Sun, Aug 6-25. Open until 10pm. Priv rm: 35. Garage pkg. V, AE, DC.

In a rustic atmosphere conducive to a hearty tuck-in, Dominique Morin treats his customers to cassoulet (a trifle overcooked on our last visit), pipérade landaise, braised duck with wild mushrooms, foie gras, and a rather pricey array of Southwestern wines. Do not overlook the collection of Armagnacs, a perfect way to end a meal in this friendly, relaxed restaurant. **C** 280-380 F. **M** 180 F (wine incl).

13 Le Bistrot Blanc

52, rue Blanche
42 85 05 30

Closed Sat, Sun, Aug. Open until 10pm. Priv rm: 30. V, AE, MC.

Bruno Borni, a Marseille native who held the rank of sauce chef at La Tour d'Argent (his sauces are indeed excellent: concentrated, light, and fragrant), cooks with a lilting Provençal accent. Recommended are his fricasséed scallops in tomato coulis, red-mullet fillets with a zingy garnish of tapenade, pigeon baked in a salt crust and, to finish, the citrus fruit "marvel." Charming atmosphere; limited cellar. **C** 250-350 F. **M** 85 F.

15 La Casa Olympe

48, rue St-Georges
42 85 26 01,
fax 45 26 49 33

Closed 1st 3 wks of Aug, Christmas wk. Open until 11pm. No pets. V.

Olympe is back, now occupying the former Casa Miguel, long the city's cheapest deal, with a philanthropically priced 5 F set meal. The wonderful menu reflects Olympe at her best, as though she knew only one way to cook: the right way. Her fans rejoiced to rediscover tried-and-tested favorites like tuna with bacon and onions, guinea-hen ravioli au jus, and spiced roast duckling, as well as such cheeky newcomers as croustillants de boudin au mesclun, chestnut-flour galette topped with spinach and a poached egg, or braised rabbit perfumed with basil on a golden bed of polenta. There is also a marmite brimming with herbed shellfish and tomatoes, whole roast sea bream with rosemary splendidly served on a copper platter, and a magnificent veal chop emboldened with a soupçon of chopped chili and a creamy lemon sauce. Homey desserts include rice pudding and gingerbread with custard sauce. The wine list is similarly unpretentious and appealing. The premises are small (not to say cramped) though prettily painted in warm tones of yellow and burnt sienna. **C** 220-250 F. **M** 180 F (weekdays).

12/20 La Champagne

10 bis, pl. de Clichy
48 74 44 78

Open daily until 3am. Priv rm: 30. Air cond. No pets. V, AE, DC.

Until the small hours you can join the carefree, festive crowd that pays high prices for homard flambé, onion soup, oysters, and sauerkraut at this effervescent restaurant. Ask for a table in the attractive upstairs room. **C** 250-500 F. **M** 119 F, 149 F.

13 Charlot

"Roi des Coquillages," 81, bd de Clichy (pl. de Clichy)
48 74 49 64

Open daily until 1am. Priv rm: 30. Air cond. Valet pkg. V, AE, DC, MC.

A fine view of the Place de Clichy, a warm welcome, and attentive service will take your mind off the overbearing Art Deco interior. Sparkling fresh oysters, spectacular shellfish assortments, a generous bouillabaisse à la marseillaise, and lobsters prepared every possible way are the staples here. **C** 300-500 F. **M** 185 F (Apr-Sep), 225 F (Oct-Mar).

13 I Golosi
6, rue de la Grange-Batelière
48 24 18 63

Closed Aug. Open until 11pm. Air cond. Pkg. V, MC.

Enter this new bistro *a vino* from the Passage Verdeau. You'll discover two levels decorated in a style we can only call "1950s Italian," where you can order cold rabbit herbed with wild thyme, chicken dressed with balsamic vinegar, clove-scented beef stew, and zuppa inglese, all accompanied by irresistible wines (Chardonnay, Barbaresco, Moscato d'Asti) assembled by a passionate oenophile who knows what he's about. **C** 120-140 F.

12/20 Le Grand Café Capucines
4, bd des Capucines
47 42 19 00

Open daily 24 hours. Terrace dining. Air cond. Garage pkg. V, AE, DC, MC.

The waiter won't pull a face if you order just one course—a shellfish assortment, for example, or salmon tartare, or a grilled pig's trotter. The extravagant décor is a replica of a Roaring Twenties *café boulevardier*. **C** 200-350 F. **M** 119 F (dinner), 185 F.

13 A la Grange Batelière
16, rue de la Grange-Batelière
47 70 85 15

Open daily until 10:30pm. Terrace dining. V, MC.

Given the dog-eared surroundings, you may be surprised by the high prices charged here. But Jacques Meunier puts truffles in his scallop cassolette, foie gras beside his artichoke compote, and regularly lists wild duck (cooked with gingerbread and buckwheat honey) and turbot (enriched with goose fat and braised cabbage) on his menu. Appraisers from the Drouot auction houses and financial wizards from neighboring banks all eat here: and they know value when they see it! **C** 350-400 F. **M** 280 F (dinner), 198 F.

16 Les Muses
Hôtel Scribe,
1, rue Scribe
44 71 24 26

Closed Sat, Sun, hols, Aug. Open until 10:30pm. Priv rm: 80. Air cond. No pets. Valet pkg. V, AE, DC.

The muse of interior design was off duty the day the Hôtel Scribe's basement restaurant was decorated. On the other hand, chef Philippe Pleuen seems privy to a regular fount of inspiration, judging by his inventive, fresh-flavored cuisine. His duck liver with potatoes, succulent beef fillet with artichokes, and chocolate croustillant with mandarin-orange sorbet are well worth the trip down from street level. There's a fine cheese board too, and an array of alluring sweets. The wine list is notable for balance rather than length. **C** 300-400 F. **M** 210 F.

13 L'Œnothèque
20, rue St-Lazare
48 78 08 76

Closed Sat, Sun, 2nd wk of Feb school hols, May 1-8, Aug 7-28. Open until 10:30pm. Air cond. V, MC.

Daniel Hallée was the sommelier at Jamin before he opened his restaurant-cum-wine shop. Grand vintages at attractive prices and interesting lesser-known growths partner such market-fresh offerings as foie gras en terrine, grilled squid, and prime rib with bone marrow. Superb collection of Cognacs. **C** 200-350 F.

13 Au Petit Riche
25, rue Le Peletier
47 70 68 68

Closed Sun. Open until 12:15am. V, AE, DC, MC.

The brass trim, mirrors, and woodwork of this nostalgic bistro are sparkling once again. This is a popular after-theater spot for tasty coq au vin de Chinon, calf's head with sauce gribiche, sole meunière, and delicious wines from the Touraine region. **C** 200-300 F. **M** 160 F.

13 Le Saharien
36, rue Rodier
42 85 51 90,
fax 45 86 08 35

Closed Sun. Open until 11pm. Air cond. Pkg. V.

Wally has pitched his tent not far from Pigalle, in a bright, cozy setting accented with carved screens, crimson carpets, and Tuareg-style seating. Topping the list of specialties is his excellent Saharan couscous (no broth, no vegetables), but you can also sample a wonderful dish of mutton with caramelized skin, pigeon pastilla, and honey cake perfumed with orange-flower water. **M** 240 F (wine incl), 150 F (week-day lunch).

17 **La Table d'Anvers**
2, pl. d'Anvers
48 78 35 21,
fax 45 26 66 67
Closed Sat lunch, Sun. Open until 10:30pm. Priv rm: 40. Air cond. Garage pkg. V, AE.

While so many chefs fall back on a "safe," reassuring repertoire of neo-bourgeois and bistro dishes to hide their lack of inspiration, Christian Conticini invents and reinvents flavor combinations with a wizardry that is nothing short of staggering. If you're tempted by the prospect of a real gastronomic adventure, we suggest you trek up to his Table at the foot of Montmartre and prepare for a feast! Choose one of the intriguing "theme" menus (featuring novel vegetables, or rare spices, "just desserts"...), or explore an exciting *carte* that is keyed to the seasons. The options are all so enticing that we usually just close our eyes and pick at random! You could start with a tartelette au thon (tuna) surrounded by spring vegetables dressed in a zesty anchovy and green-peppercorn vinaigrette, or lobster gnocchi with divine baby peas (ineffably tender because they've been peeled!) in a rose-mary-scented chicken jus, or a brilliantly conceived ravigote that brings together oysters, calf's head, cabbage, and tomato—an amazing harmony of briny and tart flavors, smooth and crisp textures. There follows (for example) grilled red mullet seasoned with artichoke pistou in a saffron-spiced bouillon, or pearly-fleshed sea bass with fava beans and grated fennel, the latter's anise undertones accented by a delicate touch of licorice. Other uncommonly delectable couplings are Conticini's saddle of rabbit with Reblochon cheese atop olive-studded polenta, or his exotically perfumed canard à l'orientale escorted by couscous and spiced chickpeas.

We could go on about these thrilling inventions, but we must leave room to mention the fabulous cheeses, and the astonishing desserts crafted by Christian's brother, Philippe Conticini. Don't be put off by Philippe's imposing waistline: his chocolate-banana-coffee "combo," his macaron au fromage frais, lait d'amande, et griotte, or mango-rhubarb puff pastry with a hint of cinnamon are all light as a summer breeze. An improved cellar now includes some attractive bottles priced under 100 F. **C** 400-600 F. **M** 250 F (lunch, wine incl), 160 F (lunch), 190 F (dinner).

12/20 **La Taverne Kronenbourg**
24, bd des Italiens
47 70 16 64,
fax 42 47 13 91
Open daily until 3am. Priv rm: 100. Air cond. Garage pkg. V, AE, DC, MC.

The last of the *cafés-concerts* on the Grands Boulevards (live music nightly) serves robust, unpretentious brasserie fare: shellfish, pork knuckle with cabbage, sauerkraut, and fine Alsatian wines. **C** 190-300 F. **M** 130 F (wine incl).

16 **Venantius**
Hôtel Ambassador,
16, bd Haussmann
48 00 06 38,
fax 42 46 19 84
Closed Sat, Sun, Feb 17-27, Jul 28-Aug 28. Open until 10:30pm. Air cond. Valet pkg. V, AE, DC, MC.

Influenced, no doubt, by the dining room's opulent *fin de siècle* décor, chef Gérard Fouché laces his menu with references to the elaborate cuisine of Carême and Escoffier. Still, he's no prisoner of the culinary past, for his more modern, personal creations display plenty of panache. Cases in point: his remarkable duck foie gras flanked by a peppery pineapple marmalade, crab gazpacho zipped up with fresh coriander, a splendid sole stuffed with celery root rémoulade, and breast of Bresse chicken cooked to perfect juiciness in a crust of Breton sea salt. Yet even dishes like these bear occasional traces of lily-gilding.

Sooner or later, Fouché will have to choose between retrospective or forward-looking cuisine. We hope it's the latter, since his flawless technique marks him as a potential three-toque winner. Dining à la carte is an expensive proposition; happily, the 210 F set meal offers an appealing alternative. Ever-so-solemn service. **C** 400-600 F. **M** 210 F (coffee incl).

Gault Millau's ratings are based solely on the restaurants' cuisine. We do not take into account the atmosphere, décor, service and so on; these are commented upon within the review.

10th arrondissement

12/20 Brasserie Flo

7, cour des Petites-Écuries
42 46 15 80

Open daily until 1:30am. Air cond. Pkg. V, AE, DC, MC.

The quintessential Alsatian brasserie, Flo is a jewel: nowhere else will you find the same vivacious atmosphere, superb décor, lively patrons, and delicious sauerkraut, best washed down with carafes of frisky Riesling. **C** 200-300 F. **M** 185 F (from 10pm, wine incl), 109 F (wine incl).

(14) Au Châteaubriant

23, rue Chabrol
48 24 58 94

Closed Sun, Mon, 1 wk in winter, Aug. Open until 10:15pm. Air cond. V, AE.

From the name you'd never guess that this little dining room tucked away near the Gare de l'Est is a noted Italian restaurant. Save for the rotating roster of daily specials, the menu is immutable. Familiar though they may be, the sardine lasagne with eggplant and the millefeuille de filet de veau are still perfectly delicious and courteously served. Tempting desserts; high prices. **C** 250-350 F. **M** 149 F.

12/20 Les Deux Canards

"Chez Catherine,"
8, rue du Faubourg-Poissonnière
47 70 03 23

Closed Sat lunch, Sun. Open until 10pm (w-e 10:30pm). Air cond. Pkg. V, AE, DC, MC.

The naïve charm of this dining room crammed with ducks is sure to win you over. The voluble owner (a former dentist) does not allow smoking—*nous aimons les fumeurs, pas la fumée*—so diners may enjoy the delicious duck terrine, sardines with pesto, Barbary duck à l'orange, and Provençal mussels in an unpolluted atmosphere. Admirable cellar. **C** 150-250 F. **M** 130 F.

12/20 Julien

16, rue du Fg-St-Denis - 47 70 12 06, fax 42 47 00 65

Open daily until 1:30am. Air cond. Valet pkg. V, AE, DC, MC.

For the pleasure of dining in these exuberant surroundings (vintage 1880), we are willing to put up with mediocre food; frankly, the kitchen turns out more than its share of botched dishes. But if you stick to the oysters, the cassoulet, or eggs poached in red wine, you'll probably leave with a pleasant memory. **C** 220-280 F. **M** 109 F (wine incl).

(13) Le Louis-XIV

8, bd St-Denis
42 08 56 56

Closed Jul-Aug. Open until 1am. Priv rm: 120. Terrace dining. Valet pkg. V, AE, DC.

The décor is more Louis XV (Pompadour period!) than Louis XIV, but no one seems to mind. The festive, dressy clientele that dines here is too busy tucking into succulent roast duck, roast lamb, roast pigeon, or juicy ribs of beef—preceded, ideally, by a spar-kling assortment of fresh shellfish. Jolly ambience, good cellar. **C** 300-550 F. **M** 150 F & 170 F (wine incl).

(14) La P'tite Tonkinoise

56, rue du Faubourg-Poissonnière
42 46 85 98

Closed Sun, Mon, Dec 22-Jan 6, Aug 1-Sep 15. Open until 10pm. Garage pkg. V.

Old Indochina hands come regularly for a whiff of the nostalgia that is virtually palpable in this quiet establishment. The chef is a pony-tailed titan, while his wife is indeed a tiny Tonkinoise. Their Vietnamese menu is packed with haunting, exotic flavors: crisp egg rolls, giant grilled shrimp in an extraordinary rice sauce (they're not on the menu—you have to ask for them), a huge dried-noodle cake studded with shrimp and vegetables (my-sao), a juicy duck breast rubbed with five-spice powder, and a savory chicken wing stuffed with onion curry. If they keep it up, they'll soon be topped with two toques! **C** 200-280 F.

12/20 Terminus Nord

23, rue de Dunkerque - 42 85 05 15

Open daily until 12:30am. Priv rm: 11. Air cond. V, AE, DC, MC.

Now part of the brasserie group of which Flo (see above) is the flagship, the Terminus serves exactly the same food as the rest of the fleet. Enjoy the lively atmosphere, the gay 1925 décor, and look no farther than the sauerkraut, briny oysters, and grilled meats for a satisfying meal. Nimble service. **C** 190-300 F. **M** 95 F (from 10pm, wine incl), 99 F & 141 F (wine incl).

11th arrondissement

L'Aiguière

(14) 37 bis, rue de Montreuil - 43 72 42 32, fax 43 72 96 36

Closed Sat lunch, Sun. Open until 10:30pm. Priv rm: 80. Air cond. Pkg. V, AE, DC, MC.

Elegant down to the last meticulous detail, this little restaurant serves romantic dinners with candlelight and piano music. The chef spurns simplicity, but his first-rate ingredients are prepared with care: try the scrambled eggs with lightly smoked salmon, crisp-skinned porgy fillet with spinach and a tasty herbed flan, or delicious bœuf à la paysanne, then finish with a a chaud-froid of pears in puff pastry. **C** 300-400 F. **M** 248 F (wine incl), 125 F, 175 F.

Les Amognes

(14) 243, rue du Fg-St-Antoine - 43 72 73 05

Closed Sun, Mon, 1st 3 wks of Aug. Open until 11pm. Terrace dining. V.

Thierry Coué has crossed rich and costly ingredients off his shopping list. The food he serves in his country-style dining room is hearty and full of earthy flavors. Take his creamy split-pea soup: it boasts baby vegetables so fresh you'll be inspired to plant your own! And the succulent roast rack of lamb is ideally accompanied by garlic gnocchi and fragrant white beans. In game season, don't miss the wild-rabbit terrine or the pheasant risotto. The cellar is filled with interesting finds, and the service is gratifyingly attentive. **M** 160 F.

Astier

(13) 44, rue J.-P.-Timbaud
43 57 16 35

Closed Sat, Sun, Dec 21-Jan 5, end Apr-Aug. Open until 11pm. Air cond. V, AE.

For 130 F, Jean-Luc Clerc will set you up with a slab of savory chicken-liver terrine, followed by rabbit in mustard sauce or a duo of sea whelks and shrimp, nicely aged cheeses, and rich chocolate mousse for dessert. The bistro atmosphere is good-humored and noisy. Intelligent, wide-ranging cellar. **M** 130 F.

La Belle Époque

(14) Holiday Inn, 10, pl. de la République
43 55 44 34,
fax 47 00 32 34

Closed Sat lunch, Sun, Aug. Open until 10:30pm. Terrace dining. Air cond. No pets. V, AE, DC.

Deft technique and focused flavors mark Alain Gruet's foie gras de canard on a bed of crisp greens, spiced veal with sweet peppers, sea bream with sautéed herb-strewn pasta, and delicate tart of saffron-tinged apples and chocolate. Remarkable service in a handsome paneled dining room with an enclosed terrace. Serious cellar. **C** 250-350 F.

12/20 Chardenoux

1, rue J.-Vallès
43 71 49 52

Closed Sat, Sun. Open until 10pm. V, AE.

In the heart of the old cabinet-makers' district, this graceful corner bistro (a registered Belle Époque building) flaunts its charms of marble, fanciful moldings, and etched glass. It's a setting peculiarly suited to Bernard Passavant's simple, generous cooking: eggs poached in red wine, daube de bœuf à la provençale, and the like. Connoisseur's cellar. **C** 200-270 F.

Les Folies

(13) "Chez Rosine,"
101, rue de St-Maur
43 38 13 61

Closed Sat lunch, Sun, Aug 10-27. Open until 11pm (Sat dinner 11:30pm). Priv rm: 30. V, AE, DC, MC.

'Twould be folly indeed to overlook this creditable Cambodian spot, where Rosine prepares a fragrant repertoire of Southeast Asian dishes. Before proceeding to the charcoal-grilled marinated meats, try the subtly perfumed soupe ma-chou or the sautéed mussels redolent of basil, garlic, chilis, lemongrass, and peppermint. Advanced students of Cambodian cooking won't want to miss Rosine's na-tong (catfish), or her blue Mekong shrimp. **C** 180-230 F. **M** 98 F, 128 F (wine incl).

Keur Makha

(13) 5, rue Guillaume-Bertrand
43 57 43 95

Closed Mon. Open until 1am. Air cond. V, AE.

Africans in Paris (and others in search of exotic tastes) favor this address, where Makha himself will guide you through the menu of soyas (skewered veal or fish), womoyo (sea bream with a hot tomato sauce), n'dolé (greens with beef or shrimp), and spicy marinated chicken that is charcoal-grilled to juicy tenderness. The cooking is skillful, the spicing hot but not incendiary. **C** 250-300 F.

Mansouria

11, rue Faidherbe
43 71 00 16,
fax 40 24 21 97

Closed Mon lunch, Sun. Open until 11:30pm. Terrace dining. No pets. V.

The trendy Bastille crowd comes here for a taste of Morocco: honeyed pumpkin purée, Moroccan crêpes, a light and flavorful couscous, and mellow, long-simmered tagines. Charming reception and service. **C** 200-300 F. **M** 99 F & 135 F (lunch), 280 F (wine incl), 164 F.

Chez Philippe

106, rue de la Folie-Méricourt
43 57 33 78

Closed Sat, Sun, hols, Aug. Open until 10:30pm. Air cond. Garage pkg. V, AE.

The menu written in purple ink is nothing if not eclectic: herrings Bismarck, grilled lobster, a monumental cassoulet, paella (the best in Paris), York ham with macaroni au gratin, beef bourguignon, turbot Dugléré, rock lobster in Port, and old-fashioned braised hare. Believe it or not, it's all delicious and satisfying. Best of all, these earthy delights are served in the most convivial setting imaginable, complete with a jovial host. Great Burgundies at giveaway prices only add to the gaiety. **C** 300-450 F.

Le Repaire de Cartouche

99, rue Amelot or 8, bd des Filles-du-Calvaire - 47 00 25 86

Closed Sat lunch, Sun, Jul 25-Aug 22. Open until 10:30pm. Priv rm: 25. V, AE, DC, MC.

Emmanuel Salabert, an experienced, skillful chef, presides over this shrine to Southwestern cuisine. Settle down in the wood-paneled dining room and sample the foie gras steamed in a cabbage leaf, steamed mussels in a creamy sauce, pork with prunes and celery, and the flaky Landais apple pie laced with Armagnac. Interesting cellar, manageably priced. **C** 250-350 F. **M** 220 F (Sat), 150 F & 350 F (weekdays).

La Table Richelieu

276, bd Voltaire
43 72 31 23

Closed Sat lunch. Open until 11pm. Priv rm: 40. Air cond. V, AE, MC.

For fresh seafood, you couldn't do much better than this bright, comfortable restaurant, where Daniel Rousseau treats customers to sparkling shellfish assortments and delicious little red mullet sautéed with Provençal herbs. He's no slouch with meat either, witness his escalopes of foie gras with caramelized endive, or the cunning sausage of veal sweetbreads and fillet flavored with a whisper of lemon and vanilla. Tasty desserts. **C** 300-400 F. **M** 145 F (weekday lunch, wine incl), 200 F, 260 F.

Thaï Éléphant

43-45, rue de la Roquette
47 00 42 00,
fax 47 00 45 44

Closed Sat lunch, May 1, Dec 25-28. Open until midnight. Priv rm: 30. Air cond. V, AE, DC, MC.

Filled with flowers, pagodas, and innumerable cheerful waiters, the Thaï Éléphant is not your run-of-the-mill Asian eatery. The menu is miles long, and many of the dishes are fiercely fiery (the hottest are marked with three red elephants). The shrimp curry is quite fine, and so are the Fomyang soup and the garlicky pork. For dessert, try the delicious jasmine tart. **C** 250-370 F. **M** 150 F (weekday lunch), 265 F, 295 F.

Le Villaret

13, rue Ternaux
43 57 75 56

Dinner only. Closed Sun, hols, 2 wks at Christmas, 12 days in May, Aug. Open until 1am. V.

The former owner of the well-known Astier (see above) recently launched this engaging bistro, where simple, scrupulously prepared food is served with bargain-priced wines. It's a winning formula! On the menu you'll find splendid foie gras, a succulent civet of pork jowls, and a light pear clafoutis. The spacious, beamed dining room is invariably crowded until late at night: don't forget to reserve your table. **C** 180-220 F.

12th arrondissement

11/20 L'Ébauchoir

43, rue des Citeaux
43 42 49 31

Closed Sun. Open until 10pm. No pets. V.

Here's a big, boisterous neighborhood bistro where the Bastille's trendier denizens regularly tuck into crab soup, calf's liver glazed with honey and coriander, tuna with orange-butter sauce, and old-fashioned molded rice pudding. **C** 150-200 F. **M** 60 F (lunch).

(13) La Flambée

4, rue Taine
43 43 21 80

Closed Sun, 1 wk at Christmas, Aug 1-21. Open until 10pm. Terrace dining. Air cond. Pkg. V, AE, MC.

The dining room shows some signs of wear, but never mind. Michel Roustan warms things up nicely with his traditional Southwestern charcuteries, tasty confit de canard with sautéed potatoes, and excellent warm apple tart. The good wines are moderately priced. **C** 240-320 F. **M** 80 F (lunch, wine incl), 125 F & 185 F (wine incl).

(13) La Frégate

30, av. Ledru-Rollin
43 43 90 32

Closed Sat, Sun, Aug 1-22. Open until 10:30pm. Air cond. V, AE.

The huge menu of this friendly haven for bons vivants is dedicated to seafood. Pierre Goueffon turns out a laudable salad of warm scallops set atop truffled lamb's lettuce, a médaillon of monkfish strewn with morsels of fresh crab, and John Dory simmered in aromatic olive oil. Wind up your feast with one of the alluring desserts (lime soufflé and sorbet, strawberry chaud-froid...). Astutely chosen wines. **C** 350-450 F. **M** 150 F (lunch), 200 F, 300 F.

(14) La Gourmandise

271, av. Daumesnil
43 43 94 41

Closed Sun, Mon dinner, Aug 6-28. Open until 10:30pm. Priv rm: 50. Garage pkg. V, AE.

Gourmand or gourmet, you'll be tempted to indulge in Alain Denoual's cuisine, served in surroundings that some find a trifle pompous. Others question the high prices charged for meager portions. But no one contests the quality of Denoual's warm fish terrine with shellfish fumet or mustardy saddle of tender rabbit, or the dreamy cinnamon ice cream with an apple sablé. It's a shame, though, that Denoual's creative fire is burning so low these days. With just a bit more spark, this food would be worth two toques. **C** 330-450 F. **M** 165 F, 135 F, 220 F, 320 F.

11/20 Les Grandes Marches

6, pl. de la Bastille
43 42 90 32,
fax 43 44 80 02

Open daily until 1am. Terrace dining. Air cond. Garage pkg. V, AE, DC.

Restored around the same time as the Opéra Bastille was built, this posh brasserie is a fine spot for a post-performance supper. Oysters and other shellfish, steaks, and a splendid turbotin (for two) are all good bets. **C** 250-350 F. **M** 168 F.

12/20 Le Mange-Tout

24, bd de la Bastille
43 43 95 15

Closed Sun, 1 wk in Aug. Open until 11pm. Priv rm: 18. Terrace dining. Pkg. V, AE, MC.

Uncomplicated cooking, served with a smile and a generous hand. Scrambled eggs with morels, skate with capers, andouillette sausage, and clafoutis are the mainstays of a traditional menu. **M** 98 F (weekdays, Sat lunch), 195 F (wine incl), 130 F, 160 F.

(13) D'Oggi

27, rue de Cotte
43 41 33 27

Closings not available. Open until 11pm. No pets. V, DC, MC.

Watch your step on the steep stairway that leads down to this tiny vaulted cellar! Once safely seated amid the crowd of happy diners, you'll enjoy delicious pasta, tasty Italian charcuterie, and an admirable tiramisù. The lunch menus are unbeatably priced, but even the à la carte tariffs are easy to take. **C** 180 F. **M** 60 F & 80 F (lunch exc Sun).

(15) L'Oulette

15, pl. Lachambeaudie - 40 02 02 12

Closed Sat lunch, Sun. Open until 10:15pm. Terrace dining. V, AE, MC.

A charmless cohort of office blocks contributes precious little warmth to the surroundings, and the large, dull dining room does nothing to dispel the chill. Happily, Marcel

Baudis can be relied upon to kindle a glow with his subtle, spirited Southwestern cooking. He ignited our enthusiasm recently with a savory chestnut bouillon enriched by tender morsels of guinea hen, an impeccably prepared John Dory in a lively sauce au verjus, and an effiloché de queue de bœuf full of robust, beefy flavor. These earthy yet perfectly modern dishes were followed by pears in flaky pastry (a pleasing variation on tourtière landaise, usually filled with apples) and a luscious sablé aux pommes caramélisées. The cellar is awash in sturdy wines from the Quercy and thereabouts; the service is very attentive. **C** 300-400 F. **M** 230 F (wine incl), 160 F.

13 La Plantation Paris

5, rue J.-César
43 07 64 15,
fax 40 19 92 56

Closed Sun. Open until 11pm. Priv rm: 12. V, AE.

Nouvelle cuisine, Creole-style: blaff de bulots (sea whelks marinated in lime juice and chilis), chicken in pan juices deglazed with pineapple vinegar, and duck with mangoes are expertly handled dishes full of vivid tropical flavors. Watch out for the wines, though: they considerably boost the bill. **C** 220-300 F. **M** 90 F (weekday lunch), 240 F (exc lunch).

15 Au Pressoir

257, av. Daumesnil
43 44 38 21,
fax 43 43 81 77

Closed Sat, Sun, 1 wk at Feb school hols, Aug. Open until 10:30pm. Priv rm: 35. Air cond. Valet pkg. V, MC.

Forgotten by most Parisians since the Colonial Exposition closed 60 years ago, the Porte Dorée district is home to a covey of fine restaurants. Le Pressoir numbers among them: chef Henri Séguin cooks with fine ingredients and a generous spirit, shown to advantage in his roast scallops with pumpkin, braised ox jowl with a suave cèpe coulis, and (in season) a sumptuous hare à la royale. The wine list offers a wealth of appealing choices, and the service is most accommodating. The décor, which was degenerating from dog-eared to dilapidated, recently received a facelift. **C** 450-580 F. **M** 390 F.

14 Le Quincy

28, av. Ledru-Rollin
46 28 46 76

Closed Sat, Sun, Mon, Aug 15-Sep 15. Open until 10pm. Air cond. No cards.

Bobosse, the jovial host, keeps things lively in this picturesque Parisian *bouchon*. The zestful bistro cooking, rooted in the Berry and Vivarais regions, is overseen by Jean-Pierre Rouat. We can vouch for his famously tasty farmhouse terrine served with garlicky cabbage, lusty beef-muzzle salad, exemplary chicken fricassée, boiled crayfish, and the best stuffed cabbage in town! To wash down these hearty victuals, there are delicious wines from the Loire and the Rhône Valley. **C** 300-400 F.

13 Sipario

69, rue de Charenton - 43 45 70 26,
fax 43 45 43 48

Closed Sun. Open until midnight. V, AE, DC, MC.

Sipario is nosing out of a steep decline, we're happy to say. If you're fond of rustic Italian fare, you'll like the excellent speck (smoked country ham), pappardelle sauced with duck juices and bits of the fowl's tender meat, and the richly flavored braised spiced beef. There's a Sicilian white wine on offer with a refreshing, sprightly bouquet. **C** 160-240 F. **M** 100 F (lunch), 220 F.

12/20 Le Train Bleu

Gare de Lyon,
20, bd Diderot
43 43 09 06,
fax 43 43 97 96

Open daily until 10pm. Priv rm: 100. Garage pkg. V, AE, DC.

The feast is for your eyes only: an extravagant, colossal, delirious, dazzling décor. Food at Le Train Bleu, though on the upswing, is still of the overpriced "standard French" variety. **C** 300-400 F. **M** 260 F (wine incl).

16 Au Trou Gascon

40, rue Taine
43 44 34 26,
fax 43 07 80 55

Closed Sat, Sun, Christmas wk, Aug. Open until 10pm. Air cond. Pkg. V, AE, DC, MC.

Can it be true, as some readers have said, that sauces are heavy and dishes occasionally botched at the Trou Gascon? You couldn't prove it by us. Our most recent repast found us raving, as usual, over the well-cured Chalosse ham, the warm pâté de cèpes in a bright-green parsley jus, the truffled chop of milk-fed veal with macaroni gratin, and the rich duck and pork cassoulet. To accompany this robust cooking, Nicole Dutournier recommends wonderful Madirans and Jurançons. True, the bistro décor is faintly frayed; the menu hasn't budged for years; and the prices (save for the lunch-hour set menu) are far from rustic. But as for the cooking, the Trou's two toques are safe! **C** 350-450 F. **M** 180 F (weekday lunch), 380 F (weekdays).

12/20 Les Zygomates

7, rue de Capri
40 19 93 04

Closed Sat lunch, Sun, Dec 27-Jan 3, Aug 1-24. Open until 10:15pm. No pets. V.

Lots of bright ideas come out of this kitchen: for starters, there's an earthy salad of pork tongue, followed by grenadier (a firm-fleshed fish) with red-wine butter or pig's tail with morels, and gingerbread ice cream for dessert. Expect a cordial welcome into the incredible dining room—formerly a butcher shop—full of *fin de siècle* details. **C** 200-250 F. **M** 125 F.

13th arrondissement

13 Auberge Etchegorry

Hôtel Vert Galant,
41, rue Croulebarbe
44 08 83 51

Closed Sun. Open until 10:30pm. Priv rm: 30. Terrace dining. Air cond. V, AE, DC.

Come here for hearty Basque food and wines. A cheerful *patron* plates up excellent regional charcuterie, tasty stuffed squid, and generously served quail paupiettes au foie gras. Lots of charm, and a lively atmosphere. **C** 250-350 F. **M** 155 F & 200 F (wine incl), 135 F.

13 Entoto

143, rue Léon-Maurice-Nordman
45 87 08 51

Closed Jul 20-Aug 9. Open until 7:30pm. No pets. No cards.

Entoto, or the vegetable kingdom. Spinach, pink lentils (in a delicious purée sparked with lime juice), pumpkin, and cracked wheat all feature prominently in the fiercely spiced dishes of Ethiopian cuisine. But meat-eaters will find their happiness too, in beef tartare, chopped lamb's tripe sautéed in butter, or guinea fowl ragoût served on a huge crêpe that does double duty as plate and bread. Charming décor. **C** 200-300 F.

13 Les Marronniers

53 bis, bd Arago
47 07 58 57,
fax 43 36 85 20

Closed Sun, Jul 28-Sep 10. Open until 11pm. Terrace dining. Air cond. Valet pkg. V, AE, DC, MC.

In fine weather one may choose between a table in the pretty pink interior or one on a pleasant patio under the eponymous chestnut trees. The *plats du jour* are usually the best part of chef Lorenzati's reliably appealing menu. Look for a good terrine of duck and wild mushrooms, Auvergne-style turbot, or an exemplary blanquette of baby lamb. Traditional cellar; efficient service. **C** 300-360 F. **M** 200 F (wine incl).

14 Le Petit Marguery

9, bd de Port-Royal
43 31 58 59

Closed Sun, Mon, Dec 23-Jan 2, Aug. Open until 10:15pm. Priv rm: 20. V, AE, DC, MC.

Michel and Jacques Cousin cook in a virile vein (game, offal, fresh fish, regional dishes) for an appreciative and very faithful public. Their bright, old-fashioned bistro is a most convivial spot. Alain Cousin directs the fleet-footed waiters who deliver generous platefuls of braised wild mushrooms, earthy terrine de boudin, cod gratin with oysters and asparagus, or partridge purée with juniper berries, as well as robust bourgeois classics like tuna stewed in Brouilly wine with fresh pasta. The single-price menus help keep costs down. **M** 160 F (lunch), 200 F, 320 F, 450 F.

13 Tang

44, av. d'Ivry
45 86 88 79

Open daily until 10pm. No pets. V, AE.

Looks aren't everything. What this huge Asian eatery most closely resembles is a soup kitchen, but the food is authentic, interesting, and incredibly low-priced (the average main dish goes for 40 F). Good bets from the extensive menu are jellyfish with 100-year-old eggs, most of the dim-sum, the spicy Szechuan shrimp, duck with black mushrooms, gingered crab, and fresh, perfectly seasoned four-meat noodles. We should warn you: the language barrier can be daunting—but go ahead and try your luck! **C** 150 F.

14 Les Vieux Métiers de France

13, bd A.-Blanqui
45 88 90 03,
fax 45 80 73 80

Closed Sun, Mon. Open until 10:30pm. Priv rm: 16. Air cond. V, AE, DC, MC.

Onto an austere modern building, chef Michel Moisan (with considerable help from his friends) has grafted the most amazing medieval décor of sculpted wood, stained glass, ancient beams, and antique paintings. What saves all this quaintness from tipping over into kitsch is Moisan's flavorful, personalized cuisine: rabbit with lentils en vinaigrette, seafood minestrone, spiced shoulder of lamb with pearl barley and an array of luscious desserts. The cellar is an oenophile's dream. **C** 350-450 F. **M** 165 F, 300 F.

14th arrondissement

14 L'Amuse-Bouche

186, rue du Château
43 35 31 61

Closed Sat lunch, Sun, Aug 1-15. Open until 10:30pm. V, AE.

Gilles Lambert's alert and graceful cuisine has won him the loyalty of a glossy clientele. Book a table in the elegant apricot-colored dining room and enjoy his marinated scallops and mussels with watercress, pikeperch in a Madiran sauce, or chicken breast stuffed with foie gras, then finish with a superb gâteau mousseux au chocolat amer. Succinct, well-designed wine list. **C** 280-380 F. **M** 160 F.

13 L'Angélus

12, rue Joannès
45 41 51 65

Closed Aug. Open until 10:15pm. Priv rm: 42. V, MC.

The spiffy bistro setting is accented with posters glorifying the magicians of yesteryear (one of the owners is a former illusionist). But there's no sleight of hand in the kitchen, just prime produce prepared with a light touch. We're partial to the flavorful, attractively presented foie gras, the fresh and tasty grilled sole, and the novel gâteau Belle-Hélène made with chocolate and pears. Well-annotated wine list, dominated by Burgundy and Bordeaux. **M** 72 F (lunch exc Sun, wine incl), 118 F (wine incl), 142 F.

13 Les Armes de Bretagne

108, av. du Maine
43 20 29 50,
fax 43 27 84 11

Closed Sat lunch, Sun (exc hols), Aug. Open until 11pm. Priv rm: 40. Air cond. Valet pkg. V, AE, DC, MC.

Here is an establishment that proudly upholds the old-fashioned traditions of hospitality, service, and French culinary showmanship in a luxurious Second Empire dining room. Top-quality seafood from Brittany stars in William Dhenin's best dishes: fresh oysters, sea bass en croûte with beurre blanc, crêpes aux langoustines, and grilled lobster. **C** 300-450 F. **M** 200 F.

13 Auberge de l'Argoat

27, av. Reille
45 89 17 05

Closed Sat, Sun, Aug 12-20. Open until 10pm. V, AE, MC.

Here's a welcoming, unpretentious little seafood spot, situated across from the Parc Montsouris. Jeannine Gaulon greets diners warmly, while in the kitchen her chef cooks up soupe de poissons, langoustine and artichoke salad, sole à la bretonne, and grilled sea bream. A few meat dishes round out this agreeable bill of fare. **C** 250-320 F. **M** 100 F (lunch), 180 F.

11/20 Le Bar à Huîtres

112, bd du Montparnasse - 43 20 71 01,
fax 43 21 35 47

Open daily until 2am. Terrace dining. V, AE, MC.

At this popular oyster bar you can, if you wish, order and eat just one oyster—but that would be a shame. Six or a dozen Belons, fines, or spéciales would surely be more satisfying, as are the gargantuan shellfish platters (190 to 590 F). The cooked fish dishes, however, are skippable. Interesting cellar of white wines. **C** 220-300 F. **M** 98 F, 128 F, 198 F.

12/20 Bistrot du Dôme

1, rue Delambre
43 35 32 00

Open daily until 11pm. V, AE.

Flipping-fresh seafood is presented with becoming simplicity at this fashionable spot: featured are crispy fried smelts, tuna with sauce vierge, and lotte in a garlicky cream sauce.

Intelligent wine list; merry ambience. **C** 230-300 F.

16 La Cagouille

Opposite 23 rue de l'Ouest, 12, pl. C.-Brancusi
43 22 09 01

Closed Dec 24-Jan 3. Open until 10:30pm. Priv rm: 16. Terrace dining. V, AE.

Gérard Allemandou has a rare talent for drawing hordes of seafood lovers to the most improbable locations. A few years ago, not even Parisian taxi drivers had heard of the Place Brancusi. Now the address is noted in every restaurant guide in the city, thanks to La Cagouille. At this *bistro du port*, dishes made from the very freshest fish and shellfish (delivered direct from Atlantic ports) are chalked on a blackboard: depending on the day's catch, they might include exquisite tiny squid in a garlicky sauce of their own ink, baked black scallops from Brest, fresh fried anchovies, shad in beurre blanc sauce, herbed brill, plump mackerel with mustard sauce, or thick, juicy sole. If you are content to drink a modest Aligoté or Quincy, your bill will hover around 300-350 F. But beware if you succumb to the temptations of the finest Cognac collection in Paris (and maybe the world). **C** 270-380 F. **M** 250 F (wine incl), 150 F.

14 Le Caroubier

122, av. du Maine
43 20 41 49

Closed Sun dinner, Mon, Aug. Open until 10:30pm. Air cond. V.

Do you like couscous? Here you'll find the genuine article: homemade, hand-rolled, and fragrant with spices. Also on hand are a lively eggplant salad, savory pastillas, and succulent tagines, simmered in the best Moroccan tradition. Heartwarming welcome. **C** 180-220 F. **M** 130 F.

14 La Chaumière des Gourmets

22, pl. Denfert-Rochereau
43 21 22 59

Closed Sat lunch, Sun, Aug. Open until 10:30pm. Priv rm: 20. Terrace dining. V, AE.

The Chaumière's friendly, provincial dining room still features faded wallpaper, the staff carries on with imperturbable diligence, the wine list remains small, and the house repertoire invariably classic. But in this case, no news really is good news: the delicious salade de ris de veau, the expertly grilled red mullet with ratatouille, and the famously tasty apple tart attest to Jean-Paul Huc's unfailing consistency and flair. **C** 300-450 F. **M** 165 F, 240 F.

12/20 La Coupole

102, bd du Montparnasse - 43 20 14 20, fax 43 35 46 14

Closed Dec 24. Open until 2am. Air cond. V, AE, MC.

This Montparnasse landmark, respectfully restored and run by the Flo brasserie group, survives with its mystique intact. The menu bears Flo's unmistakable stamp: exemplary shellfish assortments, grilled meats, and carafes of sprightly house Riesling are delivered by swift, efficient waiters. **C** 250-350 F. **M** 85 F (lunch exc Sun), 109 F (wine incl).

16 Le Dôme

108, bd du Montparnasse - 43 35 25 81, fax 42 79 01 19

Closed Mon. Open until 12:45am. Priv rm: 10. Air cond. V, AE, DC, MC.

Le Dôme is the capital's top seafood brasserie, with a neo-Art Deco interior, booths that provide cozy comfort and privacy for the high-powered patrons (they include President Mitterrand and Mayor Chirac—who don't, of course, sit together), and a wonderful *carte* prepared by chef Franck Graux. In addition to impeccably fresh oysters and the justly famous lobster salad in a truffled dressing, there is a velvety bouillon de langoustines aux champignons, a hefty turbot hollandaise, sea bass in chive vinaigrette, and bouillabaisse that bears comparison with Marseille's best. Precise, cheerful service, and a cellar filled with bottles that incite you to splurge. **C** 450-600 F.

12/20 Giovanna

22, rue E.-Jacques
43 22 32 09

Closed Sat lunch, Sun, Dec 24-Jan 2, Aug 5-31. Open until 10pm. V, MC.

You, your companion, and sixteen other diners can tuck into perfectly wrought fresh pasta and other tasty Italian dishes in this minute *trattoria*. Don't overlook the osso buco. **C** 150-200 F (lunch). **M** 65 F (lunch).

Prices in red draw attention to restaurants that offer a particularly good value.

14

Aux Iles Marquises

15, rue de la Gaîté
43 20 93 58

Closed Sat lunch, Sun, Aug 1-16. Open until 11:30pm. Priv rm: 15. V, AE, MC.

Once a favorite haunt of Édith Piaf and her friends, the Iles Marquises is decked out with salty nautical décor (shrimp-colored walls with seascape frescoes). Owner-chef Mathias Théry offers a creditable 150 F menu that brings zesty marinated scallops, sea-bream fillet with fresh pasta, then dessert, coffee, and petits-fours. But this good food deserves a better cellar. **C** 250-400 F. **M** 130 F, 150 F.

12/20

Justine

Hôtel Méridien,
19, av. du Cdt-Mouchotte
44 36 44 00,
fax 44 36 49 03

Open daily until 11pm. Air cond. No pets. Valet pkg. V, AE, DC.

A pretty winter garden in the Méridien Montparnasse is the backdrop to an attractive buffet, one of the best bargains in Paris. For 195 F you can help yourself to any amount of soup, crudités, mixed salads, terrines, and tasty *plats du jour* followed by very good cheeses and desserts. **C** 250-300 F. **M** 195 F (buffet).

14

Lous Landés

157, av. du Maine
45 43 08 04

Closed Sat lunch, Sun, Aug. Open until 10:30pm. Priv rm: 14. Air cond. V, AE, DC, MC.

Hervé Rumen's Southwestern specialties range from the frankly robust to more refined versions of country cooking. Taste his truffled escalopes de foie gras au jus de canard, tender Landais squab flavored with three kinds of garlic, or his world-class cassoulet. Desserts are all you would expect from a former colleague of Christian Constant, and the wine list offers some excellent Cahors and Madirans. Marie-Thérèse, a charming hostess, welcomes guests into the pretty green dining room. **C** 300-400 F. **M** 190 F, 300 F.

13

Le Moniage Guillaume

88, rue de la Tombe-Issoire
43 22 96 15

Closed Sun. Open until 10:15pm. Priv rm: 30. Terrace dining. Valet pkg. V, AE, DC, MC.

Michel and Nelly Garanger work hard to please their patrons, providing a warm welcome and top-quality cuisine. Michel chooses superlative seafood for his classic, expertly handled dishes: beechwood-smoked salmon prepared on the premises, baked turbot, swordfish with a bright garnish of tomato fondue and zucchini, lobster fricassée, and a satisfying warm apple tart. Wide-ranging cellar. **C** 350-500 F. **M** 180 F, 240 F.

17

Montparnasse 25

Hôtel Méridien,
19, rue du Cdt-Mouchotte
44 36 44 25,
fax 44 36 49 03

Closed Sat, Sun, Dec 23-Feb 2, Jul 29-Aug 29. Open until 10:30pm. Priv rm: 22. Air cond. No pets. Valet pkg. V, AE, DC.

Unlike so many hotel restaurants, which are little more than a convenience for in-house patrons, the Méridien boasts a magnetic menu that draws gourmets from all over Paris. The Art Deco interior opens onto a tiny garden, and the well-spaced tables are just what executives desire for their power lunches. Yet even the most intense negotiations come to a halt when the waiter presents chef Jean-Yves Guého's ingenious, imaginative dishes. This triple-toque winner cooked for years at the Hong Kong Méridien, and it shows in his Cantonese-style sweet-and-sour brill, spiced duck with basil, and rack of lamb in a spiced crust with a jus redolent of Thai herbs. He also entices appetites with his rack of milk-fed veal perfumed with an elusive hint of juniper, scallops encased in a crisp, paper-thin buckwheat crêpe, or tender morsels of pork paired with crayfish in a barley bouillon. The 230 F single-price menu offered at lunch is a steal, and so is the slightly more expensive version offered at dinner, which also includes selections from a monumental cheese board. Sommelier Gérard Margeon presides over a cellar awash in remarkable (and affordable) growers' wines. **C** 420-600 F. **M** 230 F (lunch), 290 F & 380 F (dinner).

Restaurant names in red draw attention to restaurants that offer a particularly good value.

Vittel
Grande Source
SOURCE
Perrier
DECLAREE
D'INTERET PUBLIC
33cl

Pavillon Montsouris

20, rue Gazan
45 88 38 52,
fax 45 88 63 40

Open daily until 10:30pm. Priv rm: 40. Terrace dining. No pets. Valet pkg. V, AE, DC, MC.

A walk across the Parc Montsouris at sunset will help you work up an appetite for a fine feast in this turn-of-the-century greenhouse overlooking the park, once a favorite rendezvous of the beautiful spy, Mata Hari. Stéphane Ruel's 255 F menu adds allure to this charming Parisian spot, bringing plenty of custom for his saddle of rabbit with potato salad, sea bass with shallots, veal sweetbreads and kidney in a caramelized garlic cream sauce, and for dessert, a sinful chocolate galette with pistachio ice cream. For even less money (189 F), you can treat yourself to the likes of a keen-flavored salad of skate dressed with lime, lamb's sweetbreads with garlicky cucumbers, and a flaky mango pithiviers. Yvan Courault, who used to manage the Grand Véfour, excels in the gracious art of welcoming guests. **C** 255-280 F. **M** 189 F, 255 F.

Les Petites Sorcières

12, rue Liancourt
43 21 95 68

Closed Sat lunch, Sun. Open until 10:30pm (by reserv). Terrace dining. V, MC.

Christian Teule, a talented chef of the Robuchon school, fills up his pocket-sized restaurant with an appealing 120 F lunch menu that on a given day might feature house-made jambon persillé followed by duck pot-au-feu with fava beans and pinenuts, with apple tart or baba au rhum for dessert. A la carte choices are more elaborate but no less savory: we especially like the fresh sardine croustillant with anchovy butter, the spiced lamb pie, and the vanilla-scented apricot tart. Good wines are available by the carafe. **C** 180-240 F. **M** 120 F (lunch).

La Régalade

49, av. J.-Moulin
45 45 68 58,
fax 45 40 96 74

Closed Sat lunch, Sun, Mon, at Christmas, Easter, Aug. Open until midnight. Air cond. No pets. V.

Don't neglect to book your table in advance, for this antique bistro fills up fast. Here's why: Béarn native Yves Camdeborde (ex-Crillon, no less) serves first-rate cooking that is eminently affordable as well. Regionally rooted but modern in outlook, the menu proposes a sapid terrine of oxtail and leek, calf's liver presented in a thick, rosy-pink slice, succulent wood pigeon barded with bacon, and a comforting assortment of homey desserts. The frisky wines sell for giveaway prices, and the atmosphere at the close-set tables where Claudine Camdeborde seats her guests is merry indeed. **M** 150 F.

Au Vin des Rues

21, rue Boulard
43 22 19 78

Lunch only (& dinner Wed & Fri by reserv). Closed Feb 26-Mar 6, Aug 6-Sep 4. Terrace dining. No cards.

Ex-baker Jean Chanrion's bustling, friendly bistro offers an exemplary Lyonnais repertoire, ranging from pot-au-feu to coq au Beaujolais and salt cod à la lyonnaise. The Beaujolais and Mâconnais wines are sold by the *pichet*, of course. **C** 150-200 F.

Vishnou

13, rue du Cdt-Mouchotte
45 38 92 93,
fax 44 07 31 19

Closed Sun. Open until 11:30pm (Fri & Sat midnight). Priv rm: 50. Terrace dining. Air cond. Pkg. V, AE, DC.

Silken saris line the walls of this uncommonly luxurious Indian eating house. A distinguished-looking staff serves forth fragrant dishes that are finely wrought and full of exotic flavors. Savor the subtle Hyderabadi beef, a good vegetable curry, or take advantage of the fine 150 F lunch: shrimp salad, chicken tandoori, basmati rice, and poppadums are followed by a delicious besan barfi for dessert. Amazingly, the wine list is diverse and informative. **C** 250-400 F. **M** 95 F & 150 F (lunch, wine incl), 230 F (dinner, wine incl), 220 F.

15th arrondissement

L'Agape

281, rue Lecourbe
45 58 19 29

Closed Aug 6-26. Open until 10:30pm. Terrace dining. V.

The place needs some fixing up, and the staff needs some breaking in, but chef-owner Marc Lamic hit his stride right off the bat. His appealing menu brims with bright ideas and flavors: we gobbled up his delicious confit de canard served with a cold potato terrine, the tasty sculpin fillet encased in a sesame crust, and the savory stuffed saddle of rabbit garnished with ratatouille ravioli. Desserts are more down-to-earth, but then so are the prices. **M** 120 F (exc Sun).

12/20 Le Barrail

17, rue Falguière
43 22 42 61,
fax 42 79 93 91

Closed Sat, Sun. Open until 10pm. Priv rm: 12. Air cond. V, AE, MC.

An attractive spot done up in soft pink tones. Alain Magne's cooking is low-key, but the prices are fairly high-tone, owing to a lavish use of truffles, foie gras, langoustines, and other luxuries. Good bets are the salmon and leek lasagne and the savory sautéed beef with carrots. **C** 230-350 F. **M** 110 F (weekdays, wine incl), 140 F (weekday lunch), 160 F.

Bistro 121

121, rue
de la Convention
45 57 52 90,
fax 45 57 14 69

Open daily until midnight. Air cond. V, AE, DC, MC.

This 30-year-old bistro decorated in what is by now a dated "modern" style by Slavik, serves the sort of classic, heavily sauced dishes that some people will always imagine is "real" French cooking. André Jalbert pleases his well-heeled, conservative public with laudable versions of foie gras chaud aux cerises, panaché de sole au homard et langoustines, and confit de canard with garlicky potatoes. While à la carte prices are steep, the two set menus offer reliable value. **C** 270-380 F. **M** 200 F (winter, exc Sun dinner), 200 F (wine incl), 150 F (summer).

12/20 Le Bouchut

9, rue Bouchut
45 67 15 65

Closed Sat lunch (dinner May-Jul), Sun, Aug. Open until 10pm. Terrace dining. Air cond. V, AE, MC.

This intimate little spot, set back from the Avenue de Breteuil, caters to faithful customers who return again and again for Philippe Metais's sea bream seasoned with fennel-flavored oil or parmentier de gésiers de canard confit (duck gizzards topped with fluffy mashed potatoes). For dessert, there's a pretty assortment of strawberry sweets. The fine cellar highlights wines from the Loire Valley. **C** 220-320 F. **M** 120 F (lunch, wine incl), 158 F (wine incl).

12/20 Casa Alcade

117, bd de Grenelle
47 83 39 71

Open daily until 10:30pm. Priv rm: 40. Air cond. V, MC.

A lively *bodega* offering zesty Basque and Spanish fare. Try the excellent pipérade, marinated anchovies, generously served paella, or codfish à la luzienne. The wine list features fine bottles from beyond the Pyrenees. **C** 230-330 F. **M** 120 F (weekday lunch, Sat), 160 F.

Les Célébrités

Hôtel Nikko,
61, quai de Grenelle
40 58 20 00,
fax 45 75 42 35

Closed Aug 1-31. Open until 10pm. Priv rm: 22. Air cond. Heated pool. Valet pkg. V, AE, DC, MC.

Even for inveterate quibblers like us, it isn't easy to find something to criticize at Les Célébrités. The dining room turned toward the Seine is a paragon of hushed elegance; the menu strikes a studied balance between modernized traditional dishes, updated haute-cuisine classics, and fashionable low-fat fare; no rough edges mar Jacques Sénéchal's virtuoso handling of flawless seasonal foodstuffs. His dishes are characterized by refined yet definite flavors, witness the lobster steamed over Sauternes wine, full-flavored lamb with fava beans, or celestially succulent chop of milk-fed veal. For dessert, there's a sublime chocolate-mocha tartlet. As for the cellar, it's beyond reproach: astutely assembled, appealing and, all in all, affordably priced. Speaking of affordable, the prix-fixe menu still tariffed at 280 F is a very good deal indeed. **C** 380-650 F. **M** 280 F, 370 F.

Le Clos Morillons

50, rue des Morillons - 48 28 04 37

Closed Sat lunch, Sun, 2 wks mid Aug. Open until 10pm. Air cond. V, AE, MC.

The French colonial décor of this charming establishment transports you to the tropics. The feeling lingers as you peruse the menu, for Philippe Delacourcelle's repertoire is redolent of exotic spices. Among the original, expertly rendered dishes are sole with sweet lime leaves, calf's liver scented with cinnamon, suavely spiced snails, and gingered veal with puréed almonds. Delectable desserts and a fine selection of wines priced under 100 F complete the picture. **C** 280-350 F. **M** 160 F, 285 F (weekdays, Sat dinner).

14 **La Dinée**
85, rue Leblanc
45 54 20 49,
fax 40 60 74 88

Closed Jul 29-Aug 22. Open until 10:30pm. Priv rm: 16. Garage pkg. V, AE, MC.

Christophe Chabanel won his toque at the tender age of 22. Here in his new digs, a pluperfect neighborhood restaurant, he continues to impress us with his finely honed technique and inventive, modern cooking. Among the excellent options on offer, we recommend the delicious terrine of lambs' tongues with Italian parsley, the warm salad of quail and artichokes in a vivid beet jus, and perfectly roasted pikeperch garnished with a zesty anchoïade and skewered squid. **C** 250-300 F. **M** 260 F (weekday dinner, Sun), 160 F (weekday lunch).

13 **L'Épopée**
89, av. E.-Zola
45 77 71 37

Closed Sat lunch, Sun. Open until 10:30pm. Terrace dining. V, AE, MC.

A most engaging little restaurant, owned by veteran maître d' Yves Millon. His chef, Patrick Léger, executes a concise *carte* of sophisticated, subtly flavorful dishes: crab millefeuille, veal noisettes sauced with an unctuous foie gras emulsion, and lamb fillet encased in a fragrant sage crust. Léger's desserts are (naturally!) light and ethereal; try his spiced berry soup laced with red wine. To drink, order a tasty Coteaux-du-Tricastin red from the Domaine de Grangeneuve—it's a terrific value. **C** 210-330 F. **M** 168 F.

12/20 **Erawan**
76, rue de la Fédération - 47 83 55 67

Closed Sun, Aug. Open until 10:30pm. Air cond. No pets. V, AE, MC.

Lots of regulars crowd into Erawan's little dining rooms to feast on Thai cuisine tailored for Western palates—hot it's not! Recommended are the pork-rind salad with fresh herbs and fried rice, baked cod strewn with lemon leaves in a spicy sauce, and the delicious Thai fondue. **C** 220-300 F. **M** 75 F (lunch), 106 F, 138 F, 146 F, 172 F.

12/20 **La Farigoule**
104, rue Balard
45 54 35 41

Closed Mon dinner, Sun, Aug 12-28. Open until 10pm. Garage pkg. V, AE.

Jean Gras is a colorful sexagenarian who concocts the best, most fragrant bouillabaisse in Paris. His bourride (a garlicky fish soup) isn't half bad either, and he stirs up a rousing rendition of sheep's tripe and trotters à la marseillaise. Every dish is served with a smile and a lilting Provençal accent. **C** 250-350 F.

14 **Fellini**
58, rue de la Croix-Nivert - 45 77 40 77

Closed Sat lunch, Sun, Aug. Open until 10:45pm. Air cond. No pets. V, MC.

Giuseppe hails from sunny Napoli, where he learned to cook in a fresh, forthright style that warms our hearts. Pull up a seat in his friendly trattoria, and sample his warm salad of baby squid and white beans drizzled with olive oil, or house-made fettuccine showered with strips of prosciutto, pancetta, olives, and cauliflower. His tiramisù is the lightest we've tried. To wash it all down, uncork a bottle of fine Italian wine from the well-stocked cellar. **C** 250-300 F. **M** 130 F (weekday lunch).

12/20 **Gulistan**
6, rue Lefebvre
48 28 04 92

Open daily until 11:30pm. Terrace dining. No pets. Pkg. V, DC, MC.

Best of show in this friendly Indian eatery are the sautéed lamb in spinach sauce, tender chicken tandoori with saffron-hued basmati rice, and ice cream studded with nuts and dried apricots. Other dishes, though just as graciously served and moderately priced, are often disappointing. **C** 180-230 F. **M** 65 F (weekday lunch), 85 F (lunch), 105 F (dinner).

14 **Kim-Anh**
15, rue de l'Église
45 79 40 96,
fax 40 59 49 78

Dinner only. Open daily until 11:30pm. Air cond. V, AE, MC.

Charming Kim-Anh runs this tidy, flower-filled little

Vietnamese restaurant while his wife, Caroline, practices her culinary craft in a lilliputian kitchen made for contortionists. She prepares her dishes with fresh herbs, delectable leaves and shoots, subtle spices, and light sauces. Try the shrimp soup flavored with tamarind, shredded beef fried with peanuts and vinegar, steamed snails Tonkin, a wonderfully piquant stuffed crab, and the best egg rolls in town. Quite a fine wine selection and some surprisingly good desserts. **C** 260-320 F. **M** 220 F.

Morot-Gaudry

17

8, rue de la Cavalerie
45 67 06 85,
fax 45 67 55 72

Closed Sat, Sun. Open until 10pm. Priv rm: 28. Terrace dining. Air cond. V, AE, MC.

It would be hard to find a more ample or appetizing lunch for 220 F (a price unchanged for years) than the one served at Jean-Pierre Morot-Gaudry's rooftop restaurant. It commences with a lusty calf's foot croustillant, then proceeds to rabbit stewed in white wine with wild thyme, and concludes with a selection of cheeses and a tartelette de poires Bourdaloue. Included in the price is one of a dozen delicious wines. But Morot-Gaudry's à la carte menu also has its charms: we're thinking of his foie gras en terrine laced with sweet wine, the fricassée of snails and salsify with a lively touch of mustard, scallops in a bright, creamy parsley sauce, salmon and smoky bacon with crisp sautéed cabbage, or tender Normandy beef pan-roasted in a richly flavored sauce of vintage Médoc.

Some impressive and costly wines are proposed, such as a Montrachet "Marquis de Laguiche" or a Gruaud-Larose '28. But what thrills us *chez* Morot-Gaudry is the selection of Jurançons, Chinon Vieilles Vignes, Savennières, and Vouvrays which give enormous pleasure without breaking the bank. Danièle Morot-Gaudry's welcome is wonderful, and from the verdant terrace you can glimpse a corner of the Eiffel Tower. **C** 400-500 F. **M** 220 F (lunch, wine incl), 390 F.

Le Moulin

13

70, rue Vouillé
48 28 81 61

Closed Sat lunch, Sun dinner. Open until 10:30pm. Priv rm: 25. V, AE, MC.

A quiet, unassuming sort of spot, where quality ingredients are handled with care and respect. A courteous, diligent staff serves forth the chef's bracing tuna tartare sparked with lemon, delicious fricassée de sole et de langoustines, filet mignon Rossini au jus de truffe, and for dessert, tender crêpes wrapped around a smooth praline filling. **C** 300-400 F. **M** 130 F, 150 F.

L'Oie Cendrée

13

51, rue Labrouste
45 31 91 91

Closed Sat, Sun lunch, Dec 24-Jan 5, Aug 1-22. Open until 9:30pm. V, MC.

This family-style dining room is conducive to relaxed, casual dining and the menu provides the wherewithal for a hearty tuck-in. Duck, in every permutation, is the specialty of the house. For top value, choose the 125 F set meal, which brings escargots in crisp pastry with a garlicky cream sauce, magret de canard (duck breast) au gros sel, and warm chocolate-walnut cake. The wine list presents a small selection of regional bottlings. **C** 250-280 F. **M** 95 F (Sat), 125 F.

L'Os à Moelle

13

3, rue Vasco-de-Gama - 45 57 27 27

Closed 2 wks in Aug. Open until 10:30pm. V, MC.

Thierry Faucher gives his customers terrific value for their money, with imaginative, oft-renewed menus inspired by whatever looks fresh and fine at the market. The 140 F set meal, for example, might bring an asparagus feuilleté with coddled eggs or a lively mackerel salad scented with tarragon, with salmon and lentils or guinea fowl and cabbage for a main course, and prune pie for dessert. The 180 F dinner is equally alluring, with the likes of creamy scrambled eggs and meadow mushrooms, tuna-topped pizza showered with basil, squid risotto enriched with lobster cream, and caramelized melon with chocolate quenelles and saffron sauce. With regional wines are uniformly priced (70 F a bottle, 140 F a magnum), this one looks like a real winner! **M** 180 F (dinner), 140 F (lunch).

Le Père Claude

14

51, av. de La Motte-Picquet
47 34 03 05

Open daily until midnight. Terrace dining. Air cond. V, AE, MC.

Claude Perraudin lives like a monk (albeit of the

Rabelaisian variety), his existence devoted to feeding his flock of faithful patrons. Working seven days a week (until midnight) in his newly enlarged brasserie, Father Claude oversees a gargantuan rotisserie, where strings of sausages, plump poultry, racks of lamb, and suckling pigs spin slowly on the spit as they roast to crisp, tender perfection. And there are oceans of tasty wine to wash it all down. The prices? Blessedly low, of course. **C** 220-320 F. **M** 92 F (weekdays), 115 F (w-e), 250 F, 140 F.

Le Petit Plat

14

49, av. Émile-Zola
45 78 24 20,
fax 45 78 23 13

Closed Dec 24-Jan 1. Open until 11pm. Priv rm: 43. Terrace dining. Air cond. V, MC.

Clémentine Gault (our friend Henri's daughter) and the Lampréia brothers present a mouthwatering menu of utterly simple, totally delicious fare. In season, look for the full-flavored tomatoes à la provençale; any time of year, you're likely to find fresh cockles and mussels in a fragrant broth, succulent veal breast with slow-roasted vegetables, and fresh pasta showered with bits of smoky bacon. Henri Gault personally composed the attractive wine list. **C** 170-220 F. **M** 130 F (lunch, exc Sun).

La Petite Bretonnière

16

2, rue de Cadix
48 28 34 39

Closed Sat lunch, Sun, Aug. Open until 9:30pm. Garage pkg. V.

What with the Porte de Versailles exhibition halls just around the corner, we wonder why this bright, charming spot doesn't fill up with visitors from the trade fairs? They surely couldn't find better food than at La Petite Bretonnière. Alain Lamaison's dishes are lively and daring, particularly in their treatment of vegetables and fruit. He deserves a wider audience for his wonderful white-bean soup enriched with morsels of langoustine and chorizo, pan-roasted scallops swathed in a surprisingly spiced lamb jus and garnished with grape-studded couscous, and his succulent farm pigeon flanked by silken puréed dates. Madirans and Bordeaux are the highlights of a rich cellar. Impeccable welcome and service. **C** 400-500 F. **M** 200 F (lunch).

Rascasson

13

148, rue de Vaugirard - 47 34 63 45,
fax 47 34 39 45

Closed Sat lunch, Sun, Aug. Open until 10pm. Priv rm: 40. Terrace dining. Air cond. V.

Once a pizzeria, now a winsome little seafood spot, the Rascasson is a good place for fresh fish with a Provençal accent. Michel Garbi turns out wonderfully crispy fried rockfish, red mullet enhanced by a zesty marinade, baked rascasse (sculpin), and for dessert, a fine cinnamon-nut cake. The cellar offers a good choice of affordable bottles. **M** 135 F.

Le Relais de Sèvres

Hôtel Sofitel,
8-12, rue L.-Armand
40 60 30 30,
fax 45 57 04 22

Closed Sat, Sun, at Christmas, Aug. Open until 10pm. Priv rm: 15. Air cond. Heated pool. Valet pkg. V, AE, DC, MC.

For its flagship restaurant, the Sofitel chain chose a décor that spells *good taste* in capital letters: blond woodwork, pale-blue fabric on the walls, Champagne-colored napery, Louis XV chairs... A new chef has just taken over the kitchen (the talented Martial Enguehard has set off to open a place of his own), so we'll wait until he has found his bearings to rate his cuisine. The Relais still boasts a splendid, reasonably priced cellar and an admirably trained staff. **C** 350-550 F. **M** 300 F (wine incl).

Restaurant de La Tour

13

"Roger Conticini,"
6, rue Desaix
43 06 04 24

Closed Sat lunch, Sun, Aug. Open until 10:30pm. V.

Roger Conticini (his sons run the triple-toque Table d'Anvers in the ninth arrondissement) is at the helm of this engaging little restaurant. The dishes on his trio of single-price menus change often, but all have an earthy, raffish appeal: sardine galette with fresh vegetables, a lusty salad of pig's ear and trotter, mustard-roasted mackerel flanked by potatoes whipped with pungent olive oil, and a famously good blanquette of veal and chicken with basmati rice. Tasty little wines sell for under 100 F. Nice going, Roger! **C** 210-

330 F. **M** 165 F (dinner), 108 F & 138 F (lunch).

14

Sawadee

53, av. Émile-Zola
45 77 68 90

Open daily until 10:30pm. No pets. V, AE, MC.

We think Sawadee is the best Thai restaurant in the city. Spacious, over-decorated, very lively, it offers an immense list of specialties full of unexpected flavors. The salad of pork rinds and fried rice, the skewered shellfish, mussels in a fiery sauce, cod with seaweed and wild lemon, duck perfumed with Thai basil, and coconut ice cream all come highly recommended. With a bottle of good Thai beer, your tab will hover around 200 F. **C** 260 F. **M** 75 F (lunch exc Sun), 106 F, 138 F, 146 F, 172 F.

14

Aux Senteurs de Provence

295, rue Lecourbe
45 57 11 98

Closed Sat lunch, Sun, Aug 7-21. Open until 10pm. Terrace dining. V, AE, DC, MC.

Serge Arce turns out a delicate, freshly fragrant version of Provençal cuisine. Sun-kissed ingredients lend an authentic Southern savor to his tuna in a tarragon marinade (as pretty as it is appetizing), roast galinette (a Mediterranean fish) à la niçoise enhanced by a perfect vegetable brunoise, and generous bouillabaisse. The cellar is modest, but the surroundings are neat and cheerful, with cork-covered walls and jaunty nautical prints. **C** 250-380 F. **M** 152 F.

15

Pierre Vedel

19, rue Duranton
45 58 43 17,
fax 45 58 42 65

Closed Sat lunch (& dinner in summer), Sun, Christmas wk. Open until 10:15pm. No pets. Garage pkg. V.

Be sure to book your table, because Pierre Vedel's warm Parisian bistro is invariably jam-packed. Little wonder the place is popular, with dishes like shellfish ravioli, chicken-liver terrine with lobster coulis, and sweetbreads en blanquette with wild mushrooms on the menu. True to his Southern roots, Vedel also prepares an admirably authentic bourride de lotte à la sétoise (a garlicky monkfish soup), and a satisfying nougat glacé studded with candied fruit. If you order one of the more modest growers' wines from the interesting list, you can rest assured that the bill won't be too bad. **C** 250-350 F.

16th arrondissement

14

Amazigh

2, rue La Pérouse
47 20 90 38

Closed Sat lunch, Sun. Open until 11pm. Air cond. V, AE, DC, MC.

A Moroccan restaurant with a bill of fare that grazes the two-toque level. Best of show are the savory briouates (deep-fried pastries) filled with shellfish, the eggplant salad sparked with coriander (zalouk), lamb tagine with fried eggplant, and the sumptuous "grand couscous." Also worthy of interest are the tasty stuffed sardines, lamb's brains in tomato sauce, cinnamon-scented oranges, and buttery puff pastry layered with almond cream. Like the setting, the service is pretty posh. **C** 300-400 F.

13

L'Antre du Roi Philène

16, rue Lauriston
45 00 25 03,
fax 45 00 25 77

Closed Sat, Sun, Dec 22-29, Aug 1-24. Open until 10:15pm. V, AE, DC, MC.

The mythic king in question loved to dip his spoon into a bowlful of soup, and various *potages* are indeed a prominent feature of this cozy pink-and-white restaurant. Also on hand is a selection of French and Italian offerings: asparagus millefeuille, saffron-spiced truffle risotto, and beef poached in a savory broth. Good cellar. **C** 300-350 F. **M** 139 F, 175 F, 320 F.

13

La Baie d'Ha' Long

164, av. de Versailles - 45 24 60 62,
fax 42 30 58 98

Closed Sun, Jul 25-Aug 30. Open until 10pm. Priv rm: 20. Terrace dining. Air cond. No pets. V, AE.

Roger, the proprietor of this small Vietnamese spot, is far more interested in his collection of birds and exotic fish than in food. It's his wife, Nathalie, who toils away in the kitchen producing delicious, exotic dishes from her native Vietnam: spicy soups, brochettes perfumed with fresh herbs, duck grilled with ginger. Generous portions. The cellar holds some surprisingly good wines. **C** 180-240 F. **M** 99 F (weekday lunch).

Bellini

(14)

28, rue Le Sueur
45 00 54 20

Closed Sat lunch, Sun, Aug 1-28. Open until 10:30pm. Air cond. V, AE, MC.

Comfy banquettes, smoked mirrors, gray marble, and peach-toned walls create a cozy setting for Bellini's somewhat Frenchified Italian fare. Diaphanous slices of excellent prosciutto di Parma lead into such savory dishes as sautéed squid seasoned with balsamic vinegar, golden tagliatelle topped with your choice of truffles, cèpes, or clams, and red mullet with tangy tapenade. For dessert, we're partial to the incredibly light tiramisù. The cellar harbors appealing wines from Friulia, Tuscany, and the Veneto. **C** 275-330 F. **M** 180 F.

Le Bertie's

(14)

Hôtel Baltimore,
1, rue Léo-Delibes
44 34 54 34,
fax 44 34 54 44

Open daily until 10:30pm. Priv rm: 14. Air cond. V, AE, DC, MC.

When Le Bertie's opened not long ago, a major London daily ran this tongue-in-cheek headline: "Finally! A good meal in Paris!" The dining room of the Hotel Baltimore cultivates a clubby British look that Parisians adore. And yes, the menu is English—but the potted crab, celery and Stilton soup, fish and chips with tartar sauce, grilled sirloin steak, bread-and-butter pudding, and the rest are prepared by a French chef! The maître d' will astound you with his knowledge of Britain's 400 cheeses; the wine steward will amaze you with his list of twenty prime clarets all priced at just 190 F. And after your meal, you can linger contentedly over a rare whisky or vintage Port. **C** 280-320 F. **M** 160 F, 195 F.

Bistrot de l'Étoile-Lauriston

(14)

19, rue Lauriston
40 67 11 16,
fax 45 00 99 87

Closed Sat lunch, Sun. Open until midnight. Air cond. V, AE, MC.

This big, bright bistro continues on its successful career. Chef William Ledeuil handles the neo-bourgeois repertoire with admirable ease, offering rabbit persillé or a vibrant vegetable salad showered with Parmesan to start, followed by steak à la bordelaise or stuffed veal shank simmered in a sparky vinegar sauce. For dessert, we warmly recommend the apple-rhubarb crumble. **C** 190-280 F.

La Butte Chaillot

(14)

110 bis, av. Kléber
47 27 88 88,
fax 47 04 85 70

Open daily until midnight. Priv rm: 20. Air cond. V, AE, MC.

Chef and restaurateur Guy Savoy turned an unpromising site (a former bank) into a fashionable restaurant with a star-studded clientele. The keys to his success are a clever contemporary décor, a swift and stylish staff, and—best of all—an ever-changing roster of irresistible dishes: succulent spit-roasted poultry with perfect whipped potatoes, veal breast perfumed with rosemary and olive oil, and lots of luscious desserts. **C** 250-320 F. **M** 160 F (weekday dinner), 110 F (weekday lunch), 200 F.

Paul Chène

(13)

123, rue Lauriston
47 27 63 17

Closed Sat lunch, Sun, Dec 24-Jan 2, Jul 30-Aug 22. Open until 10:30pm. Priv rm: 30. Air cond. Pkg. V, AE, DC.

Elbowroom is at a premium in Paul Chène's two faded dining rooms, but the owners are unstinting with their hospitality, and the kitchen too has a generous spirit. You're sure to relish mackerel marinated in Muscadet, tasty foie gras, langoustine feuilleté, or beef simmered in red wine. The cellar boasts a varied, judicious selection, yet the house Bordeaux is not to be neglected. **C** 350-450 F. **M** 250 F.

Conti

(16)

72, rue Lauriston
47 27 74 67,
fax 47 27 37 66

Closed Sat, Sun, Dec 30-Jan 8, Aug 5-28. Open until 10:30pm. Air cond. V, AE, DC.

Along with Pascal Fayet of Sormani (see seventeenth arrondissement), Michel Ranvier is the city's leading French exponent of Italian cooking. Perhaps a shade less creative than Fayet, Ranvier nevertheless gives his repertoire a vigorous, vibrant zest. Examples? Here are a few: scallops in a sauce laced with Vin Santo, slivers of wee violet artichokes with bresaola in white-truffle dressing, sea bream with saffron-spiced potatoes, and tender baby lamb sparked with anchovies. Ranvier's pastas are anything but run-of-the-mill: they're filled and sauced with foie gras, or bottarga, or pumpkin and marjoram... The list of fine Italian wines is a wonder to behold, and the staff that moves discreetly about the red-and-black dining room provides exemplary service. **C** 350-450 F. **M** 265 F (lunch).

13

Le Cuisinier François

19, rue Le Marois
45 27 83 74

Closed Sun dinner, Mon, Aug. Open until 10:30pm. V, MC.

After his stints at La Tour d'Argent, Robuchon, and with Boyer in Reims, Thierry Conte did not, as one might expect, open a place with his name in large letters over the door. Instead, the times being what they are, he settled for an establishment of modest proportions (just 26 seats) and a menu that is most moderately priced. A delicious terrine of lambs' tongues and leeks, braised pollack with fresh herbs, and a papillote of lavender-scented fruit are typical of the modern, uncomplicated dishes on offer. **C** 220 F. **M** 140 F.

13

Duret Mandarin

34, rue Duret
45 00 09 06

Open daily until 11pm. Priv rm: 60. Air cond. Valet pkg. V, MC.

Just between us, this place really rates closer to two toques, but we don't want the Tang family to get flustered by success. They work hard to deliver (with a smile!) such classic Asian favorites as crispy egg rolls, deep-fried dumplings, and stuffed crab, and such interesting options as steamed scallops with black-bean sauce, "special" roast chicken, and langouste or monkfish spiced with ginger. Here, by the way, we tasted the best Peking duck in town, with optimally crisp skin (order it when you book your table). **C** 160-260 F. **M** 79 F & 95 F.

13

Fakhr el Dine

30, rue de Longchamp
47 27 90 00,
fax 47 27 11 39

See *8th arrondissement.*

18

Faugeron

52, rue de Longchamp
47 04 24 53,
fax 47 55 62 90

Closed Sat (exc dinner Oct-Apr), Sun, Dec 23-Jan 2, Aug. Open until 10pm. Priv rm: 14. Air cond. No pets. Valet pkg. V, AE, MC.

The dining room's blue-and-saffron color scheme may not be to everyone's taste, but then one doesn't come here to eat the décor! What attracts us is the calm, unruffled ambience and, of course, the subtly inventive cooking of Henri Faugeron. He's a modest, even self-effacing chef, not at all obsessed by novelty. The bases of his repertoire are solidly classic, and he would rather heighten and balance the flavors of superb ingredients than create "surprise" effects.

Sterling craftsmanship marks a menu that features scallops poised on a delicate celery cream sauce, escalope de foie gras breaded à la Wiener Schnitzel (a tribute to Austria, Faugeron's second home), lobster tournedos enlivened with Moroccan spices, suprême of guinea fowl in a truffled jus, and a memorable combination of tender dilled rabbit tucked under a fluffy potato blanket. Faugeron's pear millefeuille with honey-cream sauce or macaron with caramelized pineapple are final flourishes to be savored along with the last drops of a great Bordeaux, a voluptuous Burgundy, or a more modest Chinon or Sancerre, chosen by world-class sommelier Jean-Claude Jambon.

Under the smiling supervision of hostess Gerlindé Faugeron, a whole squadron of courteous (but never obsequious) waiters tends to the high-class clientele. **C** 500-900 F. **M** 340 F (lunch, wine incl), 550 F (dinner, wine incl), 720 F (all-truffle), 290 F (lunch), 320 F (dinner).

17

Jean-Claude Ferrero

38, rue Vital
45 04 42 42,
fax 45 04 67 71

Closed Sat (exc dinner in winter), Sun, May 1-15, Aug 8-Sep 5. Open until 10:30pm. Priv rm: 35. Valet pkg. V, AE.

"All-truffle" or "all-mushroom" menus are now a staple in restaurants throughout France. Jean-Claude Ferrero, who started the vogue, is pleased to see that his idea has caught on. Encouraged by diners' enthusiasm, he's dreamed up still more thematic variations, such as

hunt and other seasonal menus, and so keeps his Second Empire *hôtel particulier* filled with a faithful, very Parisian crowd sprinkled with ambassadors and cabinet ministers.
Ferrero's spirited cooking displays a pronounced Southern tilt, evident in his soupe de poisson à la provençale, mussel gratin, and red mullet escorted by tangy tomato jam. More classically French and full of lusty flavor are his volaille en vessie aux asperges (chicken cooked to ideal juiciness in a pork bladder then garnished with asparagus tips), calf's head rémoulade, and bœuf aux carottes in a deep, winy sauce. Ferrero's inspiration fails, however, when it comes to sweets; crêpes au Grand Marnier or baked Alaska (no less) are oddly banal codas to otherwise remarkable meals. **C** 400-700 F. **M** 200 F (weekday lunch), 280 F, 350 F.

Gastronomie Quach

(14)

47, av. R.-Poincaré
47 27 98 40

Open daily until 11pm. Priv rm: 60. Air cond. V, AE, DC, MC.

Aquariums decorate this posh dining room where Monsieur Quach serves Cantonese and Vietnamese dishes that have their good days and their bad: prawns grilled with lemongrass, squid with red peppers, and grilled lamb with five spices can be delicious or bland, depending. But it's the Peking duck that keeps the glossy patrons coming back for more. Served, as it should be, in three separate courses, the duck is indeed a delight. Prices are quite reasonable—for the neighborhood. **C** 220-300 F. **M** 92 F (weekday lunch), 109 F.

Chez Géraud

(14)

31, rue Vital
45 20 33 00

Closed Sat (exc dinner Oct-Feb), Sun, Aug. Open until 10pm. V, AE, MC.

Right across the street from Jean-Claude Ferrero, Gérard Rongier's converted bakery is one of the coziest spots in Passy, with banquette seating, Sarreguemines tiles, immaculate napery, and an affable staff. Géraud packs in an appreciative audience with a zesty menu that presents parsleyed oxtail terrine, veal kidney roasted in its own fat, and succulent roast Bresse pigeon with fresh baby peas. Fans of Côtes-du-Rhône, Savigny-lès-Beaune, or Pineau des Charentes (the latter a golden nectar to sip as an apéritif) will love the list of fine growers' wines. **C** 250-350 F. **M** 200 F.

Le Grand Chinois

(13)

6, av. de New-York
47 23 98 21

Closed Mon, Aug. Open until 11pm. Priv rm: 25. V, AE, DC.

Don't come here for the décor, unless your taste runs to walls plastered with autographed celebrity photos. Come instead for the ginger-spiced hot oysters, the superb dim-sum, sautéed shrimp, and eels with onions. Though the chef isn't perfectly consistent, he also turns out a creditable salmon in sweet-and-sour sauce, hacked pigeon, and crab steamed in bok-choy leaves. What's more, the wine list is amazingly good. Owner Colette Tan welcomes guests and oversees the stylish service. **C** 300-400 F. **M** 120 F (weekday lunch, Sat), 354 F (for 2 pers), 1,330 F (for 4 pers).

La Grande Cascade

(16)

Bois de Boulogne, near the racetrack
45 27 33 51,
fax 42 88 99 06

Closed Dec 20-Jan 20. Open until 10:30pm. Priv rm: 50. Garden dining. Valet pkg. V, AE, DC, MC.

The setting of this former pleasure pavilion is extravagantly Belle Époque. In contrast, the cuisine of Jean Sabine and Frédéric Robert, a couple of enlightened culinary classicists, is reassuring and discreet. You'll be charmed by their crab ravioli in a saffron-stained fumet, sweetbreads in a puff-pastry shell (vol-au-vent) cloaked with a truffled Madeira sauce, and a lovely vanilla-lime mille-feuille. The cellar houses 80,000 bottles, service is formal, and prices are dizzying! **C** 500-750 F. **M** 550 F (dinner), 285 F (exc Sun).

Lac Hong

(14)

67, rue Lauriston
47 55 87 17

Closed Aug. Open until 10:45pm. No pets. V, MC.

Vietnam's cuisine may be the most delicately flavorful in all of Southeast Asia. Should you wish to test that proposition, just taste the remarkable dishes served forth by Phan Huu Hau, the voluble owner of this minuscule establishment. Start with a salad of grilled scampi and green papaya, then proceed to escargots perfumed with Chinese basil, crisp rice crêpes stuffed with shrimp, steamed smoked duck with fish sauce, grilled chicken redolent of five-spice powder, or the excellent salt-and-pepper shrimp. Even the Cantonese rice is exquisite: flawlessly cooked and bursting with flavor. The second toque is not far off... **C** 260 F. **M** 89 F (weekday lunch).

Oum el Banine

16 bis, rue Dufrenoy
45 04 91 22,
fax 45 03 46 26

Closed Sat lunch, Sun, Aug 10-25. Open until 11pm. Air cond. V, AE, MC.

To enter, knock on the heavy wooden door, just as you would in Morocco. Maria Seguin, a native of Fès, practices authentic Fassi cuisine, whose secrets are handed down from mother to daughter. Five types of couscous are on offer (including the refined Fès version, with caramelized onions and grapes), as well as six kinds of lamb tagine (with olives and pickled lemons, peppers and tomato, zucchini and thyme, etc.). More rarely seen, but typically Moroccan are brains in a piquant tomato sauce, spiced tripe, and calf's foot with chickpeas. **C** 250-300 F. **M** 150 F.

Restaurant names in red draw attention to restaurants that offer a particularly good value.

Le Pavillon des Princes

69, av. de la Porte-d'Auteuil
47 43 15 15,
fax 46 51 16 94

Open daily until 10:30pm. Priv rm: 120. Terrace dining. Pkg. V, AE, DC, MC.

The dining room's high-kitsch décor shouldn't spoil your appetite for Patrick Lenôtre's tasty bourgeois-style cooking. An enticing single-price menu (180 F) shows what this chef can do: among the options are a savory duck-liver terrine, lightly smoked rainbow trout, sea bass perfumed with tarragon, veal shanks au pistou, duck served in two courses, and a spicy tarte feuilletée. Fine cellar, with an emphasis on Bordeaux. You can be sure of a warm welcome when you arrive, and the attentions of a classy staff while you dine. **M** 180 F, 270 F.

Le Pergolèse

40, rue Pergolèse
45 00 21 40,
fax 45 00 81 31

Closed Sat, Sun, Aug. Open until 10:30pm. Priv rm: 25. V, AE, MC.

Albert Corre keeps on his culinary toes by devising a new 230 F menu every single day. It's a policy that keeps patrons coming back: some for the good value, others for the sheer enjoyment of discovering what Corre has in store. It might be a ragoût of woodland mushrooms, pearly scallops with sautéed leeks, saffron-tinted lobster navarin, braised sweetbreads with capers, or for dessert a pluperfect imparfait au praliné. The pastel-pink décor isn't wildly original but it's elegant and well-bred (like the service and the clientele). **C** 340-480 F. **M** 230 F, 300 F.

Le Port Alma

10, av. de New-York
47 23 75 11

Closed Sun, Aug. Open until 10:30pm. Priv rm: 15. Air cond. V, AE, DC, MC.

Paul Canal isn't one to blow his own horn, but Parisian seafood buffs know that he has few peers when it comes to cooking fish and crustaceans. You can count on Canal to pick the best of the day's catch, and prepare his prime specimens with a light, skilled hand. His crab ravioli, prawn croustillant, and fillet of John Dory are fresh as can be, with no superfluous sauces to mask their flavors. Desserts, too, are uniformly delicious, and the superb cellar holds plenty of half-bottles. **C** 300-500 F. **M** 200 F (lunch).

Le Pré Catelan

Bois de Boulogne
Route de Suresnes
45 24 55 58,
fax 45 24 43 25

Closed Sun dinner, Mon, Feb 27-Mar 13. Open until 10pm. Priv rm: 40. Garden dining. Valet pkg. V, AE, DC, MC.

Fine cuisine is the Pré Catelan's main drawing card, of course, but high praise is surely due to decorator Christian Benais, whose transformation of this Second Empire landmark is nothing short of inspired. From on high, splendid reliefs by Caran d'Ache gaze down at plush beige carpet studded with green cabochons, billowing draperies of raw linen and taffeta, and tables skirted in scarlet damask. The effect is pure magic. In winter, a warming blaze crackles in the fireplace; and on balmy days, the scene shifts to the garden, where tables are set beneath fluttering parasols. Chef Roland Durand's spirited cuisine, at once rousingly rustic and urbane, is ideally suited to this setting. Typical of his lively style are mackerel rillettes with green-bean salad, lightly cooked salmon given a jolt of black pepper and a smoky jus of grilled bell peppers, calf's head in a pungently herbal ravigote sauce, a startlingly good dish of langoustines in black risotto sparked with Thai basil, or John Dory in a fragrant bouillabaisse fumet. The sweets here are better than ever; our current favorite is the gingered nougat glacé. The cellar affords a remarkable choice of wines, prudently priced. **C** 500-960 F. **M** 270 F (weekday lunch), 400 F, 690 F.

16 Prunier-Traktir

16, av. Victor-Hugo
45 00 89 12

Open daily until 11:30pm. Priv rm: 10. Air cond. Valet pkg. V, AE, DC, MC.

The rebirth of Prunier-Traktir caused great rejoicing among Paris's pearls-and-tweed set, who regarded the demise of this once-brilliant seafood house as a personal loss. The man behind this revival is none other than Jean-Claude Vrinat, of Taillevent. From the moment he opened the doors of a scrubbed and polished Prunier, former habitués took the dining room by storm, thrilled to be back at their old tables amid the beautifully restored Art Deco mosaics. The menu, too, is much as they remember it. Vrinat placed a Taillevent alumnus in the kitchen, and charged him with resuscitating the classic house repertoire. He does an admirable job with the lobster bisque, codfish brandade, sea bass "Émile Prunier," scallops in an aromatic broth, and assortments of bracingly fresh shellfish. There's an excellent cellar, with bottles starting at around 100 F (some wines are available by the glass). And the newly refurbished upstairs dining room now provides space for additional elegant patrons. **C** 300-500 F.

16 Le Relais d'Auteuil

"Patrick Pignol,"
31, bd Murat
46 51 09 54,
fax 40 71 05 03

Closed Sat lunch, Sun, 1st wk of Aug. Open until 10:30pm. Air cond. Valet pkg. V, AE, MC.

Food-lovers warmly recommend this restaurant to their friends, for Patrick Pignol's imaginative, resolutely modern cuisine is a treat to discover. Uncompromising in his choice of ingredients, he follows the seasons to obtain the very freshest, finest produce. In summer, he'll feature tiny violet artichokes and other vegetables at the peak of their flavor; in fall, look for sage-scented braised partridge; winter might bring a mammoth sole in a sauce of lightly salted butter and fiery Szechuan pepper, while spring provides the pleasures of baby lamb and new garlic. If Pignol would just keep a tighter rein on his prices, our happiness would be complete! **C** 500-550 F. **M** 230 F (lunch), 390 F, 480 F.

12/20 Le Relais du Bois

Bois de Boulogne, Croix-Catelan, route de Suresnes
42 88 08 43,
fax 45 25 95 56

Closed Sun dinner. Open until 10:30pm. Terrace dining. No pets. V.

This rustic rendezvous—a Second Empire hunting pavilion where naughty ladies and gentlemen once engaged in rather outrageous behavior—is now the backdrop for tame family parties and corporate banquets. The comfortable dining room has its charms, but the huge summer garden is truly delightful. Good—if unexciting—food: fish soup, pot-au-feu, grilled steak, confit de canard. **C** 150-250 F.

14 Le Relais du Parc

Le Parc Victor-Hugo,
55-57, av. Raymond-Poincaré
44 05 66 10,
fax 44 05 66 00

Open daily until 10:30pm. Terrace dining. Air cond. Valet pkg. V, AE, DC, MC.

Le Relais du Parc holds a winning hand: set in the luxurious new Parc Victor-Hugo hotel, it sports a British colonial setting (straight *Out of Africa*) designed by Nina Campbell and boasts a menu conceived and supervised by none other than Joël Robuchon. The cashmere-and-tweed types who live or work hereabouts have made Le Relais their headquarters. They certainly don't mind paying bistro prices for attractive fare like warm mackerel tart, duck parmentier, spit-roasted duck, or a wine-dark civet de lapin accented with smoky bacon. Dessert brings ably executed standards—floating island, cup custards, tarte aux pommes—and there's a fascinating, affordable wine list. **C** 250-350 F.

19.5

Robuchon

55, av. R.-Poincaré
47 27 12 27,
fax 47 27 31 22
Closed Sat, Sun, Jul 8-Aug 6. Open until 10:15pm. Priv rm: 12. Air cond. Valet pkg. V.

Dining at Joël Robuchon's new restaurant is no simple proposition. No, it's an experience fraught with anxiety, anticipation, excitement, and high emotion! Just consider: after months of waiting, your name finally reaches the top of the interminable reservation list—at last one of the dining room's 45 seats is destined for you! On the appointed day, you arrive at the monumental entrance of Robuchon's Belle Époque town house, where you must ring the bell, identify yourself to the hostess, cross a gallery adorned with precious Daum and Gallé glass, then climb the magnificent (listed!) wrought-iron staircase to the landing, where Madame Robuchon tots up tabs and answers the telephone behind a fabulous Majorelle desk. Dining-room director Jean-Jacques Caimant—or one of his maître d's—will then escort you to the holy of holies.

Now for the bittersweet predicament of composing a meal from Robuchon's thrilling menu. Should you begin with a lightly truffled crème de haricots de Vendée (an apotheosis for the humble white bean), or the truffled pig's trotter sliced and served beside a salad of chestnuts dressed with a vinaigrette of Sherry vinegar, truffle oil, truffle jus, and crushed chestnuts? Or would it be wiser to start with the stunning tomato millefeuille layered with a sublime mélange of crabmeat, watercress, and herbs? The dilemmas don't stop there. For you'll have to eliminate either the huge langoustines seared in goose fat then fricasséed with lobster coral and morels, or the fantastic rock lobster roasted with cumin and rosemary, its rare savor heightened further with chopped truffles and aged Parmesan, or the deceptively simple whiting fillet, a marvel of delicacy enhanced with tomato confit, asparagus tips, and baby fennel, or else the farm-bred guinea fowl roasted to succulence and set atop a slice of flash-seared foie gras.

Don't even hope that choosing a dessert will be easier (here, we'll help you: order the divine walnut croustillant in a pool of dark-chocolate sauce). Afterward, when you repair downstairs to the spacious new *salon-fumoir*, you can recollect in tranquillity, over coffee and liqueurs, the gastronomic masterworks just sampled, and plan, perhaps, your next dinner *chez* Robuchon—necessarily some months hence, when your name again reaches the top of the waiting list! **C** 750-1,500 F.

16

Le Toit de Passy

94, av. Paul-Doumer
45 24 55 37,
fax 45 20 94 57
Closed Sat lunch, Sun. Open until 10:30pm. Priv rm: 25. Terrace dining. Air cond. Garage pkg. V, AE, MC.

On a fine day, the terrace is unquestionably the place to sit, for the unimpeded view of Passy's rooftops. Yet the dining room, accented with plants and partitions, graced with well-spaced tables and flattering lights, is a comfortable, elegant setting in which to enjoy Yannick Jacquot's subtly imaginative cuisine. Excellent meals can be made of his duck pâté enriched with foie gras and flanked by a complementary céleri rémoulade; ultrafresh langoustines in a suave citrus butter or squab roasted to succulence in a sea-salt crust and escorted by buttery braised cabbage; and the assiette of dainty chocolate sweets. The cellar holds 45,000 bottles, so the wine list will take some perusing. **C** 420-600 F. **M** 195 F (weekday lunch), 295 F, 380 F, 495 F.

13

Villa Vinci

23, rue Paul-Valéry
45 01 68 18
Closed Sat, Sun, Dec 25-Jan 1, Aug. Open until

10:30pm. Priv rm: 50. Air cond. V, AE.

Business people at lunch and an up-market local clientele in the evening frequent the Villa Vinci, a comfortable restaurant luxuriously decked out in frills and velvet. Chef Marc Schwartz sends out painstakingly prepared Italian dishes that get us salivating in no time flat: truffled lamb's-lettuce salad, scallops with garlicky aïoli and fettuccine, red mullet with basil in tomato purée, veal piccata with wild mushrooms, and scrumptious desserts. Jacky Fayet is a genial, attentive host, who gains our approval for lowering his prices this year. **C** 260-350 F. **M** 175 F (lunch).

Vivarois

192, av. V.-Hugo
45 04 04 31,
fax 45 03 09 84

Closed Sat, Sun, Aug. Open until 10pm. Air cond. Garage pkg. V, AE, DC, MC.

Claude Peyrot hasn't upped his prices in three years. Merely by holding steady, they are now lower than those posted in many a lesser establishment. Few sophisticated diners-out would bat an eye, nowadays, at paying 245 F for turbot with wild mushrooms, or 215 F for coq au vin stewed in genuine Pommard wine. So when these dishes are prepared by a four-toque chef whose cooking is perhaps the most intelligent and subtle in town, the prices seem—almost—cheap.

Claude Peyrot carries on imperturbably, polishing a concise *carte* which he enriches daily with a half-dozen dishes created on the spur of the moment. The maître d'hôtel might announce the presence of a mousse d'étrilles (a crabmeat concoction that is both ineffably light and rich), potato galettes with foie gras and truffles, or, in hunting season, hare à la royale with a superb quince compote: a regal dish indeed that will forever haunt our gastronomic memory. Even if the aforementioned are not available when you visit Vivarois, Peyrot's feuilleté de truffe and his oxtail braised with mustard—both deserve to go down in culinary history—will surely be on offer, along with a splendid herb-scented roast lobster or poularde au vinaigre. This chef's unrivaled technique, his singular sensitivity and grace, give every dish he produces a distinctive signature that is uniquely Peyrot's. To add to the pleasure, there are wines, magnificent and modest, of the sort kind that every connoisseur yearns to discover, amassed by sommelier extraordinaire Jean-Claude Vinadier. **C** 560-800 F. **M** 345 F (lunch).

17th arrondissement

Amphyclès

78, av. des Ternes
40 68 01 01,
fax 40 68 91 88

Closed Sat lunch, Sun. Open until 10:30pm. Priv rm: 25. Air cond. Valet pkg. V, AE, DC, MC.

Joël Robuchon initiated Philippe Groult in the art of harmonizing rustic with recherché flavors, to create a rich, diverse palette of tastes. The master is justly proud of his former star pupil, for here at Amphyclès "city" and "country" dishes coexist deliciously in Groult's distinctive, personal

New Bridge is old

Despite its name, the *Pont-Neuf* ("new bridge") is the oldest bridge in town. Completed in 1604, it was the first in Paris to be built without houses blocking the view of the river. It even had sidewalks—quite a novelty at the time—and a series of semicircular bays whose stone benches still make an ideal stopping place during a romantic stroll. In its early days, the bridge buzzed with a gaudy population of charlatans, traders, and troubadours (who satirized unpopular politicians or the king's latest mistress). The Pont-Neuf's most recent claim to fame came in 1985 when the American sculptor Christo wrapped it lovingly in bridal white to fashion a two-week work of art.

repertoire. It successfully embraces both slow-simmered lamb à l'ancienne and a frothy crab soup lavished with caviar; rack of veal ménagère as well as Bresse chicken poached in an elaborate spiced bouillon; and casseroled lamb's trotters alongside smothered lobster and morels with a foie gras–enriched macaroni gratin. Groult takes special care with vegetable garnishes: his marvelous salads of fresh herbs, a wonderfully smoky split-pea mousseline, or white beans whipped with cream and Parmesan are all delectable enough to make a meal on their own! We should note too that Groult's themed menus—all-truffle, all-mushroom, all-shellfish or game—attract brilliant tables of Parisian gourmets who run up astronomical bills, with the help of costly bottles from the much-improved cellar. **C** 500-850 F. **M** 260 F (lunch), 580 F, 780 F.

18

Apicius

122, av. de Villiers
43 80 19 66,
fax 44 40 09 57

Closed Sat, Sun, Aug. Open until 10pm. Air cond. Valet pkg. V, AE, DC, MC.

We know lots of high-class restaurants where the food is perfectly fine—but the ambience is stuffy and dull. At Jean-Pierre Vigato's Apicius, not only is the food simply fabulous, the atmosphere is as warm as can be. The charm begins to operate from the moment Madeleine Vigato welcomes you into the spectacularly flower-decked dining room, and the urbane sommelier suggests a suitable wine to sip while you peruse the menu.

We've been singing Vigato's praises long enough to feel we needn't repeat ourselves. Though his core repertoire doesn't change much from one year to the next, Vigato keeps himself sharp by offering a half-dozen different starters and entrées each day, (which Madeleine describes at each table in luscious detail). But who would need prodding to reorder such inspiring house classics as Vigato's escalope de foie gras with black-radish confit in a suave sweet-and-sour sauce? Or his unforgettably fragrant truffle risotto? Likewise, plump prawns flash-fried in a diaphanous batter of spices, Japanese flour, and egg white are well worth eating more than once! As is the cod with crumbled potatoes: Vigato's treatment puts that humble fish into the same noble league as turbot and sole. We can also confidently recommend the spit-roasted sweetbreads with creamy whipped potatoes, the sumptuous tourte de canard, and any of the divine game dishes Vigato prepares during the hunt season. With equal conviction we say that his sweets—an incredible gratin de café moka, crackling licorice custard, an ineffable caramel extravaganza—will provide you with a moment of unalloyed bliss. **C** 550-850 F. **M** 520 F.

16

Augusta

98, rue de Tocqueville - 47 63 39 97,
fax 42 27 21 71

Closed Sat lunch (& dinner May 1-Sep 30), Sun, 2 wks in Aug. Open until 10pm. Air cond. V, MC.

Scrupulously seasonal, rigorously precise, based on the freshest seafood: Lionel Maître's cuisine is all this and more. The clear, direct flavors of his shellfish salad, rockfish soup, fricassée de coquilles Saint-Jacques, sea bass with fava beans in an herbal jus, or langoustines with mellow garlic purée incite us to unashamed gorging! Remarkable wine list; young, eager staff. **C** 410-600 F.

14

Billy Gourmand

20, rue de Tocqueville - 42 27 03 71

Closed Sat lunch (& dinner Jul-Sep), Sun, hols. Open until 10pm. Priv rm: 14. V, AE, MC.

Chef Philippe Billy presents his polished, attractively presented cuisine in a spacious and sprightly dining room decorated with mirrors and plants. Not one to rest on his laurels, he comes up with a new single-price menu each week. On a recent visit it delivered fresh crab ravioli swathed in a mushroom cream sauce, pikeperch in red-wine sauce with a fennel and macaroni gratin, and a frozen prune feuilleté. The engaging *patronne* oversees a fine cellar of Loire Valley wines. **C** 270-410 F. **M** 150 F.

13 Le Bistrot d'à Côté

10, rue G.-Flaubert
42 67 05 81,
fax 47 63 82 75

Open daily until 11pm. Terrace dining. Air cond. Valet pkg. V, AE, MC.

All you want from a bistro: hustle, bustle, and cheeky waiters. Who wouldn't be won over by the simple, savory pleasures of such Lyonnais-style specialties as chicken-liver terrine, pork-and-beef sausage (sabodet), or grilled fresh tuna? The wines, however, are too expensive for this sort of establishment. **C** 250-330 F.

13 Le Bistrot de l'Étoile-Niel

75, av. Niel
42 27 88 44,
fax 42 27 32 12

Closed Sun lunch. Open until midnight. Terrace dining. Air cond. Valet pkg. V, AE.

Here's your typical cheerful neighborhood bistro—except that it's owned and supervised by Guy Savoy. Handily prepared and served with a smile, the fresh sardines showered with basil, comforting blanquette de veau and other *plats du jour*, the chocolate tourte and house Merlot have won a loyal following. **C** 190-280 F. **M** 170 F (Sun dinner).

13 Le Bistrot de l'Étoile-Troyon

13, rue Troyon
42 67 25 95

Closed Sat lunch, Sun. Annual closings not available. Open until midnight. Air cond. V, AE, MC.

Guy Savoy can keep a close eye on the first-born of his bistro annexes, for it stands just across the street from his four-toque restaurant. In the small, convivial dining room you can treat yourself to such heartwarming bourgeois classics as herbed lamb noisettes, duck with red beans, pan-roasted sea trout, and chocolate fondant. Good growers' wines; democratic prices. **C** 250-280 F.

13 Caves Pétrissans

30 bis, av. Niel
42 27 52 03,
fax 40 54 87 56

Closed Sat, Sun, hols, last wk of Feb, 1st 4 wks of Aug. Open until 10:30pm. Priv rm: 12. Terrace dining. V, AE, MC.

Four generations of Pétrissans have overseen this wine shop-cum-restaurant, where patrons linger happily over Jacques Bertrel's tasty cooking. The quality ingredients are simply prepared and generously served; try the tête de veau sauce ravigote, spareribs with buttery braised cabbage, poulet au vinaigre de cidre, and velvety crème brûlée. **C** 250-340 F. **M** 155 F.

13 Charly de Bab-el-Oued

95, bd Gouvion-St-Cyr - 45 74 34 62,
fax 45 74 35 36

Open daily until 11:30pm. Air cond. No pets. V, AE, DC, MC.

An inviting place to dream of the *Arabian Nights* amid colorful tiles, cedarwood, and palm trees. Feast on Claude Drigués's excellent couscous, pastillas, and tagines, followed by sweet Eastern pastries made on the premises. Perfect service. **C** 220-270 F. **M** 200 F.

12/20 Les Cigales

127, rue Cardinet
42 27 83 93

Dinner & groups by reserv. Closed Sat, Sun, Aug. No pets. V.

A quintessential neighborhood bistro, serving a roster of tasty, clever dishes. The décor plays the Provençal card to the hilt (sun-yellow walls, photos of the Riviera...), and so does the bright bill of fare: tomatoes stuffed with creamy goat cheese, grilled sea bream anointed with virgin olive oil, pasta dressed with pistou are all handily turned out by the young *patronne*. All she needs to do now is put together a decent regional cellar. **C** 190-250 F. **M** 60 F, 119 F.

17 Clos Longchamp

Hôtel Méridien, 81, bd Gouvion-St-Cyr
40 68 30 40,
fax 40 68 30 81

Closed Sat, Sun, last wk of Dec, Jul 29-Aug 30. Open until 10:30pm. Priv rm: 18. Air cond. Valet pkg. V, AE, DC, MC.

We can't figure out why a certain red-jacketed restaurant guide bumped a star from chef Jean-Marie Meulien's rating. After a serious illness he has bounced back, as energetic as ever, with an exciting menu that combines the flavors of the Mediterranean with the spices of Southeast Asia. Meulien is a master craftsman, in the mold of his mentor, Louis Outhier. He recently tempted us with a procession of technically flawless, delightfully sun-kissed dishes: plump pink shrimp atop an exquisite salad dressed with Champagne vinegar, a deeply flavorful snail and chestnut soup, scallops fired up with Thai spices, sea bass with toasted buckwheat, terrine of duck liver laced with Beaumes-de-Venise wine, and stunning squash blossoms stuffed with cardamom-spiced salmon. A similarly exotic mood inspires the delicate desserts. Award-winning sommelier Didier Bureau administers a cellar of rare and delicious wines, one of which is sure to complement your meal. The Méridien's exuberant central garden has flourished so well you would think you were in a sunnier clime; it almost makes you forget the strange, banana-shaped dining room! **C** 450-600 F. **M** 260 F (lunch), 470 F (dinner).

13 Le Col-Vert

18, rue Bayen
45 72 02 19

Closed Sat lunch, Sun, Aug 1-28. Open until 10:30pm (Fri & Sat 11pm). Priv rm: 25. Air cond. Garage pkg. V, MC.

Franck Descas is a young chef with impressive credentials and a sprightly, original style. Exotic notes from his native Antilles crop up in dishes like foie gras carpaccio served with a salad of chayote squash, tiny scallops in a dressing brightened with a dash of lime juice, or his novel fish "sausage" with tangy coarse-grain mustard and a garnish of sweet potatoes. His cooking still has a few rough edges, but we applaud his fresh, personal approach—a rarity these days! **C** 250-370 F. **M** 150 F.

11/20 Le Congrès

80, av. de la Grande-Armée
45 74 17 24

Open daily 24 hours. Air cond. V, AE, DC, MC.

A huge barracks-like brasserie, open all day and all night, vigilant about the consistent quality of its classics: shellfish (fresh all year) and large slabs of charcoal-grilled meat. Good tarte Tatin; decent selection of house wines. **C** 220-270 F. **M** 179 F (wine incl).

13 Dessirier

9, pl. du Mal-Juin
42 27 82 14,
fax 47 63 98 79

Closed Sun, Aug. Open until 11:30pm. Priv rm: 20. Terrace dining. Valet pkg. V, AE, DC, MC.

A favorable wind has blown this venerable seafood brasserie back into our Guide. The new chef relies on the sound principles of simplicity and accurate timing to produce an unctuous, full-flavored lobster bisque and a particularly tasty cod with tapenade. Desserts, however, still need work. A carafe of house Chablis is a welcome alternative to the costly wine list. Jolly service. **C** 300-450 F. **M** 200 F.

13 L'Écrin d'Or

35, rue Legendre
47 63 83 08

Closed Sat lunch, Mon, Aug 8-29. Open until 11pm. Priv rm: 16. Air cond. Garage pkg. V, AE, MC.

Huge mirrors, moldings, Venetian chandeliers, and great swathes of velvet hangings make this a supremely comfortable restaurant. The discreet, delicate cooking of the young chef, Gilles Cendres, adds to the charm. Sample his warm beef salad sparked with raspberry vinegar, turbot in a lovely dill-butter sauce, and ethereal soufflé au Grand-Marnier. Judicious cellar. **C** 250-340 F. **M** 95 F, 155 F.

13 Épicure 108

108, rue Cardinet
47 63 50 91

Closed Sat lunch, Sun, Aug 7-19. Open until 10pm. V.

Here's a quiet little restaurant with a pastel interior (in need, we think, of a brush-up) owned by Japanese chef Tetsu Goya. We were a trifle disappointed this year by the pale flavors of his otherwise well-wrought cuisine: oxtail en gelée with foie gras, "boudin blanc" of fish and frogs' legs with lentils, Barbary duck en choucroute (excellent sauerkraut), veal cooked in Riesling, and chestnut financier for dessert. **M** 170 F, 230 F.

16 L'Étoile d'Or

Hôtel Concorde-La Fayette,
3, pl. du Gal-Kœnig
40 68 51 28,
fax 40 68 50 43

Closed Sat, Sun, hols, 1 wk in Feb, Aug. Open until 10:30pm. Priv rm: 35. Air cond. Valet pkg. V, AE, DC, MC.

Jean-Claude Lhonneur, formerly of Le Grand Véfour and La Tour d'Argent, has turned L'Étoile d'Or into one of the best hotel restaurants in town. A bold approach to harmonizing flavors, admirably accurate cooking times, and fragrant, feather-light sauces are the three solid bases of an alluring repertoire. We know: it isn't easy to find this handsome, wood-paneled dining room, hidden in the labyrinth of the Hôtel Concorde; paying the bill isn't so simple either. But if you make the effort, your reward will be (for example) meltingly savory duck liver in a jus based on Banyuls wine, or a bosky mushroom confit spiked with Calvados, then smothered sea bass perfumed with truffled oil, irresistible stewed ox jowls en ravigote, and a chocolate soufflé that the waiter swears is the best in Paris! These delights are delivered by an exceptionally well trained staff. As for the cellar, it holds few bargains but there are many half-bottles in stock. **C** 400-700 F. **M** 270 F.

16 Faucher

123, av. de Wagram
42 27 61 50,
fax 46 22 25 72

Closed Sat lunch, Sun, wk of Aug 15. Open until 10pm. Terrace dining. Valet pkg. V, AE.

Gérard and Nicole Faucher have inaugurated a new price policy at their bright and lovely restaurant. Set meals have been abolished, and à la carte tariffs have come down some 50 percent. Faucher has crossed a few costly items off of his shopping list, but otherwise his cuisine is just as vivid and modern as ever. In fact, he's managed to preserve a few of his signature dishes on the new menu, including the millefeuille of thinly sliced raw beef and spinach leaves and the short ribs en pot-au-feu with a truffled jus. Alongside these veterans, you'll find oxtail ravioli in a savory bouillon and a lusty pairing of veal kidney and andouillette sausage with a potato croustillant. Good desserts and wines from a revised, less expensive cellar complete the picture. Nicole Faucher continues to greet guests with a smile in the cheerful yellow dining room embellished with paintings and elegant table settings. **C** 220-290 F.

11/20 Chez Fred

190 bis, bd Pereire
45 74 20 48

Closed Sun, 2 wks mid Aug. Open until 11pm. Terrace dining. V, AE, DC, MC.

An influx of trendies has not spoiled the service, the simplicity of the setting, or the heartwarming sincerity of Fred's cuisine: bacon with lentils, pot-au-feu, and blanquette de veau. No-nonsense wines sold by the *pichet.* **C** 210-260 F. **M** 145 F.

14 La Gazelle

9, rue Rennequin
42 67 64 18,
fax 42 67 82 77

Closed Sat lunch, Sun. Open until 11:30pm. V, AE, DC, MC.

With its star-studded ceiling, this is the prettiest African restaurant in Paris. La Gazelle boasts a surprising range of intensely tasty dishes prepared by proprietress-chef Marie Koffi-Nketsin, who comes from Cameroon: try her stuffed crab, fish with seven spices, chicken in peanut sauce, and marinated kid baked en papillote with African corn. Crocodile also features on the menu—connoisseurs, take note! Slow-paced but cheerful service. **C** 130-220 F. **M** 130 F & 150 F (weekdays, Sat dinner, wine incl), 95 F (weekday lunch, wine incl).

14 Chez Georges

273, bd Pereire
45 74 31 00,
fax 45 74 02 56

Closed Aug. Open until 11:30pm. Priv rm: 30. Terrace dining. V.

A good French bistro can survive any crisis, be it a change in fashion or a market crash. Chez Georges has seen it all, but the bustling atmosphere and comforting cuisine (roast lamb with tender beans, the famous house ribs of beef, joue de bœuf braisée) remain unchanged. So, alas, do the high prices. **C** 240-350 F. **M** 170 F.

13 Goldenberg

69, av. de Wagram
42 27 34 79,
fax 42 27 98 85

Open daily until 11:30pm. Priv rm: 60. Terrace dining. Pkg. V.

Patrick Goldenberg creates a typically Yiddish atmosphere of good humor and nostalgia, Jewish jokes and anecdotes in which to enjoy delicious Kosher cooking rooted in the traditions of Russia, Hungary, Romania, Bulgaria... There's smoked and corned beef, wonderful corned goose breast, kneidler in chicken broth, veal sausage, and other Central European classics. For dessert, don't miss the poppyseed strudel. There's also a delicatessen for take-out, and a sunny terrace for fine weather. **C** 150-250 F. **M** 98 F.

15/20 **Graindorge**
15, rue de l'Arc-de-Triomphe
47 54 00 28,
fax 44 09 84 51
Closed Sun. Open until 11pm. Priv rm: 35. Air cond. Garage pkg. V, AE.

When Bernard Broux (long-time chef at Le Trou Gascon) opened a place of his own, he forsook the Southwest and its earthy tastes in favor of the cuisine of his native Flanders. Broux's menu celebrates hearty Northern savors with a terrine of smoked eel and baby leeks, chicken breast and vegetables in a creamy waterzoï sauce, and strawberries in a sabayon spiked with raspberry-flavored kriek beer. While the wine list merits your attention, beer lovers will be knocked out by the superb selection of rare brews. **C** 250-350 F. **M** 130 F & 160 F (weekday lunch), 185 F.

15/20 **Guyvonne**
14, rue de Thann
42 27 25 43,
fax 42 27 25 43
Closed Sat, Sun, Dec 25-Jan 1, Jul 31-Aug 28. Open until 9:45pm. Priv rm: 11. Terrace dining. No pets. Pkg. V, AE, MC.

Guy Cros's cooking is as appealing as ever, but his repertoire seems to be shrinking. On our last visit to his intimate, country-style dining room, we were startled to learn that only three of the starters listed were actually available; the choice of desserts seemed awfully brief, too. But as usual, our mood soared as we tucked into the langoustines with fresh artichokes and chanterelles, baby skate in a ginger-spiced sauce, and scrumptious chocolate mousseline layered with mocha spongecake. The cellar is still stocked with first-rate Bordeaux. **C** 300-380 F. **M** 180 F.

13/20 **Chez Laudrin**
154, bd Pereire
43 80 87 40
Closed Sat lunch, Sun. Open until 10:30pm. Air cond. V, AE, MC.

Age settles gently but graciously over Jacques Billaud's "yacht-club" dining room, his regional repertoire, and the mustachioed grin with which he has greeted customers for decades. Wines are served by the magnum and charged by "the centimeter" (so you only pay for what you drink). Some of the best tripe dishes in Paris are made in this kitchen, as well as cod with aïoli, pan-roasted sole, duck breast with cabbage, and a hearty bourride de lotte (fish soup). To finish on a high note, order the flaky apple feuilleté. **C** 320-430 F. **M** 180 F, 250 F.

12/20 **Chez Léon**
32, rue Legendre
42 27 06 82
Closed Sat, Sun, Feb 15-24, Aug. Open until 9:45pm. Priv rm: 20. Pkg. V, DC.

A traditional bistro with the usual unvarying roster of robust food—terrines, saucisson chaud, tête de veau vinaigrette, duck confit, and cassoulet. For dessert, look no farther than the homey floating island. Service is pleasant, and so are the Beaujolais wines. **C** 220-280 F. **M** 140 F, 170 F.

14/20 **Le Madigan**
22, rue de la Terrasse - 42 27 31 51
Closed Sat lunch, Sun, Aug 8-Sep 5. Open until 9:30pm. Terrace dining. Air cond. V, AE, DC, MC.

After dinner, when it's time for liqueurs, Le Madigan's sober yet sumptuous dining room is transformed into a concert hall. Hopeful young talents and international prize-winners take their place at the Steinway grand for what are often remarkable recitals. The prelude to these musical soirées is chef Jean-Michel Descloux's fine-tuned cuisine. He turns out a sparkling duet of sole aïoli and potato salad, braised sweetbreads with a Parma-ham jus, and vanilla vacherin. With a selection from the abundantly annotated wine list, you're in for a harmonious evening. **C** 320-560 F. **M** 150 F & 250 F (lunch), 180 F & 280 F (dinner).

16/20 **Le Manoir de Paris**
6, rue Pierre-Demours
45 72 25 25,
fax 45 74 80 98
Closed Sat lunch, Sun. Open until 10:30pm. Priv rm: 60. Air cond. Valet pkg. V, AE, DC.

Francis Vandenhende and his wife, Denise Fabre (a bred-in-the-bone Niçoise), were among the first in Paris to introduce the sunny savors of the South into their kitchen. Since then, Mediterranean madness has overrun the city's restaurants, and the perusal of a Provençal menu no longer elicits the same thrill of surprise.

Chef Gilles Mery is obviously at ease with the Southern repertoire, though he tends to fuss and complicate his cooking. Some of his dishes merit three toques; others do not. On the debit side are aiguillettes of duck breast encumbered by too many garnishes; a leek and scallop velouté with crayfish and a drizzle of orange oil that—incredibly!—lacks flavor as well as consistency; and a Banyuls sorbet with chocolate chips and walnut sauce—take it back to the drawing board!
To his credit, Mery also delivers sprightly coddled eggs with caper blossoms and pepper confit, risotto enriched with a wonderfully appetizing garnish of chorizo and codfish, sea bream stewed in red wine with a zesty touch of anchovy, and roast squab set atop golden grilled polenta accompanied by tart-sweet green grapes. These lusty creations are staples on the 240 F prix-fixe lunch (surely one of the best deals in the area), which is best partnered by a Côtes-du-Rhône from Remi Aspect's splendid cellar. **C** 350-500 F. **M** 240 F & 295 F (lunch), 260 F & 390 F (dinner).

13 La Niçoise

4, rue Pierre-Demours
45 74 42 41

Closed Sat lunch, Sun. Open until 11pm. Priv rm: 60. Air cond. V, AE, DC.

Traditional Niçois specialties served in a picture-postcard setting that's reminiscent of Nice at holiday time. Prime ingredients are prepared with touching sincerity, to yield ricotta ravioli in a creamy pistou sauce, old-fashioned simmered tripe redolent of fresh bay leaves, and nougat glacé perfumed with orange-flower water. Perfect Provençal cellar. **M** 145 F (wine incl), 165 F.

16 Le Petit Colombier

42, rue des Acacias
43 80 28 54

Closed Sun lunch, Sat. Open until 10:30pm. Priv rm: 35. Air cond. Garage pkg. V, AE, MC.

Bernard Fournier, official defender of French gastronomy for the EU in Brussels, is first and foremost a model restaurateur. With loving devotion he watches over his *fin de siècle* "provincial" inn, a family heirloom which he runs with the energy of three men. Bernard is Johnny-on-the-spot at market, selecting only prime ingredients; at the stoves, executing a *carte* that changes daily; and at tableside, lending an attentive ear to his guests.
The reward for his vigilance is a loyal clientele of contented gourmands who tuck in joyfully to such spirited, full-bodied dishes as hare terrine à l'ancienne enriched with foie gras, pikeperch with shallot-butter sauce, milk-fed veal chops tenderly braised en cocotte, or squab in a tight, truffled jus. Each day also brings a fabulous roast—succulent ribs of beef, for example, or poularde truffée aux petits légumes—carved and served at the table. Nor should we neglect to celebrate Fournier's seasonal game menu, nor the business lunch which is one of the best (and least known) bargains in the city. To toast all these delights, there is a splendiferous cellar with some 50,000 bottles. **C** 400-500 F (dinner). **M** 200 F (lunch), 350 F (dinner).

12/20 Le Petit Salé

99, av. des Ternes
45 74 10 57,
fax 45 74 31 96

Open daily until 11:30pm. Priv rm: 8. Terrace dining. V, AE, DC, MC.

Petit salé—streaky bacon with lentils—is still the cornerstone of the generous house repertoire. In this vintage 1930s setting, you can also opt for beef-muzzle vinaigrette, sole meunière, pot-au-feu, or brandade de morue (puréed salt cod), to be washed down with a frisky red Anjou sold *au compteur* (you pay only for what you drink). **C** 200-250 F.

13 La Petite Auberge

38, rue Laugier
47 63 85 51

Closed Sun dinner, Mon lunch, Aug 1-16. Open until 10:30pm. Priv rm: 14. V, MC.

An alumnus of Bocuse's kitchen offers a ducky 160 F menu (terrine de foie gras de canard, pot-au-feu de canard, and vanilla custard) as well as pricier scallops with Belgian endive or squab au jus available à la carte. **C** 260-330 F. **M** 160 F.

The **C** (A la carte) *restaurant prices given are for a complete three-course meal for one, including a half-bottle of modest wine and service.* **M** (Menu) *prices are for a complete fixed-price meal for one, excluding wine (unless otherwise noted).*

15

Petrus

12, pl. du Maréchal-Juin - 43 80 15 95, fax 43 80 06 96

Closed Aug 10-25. Open until 11pm. Priv rm: 22. Air cond. Valet pkg. V, AE, DC, MC.

Young Jacky Louazé is the new skipper aboard the good ship Petrus. At the tender age of 26, he's already learned to handle seafood with discretion and restraint, serving forth a superb carpaccio of sea bream, bass, and salmon, a golden heap of crisp-fried whitebait, gingered tuna cooked as rare as you like, and a sole of pristine freshness caught off the coast of the Ile d'Yeu. To begin, we always choose a dozen or so glossy Marennes oysters, and to finish, we just as invariably order the chocolate soufflé. Fine selection of white wines; attentive service. **C** 350-500 F. **M** 250 F, 350 F.

15

Il Ristorante

22, rue Fourcroy 47 63 34 00

Closed Dec 24-Jan 1, Aug 13-29. Open until 10:45pm. Air cond. Garage pkg. V, AE.

We can't resist the charm of the Anfuso clan, who welcome guests into their Venetian-style dining room with heartwarming hospitality. You, too, will succumb when you taste Rocco Anfuso's vibrant, high-spirited *cucina*. Outstanding features of a recent feast were fettuccine with cuttlefish in a dusky sauce of the creatures' ink, rosy lamb under a mantle of tender eggplant, filet mignon with walnut pesto, and cinnamon ice cream with green-apple coulis. The Italian wines are seductive and attractively priced. **C** 210-310 F. **M** 165 F.

18

Michel Rostang

20, rue Rennequin 47 63 40 77, fax 47 63 82 75

Closed Sat lunch, Sun, Aug 1-15. Open until 10:15pm. Priv rm: 25. Air cond. Valet pkg. V, AE, MC.

Michel Rostang is inspired by the culinary heritage of Lyon, Provence, and his native Dauphiné, where powerful flavors and a forthright approach to food are the rule. Yet Rostang is not a "regional" chef. He applies his own standards and measures to the traditional country cooking of France, while reserving plenty of leeway for improvisation. The result is a mostly rousing yet nuanced cuisine, whose flavors usually dovetail with admirable precision. "Mostly"? "usually"? All right, we'll stop hedging. We had a few disappointing meals here this year, particularly the more recent ones. We saw shortcuts and even some unmistakable signs of carelessness: a scorched gratin dauphinois, a soggy tart... What's more, the 298 F set lunch doesn't seem like such a bargain, with dishes that rate only a couple of toques. Given the reputation—and prices—of this establishment, patrons have a right to expect a near-perfect dining experience. So Michel Rostang is back down to three toques from the four he's worn since 1992.

Don't misunderstand: there's still plenty to like *chez* Rostang. Flavors, colors, and textures compose an irresistible bouquet in his artichoke galettes lavished with fresh truffles, or in the vivid pumpkin soup dotted with chèvre-stuffed ravioli. Irreproachable too are the pan-roasted lobster en anchoïade, the thick, juicy braised sole with a zesty black-olive compote and Swiss chard in a savory jus, and the beautifully conceived pastorale d'agneau de Provence: the lamb's tongue, noisettes, sweetbreads, and trotters are steeped in a deliciously aromatic jus.

As always, Marie-Claude Rostang welcomes guests graciously into the Rostangs' newly redecorated dining room, and Alain Ronzatti continues to preside over the connoisseur's cellar. **C** 700-900 F. **M** 298 F (lunch), 520 F, 720 F.

14

Rôtisserie d'Armaillé

6, rue Armaillé 42 27 19 20

Closed Sat lunch, Sun. Open until 11pm (w-e 11:30pm). Priv rm: 85. Air cond. V, AE, MC.

Jacques Cagna reprises the bistro formula he successfully inaugurated at La Rôtisserie d'en Face (sixth arrondissement). For 195 F you can choose from a wide array of starters and desserts as well as a main course of spit-roasted poultry or meat. Delicious, affordable wines. **C** 300 F. **M** 195 F.

Restaurant names in red draw attention to restaurants that offer a particularly good value.

Guy Savoy

18, rue Troyon
43 80 40 61,
fax 46 22 43 09

Closed Sat lunch, Sun. Open until 10:30pm. Priv rm: 30. Air cond. Valet pkg. V, AE.

An arsonist set fire to Guy Savoy's restaurant in November 1993. Typically, in less time than it would take most of us to choose new wallpaper, Savoy raised the curtain on a splendid and highly original interior. Beneath a Bedouin-style canvas-swathed ceiling (to replace the elegant *verrière* that melted in the blaze) the room is accented with impressive pieces of African sculpture and fine paintings—it's a smashing success.

How on earth, people wonder, does he do it? Guy Savoy has the uncanniest way of turning an ordeal into opportunity. Even his cooking has gained a fresh, creative edge. Just look at this year's imaginative *carte*: there's a croustillant of calf's foot and peppery black radish on a salad of fresh herbs dressed with a a vibrant parsley jus; a potée of poached fresh vegetables anointed with a powerfully aromatic truffle jus; a hauntingly delicious pheasant and bean soup; roast John Dory accented with crisp, faintly bitter sautéed dandelion greens and sage-scented potatoes. And every day the menu is enriched with a complement of inspired offerings that change according to Savoy's mercurial moods!

We've heard some people complain that Savoy's portions are too small; they may have a point. But we applaud the idea of allowing diners to order desserts by the half-helping: thus, for the same money, you can sample both the spiced-cocoa pain perdu and the tingly grapefruit terrine with tea-scented sauce; or else the chocolate fondant with praline feuilleté and the vanilla millefeuille with a bright berry coulis. The wines, delicate or full-bodied (and uniformly expensive), are overseen by Éric Mancio, a sommelier with the soul of a poet. **C** 700-1,000 F. **M** 750 F.

Sormani

4, rue du Général-Lanrezac
43 80 13 91

Closed Sat, Sun, hols, end Dec, Easter, 1st 3 wks of Aug. Open until 10:30pm. Priv rm: 18. Terrace dining. Air cond. Valet pkg. V, AE.

Scion of an Italo-French family of restaurateurs, Pascal Fayet has culinary talent coursing through his veins! He's taken that innate aptitude and amplified it with a virtuosity and artistic temperament all his own.

Fayet's Italian cuisine is emphatically not the textbook version. His menu fairly crackles with brilliant inventions that will set you to salivating before you've even taken a bite! You could compose a stupendous meal from such offerings as diaphanous ravioli stuffed with sea urchins or truffled goat cheese; pearly raw scallops paired with wee purple artichokes; a "pizza" topped with onion purée, lobster, and arugula; tender tagliatelle enriched with bacon and white beans; a sumptuous white-truffle risotto; veal kidney arranged on a crisply golden polenta galette; or (Fayet's masterpiece) a fat black truffle swathed in a paper-thin slice of veal. An even more exciting alternative is to give Fayet an idea of your tastes and your appetite, then let him improvise a personalized feast just for you. Believe us, it will be a gastronomic memory to treasure! Speaking of treasures, Sormani's cellar holds some fabulous bottles, including a Santa Cristina Chianti and a Venetian Pinot Grigio from Peppoli Antinori. **C** 400-600 F. **M** 350 F (lunch, wine incl), 400 F, 450 F, 500 F (wine incl).

La Soupière

154, av. de Wagram
42 27 00 73,
fax 46 22 27 09

Closed Sat lunch, Sun, Aug 8-21. Open until 10:30pm. Priv rm: 6. Terrace dining. Air cond. V, AE, MC.

Christian and Camille Thuillart pamper their guests in a pretty *trompe-l'œil* dining room. There's nothing deceptive about the cooking, however: chef Christian's forthright repertoire features juicy pikeperch cooked in its skin, calf's liver in a sauce deglazed with balsamic vinegar, and succulent duck with fresh pasta. A passionate connoisseur of rare and expensive mushrooms, he has built special menus around truffles and morels, served when their season is at its height. **C** 250-350 F. **M** 185 F (Sat dinner), 130 F, 160 F, 250 F & 270 F (weekdays).

Le Sud Marocain

(14)

10, rue Villebois-Mareuil
45 72 35 76

Closed Aug. Open until 10:30pm. Priv rm: 10. Air cond. V, AE, DC, MC.

Here's a rare find! This tiny restaurant (it holds just 25), run by a *patron* who looks just like Chico Marx, serves sensational marinated sardines with ratatouille, a light, fragrantly herbal harira soup, several excellent tagines (chicken and olives, lamb with prunes...), and a first-rate couscous royal. **C** 165-215 F.

La Table de Pierre

(14)

116, bd Pereire
43 80 88 68

Closed Sat lunch, Sun. Open until 11pm (summer 11:30pm). Terrace dining. Air cond. V, AE, MC.

Pierre Darrieumerlou's table fairly groans beneath the weight of generously served Basco-Béarnais fare. Come with a healthy appetite, and order the lively hot peppers stuffed with codfish, the confit de canard aux cèpes, or tender Pyrenees lamb escorted by toothsome white beans. You can count on a warm welcome at this crowded, cheerful spot. **C** 280-380 F. **M** 210 F.

Taïra

(14)

10, rue des Acacias
47 66 74 14

Closed Sat lunch, Sun, Aug 15-22. Open until 10:30pm. Air cond. V, AE, DC, MC.

Taïra Kurihara is endowed with an authoritative technique and a vigorous temperament, qualities that give his cuisine a keen, zestful edge. The best dishes point up his Japanese roots; we recommend the crunchy vegetables drizzled with prawn oil, flash-seared tuna perfumed with icy basil oil, and John Dory finished with a vibrant and unusual caramelized prawn sauce. The salmon "tataki" (served practically raw, just faintly warm, with a piquant vinaigrette) are not everyone's cup of green tea, but we think they're terrific! Fine, affordable cellar; comfortable, pearl-gray décor. **C** 300-450 F. **M** 320 F (exc weekday lunch), 150 F, 170 F.

12/20 Le Timgad

21, rue Brunel
45 74 23 70,
fax 40 68 76 46

Open daily until 11pm. Priv rm: 10. Air cond. No pets. Garage pkg. V, AE, DC.

Le Timgad could be a palace in Fès, with its extravagant décor of arabesques and enameled tiles. Ahmed Laasri sends forth some very good couscous, but don't neglect his pigeon pastilla, chicken tagine with olives, or succulent spit-roasted lamb. There's a comprehensive cellar of North African wines, and excellent service. It's wise to book in advance at this popular spot. **C** 260-340 F.

La Toque

(13)

16, rue de Tocqueville - 42 27 97 75

Closed Sat, Sun, Dec 24-Jan 3, Jul 23-Aug 23. Open until 9:30pm. Air cond. Pkg. V, MC.

The room is tiny and so are the tables at Jacky Joubert's little restaurant. But the 150 F set meal is gratifyingly generous, bringing a good warm pâté of red mullet and asparagus, boned and stuffed guinea fowl with a tasty garnish of apples and grapes, a selection of cheeses, and a delectable chocolate cake followed by petits-fours. We wish the wine list were more precise, though, and that the service were speedier. **C** 250-320 F. **M** 150 F, 210 F.

18th arrondissement

A. Beauvilliers

52, rue Lamarck
42 54 54 42,
fax 42 62 70 30

Closed Mon lunch, Sun. Open until 10:45pm. Priv rm: 45. Garden dining. Air cond. No pets. Garage pkg. V, AE, DC, MC.

Édouard Carlier quickly recovered his sang-froid, after an explosion nearly deprived the city of one of its loveliest restaurants. All is back in order now, and Carlier is again surrounded by his collections of nineteenth-century portraits, Carpeaux terracottas, nostalgic bridal garlands, and by his beautifully dressed tables and fanciful floral displays. If ever a restaurant was designed for *fêtes* and celebrations, this is it. Indeed, show-business personalities, celebrity chefs, and political figures regularly scale the Butte Montmartre to toast their triumphs with Beauvilliers's best Champagne.

So why, you're wondering, has the rating been suspended? We'll tell you. After receiving an ominous number of letters that complained of erratic cooking, interminable waits, and sniffy service, we dispatched our investigators to the scene. They returned with mixed impressions. One noted that a famous name or face was indeed a sure ticket to good service and hospitality; another was disappointed by his marinated salmon with caviar cream, a skinny veal chop, and humdrum fruit tart. Even the set lunch, which we've long cited as an example, scored low, owing to a mundane salad of squid and mushrooms, an overcooked tournedos of hake and smoked bacon... Naturally, we'd rather go on praising the brilliant cuisine bourgeoise that Beauvilliers has delivered for years: the superb foie gras in shimmering Sherry aspic, mallard duck in a sauce spiked with single-malt whisky, flanked by exquisite spätzle and onion marmalade, and the rest of the appetizing roster. But we owe it to Carlier, a perfectionist with the highest standards of refinement, to issue this warning call. **C** 550-900 F. **M** 300 F (lunch, wine incl), 185 F (weekday lunch), 320 F (weekday dinner).

(13) Charlot Ier

"Les Merveilles des Mers,"
128 bis, bd de Clichy - 45 22 47 08,
fax 44 70 07 50

Open daily until 1am. Air cond. Garage pkg. V, AE, DC, MC.

The traditional house repertoire of seafood classics (bouillabaisse, braised skate, red mullet in aromatic stock) has been beefed up with a few meat dishes, but the best bets here remain the simplest preparations, starting with the extraordinary assortments of briny fresh shellfish. **C** 290-420 F. **M** 190 F.

12/20 Chez Frézet

181, rue Ordener
46 06 64 20,
fax 46 06 10 79

Closed Sat lunch, Sun. Open until 10:30pm. Priv rm: 90. Garden dining. Pkg. V, AE, MC.

Christian Marie's pocket-sized establishment overlooks a minuscule back garden, which you may admire while enjoying his market-fresh specialties. The 145 F set meal includes an apéritif and a carafe of Côtes-du-Rhône, as well as foie gras de canard en salade, fresh fillet of fish in a deliciously creamy sauce, and an apple-stuffed crêpe. **C** 220-400 F. **M** 145 F (wine incl), 180 F.

12/20 La Galerie

16, rue Tholozé
42 59 25 76

Closed Sun. Open until 11pm. No pets. V.

A miniature gallery, with a cozy, appealing air. The owners give guests a warm welcome and good value for their money, with a trio of simple but satisfying single-price menus. For lunch, there's a salad of andouille sausage showered with shallots, a brace of tender lamb chops, and a smooth crème caramel. The food is carefully prepared, and garnishes are so generous as to be excessive—but that's a small quibble indeed. **M** 68 F (lunch), 115 F & 139 F (dinner).

(13) Langevin

"Au Poulbot Gourmet," 39, rue Lamarck - 46 06 86 00

Closed Sun dinner (Oct-May). Open until 10:15pm. V.

A glass-enclosed terrace gives patrons a wide-angle view of this picturesque corner of Montmartre. Normandy native Jean-Paul Langevin serves cuisine based on top-notch seasonal ingredients, with a few discreet nods to traditional country cooking. Try his tomatoes stuffed with curried snails, sole paupiettes stuffed with mussels in a lush sauce poulette, and the yummy frozen charlotte aux deux chocolats sauce pistache. Judicious cellar. **C** 270-340 F. **M** 115 F (lunch, wine incl), 198 F (wine incl).

11/20 Chez Marie-Louise

52, rue Championnet - 46 06 86 55

Closed Sun, Mon. Open until 10pm. No pets.

Lobster salad, veal chop grand'mère, lotte with fresh pasta, clafoutis of seasonal fruits—here's honest bistro cooking, unchanged for 30 years, served amid copper saucepans and prints of carousing monks. **C** 200-240 F. **M** 130 F.

12/20 Aux Négociants

27, rue Lambert
46 06 15 11

Closed Sat, Sun, Aug, hols. Open until 10:30pm. No pets. No cards.

Jean Navier serves a wonderful selection of modest but tasty growers' wines, with an emphasis on the Loire. Wine lovers should sample a Jasnières or a Bourgeuil at the bar, but the Rhône wines are velvet on the tongue when married to the robust dishes produced by *la patronne*. Forget frills like tablecloths and concentrate instead on robust rillettes, boudin maison, farm chicken, and cassoulet. **C** 150-200 F.

14 Le Restaurant

32, rue Véron
42 23 06 22,
fax 42 23 36 16

Closed Sun. Open until 11pm. V, AE, MC.

Yves Peladeau worked his way up from busboy to owner-chef of his Restaurant at the foot of the Butte Montmartre. The dining room is as modern, bright, and à *la mode* as the imaginative menu: give your taste buds a treat with the marinated sardines, nicely seasoned marinated salmon, and a savory honey-roasted duck spiced with coriander. Small but intelligent wine list (note Charles Joguet's Chinon). The cheapest set meal is a real bargain. **C** 200-280 F. **M** 70 F, 120 F.

12/20 Wepler

14, pl. de Clichy
45 22 53 24,
fax 44 70 07 50

Open daily until 1am. Air cond. Garage pkg. V, AE, DC, MC.

A deluxe brasserie providing reliable food and good service. The shellfish is some of the freshest in Paris; other interesting options are the hearty (and truly delicious) headcheese, grilled salmon béarnaise, and a copious choucroute garnie. Fine bouillabaisse, too. **C** 200-400 F. **M** 150 F.

19th arrondissement

13 Le Bistrot Roumain

1, rue de Bellevue
42 41 73 03

Closed Sun, Mon, Aug. Open until 11pm. No pets. V, MC.

Warming, sincere Romanian fare is served here in an adorable farmhouse setting. Try the sturdy stuffed cabbage, the colossal grilled-pepper salad, spicy Transylvanian goulash, Moldavian meat and kidney stew, and baby chicken with garlic sauce. Drink a nice, round Romanian Cabernet, then finish up with the good poppyseed cake. **C** 200 F. **M** 90 F (weekday lunch).

15 Au Cochon d'Or

192, av. Jean-Jaurès
42 45 46 46,
fax 42 40 43 90

Open daily until 10:30pm. Priv rm: 40. Air cond. Valet pkg. V, AE, DC, MC.

Times have changed since the Ayral family set up shop here in 1924. The nearby slaughterhouses are now defunct; butchers and meat-packers have given way to the cultured, worldly crowd disgorged by the Cité des Sciences at La Villette. But the restaurant has evolved along with its clientele. Under René Ayral's management, the kitchen continues to grill, roast, and fry the choicest morsels of beef: filet mignons, prime ribs, and sirloin steaks. Earthier choices include calf's head en salade with a mustardy dressing, pigs' trotters served with sauce Choron, or boudin and apples. An excellent sommelier oversees the wines. **C** 350-500 F. **M** 240 F.

12/20 Dagorno

190, av. Jean-Jaurès
40 40 09 39,
fax 48 03 17 23

Open daily until 12:15am (Fri & Sat 1am). Priv rm: 80. Air cond. Valet pkg. V, AE, MC.

Quite a contrast with the futuristic Cité des Sciences, this opulent brasserie actively cultivates its old-fashioned image, offering decent, uncomplicated food. You won't be disappointed by the fresh shellfish assortments, calf's head sauce gribiche, cervelle meunière, or the enormous côte de bœuf sauce bordelaise, but the foie gras en salade is bland, and the wines are too costly. **C** 250-450 F. **M** 158 F (wine incl).

12/20 L'Oriental

58, rue de l'Ourq
40 34 26 23

Closed Sun. Open until 11pm. Priv rm: 48. Air cond. No pets. V, MC.

In this tiny Lebanese eatery you can gorge on generously served mezes, delicious hummus with minced lamb, spicy sausages, and tasty marinated chicken. Unbeatable prices. And there's a fruity red Kefraya '92 on the wine list that partners the food perfectly. **C** 100-175 F. **M** 75 F (exc Sat dinner), 125 F & 175 F (wine incl), 90 F.

Gault Millau's ratings are based solely on the restaurants' cuisine. We do not take into account the atmosphere, décor, service and so on; these are commented upon within the review.

15 Le Pavillon Puebla

"Christian Vergès," Parc des Buttes-Chaumont
42 08 92 62, fax 42 39 83 16

Closed Sun, Mon. Open until 10pm. Priv rm: 90. Garden dining. Pkg. V, AE, MC.

This stylish Napoléon III hunting lodge stands swaddled in greenery at the foot of the Buttes Chaumont park. Owner-chef Christian Vergès remains true to his Catalan roots, producing a menu full of sun-drenched, rousing flavors. The spiced squid in their ink, grilled red mullet with eggplant confit, the lively fricassée of weevers and scampi with fennel and a whiff of anise, and the lush lobster au banyuls will transport you to the Côte Vermeille. One of the city's best crème brûlées is made here and some splendid Banyuls can be found on the extensive wine list. **C** 380-500 F. **M** 180 F, 230 F.

12/20 Le Sancerre

13, av. Corentin-Cariou - 40 36 80 44, fax 42 61 19 74

Closed Sat, Sun, Aug. Open until 10:30pm. Pkg. V, AE, DC, MC.

A nostalgic atmosphere reigns at this likeable bistro, a vestige of the old abattoir district of La Villette. The bill of fare features prodigious portions of tasty charcuterie, beef rib sprinkled with coarse sea-salt, and juicy double lamb chops. As for wines, look no further than the wonderful Morgon and Sancerre sold by the centimeter (you pay only for what you drink from the bottle placed on the table). It is wise to book ahead for lunch. **C** 200-320 F. **M** 169 F (weekdays), 110 F.

20th arrondissement

14 Aux Allobroges

71, rue des Grands-Champs
43 73 40 00

Closed Sun, Mon, Aug. Open until 10pm. V.

Olivier and Annette Pateyron have given their little restaurant a spruce new look and a fantastic new menu. It's worth the trip out to the twentieth arrondissement to savor Olivier's plump langoustines poised on a colorful bed of ratatouille, braised lamb with garlic confit, and sautéed yellow plums flambé. The little 83 F set meal also has its charms, what with the tomates confites swirled with green-olive cream, steak with shallots or coriander-spiced skate, followed by cheese *and* dessert. A la carte prices are equally clement, inciting one to splurge on lobster and lotte perfumed with tarragon or Barbary duck enhanced with spices and nuts. Only the wine list needs improvement. **C** 200-250 F. **M** 83 F, 150 F.

13 Aux Becs Fins

44, bd de Ménilmontant
47 97 51 52

Closed Sun, Sep 11-20. Open until 9:30pm. Priv rm: 15. Terrace dining. V, AE.

This winsome little bistro runs alongside the Père Lachaise cemetery. The colorful owner (Édith Lefebvre) relies on a faithful clientele of regulars who don't mind the eccentric décor. The cuisine is back on course, and the toque again firmly in place. We recommend the bountiful terrines, juicy grilled meat and fish, the cassoulet "mère Édith," and the tasty (though costly) wines. Adorable service. **C** 230-350 F. **M** 180 F, 240 F.

12/20 A la Courtille

1, rue des Envierges
46 36 51 59

Open daily until 11pm. Terrace dining. V.

Enjoy a spectacular view of the city from the terrace of this elegant bistro. Even better than the food (which is pretty good: marinated sardines, duck breast with fresh figs, crème brûlée...) is the wine list, compiled with admirable expertise by Bernard Pontonnier and Francis Morel. **C** 200-230 F. **M** 70 F & 100 F (lunch exc Sun).

We're always happy to hear about your discoveries and receive your comments on ours. We want to give your letters the attention they deserve, so when you write to Gault Millau, please state clearly what you liked or disliked. Be concise but convincing, and take the time to argue your point.

THE SUBURBS

ASNIÈRES
92600 - (Hauts-de-Seine)
Paris 9 - Argenteuil 6 - Saint-Denis 8

14 Le Van Gogh
2, quai Aulagnier
47 91 05 10,
fax 47 93 00 93

Closed Sat, Sun, Feb 24-Mar 14, Aug 6-22. Open until 10pm. Priv rm: 60. Terrace dining. Air cond. No pets. Valet pkg. V, AE, DC, MC.

Robert and Pierrette Daubian have dropped anchor in this ultramodern establishment on Robinson Island. The dining room resembles the interior of a luxury liner, with portholes and bay windows offering views of the Seine. The cuisine looks out to sea, with dishes like lobster and prawn feuilleté, and filet de bar royal cooked with the freshest produce. Desserts are superb (try the delicious berry gratin with Champagne), and there are fine Bordeaux to wash it all down. **C** 270-450 F.

BOULOGNE-BILLANCOURT
92100 - (Hauts-de-Seine)
Paris (Porte de St-Cloud) 10 - Versailles 11

14 L'Auberge
86, av. J.-B.-Clément
46 05 22 35,
fax 46 05 23 16

Closed Sat lunch, Sun, hols, Jul 28-Aug 21. Open until 9:45pm. Priv rm: 30. Terrace dining. Air cond. Pkg. V, AE, DC.

The bright, tidy little dining room of this mellow provincial dwelling draws a public of well-heeled executive types. We share their enthusiasm for Jean-Pierre Roy's varied, deftly crafted menu featuring a country-style goose terrine studded with grapes, pan-roasted red mullet with a colorful fricassée of peppers and olives, and a curious chocolate dessert served with tarragon cream sauce. The cache of Jura wines in the cellar (which is otherwise strong on Bordeaux) is a relic of the days when the restaurant specialized in food from Franche-Comté. **C** 320-400 F. **M** 150 F, 190 F (wine incl).

14 La Bretonnière
120, av. J.-B.-Clément
46 05 73 56

Closed Sat, Sun. Open until 9:45pm. V, AE, DC, MC.

A former head waiter, René Rossignol switched to cuisine and brought this restaurant back up to standard. In fact, Rossignol cooks as the nightingale sings: naturally and exquisitely. His new single-price menu lists such fine traditional offerings as wild-duck terrine laced with white rum, lightly cooked salmon with lentils and smoky bacon, and delicate œufs à la neige with pralines. Interesting cellar. **M** 155 F (base price).

16 Au Comte de Gascogne
89, av. J.-B.-Clément
46 03 47 27,
fax 46 04 55 70

Closed Sat lunch, Sun. Open until 10:30pm. Garden dining. Air cond. Valet pkg. V, AE, DC, MC.

Three palm trees, a fountain, and lots of flowers make it feel like spring all year in the delightful courtyard garden. Business lunches here are actually enjoyable, while dinner in the suburbs becomes an exotic outing. Gérard Vérane, the jovial Gascon who created this tropical greenhouse, recently handed over the kitchen to Henri Charvet, who once served the best meals in Aix-en-Provence. The Gascon flavor lingers on in the half-dozen variations on foie gras, including the wonderful smoked duck foie gras with cucumber and bacon, and in the world-class collection of Armagnacs. But what really captures our attention are the sun-kissed Provençal dishes: John Dory with fennel-stuffed peppers and tiny artichokes, lobster soup with ravioli filled with green-tomato "jam," red mullet braised in a basil jus flanked by delicious stuffed vegetables, and steamed cod drizzled with Maussane olive oil. Sommelier Patrice Marchand, will help you choose from among the 100,000 wines on offer. **C** 500-700 F. **M** 240 F (lunch).

12/20 La Tonnelle de Bacchus
120, av. J.-B.-Clément
46 04 43 98

Closed Sat, Sun, Christmas-beg Jan, May. Open until 10pm. Priv rm: 15. Terrace dining. V, AE, DC, MC.

Here's an adorable vintage bistro with a shady summer terrace, where customers divide their interest among a fresh salmon tartare, hearty confit de canard, and cinnamon-scented apple crumble, all washed down with delicious wines, some of which are served by the glass. **M** 120 F.

CHÂTEAUFORT
78117 - (Yvelines)
Paris 28 - Versailles 10 - Orsay 11

16 La Belle Époque
10, pl. de la Mairie
39 56 21 66,
fax 39 56 87 96

Closed Sun dinner, Mon. Annual closings not available. Open until 10pm. Terrace dining. Pkg. V, AE, DC, MC.

Alain Rayé made the transition from urban chef to culinary country squire with nary a hitch. His village inn overflows with turn-of-the-century charm, and his menu sparkles with full-flavored enticements. He won us over (and earned an extra point) with an excellent croustillant of foie gras garnished with Port-glazed pears, John Dory paired with zingy pickled lemons, and exquisite Gâtinais rabbit with caramelized eggplant and fabulous olive fritters. Leading the list of luscious desserts was a glorious gâteau de pommes à l'orange. Stupendous, high-priced cellar. The professional service is warmed by the smiling presence of Brigitte Rayé. **C** 400-550 F. **M** 210 F, 250 F, 350 F.

CHAVILLE
92370 - (Hauts-de-Seine)
Paris 13 - Versailles 9 - Meudon 1

14 La Tonnelle
29, rue Lamennais
47 50 42 77

Closed Sun dinner, Mon. Open until 10pm. Terrace dining. Air cond. V, AE, MC.

Here, on the edge of the wood, stands a flower-decked hunting pavilion with an adorable scrap of a garden. Philippe Joubin presents his forthright, generous cuisine on a pair of well-designed menus. Featured are a robust cassolette of escargots poached in Chablis, lamb noisettes in a zesty mustard sauce, and an old-fashioned rum-soaked savarin. Game, of course, is highlighted in season. Good cellar. Host Franck Aubert extends a heart-warming welcome. **M** 185 F, 245 F.

CHENNEVIÈRES-SUR-MARNE
94430 - (Val-de-Marne)
Paris 17 - Lagny 20 - Coulommiers 51

14 L'Écu de France
31, rue de Champigny - 45 76 00 03

Closed Sun dinner, Mon, 1st wk of Sep. Open until 9:30pm. Priv rm: 50. Terrace dining. No pets. Pkg. V.

From the pink dining room you have a grand view of the River Marne, which you can admire along with Alain Desmots's fresh, skillful cooking. Order his dainty "purses" filled with poached oysters in Sherry cream, followed by thyme-rubbed lamb with a Niçois garnish, and Tahitian vanilla ice cream. The list of fine wines and vintage brandies will encourage you to indulge. **C** 300-350 F.

14 Au Vieux Clodoche
18, rue de Champigny - 45 76 09 30,
fax 45 94 25 53

Closed Tue dinner, Feb 17-24. Open until 10:30pm (summer 11pm). Priv rm: 200. Terrace dining. Garage pkg. V, AE, DC, MC.

This charming eatery on the banks of the Marne has no difficulty attracting diners from the posh villas and estates nearby, despite the menu's punishing prices. But the patrons must feel that they get their money's worth, and indeed Brigitte Huerta's good cooking has plenty of appeal: lemon-marinated salmon, rack of spring lamb (in season, of course) with a delectable potato and asparagus tourte, and dark-chocolate tart with coffee ice cream are representative. **C** 380-520 F.

CHESNAY (LE)
See Versailles

CHEVILLY-LARUE
94550 - (Val-de-Marne)
Paris 12 - Antony 5 - Créteil 11

13 Chez Fernand
248, av. de Stalingrad - 46 86 11 77

Closed Sun, Mon, Aug. Open until 10:30pm. Pkg. V.

Fernand Asselinne transferred one of his pair of Parisian restaurants out here to the suburbs. Somewhere en route, the former working-class bistro turned into a neo-Norman *auberge* that Maupassant himself (we're certain) would have admired. It's a cozy, comfortable place to enjoy such tasty, down-to-earth fare as oxtail salad ravigote, tripes au cidre et calvados, excellent Camemberts matured on the premises, and fabulous house-made bread. Though small, the cellar is well designed; and the service is friendly as can be. **C** 250-350 F. **M** 135 F.

CLICHY

92110 - (Hauts-de-Seine)
Paris 7 - Saint-Germain-en-Laye 17

La Barrière de Clichy

1, rue de Paris
47 37 05 18,
fax 47 37 77 05

Closed Sat lunch, Sun, 2 wks in Aug. Open until 10pm. Priv rm: 15. Air cond. Pkg. V, AE, DC, MC.

Superchefs Guy Savoy and Bernard Loiseau cut their teeth in the Barrière's kitchen, now manned by Gilles Le Gallès, who trained with Loiseau. By now we're familiar with Gilles's menu—mussel soup, snail fricassée, turbot en papillote, roasted lamb with garlic jus, and so on—but they are fine dishes all, beautifully served in a fresh setting that's full of charm. The two least expensive set meals are deservedly popular (they'd be more so, we bet, if wine were included too). **C** 300-400 F. **M** 150 F (weekday dinner), 220 F (weekdays), 370 F.

La Bonne Table

119, bd J.-Jaurès
47 37 38 79

Closed Sat lunch, Sun, Aug. Open until 9pm. V, MC.

Gisèle Berger is a true *cordon bleu*, respected for her talent and adherence to tradition. We find her prices a bit high for the suburbs, but the top-quality seafood Gisèle demands for her dishes doesn't come cheap. You'll enjoy her coquilles Saint-Jacques en persillade, superb Breton lobster, brandade en aïoli, bouillabaisse, and apple tart. René, the *patron*, serves his wines a trifle too cold, but his welcome is always nice and warm. **C** 340-460 F.

La Romantica

73, bd J.-Jaurès
47 37 29 71,
fax 47 37 76 32

Closed Sat lunch, Sun. Open until 10:30pm. Priv rm: 15. Terrace dining. Valet pkg. V, AE.

Claudio Puglia is a virtually self-taught cook, but his lack of culinary diplomas is more than compensated by his vibrant passion for *la bella cucina*. He tirelessly seeks out the most select olive oils and the finest Italian wines and cheeses to enhance his innovative dishes. Puglia's originality dazzles the palate with a saffron-tinged spinach risotto, a carpaccio like none you've ever tasted (especially those pale French copies so inexplicably popular these days), lasagne without a trace of heavy, overcooked tomato sauce, or sweet-and-savory lotte with raisins, pine nuts, and raspberries. And—of course!—there are a thousand and one different hand-fashioned pastas. The most spectacular is surely the silken-textured fettuccine tossed with sage and prosciutto, then presented in a hollowed-out Parmesan cheese flamed with Cognac! In summer, these *delizie* are served on a romantic garden patio, where you will be warmly welcomed by your hostess, Laetitia Puglia. **C** 260-360 F. **M** 175 F, 280 F, 350 F.

Prices in red draw attention to restaurants that offer a particularly good value.

COURBEVOIE

92400 - (Hauts-de-Seine)
Paris 11 - St-Germain-en-Laye 13

Les Feuillantines

23, pl. de Seine,
La Défense 1
47 73 88 80,
fax 40 90 96 03

Closed Sat, Sun. Priv rm: 10. Terrace dining. Air cond. Garage pkg. V, AE, DC, MC.

A largely business clientele enjoys a view of the Seine and the Ile de la Jatte from the third-floor terrace of Les Feuillantines. The menu is rather long and expensive, but proposes delicate, handily executed dishes like a crab-stuffed lettuce hearts, caramelized langoustines touched with gentle spices, crisp and airy lamb's brain beignets, and luscious lemon-filled crêpes. **C** 280-400 F. **M** 200 F (wine incl), 220 F.

La Safranée sur Mer

12, pl. des Reflets,
La Défense 2
47 78 75 50,
fax 47 76 46 20

Closed Sat, Sun, Dec 24-Jan 2, Aug. Open until 10:30pm. Priv rm: 30. Terrace dining. Air cond. Valet pkg. V, AE, DC.

With its luxurious wood-paneled décor and fine service, this seafood restaurant is a favorite lunch venue for business people with clients to impress. The chef purchases premium ingredients to prepare his saffron-stained sole with crisp haricots verts, or spiced, smoked swordfish with fresh pasta, or lobster roasted with herbs). Live music is often presented in the evening.

C 360-500 F. **M** 200 F (dinner, wine incl), 190 F (wine incl), 250 F.

CRÉTEIL
94000 - (Val-de-Marne)
Paris 12 - Evry 20 - Melun 35 - Bobigny 17

Le Cristolien
13
29, av. P.-Brossolette
48 98 12 01,
fax 42 07 24 47

Closed Sat lunch, Sun. Open until 10pm. Priv rm: 25. Terrace dining. Air cond. Garage pkg. V, MC.

The terrace is brand-new, and so is the single-price menu just introduced by chef Alain Donnard. What a pity that these laudable efforts haven't produced more convincing results. Our mussel gratin, dry and stingily served, preceded tender roast lamb flanked by bland scalloped potatoes, and an iced apple tart that was merely inoffensive. On balance, we've decided to take away a point. **M** 195 F.

CROISSY-BEAUBOURG
77183 - (Seine-et-Marne)
Paris 29 - Melun 34 - Meaux 30

L'Aigle d'Or
8, rue de Paris
60 05 31 33,
fax 64 62 09 39

Closed Sun dinner, Mon. Open until 9:15pm. Priv rm: 40. Garden dining. Pkg. V, AE, DC.

Last year we sang the Aigle's praises, but this time around it's a different tune. Host Jean-Louis Giliams, brother of owner-chef Hervé Giliams, recently passed away, leaving this establishment at sixes and sevens. After an uneven, mostly disappointing meal, we think it's best to suspend our rating until the kitchen and dining room get their act together again. **C** 450-550 F. **M** 250 F, 450 F.

DISNEYLAND PARIS
See Marne-la-Vallée

GARENNE-COLOMBES (LA)
92250 - (Hauts-de-Seine)
Paris 12 - Courbevoie 2 - Pontoise 29

Auberge du 14-Juillet
14
9, bd de la République - 42 42 21 79

Open daily until 9:30pm. V, AE, DC, MC.

The inn's patriotic sign and classic cooking are both quintessentially French. Chef Jean-Pierre Baillon goes beyond the call of duty to prepare admirably fresh, fine-tuned dishes like crab ravioli, pale-pink veal chops ideally partnered with bosky morels, and fresh cod with potatoes and onions. His son turns out the tasty desserts. Charming welcome. **C** 300-450 F. **M** 170 F, 280 F.

Aux Gourmets Landais
15
Hôtel de Paris, 5, av. Joffre - 42 42 22 86

Closed Sun dinner, Mon, Aug 15-Sep 15. Open until 10:45pm. Priv rm: 35. Terrace dining. Pkg. V, AE, DC, MC.

This comfortable establishment boasts a bit of a garden, and enough greenery to help one forget the surrounding bleakness of downtown Colombes. Alain Velazco cooks with the same charming Southwestern accent that lilts in his conversation. Sample his sturdy cassoulet made with five kinds of meat, his salade landaise enriched with superb foie gras, or his homey poulet en fricassée. His occasional forays into seafood are

> ## The toque, circa 1700
>
> **Have you ever wondered about the origin of that towering, billowy (and slightly ridiculous) white hat worn by chefs all over the world? Chefs have played an important role in society since the fifth century B.C., but the hats didn't begin to appear in kitchens until around the eighteenth century A.D. The toque is said to be of Greek origin: many famous Greek cooks, to escape persecution, sought refuge in monasteries and continued to practice their art. The chefs donned the tall hats traditionally worn by Orthodox priests, but to distinguish themselves from their fellows, they wore white hats instead of black. The custom eventually was adopted by chefs from Paris to Peking.**

equally successful, witness the salmon ravioli or the prawns with leeks and asparagus. For dessert, we cannot be warm enough in our recommendation for Velazco's apple tourtière spiked with Armagnac. Wide-ranging cellar. **C** 320-450 F. **M** 160 F (dinner, wine incl), 120 F (lunch), 200 F.

ISSY-LES-MOULINEAUX

92130 - (Hauts-de-Seine)
Paris (Pte de Versailles) 1 - Boulogne-B. 1

12/20 Coquibus

16, av. de la République - 46 38 75 80

Closed Sat lunch, Sun. Open until 10:30pm. Priv rm: 28. Terrace dining. Garage pkg. V, AE, MC.

The sign and the winsome dining room evoke Montmartre, oddly enough, but the hearty, homestyle cooking shows a Southwestern slant, witness the 150 F menu's ox jowls in aspic with a zesty sauce gribiche, pan-roasted squid emboldened with coriander, and suave crème brûlée. **C** 200-350 F. **M** 150 F.

14 Manufacture

20, esplanade de la Manufacture
40 93 08 98

Closed Sat lunch, Sun. Open until 10:30pm. Terrace dining. Air cond. V, AE.

Jean-Pierre Vigato, who also runs the three-toque Apicius in Paris, hasn't opened a second restaurant just to make more money; he sees it as an outlet for another aspect of his personality. La Manufacture is a bright, spacious restaurant converted from an old tobacco factory. Vigato's former number two, David Van Laer, cooks up an appetizing single-price menu that proposes (for example) tomato mousse and gazpacho both vigorously perfumed with basil, and calf's head, tongue, and brains in a piquant sauce ravigote followed by a selection of goat cheeses and iced praline swirled with raspberry fondue—the food is lively, colorful, and most reasonably priced. Short but pertinent wine list; cheerful service. **M** 180 F.

14 L'Olivier

22, rue Ernest-Renan
40 93 42 00,
fax 40 93 02 19

Closed Sat, Sun. Open until 10pm. Priv rm: 15. V, AE, DC.

After long years of working in other men's kitchens, Marcel Goareguer decided to strike out on his own. His restaurant has already been enthusiastically adopted by local business lunchers, owing to Goareguer's generous, scrupulously handled cuisine. Start with a fine scallop and crab terrine, then try the beef fillet in a peppery sauce accented with nasturtium blossoms. For dessert, there's a delicious pear pudding with cider-spiked custard sauce. The welcome and service, incidentally, couldn't be better. **C** 290-350 F. **M** 175 F.

LEVALLOIS-PERRET

92300 - (Hauts-de-Seine)
Paris (Porte de Champerret) 8 - Neuilly 4

13 La Cerisaie

56, rue de Villiers
47 58 40 61

Open daily until 10pm. Priv rm: 18. Pkg. V, AE.

The handsomely decorated two-level dining room looks out over a pretty square, but we have eyes only for Gilles Bordereau's appetizing salad of sweetbreads spiced with paprika, rich lobster fricassée, and rosy calf's liver with onion confit. The welcome is warm, but the wine list is confusing. **C** 350-450 F. **M** 190 F (exc weekday lunch), 230 F.

14 Gauvain

11, rue L.-Rouquier
47 58 51 09

Closed Sat, Sun, Aug. Open until 10pm. Priv rm: 25. Air cond. V, AE, MC.

A commendable establishment, driven by the talent of a creative chef whose personal, regularly renewed repertoire delights his loyal following of executives and locals. From the appetizing dishes on offer, choose a generous salade landaise or tiny scallops in an aromatic broth, then proceed to sea bream with a coarse-grain mustard sauce or saddle of lamb perfumed with cardamom, and round things off with a satisfying walnut crème brûlée. **C** 180-250 F. **M** 159 F.

14 Le Petit Poste

39, rue Rivay
47 37 34 46

Closed Sat lunch, Sun, 1 wk at Christmas, 3 wks in Aug. Open until 10:30pm. Priv rm: 12. Air cond. Garage pkg. V, AE, DC, MC.

Fifteen tables crowded around the bar—this is exactly the type of bistro Brassens used to write about in his songs. Now it is a favorite with the good people of Levallois, who come to enjoy the cooking of Pierre-Jean Leboucher, formerly of Lucas-Carton and La Marée. His scallops poached in Vouvray, rabbit with bacon and potatoes, and crêpes à la paresseuse display plenty of originality and finesse. Alert service; expensive cellar. **C** 250-300 F.

La Rôtisserie

(14)
24, rue A.-France
47 48 13 82

Closed Sun. Open until 10pm. Air cond. V, AE, MC.

A former hangar has been converted into a bilevel loft-brasserie with Art Deco fittings, to serve as the scene for Daniel Ballester's remarkably generous cooking. A 150 F single-price menu offers the likes of crab ravioli, foie gras flan with a pungent truffle jus, a puffy omelette stuffed with marrow and napped with sauce bordelaise, or succulent roast chicken and whipped potatoes flavored with olive oil. Excellent desserts conclude these satisfying repasts. Unbeatable value. **M** 150 F.

LOUVECIENNES

78430 - (Yvelines)
Paris 24 - Versailles 7

Aux Chandelles

(13)
12, pl. de l'Église
39 69 08 40

Closed Sat lunch, Wed, Aug 8-22. Open until 10pm. Terrace dining. Pkg. V, AE.

The upstairs dining room offers a view of an enclosed garden. The young owner-chef, Stéphane Dohollon, who studied with Gérard Besson, produces dishes that are so delicate you could almost accuse him of pretension. The set meals are excellent value, particularly the 260 F menu which includes wine. Worth trying this year are rabbit aspic dressed with truffle vinaigrette, turbot baked with citrus fruit, and fresh pineapple poached in tarragon syrup. Perfect, courteous service in an ideal setting for romantic dinners. **C** 300-400 F. **M** 260 F (wine incl), 160 F.

MAISONS-LAFFITTE

78600 - (Yvelines)
Paris 21 - Pontoise 18 - St-Germain-en-L. 8

Le Laffitte

(14)
5, av. de St-Germain
39 62 01 53

Closed Sun dinner, Mon, Aug. Open until 10pm. Air cond. Garage pkg. V, AE.

Offering good seafood, classic cooking, and an oft-renewed list of carefully prepared dishes, André Laurier's restaurant is an address worth noting and just the place for hearty appetites. Fine raw materials go into his rich saucisson de canard et foie gras, scallops in Champagne, and lamb charlotte with pesto sauce. Desserts are a hair less convincing, however, and the wines are quite expensive. Hospitable welcome; exemplary service. **C** 290-420 F. **M** 195 F (wine incl), 320 F.

Le Tastevin

(15)
9, av. Eglé
39 62 11 67

Closed Feb school hols, Aug 16-Sep 4. Open until 10pm. Priv rm: 25. Garage pkg. V, AE, DC.

Michel Blanchet's patrons are nothing if not faithful (no, that's not quite true: they are also—necessarily—rich). They generously forgive him when he serves the sort of meal for which we cut off his toques last year! Well, this year we too are in a forgiving mood, having dined wonderfully well on a mouthwatering gâteau of foie gras with fresh morels, a lovely and delicious marinière of fresh shellfish, a flawlessly prepared fillet of pikeperch with a tart touch of sorrel, and a first-class cheese board. Blanchet wins back his toques and our esteem. There is a down side, though: prices are incredibly steep, to the point of indecency. Le Tastevin's exceptional wine list, with prime offerings from every region, is simply out of reach for all but the wealthiest connoisseurs. **C** 400-600 F. **M** 230 F (weekday lunch), 520 F (tasting menu).

La Vieille Fontaine

(14)
8, av. Grétry
39 62 01 78,
fax 39 62 13 43

Closed Mon. Open until 10:30pm. Priv rm: 60. Garden dining. V.

Manon Letourneur and François Clerc have renounced *grande cuisine*, its works and pomps (and towering *additions*) to embrace a new faith: the 160 F single-price menu. François Clerc and his team put just as much care into the preparation of their new bourgeois repertoire as they did into the costly, sophisticated dishes of yore. You'll feel no regrets for yesterday when you fork into the lusty millefeuille layered with peppers and house-smoked cuttlefish, tender pork shanks basted with beer, spit-roasted meats, and delicious desserts (there's a yummy baked peach swirled with caramel). The romantic setting hasn't changed an iota, nor has the gracious hospitality of Manon Letourneur. **M** 160 F.

MARLY-LE-ROI
78160 - (Yvelines)
Paris 25 - Versailles 9

14 Le Village
3, Grande-Rue
39 16 28 14,
fax 39 58 62 60

Closed Sun dinner, Mon. Open until 10:15pm. Priv rm: 30. Pkg. V, AE.

This seventeenth-century house stands in the center of an enchanting Ile de France village. The dining room now sports a fresh, new look that complements chef Claude Boulic's clever, harmonious cuisine. This year, try his delicate tartare of fresh vegetables and marinated fish, the perfectly seasoned fillet of Charolais beef with melting shallots, and the high, handsome strawberry soufflé. Splendid cellar of Bordeaux. **C** 360-450 F. **M** 148 F (wine incl).

MARNE-LA-VALLÉE
77206 Marne-la-Vallée – (Seine/Marne)
Paris 28 - Meaux 28 - Melun 40

In nearby Disneyland Paris

(Access by A4)
77206 Marne-la-Vallée – (Seine/Marne)

13 Auberge de Cendrillon
In the Park,
Fantasyland
64 74 22 02

Open until 10pm. Terrace dining. Air cond. No pets. Pkg. V, AE, DC, MC.

Cinderella presides over this fairytale inn, decorated with portraits of handsome princes, lovely princesses, splendid carriages, and the rest. One can dine quite honorably here on the 110 F set menu, or choose from the short, simple *carte*. Offerings include a decent foie gras, an impeccable loin of lamb, and tasty Angus beef. It is now possible to enjoy a French or Californian wine with your meal. **C** 230-300 F. **M** 45 F (children), 110 F, 145 F, 175 F.

13 Blue Lagoon
In the Park,
Adventureland
64 74 20 47,
fax 64 74 38 13

Closed 2 days a wk mid Sep-mid Jun. Open until 10pm. Air cond. No pets. Pkg. V, AE, DC, MC.

Palm trees and a tropical lagoon are the setting for agreeably spicy dishes: swordfish with pink peppercorns, chicken curry, banana cake with pineapple sauce. Nearby are the boats that ferry passengers into the *Pirates of the Caribbean*, one of the park's most popular attractions. **C** 200-250 F. **M** 260 F, 145 F, 190 F.

14 California Grill
Disneyland Hotel
60 45 65 76,
fax 60 45 65 33

Open daily until 11pm. Priv rm: 176. Air cond. No pets. Heated pool. Valet pkg. V, AE, DC, MC.

The "gastronomic" restaurant of the Disneyland Hotel offers American-style dishes based on quality ingredients. In his ultramodern kitchens, the chef and his team prepare warm goat-cheese tart, salmon with a maple-syrup glaze and, for dessert, an ethereal honey-walnut millefeuille. Perfect service. A few inexpensive items are on hand for a quick meal: gourmet sandwiches, shrimp pizza, and the like. **C** 300-450 F. **M** 195 F, 295 F (dinner).

13 Key West Seafood
Festival Disney
70 45 70 60,
fax 70 45 70 55

Open daily until 11pm. Priv rm: 120. Terrace dining. Air cond. No pets. Pkg. V, AE, DC, MC.

Overlooking the (artificial) lake is a huge space decked out to resemble an unpretentious Florida fish house. The menu features clam chowder, garlic bread, "catch of the day," and Key Lime pie. As in most of the other Disneyland restaurants, prices are lower now than when the park first opened. The wine cellar is Californian. **C** 150-200 F. **M** 110 F.

12/20 Los Angeles Bar
Festival Disney
60 45 71 14

Open daily until midnight. Terrace dining. Air cond. No pets. Pkg. V, AE, DC, MC.

Also lakeside is this bright, airy, and modern dining room where you can enjoy pastas, pizzas, and steaks grilled to order (a pity that bottled steak sauce is the only condiment proposed). Warm, friendly "American-style" service. **C** 120-200 F. **M** 45 F (children).

Red toques signify modern cuisine; white toques signify traditional cuisine.

FORMIDABLE!
BAL DU
Moulin Rouge
PARIS
LE PRESTIGIEUX CABARET DE PARIS
MONTMARTRE • PLACE BLANCHE •
82 BOULEVARD DE CLICHY • 75018 PARIS
Tel. (1) 46 06 00 19 Fax. (1) 42 23 02 00
Telex. 281498 F

11/20 **Parkside Diner**
New York Hotel
60 45 73 00
Open daily until 11pm. Air cond. V, AE, DC, MC.
Good, simple American food. The 145 F single-price menu includes options like hamburgers, pasta, poached salmon, grilled steaks, and caloric desserts (cheesecake, banana cream pie...). **C** 150-200 F. **M** 95 F, 145 F.

11/20 **Silver Spur Steakhouse**
In the Park, Frontierland
64 74 24 57
Closed 2 days a wk mid Sep-mid Jun. Open until 10pm. Air cond. No pets. Pkg. V, AE, DC, MC.
Hearty appetites meet their match here, with huge portions of barbecued chicken wings and prime ribs of beef served in a reconstituted Wild West saloon. **C** 150-250 F. **M** 45 F (children), 110 F, 175 F.

11/20 **Walt's An American Restaurant**
In the Park, Main Street
64 74 12 97, fax 64 74 38 13
Closed 2 days a wk mid Sep-mid Jun. Open until 10pm. Priv rm: 30. Terrace dining. Air cond. No pets. Pkg. V, AE, DC, MC.
A stairway decorated with photographs of Walt Disney leads to a series of charming little dining rooms; the menu lists uncomplicated fare (lobster, main-dish salads, grilled meats) that is elegantly served. Cheerful staff. **C** 200-250 F. **M** 45 F (children), 145 F.

12/20 **Yacht Club**
Newport Bay Club
60 45 55 00
Dinner only. Open daily until 11pm. Air cond. No pets. V, AE, DC, MC.
Swordfish steak and grilled Maine lobster are featured in this huge, blue dining room; but in high season, you'll need the patience of a saint to obtain a table, for the queues are beyond belief. **M** 95 F, 145 F (dinner), 150 F.

MARNES-LA-COQUETTE
92430 - (Hauts-de-Seine)
Paris 15 - Versailles 4 - Vaucresson 1

11/20 **Les Hirondelles**
18, rue G.-et-X.-Schlumberger
47 41 00 20
Closed Sun dinner, Wed, Aug 4-Sep 1, Dec 24-Jan 2. Open until 9:30pm. V, MC.
Traditional cooking prevails at this friendly little bistro, but sometimes the chef decides to surprise his customers with a deftly grilled salmon and cèpes à la provençale. The Sunday lunch menu is a delight: zucchini fritters, pot-au-feu, and dessert for just 80 F. **C** 150-250 F. **M** 52 F (lunch, exc Sun), 80 F (Sun).

12/20 **La Tête Noire**
6, pl. de la Mairie
47 41 06 28
Closed Sun dinner, Mon. Open until 10pm. Priv rm: 30. Terrace dining. Pkg. V, AE.
A pretty view of a leafy little square and the minuscule church just opposite adds to the charm of this establishment, which is popular with the local gentry. The chef must have been distracted on our last visit, for he served us a scampi salad doused with too much vinaigrette followed by overcooked scallops. Off with the toque, despite good petits-fours and excellent house-made bread. **C** 260-360 F.

MEUDON
92190 - (Hauts-de-Seine)
Paris 12 - Versailles 10 - Boulogne 3

14 **Relais des Gardes**
42, av. du Général-Gallieni
45 34 11 79, fax 45 34 44 32
Closed Sat lunch, Sun dinner. Open until 10pm. V, AE, MC.
Patrick Pierre is the new chef on duty at this handsome brick Relais, where a classical repertoire and style still reign supreme. Yet an occasional—and welcome—creative touch lends extra interest to the oxtail terrine with butter-stewed leeks, langoustines in an agreeably tart little sauce, and crêpes gratinées filled with passionfruit. The service is not flawless, but the cellar (though expensive) is a thing of beauty, with especially fine Bordeaux. The 190 F menu is always worth a look. **C** 300-450 F. **M** 190 F.

MONTMORENCY
95160 - (Val-d'Oise)
Paris 18 - Pontoise 20 - Enghien 3

12/20 **Au Cœur de la Forêt**
Av. du Repos-de-Diane
39 64 99 19
Closed Thu, dinner Sun & Mon, Feb 17-27, Aug 16-31.

Open until 9:30pm.Terrace dining. Pkg. V, MC.

Next time you go walking in the Montmorency forest, ferret around until you find this establishment hidden among the trees. You'll enjoy the family atmosphere and the nicely crafted, seasonal cuisine, for example a pan-roasted red mullet with parsley and a decent Black Forest cake. Prices, however, are getting out of hand—particularly in view of the small portions! Slow-paced service. **C** 280-400 F. **M** 130 F, 190 F.

NEUILLY-SUR-SEINE

92200 - (Hauts-de-Seine)
Paris (Porte de Neuilly) 8 - Versailles 16

13 Le Bistrot d'à Côté

4, rue Boutard
47 45 34 55,
fax 47 45 15 08

See *Paris 17th arr.*

12/20 Bistrot Saint-James

2, rue du Général-Henrion-Berthier
46 24 21 06

Closed hols. Open until 10pm. Terrace dining. V, MC.

Sparkling-fresh ingredients go into the appealing dishes featured on this bistro's varied menu. Recent choices have included a lively terrine of goat cheese and red peppers, fish quenelles with fresh tagliatelle, and a creditably crisp millefeuille. There are tasty Bordeaux wines on hand to help these good meals along. **C** 170-270 F.

12/20 Brasserie des Arts

2, rue des Huissiers
46 24 56 17

Closed Sun. Open until 10:30pm. Pkg. V, AE, DC, MC.

A simple and unpretentious address often filled with celebrities from this chic suburb. They come for the brioche with bone marrow, chicken-liver terrine, thyme-scented roast rack of lamb, shellfish platters, and crème brûlée. The prices are geared to local incomes. **C** 200-300 F. **M** 149 F, 175 F (Sat, weekday dinner, wine incl).

13 Café de la Jatte

60, bd Vital-Bouhot
47 45 04 20,
fax 47 45 19 32

Open daily until midnight. Terrace dining. Air cond. Valet pkg. V, AE, DC.

The décor revolves around the giant skeleton of a pterodactyl surrounded by a jungle of plants. Wicker furniture, gay colors, and lots of space and light provide the rest of the atmosphere. Young waiters zoom around serving plentiful, fresh, and surprisingly well-presented dishes to tables of tanned people "in advertising": raw tuna with sesame seeds, curried chicken with baby spinach, spiced salmon with sorrel salad. The cellar could be a little more inventive. **C** 250-350 F. **M** 100 F (weekday lunch).

13 Carpe Diem

10, rue de l'Église
46 24 95 01

Closed Sat lunch, Sun, Aug 1-28. Open until 9:30pm. Air cond. V, AE, DC.

This little bistro's faithful customers are obviously drawn to the warm, simple décor, the *patronne*'s gentle attentions, and the diligent service. Serge Coquoin's soigné menu features a crab and asparagus gratin, a grilled veal chop garnished with a quiche of calf's liver and kidneys, and a delicate chocolate raviole with praline sabayon sauce. **C** 300-400 F. **M** 180 F (dinner).

14 A La Coupole

3, rue de Chartres
46 24 82 90

Closed 2 wks in Aug. Open until 10pm. No pets. V, AE, MC.

Dominique Roudin is the smiling hostess who welcomes guests into this cozy Coupole. Her husband, Pascal, works away in the kitchen, cooking up perfectly seasoned lentil salad enriched with meaty duck gizzards, calf's head with steamed potatoes in a first-class sauce vinaigrette, and satisfying apple marmalade showered with toasted almonds. More good news: the attractive wine list is moderately priced. **C** 150-250 F.

13 Jacqueline Fénix

42, av. Charles-de-Gaulle
46 24 42 61,
fax 46 40 19 91

Closed Sat, Sun, Aug. Open until 10pm. Priv rm: 40. Air cond. Garage pkg. V, AE, MC.

Headquarters for Neuilly's business-lunch crowd (lots of film and ad executives), Jacqueline Fénix offers a soothing setting, attentive service, and the classic cooking of chef Dominique Dubray. He makes the most of premium ingredients, creating elegant, harmonious meals such as the one we enjoyed recently, which featured oven-roasted sea bream, crisp-skinned red mullet with basil, and poached fruit in a spicy ginger syrup. Exciting cellar. **M** 265 F, 395 F.

14 Les Feuilles Libres

34, rue Perronet
46 24 41 41

Closed Sat lunch, Sun, Aug 1-20. Open until 10pm. Priv rm: 6. Terrace dining. Air cond. V, AE, DC.

Laurent Phelut is the new man in the kitchen, with a program sure to pique your interest. It embraces fricasséed artichokes topped with shavings of Parmesan and curls of foie gras, a winy pork civet, and a delicious chaud-froid of tart cherries with almond-milk ice cream. The wine list is worthy of your perusal. Guests are courteously welcomed and briskly served in this comfy, country-style dining room. **C** 330-450 F. **M** 195 F (wine incl).

13 Focly

79, av. Charles-de-Gaulle
46 24 43 36

Open daily until 11pm. Air cond. Pkg. V, AE, MC.

No dragons or pagodas in the conservative dining room, no outlandish listings on the menu. Focly serves a classic repertoire of sautéed crab with crispy noodles, rice with shellfish, curried lamb, and ginger ice cream, all skillfully prepared. The salt-and-pepper scampi are easily worth two toques; and the prices are most reasonable. **C** 180-260 F. **M** 130 F, 140 F (weekday lunch).

13 La Guinguette de Neuilly

Ile de la Jatte,
12, bd de Levallois
46 24 25 04

Closed at Christmas, New Year's day. Open until 11pm. Garden dining. Air cond. V.

Trendy artists are drawn to this old barge and its handful of tables for a cuisine that is forthright and full-flavored: terrine aux trois viandes, streaky bacon with lentils, and veal curry with fiery chilis. In fine weather, ask for a table on the terrace by the Seine. **C** 200-270 F.

12/20 Chez Livio

6, rue de Longchamp
46 24 81 32

Closed Sat & Sun (in Aug), at Christmas, New Year's day. Open until 10:45pm. Priv rm: 18. Garden dining. Air cond. V, AE.

A real Italian trattoria in the heart of Neuilly, manned by the Innocenti clan. Here you'll find generous and simple cuisine featuring ravioli al magro, gnocchi with basil, risotto with wild mushrooms, osso buco, and *tutti quanti*. The roof of the dining room rolls back so that you can dine under a canopy of blue sky or stars. Reservations (sometimes hard to come by) are a must. **C** 150-250 F. **M** 110 F (weekday lunch).

14 San Valero

209 ter, av. Charles-de-Gaulle
46 24 07 87,
fax 47 47 83 17

Closed Sat lunch, Sun, Dec 24-Jan 1. Open until 10:30pm. No pets. V, AE, DC, MC.

Come for a fiesta and a feast at Valero's Spanish restaurant: the menu offers paella of course, but also more authentic dishes such as quails en escabeche, scallops in a garlicky sauce with dried tuna, and baby lamb marinated in herbs, a specialty of the Rioja region. The Spanish offerings on the wine list are worthy of your attention. **C** 280-320 F. **M** 150 F (weekdays), 190 F.

13 Sébillon

"Paris-Bar," 20, av. Ch.-de-Gaulle
46 24 71 31,
fax 46 24 43 50

Open daily until midnight. Priv rm: 15. Valet pkg. V, AE, DC, MC.

The chefs come and go, the menu stays the same. The specialties of the house are the famous Sébillon roast lamb and the giant éclair. Add to that the magnificent rib of beef and the tarte Tatin "à l'ancienne," as well as some good, fresh seafood, and a thick salmon steak grilled with fennel. A selection of nice Loire wines at affordable prices. **C** 250-350 F.

12/20 La Tonnelle Saintongeaise

32, bd Vital-Bouhot
46 24 43 15,
fax 46 24 36 33

Closed Sat, Sun, Aug 1-22, Dec 24-Jan 2. Open until 10pm. Priv rm: 35. Terrace dining. V, MC.

In summer, crowds tend to gather under the trees and parasols of this Ile de la Jatte terrace. The cuisine is pleasant enough, without being challenging. There are poached eggs bordelaise to start, followed by (for example) confit de canard with garlicky potatoes or five kinds of fish in a buttery sauce. The cellar leans heavily toward Bordeaux. **C** 250-350 F. **M** 160 F, 215 F.

ORLY

94396 - (Val-de-Marne)
Paris 16 - Villeneuve-St-Georges 12

Maxim's

(15)

Aérogare d'Orly-Ouest - 46 87 16 16, fax 46 87 05 39

Closed Sat, Sun, hols, Aug. Open until 10:30pm. Priv rm: 25. Air cond. Pkg. V, AE, DC, MC.

A complete overhaul has resurrected Maxim's Orly, even giving it some of the cachet of the illustrious mother house. Gil Jouanin, a talented *cuisinier* formerly of the Café de la Paix, is in command of the kitchen. The proximity of the runways seems to have inspired him to reach for new culinary heights, for he makes the most of excellent ingredients in subtle dishes like lobster salad dressed with a snappy orange vinaigrette, artichokes lavished with curls of foie gras, or fillet of Charolais beef with roasted shallots and bone-marrow canapés in a powerfully flavored wine sauce. For dessert, we're partial to the delightful marzipan and pecan parfait. The 30,000-bottle cellar holds wines in every price range, from modest to outrageous. Next door, the Grill serves a quality set menu, including wine, for 260 F. **C** 450-550 F. **M** 290 F (coffee incl).

The prices in this guide reflect what establishments were charging at press time.

PERREUX (LE)

94170 - (Val-de-Marne)
Paris 15 - Créteil 11 - Vincennes 6

Les Magnolias

(14)

48, av. de Bry
48 72 47 43, fax 48 72 22 28

Open daily until 10pm. Priv rm: 20. Air cond. V, AE.

A brilliant and inviting room is concealed behind Les Magnolias' rather graceless façade. Chef Gérard Royant presents an interesting, appetizing single-price menu that features cool crab aspic made cooler still by a ginger-spiced cucumber granita, followed by veal sweetbreads and kidney in a Sherried sauce, and gingerbread cake with a bright apricot coulis. Expensive wine list; warm welcome. **C** 320-400 F. **M** 190 F, 290 F (weekdays, Sat dinner), 350 F (weekday lunch, wine incl).

PONTAULT-COMBAULT

77340 - (Seine/Marne)
Paris 26 - Melun 29 - Coulommiers 41

Le Canadel

(13)

Aire des Berchères, Saphir Hôtel
64 43 45 47, fax 64 40 52 43

Closed Sat, Sun, Aug. Open until 10pm. Priv rm: 10. Air cond. Heated pool. Pkg. V, AE, DC, MC.

Jean-Pierre Piovan's cooking is rich and admirably traditional: lobster in a satiny sabayon perfumed with basil, roast noisettes of lamb topped with rounds of molten goat cheese, and a delectable banana feuilleté flambé alighted on a pool of coconut velouté sauce. The décor is luscious too: chandeliers, murals, stucco columns, comfortable chairs, and well-spaced tables. Smooth service; top-notch cellar. **C** 310-410 F. **M** 235 F (wine incl), 225 F.

PORT-MARLY (LE)

78560 - (Yvelines)
Paris 21 - Versailles 10 - Louveciennes 3

Auberge du Relais Breton

(13)

27, rue de Paris
39 58 64 33, fax 39 58 35 75

Closed Sun dinner, Mon, Aug. Open until 9:30pm (Fri & Sat 10pm). Priv rm: 35. Garden dining. V, AE.

Here is an attractive place for a winter meal when a fire is roaring in the immense fireplace, but not to be overlooked in summer when you can sit in the lovely garden and enjoy rather staid, but fresh and carefully executed cuisine. We liked the salad of scallops and lamb's lettuce dressed with delicate hazelnut oil, suprême de turbot aux deux coulis, and the braised sweetbreads with morels. Desserts are so-so, but the cellar is judiciously stocked. **C** 240-320 F. **M** 219 F (wine incl), 159 F.

PUTEAUX

92800 - (Hauts-de-Seine)
Paris 10 - St-Germain-en-Laye 11

Les Communautés

(15)

Sofitel Paris CNIT, Paris-La-Défense, in the CNIT, 2, pl. de La Défense
46 92 10 10, fax 46 92 10 50

Closed Sat, Sun, hols, Aug 1-15. Open until 10:30pm. Priv

rm: 30. Air cond. Valet pkg. V, AE, DC, MC.

Pierre Miécaze is well into his stride here at the Sofitel, continuing his quest for bold new flavor harmonies. The results of his research are dazzling, even astonishing. If it's still available when you visit (Miécaze constantly revamps his menu) do try the chartreuse of wild mushrooms with foie gras. Or enjoy the tender roast duck breast embellished with a tangy fruit compote and a spicy sauce. This vibrant cuisine is well served by the elegant surroundings of the Sofitel dining room, the superb cellar, and the polished staff. **C** 280-380 F. **M** 150 F, 270 F (dinner).

14

Les Deux Arcs

Sofitel Paris-La Défense,
34, cours Michelet,
La Défense 10
47 76 44 43,
fax 47 73 72 74

Closed Sat, Sun. Open until 10:30pm. Priv rm: 100. Terrace dining. Air cond. Valet pkg. V, AE, DC.

The elder of the two Sofitel hotels at La Défense is home to a quiet, comfortable restaurant, where wheeler-dealers can talk business in peace while enjoying Éric Corailler's deft and delicious cuisine. He makes a superb persillé de homard—lobster in parsley aspic—perfumed with fresh marjoram, as well as savory ricotta-stuffed rabbit with pasta au pistou, and a sweetly spiced pear gratin enriched with honey butter. The cellar is way too expensive, but a few wines are served by the glass. **C** 300-400 F. **M** 340 F (weekday lunch), 275 F, 290 F.

15

Fouquet's Europe

In the CNIT,
2, pl. de la Défense,
Paris-La Défense
46 92 28 04,
fax 46 92 28 16

Closed Sat, Sun. Open until 10:30pm. Priv rm: 300. Terrace dining. Air cond. No pets. Valet pkg. V, AE, DC.

The stark and austere CNIT tower at La Défense is the last place you would expect to find modern French cooking that pays homage to its regional roots. But that is just the sort of satisfying food that young Alexandre Faix is regaling his patrons with at Fouquet's Europe. An exceptionally bright pupil of the great Robuchon, Faix cooks with imagination, enthusiasm, and—this is his secret—a rare sense of split-second timing. His dishes are invariably perfectly cooked. You'll see we aren't exaggerating when you taste the rascasse fillet fired up with a jolt of hot chili, tender leg of farm chicken paired with spelt, rosemary-roasted red mullet served with a vivid ratatouille, or rich shortbread topped with apples and rhubarb. Opulent cellar; top-drawer service. **C** 400-550 F. **M** 280 F.

ROISSY-EN-FRANCE

95700 - (Val-d'Oise)
Paris 26 - Meaux 36 - Senlis 28

Maxim's

Aéroport Charles-de-Gaulle
48 62 16 16,
fax 48 62 45 96

Lunch only. Open daily. Air cond. Pkg. V, AE, DC, MC.

It had to happen: what with all those planes boarding for immediate departure, Maxim's talented chef decided one day that he too should take off for new horizons! So a new team is at the controls here now, but we'll wait to judge their efforts until they reach their cruising speed. On the menu, however, you'll find a marinière of prawns flavored with Thai herbs, roast pigeon lacquered with a honey-spice glaze, and peaches wrapped up in a crêpe "purse" and swirled with blackberry coulis. The service is obliging and discreet, and the cellar presents a goodly number of growers' wines in half-bottles. **C** 370-630 F. **M** 280 F.

ROMAINVILLE

93230 - (Seine-St-Denis)
Paris 10 - Livry-Gargan 9

15

Chez Henri

72, route de Noisy
48 45 26 65,
fax 48 91 16 74

Closed Sat lunch, Mon dinner, Sun, hols, Aug. Open until 9:30pm. Priv rm: 18. Air cond. Pkg. V, AE, MC.

Chef Henri Bourgin is back on track, as our most recent meal amply attested. We could barely restrain ourselves from begging for seconds (or thirds) of his zesty shrimp salad embellished with tomato-basil sorbet, his saddle of rabbit stuffed with snails and escorted by a ragoût of woodland mushrooms, and delicate cream-cheese mousse laced with lime. The second toque sits firmly once again on Henri's head! Connoisseur's cellar; convivial atmosphere in a comfortable, flower-filled dining room. **C** 300-400 F. **M** 150 F.

RUNGIS
94150 - (Val-de-Marne)
Paris 13 - Corbeil 26 - Longjumeau 10

La Rungisserie
Pullman Paris-Orly, 20, av. Charles-Lindbergh - 46 87 36 36, fax 46 87 08 48
Closed lunch Sat & Sun. Open until 11pm (hols 10pm). Air cond. Pkg. V, AE, DC, MC.

A huge and happy hotel restaurant in a soothing, modern setting. A new chef has just moved into the kitchen, so we'll give him time to get his bearings before we judge his cooking. **C** 300-520 F. **M** 150 F (dinner w-e), 185 F (weekdays).

SAINT-CLOUD
92210 - (Hauts-de-Seine)
Paris 12 - Boulogne 3 - Versailles 10

11/20 Quai Ouest
1200, quai Marcel-Dassault
46 02 35 54,
fax 46 02 33 02
Open daily until midnight. Terrace dining. Air cond. Valet pkg. V, AE, DC, MC.

Lots of young, permatanned faces at this trendy spot, a New York–style eatery with a terrace overlooking the Seine. A squadron of smiling waiters delivers fresh, prettily presented salmon tartare, honey-glazed swordfish, and chicken fricassée. **C** 200-300 F.

SAINT-DENIS
93200 - (Seine-St-Denis)
Paris 10 - Argenteuil 10 - Chantilly 30

Melody
15, rue G.-Péri
48 20 87 73
Closed Sat lunch, Sun, 1 wk at Easter, Aug. Open until 10pm. V, MC.

What a contrast between Melody's restrained beige setting and the unbridled fantasy that comes out of the kitchen! After a longish rough patch, the chef is back in top condition, dreaming up such exciting dishes as a ragoût of langoustines and chicken giblets, or a bold upside-down tart of pears and pigeon gizzards (it's delicious!) sprinkled with a touch of caramel vinegar. Traditionalists can always fall back on the savory rack of Causses lamb. The set meals offer top value. **C** 190-250 F. **M** 102 F, 112 F.

12/20 La Table Gourmande
32, rue de la Boulangerie - 48 20 25 89
Closed Sun, Mon dinner, Tue, Wed. Open until 9:30pm. Pkg. V, MC.

Good restaurants are not exactly thick on the ground out here, so we're happy to tell you about this place. The cooking is fresh and skillful, the surroundings are cheerful. Order the sea bream with sorrel or the baked sea bass with asparagus. **C** 200-300 F. **M** 98 F.

The prices in this guide reflect what establishments were charging at press time.

SAINT-GERMAIN-EN-LAYE
78100 - (Yvelines)
Paris 21 - Chartres 81 - Dreux 70

Cazaudehore
Hôtel La Forestière
1, av. du Président-Kennedy
34 51 93 80,
fax 39 73 73 88
Closed Mon (exc hols). Open until 10pm. Priv rm: 140. Garden dining. Pkg. V, AE, MC.

On the edge of the forest in a wonderful setting of greenery and flowers sits this charming establishment decorated with old prints and English chintzes; for summer dining, there's a huge terrace that looks out over the trees. It is at this point that the superb and unshakeable "Cazau" sometimes goes off track, its luxurious cuisine suffering under the pressure of numbers. Still, when the chef decides to keep things simple, he turns out a reliable salade de tripes en cressonnette, farm chicken with pot-au-feu vegetables, and a lush licorice macaroon. Superb cellar, stylish service. **C** 310-580 F. **M** 360 F (week-end, wine incl), 250 F (weekday lunch).

Le Pavillon Henri-IV
21, rue Thiers
39 10 15 15,
fax 39 73 93 73
Open daily until 10:30pm. Terrace dining. Air cond. Pkg. V, AE, DC, MC.

Neither the staff nor the patrons appear to be having much fun, but the cuisine fully merits a gourmet's attention. It encompasses dishes so classic as to have nearly disappeared from most modern menus, all deftly prepared. As a result, a meal here resembles nothing so much as a trip to some gastronomic museum; the attractive wine list is a plus. **C** 250-450 F. **M** 240 F (weekday lunch), 640 F.

SAINT-OUEN
93400 - (Seine-St-Denis)
Paris 7 - Saint-Denis 4 - Chantilly 34

14

Le Coq de la Maison Blanche
37, bd J.-Jaurès
40 11 01 23,
fax 40 11 67 68

Closed Sun. Open until 10pm. Priv rm: 120. Terrace dining. Valet pkg. V, AE.

A covered terrace has been added to extend the 1950s-style dining room, and an oyster bar now provides premium shellfish in season. If the François family would go a step farther and add a bit more zest to the cooking, all would be well. For while we have no complaints about the good asparagus hollandaise or the codfish and vegetables with sauce aïoli, we found the sweetbreads unexciting on a recent visit, and the spit-roasted kid too dry (it badly wanted basting). Still, Alain François is a jovial host who cultivates a convivial atmosphere in this appealing, almost provincial restaurant. **C** 280-370 F.

This symbol stands for "Les Lauriers du Terroir", *an award given to chefs who prepare traditional or regional recipes.*

SÈVRES
92310 - (Hauts-de-Seine)
Paris 12 - Boulogne 3 - Versailles 8

11/20 Phileas Fogg
5, pl. P.-Brossolette
46 26 48 80

Closed Sun dinner, Mon. Open until 10:30pm. Terrace dining. V, AE, DC, MC.

Travel no farther than Sèvres railway station to go around the world in 80 dishes. The cooking is nicely handled by the wife of a former scriptwriter for the vintage series *The Avengers*, rerun ad nauseam on late-night French television. Try the tasty bagna cauda, beef braised in Guinness, or murghi sheer (Indian chicken with an almond cream sauce). Simple setting and a smiling welcome. Superb whiskies. **C** 160-250 F. **M** 79 F (lunch exc Sun).

SURESNES
92150 - (Hauts-de-Seine)
Paris (Pte Maillot) 11 - Boulogne 6

13

Les Jardins de Camille
70, av. Franklin-Roosevelt
4 5 06 22 66,
fax 47 72 42 25

Closed Sun dinner. Open until 11pm. Priv rm: 70. Terrace dining. Valet pkg. V, AE.

From the terrace guests can admire a panoramic view of Paris, but the dining room is inviting too, with its bright and cheerful décor. We're handing the chef a toque for the savory, straightforward dishes listed on his terrific 150 F menu. They include excellent jambon persillé (the aspic is made with sprightly Aligoté wine), satisfying bœuf bourguignon, and a scrumptious gingerbread sorbet spiked with rum and raisins. The cellar is splendid and accessibly priced. Attentive service. **M** 150 F.

13

Le Pont de Suresnes
58, rue Pasteur
45 06 66 56,
fax 45 06 65 09

Closed Sat lunch, Sun, Aug 15, Dec 25. Open until 11:15pm. Priv rm: 60. Terrace dining. Air cond. Valet pkg. V, AE.

The ubiquitous Guy Savoy designed the menu, and Paris-Dakar daredevil Hubert Auriol serves as celebrity host at this hip, glossy restaurant. The loft-like space is further extended by a terrace planted with rosebushes, and a merry ambience prevails as bright young things tuck happily into such tasty, uncomplicated dishes as duck and artichoke terrine served with onion confit, gurnard in a flavorful shellfish jus, and banane en papillote. **C** 230-330 F. **M** 170 F.

VANVES
92170 - (Hauts-de-Seine)
Paris 8 - Nanterre 12

13

Le Pavillon de la Tourelle
10, rue Larmeroux
46 42 15 59,
fax 46 42 06 27

Closed Sun dinner, Mon. Annual closings not available. Open until 10pm. Priv rm: 100. Terrace dining. Pkg. V, AE, DC, MC.

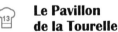

Akio Ikeno, a chef trained by Paul Bocuse, presents a repertoire of delicate dishes like sweetbreads swaddled in a cabbage leaf, steamed sea bass with sauce vierge, and a dainty molded chartreuse à l'orange. The elegant dining room is a perfect setting for this polished cuisine. **C** 350-550 F. **M** 195 F (exc hols).

VARENNE-ST-HILAIRE (LA)

94210 - (Val-de-Marne)
Paris 16 - Lagny 22 - St-Maur 3

La Bretèche

171, quai de Bonneuil - 48 83 38 73, fax 42 83 63 19

Closed Sun dinner, Mon, Feb school hols. Open until 10pm. Priv rm: 16. Terrace dining. V, AE, MC.

Choose a table on the terrace or in the bright, pink-hued dining room to savor Philippe Regnault's ably prepared tuna in a beurre blanc sauce accented with chives, casseroled lamb's kidneys with glazed shallots, and pear feuilleté swirled with ginger-spiced caramel. Extensive cellar; gracious welcome. **C** 300-350 F. **M** 160 F.

Le Pavillon Bleu

66, promenade des Anglais
48 83 10 56, fax 43 97 21 21

Open daily until 11pm.Terrace dining. V, AE, DC.

If the weather is fine, opt for a seat on the elegant covered terrace of this riverside establishment. The cooking here is conservative but capably handled: we like the garlicky salad of peppers and marinated anchovies, the smooth codfish brandade, and the pleasingly tart apple charlotte. Too bad that the cellar is so pricey! **C** 350-450 F. **M** 159 F.

Regency 1925

96, av. du Bac
48 83 15 15, fax 48 89 99 74

Closed Dec 24-26. Priv rm: 30. Air cond. Pkg. V, AE, DC.

Michel Croisille does an excellent job of running this engaging brasserie. The atmosphere is warm, the staff swift and smiling. If only the prices were just a wee bit more clement... Fish and game are the main attractions here; don't miss the scallops roasted with cèpes or the simple yet delicious marinière of shellfish. **C** 350-450 F. **M** 140 F.

VERSAILLES

78000 - (Yvelines)
Paris 23 - Mantes 44 - Rambouillet 31

11/20 Brasserie du Théâtre

15, rue des Réservoirs - 39 50 03 21, fax 39 50 74 32

Open daily until midnight (w-e 1am). Terrace dining. V, AE, DC, MC.

Classic brasserie food (fresh shellfish, pepper steak, sauerkraut, steak tartare), served in a supremely Gallic décor of mirrors, glowing woodwork, and leather banquettes. **C** 160-260 F.

Brasserie La Fontaine

Trianon Palace,
1, bd de la Reine
30 84 38 47, fax 30 21 01 22

Open daily until 10:30pm. Terrace dining. Air cond. Valet pkg. V, AE, DC, MC.

This brasserie annex of the famed Trois Marches (see below) bears the visible stamp of master chef Gérard Vié. He oversees the work of young Emmanuel Laporte, who executes an enticing menu that features a magnificent beef daube served with polenta, a light and lively terrine of skate and baby spinach, rabbit with a snappy garnish of basil-scented artichokes, and a suave pistachio custard with dark-chocolate sauce. The superb old-fashioned décor is accented with a series of amusing animal portraits. **C** 250 F. **M** 165 F.

12/20 Au Chapeau Gris

7, rue Hoche
39 50 10 81

Closed Tue dinner, Wed, Jul. Open until 10pm. Priv rm: 70. Pkg. V, AE, DC, MC.

As the ancient exposed beams attest, this is the oldest restaurant in Versailles, and it attracts an extremely posh crowd. The cuisine is honest enough and reliably fresh, though not always precise. Traditional dishes are the house specialty: sweetbread salad with Sherry dressing, rabbit with langoustines, and iced Cointreau soufflé. Exceptional wine list. Classic, thoroughly professional service. **C** 300-400 F. **M** 155 F.

La Grande Sirène

25, rue du Mal-Foch
39 53 08 08, fax 39 53 37 15

Closed Sun, Mon, Apr 18-27, Aug. Open until 10pm. Priv rm: 25. Air cond. No pets. Garage pkg. V, AE, DC, MC.

On the first floor of this Prussian-blue building, the

series of dining rooms done up in eggshell, yellow, salmon, and ivory are the very epitome of *bon goût* as envisioned by the Versaillais. The service is similarly distinguished, the cellar is exciting, and the welcome urbane. How about the food, you say? It's unpretentious and delicious, with an emphasis on fish. But we've suspended the rating because a new chef has just moved into the kitchen. We'll let you know soon how he scores. **C** 400-500 F. **M** 148 F (lunch, wine incl), 228 F (dinner), 178 F, 245 F (lunch).

13 Le Lac Hong

Opposite the Minière ponds, 18, rue des Frères-Caudron,
D 91 - 30 44 03 71

Closed Wed, Aug 15-Sep 15. Open until 9:30pm. Pkg. V.

Fine Chinese-Vietnamese cuisine at low prices (caramelized fresh tuna, quail with five-spice powder, grilled crab). Exceptionally affordable wines, charming welcome. **C** 110-160 F.

14 La Marée de Versailles

22, rue au Pain
30 21 73 73,
fax 39 50 55 87

Closed Mon dinner, Sun, Dec 24-Jan 2, Aug 1-21. Open until 10:30pm. Air cond. V.

Unlike its big sister, La Grande Sirène, who goes in for expensive seafood and high-ticket wines, this shipshape little establishment is far more modest in its aims. But the fish served here is sparkling fresh and perfectly prepared by chef Éric Rogoff. He earns an extra two points and a toque for his turbot baked in veal juices, sweet-and-sour John Dory, the fabulous grilled sole with tarragon butter, and generous "shellfish" set menu. Skilled, stylish service. **C** 220-280 F. **M** 240 F.

12/20 Le Pot-au-Feu

22, rue de Satory
39 50 57 43,
fax 39 49 04 66

Closed Sat lunch, Sun, Aug 15-30, Dec 24-28. Open until 10pm. Priv rm: 10. No pets. V, MC.

Pot-au-feu in its classic or seafood versions get star billing at this rose-colored bistro, but the chef's repertoire also includes mussels à la sétoise, plaice poached in hard cider, and veal confit à l'indienne. Attractive set meals. **C** 270-370 F. **M** 115 F, 175 F.

15 Le Potager du Roy

1, rue du Mal-Joffre
39 50 35 34,
fax 30 21 69 30

Closed Sun dinner, Mon. Open until 11pm. Priv rm: 15. Air cond. V, AE.

Philippe Letourneur has moved into high gear, presenting a devilishly clever repertoire full of precise, clear-cut flavors. We recently spied the mayor of Versailles, Monsieur Damien (a connoisseur of fine dining), at Le Potager du Roy, taking visible pleasure in a lusty dish of cabbage stuffed with bone marrow, while we enjoyed an exquisite chestnut bouillon accented with morsels of quail meat, ox jowls braised in red wine with cumin-spiced carrots, and a splendid portion of roast lamb escorted by a vegetable tian. All these good things fully deserve a second toque, which we're pleased to award this year. Note that the second of the two set meals is one of the best deals in Versailles. **C** 280-380 F. **M** 120 F (exc Sun), 169 F.

12/20 Le Quai n°1

1, av. de St-Cloud
39 50 42 26

Closed Sun dinner, Mon. Open until 11pm. Priv rm: 35. Terrace dining. Air cond. V, MC.

A dependable address for fresh shellfish and decent seafood dishes at reasonable prices. Among the better offerings are a spicy fish soup, a refreshing salad of whelks with mayonnaise, and plaice in a sauce enriched with meat jus. Amusing nautical décor; casual service. **C** 250-400 F. **M** 115 F, 160 F.

14 Le Rescatore

27, av. de St-Cloud
39 50 23 60

Closed Sat lunch, Sun. Open until 10pm. Priv rm: 45. Air cond. Garage pkg. V, AE.

Jacques Bagot is a native of the Norman port of Granville; his speciality is vibrantly fresh fish and seafood prepared in refined, imaginative ways. Try the unusual combination of oysters and duck breast called rôti d'huîtres au magret, a spice-stuffed turbot, or a keen-flavored ballottine of prawns with ratatouille. Fine cellar. **C** 300-480 F. **M** 145 F, 200 F, 235 F, 345 F.

18 Les Trois Marches

Trianon Palace,
1, bd de la Reine

39 50 13 21,
fax 30 21 01 25
Closed Sun, Mon, Aug. Open until 10pm. Priv rm: 20. Terrace dining. Air cond. Heated pool. Valet pkg. V, AE, DC, MC.

Gérard Vié is as happy as a king in the splendiferous kitchens of the Trianon Palace, where he and his *brigade* benefit from the most technically sophisticated equipment imaginable. With his every material need thus tended to, Vié can devote his full attention to cooking. This year, he's enriched his repertoire with such regal offerings as boudin blanc à la royale, leg of lamb à la Mailly, and parsleyed capon—dishes that once delighted the kings of France! But don't worry: Vié's cuisine hasn't got lost in a time warp. He continues to create such modern marvels as plump snails with green lentils redolent of star anise, or spiced lobster with a suave confit of turnips and figs, or Belon oysters and foie gras steamed over seaweed, or spice-glazed pigeon garnished with dried apricots and walnuts.

Vié also excels with simpler country-style offerings, full of provincial goodness—beef braised with carrots, cassoulet with Couïza sausages, guinea hen with crisp-tender cabbage. And his desserts are a dream: the green-walnut ice cream with caramelized crème chiboust is just one outstanding example of this *pâtissier*'s art.

The brilliant young sommelier will uncork a perfect (and probably pricey) partner to complement Vié's creations, and Robert, the veteran maître d'hôtel, will make certain that that every detail of your meal is memorable. **C** 600-850 F. **M** 260 F (weekday lunch), 395 F, 495 F, 595 F, 750 F.

In nearby Le Chesnay

(NE)
78150 Versailles – (Yvelines)

12/20 Le Chesnoy

24, rue Pottier
39 54 01 01
Closed Sun dinner, Mon, Aug 2-22. Open until 10pm. Garden dining. Air cond. V, AE, DC.

Chef Georges Torrès cooks in a fresh, generous vein; his new single-price menu proposes an earthy salad of lamb's sweetbreads and bone marrow, grilled red mullet with tangy eggplant caviar, and apple craquant subtly perfumed with rosemary. Attractive cellar. **M** 168 F.

13 Le Connemara

41, route de Rueil
39 55 63 07
Closed Sun (exc 1st & 2nd Sun of the month), Mon, 2nd wk of Feb school hols, Aug 1-20. Open until 9:30pm. Priv rm: 15. V, AE.

A little sprucing up wouldn't hurt the salmon-hued dining room, and a touch more precision could only help chef Pascal Eynard-Machet's cooking. Classic desserts; the wine list is compiled mostly from shippers' catalogs. **C** 250-400 F. **M** 155 F.

13 L'Étoile de Mer

Pl. du Nouveau-Marché, 17, rue des Deux-Frères
39 54 62 70
Closed Mon, Sat lunch, Sun dinner, Tue, Wed. Open until 9:30pm. Pkg. V.

L'Étoile de Mer's intimate, modern dining room opens onto the town marketplace. The view features a crowded lobster tank, and beyond it, the fishmonger's shop attached to the restaurant. This is where chef Antoine Vieira takes the freshest, best fish and shellfish, and transforms them into appetizing assortments and cooked dishes. You're sure to like his smooth crab soup, octopus à la portuguaise, and tasty mussels marinière. Charming welcome. Tiny wine cellar. **C** 190-400 F.

VILLENEUVE-LA-GARENNE

92390 - (Hauts-de-Seine)
Paris 11 - St-Denis 2 - Pontoise 22

15 Les Chanteraines

Av. du 8-Mai-1945
47 99 31 31,
fax 41 21 31 17
Closed Aug 16-31. Open until 10pm. Priv rm: 25. Terrace dining. Garage pkg. V, AE, MC.

Jovial Roland Nohé is at the helm of this elegant seafood restaurant set in Villeneuve's verdant park. His youthful chef, Jean-Claude Cahagnet, shows culinary skills that would do credit to a far more mature *cuisinier*. He carries off two toques and our congratulations for his parsleyed crab dressed with herb vinaigrette, perfectly cooked cod steak enhanced with a vibrant basil sauce, and splendid langoustines au caviar. For dessert, the baba au rhum is a must! **C** 260-400 F. **M** 170 F (weekdays, Sun lunch).

HOTELS

INTRODUCTION

Paris hotel rooms come in every possible style, size, and price range. But whatever the category of the room you seek, remember to book well in advance to get exactly what you want. Our selection ranges from sumptuous suites to far humbler lodgings, but note that certain hoteliers put as high a price on charm or modern facilities as others do on pure luxury, so don't assume that "charming" means "cheap." The prices quoted include taxes and service. Hotels are classified as follows: *Luxury*, *First Class*, *Classic*, *Charming*, *Practical*, *Airport*, and *The Suburbs*.

RESERVATION SERVICE

L'Office du Tourisme de Paris can arrange a same-day reservation at any hotel in Paris or the rest of France. The service costs 8 to 55 F, depending on the hotel. The friendly hostesses also provide tourist information for Paris and France. All you need to do is drop in (don't telephone) at one of the locations listed in *Basics* under Tourist Information.

NO ROOM AT THE INN?

If your every attempt to find a hotel room has failed, you needn't panic. Here are two companies that can track down a room for you or even rent you a high-class studio or apartment. The latter come with every guarantee of home comforts, security, and such options as maid, laundry, and repair services. Prices range from 450 to 2,500 F and up, depending on the size and accommodations. Town houses and houseboats are available as well! Just contact: *Paris-Séjour-Réservation*, 90, avenue des Champs-Élysées, Paris 8th arr., tel. 42 56 30 00, Monday through Friday 9am-7pm, Saturday 10am-1pm and 2pm-6pm; or *Parissimo*, 9, avenue de La Motte-Picquet, Paris 7th arr., tel. 45 51 11 11, fax 45 55 55 81, Monday through Friday 9:30am-1pm and 2:30pm-7pm.

APARTMENT HOTELS

At the apartment hotels listed below, you'll enjoy the same service you would find in a hotel, for a lower price. Rates start at about 600 F per night for a studio for two.

• *Carré d'Or*, 46, av. George-V, 8th arr., 40 70 05 05, fax 47 23 30 90. 23 stes 2,850-18,950 F. Air cond. No pets. Valet parking. All cards.

• *Les Citadines-Austerlitz*, 27, rue Esquirol, 13th arr., 44 23 51 51,

fax 45 86 59 76. 2 apts 920 F. 47 studios 490-610 F. Parking. All cards.
• *Les Citadines-Bercy,* 14-18, rue de Chaligny, 12th arr., 40 01 15 15, fax 40 01 15 20. 97 apts 460-1,230 F. Parking. All cards.
• *Les Citadines-Montparnasse,* 67, av. du Maine, 14th arr., 40 47 41 41, fax 43 27 29 94. 72 studios 440-1,500 F. Conf. Garage parking. All cards.
• *Les Citadines-Opéra,* 18, rue Favart, 2nd arr., 44 50 23 23, fax 44 50 23 50. 76 apts 590-1,115 F. Air cond. Conf. Parking. All cards.
• *Les Citadines-Trocadéro,* 29 bis, rue Saint-Didier, 16th arr., 44 34 73 73, fax 47 04 50 07. 97 apts 520-1,590 F. Garage parking. All cards.
• *Flatotel,* 14, rue du Théâtre, 15th arr., 45 75 62 20, fax 45 79 73 30. 247 rms & apts 490-3,900 F. Parking. All cards.
• *Flatotel Porte de Versailles,* 52, rue d'Oradour-sur-Glane, 15th arr., 45 54 93 45, fax 45 54 93 07. 179 rms & apts 650-1,650 F. Parking. All cards.
• *Métropole Opéra,* 2, rue de Gramont, 2nd arr., 42 96 91 03, fax 42 96 22 46. 24 apts 950-1,550 F. 9 studios 600-790 F. Air cond. Conf. Parking. All cards.
• *Orion Paris-Les-Halles,* 4, rue des Innocents, 1st arr., 45 08 00 33, fax 45 08 40 65. 55 apts 980 F. 134 studios 690 F. 1 apt for disabled. Conf. Parking. All cards.
• *Orion La Défense,* 8, bd de Neuilly, La Défense 1, 92400 Courbevoie, 47 62 55 55, fax 47 78 95 00. 104 apts 760 F. 130 studios 495 F. Conf. Parking. All cards.
• *Résidence du Roy,* 8, rue François-Ier, 8th arr., 42 89 59 59, fax 40 74 07 92. 28 apts & 7 rms 1,220-2,980 F. Air cond. Conf. Valet pkg. All cards.

SYMBOLS & ABBREVIATIONS

Our opinion of the comfort level and appeal of each hotel is expressed in the following ranking system:

 Very luxurious

 Luxurious

 Very comfortable

 Comfortable

 Very quiet

Symbols in red denote charm.

Rms: rooms. **Stes:** suites. **Air cond:** air conditioning.
Half-board: rate per person for room, breakfast, and one other meal (lunch or dinner).

LUXURY

Le Bristol

8th arr. - 112, rue du Fg-St-Honoré - 42 66 91 45, fax 42 66 34 16

Open year-round. 41 stes 6,500 F. 154 rms 2,500-3,600 F. Restaurant. Air cond. Conf. Heated pool. No pets. Valet pkg. V, AE, DC, MC.

The elegant décor (genuine period furniture, as well as lovely reproductions), the comfortable rooms, the lavish suites, and the prestigious clientele make Le Bristol one of the rare authentic luxury hotels in Paris (as well as one of the most expensive). The Bristol's two distinct wings comprise 35 newer, modern suites housed in a former Carmelite convent, and 150 more traditionally decorated rooms and suites. Among the innumerable amenities are video surveillance, ultramodern conference rooms, a heated swimming pool, a superb laundry service, and a hair salon. An elegant restaurant (Le Bristol) opens onto the lawn and flowers of a formal French garden, see *Restaurants*. The staff is both cordial and impressively trained.

Hôtel de Crillon

8th arr. - 10, pl. de la Concorde - 44 71 15 00, fax 44 71 15 02

Open year-round. 45 stes 4,850-26,800 F. 118 rms 2,450-3,950 F. Restaurants. Air cond. Conf. Valet pkg. V, AE, DC.

The Crillon is housed in an honest-to-goodness eighteenth-century palace. Indeed, the accommodations are truly fit for a king, with terraces overlooking the Place de la Concorde, sumptuous public rooms, and an exquisitely trained staff. The guest rooms, though not always immense or well soundproofed, are beautifully decorated; the suites offer all the splendor one could hope for. Everywhere the eye rests on Louis XVI–style furniture, silk draperies, pastel walls, and woodwork ornamented with gold leaf, Aubusson rugs, and polished marble. Relais et Châteaux. Restaurants: Les Ambassadeurs and L'Obélisque, see *Restaurants*.

George-V

8th arr. - 31, av. George-V - 47 23 54 00, fax 47 20 40 00

Open year-round. 50 stes 5,700-15,500 F. 248 rms 1,800-3,900 F. Restaurant. Air cond. Conf. Valet pkg. V, AE, DC, MC.

The management has made a Herculean attempt to instill new life and spirit into this landmark. The bar and the restaurant (Les Princes, see *Restaurants*; both open onto a delightful patio) have been redecorated, a Grill has been added, and many of the rooms have been renovated, with as much concern for elegance as for modernity (electronic panels located at the head of the beds allow guests to close the venetian blinds, control both the television and the air conditioning, call room service, and so on). The Galerie de la Paix (now home to a chic tea room), as well as the pictures, rare ornaments, and lovely furniture in the public rooms radiate the legendary George-V charm. But such surroundings cry out for absolutely first-rate service which, alas, is not always provided here.

Le Grand Hôtel

9th arr. - 2, rue Scribe - 40 07 32 32, fax 42 66 12 51

Open year-round. 35 stes 3,500-15,000 F. 479 rms 1,550-2,500 F. Rms for disabled. Restaurant. Air cond. Conf. Valet pkg. V, AE, DC, MC.

The renovation of this grand hotel, built in 1862, is now complete. In the past ten years, this monumental Second Empire building has recovered all the splendor it displayed when Empress Eugénie inaugurated it. The huge central lobby, capped by a glittering glass dome, is a wonder to behold. Guest rooms provide everything the international traveler could require in the way of amenities, as well as the most up-to-date business equipment, a health club, and much more. Excellent bar.

Inter-Continental

1st arr. - 3, rue de Castiglione - 44 77 11 11, fax 44 77 14 60

Open year-round. 58 stes 2,800-20,000 F. 392 rms 1,750-2,500 F. Restaurants. Air cond. Conf. V, AE, DC, MC.

Garnier, the architect of the Opéra, designed this vast hotel; three out of its seven spectacular salons are listed as historic monuments. With its remarkably equipped conference rooms, it responds perfectly to the business world's needs. As for charm and comfort, you'll find them both in the lovely patio filled with flowers, in the décor, and the incomparable loveliness of many of the rooms (though some are tiny and dark), as well as in the small singles located in the attic, from which there is a fine view of the Tuileries. Bathrooms are often old-fashioned and on the small side. The suites (with Jacuzzi) are luxurious. Two restaurants and a bar.

Meurice

1st arr. - 228, rue de Rivoli - 44 58 10 10, fax 44 58 10 15

Open year-round. 28 stes 5,000-15,000 F. 152 rms 2,200-3,600 F. Restaurant. Air cond. Conf. Valet pkg. V, AE, DC, MC.

The Meurice has undergone substantial renovation in the past few years, to restore its glamour and prestige. Most recently, the admirable salons on the main floor were refurbished; the guest rooms and suites (which offer a view of the Tuileries) were equipped with air conditioning and tastefully redecorated; and the pink-marble bathrooms are now ultramodern. The Meurice ranks as one of the best grand hotels in Paris. An elegant restaurant, Le Meurice, see *Restaurants*, is lodged in the Salon des Tuileries, which overlooks the gardens. Tea and cocktails are served to the sound of quiet piano music in the Salon Pompadour. A free secretarial service is available, and guests have use of the hotel's box at the Longchamp racetrack during the season.

Plaza-Athénée

8th arr. - 25, av. Montaigne - 47 23 78 33, fax 47 20 20 70

Open year-round. 42 stes 5,920-10,050 F. 169 rms 2,740-4,750 F. Restaurant. Air cond. Conf. Valet pkg. V, AE, DC, MC.

Discretion, efficiency, and friendly courtesy are the Plaza's trademarks. The rooms and suites are bright, generous in size, and fitted with every amenity. The rooms overlooking Avenue Montaigne are perfectly soundproofed. At about 11am, guests gather in the bar (Plaza-Bar Anglais, where Mata Hari was arrested); and, from 4pm to 7pm in particular, you'll see them in the gallery (of which Marlene Dietrich was particularly fond). The Régence restaurant is located just across from the wonderful patio, where tables are set in the summer among cascades of geraniums and ampelopsis vines, see *Restaurants*. Dry-cleaning services are provided, and there is a beauty salon on the premises.

Hôtel Prince de Galles

8th arr. - 33, av. George-V - 47 23 55 11, fax 47 20 96 92

Open year-round. 30 stes 6,500-18,000 F. 140 rms 1,900-3,500 F. Restaurant. Half-board 1,210-1,435 F. Air cond. Conf. Valet pkg. V, AE, DC, MC.

Extensive renovations have restored the brilliance of this renowned hotel, built in the Roaring Twenties. Marble expanses stretch as far as the eye can see, walls are accented by handsome prints, and guest rooms have been outfitted with minibars, safes, and a flock of new facilities. We only wish that the lovely old mosaics had been preserved. As ever, the hotel's open-roofed patio is a delightful place to have lunch on a warm day; the paneled Regency Bar is another pleasant spot, dis-

Chic Champs

The cars that long encumbered the Champs-Élysées have now been banished to underground lots, and the recaptured space turned into a walkway shaded by hundreds of newly planted plane trees. Sleek benches and sculptural stoplights designed by Jean-Michel Wilmotte (his credentials include furnishings for the Louvre and the Élysée Palace) also enhance the Champs' refurbished image. And everyone agrees that the new sidewalks, with their subtle tones of gray, are the summum of elegance. There's just one problem: it's nearly impossible to remove chewing gum from the expensive granite paving stones!

tinguished by excellent service. Restaurant: Le Jardin des Cygnes, see *Restaurants.*

Raphaël

16th arr. - 17, av. Kléber - 44 28 00 28,
fax 45 01 21 50

Open year-round. 35 stes 3,000-7,000 F. 52 rms 2,000-2,500 F. Restaurant. Air cond. Conf. Valet pkg. V, AE, DC, MC.

Built between the wars, the Raphaël has maintained an atmosphere of refinement and elegance. The Oriental rugs strewn upon the marble floors, the fine woodwork, old paintings, and period furniture make Le Raphaël a luxurious place to stay, preferred by a wealthy, well-bred clientele. The spacious rooms are richly furnished in various styles; the wardrobes and bathrooms are immense. Suite 601 boasts a huge terrace and a view of the Arc de Triomphe. Top-drawer reception and service, of course.

Résidence Maxim's de Paris

8th arr. - 42, av. Gabriel - 45 61 96 33,
fax 42 89 06 07

Open year-round. 33 stes 3,500-15,000 F. 4 rms 1,900-2,250 F. Restaurant. Air cond. Conf. Valet pkg. V, AE, DC, MC.

Pierre Cardin himself designed the hotel of his dreams, a small but palatial establishment that may well be the world's most luxurious. The landings of each floor are decorated like elegant salons, with beautiful and unusual antique pieces and paintings. Polished stone and sumptuous murals adorn the bathrooms. The suites must be seen to be believed, particularly those on the top floor, which are lacquered in vivid colors and furnished with pieces designed by Cardin. Obviously, accommodations like these are well beyond the bank balances of most mortals.

Ritz

1st arr. - 15, pl. Vendôme - 42 60 38 30,
fax 42 60 23 71

Open year-round. 45 stes 5,600-49,260 F. 142 rms 2,450-4,150 F. Restaurant. Air cond. Conf. Heated pool. No pets. Valet pkg. V, AE, DC, MC.

The world's most famous hotel is poised to enter the 21st century with state-of-the-art facilities, but without having betrayed the distinctive character that won the Ritz its reputation. Even if nowadays you can change the video program or make a phone call without leaving your bed or marble bath (Charles Ritz was the first hotel owner to provide private bathrooms for his clients), nothing has altered the pleasure of stretching out on a wide brass bed surrounded by authentic antique furniture. Add to that a full view of one of the city's most spectacular squares, in an atmosphere of old-fashioned luxury so enveloping that a new word ("ritzy") had to be coined for it. The liveried staff knows the difference between courtesy and obsequiousness. Recent improvements include an eighteen-meter swimming pool, a squash court, a health club modeled on a thermal spa of antiquity, and a rooftop heliport. The restaurant, L'Espadon, see *Restaurants,* has its own garden. Additional entertainment possibilities include a nightclub and several bars.

Royal Monceau

8th arr. - 37, av. Hoche - 42 99 88 00,
fax 42 56 90 03

Open year-round. 39 stes 3,400-15,000 F. 180 rms 1,950-3,150 F. Rms for disabled. Restaurants. Air cond. Conf. Heated pool & beauty center. Valet pkg. V, AE, DC, MC.

This large, luxurious, and discreet hotel attracts politicians, foreign business people, and entertainers with spacious rooms, magnificent marble bathrooms, and all the usual ingredients of hotel comfort (including excellent room service). Extras include a fashionable piano bar, a spacious health club (with sauna, Jacuzzi, swimming pool, and a massage service), ultramodern conference rooms, and a well-equipped "business club." The rooms overlooking the charming flowered patio are the most sought-after by the hotel's habitués. Restaurants: Le Carpaccio and Le Jardin du Royal Monceau, see *Restaurants.*

Westminster

2nd arr. - 13, rue de la Paix - 42 61 57 46,
fax 42 60 30 66

Open year-round. 18 stes 2,700-4,300 F. 84 rms 1,600-2,000 F. Restaurant. Air cond. Conf. Valet pkg. V, AE, DC, MC.

Here is a charming midsize luxury hotel advantageously situated between the Opéra and the Place Vendôme. The pink-and-beige-marble lobby is splendid and luxurious; the bar (with piano) is more than comfortable. Conference rooms are superbly equipped. As for the guest rooms, they are handsomely decorated with attractive fabrics, chandeliers, and Louis XV–style furnishings and are fitted with minibars, safes, and satellite TV. The marble bathrooms and suites have just been renovated. Restaurant: Le Céladon, see *Restaurants*.

FIRST CLASS

Ambassador

9th arr. - 16, bd Haussmann
44 83 40 40, fax 42 46 19 84
Open year-round. 9 stes 2,000-3,500 F. 289 rms 1,200-1,800 F. Restaurant. Air cond. Conf. Valet pkg. V, AE, DC, MC.

A fine traditional hotel, proud of its luxurious fittings. The relatively spacious guest rooms have been modernized in excellent taste with sumptuous fabrics, thick carpeting, and Art Deco furniture. The lobby and public rooms are imposing: pink-marble columns topped with gilded Corinthian capitals, marble floors, and Aubusson tapestries on the walls. The penthouse suites look out over Sacré-Cœur. Restaurant: Venantius, see *Restaurants*; and a handsome Art Deco bar.

The prices in this guide reflect what establishments were charging at press time.

Baltimore

16th arr. - 88 bis, av. Kléber - 44 34 54 54,
fax 44 34 54 44
Open year-round. 1 ste 3,500 F. 104 rms 1,600-2,500 F. Restaurant. Air cond. Conf. Pkg. V, AE, DC.

Six fully equipped meeting rooms are located on the lower level; the largest and most luxurious is the former vault room of the Banque Nationale de Paris. The comfortable guest rooms are decorated with understated elegance, in keeping with the neighborhood and the tastes of the clientele. Restaurant: Le Bertie's, see *Restaurants*.

Beverly Hills

8th arr. - 35, rue de Berri - 53 77 56 01,
fax 42 56 52 75
Open year-round. 14 stes 2,500-9,900 F. Air cond. Conf. V, AE, DC, MC.

The extravagant décor of marble, mirrors, and precious woods reeks of money: this apartment-hotel is designed for millionaires, emirs, and merchant princes who want to wallow in luxury. Security is provided for with total electronic surveillance. The huge suites offer every imaginable amenity, from dining rooms to wide-screen TV.

Hôtel Balzac

8th arr. - 6, rue Balzac - 45 61 97 22,
fax 42 25 24 82
Open year-round. 14 stes 3,000-6,000 F. 56 rms 1,650-2,200 F. Restaurant. Air cond. Garage pkg. V, AE, DC, MC.

A quietly luxurious establishment near the Place de l'Étoile, frequented by celebrities and jet-setters. The huge rooms are decorated in delicate tones, with lovely furniture, beautiful chintzes, and thick carpeting. Most have king-size beds, all have superb modern bathrooms. Unobtrusive yet attentive staff. Restaurant: Bice, see *Restaurants*.

Hidden treasures in the Marais

Since 1960, many of the aristocratic homes in the Marais district (which started out life as a swamp) have been restored to their former glory. Just 35 years ago, the splendid *hôtels particuliers*—town houses—were practically invisible, lurking behind blackened and weather-beaten façades. Nowadays, one may spend a marvelous afternoon taking in such architectural treasures as the Hôtel Carnavalet at 23, rue de Sévigné, the Roman-inspired Hôtel d'Hallwyll at 28, rue Michel-le-Comte, and the imposing Hôtel de Soubise at 60, rue des Francs-Bourgeois.

California

8th arr. - 16, rue de Berri - 43 59 93 00, fax 45 61 03 62

Open year-round. 13 stes 3,000-6,000 F. 160 rms 1,100-2,200 F. Restaurant. Half-board 1,470-2,480 F. Air cond. Conf. Valet pkg. Fitness club. V, AE, DC, MC.

A light-filled lobby and a sunny lounge provide a good first impression. The cheerful, adequately sized rooms are decorated with chintzes, paintings, and prints. All boast spacious marble bathrooms. Extremely pleasant service. Accommodations overlooking the courtyard are amazingly quiet, despite the proximity of the Champs-Élysées.

Caron de Beaumarchais

4th arr. - 12, rue Vieille-du-Temple
42 72 34 12,
fax 42 72 34 63

Open year-round. 19 rms 620-690 F. Air cond. Pkg. V, AE, DC, MC.

Here's a find: a hotel overflowing with charm, set in the heart of the Marais district. The lobby's eighteenth-century atmosphere is underscored by a stone floor, Louis XVI fireplace, beamed ceilings, and handsome antique furniture. The perfectly comfortable rooms are equipped with air conditioning and double glazing for cool quiet in summer.

Castille

1st arr. - 37, rue Cambon - 44 58 44 58, fax 44 58 44 00

Open year-round. 17 stes 2,200-3,000 F. 70 rms 1,300-2,200 F. Rms for disabled. Restaurant. Air cond. Conf. Valet pkg. V, AE, DC, MC.

After a thorough renovation, this hotel next door to Chanel and just opposite the Ritz provides even more luxurious amenities. Tasteful, elegant décor.

Château Frontenac

8th arr. - 54, rue Pierre-Charron - 47 23 55 85, fax 47 23 03 32

Open year-round. 4 stes 1,600-1,650 F. 102 rms 890-1,400 F. Restaurant. Air cond. Conf. No pets. V, DC.

A reasonably priced hotel (given the location), with various sizes of room done in vaguely Louis XV style. Superb marble bathrooms. The soundproofing is effective, but the rooms overlooking the Rue Cérisole are still the quietest. Attentive reception; courteous service. Restaurant: Le Pavillon Frontenac.

Chateaubriand

8th arr. - 6, rue Chateaubriand - 40 76 00 50, fax 40 76 09 22

Open year-round. 28 rms 1,000-1,400 F. Restaurant. Air cond. Garage pkg. V, AE, DC, MC.

Built in 1991, this luxury hotel tucked away behind the Champs-Élysées boasts a polychrome-marble lobby and a courteous, professional staff. Classically elegant rooms; beautiful bathrooms.

Claridge-Bellman

8th arr. - 37, rue François-Ier - 47 23 54 42, fax 47 23 08 84

Open year-round. 42 rms 950-1,350 F. Restaurant. Air cond. No pets. V, AE, DC, MC.

A small, unpretentious hotel with rooms of reasonable size, each of which boasts a special feature, be it a crystal chandelier, antique furniture, a fine print or painting, or a marble fireplace. Friendly, stylish service.

Concorde-La Fayette

17th arr. - 3, pl. du Général-Kœnig
40 68 50 68,
fax 40 68 50 43

Open year-round. 27 stes 3,500-8,000 F. 947 rms 1,400-2,100 F. Restaurants. Air cond. Conf. Valet pkg. V, AE, DC, MC.

The Concorde-La Fayette is immense: a huge oval tower that houses the Palais des Congrès and its 4,500 seats; banquet rooms that can accommodate 2,000; scores of boutiques; four cinemas; nightclubs; and 1,500 parking places. The hotel's 1,000 rooms are neither spacious nor luxurious, but they offer all the modern amenities. Airport shuttles can be relied upon to stop here. Panoramic bar, three restaurants, including L'Étoile d'Or, see *Restaurants*.

Concorde Saint-Lazare

8th arr. - 108, rue St-Lazare - 40 08 44 44, fax 42 93 01 20

Open year-round. 23 stes 2,450-5,000 F. 277 rms 1,050-1,650 F. Restaurant. Air cond. Conf. V, AE, DC, MC.

An enormous hotel, built in 1889 by Gustave Eiffel. Sixty of the rooms and suites have just been fully renovated. Streetside rooms offer the most spacious accommodation. Though large, the bathrooms are a bit old-fashioned. The hotel's most arresting feature is the lobby, a listed architectural landmark, that soars three storeys up to coffered ceilings aglitter with gilt, marble, and crystal chandeliers. A magnificent billiard room on the main floor is open to the public, as are the cocktail lounge and brasserie.

Édouard-VII

2nd arr. - 39, av. de l'Opéra - 42 61 56 90,
fax 42 61 47 73
Open year-round. 4 stes 2,000 F. 66 rms 950-1,300 F. Restaurant. Air cond. Conf. V, AE, DC, MC.

The years of renovations have finally borne fruit: this hotel is now a luxurious place to stay, with individually styled rooms and beautifully crafted furniture. From the upper storeys, there is a wonderful view of the Opéra. Restaurant: Delmonico, see *Restaurants*.

Élysées Star

8th arr. - 19, rue Vernet - 47 20 41 73,
fax 47 23 32 15
Open year-round. 4 stes 2,200-3,500 F. 38 rms 1,300-1,900 F. Air cond. Conf. Valet pkg. V, AE, DC, MC.

Different decorative styles—from Louis XV to Art Deco—distinguish the various floors of this prestigious hotel near the Champs-Élysées, a paradise for business people. Superb facilities.

Golden Tulip

8th arr. - 218-220, rue du Fg-Saint-Honoré
49 53 03 03,
fax 40 75 02 00
Open year-round. 20 stes 2,300-3,700 F. 52 rms 1,550-1,850 F. Rms for disabled. Restaurant. Air cond. Conf. Heated pool. No pets. Garage pkg. V, AE, DC, MC.

Owned by a Dutch chain, this comfortable hotel is decorated in modern style using traditional materials (marble, wood, quality fabrics, *trompe-l'œil* paintings). The bright, spacious rooms offer every amenity; all are air conditioned, with splendid marble bathrooms. Restaurant: Le Relais Vermeer, see *Restaurants*.

Hilton

15th arr. - 18, av. de Suffren - 44 38 56 00,
fax 44 38 56 10
Open year-round. 32 stes 3,500-12,000 F. 424 rms 1,500-2,000 F. Rms for disabled. Restaurants. Air cond. Conf. Pkg. V, AE, DC, MC.

The city's first postwar luxury hotel is still living up to Hilton's high standards. Rooms are airy and spacious, service is courteous and deft, and children—of any age—can share their parents' room at no extra charge. Closed-circuit TV shows recent films. Ten storeys up are the two "Executive Floors," with their particularly fine rooms (spectacular views of the Seine) and special services. The Hilton houses two restaurants and three bars, as well as a hair salon and prestigious boutiques.

Lancaster

8th arr. - 7, rue de Berri - 40 76 40 76,
fax 40 76 40 00
Open year-round. 9 stes 3,600-7,300 F. 50 rms 1,750-2,550 F. Restaurant. Air cond. Conf. Valet pkg. V, AE, DC, MC.

Inhale the perfume of the immense, breathtaking bouquet of flowers in the lobby, then admire the general setting—furniture, wall hangings, paintings, ornaments—of this refined and luxurious hotel. The ravishing indoor garden, with its flowers, fountains, and statues (meals are served there on sunny days) lends an unexpected bucolic touch to this hotel located only a few steps from the Champs-Élysées. The rooms and suites all have period furniture and double windows; their comfort is much appreciated by the aristocrats, statesmen, and business tycoons who frequent the Lancaster. Excellent reception; attentive and punctual service. The small conference rooms have fine equipment.

Littré

6th arr. - 9, rue Littré
45 44 38 68,
fax 45 44 88 13
Open year-round. 4 stes 1,325-1,585 F. 93 rms 695-950 F. Conf. No pets. AE, DC, MC.

The style and décor of this four-star hotel are heavy and conservative, but the Littré's many habitués find the old-fashioned comfort and service entirely satisfactory. In the spacious, recently renovated rooms you'll find high, comfortable beds, ponderous furniture, enormous wardrobes, and huge marble bathrooms. English bar.

Lotti

1st arr. - 7, rue de Castiglione - 42 60 37 34,
fax 40 15 93 56
Open year-round. 6 stes 4,900-6,500 F. 133 rms 1,400-3,300 F. Restaurant.

Air cond. Conf. Valet pkg. V, AE, DC, MC.

This elegant hotel is popular with members of the European aristocracy. Each of the spacious rooms, whose comfort is worthy of their clientele, is individually decorated and offers excellent facilities. The restaurant, the lobby, and all the rooms were recently renovated. The charming attic rooms are reserved for non-smokers.

Louvre-Concorde

1st arr. - Pl. André-Malraux - 44 58 38 38, fax 44 58 38 01

Open year-round. 22 stes 2,500-5,000 F. 178 rms 1,300-2,000 F. Air cond. Conf. Valet pkg. V, AE, DC, MC.

From the door of this comfortable, classic hotel, you can see the gardens of the Palais-Royal, the Louvre, and the Tuileries. While most of the guest rooms are spacious and high-ceilinged, offering the décor and all the conveniences we have come to expect from this chain, others are on the small and gloomy side (though they are gradually being renovated). Brasserie, piano bar.

Hôtel Lutétia

6th arr. - 45, bd Raspail - 49 54 46 46, fax 49 54 46 00

Open year-round. 27 stes 2,500-6,000 F. 248 rms 950-1,960 F. Restaurants. Air cond. Conf. Valet pkg. V, AE, DC, MC.

A Left Bank landmark, the Lutétia is a noteworthy example of Art Deco style. Marble, gilt, and red velvet grace the stately public areas where government bigwigs, captains of industry, and well-heeled travelers come and go. Leading off the imposing entrance are the lounge, a bar, a brasserie, a restaurant (Brasserie Lutétia and Le Paris, see *Restaurants*), and conference rooms. The large and expensive suites are done up in pink, with understated furniture and elegant bathrooms—the overall look is very 1930s. As for the service, though occasionally impersonal, it is dependably efficient and precise. Renovations are currently underway.

Marignan

8th arr. - 12, rue Marignan - 40 76 34 56, fax 40 76 34 34

Open year-round. 16 stes 2,500 F. 57 rms 1,600-2,200 F. Restaurant. Air cond. Conf. Valet pkg. V, AE, DC, MC.

Strategically situated in the heart of the "Golden Triangle," between the Champs-Élysées and Avenue Montaigne, this hotel is a charming establishment, with its listed Art Deco façade and unusual interior decoration (note the Botero sculpture in the lobby). The magnificent rooms are done up in marble and expensive fabrics, with every modern comfort; some even boast a little terrace. There is a restaurant, and an attractive cocktail bar installed beneath a skylight. The high-society prices don't seem to faze the haute-couture crowd that favors the Marignan.

Montalembert

7th arr. - 3, rue de Montalembert - 45 48 68 11, fax 42 22 58 19

Open year-round. 5 stes 2,750-3,600 F. 51 rms 1,625-2,080 F. Restaurant. Air cond. Conf. V, AE, DC, MC.

The management has been unstinting in its efforts to restore this 1926 hotel to its former splendor with luxurious materials (marble, ebony, sycamore, leather), designer fabrics and linens. Guests love the huge towels, cozy dressing gowns, and premium toiletries they find in the spectacular blue-gray bathrooms. The eighth-floor suites afford a magnificent view of the city. The hotel bar is a favorite rendezvous of writers and publishers.

Pergolèse

16th arr. - 3, rue Pergolèse - 40 67 96 77, fax 45 00 12 11

Open year-round. 40 rms 850-1,500 F. Air cond. V, AE, DC, MC.

A new deluxe hotel, the Pergolèse provides a top-class address as well as smiling service and first-rate amenities for what are still (relatively) reasonable prices. Elegant furnishings and décor by Rena Dumas.

Régina

1st arr. - 2, pl. des Pyramides - 42 60 31 10, fax 40 15 95 16

Open year-round. 14 stes 2,500-3,500 F. 107 rms 1,000-1,900 F. Restaurant. Air cond. Conf. Valet pkg. V, AE, DC.

Opposite the Tuileries is one of the city's most venerable luxury hotels, with immense rooms, precious furniture (Louis XVI, Directoire, Empire) and—a practical addition—double-glazed windows. The grandiose lobby is graced with handsome old clocks that give the time of all the major European cities. A quiet bar and a little restaurant that opens onto an indoor garden are pleasant places to idle away an hour.

Royal Saint-Honoré

1st arr. - 221, rue St-Honoré - 42 60 32 79,
fax 42 60 47 44

Open year-round. 5 stes 1,600-2,200 F. 75 rms 1,200-1,400 F. Restaurant. Air cond. Conf. No pets. V, AE, DC, MC.

Closed for over a year, the Royal Saint-Honoré is back with a brighter, fresher look. The attentive staff does its utmost to make your stay enjoyable, whether you are in town for business or for pleasure. All of the rooms are spacious; some boast terraces overlooking the Tuileries. Marble bathrooms.

Saint James et Albany

1st arr. - 202, rue de Rivoli - 44 58 43 21,
fax 44 58 43 11

Open year-round. 13 stes 1,700-3,200 F. 198 rms 880-1,480 F. Restaurant. Air cond. Conf. Pkg. V, AE, DC, MC.

The hotel's energetic management strives successfully to keep the establishment's standards high. The Saint James et Albany enjoys an exceptional location across from the Tuileries, and provides studios, two-room apartments, suites, and bilevel suites equipped with kitchenettes. The rooms overlook a courtyard or an inner garden and are perfectly quiet. Other amenities include a sauna, a cozy bar with background music, and a restaurant, Le Noailles.

Saint James Paris

16th arr. - 5, pl. du Chancelier-Adenauer
44 05 81 81,
fax 44 05 81 82

Open year-round. 31 stes 2,100-3,000 F. 17 rms 1,450-1,900 F. Restaurant. Air cond. Conf. Valet pkg. V, AE, DC, MC.

A staff of 100 looks after the 48 rooms and suites—a luxury level of attention with prices fixed accordingly. The huge rooms are decorated in a low-key 1930s style, with flowers, plants, and a basket of fruit adding warmth. The marble bathrooms are equipped with Jacuzzis. Don't miss the magnificent library, which also houses the hotel's piano bar.

Scribe

9th arr. - 1, rue Scribe - 44 71 24 24,
fax 42 65 39 97

Open year-round. 11 stes 3,000-5,900 F. 206 rms 1,750-2,200 F. Rms for disabled. Restaurant. Air cond. Conf. Valet pkg. V, AE, DC, MC.

Behind the Scribe's Napoléon III façade stands a prime example of the French hotelier's art. All the rooms, suites, and two-level suites (the latter are composed of a mezzanine bedroom, a living room that doubles as a dining room/office, a bathroom, dressing room, and two entrances) are comfortably furnished in classic style, and offer huge bathrooms. Streetside rooms have double windows and either contemporary or Louis XVI-style furniture; those overlooking the courtyard are furnished with Louis-Philippe-style pieces and are perfectly quiet. A multitude of TV channels is on tap, as well as 24-hour room service. Restaurant: Les Muses, see *Restaurants*; and a bar.

La Trémoille

8th arr. - 14, rue de La Trémoille - 47 23 34 20,
fax 40 70 01 08

Open year-round. 14 stes 2,780-5,170 F. 94 rms 1,660-2,930 F. Restaurant. Air cond. Conf. Valet pkg. V, AE, DC, MC.

Cozy comfort, antique furniture, balconies with bright flower-filled window-boxes, and service worthy of a grand hotel. Several suites are quite new and remarkably comfortable; all the rooms have lovely bathrooms and modern amenities. The delightful dining room/ salon is warmed by a crackling fire in winter. Restaurant: Le Louis d'Or.

Hôtel Vernet

8th arr. - 25, rue Vernet - 44 31 98 00,
fax 44 31 85 69

Open year-round. 3 stes 3,200-3,400 F. 54 rms 1,500-2,200 F. Restaurant. Air cond. Conf. Valet pkg. V, AE, DC, MC.

The Vernet is an admirable hotel, combining the best of modern and traditional comforts. The rooms and suites are handsomely decorated with genuine Louis XVI, Directoire, or Empire furniture, and walls are hung with sumptuous blue or green fabric. Jacuzzi in all the bathrooms. Guests have free access to the luxurious Thermes du Royal Monceau health spa. Restaurant: Les Élysées du Vernet, see *Restaurants*.

Vigny

8th arr. - 9, rue Balzac - 40 75 04 39, fax 40 75 05 81

Open year-round. 11 stes 2,600-5,000 F. 26 rms 1,900-2,200 F. Restaurant. Air cond. Valet pkg. V, AE, DC, MC.

A handsome and prestigious hotel, the Vigny offers English mahogany furniture, comfortable beds, and fine marble bathrooms: the virtues of another age simplified and brought up to date. The suites provide all-out luxury. Excellent service. Lunch and light suppers are served at the bar (Le Baretto) designed by Adam Tihany. Relais et Châteaux.

Warwick

8th arr. - 5, rue de Berri - 45 63 14 11, fax 43 59 00 98

Open year-round. 5 stes 4,000-8,500 F. 142 rms 2,030-2,560 F. Restaurant. Half-board 1,960-2,940 F. Air cond. Conf. V, AE, DC, MC.

Luxurious and modern, just off the Champs-Élysées, this hotel offers bright, spacious, freshly refurbished rooms done in pastel colors and chintz. Efficient soundproofing and air conditioning. There is an attractive bar with piano music in the evening and a pleasant rooftop terrace. Room service available 24 hours a day. Restaurant: La Couronne, see *Restaurants*.

CLASSIC

Agora Saint-Germain

5th arr. - 42, rue des Bernardins - 46 34 13 00, fax 46 34 75 05

Open year-round. 39 rms 530-680 F. No pets. V, AE, DC, MC.

A very well kept establishment which was recently redecorated. Bright rooms (a dozen have just been renovated) with comfortable beds, minibar, radio, and television. Bathrooms feature such welcome amenities as hairdryers.

Alexander

16th arr. - 102, av. Victor-Hugo - 45 53 64 65, fax 45 53 12 51

Open year-round. 2 stes 1,870 F. 59 rms 830-1,300 F. Air cond. No pets. V, AE, DC, MC.

Stylish comfort and impeccable maintenance distinguish this peaceful establishment, where the rooms are redecorated regularly. There are nice big bathrooms with all modern fixtures. And you can count on a courteous reception.

Aramis Saint-Germain

6th arr. - 124, rue de Rennes - 45 48 03 75, fax 45 44 99 29

Open year-round. 42 rms 500-800 F. Air cond. Conf. No pets. V, AE, DC, MC.

These new, well-soundproofed and attractively decorated rooms have soft lighting, modern equipment, and perfect bathrooms. The service is especially attentive. Piano bar; no restaurant, but breakfast is served any time of day.

Bastille Speria

4th arr. - 1, rue de la Bastille - 42 72 04 01, fax 42 72 56 38

Open year-round. 42 rms 530-620 F. No pets. V, AE, DC, MC.

The building dates from the nineteenth century, but the rooms are modern and bright, with good equipment. Though not large, they are perfectly quiet thanks to double windows. Very pleasant reception and service.

Bradford

8th arr. - 10, rue St-Philippe-du-Roule 45 63 20 20, fax 45 63 20 07

Open year-round. 2 stes 990-1,200 F. 46 rms 620-990 F. No pets. Garage pkg. V, AE, DC, MC.

A traditional hotel, where elegant simplicity combines with exemplary service to give guests true comfort. Decorated in a predominantly Louis XVI style, the rooms are currently being renovated, but in any case they are spacious and soothing. Good singles; rooms ending with the numbers 6 and 7 are the largest.

Hôtel de la Bretonnerie

4th arr. - 22, rue Ste-Croix-Bretonnerie 48 87 77 63, fax 42 77 26 78

Closed Jul 30-Aug 27. 2 stes 900 F. 28 rms 620-750 F. No pets. V, MC.

A seventeenth-century town house, tastefully renovated and regularly redecorated. The spacious rooms are made cozy with exposed wood beams and antique furniture; the bathrooms are perfectly modern. Look forward to a friendly reception.

Britannique

1st arr. - 20, av. Victoria - 42 33 74 59, fax 42 33 82 65

Open year-round. 40 rms 600-830 F. No pets. Garage pkg. V, AE, DC, MC.

A warm welcome and good service characterize this family-run hotel. The rooms are tastefully decorated with pale walls, dark carpeting, minibar, and comfortable modern furniture. Satellite television.

Cayré

7th arr. - 4, bd Raspail - 45 44 38 88, fax 45 44 98 13

Open year-round. 126 rms 900-1,200 F. Rms for disabled. Conf. Garage pkg. V, AE, DC, MC.

A pink-and-gray marble floor, glass pillars, and red-leather furniture lend an air of luxury to the lobby. The rooms, modern and thoroughly soundproofed, are impersonal but well equipped (many were just redecorated), and feature marble bathrooms. Good service, too.

Chambellan Morgane

16th arr. - 6, rue Keppler - 47 20 35 72, fax 47 20 95 69

Open year-round. 20 rms 650-900 F. Conf. Pkg. V, AE, DC, MC.

The pink-walled rooms are dainty and fresh, with flowered curtains and functional blond-wood furniture. The tiled bathrooms are equipped with tubs large enough to relax in. Conveniently situated at a point equidistant from L'Étoile, the Champs-Élysées, and the Seine, this hotel offers everything a traveler might wish, except a warm welcome.

Colisée

8th arr. - 6, rue du Colisée - 43 59 95 25, fax 45 63 26 54

Open year-round. 45 rms 560-750 F. Air cond. V, AE, DC, MC.

Rooms are on the small side (those with numbers ending in an 8 are more spacious), but quite comfortable, with flowered wallpaper and tiled bathrooms. The four attic rooms have beamed ceilings and considerable charm. There is an inviting red-lacquered bar, but no restaurant.

Commodore

9th arr. - 12, bd Haussmann - 42 46 72 82, fax 47 70 23 81

Open year-round. 12 stes 2,300-3,700 F. 150 rms 1,100-2,050 F. Restaurant. Conf. V, AE, DC, MC.

This commendable traditional hotel is located a few steps away from the Drouot auction house. A portion of the rooms were recently renovated in a bright, elegant style (814 has a view of Sacré-Cœur). As for the others, the less said the better. All, however, are spacious; newlyweds should request the honeymoon suite, which must be seen to be believed.

Courcelles

17th arr. - 184, rue de Courcelles - 47 63 65 30, fax 46 22 49 44

Open year-round. 42 rms 610-770 F. V, AE, DC, MC.

The corridors of this immaculately kept hotel were recently renovated. All the rooms here are equipped with TV, direct-line telephones, clock-radios, and minibars. Very pleasant reception and service. Note that the bar is reserved for hotel guests only.

Duminy-Vendôme

1st arr. - 3, rue du Mont-Thabor - 42 60 32 80, fax 42 96 07 83

Open year-round. 79 rms 648-866 F. Conf. No pets. Pkg. V, AE, DC.

Duminy-Vendôme's rooms have impeccable bathrooms and 1920s-

Eau de Wallace

The 50 *Fontaines Wallace* that dot the city are an enduring symbol of Paris. These dark-green iron fountains feature decorative domes upheld by a quartet of female figures, who stand gracefully around an ever-running stream of cool water. Donated to the city in 1873 by the English philanthropist, Sir Richard Wallace, the fountains provided Parisians with pure drinking water, a commodity in dangerously short supply after the devastating Siege of the Commune in 1871.

style furnishings. Rooms on the sixth and seventh floors have slightly sloping ceilings, and those with numbers ending in 10 are larger than the rest. A small summer patio is located on the main floor, as is the rather amazing bar, swathed in red velvet.

Élysa

5th arr. - 6, rue Gay-Lussac - 43 25 31 74, fax 46 34 56 27

Open year-round. 30 rms 450-720 F. Conf. No pets. V, AE, MC.

In the heart of the Latin Quarter, near the Luxembourg Gardens. The small, inviting rooms have all just been renovated. Marble bathrooms.

Élysées-Maubourg

7th arr. - 35, bd de Latour-Maubourg 45 56 10 78, fax 47 05 65 08

Open year-round. 1 ste 1,200 F. 29 rms 560-730 F. Conf. V, AE, DC.

The 30 rooms of this hotel are decorated in classic good taste, in green, blue, or beige tones. Adequately sized, they are superbly equipped and comfortable. There is a Finnish sauna in the basement, a bar, and a flower-filled patio.

Frantour Suffren

15th arr. - 20, rue Jean-Rey - 45 78 50 00, fax 45 78 91 42

Open year-round. 1 ste 3,412 F. 407 rms 856-1,950 F. Rms for disabled. Restaurant. Air cond. Conf. No pets. Pkg. V, AE, DC, MC.

The Frantour Suffren is a large, modern hotel located next to the Seine and the Champ-de-Mars. Though somewhat impersonal, the simple rooms are regularly refurbished and offer excellent equipment. There is an attractive, plant-filled restaurant (Le Champ de Mars), and a garden where meals are served in summer.

Holiday Inn République

11th arr. - 10, pl. de la République - 43 55 44 34, fax 47 00 32 34

Open year-round. 30 stes 2,295 F. 288 rms 1,460-1,740 F. Rms for disabled. Restaurant. Air cond. Conf. V, AE, DC, MC.

The architect Davioud, who designed the Châtelet, built this former Modern Palace in 1867. Today it belongs to the largest hotel chain in the world, which completely restored and modernized it. The rooms and suites are functional, pleasant, and well soundproofed; the most attractive ones overlook the flower-filled covered courtyard. Restaurant: La Belle Époque, see *Restaurants*.

Le Jardin de Cluny

5th arr. - 9, rue du Sommerard - 43 54 22 66, fax 40 51 03 36

Open year-round. 40 rms 520-750 F. Air cond. Conf. No pets. V, AE, DC, MC.

A perfectly functional hotel in the heart of the Latin Quarter, with comfortable rooms and modern bathrooms.

Kléber

16th arr. - 7, rue de Belloy - 47 23 80 22, fax 49 52 07 20

Open year-round. 1 ste 950-1,360 F. 21 rms 690-840 F. Conf. Garage pkg. V, AE, DC, MC.

A family-run hotel managed in a thoroughly professional way, this impeccable little establishment has 22 sptoless, personalized rooms spread over six floors. All are equipped with double-glazed windows and pretty bathrooms. Bar open 24 hours a day.

Latitudes Saint-Germain

6th arr. - 7-11, rue St-Benoît - 42 61 53 53, fax 49 27 09 33

Open year-round. 117 rms 640-950 F. Rms for disabled. Air cond. Conf. No pets. V, AE, DC, MC.

This large, modern hotel, formerly a printing works, is located in the heart of Saint-Germain-des-Prés; its gracious turn-of-the-century façade has been preserved. The spacious rooms are well equipped and have just been freshly painted and carpeted. A cellar jazz club provides hot and cool live music every night except Sunday.

Lenox

14th arr. - 15, rue Delambre - 43 35 34 50, fax 43 20 46 64

Open year-round. 6 stes 930-960 F. 46 rms 520-640 F. V, AE, DC, MC.

In the heart of Montparnasse, a peaceful hotel with a cozy sort of charm. The penthouse suites have fireplaces, and are most attractive. Rooms vary in size, yet are uniformly comfortable and well maintained. Light meals are served at the bar until 2am (there is no restaurant).

Madison

6th arr. - 143, bd St-Germain - 40 51 60 00, fax 40 51 60 01

Open year-round. 55 rms 750-1,485 F. Air cond. V, AE, DC.

A comfortable hotel in the heart of Saint-Germain, decorated with a sprinkling of antique pieces; the bathrooms are done up in pretty Provençal tiles. Very well equipped: double glazing, air conditioning, minibar, satellite TV, etc. Smiling service and a generous breakfast buffet.

Méridien Étoile

17th arr. - 81, bd Gouvion-Saint-Cyr 40 68 35 35, fax 40 68 31 31

Open year-round. 18 stes 3,800-7,500 F. 1,007 rms 1,450-2,150 F. Rms for disabled. Restaurants. Air cond. Conf. Valet pkg. V, AE, DC, MC.

This Méridien is the largest hotel in Western Europe, and one of the busiest in Paris. The rooms are small but remarkably well equipped. A variety of boutiques, a nightclub, the Hurlingham Polo Bar, and four restaurants liven things up (for the excellent Clos Longchamp, see *Restaurants*), as does the popular cocktail lounge where top jazz musicians play (Club Lionel Hampton, see *Nightlife*). Other services include spacious conference rooms, a sauna, and travel agencies.

Méridien Montparnasse

14th arr. - 19, rue du Commandant-Mouchotte 44 36 44 36, fax 44 36 49 00

Open year-round. 35 stes 3,500-4,500 F. 920 rms 1,650 F. Rms for disabled. Restaurants. Air cond. Conf. No pets. V, AE, DC, MC.

Luxurious, soigné, and comfortable—that's the Méridien in a nutshell. Try to reserve one of the newer rooms, which are particularly bright and spacious. Or the Presidential Suite, if your means permit. Certain rooms are for nonsmokers only; all afford good views of the city. For fine dining there are two restaurants: Justine and Montparnasse 25, see *Restaurants*; bar; boutiques.

Montana-Tuileries

1st arr. - 12, rue St-Roch - 42 60 35 10, fax 42 61 12 28

Open year-round. 25 rms 580-1,050 F. V, AE, DC, MC.

This very chic little hotel doesn't actually overlook the Tuileries, but they are only a stone's throw away. All double rooms, well equipped. Numbers 50 and 52 have balconies.

Napoléon

8th arr. - 40, av. de Friedland - 47 66 02 02, fax 47 66 82 33

Open year-round. 2 stes 3,750-4,500 F. 100 rms 800-1,650 F. Restaurant. Air cond. Conf. Valet pkg. V, AE, DC, MC.

Admirably situated, this fine hotel provides top-flight service along with excellent equipment and amenities. The spacious rooms have classic décor, and offer good value in this up-market neighborhood. The pleasant banquet rooms (L'Étoile, for example) are much in demand for receptions and conferences.

Hôtel des Nations

5th arr. - "Neotel," 54, rue Monge 43 26 45 24, fax 46 34 00 13

Open year-round. 38 rms 550-600 F. No pets. No cards.

New carpeting and fabric wallcoverings were installed not long ago at this well-kept, functional hotel. Tiled bathrooms, double glazing. Some rooms look out over a garden that in summer is filled with flowers. Courteous service.

Nikko

15th arr. - 61, quai de Grenelle - 40 58 20 00, fax 45 75 42 35

Open year-round. 7 stes 3,500-8,700 F. 763 rms 1,430-1,910 F. Restaurants. Air cond. Conf. Heated pool. Valet pkg. V, AE, DC, MC.

Thirty-one floors piled up to resemble an immense beehive. You can opt either for vaguely Japanese-style or modern, ultrafunctional rooms; the large porthole windows overlook the Seine and the Pont Mirabeau. The six upper floors are reserved for luxury rooms with personalized service. Bou-tiques, conference rooms, a heated swimming pool with sauna, fitness club, and a massage service are just some of the Nikko's attractive features. You'll also find an inviting bar, restaurants (Les Célébrités, see *Restaurants*), and a brasserie within the complex.

Prices for rooms and suites are per room, not per person. Half-board prices, however, are per person.

Novotel Les Halles

1st arr. - Pl. Marguerite-de-Navarre
42 21 31 31,fax 40 26 05 79
Open year-round. 5 stes 1,520 F. 280 rms 850-930 F. Rms for disabled. Restaurant. Air cond. Conf. Garage pkg. V, AE, DC.

This ultramodern building constructed of stone, glass, and zinc is located in the heart of the former market district, near the Pompidou Center and the Forum des Halles. The huge rooms offer perfect comfort, but their air conditioning prevents you from opening the windows. The restaurant is open from 6am to midnight, and there is a terrace bar. The conference rooms can be tailored to size by means of movable partitions. Other services include a travel agency and a duty-free shop.

Le Parc Victor-Hugo

16th arr. - 55-57, av. R.-Poincaré - 44 05 66 66, fax 44 05 66 00
Open year-round. 17 stes 2,650 F. 103 rms 1,690-2,300 F. Restaurants. Air cond. Conf. Valet pkg. V, AE, DC, MC.

Celebrity decorators were called in to refurbish this elegant hotel, which just inaugurated an additional wing. Supremely comfortable, the rooms boast the most refined appoint-ments and every imaginable amenity. The public rooms are furnished with admirable pieces and accented with beautiful sculpture. A large, glorious indoor garden is planted with rare specimens. Restaurant: Le Relais du Parc, see *Restaurants*.

Paris Saint-Honoré

8th arr. - 15, rue Boissy-d'Anglas
44 94 14 14,fax 44 94 14 28
Open year-round. 7 stes 1,580 F. 112 rms 800-1,055 F. Air cond. V, AE, DC, MC.

Comfortable and functional, favored by business travelers and visitors to the nearby American Embassy, this well-renovated hotel houses seven storeys of pleasant, modern rooms with impeccable bathrooms. The bar, open from 10am to 2am, is decorated with marquetry from the trains of the *Compagnie Internationale des Wagons Lits*. No restaurant, but light meals are available around the clock from room service.

Quality Inn-Rive Gauche

6th arr. - 92, rue de Vaugirard - 42 22 00 56, fax 42 22 05 39
Open year-round. 7 stes 760-920 F. 127 rms 650-895 F. Rms for disabled. Air cond. Garage pkg. V, AE, DC, MC.

Part of an American chain with about 1,000 hotels worldwide, this is a quiet, functional establishment. Well-equipped rooms with minibar and satellite TV, some furnished in cruise-liner style. Piano bar filled with plants. Substantial breakfasts are served until 11am. Impeccable service.

Résidence Bassano

16th arr. - 15, rue de Bassano - 47 23 78 23, fax 47 20 41 22
Open year-round. 3 stes 1,600-1,950 F. 27 rms 750-1,150 F. Air cond. V, AE, DC, MC.

Housed in a building of Haussmann vintage, the rooms are not all equally attractive. Yet most are bright and all are thoughtfully designed and equipped, enhanced with Art Deco-style furniture. Among the amenities are a sauna, Jacuzzi, and 24-hour room service.

Résidence Monceau

8th arr. - 85, rue du Rocher - 45 22 75 11, fax 45 22 30 88
Open year-round. 1 ste 860 F. 50 rms 675 F. Restaurant. Conf. No pets. V, AE, DC, MC.

Though it lacks atmosphere, the Résidence Monceau is functional and well kept, and employs a helpful, courteous staff. All the rooms have private bathrooms, TVs, minibars, and automatic alarm clocks. Good privacy; breakfast is served on a patio. No restaurant, but snacks are available at the bar.

Résidence Saint-Honoré

8th arr. - 214, rue du Fg-St-Honoré - 42 25 26 27, fax 45 63 30 67
Open year-round. 91 rms 750-990 F. Air cond. V, AE, DC, MC.

A surprising range of styles has been used in the gradual renovation of the spacious rooms, which are more comfortable than luxurious. Dynamic management, uncommonly courteous staff. The Saint-Honoré auction rooms are situated on the hotel's lower level.

Rond-Point de Longchamp

16th arr. - 86, rue de Longchamp - 45 05 13 63, fax 47 55 12 80

Open year-round. 1 ste 900-1,200 F. 56 rms 672-1,000 F. Restaurant. Air cond. Conf. Pkg. V, AE, DC, MC.

The sizeable, comfortable rooms are nicely fitted and prettily decorated (gray carpeting, burr-walnut furniture), and have marble bathrooms. There is an elegant restaurant with a fireplace, as well as a billiard room.

Saint-Ferdinand

17th arr. - 36, rue St-Ferdinand - 45 72 66 66, fax 45 74 12 92

Open year-round. 42 rms 730-880 F. Air cond. V, AE, DC, MC.

This small, functional hotel is of recent vintage. The rooms are tiny (the bathrooms even more so), but they are refurbished regularly and well equipped, with television, minibar, safe, and hairdryer. Soothing décor.

Saxe-Résidence

7th arr. - 9, villa de Saxe - 47 83 98 28, fax 47 83 85 47

Open year-round. 3 stes 845 F. 52 rms 623 F. No cards.

Situated between two convents and a bouquet of secret gardens, this hotel is miraculously quiet. The rooms are constantly updated, and there is a 1950s-style bar. Even the singles are of decent size. Courteous reception.

A red hotel ranking denotes a place with charm.

Hôtel de Sévigné

16th arr. - 6, rue de Belloy - 47 20 88 90, fax 40 70 98 73

Open year-round. 30 rms 640-760 F. Pkg. V, AE, DC, MC.

A classic hotel. The modern, comfortable rooms are soundproof and with minibars and individual safes. Friendly service and reception.

Sofitel

15th arr. - 8-12, rue Louis-Armand - 40 60 30 30, fax 45 57 04 22

Open year-round. 14 stes 1,400-1,600 F. 522 rms 980 F. Restaurants. Air cond. Conf. Heated pool. Valet pkg. Helipad. V, AE, DC.

Thirty-seven meeting and conference rooms (with simultaneous translation available in five languages) are connected to a central administration office. The hotel also features recreational facilities (exercise room, sauna, and a heated swimming pool with sliding roof on the 23rd floor), and a panoramic bar. The rooms, all equipped with magnetic closing systems, are functional (some are on the small side). Restaurant: Le Relais de Sèvres, see *Restaurants*.

Sofitel Paris Saint-Jacques

14th arr. - 17, bd St-Jacques - 40 78 79 80, fax 45 88 43 93

Open year-round. 14 stes 1,825-2,000 F. 783 rms 930-1,360 F. Rms for disabled. Restaurant. Half-board 1,080-1,515 F. Air cond. Conf. Valet pkg. V, AE, DC, MC.

The Sofitel Saint-Jacques is conveniently close to Orly airport. It offers good-sized rooms with comfortable bathrooms, air conditioning, and blackout blinds that allow long-distance travelers to sleep off their jet lag. For entertainment, there are bars and restaurants; or you could ask one of the staff members to show you the "Deluxe" suite, which has often served as a setting for films.

Sofitel Arc-de-Triomphe

8th arr. - 14, rue Beaujon - 45 63 04 04, fax 42 25 36 81

Open year-round. 6 stes 1,950-3,200 F. 129 rms 800-1,500 F. Restaurant. Air cond. Conf. Pkg. V, AE, DC.

This solid, austere building, dating from 1925, houses a comfortable hotel that is not, however, long on charm. But the facilities (ultramodern equipment for the business clientele) are first-rate, and are constantly being updated. The largish, bright rooms are decorated with functional furniture (minibars, TVs, and video programming). Room service. Restaurant: Clovis, see *Restaurants*.

Splendid Étoile

17th arr. - 1 bis, av. Carnot - 45 72 72 00, fax 45 72 72 01

Open year-round. 7 stes 1,600 F. 50 rms 880-1,158 F. Restaurant. Air cond. Conf. No pets. V, DC, MC.

The Splendid Étoile features 57 well-maintained, comfortably furnished, good-sized rooms and suites, all with double glazing (some afford views of the Arc de Triomphe). Attractive English-style bar. Restaurant: Le Pré Carré.

Terrass' Hôtel

18th arr. - 12, rue Joseph-de-Maistre
46 06 72 85,
fax 42 52 29 11

Open year-round. 13 stes 1,500 F. 88 rms 900-1,190 F. Restaurant. Half-board 695-910 F. Air cond. Conf. Pkg. V, AE, DC.

A just-completed renovation has spruced up this excellent hotel. Located at the foot of the Butte Montmartre, the Terrass offers a majestic view of almost all of Paris. Rooms are comfortable and nicely fitted, with some attractive furniture and Italian-tile bathrooms. Up on the seventh floor, the panoramic terrace doubles as a bar in summer.

Vert Galant

13th arr. - 41, rue Croulebarbe - 44 08 83 50,
fax 44 08 83 69

Open year-round. 15 rms 400-500 F. No pets. Pkg. V, AE, DC.

Now for something completely different: this delightful country *auberge* provides adorable rooms (with kitchenette) overlooking an indoor garden where grapes and tomatoes grow! Quiet; good value. Restaurant: Auberge Etchegorry, see *Restaurants*.

Victoria Palace

6th arr. - 6, rue Blaise-Desgoffe - 45 44 38 16,
fax 45 49 23 75

Open year-round. 110 rms 750-1,300 F. Conf. Garage pkg. V, AE, DC, MC.

A reliable establishment, freshly renovated in 1993. The rooms are sizeable and comfortable, with really spacious closets and good bathrooms. Bar and restaurant. The elevator is brand-new.

Vieux Paris

6th arr. - 9, rue Gît-le-Cœur - 43 54 41 66,
fax 43 26 00 15

Open year-round. 7 stes 1,270-1,470 F. 13 rms 990-1,170 F. No pets. V, AE.

Here's a hotel that wears its name well, for it was built in the fifteenth century. An overhaul in 1991 turned the Vieux Paris into a luxurious stopover, whose comfort and first-rate amenities fully justify the high rates. Rooms are handsomely furnished and perfectly quiet, with Jacuzzis in every bathroom. Warm reception.

Yllen

15th arr. - 196, rue de Vaugirard - 45 67 67 67,
fax 45 67 74 37

Open year-round. 1 ste 910-995 F. 39 rms 490-670 F. Garage pkg. V, AE, DC, MC.

Yllen's modern, functional rooms have understated décor and are well soundproofed—but they are quite small. Corner rooms (those with numbers ending in 4) on the upper floors are the best. Energetic management, friendly reception.

Waldorf Madeleine

8th arr. - 12, bd Malesherbes - 42 65 72 06,
fax 40 07 10 45

Open year-round. 45 rms 950-1,200 F. Air cond. No pets. Pkg. V, AE, DC, MC.

This handsome freestone building houses an elegant lobby (notice the Art Deco ceiling) and rooms of exemplary comfort, with double glazing and air conditioning. You can count on a smiling reception.

Le Zéphyr

12th arr. - 31 bis, bd Diderot - 43 46 12 72,
fax 43 41 68 01

Open year-round. 89 rms 530-720 F. Rms for disabled. Restaurant. Air cond. Conf. Garage pkg. V, AE, DC, MC.

Practically next door to the Gare de Lyon, the Zéphyr is a newly renovated hotel with good equipment. Rooms are bright and neat, the wel-

For whom the clock tolls

The first public clock in Paris, dating from 1370, is still ticking away on a turret of the *Conciergerie* (a medieval fortress on the Ile de la Cité). The clock's darkest hour was during the Revolution, when its chimes told thousands of unfortunate inmates of this palace-turned-prison that their time was up. Prisoners condemned at the courthouse next door spent their last night at the Conciergerie before heading to the guillotine at dawn. Among the famous victims were Queen Marie-Antoinette and the revolutionary leaders Danton and Robespierre.

come is friendly, and service is reliably prompt. Quality breakfasts.

CHARMING

Abbaye Saint-Germain

6th arr. - 10, rue Cassette - 45 44 38 11, fax 45 48 07 86

Open year-round. 4 stes 1,750-1,900 F. 42 rms 840-1,450 F. Air cond. No pets. V, AE, MC.

Set back from the street, this serene eighteenth-century residence located between a courtyard and a garden offers well-kept, elegantly decorated rooms which are not, however, particularly spacious; the most delightful are on the same level as the garden (number 4 even has a terrace).

Agora

1st arr. - 7, rue de la Cossonnerie - 42 33 46 02, fax 42 33 80 99

Open year-round. 29 rms 370-595 F. No pets. V, AE.

In the heart of the pedestrian district of Les Halles, these rooms are exquisitely decorated and well soundproofed, with newly renovated bathrooms. Lovely pieces of period furniture and engravings are everywhere; the cleanliness is impressive. Cheerful reception.

Hôtel de l'Alligator

14th arr. - 39, rue Delambre - 43 35 18 40, fax 43 35 30 71

Open year-round. 35 rms 430-650 F. Conf. Pkg. V, AE, DC, MC.

Practical, welcoming, and attractive to boot. Rooms are small (balconies on the fifth and sixth floors), but trim and comfortable with good equipment. The breakfast room boasts a skylight and furniture designed by Philippe Starck.

Angleterre

6th arr. - 44, rue Jacob - 42 60 34 72, fax 42 60 16 93

Open year-round. 3 stes 1,000-1,100 F. 27 rms 600-1,100 F. Rms for disabled. No pets. V, AE, DC, MC.

Hemingway once lived in this former British Embassy, built around a flower-filled patio. The impeccable rooms are fresh and appealing; some are quite spacious, with high beamed ceilings. Large, comfortable beds; luxurious bathrooms. Downstairs, there is a bar and lounge with a piano.

Atala

8th arr. - 10, rue Chateaubriand - 45 62 01 62, fax 42 25 66 38

Open year-round. 1 ste 1,500 F. 48 rms 700-1,300 F. Restaurant. Air cond. Conf. Pkg. V, AE, DC, MC.

In a quiet street near the Champs-Élysées, this hotel provides cheerfully decorated rooms that open onto a verdant garden. Balconies and terraces come with rooms on the sixth and eighth floors. L'Atalante, the hotel's bar and restaurant, offers garden dining in fine weather. Excellent service.

De Banville

17th arr. - 166, bd Berthier - 42 67 70 16, fax 44 40 42 77

Open year-round. 39 rms 550-700 F. Restaurant. V, AE, MC.

A fine small hotel that dates from the 1930s. There are flowers at the windows (some of which open to panoramic views of Paris) and all manner of pleasing details in the bright, cheerful rooms. Accommodations are large, and blessedly quiet thanks to thick carpeting. Marble or tile bathrooms. Excellent English breakfasts.

Beau Manoir

8th arr. - 6, rue de l'Arcade - 42 66 03 07, fax 42 68 03 00

Open year-round. 3 stes 1,350-1,465 F. 29 rms 995-1,155 F. Air cond. V, AE, DC, MC.

The opulent décor—it features *Grand Siècle* wall hangings—is somehow reminiscent of Versailles. But the Beau Manoir is just steps away from the Madeleine, in the city's fashionable shopping district. Some of the luxurious rooms overlook pretty indoor gardens. Uncommonly delicious breakfasts are served in the hotel's vaulted cellar.

Belle Époque

12th arr. - 66, rue de Charenton - 43 44 06 66, fax 43 44 10 25

Open year-round. 4 stes 850-1,250 F. 26 rms 500-670 F. Restaurant. Half-board 410-495 F. Conf. Valet pkg. V, AE, DC.

Not far from the Gare de Lyon, this well-kept hotel is furnished and decorated in 1930s style. Comfortable beds, modern bathrooms, and double glazing throughout. Pretty garden courtyard. The bar is open from noon to 10pm; a restaurant serves breakfast and light meals.

Bersoly's Saint-Germain

7th arr. - 28, rue de Lille - 42 60 73 79,
fax 49 27 05 55
Closed Aug. 16 rms 580-680 F. V, MC.

Writers, artists, and antique dealers frequent this hotel, whose furniture is largely provided by the nearby "golden triangle" of antique shops. Rooms are named for famous artists, and reproductions of their paintings adorn the walls. Breakfast is served in the attractive vaulted basement. Faultless reception.

Brighton

1st arr. - 218, rue de Rivoli - 42 60 30 03,
fax 42 60 41 78
Open year-round. 1 ste 1,420 F. 69 rms 430-900 F. No pets. V, AE, DC, MC.

A dream setting opposite the Tuileries, near the Louvre, is offered at very reasonable prices. The large rooms on the Rue de Rivoli have wonderful views, high molded ceilings, huge brass beds, nineteenth-century furniture, and good-sized bathrooms. The little attic rooms are especially good value.

Centre-Ville Étoile

17th arr. - 6, rue des Acacias - 43 80 56 18,
fax 47 54 93 43
Open year-round. 20 rms 690-950 F. Restaurant. Air cond. Pkg. V, AE, DC, MC.

A modern hotel with lots of personality and an intimate, comfortable atmosphere. Entirely decorated in black and white with Art Deco touches, the attractive, contemporary rooms boast minitels (electronic telephone directories), satellite TV, and spotless tiled bathrooms.

Crystal Hotel

6th arr. - 24, rue St-Benoît - 45 48 85 14,
fax 45 49 16 45
Open year-round. 1 ste 900-1,140 F. 25 rms 550-840 F. Conf. V, AE, DC.

A charming small hotel with a friendly atmosphere, favored by artists and writers. The rooms are decorated with designer fabrics and wallpaper, and the occasional piece of antique furniture. Thoughtfully equipped bathrooms. Deep, comfy Chesterfield sofas provide a welcoming touch in the lobby.

Danemark

6th arr. - 21, rue Vavin - 43 26 93 78,
fax 46 34 66 06
Open year-round. 15 rms 590-760 F. V, AE, DC, MC.

This small hotel was carefully renovated in 1930s style. Although the rooms are not very large, they are elegantly furnished, with pleasant lighting, mahogany, ash, or oak furniture and gray-marble bathrooms (number 10 has a Jacuzzi). Charming public rooms.

Les Deux Iles

4th arr. - 59, rue St-Louis-en-l'Ile - 43 26 13 35,
fax 43 29 60 25
Open year-round. 17 rms 700-810 F. Garage pkg. No cards.

This particularly welcoming hotel, like many buildings on the Ile-Saint-Louis, is a lovely seventeenth-century house. You'll sleep close to the Seine in small, pretty rooms decorated with bright fabrics and painted furniture.

Esméralda

5th arr. - 4, rue Saint-Julien-le-Pauvre
43 54 19 20,
fax 40 51 00 68
Open year-round. 18 rms 170-510 F. No cards.

It isn't easy to book a room here, for the Esméralda's reputation for charm and value is known worldwide. The owner, artist Michèle Bruel, has given her hotel a rare personality with paintings, real or *faux* antiques, and curiosities galore. The rooms are quite small but comfy; the best afford romantic views of Notre-Dame.

L'Hôtel

6th arr. - "Guy-Louis Duboucheron", 13, rue des Beaux-Arts - 43 25 27 22,
fax 43 25 64 81
Open year-round. 3 stes 2,800-3,800 F. 24 rms 950-2,300 F. Restaurant. Air cond. Conf. V, AE, DC, MC.

"L'Hôtel" provides top-notch amenities and service, of course, but it's the charm of the place that accounts for its enduring popularity. The décor of this delightful Directoire-style building resembles no other—whether it's number 16, the room once occupied by Oscar Wilde, the Imperial room (decorated in a neo-Egyptian style), the Cardinale room (swathed in purple), or number 36, which contains the Art Deco furniture from the home of music-hall star Mistinguett. The seventh floor houses two lovely suites. The atmosphere here reproduces that of a private home and is truly unlike what one usually finds in a hotel. Restaurant: Le Bélier, see

Restaurants, piano bar on the premises.

Duc de Saint-Simon

7th arr. - 14, rue St-Simon - 44 39 20 20, fax 45 48 68 25

Open year-round. 5 stes 1,865 F. 29 rms 1,065-1,465 F. Air cond. No pets. No cards.

Set back from the street between two gardens, this quiet, elegant nineteenth-century building houses a most appealing hotel. Fully renovated by its Swedish owners, it provides discreet luxury and comfort, with antiques, fine paintings and objets d'art, good lighting, and enchanting décor. The four rooms on the second floor have terraces that overlook the garden. Room 41, in the annex, boasts an imposing canopied bed. There is a bar, but no restaurant.

Ducs d'Anjou

1st arr. - 1, rue Ste-Opportune - 42 36 92 24, fax 42 36 16 63

Open year-round. 38 rms 390-565 F. V, AE, DC, MC.

Located on the delightful small Place Sainte-Opportune, this ancient building has been restored from top to bottom. The rooms are small (as are the bathrooms) but quiet; rooms 61 and 62 are larger, and can comfortably accommodate three people. Rooms overlooking the courtyard are a bit gloomy.

Éber Monceau

17th arr. - 18, rue Léon-Jost - 46 22 60 70, fax 47 63 01 01

Open year-round. 5 stes 1,000-1,300 F. 13 rms 480-630 F. No pets. Garage pkg. V, AE, DC, MC.

This former bordello has been totally renovated, and "adopted," so to speak, by people in fashion, photography, and the movies. Rooms are on the small side, but they are tastefully decorated and furnished, with good bathrooms. A large, two-level suite on the top floor has a lovely terrace. Breakfast is served on the patio in summer.

Élysée

8th arr. - 12, rue des Saussaies - 42 65 29 25, fax 42 65 64 28

Open year-round. 2 stes 1,270 F. 30 rms 540-950 F. Air cond. No pets. V, AE, DC, MC.

An intimate, tastefully renovated hotel where you will receive a most pleasant welcome. All the rooms are different (room 301 is especially elegant); the two suites under the eaves are much in demand. There's an inviting lounge with a fireplace, and an attractive bar.

Ermitage Hôtel

18th arr. - 24, rue Lamarck - 42 64 79 22, fax 42 64 10 33

Open year-round. 12 rms 395-440 F. No pets. No cards.

This charming hotel occupies a little white building behind the Basilica of Sacré-Cœur. The personalized décor in each room is punctuated by an antique or *bibelot*. Pretty bathrooms. There is a garden and a terrace for relaxing after a busy day, and you can expect a friendly reception.

Étoile Park Hotel

17th arr. - 10, av. Mac-Mahon - 42 67 69 63, fax 43 80 18 99

Closed Jul 20-Aug 20. 28 rms 484-760 F. No pets. Pkg. V, AE, DC, MC.

Modern and decorated in understated good taste, this hotel offers refined guest rooms (ten were just refurnished this year) and comfortable, well-designed bathrooms. Extremely good-humored reception.

Étoile-Pereire

17th arr. - 146, bd Pereire - 42 67 60 00, fax 42 67 02 90

Open year-round. 5 stes 956 F. 21 rms 506-706 F. No pets. Garage pkg. V, AE, DC, MC.

Attention to detail is a priority at this welcoming hotel. Located at the back of a quiet courtyard, the spacious, pastel rooms are most attractive, with garden views. Both the atmosphere and service are charming and cheerful.

Ferrandi

6th arr. - 92, rue du Cherche-Midi - 42 22 97 40, fax 45 44 89 97

Open year-round. 1 ste 950-1,250 F. 41 rms 440-950 F. V, AE, DC, MC.

In a quiet street near Montparnasse, with a reception area that matches the charm of the rooms. Some of the guest rooms have four-poster beds, others a fireplace. All have good bathrooms (with hairdryers) and double glazing. Delightful welcome.

Garden Élysée

16th arr. - 12, rue St-Didier - 47 55 01 11, fax 47 27 79 24

Open year-round. 48 rms 900-1,600 F. Rms for disabled. Restaurant. Half-board 1,180-1,730 F. Air cond. Conf. No pets. Valet pkg. V, AE, DC, MC.

All the facilities of a luxury hotel in a bucolic garden setting, between the Trocadéro and the Champs-Élysées. Housed in a new building set back from the street are elegant, unusually spacious rooms with modern marble or tile baths. The 1930s décor is fresh and appealing, and the equipment is particularly fine (satellite television, individual safes, Jacuzzi).

Hameau de Passy

16th arr. - 48, rue de Passy - 42 88 47 55, fax 42 30 83 72

Open year-round. 32 rms 485-560 F. V, AE, DC, MC.

Tucked away in a flower-filled cul-de-sac, this exceptionally quiet hotel was modernized in 1990. Roughcast walls and stained-wood furniture decorate the comfortable rooms (some connecting) that overlook the garden. Bright, tidy bathrooms; smiling service and reception.

Hôtel du Jeu de Paume

4th arr. - 54, rue St-Louis-en-l'Ile - 43 26 14 18, fax 40 46 02 76

Open year-round. 32 rms 795-1,340 F. Conf. V, AE, DC, MC.

This is a seventeenth-century building with a splendid wood-and-stone interior, featuring a glass elevator that ferries guests to their bright, quiet rooms. There is a pleasant little garden, too.

Left Bank Saint-Germain

6th arr. - 9, rue de l'Ancienne-Comédie 43 54 01 70, fax 43 26 17 14

Open year-round. 1 ste 1,400 F. 30 rms 850-990 F. Air cond. V, AE, DC, MC.

An eighteenth-century building, with loads of charm. The tasteful but rather repetitive décor features custom-made walnut furniture in Louis XIII style, lace bedspreads, brass lamps, and marble bathrooms.

Hôtel du Léman

9th arr. - 20, rue de Trévise - 42 46 50 66, fax 48 24 27 59

Open year-round. 24 rms 390-730 F. Garage pkg. V, AE, DC, MC.

This charming, out-of-the-ordinary small hotel has been tastefully renovated. Tuscany marble inlays enhance the modern décor in the lobby. The tiny rooms are pleasantly decorated with attractive bedside lamps and original drawings and watercolors. A generous buffet breakfast is served in the vaulted basement.

Lenox

7th arr. - 9, rue de l'Université - 42 96 10 95, fax 42 61 52 83

Open year-round. 2 stes 960 F. 32 rms 580-780 F. Restaurant. No pets. V, AE, DC.

These petite but most attractive rooms are decorated with elegant wallpaper and stylish furniture; numbers 22, 32, and 42 are the most enchanting. On the top floor are two split-level suites with exposed beams and flower-filled balconies. The elegant bar stays open until 2am.

Lido

8th arr. - 4, passage de la Madeleine 42 66 27 37, fax 42 66 61 23

Open year-round. 32 rms 800-930 F. Air cond. V, AE, DC, MC.

A laudable establishment, situated between the Madeleine and the Place de la Concorde. The lobby is most elegant, with Oriental rugs on the floor and tapestries on the stone walls. The guest rooms, decorated in pink, blue, or cream, have comfortable beds with white lace covers, modern bathrooms, and double-glazed windows. The staff is thoughtful and courteous.

Lutèce

4th arr. - 65, rue St-Louis-en-l'Ile - 43 26 23 52, fax 43 29 60 25

Open year-round. 23 rms 680-830 F. No cards.

A tasteful, small hotel for people who love Paris, this handsome old house has some twenty rooms (there are two charming mansards on the sixth floor), with whitewashed walls and ceiling beams, decorated with bright, cheerful fabrics. The bathrooms are small but modern and impeccably kept. The lobby features lavish bouquets and a stone fireplace which is often used in winter.

Majestic

16th arr. - 29, rue Dumont-d'Urville

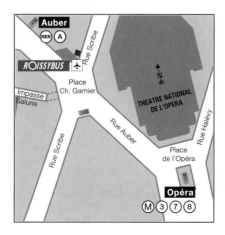

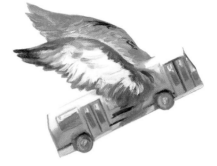

45 00 83 70,
fax 45 00 29 48
Open year-round. 3 stes 1,800-2,000 F. 27 rms 1,150-1,450 F. Air cond. V, AE, DC, MC.

Rooms in this exemplary hotel are redecorated by turns, and all boast comfortable beds, fine furniture, and thick carpeting. On the top floor, a lovely penthouse features a small balcony filled with flowers. Old-World atmosphere.

Les Marronniers

6th arr. - 21, rue Jacob - 43 25 30 60,
fax 40 46 83 56
Open year-round. 37 rms 510-1,020 F. Conf. No pets. Pkg. No cards.

Set back slightly from the Rue Jacob, this delightful hotel is blessed with a small garden shaded by two chestnut trees. Choose a room just above this garden, or one of the rather bizarre but absolutely adorable (and bright) attic rooms on the seventh floor, which have views of the belfry of Saint-Germain-des-Prés. Peace and quiet are assured. Breakfast is served on a bright (weather permitting!) glass-enclosed veranda.

Libertel Moulin

9th arr. - 39, rue Fontaine - 42 81 93 25,
fax 40 16 09 90
Open year-round. 50 rms 550-950 F. Conf. Pkg. V, AE, DC, MC.

A hotel full of charm and surprises near the Place Pigalle, with an appealing Pompeii-style lobby and rooms of varying sizes (some are extended by a small terrace overlooking the inner courtyards). An excellent buffet-style breakfast is served until 11am.

Le Notre-Dame Hôtel

5th arr. - 1, quai St-Michel - 43 54 20 43,
fax 43 26 61 75
Open year-round. 3 stes 1,050 F. 26 rms 590-790 F. V, AE, DC, MC.

Situated in a noisy area, but the hotel is protected by effective double glazing. The sixth floor houses three split-level attic rooms with red carpeting, rustic furniture, marble bath, and a mezzanine that affords superb views over Notre-Dame and the Seine.

Panthéon

5th arr. - 19, pl. du Panthéon - 43 54 32 95,
fax 43 26 64 65
Open year-round. 34 rms 635-750 F. Conf. No pets. Garage pkg. V, AE, DC, MC.

Clever use of mirrors makes the entrance, lounge, and bar seem bigger. The elegant rooms are quite spacious, decorated in Louis XVI or Louis-Philippe style, with pastel wallcoverings. Room 33 has a grand four-poster bed; all rooms are equipped with minibars and cable TV.

Pavillon de la Reine

3rd arr. - 28, pl. des Vosges - 42 77 96 40,
fax 42 77 63 06
Open year-round. 20 stes 1,950-3,100 F. 35 rms 1,300-1,700 F. Rms for disabled. Air cond. Valet pkg. V, AE, DC, MC.

Part of the hotel dates from the seventeenth century, while the rest is a clever "reconstitution." The rooms and suites, all equipped with marble bathrooms, are tastefully decorated. The furnishings are an artful blend of authentic antiques and lovely reproductions. Accommodations overlook either the Place des Vosges and its garden or a quiet inner patio filled with flowers.

Regent's Garden Hotel

17th arr. - 6, rue Pierre-Demours
45 74 07 30,
fax 40 55 01 42
Open year-round. 39 rms 640-930 F. Garage pkg. V, AE, DC, MC.

This handsome Second Empire building, just a stone's throw from the Place de l'Étoile, offers large, nicely proportioned rooms with high, ornate ceilings; some have fireplaces. Comfortable and well kept, the hotel also boasts a gorgeous flower garden.

Relais Christine

6th arr. - 3, rue Christine - 43 26 71 80,
fax 43 26 89 38
Open year-round. 13 stes 2,150-2,700 F. 38 rms 1,520-1,700 F. Air cond. Conf. Pkg. V, AE, DC.

This Renaissance cloister was transformed into a luxury hotel in the early 1980s. While it has retained some of the peace of its earlier vocation, the hotel now possesses all the comfort and elegance of the present age, from double glazing to perfect service. The rooms are all decorated in individual styles, with Provençal prints and pink Portuguese marble baths. The best rooms are the two-level suites and the ground-floor room with private terrace, but all are spacious, comfortable, quiet, and air conditioned. Courteous reception.

Relais Saint-Germain

6th arr. - 9, carrefour de l'Odéon
43 29 12 05,
fax 46 33 45 30
Open year-round. 1 ste 1,880 F. 20 rms 1,250-1,580 F. Air cond. V, AE, DC.

A handful of rooms were just added to this tiny hotel; all the accommodations are personalized and decorated in luxurious style, with superb furniture, lovely fabrics, exquisite lighting, and beautiful, perfectly equipped marble bathrooms. The tall, double-glazed windows open onto the lively Carrefour de l'Odéon. You are bound to fall in love with Paris staying at this tiny jewel of an establishment. Exemplary service.

Saint-Grégoire

6th arr. - 43, rue de l'Abbé-Grégoire
45 48 23 23,
fax 45 48 33 95
Open year-round. 1 ste 1,290 F. 19 rms 760-890 F. Air cond. Pkg. V, AE, DC, MC.

The cozy lounge is warmed in winter by a fireplace and there's a small garden for fine days. The rooms are painted in subtle shades of yellow and pink, with matching chintz curtains, white damask bedspreads, and some fine antique furniture. Double glazing and modern bathrooms. Perfect breakfasts.

Saint-Louis

4th arr. - 75, rue St-Louis-en-l'Ile - 46 34 04 80,
fax 46 34 02 13
Open year-round. 21 rms 670-770 F. V, MC.

Elegant simplicity characterizes this appealing hotel, where attention to detail is evident in the gorgeous flower arrangements and polished antiques. Small, perfectly soundproofed rooms offer comfortable beds and thick carpeting underfoot. The modern bathrooms are pretty indeed.

Saint-Louis-Marais

4th arr. - 1, rue Charles-V - 48 87 87 04,
fax 48 87 33 26
Open year-round. 15 rms 510-710 F. V, MC.

Reasonable prices and a delightful reception at this former convent annex in the heart of historic Paris. Each room is different, but all are charming and comfortable. Numbers 18 and 20 have *trompe-l'œil* décor.

Saint-Merry

4th arr. - 78, rue de la Verrerie - 42 78 14 15,
fax 40 29 06 82
Open year-round. 11 rms 400-1,000 F. Pkg. No cards.

A former presbytery, this seventeenth-century building is home to an original collection of Gothic furniture, which the owner has been buying at auctions for over 30 years. The telephone booth near the reception desk is a former confessional! Rooms are mostly small, with bathrooms not much bigger than closets, but the charm of the place is such that you have to book well in advance for the summer.

Sainte-Beuve

6th arr. - 9, rue Ste-Beuve - 45 48 20 07,
fax 45 48 67 52
Open year-round. 5 stes 1,600-1,650 F. 23 rms 700-1,300 F. No pets. V, AE, MC.

The Sainte-Beuve is a tasteful, harmonious example of the neo-Palladian

Look for the Golden Onions

The Cathedral of Saint Alexander Newsky reigns over Paris's White Russian enclave in the eighth arrondissement. Built in 1861 with funds donated by Czar Alexander II, the church is distinctively Byzantine, decorated with beautiful icons and with a trio of golden "onions." After services (which are recited in Slavonic) it is customary to repair across the street to the authentically Russian Bar Daru (19, rue Daru), for blinis and salmon or caviar, a tot of vodka, and nostalgic conversation. The best time to visit is at the Orthodox Easter, when the whole neighborhood joins in the festivities.

style of decoration, promoted in particular by David Hicks. In the guest rooms soft colors, chintzes, and the odd antique create a soothing atmosphere. Most attractive too are the marble-and-tile bathrooms, and the elegant lobby with its comfortable sofas arranged around the fireplace.

Hôtel des Saints-Pères

6th arr. - 65, rue des Saints-Pères - 45 44 50 00, fax 45 44 90 83

Open year-round. 4 stes 1,500 F. 35 rms 450-1,500 F. Air cond. No pets. V, AE.

Situated in two buildings, with all the quiet, elegantly furnished rooms overlooking a garden. Suite 205 is particularly attractive, and two new rooms with charming beams were just added . Downstairs is a pretty breakfast room, and a bar that opens onto the garden. Professional service.

San Régis

8th arr. - 12, rue Jean-Goujon - 44 95 16 16, fax 45 61 05 48

Open year-round. 10 stes 3,050-5,300 F. 34 rms 1,600-2,750 F. Restaurant. Air cond. No pets. Valet pkg. V, AE, DC, MC.

This jewel of a hotel, much appreciated by celebrities from the worlds of show business and *haute couture*, provides a successful mix of traditional comfort and the latest technology. Beautifully kept rooms boast splendid period furniture and paintings, sumptuous bathrooms, and lots of space, light, and character. The staff is irreproachable.

Select Hotel

5th arr. - 1, pl. de la Sorbonne - 46 34 14 80, fax 46 34 51 79

Open year-round. 1 ste 980-1,300 F. 67 rms 530-890 F. Air cond. V, AE, DC.

A glass-roofed atrium with an abundance of plants has been built at the heart of this attractive hotel next door to the Sorbonne. The pleasant, spacious rooms are functionally furnished. Generous buffet breakfast; bar.

Suède

7th arr. - 31, rue Vaneau - 47 05 18 65, fax 47 05 69 27

Open year-round. 1 ste 1,040-1,295 F. 40 rms 510-780 F. Restaurant. No pets. V, AE, DC, MC.

Decorated in tones of gray in a refined but rather austere Empire style, the guest rooms are quiet and nicely equipped. Streetside rooms are a trifle gloomy. Though smaller, those overlooking the indoor garden are much more cheerful, and from the sixth floor, they offer a view of the the Matignon gardens—and, on occasion, the prime minister's garden parties!

Tamise

1st arr. - 4, rue d'Alger - 42 60 51 54, fax 42 86 89 97

Open year-round. 18 rms 480-700 F. V, MC.

Designed by the architect Visconti and situated just twenty yards from the Tuileries, this tiny establishment offers authentic luxury at astonishingly low rates (note the pretty English furniture—in keeping with the hotel's name which is French for "Thames").

Trois Collèges

5th arr. - 16, rue Cujas - 43 54 67 30, fax 46 34 02 99

Open year-round. 44 rms 360-750 F. Pkg. V, AE, DC, MC.

Benedictine monks once inhabited this hotel; Rimbaud wrote about it, and García Márquez signed the guest list. Situated in the center of the Latin Quarter, the hotel offers elegant rooms decorated with blond-wood furniture and attractive posters. Note the ancient well (over 70 feet deep) in the atrium lobby. Tea room.

Université

7th arr. - 22, rue de l'Université - 42 61 09 39, fax 42 60 40 84

Open year-round. 27 rms 550-1,300 F. Air cond. No pets. V, AE, MC.

Comfortable beds and modern bathrooms are featured in an intelligently renovated seventeenth-century residence that is most appealing with its beams, half-timbering, and period furniture. The rooms are provided with comfortable beds and pretty wallcoverings. Rooms on the first floor have unusually high ceilings, while the fifth-floor suites boast flower-decked terraces.

Varenne

7th arr. - 44, rue de Bourgogne - 45 51 45 55, fax 45 51 86 63

Open year-round. 24 rms 470-650 F. V, AE, MC.

A cheerful reception is assured at this small hotel whose provincial air is underlined by a courtyard filled with flowers and trees (where breakfast and drinks are served on sunny days). The rooms overlooking the street have double windows.

Villa des Artistes

6th arr. - 9, rue de la Grande-Chaumière
43 26 60 86,
fax 43 54 73 70
Open year-round. 59 rms 650-850 F. Air cond. No pets. V, AE, DC, MC.

An oasis of calm amid the noise and bustle of Montparnasse. Luxury, quiet, and comfort are assured in this hotel, built around a garden patio. Excellent value for this district.

La Villa Maillot

16th arr. - 143, av. de Malakoff - 45 01 25 22,
fax 45 00 60 61
Open year-round. 3 stes 2,300-2,500 F. 39 rms 1,300-1,500 F. Rms for disabled. Restaurant. Half-board 1,547-1,857 F. Air cond. Conf. Valet pkg. V, AE, DC.

Formerly an embassy, this recent conversion is sophisticated and modern: an exemplary establishment. The very comfortable rooms (some equipped with a kitchenette camouflaged in a closet), have a gray-and-beige color scheme that gives them an Art Deco feel. Pink-marble bathrooms; wonderful breakfast buffet served in an indoor garden.

La Villa Saint-Germain

6th arr. - 29, rue Jacob - 43 26 60 00,
fax 46 34 63 63
Open year-round. 3 stes 1,950 F. 28 rms 800-1,600 F. Air cond. V, AE, DC, MC.

A laser beam projects room numbers onto the doors; the bathroom sinks are crafted of chrome and sanded glass; orange, violet, green, and red leather furniture stands out vividly against the subdued gray walls: Marie-Christine Dorner has created a high-tech environment for this new hotel, which attracts a trendy, moneyed clientele. Jazz club on the lower level (La Villa), with name performers.

PRACTICAL

Alison

8th arr. - 21, rue de Surène - 42 65 54 00,
fax 42 65 08 17
Open year-round. 35 rms 440-730 F. V, AE, DC, MC.

The 35 modern, functional rooms are bright and cheerful, with tidy, tiled bathrooms. Bar and lounge on the ground floor. Two mansard rooms on the top floor can be combined to form a suite. Bar.

Ambassade

16th arr. - 79, rue Lauriston - 45 53 41 15,
fax 45 53 30 80
Open year-round. 38 rms 400-545 F. V, AE, DC, MC.

The rooms behind a lovely façade are decorated with printed wallpaper and lacquered cane furniture. Small gray-marble bathrooms. Ask for a room overlooking the courtyard and you'll think you're in the country.

Aurore Montmartre

9th arr. - 76, rue de Clichy - 48 74 85 56,
fax 42 81 09 54
Open year-round. 24 rms 350-420 F. Rms for disabled. Conf. V, AE, DC, MC.

A simple hotel offering smallish rooms (those on the sixth floor are larger), all soundproofed and perfectly kept. Minibar. Friendly reception.

Beaugrenelle Saint-Charles

15th arr. - 82, rue St-Charles - 45 78 61 63,
fax 45 79 04 38
Open year-round. 51 rms 380-450 F. Conf. V, AE, DC, MC.

Near the Beaugrenelle shopping complex, this friendly hotel provides modern, well-equipped rooms decorated in restful colors. Breakfast is served in the rooms upon request. Good value.

Bergère

9th arr. - 34, rue Bergère - 47 70 34 34,
fax 47 70 36 36
Open year-round. 135 rms 550-990 F. No pets. V, AE, DC.

All the quiet rooms (most of which overlook a courtyard garden) have been freshened up and modernized, including the bathrooms. The setting is modern and simple, with mostly country-style furniture. Fine equipment; inviting public rooms.

Du Bois

16th arr. - 11, rue du Dôme - 45 00 31 96,
fax 45 00 90 05
Open year-round. 41 rms 410-590 F. Garage pkg. V, AE, MC.

This simple hotel offers excellent value. In addition to a warm welcome, guests find small, well-kept rooms which were attractively redecorated not long ago with Laura Ashley fabrics and wallpaper.

A red hotel ranking denotes a place with charm.

Hôtel des Chevaliers

3rd arr. - 30, rue de Turenne - 42 72 73 47, fax 42 72 54 10
Open year-round. 24 rms 560-610 F. V, AE, MC.

In the heart of the Marais, a small hotel frequented by actors and movie folk. The small rooms are bright and pleasantly furnished; some have just been redecorated. Warm reception.

Claret

12th arr. - 44, bd de Bercy - 46 28 41 31, fax 49 28 09 29
Open year-round. 52 rms 350-550 F. Restaurant. Half-board 320-650 F. Conf. Garage pkg. V, AE, DC.

This neat, modernized hotel (formerly a *gendarmerie*) offers a family atmosphere and a wine bar in the basement. Each meticulously maintained room is named for a wine region of France. Brand-new bathrooms.

Hôtel du Collège de France

5th arr. - 7, rue Thénard - 43 26 78 36, fax 46 34 58 29
Open year-round. 2 stes 1,030-1,130 F. 25 rms 480-580 F. No pets. Garage pkg. V, AE, MC.

The simple rooms of the Hôtel du Collège de France, located on a quiet little street, are tidy and comfortable. Most charming are the attic rooms, with their wooden beams and a view of the towers of Notre-Dame.

The prices in this guide reflect what establishments were charging at press time.

Étoile

17th arr. - 3, rue de l'Étoile - 43 80 36 94, fax 44 40 49 19
Open year-round. 25 rms 580-780 F. Conf. V, AE, DC, MC.

L'Étoile is strategically located between the Place de l'Étoile and the Place des Ternes. Rooms are clean, modern, and functional (renovated in 1991). A little pricey, though, for the level of comfort and service. Buffet breakfast. Courteous reception.

Favart

2nd arr. - 5, rue de Marivaux - 42 97 59 83, fax 40 15 95 58
Open year-round. 37 rms 500-620 F. Conf. Pkg. V, AE, DC, MC.

Goya stayed here when he fled to Paris in 1824. Set on a quiet square opposite the Opéra Comique, this hotel exudes a certain faded charm. Reasonable rates.

Flora

10th arr. - 1-3, cour de la Ferme-Saint-Lazare 48 24 84 84, fax 48 00 91 03
Open year-round. 45 rms 385-580 F. V, AE, DC, MC.

Near the Gare du Nord and the Gare de l'Est, the Flora offers pleasant, well-equipped, modern rooms decorated in pastel shades.

Folkestone

8th arr. - 9, rue Castellane - 42 65 73 09, fax 42 65 64 09
Open year-round. 2 stes 1,020 F. 48 rms 700-800 F. No pets. V, AE, DC, MC.

The beamed rooms, decorated with fabric wallcoverings or Japanese grass paper, have Art Deco armchairs and comfortable beds. Generous buffet breakfasts, with sweet rolls and pastries baked on the premises. Gracious reception.

Fondary

15th arr. - 30, rue Fondary - 45 75 14 75, fax 45 75 84 42
Open year-round. 20 rms 375-405 F. Pkg. V, AE, MC.

A neat and tidy hotel with polished wood floors. The rooms are decorated in cheerful colors, with bamboo furniture; some have terraces. Service is warm and efficient.

Grands Hommes

5th arr. - 17, pl. du Panthéon - 46 34 19 60, fax 43 26 67 32
Open year-round. 1 ste 750-850 F. 31 rms 615-750 F. Conf. V, AE, DC.

Opposite the Panthéon. The fairly spacious rooms are decorated with pink, cream, or floral fabric wallcoverings. Room 22 has a canopied brass bed, 60 and 61 boast balconies and pleasant views. Cable TV, minibar. The staff is friendly and efficient.

Ibis Paris-Jemmapes

10th arr. - 12, rue Louis-Blanc - 42 01 21 21, fax 42 08 21 40
Open year-round. 50 rms 440 F. Conf. Garage pkg. V, AE, DC, MC.

Near the Canal Saint-Martin, this well-designed business hotel is perfectly tailored for a busy clientele attending conventions and seminars. The rooms are spacious, modern, and fully equipped. Generous breakfast buffet. The management is friendlier and more attentive than in most chain hotels.

Ibis Paris-Bercy

12th arr. - 77, rue de Bercy - 43 42 91 91, fax 43 42 34 79

Open year-round. 368 rms 450 F. Restaurant. Conf. Pkg. V, AE, DC, MC.

This very professional establishment, surely one of the best in the chain, has a superb marble lobby. Guest rooms have blue-and-white décor and dark carpeting. One room on each floor is reserved for the disabled. Plain, well-kept bathrooms. Elegant bar; pleasant restaurant.

Idéal Hôtel

15th arr. - 96, av. Émile-Zola - 45 79 09 79, fax 45 79 73 59

Open year-round. 35 rms 350-430 F. Garage pkg. V, AE, DC, MC.

Here's an establishment that lives up to its name. Fully renovated, it stands at equal distance from the Eiffel Tower and the Porte de Versailles exhibition center. Spruce décor; exceptional comfort. Rates are remarkably reasonable.

Istria

14th arr. - 29, rue Campagne-Première 43 20 91 82, fax 43 22 48 45

Open year-round. 26 rms 460-580 F. V, AE, DC, MC.

Elm furniture and pastel colors grace the rooms and bathrooms of this well-kept hotel, where Mayakovski, Man Ray, and Marcel Duchamp once slept. The building is fully modernized.

Le Jardin des Plantes

5th arr. - 5, rue Linné 47 07 06 20, fax 47 07 62 74

Open year-round. 33 rms 420-640 F. Restaurant. Conf. V, DC, MC.

This hotel, set in a quiet street behind the Botanical Gardens, has appealing, delightfully decorated rooms—flowers and floral motifs abound. On the fifth floor, there is a terrace with a lovely view; in the basement, a sauna and an ironing room. Restaurant–tea room on the ground floor.

Les Jardins d'Eiffel

7th arr. - 8, rue Amélie - 47 05 46 21, fax 45 55 28 08

Open year-round. 80 rms 560-860 F. Rms for disabled. Air cond. Conf. Garage pkg. V, AE, DC, MC.

Some rooms are awaiting renovation, but 44 have already been redecorated in attractive colors and re-equipped with double glazing, minibars, hairdryers, and trouser presses. The upper floors overlook the Eiffel Tower. Sauna, many services and amenities, charming reception.

Hôtel Le Laumière

19th arr. - 4, rue Petit 42 06 10 77, fax 42 06 72 50

Open year-round. 54 rms 255-370 F. Pkg. V, MC.

This meticulously kept small hotel is located a few steps away from the Buttes-Chaumont park, in a district where modern hotels are not exactly plentiful. Convenient for the La Villette exhibition center. Rooms are small (those on the courtyard are larger), well soundproofed, and moderately priced.

Longchamp

16th arr. - 68, rue de Longchamp - 47 27 13 48, fax 47 55 68 26

Open year-round. 1 ste 900 F. 22 rms 600-750 F. V, AE, DC, MC.

The quiet, comfortable rooms are not large, but they are equipped with minibar, direct-line telephone, and television with two channels in English. Intimate atmosphere, charming reception.

La Louisiane

6th arr. - 60, rue de Seine - 43 29 59 30, fax 46 34 23 87

Open year-round. 80 rms 405-710 F. No pets. V, AE, DC, MC.

An artistic clientele (writers, dancers, models, musicians) frequents this large Art Deco hotel that stands right in the middle of the Buci street market. Regulars know they will find a warm reception, and rooms that are simple and comfortable, either painted or hung with Japanese grass paper.

Luxembourg

6th arr. - 4, rue de Vaugirard - 43 25 35 90, fax 43 26 60 84

Open year-round. 33 rms 600-780 F. V, AE, DC, MC.

Near the Luxembourg Gardens, in the heart of the Latin Quarter. The pleasant rooms, refurbished in 1993, have minibar, hairdryer, and individual safe; small bathrooms. Gracious reception by the charming owner.

Magellan

17th arr. - 17, rue Jean-Baptiste-Dumas

45 72 44 51,
fax 40 68 90 36
Open year-round. 75 rms 400-590 F. No pets. Garage pkg. V, AE, DC, MC.

Business people will appreciate the quiet and comfort of the functional rooms (renovated in 1993) offered by this creditable hotel, known for the regularity and quality of its service. Attractive garden. Bar; no restaurant.

Marais

3rd arr. - 2 bis, rue de Commines - 48 87 78 27,
fax 48 87 09 01
Open year-round. 39 rms 360-480 F. Conf. V, AE, MC.

A simple, neat hotel between Bastille and République offers small, bright, modern rooms. The connecting rooms on the first, second, and fifth floors are ideal for families.

Marsollier Opéra

2nd arr. - 13, rue Marsollier - 42 96 68 14,
fax 42 60 53 84
Open year-round. 29 rms 480-760 F.

A blessedly peaceful hotel in the heart of Paris. Rooms on the upper floors are the most desirable: number 701 has a rather low ceiling, but it affords a splendid view of the city's rooftops. Rates are reasonable.

Mercure Pont de Bercy

13th arr. - 6, bd V.-Auriol - 45 82 48 00,
fax 45 82 19 16
Closed 3 wks in Aug, hols. 89 rms 570-670 F. Rms for disabled. Restaurant. Half-board 650-750 F. Air cond. Conf. Pkg. V, AE, DC, MC.

A modern hotel near the Bercy sports complex and the Gare d'Austerlitz, the Mercure offers easy access from the *peripherique* (the Paris ring road). Well suited to the needs of business people, the rooms are soundproofed and have a large desk area. Some rooms have a terrace.

Mercure

14th arr. - 20, rue de la Gaîté - 43 35 28 28,
fax 43 27 98 64
Open year-round. 6 stes 1,160 F. 179 rms 680-940 F. Rms for disabled. Restaurant. Air cond. Pkg. V, AE, DC.

The comfortable rooms (excellent beds) are just big enough, with double glazing, minibar, direct-line telephone, and ten television channels. Functional bathrooms; generous breakfast buffet.

Mercure-Porte de Versailles

15th arr. - 69, bd Victor - 44 19 03 03,
fax 48 28 22 11
Open year-round. 91 rms 580-980 F. Restaurant. Air cond. Conf. Pkg. V, AE, DC.

The well-designed, air-conditioned (with individual controls), and soundproofed rooms all offer modern amenities, and are regularly refurbished. The excellent bathrooms are equipped with radios, hairdryers, and magnifying mirrors. Perfect for business people (the exhibition center is close at hand).

Modern Hotel Lyon

12th arr. - 3, rue Parrot - 43 43 41 52,
fax 43 43 81 16
Open year-round. 1 ste 750-855 F. 47 rms 495-570 F. No pets. V, AE, MC.

The location is most convenient (near the Gare de Lyon). Rooms are comfortable, unpretentious, and equipped with minibars. Thoughtful service.

Neuville

17th arr. - 3, pl. Verniquet - 43 80 26 30,
fax 43 80 38 55
Open year-round. 28 rms 580-700 F. Conf. Pkg. V, AE, DC, MC.

This pleasing hotel on a quiet square offers simple rooms, tastefully decorated with floral fabrics and equipped with fine bathrooms. Pleasant salon/winter garden and basement wine bar, Les Tartines.

Le Noailles

2nd arr. - 9, rue de la Michodière - 47 42 92 90,
fax 49 24 92 71
Open year-round. 58 rms 600-850 F. Conf. V, AE, MC.

Metal, glass, and wood compose this hotel's riveting contemporary architecture. Fully renovated in 1990, the Noailles features a restful central patio and comfortable, attractive guest rooms.

Nouvel Hôtel

12th arr. - 24, av. du Bel-Air - 43 43 01 81,
fax 43 44 64 13
Open year-round. 28 rms 360-520 F. V, AE, DC, MC.

The rooms of the Nouvel Hôtel are peaceful and attractive, and all were just freshly renovated and redecorated (the prettiest is number 9, on the same level as the garden). Good bathrooms; hospitable reception.

Prices for rooms and suites are per room, not per person. Half-board prices, however, are per person.

Novanox

6th arr. - 155, bd du Montparnasse
46 33 63 60,
fax 43 26 61 72
Open year-round. 27 rms 550-680 F. V, AE, DC, MC.

The owner of this hotel, opened in 1989, has used an amusing mixture of 1920s, 1930s, and 1950s styles for the décor. On the ground floor, a large, cheerful room serves as lounge, bar, and breakfast room.

Novotel Bercy

12th arr. - 85, rue de Bercy - 43 42 30 00,
fax 43 45 30 60
Open year-round. 1 ste 1,250-1,400 F. 128 rms 710-760 F. Rms for disabled. Restaurant. Air cond. Conf. Pkg. V, AE, DC, MC.

An ultramodern steel-and-glass structure, next door to the Bercy sports complex. The rooms are furnished and equipped to the chain's standards, with minibars, direct-line telephones, and room service from 6am to midnight. In addition to meeting rooms and business facilities, there is a large terrace, used for receptions in fine weather.

Orléans Palace Hôtel

14th arr. - 185, bd Brune - 45 39 68 50,
fax 45 43 65 64
Open year-round. 92 rms 500-570 F. Restaurant. Conf. V, AE, DC, MC.

A quiet and comfortable traditional hotel that offers good value. The well-equipped and sound-proofed rooms are decorated in an austere style. Indoor garden.

Ouest Hôtel

17th arr. - 165, rue de Rome - 42 27 50 29,
fax 42 27 27 40
Open year-round. 48 rms 326-406 F. Pkg. V, AE, DC, MC.

This cozy establishment has thick carpeting, efficient double glazing, and modest, modern rooms. Five are fairly spacious, the rest are small and in some cases a trifle dark. The bathrooms are old-fashioned though well maintained.

Parc Montsouris

14th arr. - 4, rue du Parc-Montsouris
45 89 09 72,
fax 45 80 92 72
Open year-round. 7 stes 480 F. 28 rms 310-420 F. Pkg. V, AE, MC.

This small, quiet hotel, remodeled in 1992, features plainly furnished white rooms with bright, new bathrooms. The lovely Parc Montsouris is just a short walk away.

Passy Eiffel

16th arr. - 10, rue de Passy - 45 25 55 66,
fax 42 88 89 88
Open year-round. 50 rms 530-640 F. Air cond. V, AE, DC, MC.

Five storeys of spotless, comfortable rooms (though all are not equally attractive). Four are large enough to suit families. A pleasant breakfast room faces a tiny, glass-enclosed garden.

Perreyve

6th arr. - 63, rue Madame - 45 48 35 01,
fax 42 84 03 30
Open year-round. 30 rms 430-560 F. , AE, DC, MC.

Near the lovely, leafy Luxembourg Gardens, the Perreyve's 30 comfortable rooms have small but faultless bathrooms. There is a little salon on the main floor with mahogany furniture and inviting armchairs.

Hôtel de la Place du Louvre

1st arr. - 21, rue Prêtres-Saint-Germain-Auxerrois - 42 33 78 68,
fax 42 33 09 95
Open year-round. 20 rms 496-812 F. V, AE, DC, MC.

Partially renovated in 1993, this hotel is decorated with paintings and sculptures throughout. The fairly large rooms are all comfortably furnished, with good bathrooms. Five charming bilevel rooms are situated under the eaves. Breakfast is served in a vaulted cellar that dates from the sixteenth century. Guests may expect a warm welcome.

Hôtel du Pré

9th arr. - 10, rue P.-Sémard - 42 81 37 11,
fax 40 23 98 28
Open year-round. 41 rms 395-540 F. Pkg. V, AE, DC, MC.

Actually two hotels, comfortable and close to the Gare du Nord and the Gare de l'Est. Downstairs, guests have the use of a bar, a bright lounge, and a pleasant breakfast room. The guest rooms sport painted wood paneling or Japanese wallpaper, paired with cane and bamboo furniture. Good bathrooms.

Queen's Hôtel

16th arr. - 4, rue Bastien-Lepage
42 88 89 85,
fax 40 50 67 52
Open year-round. 22 rms 320-520 F. Air cond. No pets. V, AE, DC, MC.

For an "English" atmosphere and rather petite but

delightful modern rooms, try this modest little hotel with a lovely white façade and flower-filled balconies. Excellent reception.

Récamier

6th arr. - 3 bis, pl. St-Sulpice - 43 26 04 89

Open year-round. 1 ste 800-850 F. 29 rms 360-560 F. No pets. Pkg. V, MC.

Publishers, professors, and physicians jealously guard the address of this, their favorite Parisian hotel. Accommodations are quite simple, gratifyingly quiet, and superbly located next to Saint-Sulpice. To further enhance the peace (and intellectual cachet) of the place, TV has been banned from the rooms. Friendly reception.

Regyn's Montmartre

18th arr. - 18, pl. des Abbesses - 42 54 45 21, fax 42 23 76 69

Open year-round. 22 rms 380-455 F. V, AE, MC.

Each of the rooms in this quiet, well-maintained hotel has a direct-line telephone, radio, TV, and bathroom; the décor is simple but pleasant. Charming, warm-hearted reception. Good value.

Le Relais du Louvre

1st arr. - 19, rue Prêtres-Saint-Germain-Auxerrois - 40 41 96 42, fax 40 41 96 44

Open year-round. 2 stes 1,200-1,400 F. 18 rms 580-890 F. Restaurant. Pkg. V, AE, DC, MC.

The original façade of this historic building opposite the Tuileries has been preserved, but the interior is fully modernized. The rooms, decorated by Constance de Castelbajac, overflow with charm. Those with numbers ending in 1 are slightly smaller than the rest. Wonderfully hospitable reception.

Le Relais de Lyon

12th arr. - 64, rue Crozatier - 43 44 22 50, fax 43 41 55 12

Open year-round. 34 rms 426-542 F. Pkg. V, AE, DC, MC.

This pleasant hotel provides bright, comfortable, well-equipped rooms which are absolutely quiet (double glazing, blinds). Most overlook a little patch of garden, and those on the fifth floor have a terrace. Friendly reception.

Résidence des Gobelins

13th arr. - 9, rue des Gobelins - 47 07 26 90, fax 43 31 44 05

Open year-round. 32 rms 355-445 F. V, AE, DC, MC.

A delightful small hotel in a quiet street not far from the Latin Quarter and Montparnasse. The warm welcome of the young owners merits a detour. Rooms are decorated in blue, green, or orange, a different color for each floor. Terrace.

Résidence Saint-Lambert

15th arr. - 5, rue E.-Gibez - 48 28 63 14, fax 45 33 45 50

Open year-round. 48 rms 380-550 F. Pkg. V, AE, DC, MC.

This pleasant, quiet hotel near the exhibition center at Porte de Versailles has tidy, smallish but nicely equipped rooms, some overlooking the garden. A laundry and bar are on the premises.

Résidence Trousseau

11th arr. - 13, rue Trousseau - 48 05 55 55, fax 48 05 83 97

Open year-round. 11 stes 820-1,250 F. 55 rms 540-780 F. Rms for disabled. Conf. Pkg. V, AE, MC.

Completed in 1989, this self-service hotel is situated in a quiet side street not far from the Bastille. Pleasant, modern décor and all mod cons: sink, refrigerator, electric hotplates, dishes, coffee machine, and microwave oven.

Riboutté-La Fayette

9th arr. - 5, rue Riboutté - 47 70 62 36, fax 48 00 91 50

Open year-round. 24 rms 370-450 F. V, AE, MC.

This small and charming hotel faces Rue La Fayette and is located within walking distance of the Opéra, the Bourse (Stock Exchange), and the *grands boulevards.* Its quiet rooms are small and attractive. The four rooms on the top floor are the most sought-after.

Royal Médoc

9th arr. - 14, rue Geoffroy-Marie 47 70 37 33, fax 47 70 34 88

Open year-round. 41 rms 550-680 F. Restaurant. No pets. V, DC, MC.

Ten minutes away from the Opéra and close to the Bourse and main boulevards, this functional, freshly renovated hotel (with tidy rooms, direct-line telephones, and helpful, multilingual staff) is perfect for international business travelers.

Saint-Dominique

7th arr. - 62, rue St-Dominique - 47 05 51 44, fax 47 05 81 28

Open year-round. 34 rms 465-610 F. Pkg. V, AE, DC, MC.

This most modest of the three "Centre Ville" hotels is also the most charming, and the location is excellent. The delightful little rooms are cozy and comfortable.

Hôtel de Saint-Germain

6th arr. - 50, rue du Four - 45 48 91 64, fax 45 48 46 22

Open year-round. 30 rms 415-695 F. Conf. Garage pkg. V, AE, DC, MC.

This small hotel with its delightful décor and English furniture offers round-the-clock room service, babysitting, and various tours of Paris (by helicopter, minibus, or on foot).

Saint-Romain

1st arr. - 5-7, rue St-Roch - 42 60 31 70, fax 42 60 10 69

Open year-round. 34 rms 510-830 F. V, AE, DC, MC.

Recently renovated, this small hotel offers business services that many of its classier cousins do not, such as typing, photocopying, fax, and telex. Simple, comfortable rooms decorated in pretty colors, with marble baths. Breakfast is served in a beautiful vaulted cellar.

Sénateur

6th arr. - 10, rue de Vaugirard - 43 26 08 83, fax 46 34 04 66

Open year-round. 42 rms 580-1,500 F. Conf. V, AE, DC, MC.

A comfortable, modern hotel with a huge mural and plenty of greenery brightening up the ground floor. The rooms were freshly redecorated in 1993. Fine views from the top floor.

7e Art

4th arr. - 20, rue St-Paul - 42 77 04 03, fax 42 77 69 10

Open year-round. 23 rms 295-650 F. Restaurant. Conf. V, AE, DC, MC.

Posters and photographs evoking the movies—known in France as the seventh art—paper the walls. Very small but comfortable rooms with tiny, well-equipped bathrooms. No room service, but light meals are served at the restaurant (City Light).

Solférino

7th arr. - 91, rue de Lille - 47 05 85 54, fax 45 55 51 16

Closed Dec 15-Jan 5. 1 ste 750 F. 31 rms 300-650 F. Garage pkg. V, MC.

Almost opposite the Musée d'Orsay, here are simple rooms done in fresh colors, with bath or shower. There is a charming little lounge, a sky-lit breakfast room, and pretty ornaments everywhere. The Solférino is both relaxing and pleasantly old-fashioned. Friendly reception.

La Tour d'Auvergne

9th arr. - 10, rue de La Tour d'Auvergne 48 78 61 60, fax 49 95 99 00

Open year-round. 25 rms 450-650 F. Restaurant. Garage pkg. V, AE, DC, MC.

A competently run, no-nonsense hotel. Each room has décor from a different period; all are furnished with four-poster beds and double-glazed windows. A fine little establishment, ideal for business travelers.

Trocadéro

16th arr. - 21, rue St-Didier - 45 53 01 82, fax 45 53 59 56

Open year-round. 23 rms 520-620 F.

The smallish rooms are done up in soothing pale tones, and the bathrooms are well equipped. The management and staff are unfailingly cheerful. Note the relatively low prices (considering the neighborhood).

Tim'hôtel Montmartre

18th arr. - 11, rue Ravignan - 42 55 74 79, fax 42 55 71 01

Open year-round. 60 rms 440-680 F. V, AE, DC, MC.

On an adorable little square near the Bateau-Lavoir (where Picasso painted the *Demoiselles d'Avignon*), this hotel gives guests a taste of Montmartre's "village" life. Book a room on the upper floors for the best views. Entirely renovated in 1994, the rooms all have full bathrooms and cable TV.

Utrillo

18th arr. - 7, rue A.-Bruant - 42 58 13 44, fax 42 23 93 88

Open year-round. 30 rms 300-435 F. No pets. V, AE, DC, MC.

Located behind the Rue Lepic in a quaint part of Montmartre, this former boarding house (where painter Maurice Utrillo once lived) is now totally modernized. The rooms feature whitewashed walls, and the upholstery and bedding are in cheerful fabrics. The courtyard was recently renovated.

Vieux Marais

4th arr. - 8, rue du Plâtre - 42 78 47 22, fax 42 78 34 32

Closed Aug. 30 rms 385-550 F. No pets. V, MC.

You can count on a warm, friendly welcome at this small hotel. Though the neighborhood is lively, this street is relatively quiet. The well-equipped, unpretentious rooms are undergoing a thorough renovation.

Wallace

15th arr. - 89, rue Fondary - 45 78 83 30, fax 40 58 19 43

Open year-round. 35 rms 500-650 F. Restaurant. Half-board 400-600 F. Conf. Garage pkg. V, AE, DC, MC.

This hotel exudes old-fashioned charm. Most of its small but cheerful rooms overlook a quiet garden. Elegant lobby; meals on trays.

Welcome Hotel

6th arr. - 66, rue de Seine - 46 34 24 80, fax 40 46 81 59

Open year-round. 30 rms 340-515 F. No pets. No cards.

You can almost forget the busy intersection of the nearby Boulevard Saint-Germain behind the double windows of these small, cozy, tidy rooms. And if you want a taste of the bohemian life, you'll find it on the sixth floor (though you can take the elevator!) where you will discover a quaint beamed attic. Reasonable rates.

A red hotel ranking denotes a place with charm.

AIRPORTS

ORLY
94396 - (Val-de-Marne)
Paris 16 - Villeneuve-St-Georges 12

Mercure Paris-Orly-Aéroport

Orly-Ouest 429 46 87 23 37, fax 46 87 71 92

Open year-round. 1 ste 750-800 F. 193 rms 540-640 F. Rms for disabled. Restaurant. Air cond. Conf. Pkg. V, AE, DC, MC.

The hotel was recently renovated, and provides soundproof rooms decorated in lively, bright colors. The bathrooms are excellent. Rooms can be rented for the day only (10am-6pm) at special rates. Minigolf and airport shuttle bus.

Paris Orly Airport Hilton

Aérogare Orly-Sud 267 - 45 12 45 12, fax 45 12 45 00

Open year-round. 12 stes 1,300-1,500 F. 347 rms 950-1,300 F. Restaurant. Air cond. Conf. Garage pkg. V, AE, DC, MC.

Functional, comfortable rooms near the airport with a free shuttle service. Excellent facilities for conferences or seminars. Round-the-clock room service. Bar and shops.

ROISSY-EN-FRANCE
95700 - (Val-d'Oise)
Paris 26 - Meaux 36 - Senlis 28

Holiday Inn

1, allée du Verger 34 29 30 00, fax 34 29 90 52

Open year-round. 1 ste 1,800 F. 243 rms 760-1,080 F. Rms for disabled. Restaurant. Air cond. Conf. Heated pool. Garage pkg. V, AE, DC, MC.

Situated in the old village of Roissy. Rooms are large, bright, and functional. There's a health club for hotel guests (sauna, gym, Jacuzzi, etc.). Free shuttle to the terminals and the exhibition grounds at Villepinte.

Sofitel

Aéroport Charles-de-Gaulle - 48 62 23 23, fax 48 62 78 49

Open year-round. 8 stes 1,500 F. 344 rms 700-950 F. Rms for disabled. Restaurant. Air cond. Conf. Heated pool. Tennis. Valet pkg. V, AE, DC, MC.

A comfortable airport hotel with a discothèque, sauna, and coffee shop. Round-the-clock room service and a free shuttle to the airport. Entertainment facilities include a disco and piano bar, and there's a coffee shop too.

THE SUBURBS

BAGNOLET
93170 - (Seine-St-Denis)
Paris 6 - Meaux 41 - Lagny 27

Novotel Paris-Bagnolet

1, av. de la République - 49 93 63 00, fax 43 60 83 95

Open year-round. 8 stes 830 F. 611 rms 540 F. Rms for disabled. Restaurant. Air cond. Conf. Heated pool. Garage pkg. V, AE, DC, MC.

Just outside Paris, this is a good address for seminars and conferences. The rooms are modern, functional, and well sound-proofed. Piano bar.

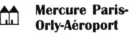

BOULOGNE-BILLANCOURT
92100 - (Hauts-de-Seine)
Paris (Porte de St-Cloud) 10 - Versailles 11

Adagio
20-22, rue des Abondances - 48 25 80 80,
fax 48 25 33 13
Open year-round. 75 rms 595-755 F. Rms for disabled. Restaurant. Pkg. V, AE, DC.

This modern, glass-and-concrete hotel has bright, spacious rooms fitted with every convenience and pleasantly furnished. The basement houses a vast complex of conference rooms. Summer terrace.

CHESNAY (LE)
See Versailles

COURBEVOIE
92400 - (Hauts-de-Seine)
Paris 11 - St-Germain-en-Laye 13

Mercure
18, rue Baudin
49 04 75 00,
fax 47 68 83 32
Open year-round. 6 stes 1,200-1,500 F. 515 rms 680-890 F. Rms for disabled. Restaurant. Air cond. Conf. Garage pkg. V, AE, DC, MC.

This ovoid concrete structure at La Défense dominates an 80-boutique shopping center. The hotel offers every expected comfort, and the management is dedicated to providing even more. Bar; shuttle service to the RER station.

CRÉTEIL
94000 - (Val-de-Marne)
Paris 12 - Evry 20 - Melun 35 - Bobigny 17

Novotel Créteil-le-Lac
N 186, rue J. Gabin
42 07 91 02, fax 48 99 03 48
Open year-round. 5 stes 6,100 F. 105 rms 450-480 F. Restaurant. Air cond. Heated pool. Pkg. V, AE, DC, MC.

The rooms in this lakeside hotel were recently modernized. Sports complex with windsurfing nearby.

DISNEYLAND PARIS
See Marne-la-Vallée

ENGHIEN
95880 - (Val-d'Oise)
Paris 18 - Argenteuil 16 - Chantilly 32

Le Grand Hôtel d'Enghien
85, rue du Gal-de-Gaulle - 34 12 80 00,
fax 34 12 73 81
Open year-round. 3 stes 1,400-2,880 F. 48 rms 700-1,200 F. Restaurant. Air cond. Conf. Golf. Valet pkg. V, AE, DC, MC.

The building is undistinguished, but it stands in lovely grounds next to the lake. The spacious, comfortable rooms are decorated with period furniture.

A red hotel ranking denotes a place with charm.

MARNE-LA-VALLÉE
77206 Marne-la-Vallée – (Seine/Marne)
Paris 28 - Meaux 28 - Melun 40

In nearby Disneyland

(Access by A4)
77206 Marne-la-Vallée – (Seine/Marne)

Cheyenne Hotel
Desperado road
60 45 62 00,
fax 60 45 62 33
Open year-round. 999 rms 400-675 F. Rms for disabled. Restaurant. Golf. No pets. Pkg. V, AE, DC, MC.

Perhaps the most amusing of all the resort's hotels: fourteen separate structures recall the frontier towns of the Far West. It's not luxurious, but the rooms are tidy and spacious. Adults can enjoy tequila and country music in the saloon-restaurant, while kids have a ball on the playground.

Disneyland Hotel
60 45 65 00,
fax 60 45 65 33
Open year-round. 21 stes 3,250-12,500 F. 479 rms

Les Jeux Sont Faits

Feeling lucky? Head for the Casino d'Enghien, a lakeside Art Deco gaming palace just outside of Paris. Ladies, you may don your diamonds (gentlemen, you must wear a tie) to bet on blackjack or baccara: fortunes are won and—mostly—lost as croupiers look on imperturbably. The casino opens daily at 4pm. To get there, either take route A1 from the Porte de Clignancourt to the Saint-Denis exit, or hop on the train at the Gare du Nord for the 15-minute trip to Enghien-les-Bains.

1,650-2,500 F. Rms for disabled. Restaurant. Air cond. Heated pool. No pets. Valet pkg. V, AE, DC, MC.

This enormous candy-pink Victorian pastiche is the *nec plus ultra* of Disneyland Paris hotels. Sumptuous suites, first-class service; but the pseudo setting and formal atmosphere are surely not everyone's cup of tea. The rates are simply staggering. Restaurants: California Grill (see *Restaurants)* and Inventions.

Newport Bay Club

60 45 55 00,
fax 60 45 55 33

Open year-round. 15 stes 1,400-2,000 F. 83 rms 625-875 F. Rms for disabled. Restaurant. Air cond. Conf. Heated pool. Golf. No pets. Pkg. V, AE, DC, MC.

Were it not so enormous, the Newport Bay Club would be an almost-convincing facsimile of a summer resort in New England. The rooms are decorated with pretty white wicker furniture. Good value for the money. Restaurant: Yacht Club, see *Restaurants.*

New York Hotel

60 45 73 00,
fax 60 45 73 33

Open year-round. 36 stes 3,000-9,000 F. 538 rms 1,025 F. Rms for disabled. Restaurants. Air cond. Conf. Heated pool. Tennis. Golf. No pets. Pkg. V, AE, DC, MC.

Manhattan in the 1930s is the theme, complete with skyscrapers, Wall Street, and Rockefeller Center—there's even an ice-skating rink in winter. The Art Deco guest rooms feature mahogany furniture, king-size beds, and impeccably equipped bathrooms. Among the many amenities are a beauty salon, athletic club, conference center, a restaurant (Parkside Diner, see *Restaurants*), and the Manhattan Jazz Club, which books top-name talent.

Santa Fe Hotel

In the Park, near the Pueblos Indian village
60 45 78 00

Open year-round. 1,000 rms 550 F. Rms for disabled. Restaurant. Air cond. No pets. Pkg. V, AE, DC, MC.

Forty-two "pueblos" make up an ersatz Indian village, dotted with giant cacti; the parking lot is built to look like a drive-in movie theater. Game rooms for the children, and there's an amusing Tex-Mex restaurant, La Cantina.

Sequoia Lodge

In the Park, near lake Buena Vista - 60 45 51 00,
fax 60 45 51 33

Open year-round. 11 stes 1,500-1,700 F. 1,000 rms 525-775 F. Rms for disabled. Restaurant. Air cond. Pool. Golf. No pets. Pkg. V, AE, MC.

Bare stone and rough-hewn wood evoke a Rocky Mountain lodge. The sequoias have yet to reach their majestic maturity, but guests will find plenty of entertainment at the hotel's restaurants, shops, piano bar, or exercise room.

NEUILLY-SUR-SEINE

92200 - (Hauts-de-Seine)
Paris (Porte de Neuilly) 8 - Versailles 16

Hôtel International de Paris

58, bd V.-Hugo
47 59 80 00, fax 47 58 75 52

Open year-round. 3 stes 1,300-2,000 F. 327 rms 600-800 F. Restaurant. Half-board 700-915 F. Air cond. Conf. Garage pkg. V, AE, DC, MC.

A large, rather graceless contemporary hotel surrounded by lawns and gardens. Elegant luxuriously renovated rooms with every amenity. Sumptuous breakfast buffet.

Le Jardin de Neuilly

5, rue P.-Déroulède
46 24 51 62,
fax 46 37 14 60

Open year-round. 30 rms 580-1,200 F. Air cond. Conf. Pkg. V, AE, DC, MC.

There is indeed a garden behind the good-looking building that houses this hotel. Rooms are fairly spacious, and furnished with attractive antique pieces. The marble bathrooms are perfectly equipped. Charming reception.

Hôtel du Parc

4, bd du Parc
46 24 32 62,
fax 46 40 77 31

Open year-round. 71 rms 310-510 F. Rms for disabled. Conf. V, MC.

Between the Porte de Champerret and La Défense, on the Ile de la Jatte facing the Seine, stands this small 1930s hotel with well-equipped, regularly renovated rooms.

PONTAULT-COMBAULT

77340 - (Seine/Marne)
Paris 26 - Melun 29 - Coulommiers 41

Saphir Hôtel

Aire des Berchères
64 43 45 47,
fax 64 40 52 43

Open year-round. 21 stes 595-870 F. 158 rms 485-530 F. Rms for disabled. Restaurant. Air cond. Conf.

Heated pool. Tennis. Pkg. V, AE, DC, MC.

A brand-new hotel next to Disneyland. Rooms are airy, pleasant, and well equipped. Facilities include conference rooms, sauna, and a superb indoor swimming pool. Grill. Restaurant: Le Canadel, see *Restaurants*.

PUTEAUX

92800 - (Hauts-de-Seine)
Paris 10 - Versailles 14

Dauphin

45, rue J.-Jaurès
47 73 71 63,
fax 46 98 08 82

Open year-round. 30 rms 470 F. Tennis. Valet pkg. V, AE, DC.

The Dauphin stands opposite the Princesse Isabelle, and is run by the same family. Generous buffet breakfasts are set up in the sitting room; guest rooms are comfortable and pretty, with cable television. Some rooms are reserved for non-smokers. Free shuttle to the RER station.

Princesse Isabelle

72, rue J.-Jaurès
47 78 80 06,
fax 47 75 25 20

Open year-round. 1 ste 950 F. 30 rms 640 F. Air cond. Tennis. Valet pkg. V, AE, DC.

The rooms of this hotel near La Défense are prettily decorated, and have bathtubs with Jacuzzi or multijet showers. Some rooms open onto the flowered patio. Note that there's a convenient free chauffeur service to the RER and Pont de Neuilly Métro station.

Sofitel Paris CNIT

Paris-La Défense, in the CNIT, 2, pl. de La Défense - 46 92 10 10,
fax 46 92 10 50

Open year-round. 6 stes 2,400-3,000 F. 141 rms 1,280-1,600 F. Rms for disabled. Restaurant. Air cond. Conf. Pkg. V, AE, DC, MC.

The hotel is aimed at business travelers. It provides huge rooms (some boast a view of the Grande Arche), luxurious bathrooms, and 24-hour room service. Restaurant: Les Communautés, see *Restaurants*.

Sofitel Paris-La Défense

34, cours Michelet, La Défense 10
47 76 44 43, fax 47 73 72 74

Open year-round. 1 ste 2,500 F. 149 rms 1,280 F. Rms for disabled. Restaurant. Air cond. Conf. Valet pkg. V, AE, DC, MC.

A creditable chain hotel, warmly decorated with gilt mirrors and pale marble. Rooms are quiet, with superb pink-marble bathrooms. Service is top-notch and breakfasts are delicious. Good facilities for conferences. Restaurant: Les Deux Arcs, see *Restaurants*.

Syjac Hôtel

20, quai de Dion-Bouton - 42 04 03 04,
fax 45 06 78 69

Open year-round. 7 stes 850-1,500 F. 29 rms 570-850 F. No pets. Pkg. V, AE, DC, MC.

This modern hotel offers a pleasant alternative to concrete high-rises. Rooms are very pleasing, large and well appointed. There are some nice two-level suites (with fireplace) overlooking the Seine, and a pretty flowered patio.

Le Victoria

85, bd R.-Wallace
45 06 55 51,
fax 40 99 05 97

Open year-round. 32 rms 395-540 F. Tennis. Garage pkg. V, AE, DC, MC.

Not far from the Arche de La Défense, this recently opened hotel offers comfortable, well-equipped rooms.

RUNGIS

94150 - (Val-de-Marne)
Paris 13 - Corbeil 26 - Longjumeau 10

Holiday Inn

4, av. Ch.-Lindbergh
46 87 26 66,
fax 45 60 91 25

Open year-round. 168 rms 795-995 F. Rms for disabled. Restaurant. Air cond. Conf. Pkg. V, AE, DC, MC.

Comfortable and well-kept rooms near Orly airport (free shuttle). From your window, you'll look down on the Rungis *halles* (the Paris wholesale food market). Shops.

Pullman Paris-Orly

20, av. Ch.-Lindbergh - 46 87 36 36,
fax 46 87 08 48

Open year-round. 2 stes 1,400 F. 188 rms 650 F. Restaurant. Air cond. Conf. Heated pool. Pkg. V, AE, DC, MC.

A reliable, comfortable chain hotel with excellent soundproofing, air conditioning, television, and direct telephone lines. Among the amenities on offer are a non-stop shuttle to and from the airports, a panoramic bar, a restaurant, sauna, shops, and a swimming pool. Deluxe rooms are available ("Privilège") and there are several lounges.

SAINT-CLOUD
92210 - (Hauts-de-Seine)
Paris 12 - Boulogne 3 - Versailles 10

Hôtel Quorum
2, bd de la République - 47 71 22 33, fax 46 02 75 64
Open year-round. 58 rms 460-570 F. Rms for disabled. Restaurant. Tennis. V, AE, DC.

A bright new hotel with modern, quietly elegant public rooms, and spacious guest rooms with gray-marble baths. The best are on the upper floors with a view over the Parc de Saint-Cloud.

Villa Henri-IV
43, bd de la République - 46 02 59 30, fax 49 11 11 02
Open year-round. 36 rms 460-550 F. Restaurant. Conf. Garage pkg. V, AE, DC, MC.

A pleasant address off the boulevard. Rooms are decorated in Louis XVI, Louis-Philippe, or Norman style and are huge, bright, and well equipped.

SAINT-GERMAIN-EN-LAYE
78100 - (Yvelines)
Paris 21 - Chartres 81 - Dreux 70

La Forestière
1, av. du Président-Kennedy - 39 73 36 60, fax 39 73 73 88
Open year-round. 5 stes 1,050-1,300 F. 25 rms 680-980 F. Restaurant. Half-board 725 F. Tennis. Pkg. V, AE, MC.

Thirty rooms and suites were recently renovated and pleasantly furnished in an old-fashioned style with fresh, spring-like fabrics. The hotel sits on extensive, flower-filled grounds at the edge of the forest. Restaurant: Cazaudehore, see *Restaurants*. Relais et Châteaux.

Le Pavillon Henri-IV
21, rue Thiers
39 10 15 15, fax 39 73 93 73
Open year-round. 3 stes 1,900 F. 42 rms 400-1,300 F. Rms for disabled. Restaurant. Half-board 670-870 F. Conf. Pkg. V, AE, DC, MC.

This is where Louis XIV was born, Alexandre Dumas wrote *The Three Musketeers*, and Offenbach composed a number of operettas. Total comfort inhabits the 45 huge rooms and suites. The public rooms are magnificent and there's a splendid view over the extensive grounds.

VÉLIZY
78140 - (Yvelines)
Paris 15 - Versailles 7 - Jouy-en-Josas 4

Holiday Inn Paris-Vélizy
22, av. de l'Europe
39 46 96 98, fax 34 65 95 21
Open year-round. 182 rms 725-1,050 F. Rms for disabled. Restaurant. Air cond. Conf. Heated pool. Golf. Garage pkg. V, AE, DC, MC.

Situated near a shopping center, the Holiday Inn offers functional rooms and excellent facilities. Free shuttle to the Pont-de-Sèvres Métro station.

VERSAILLES
78000 - (Yvelines)
Paris 23 - Mantes 44 - Rambouillet 31

Bellevue Hôtel
12, av. de Sceaux
39 50 13 41, fax 39 02 05 67
Open year-round. 2 stes 300-500 F. 24 rms 300-450 F. Rms for disabled. Pkg. V, AE, DC, MC.

The Bellevue's Louis XV/XVI-style rooms are soundproofed and well equipped (new beds) but a trifle worn, despite a recent remodeling. Located near the château and conference center.

Sofitel
2 bis, av. Paris
39 53 30 31, fax 39 53 87 20
Open year-round. 6 stes 1,200 F. 146 rms 850 F. Rms for disabled. Restaurant. Air cond. Pkg. V, AE, DC, MC.

Exceptionally well situated near the Place d'Armes and the château but set back from the street, this Sofitel offers spacious, modern rooms and prestigious amenities. Excellent reception. Piano bar.

Trianon Palace
1, bd de la Reine
30 84 38 00, fax 39 49 00 77
Open year-round. 22 stes 3,500-7,500 F. 165 rms 890-2,200 F. Restaurant. Half-board 735-1,160 F. Air cond. Conf. Heated pool. Tennis. Valet pkg. Helipad. V, AE, DC, MC.

After sprucing up the place to the tune of $60 million, owner Yusake Miyama has thrown open the gilded gates of his stupendously lavish hotel. From video-conference equipment to a medically supervised spa, it is the last word in luxury. Restaurant: Les Trois Marches, see *Restaurants*.

Le Versailles
Petite-Place, 7, rue Ste-Anne - 39 50 64 65, fax 39 02 37 85
Open year-round. 48 rms 350-510 F. Rms for disabled. Restaurant. Pkg. V, AE, DC.

Conveniently situated near the entrance to the château and facing the convention center, Le Versailles has modern rooms and recently refitted bathrooms. Garden and patio.

CAFES & QUICK BITES

CAFES

Le Bourbon

7th arr. - 1, pl. du Palais-Bourbon - 45 51 58 27
Open daily 7:30am-10:30pm (Sun 7:30am-7pm). V, AE, DC. M° Chambre-des-Députés.

Le Bourbon welcomes a smart clientele of politicians (the Assemblée Nationale is just steps away), fashion writers, and models. Drinks and light refreshments may be enjoyed, weather permitting, on the flower-decked terrace, which overlooks one of the city's loveliest squares.

Café Beaubourg

4th arr. - 43, rue Saint-Merri 48 87 63 96
Open daily 8am-1am (Sat & Sun 8am-2am). V, AE, DC, MC. M° Les Halles.

The café's soaring central space is punctuated by eight columns. To your left, as you enter, a section is reserved for the perusal of French and foreign newspapers. Relatively private spots can be found on the upper level, where the efforts of budding artists are displayed. And virtually every seat affords a view of the esplanade of the Centre Pompidou, with its buskers, fire-eaters, and mad poets. Though the coffee, salads, and croque-monsieurs are A-OK, the sandwiches are still not up to scratch. A generous brunch is served on Sundays (100 F).

Café de Flore

6th arr. - 172, bd Saint-Germain - 45 48 55 26
Open daily 7am-1:30am. V, AE. M° St-Germain-des-Prés.

Guillaume Apollinaire and Jean-Paul Sartre are gone, but writers with less illustrious reps still frequent the Flore, as do a few actors, many locals, and a plethora of tourists. The café's upper room provides larger tables where groups of habitués gather for (noisy) conversation and a glass of the house tipple, Pouilly-Fumé from Ladoucette.

Café de la Paix

9th arr. - 12, bd des Capucines - 40 07 30 20
Open daily 10am-1:30am. V, AE, DC, MC. M° Opéra.

Is it just us, or have the waiters at this Parisian landmark grown terribly blasé? Too much notoriety, too many tourists seem to have taken a fatal toll on this once-glorious café. Sneak inside for a peek at the Second-Empire restrooms (on the first floor), but avoid the crowded, noisy tables. In all fairness we must say that the coffee (six varieties) is pretty good.

La Coupole

14th arr. - 102, bd du Montparnasse - 43 20 14 20
Open daily 7:30am-2am. V, AE, DC. M° Vavin.

When the Coupole changed hands some years back, the new owners promised not to alter this hallowed monument to the creative energy of Montparnasse, its writers, artists, and hangers-on. Broadly speaking, they kept their word. The terrace of the restored and refurbished Coupole is a fine place to sit with a beer or a coffee and watch Parisian life whiz by. Note that drinks alone are not served at mealtimes; breakfast is served until 10:30am.

Deauville

8th arr. - 75, av. des Champs-Élysées - 42 25 08 64
Open daily 8am-3am. V, MC. M° George-V.

The Deauville is always one of the last spots to close on the Champs-Élysées, making it an ideal rendezvous for infatigable nighthawks. The terrace provides an excellent view on the *plus belle avenue du monde*, now broader, cleaner, greener after a thorough-going renovation.

Les Deux Magots

6th arr. - 170, bd Saint-Germain - 45 48 55 25
Open daily 7:30am-1:30am. AE. M° St-Germain-des-Prés.

Over there, a group of Japanese tourists is sipping the famous "old-fashioned chocolate"—made from chocolate bars melted in rich milk and whipped to creamy lightness. Beneath the eponymous Magots (the twin bronze figures perched at ceiling level), a German couple sips the house Muscadet. On the terrace, Americans try out their French on the weary waiters, while nattily dressed locals gossip over jugs of coffee. The legendary habitués of the post-war era have long since vanished, but an air of excitement still hovers about this quintessential Parisian café.

Fouquet's

8th arr. - 99, av. des Champs-Élysées - 47 23 70 60
Open daily 8am-2am. V, AE, DC, MC. M° George-V.

Historically, this is *the* café on the Champs-Élysées, with its sprawling terrace on the "good" side of the avenue. True, some

TV and film celebs can be spotted here, but mainly one sees tourists and other ordinary folks (who are willing, that is, to spend 25 F for a cup of coffee) soaking up the morning sun or the evening neon.

Le Majestic Café

4th arr. - 34, rue Vieille-du-Temple - 42 74 61 61
Open daily 11am-2am. V, AE, DC. M° Hôtel-de-Ville.

A hybrid, much like the neighborhood it inhabits. Le Majestic blends a certain vintage charm with a resolutely hip attitude (the latter provided by the new generation of trendy young patrons). Live rock concerts are occasionally scheduled here.

La Palette

6th arr. - 43, rue de Seine
43 26 68 15
Open 8am-2am. Closed Sun. No cards. M° Odéon.

Painters, gallery owners, antique dealers, and art students are the pillars of this venerable café, an unofficial annex of the nearby Beaux-Arts school. When the weather is clement, it's fun to grab one of the sidewalk tables that stretch halfway up the Rue Jacques-Callot, order up a beer and a *guillotine* (an open-faced ham sandwich made with chewy Poilâne bread), and take in all the details of this animated Left Bank scene.

Pause Café

11th arr. - 41, rue de Charonne - 48 06 80 33
Open 9am-1am (Sun 9am-9pm). Closed Mon. V. M° Ledru-Rollin.

Here's an inviting place to stop for a drink or a snack, and a glimpse of the Bastille's arty crowd. Architects, designers, and gallery owners meet and greet in a relaxed atmosphere we find quite *sympathique*. Suitably trendy magazines (*Globe*, *Beaux-Arts*) are thoughtfully provided for customers' perusal.

Le Sancerre

18th arr. - 35, rue des Abbesses - 42 58 08 20
Open daily 7am-1:30am. V. M° Abbesses.

As you enter, look up and admire the mermaid painted on the ceiling. This is a café with character, hard by the scenic and very lively Place des Abbesses. The patrons are a colorful mix of local tradesmen, workers, rockers, and bohemians, artists, and the odd tourist. For your refreshment, the menu offers good wines by the glass, sandwiches, and meal-sized salads.

Le Select

6th arr. - 99, bd du Montparnasse - 42 22 65 27
Open daily 8am-2:30am (Sat & Sun 8am-3:30am). V. M° Vavin.

A more select class of eccentric prefers this café to other, flashier Montparnasse venues. A funky place to rendezvous before a seafood dinner at Le Dôme.

Le Train Bleu

12th arr. - 20, bd Diderot
43 43 09 06
Open daily 9am-10pm. V, AE, DC. M° Gare-de-Lyon.

Many people know that Le Train Bleu restaurant in the Gare de Lyon boasts a stunning interior; but not everyone is aware that this Belle Époque gem is also a bar and café. Why waste time in the lugubrious bistros on the station level, when a beautiful, comfortable (though admittedly more expensive) place of refreshment awaits up one flight of stairs?

QUICK BITES

Al Diwan

8th arr. - 30, av. George-V
47 20 84 98
Open daily 8:30am-11:30pm. V, AE, DC. M° George-V.

The carry-out shop of the Al Diwan restaurant stocks all the fixings for an impromptu Lebanese picnic: choose chawarma (marinated beef), labneh (creamy cheese), makanek (spicy sausages), or felafel sandwiches on the bread of your choice, round out your basket with some baklava and walnut cakes, pick a bottle of Lebanese wine (don't forget the corkscrew), and you're set!

Ay Caramba

19th arr. - 59, rue de Mouzaïa - 42 41 23 80, fax 42 41 50 34
Open daily 7:30pm-11:30pm. V, AE, MC. M° Danube.

Even if you're feeling blue, the merry atmosphere and spicy specialties of this popular *cantina* near the Buttes Chaumont park are guaranteed to raise your spirits! Great guacamole, delicious chili, enchiladas, and more to eat on the spot or take away. A full meal will cost you around 150 F.

Find the address you are looking for, quickly and easily, in the index.

La Boutique à Sandwichs

8th arr. - 12, rue du Colisée
43 59 56 69
Open 11:45am-1am. Closed Sun, 3 wks in Aug. V. M° Saint-Philippe-du-Roule.

On the second floor of this restaurant, you might see a few famous faces seated together around raclette, vegetable soup, and other simple but tasty treats. For our part, we remain loyal to the ground floor, where some of the best sandwiches in town (15 to 30 F) are put together, featuring shrimp, chicken, and smoked ham. The excellent corned beef (pickelfleisch), served hot or cold with horseradish and pickles on Poilâne bread, bears comparison to a good New York deli version. A great spot for a quick lunch on the cheap.

Café de Mars

7th arr. - 11, rue Augereau
47 05 05 91
Open daily noon-3pm & 8pm-11:30pm (Sat 11:30am-4:30pm & 8pm-11:30pm; Sun 11:30am-4:30pm). V, MC. M° École-Militaire.

A menu that provides an engaging mix of American (spareribs, salads) and Mediterranean (breaded mozzarella with arugula, grilled scampi), a jovial atmosphere, and a cosmopolitan crowd account for the Café's continuing success. The staff goes all out to produce a traditional American brunch on Sunday.

Café Mexico

16th arr. - 1, place de Mexico
47 27 96 98
Open daily 11am-11pm. M° Trocadéro.

In choosing Le Mexico as their *cantina,* the neighborhood's gilded youth have shown that their good taste extends beyond their signed and logo'd togs. Follow their lead and try the good fresh pasta, shrimp in Sherry, platters of smoked salmon or duck breast, and the cool, inventive salads. But for dessert, sneak off to Angelina, across the street.

Fauchon

8th arr. - 30, place de la Madeleine - 47 42 60 11
Open 9:40am-7pm (mini Fauchon 9:40am-9pm; summer 9:40am-10pm). Closed Sun. V, AE, DC. M° Madeleine.

The MO for getting through this deluxe cafeteria would drive anyone (but a Frenchman!) bonkers. First you line up to choose your main dish, dessert, and coffee, then you take your ticket to the cash register (another line), queue again to retrieve your meal, and finally set off in search of a place to consume it (don't hope for a table). The up side? Well, the food is very good indeed—and so is the coffee. Figure on spending 100 to 140 F for a full meal, 12 to 35 F for a pastry and coffee.

Flora Danica

8th arr. - 142, av. des Champs-Élysées
44 13 86 25
Open daily 9am-10pm (Sun 11am-8pm). V, AE. M° George-V.

This Danish outpost at the top of the Champs-Élysées is as popular as ever. After a movie, come here for a platter of Baltic herring (smoked or with cream) and potato salad, or gravlax, or smoked salmon, along with a frosty Tuborg beer and perhaps a danish pastry. Expect to spend about 200 F.

A precarious perch

The column that towers over the *Place Vendôme* seems to be equipped with an ejector seat. More than one famous figure has experienced the precarity of that particular perch since the first version was erected in 1686. The statue of the Sun King, Louis XIV, destroyed during the Revolution, was followed by Napoléon in a number of guises, briefly interrupted by King Henri IV when the monarchy was restored in 1814. Henri, who reigned in the late sixteenth and early seventeenth centuries, was the father of the Duke of Vendôme who gave his name to this magnificent square. The present Napoléon—dressed, like the original, in Roman garb—watches over the jewelers, couturiers, and furriers of this opulent neighborhood.

Higgin's

8th arr. - 1, rue Montalivet
42 66 95 26
Open daily noon-11pm (Sun noon-5pm). M° St-Augustin.

Join TV reporters, politicians, and sports stars like Alain Prost and Yannick Noah who come here to nosh American-style on eggs Benedict (65 F), guacamole (40 F), salmon tartare (60 F), or a tall, tasty pastrami sandwich (70 F). Still hungry? Move on to a warm brownie or delicious berry millefeuille. Chilean and Australian wines wash all this cheerful fare down in a handsome 1930s-inspired "cruise ship" setting.

Lina's

2nd arr. - 50, rue Étienne-Marcel - 42 21 16 14
Open 10am-6pm. Closed Sun. No cards. M° Étienne-Marcel.
8th arr. - 8, rue Marbeuf
47 23 92 33
Open 9am-5:30pm. Closed Sun. No cards. M° Franklin-D.-Roosevelt.

The friendly, swift staff works as you watch, building delicious, visibly fresh sandwiches. Shrimp, cucumber, bacon, and pastrami are but a few of the many options which you can take out, or munch on a stool behind the broad glass shopfront. With a dessert (brownies, pecan pie, Häagen-Dazs ice cream...) and a glass of Bordeaux, you'll spend about 70 F.

Lord Sandwich

8th arr. - 134, rue du Fg-St-Honoré - 42 56 41 68
Open 10am-3pm. Closed Sat, Sun. V. M° St-Philippe-du-Roule.

Lord Sandwich serves a huge array of some of the freshest bread-and-meat combos in Paris. They range from simple BLTs to far more sophisticated compilations (special mention goes to their sweet-and-savory offerings). Vegetarians and weight-watchers can opt for a crisp, satisfying salad. The cafeteria format is reminiscent of a fast-food outfit, but there is a garden-style dining room on the upper floor.

Au Régal

16th arr. - 4, rue Nicolo
42 88 49 15
Open daily 9:30am-11pm. V, AE. M° La Muette.

A sudden craving for caviar can be satisfied (for a price!) at this traditional Russian grocery-cum-restaurant. More modestly tariffed and perfectly delicious are the salmon roe, zakuski, herring any way you like it, borscht, pirozkis, and the wonderful vatrouchka (Russian cheesecake). We hear that Brigitte Bardot occasionally comes in to feast on blinis and smoked salmon.

Thanksgiving

4th arr. - 20, rue Saint-Paul
42 77 68 29
Open daily 11am-8pm (Sun 11am-6pm). V. M° Saint-Paul.

Just across from the Village Saint-Paul antique market, you can enjoy an American-style lunch or weekend brunch featuring such familiar favorites as jambalaya, meat loaf, or barbecued spare ribs, washed down with a tasty California wine. The house sweets are typically rich and delicious: pecan pie, carrot cake, and a truly terrific cheesecake. Lots of Yankee specialties are available for take-out, and the retail grocery provides a wide array of comfort foods from back home.

Verdeau

9th arr. - 25, passage Verdeau - 45 23 15 96
Open 11:30am-6pm. Closed Sat, Sun. V, MC. M° Richelieu-Drouot.

Tucked away in an utterly charming gallery of shops, the Verdeau is now owned by a Scandinavian proprietress, Madame Knutsen. Her culinary heritage is reflected in generous platters of marinated salmon and other Northern delicacies offered here at lunch, alongside a varying rostre of *plats du jour*, tempting desserts, and excellent wines sold by the bottle or the glass. Tea and pastries are served here in the afternoon.

West Side Café

17th arr. - 34, rue St-Ferdinand - 40 68 75 05
Open 10am-6pm (Sat 11am-5pm). Closed Sun, hols. V. M° Argentine.

This American-style diner looks like something Edward Hopper might have painted. At noontime, customers cluster around the counter for tasty turkey, lox, pastrami, or guacamole sandwiches made with bagels, onion rolls, or multi-grain breads (25 to 62 F), or the hearty chicken and Far West Side salads. It's fun to munch on a brownie or some chocolate-chop cookies and contemplate this very Parisian take-off on an old Yankee tradition.

TEA ROOMS

A Priori-Thé

2nd arr. - 35-37, galerie Vivienne - 42 97 48 75
Open daily noon-7pm. V, MC. M° Pyramides.

We'd be hard pressed to come up with a prettier or more charming spot in Paris than the Passage Vivienne. You enter beneath a glass roof supported by bas-relief goddesses and horns of plenty, to reach this honey-colored room (the scrap of a terrace out front is furnished with rattan armchairs). From noon until 3pm fashion mavens, journalists, and intellectuals lunch on cold platters, tempting *plats du jour* (try the welsh rarebit), and such homey desserts as fruit crumble and pecan pie. Come teatime, you'll find a selection of teas served with scones, muffins, and jam. Brunch is served on weekends.

Angelina

1st arr. - 226, rue de Rivoli
42 60 82 00
Open daily 9:30am-7pm (Sat & Sun 9:30am-7:30pm). V, DC, MC. M° Tuileries.
9th arr. - Galeries Lafayette, 40, bd Haussmann
42 82 34 56
Open 9:30am-6:30pm. Closed Sun. V, AE, DC, MC. M° Opéra.
16th arr. - 86, av. de Longchamp - 47 04 89 42
Open daily 10am-8pm. V, MC. M° Trocadéro.
17th arr. - Palais des Congrès, Porte Maillot
40 68 22 50
Open daily 9am-8pm. V, AE, DC, MC. M° Porte Maillot.

Angelina offshoots have appeared all over town of late, but the Rue de Rivoli address is the old original—and, as far as its loyal clientele is concerned, the only true—Angelina. Populated by elderly grande dames in green hats, dandies of various ages in tweed or leather jackets, and young ladies just out of convent schools with their smartly suited mothers, this posh, genteelly faded *salon de thé* is a charming relic of Paris past. Proust, indeed, a notorious gourmand, frequented Angelina back when it was still called Rumpelmayer's. He probably adored the thick, piping-hot chocolate that is still the house specialty. If you're in the mood to gorge, order the legendary Mont-Blanc (sweet chestnut purée in a meringue shell, heaped with whipped cream) or a Conversation (puff pastry filled with marzipan and topped with meringue).

Arbre à Cannelle

2nd arr. - 57, passage des Panoramas - 45 08 55 87
Open noon-6:30pm. Closed Sun. V, MC. M° Rue Montmartre.

You'll find this grand Second Empire tea room sheltered in the newly refurbished, wonderfully luminous Passage des Panoramas. Stockbrokers and advertising types drop by here for lunch; they are joined, at teatime, by a cadre of elegant elderly ladies. We're particularly fond of the homemade apple crumble and the excellent walnut tart, perfect with one of the many fine teas.

L'Arlequin

6th arr. - 25, rue St-André-des-Arts - 43 26 48 12
Open daily noon-3:30pm & 6:30pm-11:30pm. V, MC. M° Saint-Michel.

Dominique's domain is a warm, wood-paneled room where you can be sure of a delicious lunch or cozy teatime treat. Her homemade pastries include scones, muffins, pancakes, tarts, fruit crumbles, and a delectable chocolate cake. Savor them with a steaming cup of chocolate or a premium tea from Mariage Frères.

Boissier

16th arr. - 184, av. Victor-Hugo - 45 04 87 88
Open 10am-7pm. Closed Sun. V, MC. M° Rue de la Pompe.

This elegant, traditional tea room gives onto the Square Lamartine. Inside, little girls in kilts and white ankle socks devour such house specialties as enormous chocolate bonbons and delicately flaky apple tarts. Their mothers, no doubt more concerned with their figures, order salads or a platter of Parma ham, mozzarella, tomatoes, and raw mushrooms, along with a glass of Château de Lussac. Among the pastries, our vote goes to the Breda (a rich coffee mousse) and the filbert-based Noisettine. On a blustery afternoon, nothing comforts like Boissier's divine hot chocolate (28 F), which comes in five different flavors. Tea or chocolate and a pastry will cost about 75 F.

The prices in this guide reflect what establishments were charging at press time.

Brocco

3rd arr. - 180, rue du Temple
42 72 19 81
Open daily 6:30am-7pm. M° République.

Piping-hot bittersweet chocolate, a creamy rhubarb Chiboust with a touch of lemon and a crunch of caramel, a Royal rich with praline—these are just a few of the superior sweets on offer at Brocco, an unassuming, old-fashioned pastry shop near the Place de la République.

Brûlerie de l'Odéon

6th arr. - 6, rue Crébillon
43 26 39 32
Open 10am-6:45pm. Closed Sun, Mon. No cards. M° Odéon.

You'll smell the delightful aroma of roasted coffee beans even before you step into this old-fashioned shop, founded in 1853 and still run by the same family. The coffee, indeed, is excellent (9 F) and the inexpensive, homey sweets (chocolate cake, tea bread, apple tart...) make satisfying snacks. Oh yes, and there is tea, too—more than twenty varieties in fact, including spice- and fruit-flavored brews (20 F).

La Bûcherie

5th arr. - 41, rue de la Bûcherie - 43 54 24 52
Open daily 8:45am-1am. V, AE, DC, MC. M° St-Michel.

There are surely better ways to spend a stormy weekend afternoon than before the Bûcherie's crackling fire, with a cup of fine tea, a slice of tart lemon meringue pie, a view of Notre-Dame, and a book from Shakespeare & Co. (right next door)—the trouble is, we can't think of a single one.

Cador

1st arr. - 2, rue de l'Amiral-Coligny - 45 08 19 18
Open 9am-7:30pm. Closed Mon. V, MC. M° Louvre.

Worthy of its prestigious setting just opposite the Louvre, Cador is a regal little pastry shop with a gilt décor fit for a king. Seated at pink-and-taupe marble tea tables, tourists and locals alike make short work of dainty cakes from the mouthwatering display in the window. The Petits Cadors (chocolate and orange peel on a short-pastry base) and the Mousseline, a recent creation accompanied by a luscious Grand-Marnier custard sauce, attract their fair share of customers.

Carette

16th arr. - 4, pl. du Trocadéro
47 27 88 56
Open 8am-7pm. Closed Tue. No cards. M° Trocadéro.

Carette is famous for its expensive macaroons—chocolate, vanilla, lemon—and its coffee. The wealthy heirs and heiresses of the Avenue Mozart have long come here to chat over tea. But now the younger generation has moved in; if their racket is not to your liking, just remember that Carette is also a pastry shop: you can stop by, pick up some macaroons (or a Mont Blanc, or a Parfait au Café), and go home to eat them in peace.

Casta Diva

8th arr. - 27, rue Cambacérès
42 66 46 53
Open 11:30am-6:30pm. Closed Sat, Sun. No cards. M° Miromesnil.

Lunchtime brings quite a crush into Casta Diva's Art Deco rooms. The spacious alcoves and heavy pistachio-colored curtains shelter a posh, well-shopped-for clientele—even the salads (70 F) and savory tarts are rich! Come time for tea, the atmosphere is muted and serene, ideal for enjoying a rare selection from Mariage Frères or coffee from Verlet, along with a custard-swirled chocolate-mousse cake, tarte Tatin, or chocolate-orange tart. Tea and a pastry will set you back about 60 F.

Le Chalet des Iles

16th arr. - Lac inferieur du Bois de Boulogne
42 88 04 69, fax 45 25 41 57
Open daily Mar-Dec: 9am-9:30pm. V, AE, DC, MC. M° La Muette.

Zola and Proust both frequented this picturesque Chalet, built in the mid-nineteenth century for Empress Eugénie. Though lunch and dinner are served here too, we like this spot best at teatime. After an excursion on the lake (canoe rental: 43 F per hour), we stop in here and gorge shamelessly on ice cream and plump little madeleines.

La Charlotte de l'Ile

4th arr. - 24, rue Saint-Louis-en-l'Ile - 43 54 25 83
Open 2pm-8pm. Closed Mon, Tue. V, MC. M° Pont-Marie.

Tea tins piled everywhere, posters, paintings, old mirrors, hats, bouquets of dried flowers and, yes, even a piano: such are the elements of this wonderful, artistically disordered décor. Fruit tarts sit nicely with any of the 32 teas (we like the spiced variety), served on small etched trays, in antique teapots and cups, with silver carafes for the hot water. Hot-chocolate lovers will be more than happy with the aromatic, old-fashioned version offered here.

Chocolat Viennois

17th arr. - 118, rue des Dames - 42 93 34 40
Open 10am-noon & 2:30pm-10pm. Closed Sat eve, Sun. V, AE, MC. M° Villiers.

Within this Tyrolean chalet you'll discover a gift shop, a restaurant, and a snug tea room. The latter tempts gourmands to indulge in such Austrian delights as a chocolate-and-praline Mozartkugeln, a decadent Sachertorte, or flaky apple strudel served with raspberry-rhubarb granita (all priced at around 35 F). Though the flavored coffees are a treat (13 F), we usually go whole hog—the term is well advised—and order the Viennese hot chocolate topped with a drift of sweetened whipped cream (19 F).

Concertea

7th arr. - 3, rue Paul-Louis-Courier - 45 49 27 59
Open 11:30am-7pm (Mon 11:30am-4pm). Closed Sun. V, MC. M° Rue du Bac.

If you like Mozart with your chocolate tart, Verdi with your lemon meringue pie, or Bach with your vegetable quiche, this charming spot will suit you to a... tea. Check out the menu (written on a musical staff), then enjoy the concert while sipping smoky Lapsang Souchong from Mariage Frères or nibbling on one of the fresh and delicious homemade gâteaux (38 F)

Coquelin Aîné

16th arr. - 67, rue de Passy
45 24 44 00, fax 40 50 12 91
Open 9am-7:30pm (Sun 9am-1pm). Closed Mon. V. M° Passy.

Coquelin Aîné—what a truly Parisian treat. Yes, my dear, we know exactly where we are the moment we enter this tea room and see Hermès scarves in the necks of Burberry raincoats. Sweet, snobby little things from the local private school come in for tea and a tart, éclair, meringue, or Coquelin's famed macaroon. In warm weather, we like to lunch on the terrace (145 F) and savor the view of the pretty Place de Passy.

A la Cour de Rohan

6th arr. - 59-61, rue St-André-des-Arts - 43 25 79 67
Open daily noon-7:30pm (Fri & Sat noon-10pm). V, MC. M° Odéon.

Tucked away in a little passage off the Boulevard Saint Germain is this cozy tea room that's as comfortable as a private home, with dishes designed by Cocteau, Louis XVI furniture, and fragile Limoges china. Patrons seated at chintz-skirted tables murmur quietly over lunch (good chicken-liver salad) or teatime treats (yummy rhubarb crumble), while the charming hostess attends to their comfort. The delicious homemade jams and scones are also available for take-out. Tea and a pastry will cost you about 65 F.

> *Some establishments change their closing times without warning. It is always wise to check in advance.*

Hôtel de Crillon

8th arr. - 10, pl. de la Concorde - 44 71 15 00
Open daily 3pm-6pm. V, AE, DC, MC. M° Concorde.

We prefer to use the smaller entrance on the Rue Boissy-d'Anglas to reach the Crillon's stately salon, decorated in blue velvet by designer Sonia Rykiel. We settle in, not a bit intimidated by the wealth of marble, the Baccarat crystal chandeliers, the gleaming silver tea services, nor by the elegant, elderly patrons and stiffly formal staff. With utter confidence, we order the Thé du Crillon (155 F), an extravaganza of petits-fours, glazed fruits, finger sandwiches, scones, madeleines, and financiers (wee almond cakes), as well as jam and honey, accompanied by coffee, tea, or cinnamon-scented hot chocolate. Too much, you say? Well, one can always order a simple cup of tea from the list of 40 varieties from Mariage Frères. A single selection from the tantalizing pastry trolley will cost from 55 to 75 F. When the weather is fine, tea is served in the adjoining courtyard, to the soothing strains of a harp.

Dalloyau

6th arr. - 2, pl. Edmond-Rostand - 43 29 31 10
Open daily 8:30am-7:30pm (Sat & Sun 8:30am-8pm). V, AE, MC. RER Luxembourg (B).
8th arr. - 99-101, rue du Fg-St-Honoré - 42 99 90 00
Open daily 8:30am-9pm. V, AE, DC, MC. M° Saint-Philippe-du-Roule.
15th arr. - 69, rue de la Convention - 45 77 84 27, fax 45 75 27 99
Open daily winter: 9:15am-7:30pm (Sun 8:30am-7pm;

Mon 9:30am-7:30pm); summer: 9am-8pm (Sat & Sun 8:30am-8pm). V, AE, DC, MC. M° Boucicaut.

Dalloyau will always be Dalloyau. Nothing changes here: grandmothers still chat together or bring their grandchildren in for a treat, schoolgirls still sit telling each other schoolgirl stories, and young couples still smile timidly at each other after a walk in the Luxembourg Gardens across the way. The conscientious staff serves a substantial choice of teas, fruit juices, good hot chocolate, delicate pastries, and sumptuous ice-cream concoctions. The lunchtime crowd favors fresh salads and tasty *plats du jour* that don't cost the earth.

Aux Délices de Scott

17th arr. - 39, av. de Villiers
47 63 71 36
Open 8:30am-7:30pm (Sat 10am-7pm; Mon 9am-7pm). Closed Sun. V, MC. M° Malesherbes.

Aux Délices is nothing short of an institution. The huge room, tiled in blue and sienna with ivory woodwork and endless mirrors, once hosted the likes of Sarah Bernhardt and Sacha Guitry. Tea is served with all due ceremony, and may be accompanied by ethereal macaroons, caramelized tarts, a Roxane (spongecake, almonds, filberts, and chestnut cream), or a Malgache (spongecake and chocolate buttercream), among other excellent pastries (18 to 24 F).

Find the address you are looking for, quickly and easily, in the index.

L'Ébouillanté

4th arr. - 6, rue des Barres
42 78 48 62
Open noon-9pm. Closed Mon. No cards. M° St-Paul.

You can get anything you want at Géraldine's restaurant. For lunch, try the fresh, original, meal-sized salads, or the Moroccan brik—a coddled egg or other savory filling swathed in crisp, flaky pastry. Or fortify yourself for an afternoon of sightseeing with the Very, Very Well, a cocktail of fresh-squeezed orange juice, egg yolk, milk, and crème fraîche. Afternoon tea brings an assortment of uncomplicated sweets partnered by sophisticated coffee concoctions (11 to 20 F) or expertly brewed teas (22 F).

Les Enfants Gâtés

4th arr. - 43, rue des Francs-Bourgeois - 42 77 07 63
Open daily noon-8pm. V, MC. M° Saint-Paul.

The ambience is soft, the lighting is subdued; round tables and deep armchairs stand beneath whirling ceiling fans. An ideal place for tea (or even better, hot chocolate) and conversation. If your sweet tooth demands indulgence, order the brownie (the waitress may try to convince you to order the *tarte du jour*, but stand your ground). Stiffish prices.

L'Esquisse

12th arr. - 11, pl. d'Aligre
44 73 90 04
Open 11:30am-midnight (Sun 11:30am-5pm). Closed Mon. V, AE, MC. M° Ledru-Rollin.

A visit to the colorful Marché d'Aligre could be agreeably concluded by lunch at this airy, engaging eatery, decked out in summery shades of yellow and green. A savory tart or salad, tea, and a dessert (fruit gratins, chocolate fondant, and the like) add up to a reasonably priced repast.

L'Été en Pente Douce

18th arr. - 23, rue Muller
42 64 02 67
Open daily noon-3pm & 7pm-11pm. V, MC. M° Anvers.

This old-fashioned bakery-cum-tea shop sports a genuine turn-of-the-century décor. The covered terrace, which offers a view of the charming Place

Heroic taxpayers

After the architectural free-for-all of the Middle Ages, the development of the *Place des Vosges* in the early seventeenth century heralded an era of elegance and symmetry with its arcades, stone-and-brick façades, and steep slate roofs. Despite various renovations, the 36 houses have retained their homogeneous aspect. The Place des Vosges was given its present name in 1800 in honor of the first French department to pay its taxes after the Revolution.

Utrillo, hosts a mix of tourists and Montmartre regulars who come here for such yummy treats as walnut-pear tartlets and fudgy chocolate fondants (28 F). At lunchtime, try the salmon feuilleté, which comes out of the oven all warm and golden-brown, just like the delicious bread that is still baked daily on the premises.

La Fourmi Ailée

5th arr. - 8, rue du Fouarre
43 29 40 99
Open noon-6:30pm. Closed Tue. V, AE, MC. M° Maubert-Mutualité.

From the outside, La Fourmi Ailée looks like a bookstore. Inside, why, it is a bookstore, but one that conceals a blissfully intimate tea room. Waiting on a rustic sideboard sit a fresh, fragrant spice cake, a Norman apple tart, and scones served with two kinds of jam. Wisps of steam rise from the spouts of assorted teapots set on the tables (sixteen different brews are offered). One could easily while away the better part of an afternoon in so inviting a spot, with a newly purchased volume of, say, Virginia Woolf (most of the books are by women authors, and the selection is international). Brunch is served on weekends, and in winter a crackling fire warms the room.

Les Fous de l'Ile

4th arr. - 33, rue des Deux-Ponts - 43 25 76 67
Open noon-3pm & 7pm-midnight (Sun noon-7pm). Closed Mon. V, MC. M° Pont-Marie.

The upper levels above this large, windowed room are lined with books, china is displayed in glass cases, and arty photographs hang here and there. It's a busy place, very relaxed and pleasant, with a student atmosphere. The clientele is young and cosmopolitan; the waiters officiate in T-shirts and jeans. The teas offered include Sakura (green tea flavored with cherry) and Caraïbes (scented with Caribbean flowers), both of which go well with the creamy house cheesecake. The Sunday brunch (100 to 150 F) is quite popular.

Galerie de la Paix

8th arr. - Hôtel George-V, 31, av. George-V - 47 23 54 00
Open daily 9am-7pm. V, AE, DC, MC. M° George-V.

The power tea, it seems, has ousted the power breakfast as an occasion for wheeling and dealing. An ideal place to perform this ritual of ambition is the stately *salon de thé* in the Hôtel George-V. Cement an alliance, plan a merger, or acquire an adversary's assets over a cup of Japanese Matcha Uji or Russian Czar Alexander tea (prepared according to the "five essential laws of tea brewing") accompanied by a plate of miniature French pastries or sandwiches. These delicacies are served beneath the benevolent gaze of Peace and Abundance, allegorical figures who star in the immense tapestry that is the Galerie's most prominent feature. An abundance of money is what you'll need when the bill comes: 35 to 50 F for coffee, tea, or chocolate; 50 F for fruit juice; 60 to 80 F for pastries or sandwiches.

L'Heure Gourmande

6th arr. - 22, passage Dauphine - 46 34 00 40
Open 11am-7pm. Closed Sun. V, MC. M° Odéon.

Sheltered in the picturesque Passage Dauphine is a pluperfect little tea room that offers handsome surroundings, a hospitable welcome, fabulous cheesecake, and the peace necessary to enjoy it all—stay an hour, or two hours if you like. For tea and cake, you'll pay about 75 F; a light lunch runs about 100 F.

Ladurée

8th arr. - 16, rue Royale
42 60 21 79
Open daily 8:30am-7pm (Sun 10am-7pm). V, MC. M° Madeleine.

Cherubs on faded frescoes, plush red carpet, oaken woodwork, and round tables of veined black marble are all part of the charm of this tiny institution, which is always full as a tick. Especially on Saturdays, when lovely ladies from the best neighborhoods put down their Hermès shopping bags for a few minutes to enjoy tea with a macaroon (20 F) or two (they are the best in Paris, you know). Lunchtime is surprisingly lively: choices run to the likes of omelettes, chicken, such daily specials as cassoulet, or minuscule crab and salmon sandwiches that will empty your wallet long before they fill your stomach.

Some establishments change their closing times without warning. It is always wise to check in advance.

Le Loir dans la Théière

4th arr. - 3, rue des Rosiers
42 72 90 61
Open daily noon-7pm (Sun 11am-7pm). No cards. M° St-Paul.

A teatime classic. Habitués spread their books and papers around steaming teapots or cups of rich hot chocolate, then settle in for a studious hour punctuated, perhaps, by a portion of pear charlotte or cinnamon-scented apple-walnut cake. Expect to spend 60 F for tea and a pastry, and about 80 F for a lunch of salad and a savory tart.

La Maison du Chocolat

8th arr. - 52, rue François-Ier
47 23 38 25
Open 10am-6pm. Closed Sun. V, MC. M° Franklin-D.-Roosevelt.

Both haven and heaven for the truly devout—chocoholic, that is—can be found here. La Maison du Chocolat is a tea room that lives up to its name by serving neither tea nor coffee, just hot chocolate (28 F). The luscious house drink, poured from a chocolate pot into Limoges china cups, comes in five incarnations: Guayaquil, a classic and elegant brew; Caracas, bitter, full-bodied, recommended for true lovers of chocolate; Brésilien, lightly flavored with coffee; Seville, spiced with cinnamon and vanilla; and Bacchus, laced with Antilles rum. All come accompanied with whipped cream on the side. You can also try a rich chocolate frappé, with either ice cream or sorbet. If you're still not sated, sample one of the pastries (36 F), perhaps the Gounod with bits of orange peel, or the Mokambo with its fresh raspberry flavor, or an assortment of fifteen chocolates lovingly dreamed up by Robert Linxe, the tutelary genius of the place.

Mariage Frères

4th arr. - 30, rue du Bourg-Tibourg - 42 72 28 11
Open daily noon-7pm. V, AE, MC. M° Hôtel-de-Ville.
6th arr. - 13, rue des Grands-Augustins - 40 51 82 50
Open noon-7pm. V, AE. M° Saint-Michel.

It teems with teas, teapots, teacups, tea biscuits, and tea balls—Mariage Frères is without a doubt top dog in the Paris tea-ocracy. For more than a century the firm has sold 350 kinds of tea, from the strongest Imperial Slavic blends to the most delicately perfumed varieties. Many may be sampled in the shop's rather staid tea room. They are naturally brewed with filtered water and served at the appropriate temperatures in insulated pots. The waiters, impeccably garbed in something vaguely Indian (one wonders when they have time to read their Kipling), wheel between the tables, scrupulously performing the house "ritual of tea." Delicate pastries, such as the Coup de Soleil (a berry tart with crème brûlée topping) accompany the sublime brews.

Find the address you are looking for, quickly and easily, in the index.

Grande Mosquée de Paris

5th arr. - 39, rue Geoffroy-St-Hilaire - 43 31 18 14
Open daily 10am-9:30pm. No cards. M° Jussieu.

When you emerge—skin softened, hair shining and scented—from the hammam that is part of the Paris Mosque complex, prolong your sense of well-being with a stop at the Mosque's tea room. In a cool, dim atmosphere, with music playing in the background, sample North African and Middle Eastern pastries (we like the cream-filled Cornes de Gazelle) accompanied by strong, sweet mint tea (20 F), Turkish coffee, or barley water.

Muscade

1st arr. - 36, rue de Montpensier & 67, galerie de Montpensier, jardin du Palais Royal - 42 97 51 36
Open daily noon-7pm. V, AE, MC. M° Palais-Royal.

A wall of mirror and another of window give the actors (from the nearby Comédie Française) and government officials who frequent this chic little tea room a many-angled view of the Palais-Royal gardens. In fine weather, take a cue from the regulars: lay claim to a table outside, then go inside to inspect the pastries and make your choice.

Les Nuits des Thés

7th arr. - 22, rue de Beaune
47 03 92 07
Open daily noon-7pm (Sun 11:30am-7pm). No cards. M° Rue du Bac.

The interior is ever-so-soigné: white lacquer, pink upholstery, mercury mirrors, damask tablecloths, antiques... The welcome may be cool if you aren't a regular, but the clientele is noticeably at ease, chatting about such weighty topics as dog pedigrees, boating, and the latest literary successes. One nibbles here on salads and main-dish pies and tarts of all sorts, but truth to tell, only the desserts are really exceptional (we're thinking of the caramelized cream-cheese tart and the raspberry macaroons). You'll spend something like 140 F for lunch, half that for tea and a pastry.

Pandora

2nd arr. - 24, passage Choiseul - 42 97 56 01
Open 11:30am-7pm. Closed Sat, Sun. V, MC. M° Pyramides.

Take a good look at the pastry selection as you cross the front room, then proceed to the chocolate-colored room in the back, where daylight filters down through the glass ceiling. At lunchtime, crisp toasted bread and fresh butter are already set out on the well-spaced round tables; the menu offers zucchini flan, a remarkable chicken salad, and other light dishes. Late afternoon is a quieter time, perfect for indulging in Pandora's chocolate-chestnut cake, or the rhubarb or coffee tarts. Reasonable prices. It is advisable to book in advance for lunch.

La Pâtisserie Viennoise

6th arr. - 8, rue de l'École-de-Médecine - 43 26 60 48
Open 9am-7:15pm. Closed Sat, Sun. No cards. M° Odéon.

Medical and literature students are among the enlightened crowd loyal to this Latin Quarter citadel, its seats worn smooth and shiny by generations of devotion. La Pâtisserie Viennoise opened in 1928, and the youthful ambience remains as tasteful as the cakes are tasty—the strudel and the poppy-seed cake (called *flanni*) are among our favorites. The teas are perfect and the Viennese hot chocolate is a dream; they marry beautifully with a croissant or a raisin brioche. Everything is made on the premises and everything is good. There's only one drawback: the place is always packed. But so what—just pile on in or find a stool at the bar. You'll think you've been transported from Paris to a Viennese *Konditorei*.

La Pause Gourmande

14th arr. - 27, rue Campagne-Première - 43 27 74 51
Open 9am-7pm. Closed Sat, Sun. No cards. M° Raspail.

Though the books that highlight the décor are merely *trompe-l'œil*, a cultivated ambience indeed prevails in this Montparnasse tea room. Come for a sweet snack—apple-custard or lemon-marzipan tart, chocolate or apple-pear cake—or for an inexpensive lunch. The nominal sum of 60 F entitles one to a savory tart, salad, beverage, and dessert; meal-sized salads (38 to 48 F) are also featured.

Le Plaza

8th arr. - 25, av. Montaigne 47 23 78 33
Open daily 4pm-7pm. V, AE, DC, MC. M° Champs-Élysées-Clemenceau.

Take tea in a regal setting of mirrors and tapestries at Le Plaza. While a pianist plays discreetly in the background, you can nibble on poundcake, macaroons, baba au rhum, and other such traditional treats. A cup of tea and an assortment of three—minute—pastries comes to 100 F even.

Ritz

1st arr. - Hôtel Ritz, 15, pl. Vendôme - 42 60 38 30
Open 4pm-6pm. Closed Sun. V, AE, DC, MC. M° Concorde.

A harpist adds a magical note to this enchanted garden where classical busts, plane trees, and elegant patrons create an otherworldly haven. A discreet, attentive staff serves good tea and proper little English-style sandwiches, though for our money (195 F, to be precise) only the millefeuille truly rises above the ordinary. But the atmosphere is worth the price of admission.

Rollet-Pradier

7th arr. - 6, rue de Bourgogne 45 51 78 36
Open daily 8am-7:45pm. V, MC. M° Invalides.

Georges Clemenceau was a regular here, and his favorite cake, the Fanny, is still in demand (it involves a topping of delectable chocolate ganache on a sweet meringue base). We like the newer Dauphiné, a walnut spongecake swirled with coffee-flavored buttercream. All the pastries are manageably priced at around 20 F, and they may be enjoyed with a cup of tea or (even better) with the famed *chocolat chaud maison*. A light lunch, consisting of a sophisticated salad, dessert, and coffee, comes to about 75 F.

Rose Thé

1st arr. - 91, rue St-Honoré
42 36 97 18
Open noon-6:30pm. Closed Sun. V, MC. M° Châtelet.

Your grandmother from Philadelphia would love it here: tasteful paintings, subdued lighting, antiques, lush plants, and a sideboard loaded with tempting cakes. Tea lovers will certainly fall for the rose-thé, an exquisite blend of Bulgarian rose with a touch of jasmine and lotus. Devotees of something more solid will find no fault with the old-fashioned chocolate cake made from real chocolate bars. And the hot chocolate (32 F) is not to be missed. Between noon and 2pm the regulars, including many antique dealers, come to lunch on gratins, quiches, or meat pie. In summer a sheltered terrace provides a spot of calm in the madding heart of Paris.

Le Salon de Jane

7th arr. - 27, rue Pierre-Leroux - 40 65 05 50
Open 11:30am-6:30pm. Closed Sun. No cards. M° Vaneau.

We always look forward to visiting this cozy *salon*, done up in faded pastel hues with rustic beams overhead. Jane bakes the toothsome house sweets herself: seasonal fruit tarts, poundcake, roasted apples with custard sauce, and more (25 to 30 F). She is also responsible for the savory tarts served at lunchtime in big, satisfying portions (42 F), accompanied by perfectly brewed teas or fresh-squeezed fruit juices.

Le Salon du Chocolat

8th arr. - 11, bd de Courcelles - 45 22 07 27
Open 2pm-6:30pm. Closed Sun. V, MC. M° Villiers.

In addition to intensely flavored chocolates (try the palets made with cocoas from Java, Ghana, and Colombia), the Salon also proposes decadent gâteaux (30 to 40 F). At lunch an appealing selection of hot dishes is served, but the Salon really comes into its own at teatime, offering a wide choice of brews from China and India, and a sublime version of hot chocolate, served in a delicate porcelain pot. The triple-chocolate cake, we might add, is in a class by itself. Plan to spend 60 F for a beverage and pastry.

Le Samovar d'Or

7th arr. - 59, av. de Suffren
43 06 37 36
Open 9:30am-7:30pm. Closed Mon. V, MC. M° Dupleix.

Didier Laurant learned his trade *chez* Lenôtre, and apparently studied hard and well. The proof is in his ambrosial Royal Chocolat (praline spongecake with bitter-chocolate mousse and custard sauce), the equally divine Délice de Suffren (banana mousse swirled with caramel sauce), or the refined yet rustic apple-nougat tart. These indulgences may be savored slowly on the premises, along with one of 35 teas or a cup of extraordinary hot chocolate. Lunchtime options include appetizing cold platters, *plats du jour*, and house-made ice creams. Sunday brunch is also served.

Senteurs des Thés

6th arr. - 118 bis, rue d'Assas
46 33 28 74
Open 9am-6:30pm (Sat 10:30am-6:30pm). Closed Sun. No cards. M° Notre-Dame-des-Champs.

An agreeably airy tea room with a Left Bank clientele and a decidedly feminine look. A profusion of flowers, rattan furnishings, watercolors on the walls, and delicate china on the tables create a cozy, inviting atmosphere in which to enjoy a light lunch or afternoon break. Danièle Lauret prepares simple, unpretentious dishes based on fresh ingredients (cold platters of vegetables or charcuterie, veal blanquette, or poached salmon: 65 to 75 F) and attractive, old-fashioned desserts. Teas come from the Palais des Thés and fruit juices are always fresh-squeezed, but our preferred beverage is the creamy, old-fashioned hot chocolate.

Le Stübli

17th arr. - 11, rue Poncelet
42 27 81 86
Open 9am-6:30pm (Sun 9am-12:30pm). Closed Mon. V, MC. M° Ternes.

In the ground-floor shop you can choose from among the best German and Viennese pastries in Paris—Linzertorte, Sachertorte, Black Forest cake and, of course, apple strudel (23 to 25 F). On the second floor, in the warm atmosphere of an Austrian chalet, all of these pastries and more can be tasted along with a cup of hot chocolate or Viennese-style coffee. *Stüblime*! In case you're really hungry, don't worry—there's Bavarian salad, Swabian onion tart (38 F), a Baltic platter, and the Stübli and a plate of hot beef sausage.

The Tea Caddy

5th arr. - 14, rue St-Julien-le-Pauvre - 43 54 15 56
Open noon-7pm (Sat noon-7:30pm; Sun 11:30am-7pm). Closed Wed. No cards. M° Saint-Michel.

Exposed ceiling beams and stained-glass windows foster a charming, quiet, somehow medieval atmosphere, perfectly in tune with the ancient neighborhood of Saint-Julien-le-Pauvre. The Tea Caddy attracts a young, international clientele with a pastry list that has English and Austrian accents. Sacher-torte, Linzertorte, fruit pies with cream, delicious scones, cinnamon toast, and muffins are complemented by six or seven types of tea.

Tea Follies

9th arr. - 6, pl. Gustave-Toudouze - 42 80 08 44
Open daily 9am-9pm (Sun 9am-7pm, summer 9am-midnight). V, AE.. M° St-Georges.

On warm days, tables spill out onto the chestnut-shaded terrace where lunch, tea, and Sunday brunch are served to a lively crowd of youthful habitués. When inclement weather (or a lack of terrace seats) forces customers inside, they discover a perfectly pleasant, white-walled, loft-like room enlivened with watercolors and ink drawings. Wherever you sit, you'll relish the savory tarts and delectable pastries (almond meringue, creamy cheesecake, or tartelettes filled with lemon-curd). The "light" brunch costs 70 F, the full version runs 129 F with fish, or 119 F without.

Tea and Tattered Pages

6th arr. - 24, rue Mayet 40 65 94 35
Open daily 11am-7pm. No cards. M° Duroc.

Why do we feel like donning bell bottoms and a flowered vest when we come here? Must be the atmosphere redolent of hippiedom that floats among these used English-language books and over the tea tables laden with brownies, muffins, scones, and cheesecake. The Americans, Canadians, and Brits who gather here chat and joke merrily in their native tongue(s). Tea and a cake will cost you about 50 F.

Thé Cool

16th arr. - 10, rue Jean-Bologne - 42 24 69 13
Open daily noon-7:30pm. No cards. M° Passy.

Thé Cool exudes the charm of an airy English garden—it's a haven of calm in the middle of a busy neighborhood. At lunch, enjoy the view of the pretty square opposite while tucking into an attractive platter of, say, mozzarella or salmon, or a tasty club sandwich. Those who live for teatime will rejoice at the selection of 30 rare and wonderful brews, which may be accompanied by a mouthwatering range of sweets (chocolate marquise with crème anglaise, fruit tarts, apple crumble...).

Find the address you are looking for, quickly and easily, in the index.

La Théière

14th arr. - 118, bd du Montparnasse - 43 27 22 00
Open 10:30am-7:30pm. Closed Sun. V, MC. M° Vavin.

At this mecca for tea buffs, you will also find first-rate coffees, jams, chocolates, and fresh, appealing breads, fudgy brownies, an exceptionally good pear tart, and a tea cake imported especially from England. Simple but satisfying hot dishes appear at lunchtime (salmon en papillote, savory tarts), alongside generous salads and such.

Thé S F

2nd arr. - Passage du Grand-Cerf - 40 28 08 76
Open 10am-7pm. Closed Sun. V, MC. M° Étienne-Marcel.

Sip one of 45 teas, gathered from all over the globe, as you admire the owner's collection of antique radios (to which the establishment's name makes a punning reference: Thé S F = TSF = *Télégraphie Sans Fil* = wireless, or radio...). To go with, there are such noteworthy sweets as the Volcan (a cake based on chestnut purée, flamed with rum) or the airy Vol-au-Vent filled with rhubarb and black-currants. Tea and a pastry will cost you 50-odd francs.

Toraya

1st arr. - 10, rue St-Florentin 42 60 13 00
Open 10am-6:30pm. Closed Sun. V, AE, DC, MC. M° Concorde.

Westerners may be disconcerted by the taste of green tea, which the courteous staff serves forth on a tray that is itself a work of art. Or by the pastries with such poetic names as toyamazakura (*cherry trees on the far mountain*), semi no ogawa (*red fish*), or matso no yuki (*snow-covered pines*). Strange, very strange, is the colorless agar-agar (gelatin substitute) topped with aduki-bean paste. The staff will tell you that Japanese pastry has something for all five senses: the melodious sound of the name, the treat for the eyes, the agreeable contact of the red-bean paste with the tongue and teeth, and the pleasing sound of crunching rice. There remains then only to define the pleasure of the taste. Well, it must be delicious—after all, Toraya has been purveyor to the Emperor of Japan since 1789.

Verlet

1st arr. - 256, rue St-Honoré
42 60 67 39
Open 9am-7pm. Closed Sat, Sun. No cards. M° Palais-Royal.

At Verlet, it isn't Champagne or the proximity of our beloved that goes to our head, but rather the intoxicating aromas of coffee and tea. The fragrance lures us in the door, pining for a steaming cup of *something*. This is one of the best places in Paris for either tea or coffee. Seated on the rickety chairs (which, by the way, are few in number and hotly contested at lunchtime), in an all-wood décor dating from 1880, coffee devotees sip Jamaican, an excellent Moka, or the house blend, Grand Pavois. For tea drinkers, there are more than 30 varieties, including a perfumed Chinese tea called White Flowers and a famous Darjeeling, which is particularly soft and subtle. The house pastries, salads, and sandwiches are uniformly delicious.

WINE BARS

L'Ami Pierre

11th arr. - 5, rue de la Main-d'Or - 47 00 17 35
Open daily 11am-1am. V. M° Ledru-Rollin.

A former colleague of Jacques Mélac opened this animated wine bar near the Bastille, where solid *plats du jour* are enhanced by a savvy choice of wines. The old-fashioned bistro décor exudes character—and the characters clustered around the bar supply plenty of Parisian ambience!

L'Ange-Vin-Jean-Pierre Robinot

11th arr. - 24, rue Richard-Lenoir - 43 48 20 20
Open 11am-8:30pm (Tue & Thu 11am-2am). Closed Sat, Sun. V. M° Voltaire.

The luscious dessert wines for which Anjou is famous—Montlouis, Coteaux-de-l'Aubance, Vouvray, and Coteaux-de-Layon—here get the star billing they deserve. Recent harvests have yielded some stellar examples, which owner Jean-Pierre Robinot would be only too happy to pour for you. Keep them company with a creditable *plat du jour*, or a selection from the wonderful cheese board.

Bar du Caveau

1st arr. - 17, pl. Dauphine
43 54 45 95
Open 8:30am-8pm. Closed Sat, Sun. M° Pont-Neuf.

Lawyers and judges work up a powerful thirst, what with all their pleading and sentencing. After a day in court, they can be found here, getting down to cases over a glass of Bordeaux (Château d'Arricaud, for example) and a sandwich made with excellent poached ham. Even if you aren't a member of the bar, feel free to join in or just sit quietly with your wine and a Parisian daily, presented in the old reading-room style on a thin pole. In summer the tiny sidewalk terrace on the Place Dauphine is a treat.

Au Bascou

3rd arr. - 38, rue Réaumur
42 72 69 25
Open until midnight. Closed Sat lunch, Sun. V, AE, DC. M° Arts-et-Métiers.

Jean-Guy Loustau, a burly Basque who presided for many years over the splendid cellar of Le Carré des Feuillants, is running his own show now. What a pleasure to watch a pro at work! He'll advise you on choices from the short menu, which is a far cry from your usual wine bar fare (lush shirred eggs with foie gras; spiced escargots; rabbit sauté; lentils with chorizo...). The wines are just as exciting, with bottles from all over France, especially the Southwest.

Beaujolais-Saint-Honoré

1st arr. - 24, rue du Louvre
42 60 89 79
Open daily 6am-2am. M° Louvre.

A fresh infusion of energy—in the form of a hipper, more youthful clientele—has given this landmark wine bar a new lease on life. Tasty charcuterie is perfectly partnered by good, authentic Beaujolais.

La Bergerie-Christian Baudy
16th arr. - 21, rue de Galilée
47 20 48 63
Open 8am-10pm. Closed Sun. V. M° George-V.

An award-winning wine bar, notable for its mature vintages of sweet Loire Valley wines (Coteaux-du-Layon, Bonnezeaux...), as well as lipsmacking, reasonably priced Bourgueils and Chinons. The food, which is decent if not exciting, brings in a neighborhood crowd at lunchtime.

Bistrot de la Gaîté
3rd arr. - 7, rue Papin
42 72 79 45
Open daily 7:30am-8pm. M° Réaumur-Sébastopol.

Jérôme and Mireille Constant, late of the Taverne Henri-IV (see below), are the proud new proprietors of a fine little bistro. The open-faced sandwiches of garlicky sausage or Bayonne ham (on Poilâne's bread, of course!) are accompanied by honest, straightforward wines that couldn't be more charitably priced (5.20 F for 8 cl of good Morgon or Bourgueil). We're sure that when they get the hang of their routine, the Constants will relax and crack a smile!

Bistrot des Augustins
6th arr. - 39, quai des Grands-Augustins - 43 54 41 65
Open daily 11am-2am. No cards. M° Saint-Michel.

Down at the bottom of the Boulevard Saint-Michel, amid fast-food chains and greasy spoons, stands this honest-to-god bistro, unflagging in its devotion to French culinary tradition. Robust homemade terrine, a satisfying cheese assortment, and savory ome-lets are solidly supported by a range of proprietors' wines: Lesimple's Muscadet, a honeyed Cérons, and Sinard's Côtes-du-Rhône sell for 12 to 18 F a glass.

Le Bistrot du Sommelier
8th arr. - 97, bd Haussmann
42 65 24 85
Open noon-2:30pm & 7:30pm-11pm. Closed Sat, Sun. V, AE. M° St-Augustin.

Despite the name, this is hardly a bistro; it's more like a classic restaurant. But there's certainly a sommelier: Philippe Faure-Brac, who won the crown of World's Best Sommelier in 1992. His own predilection is for wines from the Rhône Valley, of which he is a native, and "Bordeaux from the other side of the river" (Saint-Émilion, Pomerol). A valuable address for people who wish to learn more about wine and about matching wines with food. No concessions are made to accessibility or easy drinking. And prices are high.

Aux Bons Crus
1st arr. - 7, rue des Petits-Champs - 42 60 06 45
Open 11:30am-10pm (Sat 11:30am-6pm). Closed Sun. V, MC. M° Bourse.

Alice Kiberlain presides over a venerable wine bar that sports a piously preserved 1905 décor. It's a great favorite with apprentice actors from the Dramatic Arts Conservatory nearby, who along with stage technique have learned the art of eating and drinking well on the cheap. A hearty Cantal cheese fondue with potato-and-ham salad (58 F), or steak tartare maison (68 F), plus a glass of Jousselin's tasty Touraine Cabernet (12 F) still leaves plenty of change from a 100 F bill.

Le Bouchon du Marais
4th arr. - 15, rue François-Miron - 48 87 44 13
Open noon-3pm & 7pm-12:30am. Closed Sun. V, AE. M° Saint-Paul.

Inaugurated in 1992, this bar is already a classic. In a convivial atmosphere, you can down some choice Loire Valley vintages (the proprietor himself owns a vineyard in Chinon), along with the usual selection of sandwiches, grilled andouillette or, for a change of pace, the rather odorous potato-and-cheese dish known as raclette.

Ma Bourgogne
8th arr. - 133, bd Haussmann
45 63 50 61
Open 7am-10pm. Closed Sat, Sun. V, AE. M° Miromesnil.

Nothing ever seems to change at this temple to Beaujolais, a friendly place where a faithful lunchtime crowd returns religiously for coq au Juliénas, bœuf bourguignon, and parsleyed ham terrine. The owner, Burgundy-born Louis Prin, continues to purchase his wines direct from the producers, as he has done for the past 33 years. His Hautes-Côtes-de-Beaune possesses a rare finesse.

Maison Fondée en
1765
Hennessy
COGNAC
X.O
COGNAC
Hennessy

Au Bourguignon du Marais

4th arr. - 19, rue de Jouy
48 87 15 40
Open 10am-1am. Closed Sun. V, AE. M° Saint-Paul.

Jacques Bavard is a newcomer to the wine-bar scene, but he's attracted a good deal of notice. He launched a successful policy of selling first-class Burgundies at wine-shop prices (his adjoins the bar) plus a corkage fee of 35 F. In other words, bottles that usually go for twice or thrice the price in regular restaurants, are suddenly affordable here! Examples? Take Fernand Chevrot's admirable Maranges: tariffed at 72 F in the shop, it comes to 107 F if you choose to enjoy it with an assortment of charcuteries (63 F) or a *plat du jour* (70 F). Other offerings worth trying are the Santenay (131 F per bottle in the bar) and Darviot's Volnay.

La Cagouille

11th arr. - 17, rue Oberkampf - 47 00 10 33
Open 9:30am-4pm & 7pm-11pm (Sat noon-4pm). Closed Sun. V. M° Oberkampf.

A "cagouille" is a snail, in the parlance of Charentes, home of modest white wines and noble Cognacs. This friendly little provincial outpostoffers original dishes based on the region's produce, plus remarkable omelets, and an estimable selection of wines served by the glass.

La Cave Drouot

9th arr. - 8, rue Drouot
47 70 83 38
Open 7:30am-9:30pm. Closed Sun. No cards. M° Richelieu-Drouot.

This long-lived establishment across from the Drouot auction house is at once a wine bar, a brasserie, and a restaurant. The choice of edibles thus ranges from open-faced sandwiches to full-fledged *cuisine gastronomique*. Antique dealers, auctioneers, and collectors rely on Jean-Pierre Cachau to select the perfect wine to accompany their meal: perhaps the Ladoix from Burgundy, which he bottles himself; or a slightly sweet Pacherenc de Vic Bilh, from his native Béarn.

Les Caves Pétrissans

17th arr. - 30 bis, av. Niel
42 27 83 84, fax 40 54 87 56
Shop: open 10am-1pm & 3pm-8pm (Sat 10am-1:30pm). Closed Sun. Restaurant: open noon-2:30pm & 7pm-10:30pm. Closed Sat, Sun. V, AE. M° Ternes.

In the course of a century, Pétrissans has slaked the thirst of a cavalcade of literati and bon vivants. Today Christine Allemoz, great-granddaughter of founder Martin Pétrissans, runs this establishment, with her husband, a former lawyer. They've gradually transformed the wine bar that adjoins their retail shop into a full-fledged *restaurant à vins*. The wines are chosen with care: try a glass of Conti's excellent white Bergerac, Raffault's Chinon Les Galuches (both 18 F a glass), or the Cahors vinified by celebrity chef Alain Senderens (95 F per bottle). The set-price meal is tagged at 155 F, and there are lots of à la carte choices too (delicious rabbit in aspic). We would like to see smoother service, however, and an occasional smile from the staff.

Les Caves Solignac

14th arr. - 9, rue Decrès
45 45 58 59
Open noon-2pm & 7:30pm-10pm. Closed Sat, Sun. V, AE. M° Plaisance.

With a vaguely Italian décor highlighted by lots of old posters and a curious collection of antique siphons, this well-run *bistrot à vins* balances on the cusp of the fashionable. Owner Jean-François Banéat takes great pains to serve only the freshest fare (the house foie gras is a marvel) backed up by a tantalizing roster of wines. Nor does he hesitate to transfer any wine that needs it into a (lovely) decanter—a laudable practice we don't often encounter in the city's wine bars.

La Cloche des Halles

1st arr. - 28, rue Coquillière
42 36 93 89
Open 8am-10pm (Sat 10am-6pm). Closed Sun. M° Les Halles.

The wooden clock is still there, a small replica of the bronze one that used to ring to signal the closing of the market at Les Halles. Owner Serge Lesage scrupulously maintains this old bistro's tradition. There are always several special dishes in addition to the excellent open-faced sandwiches, quiches, and good wines bottled on the premises. At lunchtime, a bit of patience is in order; people stand three-deep around the bar, a friendly mix of hipsters elbow-to-elbow with police inspectors, notaries, and shopkeepers. Fully refreshed, you'll have spent a few dozen francs at most.

Clown Bar

11th arr. - 114, rue Amelot
43 55 87 35
Open noon-3:30pm & 6:30pm-1am. Closed Sun. No cards. M° Filles-du-Calvaire.

Countless drawings, figurines, and posters of clowns, clowns, clowns fill this historic establishment near the picturesque Cirque d'Hiver. While the 1919 décor alone is worth the trip, why neglect the marvelous wines (Guerbois's Touraine, Champalou's Vouvray...) and robust terrines served here? Tables are few and hotly contested, so remember to book ahead; if you smile at the staff they may—just may—smile back.

La Côte

2nd arr. - 77, rue de Richelieu
42 97 40 68
Open 7:30am-8:30pm. Closed Sat, Sun. V. M° Bourse.

The fleet-footed Fabre brothers are famed for their victories in waiters' races around the world (the object of these contests is to run to a distant finish line while holding a tray with two full glasses and a bottle of wine). Both also run Paris wine bars: this one is a simple bistro that offers uncomplicated daily specials (rabbit with mustard sauce, bœuf bourguignon), excellent cheeses, and a varied choice of wines from the Loire Valley and Beaujolais. A large, eclectic clientele moves in at lunchtime, and the staff is sometimes flustered by the crush.

Les Coteaux

15th arr. - 26, bd Garibaldi
47 34 83 48
Open 10am-10pm (Mon 10am-7:30pm). Closed Sat, Sun. V. M° Sèvres-Lecourbe.

In this bright, tiny dining room a cheerful staff serves generous charcuteries (the house terrine is plunked down on the table, so you can serve yourself!), warming *plats du jour* (we liked the sage-scented veal stew on a bed of fresh pasta), and nicely matured cheeses. Owners Bernard and Évelyne Olry have put together a small but interesting wine list that includes an ample choice of offerings by the glass.

Le Coude-Fou

4th arr. - 12, rue du Bourg-Tibourg - 42 77 15 16
Open daily noon-4pm & 6pm-2am (Sun 6pm-2am). V, AE. M° Hôtel-de-Ville.

Le Coude Fou has more elbowroom since it annexed the shop next door. The place is brighter and airier, too, a real plus for the atmosphere. Conversations flow freely among the tables, over dishes like duck pot-au-feu, foie gras, and boudin. The house usually offers about 30 wines, half of them by the glass. The Côtes-du-Rhônes and Loire Valley options are particularly well chosen, and there are some appealing little wines from Savoie. The reception and service are a tad warmer than they used to be. For a change of pace (and a 120-wine list) visit Les Fous d'en Face just across the street. It is run by wine fanatic Philippe Llorca, founder of Le Coude Fou.

La Courtille

20th arr. - 1, rue des Envierges - 46 36 51 59
Open daily noon-3pm & 8pm-11pm. V. M° Pyrénées.

Atop the picturesque heights of Belleville, a working-class district where Édith Piaf and Maurice Chevalier frolicked as kids, two noted wine wallahs, François Morel of the neighboring Cave des Envierges (see below) and his associate, Bernard Pontonnier, preside over La Courtille, a spiffy wine bar-cum-brasserie. Come on up (the view is terrific) to feast on such earthy delights as oxtail salad, boudin with caramelized apples, or blanquette de veau, all perfect foils for the astutely chosen growers' wines (we especially like Foillard's manly Morgon). Photos by Willy Ronis of Belleville in the 1950s punctuate the airy, ivory and pine-green décor.

L'Échanson

14th arr. - 89, rue Daguerre
43 22 20 00
Open noon-2:30pm & 8pm-10:30pm. Closed Sun, Mon. V. M° Denfert-Rochereau.

Luc and Véronique's eclectic wine list leans ever so slightly toward the Loire, but there are plenty Corsican, Italian, and Alsatian bottles to keep things interesting. If you ask the owners to choose for you (tell them you like to be surprised), they'll be happy to oblige. As for the food, it runs to laudably rendered brasserie favorites and a few Provençal dishes. Great desserts.

Find the address you are looking for, quickly and easily, in the index.

L'Écluse Bastille

11th arr. - 13, rue de la Roquette - 48 05 19 12
Open daily noon-1:30am. M° Bastille.

The latest link in the Écluse chain boasts the chic atmosphere, trendy clientele, stylish staff, and huge range of Bordeaux that are the company's trademarks. Sign of the times: tariffs have dropped on many of the most illustrious bottles. Lower prices have increased demand, so the wine list is in constant flux. But you can depend on discovering lots of affordable, attractive options (last holiday season, for instance, Château d'Yquem was being offered by the glass—a rare find at any price). As for the food, it is uncomplicated and fresh, based on top-quality ingredients: smoked goose breast, carpaccio, foie gras, steak tartare, and salades composées are the mainstays.

L'Écluse François-Ier

8th arr. - 64, rue François-Ier
47 20 77 09
Open daily noon-1am. M° George-V.

See *text above.*

L'Écluse Les Halles

1st arr. - 5, rue Mondétour
40 41 08 73
Open daily noon-1am. M° Étienne-Marcel.

A high-class operation like L'Écluse is rare in these parts, where tourist traps and grungy cafés abound. You'll spot the familiar façade at the end of the Rue Rambuteau, tucked behind the Forum des Halles. Inside, a comfortable room and a hospitable welcome await.

L'Écluse Grands-Augustins

6th arr. - 15, quai des Grands-Augustins - 46 33 58 74
Open daily noon-1am. M° Saint-Michel.

The old original, and still our favorite Écluse.

L'Enoteca

4th arr. - 25, rue Charles-V
42 78 91 44
Open daily noon-2am. V. M° Sully-Morland.

Should you be seized by an irresistible urge for a bottle of Brunello di Montalcino, Sassicaia, or a lush Malvasia dei Lipari, head over to the Marais and L'Enoteca, the city's first Italian wine bar. An immediate hit with journalists and political types, this engaging trattoria features succulent pasta dishes, authentic Italian snacks, and a mind-boggling, 100 percent Italian wine list. We can't think of a better place for a Sunday-night supper (neither can a lot of other folks—remember to book your table in advance).

L'Entre-Deux-Verres

2nd arr. - 48, rue Sainte-Anne
42 96 42 26
Open 11:30am-3:30pm. Closed Sat, Sun. M° Quatre-Septembre.

The food, the wines, the owners: every element of this charming establishment, lodged in an ancient coaching inn, hails from Bordeaux! Lampreys from the Gironde River are a fixture on the menu, as are wines from the family vineyards in Entre-Deux-Mers and Fronsac.

Les Envierges

20th arr. - 11, rue des Envierges - 46 36 47 84
Open noon-2am (Sat & Sun noon-8pm). Closed Mon, Tue. No cards. M° Pyrénées.

Renaissance man (he holds diplomas in philosophy and art history) and wine meister François Morel launched this, one of the city's most successful *bars à vins,* where customers may hoist a glass or buy a bottle to take home. Loire Valley wines occupy the place of honor, but Morel is not averse to promoting his finds from Roussillon or the Jura. Keeping good company with these choice tipples is Nadine's generous bistro cooking, which gets better with each passing year.

Espace Hérault

5th arr. - 8, rue de la Harpe
46 33 00 56, fax 43 29 81 34
Open noon-2pm & 7:30pm-10:30pm. Closed Sun. V, AE, DC. M° Saint-Michel.

Fragrant wines and inexpensive down-home dishes from the Languedoc-Roussillon region cop top billing at this bistro, the little brother of Le Rabelais next door. Before getting down to cases (bouillabaisse, basil-scented sardines, veal sauté), why not sharpen your appetite with a cool glass of Picpoul-de-Pinet or red Montpeyroux (12 F), accompanied by a selection of lusty tapas?

Le Griffonnier

8th arr. - 8, rue des Saussaies
42 65 17 17
Open 8am-9pm. Closed Sat, Sun. M° Champs-Élysées-Clemenceau.

Listening to the witty exchanges between the boss and his waiter is a great way to hone your repertoire of snappy comebacks in French—if, that is, you can cut through the *patron*'s Auvergnat accent! Robert Savoye's bistro is a favorite with couturiers and gallery owners, who "ooh" and "aah" over the perfectly ripened Fourme d'Ambert (a buttery blue cheese from Auvergne), while sipping heady examples from the bar's collection of Beaujolais, Loire Valley, and Mâconnais wines.

Juvenile's

1st arr. - 47, rue de Richelieu
42 97 46 49
Open noon-midnight (food served until 11pm). Closed Sun. V. M° Palais-Royal.

Juvenile's is new and improved: and the overhaul, by owner Tim Johnston's account, is not over yet—just wait till the air conditioning is installed! But with or without added creature comforts, we've always felt perfectly at ease in this hybrid wine-and-tapas bar, where the Queen's English is spoken, and American understood. The rare Sherries that headline the wine list are ideal companions to the Spanish-style bar snacks (chicken wings, marinated fish, country ham, and such) that are the house specialty. But the vineyards of southern Burgundy, the Rhône, and Bordeaux are not neglected; and the menu even sounds a British note with a yummy roast-beef sandwich and nursery desserts.

Jacques Mélac

11th arr. - 42, rue Léon-Frot
43 70 59 27, fax 43 70 73 10
Open 9am-10:30pm (Mon 9am-6pm). Closed Sat, Sun. V. M° Charonne.

Jacques Mélac turned his father's neighborhood bistro into the city's most celebrated wine bar. And even though he heads an association of Parisian wine-growers (anyone with even one little vine is eligible to join), oversees his own vineyard in Lirac, and has extended his bistro's operating hours, Mélac still brims with energy and enthusiasm. Spreading himself thin? Not at all: at virtually any time of day he can be found behind his *comptoir*, vaunting the merits of his excellent Chinons, Cahors, Chignins, or Coteaux-du-Layon. The food that goes with these heavenly wines is simple, rustic, and absolutely authentic. Try the blue-cheese omelet, the tripe from Aveyron, or the assortment of charcuterie from remote Rouergue. Reservations are not accepted, so either come early or come prepared to wait.

Millésimes

6th arr. - 7, rue Lobineau
46 34 21 15
Open daily 7pm-1am. V. M° Mabillon.

No fewer than 32 wines are offered by the glass, priced from 8 to 25 F. Some of the options are a tasty Cornas from the Tain cooperative, a sturdy Madiran, and a nicely balanced Sauternes. The charming English *patronne* also serves steaks, salads (from 35 to 75 F), and charcuterie.

Some establishments change their closing times without warning. It is always wise to check in advance.

Le Moulin à Vins

18th arr. - 6, rue Burq
42 52 81 27
Open 11am-4pm & 6pm-2am (Sat 6pm-2am). Closed Sun, Mon. M° Abbesses.

Charming Danièle Denis-Bertin presides over this convivial wine bar perched on the flank of the Butte Montmartre. Let her help you choose from among her attractive bottlings, a selection that has won the hearts and minds of the neighborhood's finicky wine buffs. The quality of the *plats du jour* has risen noticeably; so why not order a generous bœuf mode or salade de rillons, along with a glass (or three) of Guerbois's Gamay de Touraine, then finish up with a delicious sweet Jurançon? Don't be surprised if the regulars decide to strike up a song, and someone brings out an accordion—it's a great way to spend an evening in Montmartre.

Aux Négociants

18th arr. - 27, rue Lambert
46 06 15 11
Open noon-8pm (Tue, Thu & Fri noon-10:30pm). Closed Sat, Sun. No cards. M° Lamarck-Caulaincourt.

A Montmartre landmark; one of the pillars of this wine bar is a man dressed up like Aristide Bruand, complete with a jaunty red muffler tossed over his shoulder. But this is no self-consciously picturesque tourist attraction—no, Aux Négociants is a place for serious drinking, as you will observe from the mouth-watering multi-regional wine list that features (among others) bottles from Jasnières and Gaillac.

And for serious chowing down: the food is robust, all homemade, and perfectly delicious (check out the rillettes de canard and the other excellent poultry dishes).

L'Œnothèque

9th arr. - 20, rue Saint-Lazare
48 78 08 76
Open noon-2:30pm & 8pm-10:30pm. Closed Sat, Sun. V. M° Saint-Lazare.

Not so much a bar as a *restaurant à vins* (and one of the best in the city, at that), Daniel Hallée's Œnothèque offers simple yet refined cuisine that perfectly complements his fabulous wine collection. Don't miss the connoisseur's collections of Burgundies and Cognacs.

Le Pain et le Vin

17th arr. - 1, rue de l'Armaillé
47 63 88 29, fax 44 40 41 91
Open 11:30am-3pm & 7pm-12:30am. Closed Sun. V, AE. M° Argentine.

Improved service and fresher, more appealing cuisine have brought us back to this wine bar, created by four enterprising chefs (Dutournier, Morot-Gaudry, Fournier, and Faugeron). The food is hearty and simple (steak tartare, tête de veau, *plats du jour*), but the main attraction is the wine list: 120 different bottlings, chosen by the chefs themselves, of which no fewer than 40 are available by the glass.

Bernard Péret

14th arr. - 6, rue Daguerre
43 22 57 05, fax 43 20 17 64
Open 9:30am-8pm. Closed Mon. V. M° Denfert-Rochereau.

Peering into all the little food shops along this street, we always work up quite a hunger and thirst. But Bernard Péret is here to remedy that, as were his father and grandfather, with plates of zesty mountain sausage and bottles of lipsmacking Morgon. Péret's wine cellar is immense—the shop side sells wine right out onto the sidewalk—but the bistro section is tiny, with six tables and a *zinc* bar where you can sample some fifteen wines by the glass. Hard-to-please English connoisseurs in Paris, who consider Péret's Chénas and Beaujolais Nouveau the best available, can often be found here toward the end of the business day, elbow-to-elbow with the butcher and the baker, comparing the relative merits of a Fleurie and a Juliénas.

Les Pipos

5th arr. - 2, rue de l'École-Polytechnique - 43 54 11 40
Open 8am-9pm (Sat 8am-4pm). Closed Sun. No cards. M° Maubert-Mutualité.

Christine and Jean-Michel Delhoume are a couple of pros in the wine dodge, and their long experience serves their patrons well. This establishment across from the old École Polytechnique

Art on the wall

Paris is officially encouraging the revival of a forgotten art form —the painted wall. The first *mural advertisements* that emerged in the nineteenth century had some artistic merit, but as the suburbs and the Métro spread they lost their impact in a morass of mediocre slogans. In 1943 a law was passed limiting the size of such dubious decoration to a measly fifty square feet. However the work of some talented fly-by-nighters during the '60s and '70s put mural art back on the Paris map, and in 1979 companies were once again allowed to tout their wares on walls. Since 1976 the city authorities have financed the decoration of between five and seven walls a year. Artists are invited to submit designs and a jury selects which ones will give a facelift to some of the city's bleaker buildings. The best way to appreciate a wall painting is probably to come across one by chance, but here are some starters: Philippe Rebuffet's firemen at 45, rue Saint-Fargeau in the twentieth arrondissement; *trompe-l'œil* workmen putting up a sign at 52, rue de Belleville, also in the twentieth; Cueco's little girl playing in the Passage Gatbois, in the twelfth; "Shadow of a tree", a reflection of reality at 47, boulevard de Strasbourg in the tenth arrondissement.

(whose alumni are known as *Pipos*) smells of aged wood and polished metal. It makes for a warm and convivial atmosphere in which to partake of Guerbois's excellent Gamay or René Sinard's fine Côtes-du-Rhône (12 to 16 F a glass), as well as tasty *plats du jour* (49 to 56 F). Inspired by the 1910 phonograph, patrons occasionally burst into song, much to the enjoyment of the owners, who indeed seem in perfect harmony with themselves, their work, and their customers.

Le Relais Chablisien

1st arr. - 4, rue Bertin-Poirée
45 08 53 73
Open 8am-10pm. Closed Sat, Sun. V, AE. M° Châtelet.

As its name suggests, this inviting bistro near the Samaritaine promotes the wines of northern Burgundy: Aligoté (10 F a glass at the bar), Servin's crisp Chablis (14 F), a delicious Irancy (130 F a bottle), and a Givry from Parize (90 F). But owner Christian Faure is no jingoist—his wine list features fine bottles from all over France. Copious portions of eggs poached in red wine, stewed veal, winkles in Chablis with basil, and other hearty treats can be savored near the bar, or under the ancient beams of the tiny mezzanine. Reservations are recommended.

Le Relais du Vin

1st arr. - 85, rue Saint-Denis
45 08 41 08
Open 11am-1:30am. Closed Sun. V. M° Étienne-Marcel.

The Rue Saint-Denis is famed for appealing to appetites somewhere south of the taste buds, but at this Relais, only your palate will be titillated with the likes of Henri Clerc's Burgundy, a green-tinged Saint-Véran, or Guiton's Ladoix Premier Cru. Solid bistro chow is also served here, in an atmosphere reminiscent of the now-vanished Les Halles market district. Friendly prices.

Repaire de Bacchus

6th arr. - 13, rue du Cherche-Midi - 45 44 01 07
Open 10:30am-8:30pm. Closed Sun, Mon. V. M° Sèvres-Babylone.

The best butcher in town and some eminent wine writers frequent this wine shop-cum-bistro, where the "discoveries of the month" are always worth a look and a taste (recent examples have included a suave Montlouis and a floral Crozes-Hermitage blanc). A well-turned-out neighborhood crowd stops in around 1pm for a glass of something good and a plate of charcuterie.

Le Réveil du Xe

10th arr. - 35, rue du Château-d'Eau - 42 41 77 59
Open 7am-8:30pm (Tue 7am-11pm). Closed Sat, Sun. V. M° Château-d'Eau.

Every first Tuesday of the month, Marie-Catherine Vidalenc cooks up a huge pot of aligot (garlicky mashed potatoes with cheese) that brings a tear of nostalgia to the eye of every native-born Auvergnat who tastes it. Her potato pâté, stuffed cabbage, tripe, and down-home charcuteries have a similar effect. Meanwhile, Daniel Vidalenc, son and grandson of bistro proprietors, serves forth the wines he chooses, purchases, and bottles himself (the Chénas and Morgon go for 15 F a glass), as well as excellent growers' wines like Amirault's stunning Bourgueil and Delubac's Cairanne from the Côtes-du-Rhône.

Le Rouge-Gorge

4th arr. - 8, rue Saint-Paul
48 04 75 89
Open 10am-2am. Closed Sun. V. M° Saint-Paul.

After a stroll among the antique dealers (one of whom boasts an enviable collection of corkscrews), why not stop in here and see what good bottles the "theme of the week" has brought forth? Every few weeks, in fact, a different region of France is highlighted. Recently Chinon and Bourgueil were featured, to honor Rabelais's quatercentenary. Excellent Juras, not easy to find, are always on tap here. As for solid sustenance, hot dishes are served at lunchtime (and in the evening, if the noontime crowd hasn't gobbled everything up).

Le Rubis

1st arr. - 10, rue du Marché-Saint-Honoré - 42 61 03 34
Open 7am-10pm (Sat 9am-4pm). Closed Sun. No cards. M° Pyramides.

Ages ago, at this very spot, old Léon Gouin first raised the banner for good wine and excellent charcuterie. In his honor, the regulars—who range from firemen to fashion plates—continue to call the place Chez Léon. After all, the menu has never veered off course, and the selection of wines is still topnotch. The food includes a daily hot special in addition to an enticing array of open-faced sandwiches and cheese and cold meat platters. The only problem of the place is its size; Le Rubis is just too small to handle all its devotees! In the summer, after having done elbow-to-elbow combat to get a glass of wine and some food from the bar, you can carry your conquest out to the sidewalk, where upended wine casks serve honorably as tables.

Le Sancerre

7th arr. - 22, av. Rapp
45 51 75 91
Open 7am-8:30pm. Closed Sun. V, AE. M° Alma-Marceau.

Reserve a table if you want to eat lunch here; in a fancy neighborhood where good bistros are rare, this one fills up fast. And it doesn't lack for personality—the owners, the Mellot family, have plenty of that! The Mellots run the Domaine de la Moussière vineyard, and they sell their Sancerre here direct from their cellars. The menu's omelets, andouillette sausage, and pungent crottin de Chavignol goat cheese make perfect partners for the cool, flinty white wine.

Au Sauvignon

7th arr. - 80, rue des Saints-Pères - 45 48 49 02
Open daily 8:30am-10pm. No cards. M° Sèvres-Babylone.

The changing of the guard (now the "youngsters" have taken over) and the extension of the terrace have fortunately done nothing to alter the style and tone of this popular bistro. The formula for success is simple: a few good wines (oh! that Quincy!) and some appetizing tartines of tangy goat cheese and premium charcuterie (on neighbor Lionel Poilâne's excellent bread, of course).

Au Soleil d'Austerlitz

5th arr. - 18, bd de l'Hôpital
43 31 22 38
Open 6am-9pm (Sat 7am-6pm). Closed Sun. V. M° Saint-Marcel.

An estimable institution, without which the neighborhood just wouldn't be the same. Where to go after meeting a friend at the train station? Or after a meander through the nearby Jardin des Plantes? Come here, for a fruity Régnié (the most recently proclaimed *cru* of Beaujolais) or boss André Calvet's latest discovery. As for solid sustenance, you can count on earthy charcuterie from Aveyron and warming daily specials (try the bœuf bourguignon).

Taverne Henri-IV

1st arr. - 13, pl. du Pont-Neuf
43 54 27 90
Open noon-10pm (Sat noon-4pm). Closed Sun. No cards. M° Pont-Neuf.

At the tip of the Ile de la Cité, poised on the Pont-Neuf, stands Robert Cointepas's noble tavern, now a tourist attraction nearly as popular as the Pyramide du Louvre. Really: the menu's even been printed in Japanese! Still, the regulars—magistrates, police inspectors, publishers, journalists, lawyers—manage to hold their ground. They steadfastly defend their turf, their tartines of excellent cheese and charcuterie, and their access to the premium Beaujolais, Montlouis, and Bordeaux personally selected by Robert Cointepas. Each October, Cointepas (the "patriarch" of Paris wine bars) travels to the vineyards to choose his wines, then brings them back to town, bottles them himself, and pours them in peak condition for his customers all year long. You can sample his finds at lunchtime in a jolly, boisterous ambience, or in quieter surroundings after, say, 7pm when a friendly neighborhood crowd clusters round the bar.

Aux Tonneaux des Halles

1st arr. - 28, rue Montorgueil
42 33 36 19
Open 7am-1am. Closed Sun, Mon. V. M° Les Halles.

The nostalgia is thick enough to cut with a knife. Take in the pre-war décor, the ghostly photos of the now-demolished Halles, the vintage telephone booth... as you dig in to equally old-fashioned French fare: museau vinaigrette, herring fillets, charcuterie, et al. To wash them down, order a bottle of Guy Breton's Beaujolais Villages (90 F).

Le Val d'Or

8th arr. - 28, av. Franklin-Roosevelt - 43 59 95 81
Open 7:30am-9pm (Sat 9am-5pm). Closed Sun. V. M° Franklin-D.-Roosevelt.

Géraud (not Gérard, thank you) Rongier, who hails from deep in the Auvergne, is one of the grand masters of the wine profession. This little bistro near Saint-Philippe-du-Roule fills up at midday with advertising and fashion execs, civil servants from the Ministry of the Interior, and folks from the nearby TV stations, who come to sample his selections from the Loire Valley, his Côte-de-Brouilly, an exemplary Mâcon-Clessé, and a lipsmacking Aloxe-Corton. All are offered at highly competitive prices. As for more solid sustenance, Rongier makes tasty tartines with succulent hams that he poaches himself, home-prepared rillettes, and perfectly ripened cheeses.

Le Valençay

4th arr. - 11, bd du Palais
43 54 64 67
Open 8am-10:30pm. Closed Sun. V. M° Cité.

Of the many wine bars that have sprung up around the Law Courts, Le Valençay stands out. Step up to the bar along with the cohort of thirsty lawyers and judges, and plead for a glass of berry-fresh Anjou (8.50 F) or flinty Quincy (12 F) as an apéritif. Hungry? Then why not do justice to the 65 F menu that offers a starter, a steak, and a glass of red wine?

Le Verre-Bouteille

17th arr. - 85, av. des Ternes
45 74 01 02
Open noon-3pm & 7:30pm-5am (Sun brunch noon-4pm). Closed Sat. V, AE, DC. M° Ternes.

Now you know where to come at 2am when you're famished and in need of a restorative glass of wine. Simple food, speedy service, excellent wine list (Champagnes are not forgotten).

Le Vin des Rues

14th arr. - 21, rue Boulard
43 22 19 78
Open 10am-8pm. Closed Sun, Mon. No cards. M° Denfert-Rochereau.

The atmosphere of this Everyman's bistro is enlivened by Jean Chanrion's excellent choice of Beaujolais and Mâcons, and the daily specials he crafts from the best ingredients. Ah, his blanquette de veau with a little glass of Brouilly...

Willi's Wine Bar

1st arr. - 13, rue des Petits-Champs - 42 61 05 09
Open noon-11pm. Closed Sun. V. M° Bourse.

We bet even Joan of Arc and Napoléon would embrace Englishmen as *sympathiques* as Mark Williamson and Tim Johnston! They powered the the wine-bar wave that hit Paris about ten years back, and they introduced a new generation to the top wines (Cornas, Côte-Rôties, Hermitage...) from the Côtes-du-Rhône. We alway look forward to trying their most recent discoveries, from France or farther afield: the oft-renewed list boasts some gems from Australia, California, Italy, and Spain. The handsome bar and comfortable dining room attract a crowd of intellectuals, bankers, and fashion folk at midday; lots of English-speaking regulars turn up at night. The menu is mainly French, and the food, in our opinion, just gets better all the time.

NIGHTLIFE

BEER BARS

L'Académie de la Bière

5th arr. - 88 bis, bd de Port-Royal - 43 54 66 65
Open daily noon-2am (Sun noon-8pm). V. M° Port-Royal.

As the name suggests, those dedicated to the delights of King Gambrinus (the mythical inventor of beer) gather here to clink mugs into the night. University types from the neighborhood sit alone resting their eyes on the collections of bottles and labels that adorn the walls. The wooden benches are a bit hard, and at busy times elbows get pressed pretty close together, but these quibbles are small beer compared to the tasty house brew, drawn perfectly under the practiced eye of a true artist of the tap, Pierre Marion.

Le Bar Belge

17th arr. - 75, av. de Saint-Ouen - 46 27 41 01
Open 11am-3am. Closed Sun. V. M° La Fourche.

Two of the many lusty beers on tap at this authentically Flemish watering hole are a Lindermans kriek and a lambic Vieux Bruges; the superb list of bottled beers is topped by Belgium's famous Judas-sur-Lie. Like the other jolly habitués who gather here, we always order a plate of the excellent jambon d'Ardenne to accompany our brew.

La Brasserie de l'Est

10th arr. - 78, bd de Strasbourg - 46 07 00 94
Open daily 5:30am-2am. V, AE, DC. M° Gare-de-l'Est.

When you spy this big old brasserie, situated just across from the Gare de l'Est, you're likely to think it's a tourist trap. But you'd be wrong. The draft beer served here is among the best in Paris. Don't miss the bière de mars (March beer), a sure harbinger of spring. All year long, you can quaff the delicious weissbier (white beer) brewed from wheat.

Carr's

1st arr. - 1, rue du Mont-Thabor - 42 60 60 26
Open daily noon-1:30am. V, AE, DC. M° Tuileries.

Uncontestably the smartest Irish spot in town. The quasi-Victorian façade conceals a cozy interior, where customers are served by stylish waiters. The ambience is more *Financial Times* than *High Times*, but the Guinness and Kilkenny please every faction. Good food, too.

Finnegan's Wake

5th arr. - 9, rue des Boulangers - 46 34 23 65
Open daily 4pm-12:30am (Sun noon-6pm). M° Jussieu.

Though it's a recent addition to the Latin Quarter scene, Finnegan's Wake is already a popular student haunt (they work up a powerful thirst poring over dusty tomes in the library). English is spoken in this friendly Irish pub, where the draft beer is drawn as it should be: slow and easy. Folk music can be heard here, of an evening.

Flann O'Brien

1st arr. - 6, rue Bailleul
42 60 13 58
Open daily 4pm-2am. No cards. M° Louvre.

The most authentically Irish of the city's pubs. James, the owner, makes sure that the Guinness is served just as it would be in Dublin or Cork: rich, smooth, with virtually no gas bubbles.

Au Général La Fayette

9th arr. - 52, rue La Fayette
47 70 59 08
Open 10am-3am (Sat 10am-4am). Closed Sun. V. M° Cadet.

The premises have just been remodeled and enlarged, so don't hesitate to come and join the jolly jostlers around the convivial bar. Order a cool pint of Guinness or a Belgian brew, or choose an indoor or terrace table for a light meal (salads, charcuterie, herrings, cheese...). The service is simpatico, and so is the cosmopolitan clientele.

Au Gobelet d'Argent

1st arr. - 11, rue du Cygne
42 33 29 82
Open daily 4pm-2am. No cards. M° Étienne-Marcel.

This is *the* place in town for Guinness and loads of Irish ambience.

La Gueuze

5th arr. - 19, rue Soufflot
43 54 63 00, fax 43 54 12 59
Open noon-2am. Closed Sun. V, AE. RER Luxembourg (B).

What appears from the street to be a modest tavern turns out to be a huge beer hall, large enough to accommodate the entire Sorbonne! Teachers and students alike come around at noon and in the evening to sample a classic array of Belgian brews, sufficiently inclusive to satisfy any lover of fine suds. From the menu, you can choose a tartine (open sandwich) of herbed cream cheese on hearty dark bread, and wash it down with a solid Duvel beer.

The James Joyce

17th arr. - 71, bd Gouvion-St-Cyr - 44 09 70 32
Open daily noon-1:30am. No cards. M° Porte-Maillot.

The great Irish writer, who was not averse to taking a drop now and again, presides over this smart, roomy, three-level pub near the Porte-Maillot. Here you can not only quaff a Guinness or Kilkenny in uncommon comfort, but lunch or dine as well on decent *plats du jour*. Sunday brunch is a specialty, and live Irish music or jazz are featured regularly.

Kitty O'Shea's

2nd arr. - 10, rue des Capucines - 40 15 00 30
Open 12:30pm-1:30am (Sat & Sun noon-2am). V, AE. M° Opéra.

Kitty doesn't have any culinary ambitions; one comes here to put down a few Smithwicks and Guinnesses, served on tap at ideal temperature and pressure—just like in Dublin. The smoked salmon, the chicken pie, and the Irish coffee never fail to be everything the regulars expect them to be. The décor, which is half-bar, half-dining room, has its charm, and is reliably packed on weekends. The city's biggest Saint Patrick's Day party is held here annually.

Le Manneken-Pis

2nd arr. - 4, rue Daunou
48 42 85 03
Open daily 11:30am-2am. No cards. M° Opéra.

These folks are pros in the beer biz: they'll tell you all sorts of interesting facts about what you're drinking, and if they like your face, they'll let you in on some of their rarest brews. Belgian monastery beers hold the place of honor, with krieks and gueuzes galore, but the bar's selection extends to all the best French and German brews. A roster of hearty Belgian dishes—carbonnade, waterzoï, and the like—will take care of any hunger pangs. Warm wood-paneled interior; even warmer atmosphere!

La Marine

6th arr. - 59, bd du Montparnasse - 45 48 27 70
Open daily 9am-1am. No cards. M° Montparnasse.

Choose a seat on the terrace (gee, what a great view of the Tour Montparnasse!), a booth inside, or—our favorite—a stool at the bar, then set about the task of selecting your brew. The range of offerings is superb, and updated regularly, but your best bet is usually the "Beer of the Month," whatever its provenance. To go with, try a satisfying croque-monsieur made with country bread or the yummy Welsh rarebit.

L'Oiseau de Feu

11th arr. - 12, place de la Bastille - 40 19 07 52
Open daily 9am-5am. V. M° Bastille.

An off-shoot of the popular Général Lafayette tavern (see above), this spiffing establishment offers a fine selection of expertly drawn draft beers and a short menu of uncomplicated food. The view of the new Opera house is a plus—or a minus, depending on your tastes in architecture.

O'Neil

6th arr. - 20, rue des Canettes
46 33 36 66
Open daily 11am-2am. M° Mabillon.

Born in Lille a few years back, this chain of microbreweries is a growing success all over France. The beers on offer are brewed right on the premises for ultimate freshness. The selection available depends on the season, but there is always a crisp lager, a mellow amber, and a dark stout on hand. Barrels of beer can be purchased for home drinking, and there is a short list of basic dishes to keep the suds company. Convivial atmosphere.

Le Sous-Bock Tavern

1st arr. - 49, rue Saint-Honoré - 40 26 46 61
Open daily 11am-5am (Sun 3pm-5am). V. M° Louvre.

No fewer than 400 beers and 200 whiskies are on offer at this bustling bar, now a popular fixture on the Paris pub scene. The concise but appealing menu features classic brasserie fare (we can recommend the fine rillettes and civet de sanglier). For entertainment, there's a giant video screen and recorded—mainly country—music.

Find the address you are looking for, quickly and easily, in the index.

La Taverne de Nesle

6th arr. - 32, rue Dauphine
43 26 38 36
Open daily 8pm-4am (Sat 8pm-5am). No cards. M° Dauphine.

Hundreds of beers (ten on tap) including several premium Belgian krieks are served in this tavern, where you can wind up a soirée by watching ear-splitting videos or the antics of last-round revelers. Not your idea of entertainment? Then come by early, around 8pm, for an apéritif and a relaxed chat in a much calmer, more sophisticated atmosphere.

La Taverne des Halles

1st arr. - 12, rue de la Cossonnerie - 42 36 26 44
Open daily 8am-2am. V, AE, DC. M° Les Halles.

Saucy waiters whirl about the Taverne with trays of excellent draft or bottled beer, each variety served in its appropriate glass. If you crave a rare, strongly flavored brew, we recommend La Maudite from Quebec. The cheerful ambience (there's a lively terrace for fine days) attracts quite a crowd, an extra assurance that the beers are good and fresh. The food, however, is quite a bit less appealing.

Tigh Johnny

2nd arr. - 55, rue Montmartre
42 33 91 33
Open daily 4pm-12:30am. No cards. M° Les Halles.

The boisterous Irish atmosphere is accented by live music, usually ditties and ballads direct from the Emerald Isle. Guinness stout is served at precisely the right temperature, topped with the correct amount of foam.

CABARETS

Crazy Horse

8th arr. - 12, av. George-V
47 23 32 32
Open daily from 8:45pm. V, AE, DC. M° George-V.

For nearly 25 years now the "Crazy" has entertained convoys of tourists with its bevy of buxom beauties. Clad only (and only briefly!) in leather wasp-waisters, these *femmes fatales, the most sophisticated in the universe,* (so states the program) cavort and form—presumedly—erotic tableaux. But for our money (between 400 and 600 F, to be precise), the most exciting aspect of the show is the astonishingly inventive lighting, which clothes Lova Moor, Betty Buttocks, and their cohorts with laser beams. Herculean bouncers stationed at the doors make sure that the atmosphere doesn't turn too steamy. The show is stylish and professional, yes; but is it sexy...?

Lido de Paris

8th arr. - 116bis, av. des Champs-Élysées - 40 76 56 10
Open daily from 8pm. V, AE, DC. M° George-V.

Closer in spirit to an athletic event than a cabaret performance, the new *C'est Magique* revue cost $14 million to create. The fast-moving show now features even more breathtaking acts, including "Ming," a Chinese juggler with large vases, a stunning tennis racket juggler, ice skating acts, and of course, the 60 elegant Bluebell Girls donning on more contemporary costumes backed up by highly original special effects and dozens of computer operated stage sets. The Lido offers a dinner (8pm at 850 F) and two shows (10pm & midnight at 510 F). On your way out, the Lido boutique displays 140 gift items and fashion accessories to commemorate this happy experience.

Chez Michou

18th arr. - 80, rue des Martyrs
40 06 16 04
Open 9pm-1am. Closed Mon. No cards. M° Pigalle.

The camp just doesn't come any higher. Michou (the man in the blinding dinner jacket) runs a fast-paced, deliciously vulgar drag show featuring parodies of French stars of stage and screen. Even if you can't identify Mireille Mathieu or the other personalities caricatured, the actors are so outrageously funny that you'll split your sides anyway. You'll pay 550 F for dinner, drinks, and the revue.

Le Moulin Rouge

18th arr. - 82, bd de Clichy
46 06 00 19
Revue daily: 10pm & midnight. V, AE. M° Blanche.

You've all seen the movie; now you can see the genuine article—in the flesh! Tradition is everything here, and the justly famous Doriss Girls (they really *are* adorable) scrupulously respect it: twice a night, seven nights a week, they prance on stage and cancan their cans off! Dinner, served at 8pm, will set you back a cool 670 F, while the revue alone costs 465 F.

Paradis Latin

5th arr. - 28, rue du Cardinal-Lemoine - 43 25 28 28
Open: 8pm (dinner), 9:45pm (revue). Closed Tue. V, AE. M° Cardinal-Lemoine.

What can we say about a cloying floor show with dancers who look like a nice bunch of sorority sisters decked out in feathers and rhinestones? The revue is updated religiously once a year, but you can count on the usual obligatory numbers—French cancan, erotic tango, and so on, performed in a magnificent Belle Époque theater designed by Gustave Eiffel.

COCKTAIL BARS

Banana Café

1st arr. - 13-15, rue de la Ferronnerie - 42 33 35 31
Open daily 4:30pm-dawn. V, AE. M° Les Halles.

A hip, mixed (gay, straight) crowd creates an electric atmosphere that never dims, from dusk to dawn. Lethal cocktails (try the Cointreau-Caïpiranha); happy hour from 4 to 7pm.

Le Bar du Cercle Ledoyen

8th arr. - Pavillon Ledoyen, carré des Champs-Élysées
47 42 23 23
Open daily 11am-2am. V, AE, DC, MC. M° Champs-Élysées-Clemenceau.

Not just a swanky watering hole, this posh bar set in a verdant corner of the Champs-Élysées is a veritable oasis for the strung-out and stressed-out. The classy interior bears the stamp of celebrity decorator Jacques Grange. Attentive service.

Birdland

6th arr. - 8, rue Guisarde
43 26 97 59
Open 6pm-dawn (Sun 10pm-dawn). V. M° Mabillon.

The owners recently refurbished this cozy nest for jazz-loving night owls, situated in the heart of Saint-Germain-des-Prés. Sip a cocktail (a few non-alcholic offerings are available) and lend an ear to what is surely one of the finest collections of jazz recordings in town.

La Casbah

11th arr. - 18-20, rue de la Forge-Royale - 43 71 71 89
Open daily 7pm-5am. V, AE, DC, MC. M° Faidherbe-Chaligny.

A neo-Moorish nightspot with a fascinating "pre-worn" décor, La Casbah draws a hip, handsome crowd with its exotic cocktails and feverish atmosphere. You can join these trendy revelers if (and only if) the surly doorman/bouncer likes your looks.

Chapman

2nd arr. - 25, rue Louis-le-Grand - 47 42 98 19
Open 11pm-2am (Sat 5pm-2am). Closed Sun. V. M° Opéra.

Just a short putt away from the Opéra, this wood-paneled bar festooned with golfers' paraphernalia plays the "English club" card to the hilt. Bernard, the owner and chief mixologist, is an alumnus of the famed Harry's Bar. He welcomes a clean-cut crew of habitués (stockbrokers and such) with cleverly concocted cocktails and a soothing ambience.

China Club

12th arr. - 50, rue de Charenton - 43 43 82 02
Open daily 7pm-2am (Fri & Sat 10:30pm-4am). V. M° Bastille.

The chic denizens of the Bastille nightlife district like to forgather at this glamorous, multilevel club: either at the long ground-floor cocktail bar, upstairs in the smoky *fumoir* where choice Cognacs and Armagnacs are poured, or downstairs in the late-night bar (weekends only) dubbed "Le Sing Song."

Closerie des Lilas

6th arr. - 171, bd du Montparnasse - 43 26 70 50
Open daily 11am-1:30am. V, AE, DC, MC. M° Vavin.

Sure, this place once served the likes of Hemingway and Gide, though now only Jean-Édern Hallier (who?) holds court at his table by the door. But there is still a superb décor, particularly inviting in warm weather with the laurel-enclosed terrace, the high-class, polished service, and the excellent cocktails. Snobby and expensive? You bet. But remember, you're not out for a beer at the neighborhood tavern.

Le Comptoir

1st arr. - 14, rue Vauvilliers
40 26 26 66
Open daily 11am-2am (Sat & Sun 11am-4am). V. M° Les Halles.

Here's a splendid place to mingle with a very Parisian throng, and down a selection of delicious tapas accompanied by an appealing choice of spirited libations. On Friday and Saturday nights, the presence of a DJ keeps the joint jumping, but effectively thwarts any effort at conversation.

Le Dépanneur

9th arr. - 27, rue Fontaine
40 16 40 20
Open daily 24 hours. V. M° Place-de-Clichy.

"Tequila, tequila, arriba!" Here comes Miss Tequila, packing icy bottles of Jalisco in her holsters, a cartridge belt loaded with shot glasses slung across her chest, ready to serve a "rapido" to her hard-drinking customers. Strategically located within shootin' distance of the big guns on the Pigalle nightlife circuit, this neo-postmodern watering hole is open 24 hours a day, every day.

Le Forum

8th arr. - 4, bd Malesherbes
42 65 37 86
Open daily 11:30am-2am (Sat & Sun 5:30pm-2am). V. M° Madeleine.

This is the quintessential French cocktail bar, with flawless service, a lovely décor—even the cocktail shakers are works of art—and an iron-clad policy of discretion. At about seven in the evening, couples (legit and less so) drift in for an intimate chat before heading home. The 150 cocktails and the extraordinary selection of Scotch whiskies (40 single malts) are accompanied by olives and peanuts. The deep leather armchairs are comfortable, and the 1930s atmosphere soothes the spirit.

George-V

8th arr. - 31, av. George-V
47 23 54 00
Open daily 11am-1:30am. V, AE, DC, MC. M° George-V.

A bar for high-flying corporate types out to celebrate a major contract, or film producers out to sign a major backer. Famous faces? Not many... A lot of expensive suits, though, can be seen in this tony hotel bar. We wouldn't choose this spot for a tryst, but it's fine for engaging in civil conversation while nursing a whisky selected by Monsieur Jacques (he's fluently conversant on the subject of Scotch).

Le Grand Hôtel

9th arr. - Le Grand Hôtel, 2, rue Scribe
40 07 32 32
Open daily 11am-2am. V, AE, DC, MC. M° Opéra.

Come cocktail time, dandies, rich idlers, and other elegant fauna gather beneath the Grand Hôtel's immense glass-and-steel dome to see and be seen. Intimate it's not, but the scene is a hoot, and the expertly mixed drinks are served with style.

Harry's Bar

2nd arr. - 5, rue Daunou
42 61 71 14
Open daily 10:30am-4am. AE, DC. M° Opéra.

Time weighs lightly on this Parisian landmark, which looks much the same today as it did at the Liberation. The main bar is a bustling, convivial place where sports fans (particularly rugby rooters) discuss their favorite teams. The downstairs piano bar is more conducive to quiet conversation over a Blue Lagoon cocktail.

L'Hôtel

6th arr. - 13, rue des Beaux-Arts - 43 25 27 22
Open daily 7am-2am. V, AE, DC. M° Odéon.

A half-dozen tables, a few stools, the gentle

The Ile Saint-Louis opens up

Instead of huddling behind high walls as was usual for many of the capital's finest residences, the town houses here were built facing the Seine to give their occupants the benefit of a view and fresh air. King Louis XIII acquired in 1611 the two separate islands that today constitute the Ile Saint-Louis, had them joined with two stone bridges and started 50 years of building work under the supervision of architect Louis Le Vau. The result is a harmonious architectural whole best enjoyed during a leisurely stroll. The Church of Saint Louis-en-l'Ile, with its original ironwork clock and wooden sculptures, is the only monument on the island open to the public.

sound of a fountain, warm colors, a cheeky bartender... and the cocktails—such as the Bélier (vodka, Curaçao, grenadine, fruit juices)—are good, too. This is a romantic spot to wind up an evening on the town.

Hurlingham Polo Bar

17th arr. - Le Méridien, 81, bd Gouvion-Saint-Cyr
40 68 34 34
Open daily 11:30am-2am. V, AE, DC, MC. M° Porte-Maillot.

A pleasant place to hoist a "wee dram" in cheerful company. Georges and his staff will initiate you into the lore of rare old whiskies amid improbably British surroundings—leather armchairs, tartan fabrics, a gas-log fire: the works! Champagnes and judiciously chosen wines are also on offer.

Meurice

1st arr. - Hôtel Meurice, 228, rue de Rivoli - 44 58 10 60
Open daily 10:30am-2am. V, AE, DC, MC. M° Tuileries.

One visits this bar chiefly to sip tea or nibble on a toast au caviar (365 F) in a sumptuous "Pompadour" décor (Madame herself would surely have approved). But if the need for stronger stimulation should arise, the waiter can dip into a classy selection of whiskies and Armagnacs.

Le Normandy

1st arr. - Hôtel Normandy, 7, rue de l'Échelle - 42 60 30 21
Open daily 11am-midnight (Sat & Sun 11am-1pm & 6pm-midnight). V. M° Palais-Royal.

The Normandy's comfy Chesterfield armchairs don't attract the preen-and-be-seen set, but you may hear the confidential murmurings of journalists and others enjoying a pre-Comédie Française drink. This is a bar where single women can feel at ease, and the cocktails shaken up by Serge, Jean, and Xavier are as fine as every other feature of this mellow hotel bar. There is a fine choice of brandies, featuring Cognacs from Delamain and a superb Armagnac 1957, Cuvées Normandie.

La Perla

4th arr. - 26, rue François-Miron - 42 77 59 40
Open daily noon-2am. V, AE. M° Saint-Paul.

La Perla was a pioneer in the wave of Mexican bars that hit Paris a few years back. The corner premises on a charming street in the Marais give patrons a wide-angle view of the passing scene, which they may contemplate while enjoying a Dos Equis, a shot of tequila, or a margarita special. The exotic cocktails lubricate the friendly mixing that goes on here of an evening. A short menu of decent Mexican dishes is served.

Plaza Bar Anglais

8th arr. - 25, av. Montaigne
47 23 78 33
Open daily 11am-2am. V, AE, DC, MC. M° Alma-Marceau.

Classier than this, there isn't. Here is a bar where you can talk business or speak of love, safe in the knowledge that you will be neither interrupted nor importuned. Service is impeccable and discreet; in the evening, a piano provides unobtrusive background music.

Raphaël

16th arr. - 17, av. Kléber
44 28 00 28
Open daily 11am-midnight. V. M° Kléber.

The bar of the Hotel Raphaël is opulent and refined, with bronze sculptures, carved wood, plush carpets, and expertly mixed cocktails. Exclusive and deliberately expensive, this bar is a favorite watering hole for stars seeking a respite from their admiring throngs.

Rosebud

14th arr. - 11 bis, rue Delambre - 43 35 38 54
Open daily 7pm-2am. V. M° Vavin.

With each passing decade, a new generation of appreciative fans is introduced to this Montparnasse landmark, where intellectuals and other observers of the urban scene exchange ideas over a drink and a bowl of the bar's famous chili.

Le Scribe

9th arr. - Hôtel Scribe, 1, rue Scribe - 44 71 24 24
Open daily 8:30am-2am. V, AE, DC, MC. M° Opéra.

Along with the rest of the hotel, Le Scribe's bar got a much-needed facelift which transformed it into a pluperfect hotel bar, where guests and visitors may enjoy excellent cocktails, soft piano music, and private conversation in newly luxurious surroundings.

Le Vigny

8th arr. - Hôtel Vigny, 9-11, rue Balzac - 40 75 04 39
Open daily 7am-2am. V, AE, DC, MC. M° George-V.

A beautiful bar in an equally handsome hotel, just off the Champs-Élysées.

Polished wood, mellow leather, and soft lights create a luxurious setting that is dependably quiet and discreet—unless, of course, a gaggle of groupies awaiting the appearance of their idol has taken over the turf! A glass of premium whisky will set you back about 80 F.

Washington Square

8th arr. - 42, rue de Laborde
45 22 08 36
Hours vary. Closed Sun, Mon. V. M° Saint-Augustin.

A snug little spot that draws a lively crowd, with a sprinkling of sport and show-biz celebrities. In a neighborhood that is unusually sedate, this bar provides welcome signs of life after dark, with music and expertly mixed cocktails.

LIVE MUSIC

Le Baiser Salé

1st arr. - 58, rue des Lombards - 42 33 37 71
Open daily 6:30pm-6am. V. M° Châtelet.

For jazz fans eager to discover talented musicians destined for fame (if not fortune, the jazz life being what it is); years from now, you'll be able to say "I saw them play in Paris before anybody ever heard of them...". The music starts around 10pm. First drink: 70 F, 30 F thereafter.

Le Bilboquet

6th arr. - 13, rue Saint-Benoît
45 48 81 84
Open daily 10pm-dawn. V, AE, DC. M° Saint-Germain-des-Prés.

A temple of jazz since 1947, and still going strong. Le Bilboquet is a Saint-Germain landmark, where Charlie Parker, Kenny Clarke, and many have others put in appearances. The mood here is warm and intimate, the music hot and cool by turns. The restau-rant now offers a more- than-decent set menu, reasonably priced at 187 F.

Caveau de la Huchette

5th arr. - 5, rue de la Huchette - 43 26 65 05
Open daily 9:30pm-2:30am (Fri 9:30pm-3am, Sat & hol eves 9:30pm-4am). M° Saint-Michel.

This is a shrine to good old-fashioned swing, boogie, and Dixieland, situated in a cellar in the Latin Quarter. You'll feel you've been transported back to the 1950s: there's a live orchestra, clouds of smoke, romantic young tourists, graduate students who never will, and some veteran dancers with a real sense of rhythm for the jitterbug and bebop. The drinks are inexpensive, too.

Club Lionel Hampton

17th arr. - Le Méridien,
81, bd Gouvion-Saint-Cyr
40 68 30 42
Open daily from 10:30pm. V, AE, DC, MC. M° Porte-Maillot.

Opera in Paris

There's no opera at the Opéra at present: the richly ornamented Palais Garnier, for over one hundred years the city's temple of lyric art, is now the scene of ballet and other dance performances, as well as the occasional concert. The Opéra Bastille, one of President Mitterrand's most controversial contributions to Parisian architecture, now hosts the official lyric season. Lately, however, some of the most acclaimed opera productions in Paris have been staged at the Théâtre de la Ville. Other venues that regularly present operatic performances are the Théâtre des Champs-Élysées and the Opéra Comique. For information about specific productions, check *Le Monde* **or** *Le Figaro's* **magazine supplement on Wednesdays, or** *Pariscope* **or** *L'Officiel des Spectacles,* **which also appear on Wednesdays.**

Opéra Palais Garnier, **place de l'Opéra, 9th arr. Reservation: 47 42 53 71.**

Opéra de Paris Bastille, **20 rue de Lyon, 12th arr. Reservations: 44 73 13 00.**

Théâtre de la Ville, **2 place du Châtelet, 4th arr. Reservations: 42 74 22 77.**

Théâtre des Champs-Élysées, **15 avenue Montaigne, 8th arr. Reservations: 49 52 50 50.**

Opéra Comique (Salle Favart), **5 rue Favart, 2nd arr. Reservations: 42 86 88 83.**

A *Who's Who* of jazz and blues greats have played in this plush, comfortable lounge, located in one of the city's finest hotels. We can recall spending memorable evenings here with Fats Domino, Monty Alexander, John Hendrix, the Count Basie orchestra, Linda Hopkins, and many more.

Au Duc des Lombards

1st arr. - 42, rue des Lombards - 42 33 22 88
Open daily 6pm-4:30am. V. M° Châtelet.

A popular jazz venue somehow reminiscent of an English pub, where prices are comparatively low (the first drink is tariffed at 58 F). Though the audience doesn't listen in religious silence, musicians like to play here anyway because the acoustics are just right. Relaxed atmosphere, quality bands. Jam sessions on Tuesdays. The restaurant upstairs (a favorite with musicians passing through town) is open until 4am.

L'Eustache

1st arr. - 37, rue Berger
40 26 23 20
Open daily 10:30pm-2am. V. M° Les Halles.

Lots of people, lots of noise: L'Eustache is one big party, night after night, with live jazz featured from Thursday through Saturday. The more solemn sort of jazz buff spurns it absolutely, but L'Eustache does not pretend to be a concert hall. The acoustics are so-so, yet we've heard some terrific horn blowing here.

New Morning

10th arr. - 7-9, rue des Petites-Écuries - 45 23 51 41
Open daily from 8:30pm. V. M° Château-d'Eau.

Unquestionably the city's premier jazz club, the scene of unforgettable evenings with the late Chet Baker and Stan Getz, Gary Burton, Betty Carter, Oscar Peterson, Archie Shepp... Some New Age and World acts also make occasional appearances. The New Morning's 400-seat auditorium boasts surprisingly comfortable seating and superb acoustics. You can purchase tickets (110 F) at the door an hour before the gig.

Le Petit Journal Montparnasse

14th arr. - 13, rue du Commandant-Mouchotte
43 21 56 70
Open 9pm-2am. Closed Sun. M° Montparnasse.

Le Petit Journal Montparnasse features first-rate jazz musicians in a room with good sight lines, good acoustics, and a long, comfortable bar. Its sister establishment at 71, boulevard Saint-Michel, leans to swing and Dixieland bands, but the Claude Bolling Trio plays there with some regularity, as does saxophonist Benny Waters, and plenty more. Both clubs offer a constantly rotating roster of musicians for a solid selection of contemporary and vintage jazz.

Le Petit Opportun

1st arr. - 15, rue des Lavandières Sainte-Opportune - 42 36 01 36
Open 9pm-dawn. Closed Mon. V. M° Châtelet.

An evening at the Petit Op' is musically rewarding, but physically resembles a descent into hell. A dark, cramped, smoky cellar is the scene of remarkable concerts by the distinguished likes of Steve Lacy and Steve Potts, Aldo Romano, and hosts of lesser-known but always exceptional jazz musicians. Cover and first drink: 100 F. The music starts at 10:30pm.

Sunset

1st arr. - 60, rue des Lombards - 40 26 46 60
Open daily 7pm-3am. V. M° Châtelet.

Improbably neat and shipshape, this jazz cellar presents an unusual program of modern, expressive, sometimes over-the-top music. An offbeat spot for a nightcap (cover and first drink, from 88 F), where you can catch a whiff of things to come in the world of jazz. Late-night restaurant.

La Villa

6th arr. - La Villa Saint-Germain, 29, rue Jacob
43 26 60 00
Open 6pm-2am. Closed Sun. V, AE, DC, MC. M° Saint-Germain-des-Prés.

Top jazz personalities from Europe and the U.S. are charmed by this intimate club, hidden away on the lower level of a Saint-Germain hotel. Here is where the great drummer Billy Hart chose to play when he came through town a while back; Von Freeman and Ahmad Jamal also recently performed here for appreciative audiences. Concerts start around 10pm; cover and first drink will run you 120 F.

NIGHTCLUBS

L'Arc

8th arr. - 12, rue de Presbourg - 45 00 45 00
Open daily 9pm-dawn. V. M° Charles-de-Gaulle-Étoile.

It didn't take long for L'Arc to catch on among the city's better-bred nighthawks. Housed in the splendid Hôtel des Maréchaux, with a garden that overlooks the Arc de Triomphe, this semi-private club (you'll get in if the doorman likes your face) offers a restaurant, a bar with music, and a discothèque. The occasional show-biz type enlivens a dressy crowd that hails mostly from the fashion trade.

Les Bains

3rd arr. - 7, rue du Bourg-l'Abbé - 48 87 01 80
Open daily 11pm-dawn. Restaurant: open nightly from 9:30pm. V. M° Étienne-Marcel.

Stars, dandies, and young beauties who live to preen and be seen haunt this exclusive venue, where they rub shoulders (and more!) with poohbahs from the worlds of show biz, advertising, and fashion. The top models of the moment and their entourages can be seen here nightly. In order to get through the door it helps to be insanely chic, madly elegant, or wildly notorious. Otherwise, it's advisable to be (or be with) an habitué. You'll pay 140 F (one drink included) for the privilege.

Le Balajo

11th arr. - 9, rue de Lappe
47 00 07 87
Open Mon, Thu-Sat 11:30pm-dawn, Fri-Mon 3pm-6:30pm. Closed Tue, Wed. V. M° Bastille.

In the 1980s mega-DJs Serge and Albert made Le Balajo a byword among night owls from Manhattan to Tokyo, Copenhagen, and Buenos Aires. Today, a new, less determinedly hip generation dances here to mambo, *musette*, and disco rhythms under the benevolent gaze of muscle-bound bouncers whose bored faces say, "This trend, too, shall pass." Afternoon dance sessions (mostly disco and French accordion music) attract a middle-aged crowd.

Le Café Vogue

9th arr. - 50, rue de la Chaussée d'Antin - 42 85 09 13
Open 11:30pm-dawn. Closed Sun. V. M° Chaussée-d'Antin.

An upstairs restaurant, decorated like an exotic hothouse, attracts a hip young crowd sprinkled with gorgeous girl and boy models. After dinner, some of these handsome merrymakers swan off to the billiard room for drinks and a few rounds of pool; others head downstairs to the dance club, dubbed Einstein à Gogo, drawn by the irresistible beat of garage, techno, and soul sounds.

Castel

6th arr. - 15, rue Princesse
43 26 90 22
Open 9pm-5am. Closed Sun. V, AE. M° Mabillon.

But for the rare exception, this club is strictly members-only. The Castel gang numbers 3,000 and constitutes a private community of honored members: upper-crust Parisians, show-biz personalities, literary celebrities, and affiliated members who belong to other exclusive clubs. They sup (very well), drink, dance, and gossip together, far from the night's vulgar rabble. To join this late-night coterie, you need two sponsors, a file on your life history, and several thousand francs to cover application and fees. Only 50 new members are admitted per year. Now, if you are still interested, good luck!

La Chapelle des Lombards

11th arr. - 19, rue de Lappe
43 57 24 24
Open 8pm-5am (Sat 10:30pm-6:30am; Sun from 6pm). Closed Mon-Wed. M° Bastille.

This is the land of rum punch, Afro-Cuban music, the samba, and the tropics. It is here that sunshine breaks through gray Paris skies. The beat is hot, real hot. Come dance to the funky Latino beat and mingle with the happy crowd—they're on to a good thing, and they know it.

El Globo

10th arr. - 8, bd de Strasbourg - 42 01 37 33
Open 11pm-dawn. Closed Sun-Wed. V. M° Strasbourg-Saint-Denis.

Here's something a little different. On Friday nights, this unprepossessing venue turns into a bodega—*muy caliente*! Celebrities and veteran nightcrawlers cross paths in a cosmopolitan atmosphere. The *What's Up?* and *Que Pasa* soirées, on Thursday and Saturday nights respectively, are new and noteworthy nocturnal submissions, hosted by the hottest DJs in town. Admission to these fiestas costs 100 F (one drink included).

Keur Samba

8th arr. - 79, rue de La Boétie
43 59 03 10
Open daily midnight-6am. V. M° Saint-Augustin.

Le Keur starts to samba when other clubs are winding down. Even a slow night goes on until 7 or 8 in the morning, but some nights go on until 11... tomorrow. The African jet set, fashion models, diplomats, wealthy business people, and carefree youth party here, overseen by N'Diaye Kane: he keeps the dancers happy with an unending wave of West-Indian, Brazilian, and Afro-Cuban rhythms. If this sounds like your idea of a good time, don your smartest togs, put on a smile, and forget "attitude": the man at the door likes easy-going elegance.

La Locomotive

18th arr. - 90, bd de Clichy
42 57 37 37
Open 11pm-6am. Closed Mon. M° Blanche.

Young nighthawks adore the Locomotive. It's so big you can get lost in it, and it draws the rockers like moths to a flame. The menu is unchanged since the great days of rock 'n' roll... in the '60s this was the land of the Who, the Rolling Stones, and the Kinks. Today the Locomotive claims to be at the cutting edge of rock (well, that's what the bouncer told us, anyway). Dress in your best sneakers, Levi's, and a clean T-shirt and you'll fit right in with the dancing, flirting, youthful mob.

Le Palace

9th arr. - 8, rue du Fg-Montmartre - 47 70 75 02
Open daily 11:30pm-dawn. V. M° Rue Montmartre.

Once a legendary nightspot, now part of Régine's empire, Le Palace is out to recover its status on the capital's club circuit. The party never stops: the dance floor is humongous and there are two bars. In addition to special event evenings, there are tea dances on Sunday afternoons for gay men and weekend parties for ladies only in the Kit-Kat Club downstairs.

Le Queen

8th arr. - 102, av. des Champs-Élysées - 42 89 31 32
Open daily midnight-dawn. V, AE. M° George-V.

An extremely colorful crowd haunts Le Queen, probably the hottest club in town right now. The outrageously dressed, extravagantly boisterous denizens know how to have a good time! Ladies with escorts are welcome every night but Thursday, to dance to disco and funky house sounds. The themed soirées, held regularly, are not to be missed. Admission: 80 F on weekends, other nights free.

Régine's

8th arr. - 49, rue de Ponthieu
43 59 21 13
Open 9:30pm-dawn. Closed Sun. V. M° Franklin-D.-Roosevelt.

The envious (those who get turned away at the door) bad-mouth it. Régine's flamboyant friends, the silk-tie-and-satin-knickers brigade, ignore the critics and continue to spend large sums of money with total insouciance. But one unmistakable sign of the club's vitality is the fact that a younger crowd comes to dance here now: the children of film stars and the scions of wealthy fami-

Kiosques

Two popular addresses with folks who decide to go to the *theater* at the last minute. You're likely to get a good seat because this is where *tickets* that originally went to booking agencies wind up when they're not sold. They're half-price, but you'll probably have to stand in line.

8th arr. - **Place de la Madeleine.**

14th arr. - **Parvis de Montparnasse**

Open 12:30pm-8pm (Sun 12:30pm-4pm), closed Mon.

lies all seem to have membership cards in their pockets. They sail in the door, no questions asked. But for the common run of mortals, Régine's door is still irrevocably shut.

Rex Club

2nd arr. - 5, bd Poissonnière
42 36 10 96
Open 11pm-dawn. Closed Sun, Tue. V. M° Rue Montmartre.

Dance to a different beat almost every night of the week at the Rex Club's wild and woolly theme parties. Wednesday brings *Megafolies* and on Thursday, DJ Laurent Garnier hosts *Wake Up, Paris,* a soirée of garage, disco, and techno-house sounds. Grunge hounds will want to show up on Saturday for *Planet Rock,* and those who dig a tropical beat should know that Saturdays are reserved for salsa, zouk, or reggae. Admission (which includes one drink) is 60 F Tuesday through Thursday, 70 F on Friday, and 100 F on Saturday.

Some establishments change their closing times without warning. It is always wise to check in advance.

Slow Club

1st arr. - 130, rue de Rivoli
42 33 84 30
Open from 10pm. Closed Sun, Mon (exc hol eves). V. M° Louvre.

A jitterbugging couple flashes on the neon sign outside: the retro mood is set. When you hear the swing and big-band sounds inside, you may think you've walked into a 1940s time warp. The middle-aged dancers are sure they've recaptured their youth. But this is no old folks' home: there's great music on tap, performed by first-rate (mostly French) dance and Dixieland bands who have plenty of youthful fans. For a cheap and cheerful night on the town (admission is 75 F on weekends) you couldn't do better!

Studio A

8th arr. - 49-51, rue de Ponthieu - 45 61 46 47
Open 11pm-dawn. Closed Sun. V. M° Franklin-D.-Roosevelt.

Three dance floors and three bars for fun, fun, fun! Film folks and entertainers feel right at home in the circus atmosphere (complete with "wild animal cages"), where the party doesn't wind down until 10am the next day (noon on weekends)!

Le Tango

3rd arr. - 13, rue au Maire
42 72 17 78
Open 11pm-dawn. Closed Mon-Thu. V. M° Arts-et-Métiers.

Afro-Latin music is alive and well, from Wednesday to Friday in this old dance hall. Black and white members of the Paris African scene flock here to warm their hearts (and shake the rest) to the beat of biguine, samba, and salsa. If you hate nightclubs, fashion, and Top 40 hits, but love chance encounters and cha-cha, head over here for one last tango in Paris. Friday nights bring a live band and karaoke!

Le Timmy's

6th arr. - 76, rue de Rennes
45 44 22 84
Open 11:30pm-6am (Sun 5pm-midnight). Closed Mon. V. M° Saint-Placide.

This upscale address near Saint-Germain swings to an Afro-Creole beat and caters to black jet-setters. To fit in with this dressy crowd, only your smartest clothes will do. Admission free, but drinks are 120 F a pop.

SHOPS

ANTIQUES

ANTIQUE CENTERS

La Cour aux Antiquaires

8th arr. - 54, rue du Fg-St-Honoré - 42 66 38 60
Open 10:30am-6:30pm. Closed Sun, Mon, Aug. M° Concorde.

A choice selection of art and antiques is presented in these small, highly polished boutiques arranged around a delightful courtyard. The eighteen shops offer elegant merchandise ranging from inlaid furniture of the seventeenth through nineteenth centuries, to paintings, engravings, bronzes, silver, and quality *bibelots* for a demanding clientele.

Le Louvre des Antiquaires

1st arr. - 2, pl. du Palais-Royal
42 97 27 00
Open 11am-7pm. Closed Mon (Sun & Mon in Jul & Aug). M° Palais-Royal.

Le Louvre des Antiquaires, a marketplace for objets d'art, is the greatest success of its kind in France and probably the world. The former Magasins du Louvre department store, beautifully remodeled, houses some 250 dealers on three levels. These merchants are the most select, professional, and scrupulous in the trade, if not the most famous. Every piece offered for sale is absolutely authentic and of irreproachable quality. Of course, the prices reflect these high standards.

Thirty specialties are represented—from archaeological artifacts to eighteenth-century furniture, from nineteenth-century minor masters to Art Deco ornaments, from antique porcelain to rare prints, and from animal bronzes to lead soldiers and ship models, fans, rare books, and fabulous jewels. In addition, Le Louvre des Antiquaires provides a delivery service, a club, exhibition halls, and bars. Monthly exhibitions are mounted around selected themes on the second floor.

Village Saint-Paul

4th arr. - 23-27, rue St-Paul
Closed Tue & Wed. M° St-Paul.

This picturesque congregation of antique dealers was inaugurated between the Rue Saint-Paul and the Rue Charlemagne about fifteen years ago. Encompassing some 70 stands, the Village is a good source for jewelry, pictures, glass and

Le Marché aux Puces

Each weekend some 150,000 visitors trek out to Saint-Ouen, a northern suburb just beyond the eighteenth arrondissement, to the world's largest antique market. From dawn on Friday through Monday afternoon, dealers sell everything from used kitchen utensils to vintage jeans, from Art Deco clocks and *bibelots* to signed eighteenth-century secretaries. The Marché Biron boasts the classiest merchandise—crystal chandeliers, rare silver, and such; the Marché Serpette draws clients from the fashion and entertainment fields with trendy retro and Art Deco pieces; the open-air Marché Paul-Bert is an eclectic treasure trove where early birds can unearth some terrific finds; the Marché Vernaison, the heart of the flea market, numbers 400 stands hawking vintage linens, crockery, stamps, and miscellaneous collectibles; the tiny, tidy shops of the Marché Malassis present cleaned-up, restored merchandise in a modern, high-tech setting; the newest arrival, the Marché Dauphine, is still seeking to carve out its own niche.
93400 Saint-Ouen
Marché Biron: **85, rue des Rosiers;**
Marché Serpette: **110, rue des Rosiers;**
Marché Paul-Bert: **104, rue des Rosiers & 18, rue Paul Bert;**
Marché Vernaison: **99, rue des Rosiers & 136, rue Michelet;**
Marché Malassis: **142, rue des Rosiers;**
Marché Dauphine: **138, rue des Rosiers.**

crystal, country furniture, and decorative objects from the 1900–1930 period.

Village Suisse

15th arr. - 78, av. de Suffren and 54, av. de La Motte-Picquet
Open 10:30am-7pm. Closed Mon-Wed. M° La Motte-Picquet-Grenelle.

With 150 dealers offering everything from "junque" to rare and precious pieces, this "Village" is a popular attraction for dedicated antique hounds and Sunday strollers alike. Among the top merchants are Maud and René Garcia, for African art; Michel d'Istria, for sixteenth- and seventeenth-century wooden furniture from France, Spain, Italy, and England; Jeannine Kugel, for animal bronzes; and Antonin Rispal, for Art Nouveau glass by Daum, Gallé, Carabin, and Majorelle.

FRENCH ANTIQUES

ART NOUVEAU, ART DECO & 1930s

Maria de Beyrie

6th arr. - 23, rue de Seine
43 25 76 15, fax 43 29 42 57
Open 2pm-7pm (mornings by appt). Closed Sun. V, AE, DC. M° Odéon.

Lovely antiques from the turn of the century can be found in this shop, as well as pieces by the great designers from the years 1925–1930: Legrain, Rousseau, Printz, Ruhlmann, and others. And that is not to mention the architect-designed furniture, particularly pieces crafted in metal, from 1925 to 1950. You will also find the creations of the Union des artistes modernes, run by René Herbst with Le Corbusier, Chareau, Mallet-Stevens, Charlotte Periand, and Eileen Gray.

Jean-Jacques Dutko

6th arr. - 13, rue Bonaparte, corner rue des Beaux-Arts
43 26 96 13, fax 43 26 29 91
Open 10:30am-1pm & 2:30pm-7pm (Mon 2:30pm-7pm). Closed Sun. No cards. M° Saint-Germain-des-Prés.

Dutko was one of the early promoters of Art Deco, particularly at the Paris Biennale. Clustered all around him are the top designers of the period (Gray, Ruhlmann, Printz, Dunand). Modern art, Dutko's second love, is represented by paintings and sculptures by Fautrier, Bourdelle, Léger, and Poliakoff, as well as paintings and drawings by André Masson.

Félix Marcilhac

6th arr. - 8, rue Bonaparte
43 26 47 36, fax 43 54 75 13
Open 10am-noon & 2:30pm-7pm. Closed Sat, Sun. No cards. M° St-Germain-des-Prés.

Félix Marcilhac is one of the big boys in Art Deco, recognized far and wide for his expertise on Lalique and Dunand. He sells to the grandest museums in the world, and his top-quality pieces attract a knowledgeable clientele.

Le Roi Fou

8th arr. - 182, rue du Faubourg-Saint-Honoré
42 63 82 59, fax 45 63 40 57
Open 10:30am-noon & 1pm-6:30pm. Closed Sun, Mon. No cards. M° Saint-Philippe-du-Roule.

Alexandre Mai has accumulated a considerable cache of all sorts of small occasional pieces dating from 1880 through 1930: furniture, bronzes, ivories, porcelain, clocks, jardinières (flower stands), and Art Deco chandeliers. If you are willing to rummage a bit, your efforts will surely be rewarded (with a fine Tiffany lamp reproduction, for example).

DIRECTOIRE, EMPIRE, RESTORATION & CHARLES X

Raoul Guiraud

7th arr. - 90, rue de Grenelle
42 22 61 04, fax 45 39 37 90
Open 10:30am-12:30pm & 2:30pm-7pm. Closed Sun. V, AE, DC, MC. M° Rue du Bac.

A shop that showcases objects which are both beautiful and useful, such as scientific and navigational instruments, sundials, and medical equipment from the seventeenth through nineteenth centuries.

Mancel-Coti

7th arr. - 42, rue du Bac
45 48 04 34
Open 10am-1pm & 2pm-7pm. Closed Sun. No cards. M° Rue du Bac.

This is a venerable establishment reputed for its furniture, clocks, and porcelain of the Directoire, Consulate, and Empire periods. Mancel-Coti's clients are eminent connoisseurs, and have included Prince Murat and the Legion of Honor museum.

Renoncourt

6th arr. - 1, rue des Saints-Pères - 42 60 75 87
7th arr. - 7, quai Voltaire
42 60 15 63,
fax 42 60 15 14
8th arr. - 77, rue du Fg-St-Honoré - 44 51 11 60
Open 10am-12:30pm & 2pm-7pm. Closed Sun. AE. M° Saint-Germain-des-Prés, Palais-Royal, Miromesnil.

A far-ranging selection of mahogany and fruitwood furniture from the Empire, Restoration, and Charles X periods. The pieces are of the highest quality, and the Renoncourts generously take the time to share their extensive knowledge.

LOUIS-PHILIPPE, NAPOLEON III & LATE NINETEENTH CENTURY

Calvet

9th arr. - 10, rue Chauchat
42 46 12 36, fax 42 46 12 36
Open 9:30am-12:30pm & 2:30pm-6:30pm. Closed Sat, Sun. No cards. M° Richelieu-Drouot.

Calvet specializes in furniture built during the Second Empire in the manner of such great eighteenth-century masters as Reisener, Weisweler, and Gouthière. In fact, the best cabinetmakers of the 1850s and 1860s often surpassed the craftsmanship of their forebears (note the rosewood interiors of the later pieces). Calvet has dealt in these elegant antiques for three generations.

Madeleine Castaing

6th arr. - 21, rue Bonaparte
43 54 91 71
Open 10am-1pm & 3pm-7pm. Closed Sun, Mon. No cards. M° St-Germain-des-Prés.

The late, lamented Madeleine Castaing, long the doyenne of French decorators, friend to painters, patron of Soutine, was one of the very first to champion the dainty furniture pieces and decorative objects of the Second Empire. Madame Lombardini now oversees the shop, which also carries a substantial selection of carpeting and fabrics designed by Madeleine Castaing.

MEDIEVAL & RENAISSANCE

Jacqueline Boccador

7th arr. - 1, quai Voltaire
42 60 75 79, fax 42 60 31 27
Open 10:30am-7pm (Mon 2:30pm-7pm). Closed Sun. No cards. M° Palais-Royal.

Often called upon to testify as expert witness for the French Customs Service, Jacqueline Boccador (the "High Priestess of Gothic Sculpture") possesses in-depth knowledge of both medieval and Renaissance antiques. She is the author of several scholarly works on these subjects, and has a rare ability to communicate her passion for Haute Époque furniture, sculpture, and tapestries.

Bresset

7th arr. - 5, quai Voltaire
42 60 78 13, fax 42 60 59 38
Open 10am-12:30pm & 2:30pm-7pm (Mon 2:30pm-7pm). Closed Sun. No cards. M° Palais-Royal.

No one will dispute the fact that the Bressets are among the world's top specialists in medieval statuary, whether in wood or stone, unpainted or polychrome. They also sell Gothic tapestries to major museums, as well as paintings, furniture, and carved wood—wonderful cabinets encrusted with tortoiseshell or ebony—and bronze, ivory, and enameled sculpture from the Middle Ages and Renaissance. When you visit, be sure to ask to see the superb vaulted cellars on the Quai Voltaire.

Jean-Claude Edrei

7th arr. - 44, rue de Lille
42 61 28 08
Open 10am-7pm. Closed Sun. AE. M° Rue du Bac.

Here is a huge, beautiful showplace dedicated in part to the medieval period, and in particular to china and ceramics, for which Edrei is well known as a top-rank dealer. On the walls hang superb tapestries, which enhance the massive seventeenth- and eighteenth-century furniture.

Perpitch-Liova

7th arr. - 240, bd Saint-Germain
45 48 37 67, fax 42 84 04 64
Open 9am-12:30pm & 2:30pm-7pm. Closed Sun. No cards. M° Rue du Bac.

In business for more than 50 years, the House of Perpitch-Liova is renowned for its expertise on the Flemish and Italian Renaissance, as well as on French Gothic and medieval statuary. Louis XIII chairs, credenzas, and tables, including some enormous monastery pieces, and tapestries from the sixteenth and seventeenth centuries are on display in this shop situated on the corner of the Rue du Bac.

SEVENTEENTH & EIGHTEENTH CENTURIES

Didier Aaron

8th arr. - 118, rue du Faubourg-Saint-Honoré
47 42 47 34, fax 42 66 24 17
Open 10am-12:30pm & 2:30pm-6:30pm (Sat from 11am). Closed Sun. No cards. M° Miromesnil.

In London, New York, and Paris, Didier Aaron enjoys a brilliant reputation for his prestigious collection of eighteenth-century inlaid furniture and objets d'art. He has extended his interests to the purchase and sale of fine paintings and decorative pieces: his firm now includes a design office headed by celebrity decorator, Jacques Grange.

Antiquités de Beaune

7th arr. - 14, rue de Beaune
42 61 25 42, fax 42 61 24 44
Open 11am-12:30pm & 2:30pm-7pm (Mon 2:30pm-7pm). Closed Sun. No cards. M° Rue du Bac.

A noted specialist in French eighteenth-century country furniture crafted in cherry, maple, sycamore, and walnut, Madame Horowitz also possesses a large selection of German and French porcelain from the eighteenth and early nineteenth centuries.

Aveline

8th arr. - 20, rue du Cirque
42 66 60 29
Open 9:30am-1pm & 2pm-6:30pm. Closed Sun. No cards. M° Miromesnil.

Here is a respected establishment whose eighteenth-century "museum quality" furniture and paintings are indeed often purchased by major museums (the Louvre, the Getty, the Musée de Compiègne, to name but a few). Jean-Marie Rossi is also known for his collection of outstanding curiosities that are always both beautiful and strikingly original. Naturally, all of these treasures fetch stratospheric prices.

La Cour de Varenne

7th arr. - 42, rue de Varenne
45 44 65 50, fax 45 49 05 38
Open 10am-7pm (Sat 10am-6pm). Closed Sun. No cards. M° Rue du Bac.

This lovely shop opens not only onto the street but also onto a beautiful enclosed courtyard, around which stand the outbuildings of the former residence of Madame de Staël. Claude Lévy has accumulated some real treasures here, including seventeenth- and eighteenth-century clocks, and fine mahogany furniture with secret mechanisms and compartments. Despite astronomical prices, these peerless pieces find buyers from all over the globe.

Fabius Frères

8th arr. - 152, bd Haussmann
45 62 39 18, fax 45 62 53 07
Open 9:30am-noon & 2:30pm-6pm. Closed Sat, Sun. No cards. M° Saint-Philippe-du-Roule.

Since 1867 the Fabius family has been antique dealers in Paris—the business handed down from father to son (except when a son named Laurent chose the political scene instead). The firm's clients are museums and the high and mighty who appreciate the choice collection of seventeenth- and eighteenth-century furniture and objects. Also on view are impressive holdings of Second Empire pieces, as well as nine-teenth-century paintings and animal bronzes by Barye and Carpeaux.

Galerie Camoin-Demachy

7th arr. - 9, quai Voltaire
42 61 82 06
Open 10am-1pm & 2:30pm-7pm. Closed Sun. No cards. M° Palais-Royal.

This may well be the most beautiful antique shop in Paris, with magnificent pieces magnificently presented. Decorator Alain Demachy has realized his ambition: to bring together in a single setting rare and lovely furniture of the eighteenth and nine-teenth centuries (including Russian, Italian, and Austrian creations), with refined objets d'art and decorative ornaments from a wide range periods and styles. The result is strikingly luxurious and more than a bit intimidating!

Gismondi

8th arr. - 20, rue Royale
42 60 73 89, fax 42 60 98 94
Open 10am-1pm & 2pm-7pm (Sat until 6pm). Closed Sun. No cards. M° Madeleine.

Already well known among collectors for his Antibes shop, Jean Gismondi also occupies prestigious premises on the Rue Royale, supervised by his daughter, Sabrina. She admits to a pronounced predilection for dramatic baroque pieces—sumptuous German and Italian cabinets, gilded bronzes, desks by Boulle overlaid with copper and tortoiseshell—which she presents along with a stunning variety of decorative objets d'art and paintings from the seventeenth and eighteenth centuries. And the theatrical setting, with its distinctly Italian feel, is itself a marvel to behold.

Kraemer

8th arr. - 43, rue de Monceau
45 63 24 46, fax 45 63 54 36
Open 9am-7:30pm. Closed Sun. No cards. M° Miromesnil.

Evidently, it is possible to be one of the world's most respected authorities on French furniture and decorative arts of the seventeenth and eighteenth centuries, to sell to major museums and distinguished collectors, yet to remain charmingly modest. For such are the accomplishments of Philippe Kraemer and his sons, whose mind-boggling gallery is every bit as fascinating as a world-class museum.

Jean de Laminne

8th arr. - 148, bd Haussmann
45 62 08 15
Open 9:30am-12:30pm & 2:30pm-6:30pm (& by appt). Closed Sat, Sun. No cards. M° Miromesnil.

Since 1937, in his 2,000-square-foot shop, Jean de Laminne (now working in tandem with his son) has displayed stunning pieces from the eighteenth century. Devotees of Regency furniture crafted in ebony or black wood with copper finework will swoon over Laminne's superb commodes and mirrors, which still bear their original patina. The shop recently extended its activity to include wrought-iron garden furniture and curiosities from the nineteenth century, as well as seventeenth- and eighteenth-century drawings.

Michel Meyer

8th arr. - 24, av. Matignon
42 66 62 95, fax 49 24 07 88
Open 10am-1pm & 2pm-7pm. Closed Sun. No cards. M° Miromesnil.

Michel Meyer is a most perspicacious dealer, a talent that he comes by naturally, since he grew up in a family of connoisseurs, surrounded by the finest antiques. His superb inventory of furniture and objets d'art from the Age of Enlightenment is constantly replenished. Meyer cultivates a special taste for bronzes and painted ironwork, while his wife and partner concentrates on seventeenth- and eighteenth-century drawings. Meyer's global reputation makes him an influential figure at the Paris Biennale shows.

Perrin

7th arr. - 3, quai Voltaire
42 60 27 20, fax 42 61 32 61
8th arr. - 98, rue du Faubourg-Saint-Honoré (pl. Beauvau)
42 65 01 38, fax 49 24 04 08
Open 10am-1pm & 2pm-7pm (Mon 2pm-7pm). Closed Sun. No cards. M° Palais-Royal.

Perrin can be counted among the major players in the world of antiques. In a flamboyant décor of lacquer and black aluminum, Jacques Perrin stages a presentation of some spectacular pieces from the seventeenth and eighteenth centuries: Boulle commodes, Mazarin desks, and other signed masterpieces of the period.

Maurice Segoura

8th arr. - 20, rue du Faubourg-Saint-Honoré
42 65 11 03, fax 42 65 16 08
Open 9am-7pm. Closed Sun. No cards. M° Concorde.

Segoura is another major name among Parisian antique dealers. His collection, displayed on three floors, comprises furniture, objets d'art, and spectacular decorative pieces coveted by a prestigious international clientele. Segoura also buys and sells paintings by such French masters as Greuze, Watteau, and Fragonard, whose works are scattered here and there in the shop, further enhancing the incomparably beautiful furniture.

Bernard Steinitz

8th arr. - 75, rue du Faubourg-Saint-Honoré
47 42 31 94, fax 49 24 91 16
Open 9:30am-6:30pm (Sat 11am-6pm). Closed Sun. No cards. M° Miromesnil.

In New York, Steinitz is known as the "prince of antique dealers." Here in Paris, he occupies a princely four-storey showplace on the Faubourg Saint-Honoré, opposite the Bristol hotel. Among the treasures on view are signed eighteenth-century pieces from the finest craftsmen, rare Russian furniture, superb bronzes, and much more. In Steinitz's workshops, 30 select artisans maintain the highest tradition of restoration. The prices? Oh my, the prices. Let's just say they're in the highest tradition also. But one may visit simply to feast one's eyes.

FOREIGN ANTIQUES

AFRICAN, OCEANIC & PRE-COLUMBIAN

Arts des Amériques

6th arr. - 42, rue de Seine
46 33 18 31
Open 11am-1pm & 3pm-7pm (Mon 3pm-7pm). Closed Sun. No cards. M° Saint-Germain-des-Prés.

An enormous selection of primarily pre-Columbian art, from Mexico, Costa Rica, and Colombia. The stone statues and terracotta objects are all sold with a photograph and a certificate of authenticity.

Galerie Carrefour

6th arr. - 141, bd Raspail
43 26 58 03, fax 43 25 94 33
Open 9am-noon & 2pm-6pm. Closed Sun. No cards. M° Notre-Dame-des-Champs.

Established in 1930, this is the oldest primitive-art gallery in Paris. On hand is a huge, diverse, and expertly chosen collection of mostly African objects: Ibéji, Yoruba, and Dan masks, Ibo statues, Ashanti bronzes, Senufo doors, Akan jewelry, Baoulé statuettes, and more. In addition, there's a department of Mediterranean Basin antiques. The range of prices is as wide as the turnover is high.

Galerie Mermoz

8th arr. - 6, rue du Cirque
42 25 84 80, fax 40 75 03 90
Open 10am-12:30pm & 2pm-7pm. Closed Sun. No cards. M° Franklin-D.-Roosevelt.

This is a highly specialized shop with a fine reputation. The Galerie Mermoz is always represented at the Paris Biennale and the Salon de Mars, with a rigorously selected array of pre-Columbian works. Prices to match the quality.

Galerie Alain de Monbrison

6th arr. - 2, rue des Beaux-Arts
46 34 05 20, fax 46 34 67 25
Open 10am-12:30pm & 2:30pm-6:30pm. Closed Sun, Mon. No cards. M° Saint-Germain-des-Prés.

A splendid display of primitive art from Africa, Oceania, and Colombia. The gallery mounts exhibitions that are a must for serious collectors and connoisseurs.

Monday, like Sunday, is a day of rest for many shopkeepers.

March on the Arch

When Napoléon Bonaparte had the *Arc de Triomphe* **built to celebrate his battlefield victories, it stood on the outer edge of Paris and the view took in the surrounding countryside. Nowadays you look out over the ultrachic eighth and sixteenth arrondissements while to the northwest the Arch's modern cousin, the** *Grande Arche de La Défense*, **guards the city's newest business district. Twelve broad avenues compose the "star" that radiates from the** *Place de l'Étoile*, **former name of the Place Charles-de-Gaulle. The best way to appreciate this urban galaxy is to climb (or take the ele-vator) to the top of the Arc de Triomphe. At the foot of Napoléon's monument an eternal flame burns over the** *Tomb of the Unknown Soldier*, **chosen among the many unidentified victims of the tragedy that was World War I. The eternal flame symbolizes the nation's enduring sorrow and pity.**

BRITISH

British Import

92200 Neuilly - 23, bd du Parc, Ile-de-la-Jatte
46 37 27 75, fax 46 37 25 54
Open 11am-7pm. Closed Sun. V, AE, MC. M° Porte-de-Champeret.
1st arr. - 1st floor, 2, allée Topino, Louvre des Antiquaires
42 60 19 13
Open 11:30am-7pm. Closed Mon (Sun & Mon in Jul & Aug). M° Palais-Royal.
15th arr. - 78, av. de Suffren, Village Suisse - Sous-Sol n°3 & 62, pl. de Zurich
45 67 87 61
Open 2:30pm-6:30pm (Sat & Sun 11am-12:30pm & 2:30pm-6:30pm). Closed Tue, Wed. M° La Motte-Picquet-Grenelle.

Despite the name, this establishment also offers Irish, Scandinavian, and even a few French pieces. But the firm's chief claim to fame is its collection of English, mostly mahogany furniture from the eighteenth and nineteenth centuries. At the Ile de la Jatte location, a restoration workshop handles repairs and French polishing. New stock arrives regularly (approximately 100 pieces every few months).

Andrée Higgins
7th arr. - 54, rue de l'Université - 45 48 75 28
Open 9:30am-1pm & 2pm-7pm. Closed Sun. No cards. M° Rue du Bac.

Andrée Higgins pioneered the vogue for English furniture that hit Paris just after World War II. She chooses her furniture from the eighteenth and nineteenth centuries with the utmost care. The recently popular colonial style has led her to collect lovely Chinese lacquer-panel tables and secretaries, which were fashionable in England at the turn of the century. On our last visit, we also spotted some superb French furniture and most unusual lamps.

Aliette Massenet
16th arr. - 169, av. Victor-Hugo
47 27 24 05, fax 47 55 08 26
Open 10am-6:30pm. Closed Sun. V, AE, DC, MC. M° Victor-Hugo.

Every month or so, the charming Aliette takes delivery of a fresh supply of British mahogany furniture and nineteenth-century objects, tea services, table settings, porcelains, sporting prints, silver and bronze frames, pipe holders, costume jewelry, and so on. Interesting prices, particularly during the semi-annual sales held in June and October.

FAR EASTERN

Boutique du Marais
4th arr. - 16, rue de Sévigné
42 74 03 65, fax 40 29 98 28
Open 10:30am-1pm & 2pm-7pm. Closed Sun, Mon. V, AE, DC, MC. M° Saint-Paul.

Marie-Anne Baron specializes in antiques from China and Japan; her collection is eclectic, ranging from opium pipes to Japanese lacquered cupboards (Tansu). Don't miss her fine examples of southern Chinese statuary dating from the sixteenth to nineteenth centuries.

Compagnie de la Chine et des Indes
8th arr. - 39, av. de Friedland
42 89 05 45, fax 42 89 11 07
Open 9:30am-noon & 2pm-6:30pm. Closed Sun. No cards. M° Charles-de-Gaulle-Étoile.

A top-notch selection of Chinese porcelain, pottery, furniture, Indian and Khmer sculpture, paintings, and screens is displayed on three levels. Some of the objects are truly of museum quality, and the head of the shop, Jean-Pierre Rousset, can be counted on for expert advice.

Galerie Beurdeley
7th arr. - 200, bd Saint-Germain - 45 48 97 86,
fax 45 44 99 11
Open 10am-12:30pm & 2:30pm-7pm. Closed Sun. No cards. M° Saint-Germain-des-Prés.

Jean-Michel Beurdeley is recognized as one of the foremost authorities on Far Eastern art. He supplies many leading museums, and though he is rarely seen in Paris—he travels extensively—his gallery is a first-rate source for superb pieces from China and Japan. Three or four exhibitions are mounted here each year, accompanied by excellent annotated catalogs.

Gérard Lévy
7th arr. - 17, rue de Beaune
42 61 26 55,
fax 42 96 03 91
Open 2pm-6:30pm (mornings by appt). Closed Sun. V, AE, DC. M° Rue du Bac.

Lévy is a most reliable guide to the art of China, Cambodia, Japan, Korea, and Thailand. He sells major pieces to museums, but there are usually some more accessible items on display as well—always of irreproachable quality. Lévy is also an antique photograph buff, and is an official expert on the subject.

Yvonne Moreau-Gobard
6th arr. - 5, rue des Saints-Pères
42 60 88 25, fax 42 60 08 55
Open 10am-12:30pm & 2pm-7pm. Closed Sun. No cards. M° St-Germain-des-Prés.

The wife of the noted appraiser Jean-Claude Moreau-Gobard, Yvonne offers a comprehensive array of archaeological objects from China, India, and Cambodia. The number of pieces displayed here is as impressive as their quality.

Orient-Occident
6th arr. - 5, rue des Saints-Pères
42 60 77 65, fax 42 60 08 55
Open 10am-12:30pm & 2pm-7pm. Closed Sun. No cards. M°St-Germain-des-Prés.

As unassuming and media-shy as possible, Jean-Loup Despras, who reads hieroglyphs like we read the funnies, is a top specialist in Egyptian antiquities, sculpture in particular. He and his wife have shared these premises with Yvonne Moreau-Gobard (see above) for 25 years.

Janette Ostier

3rd arr. - 26, pl. des Vosges
48 87 28 57, fax 48 87 44 94
Open Thu-Fri 3pm-7pm & by appt. Closed Sun. No cards. M° Saint-Paul.

This charming little boutique is primarily devoted to Japanese art; on view are drawings, etchings, pictures, painted screens, masks, and lacquered boxes. Janette Ostier gives each client her full attention, since she receives principally by appointment.

ISLAMIC

Arts de l'Orient

6th arr. - 21, quai Malaquais
42 60 72 91, fax 42 61 01 52
Open 10:30am-12:30pm & 2:30pm-7pm. Closed Sun. No cards. M° Saint-Germain-des-Prés.

Annie Kevorkian is one of France's foremost specialists in Middle Eastern art. Her shop displays a magnificent collection of Islamic ceramics, in addition to Persian miniatures, antique glass and terracotta objects, and some exquisite bronzes.

Philippe et Claude Magloire

4th arr. - 13, pl. des Vosges
42 74 40 67
Open 1pm-6pm. Closed Sun, Mon. V, AE, DC, MC. M° Saint-Paul.

Claude and Philippe Magloire, who are geologists and collectors as well as expert appraisers attached to the French Court of Appeals, spent ten years in Iran. In 1981, they opened a gallery on the Place des Vosges to introduce and promote Iranian art, a refined but little-understood tradition in the West. Treasures such as bronzes from Luristan, Islamic ceramics (from Nishapur), and antique rugs form an impressive collection of Asian art and archaeology.

Jean Soustiel

8th arr. - 146, bd Haussmann
45 62 27 76, fax 45 63 44 63
Open 10am-1pm & 2pm-7pm. Closed Sun, Mon. No cards. M° Miromesnil.

Nineteen ninety three marked the 110th anniversary of this gallery, where four generations of the Soustiel family have promoted Islamic art. Jean Soustiel is a world-class authority on Muslim civilization from Spain to India in the vast span between the seventh and the nineteenth centuries. His exhaustive study of Islamic ceramics has become the collector's bible. Soustiel's associate, Marie-Christine David, specializes in Indian ceramics.

MEDITERRANEAN

Galerie Nina Borowski

7th arr. - 40, rue du Bac
45 48 61 60, fax 45 48 75 25
Open 11:30am-1pm & 2pm-7pm (Mon 2pm-6pm). Closed Sun. V, AE, DC, MC. M° Rue du Bac.

Daughter of the great Borowski of Basel, the erudite and charming Nina Borowski presides over a significant collection of pottery, vases, bronzes, and marbles of Greek, Roman, and Etruscan origin. Each year, she organizes an exhibit of archaeological artifacts.

Mythes et Légendes

4th arr. - 18, pl. des Vosges
42 72 63 26, fax 42 72 83 70
Open 10am-12:30pm & 2pm-7pm. Closed Sun. V, AE, DC. M° Bastille.

A fabled source for Far Eastern antiquities, located under the arcades of the Place des Vosges. Michel Cohen also displays a spectacular selection of medieval and Renaissance furniture.

A la Reine Margot

6th arr. - 7, quai de Conti
43 26 62 50, fax 43 25 59 82
Open 10:30am-1pm & 2pm-7pm. Closed Sun. V, AE, DC, MC. M° Odéon.

This is the oldest gallery of its kind in Paris. These days more and more space is being devoted to archaeological artifacts (statuettes, masks, figurines) from Greece, Persia, China, and Egypt. Gilles Cohen, the proprietor, mounts excellent exhibits each year and publishes fascinating catalogs.

RUSSIAN

Artel

6th arr. - 25, rue Bonaparte
43 54 93 77
Open 10:30am-12:30pm & 2:30pm-7pm. Closed Sun,

Mon. No cards. M° Saint-Germain-des-Prés.

Though the supply of objets d'art from czarist Russia is increasingly rare, the demand remains high. A devotee of Russian and Greek icons ranging in origin from the fifteenth to the nineteenth century, Martine Cuttat also sees to the restoration of these fragile pieces.

Vieille Cité

1st arr. - 350, rue Saint-Honoré - 42 60 67 16
Open 11am-6:30pm. Closed Sat, Sun. V, AE. M° Tuileries.

A showcase for treasures wrought of hammered silver, beautiful icons, Fabergé pieces, porcelain, Russian paintings, and a collection of delicately worked stone Easter eggs, over which presides collector and expert appraiser Alexandre Djanchieff.

SPECIALISTS

BANKING, STAMPS & STOCKS

Galerie Numistoria

2nd arr. - 76, rue de Richelieu
49 27 92 71, fax 49 27 92 18
Open 10am-7pm (Sat 11am-6pm). Closed Sun. V, AE. M° Bourse.

This huge and constantly changing presentation of all kinds of bank notes and certificates offers everything from stocks and bonds to coins and old deeds. There's no place like it this side of Ali Baba's cave.

Le Marché aux Timbres

8th arr. - Av. des Champs-Élysées, Carré Marigny
Open Thu, Sat, Sun & hols 10am-6pm. No cards. M° Champs-Élysées-Clemenceau.

On the right side of the Champs-Élysées near the corner of the Avenues Marigny and Gabriel, 70 licensed stamp sellers set up booths along the sidewalk and the alleyways. The market opens around 10am, and goes on for most of the day, as collectors buy, sell, and exchange their wares. In addition to stamps, look for antique postcards and even telephone cards, which are now considered worthy collectibles.

BRONZES

Moatti

6th arr. - 77, rue des Saints-Pères
42 22 91 04, fax 45 44 86 17
Open 10am-1pm & 2pm-7pm. Closed Sun. V, AE, DC, MC. M° Sèvres-Babylone.

In his town house on the Rue des Saints-Pères, Alain Moatti shows almost exclusively by appointment. His collection comprises what connoisseurs judge to be the world's most impressive array of Renaissance bronzes. Here prices are whispered in a way that suggests that art is above any mere monetary valuation. Every piece is guaranteed for authenticity, quality, and rarity. Meanwhile, in the upstairs gallery, Moatti's son, Emmanuel, buys and sells fine paintings from the French, Italian, and Flemish schools.

COINS & MEDALS

Sabine Bourgey

9th arr. - 7, rue Drouot
47 70 35 18, fax 42 46 58 48
Open 9am-12:45pm & 2pm-6:30pm (Fri until 5:45pm). Closed Sat, Sun. No cards. M° Richelieu-Drouot.

Located in a Belle Époque apartment opposite the sales room of the famous Drouot auction house, the Bourgey family's offices have maintained the plush, discreet ambience of an earlier age. Dedicated coin collectors will find exquisite display cases filled with rare treasures, a library of several thousand titles on the subject, and the undivided attention of Sabine Bourgey, who also initiates new clients into the mysteries of numismatics.

Numismatique et Change de Paris A. Vinchon

2nd arr. - 3, rue de la Bourse
42 97 53 53
Open 9am-12:30pm & 1:30pm-5:30pm. Closed Sat, Sun. V, DC, MC. M° Richelieu-Drouot.

To buy or sell gold coins, ingots, tokens, old bills, and bank notes, this is the place. Gold pieces purchased here are sealed in transparent plastic sachets in the presence of the buyer, a procedure that provides a valuable guarantee. If you are interested in selling gold, you should know that the shop takes a ten percent commission.

Remember that if you spend 2,000 F or more in a store, you are entitled to a full refund of the value-added tax (VAT). See Basics *for details.*

Jean Vinchon

2nd arr. - 77, rue de Richelieu
42 97 50 00, fax 42 86 06 03
Open 9am-6pm. Closed Sat, Sun. No cards. M° Bourse.

Jean Vinchon is one of the world's foremost coin experts. In the hushed atmosphere of his shop, great collectors argue the merits of individual coins each worth a fortune, while Vinchon advises those interested in less exalted pieces with the same careful attention.

CRYSTAL & GLASS

L'Arlequin

4th arr. - 19, rue de Turenne
42 78 77 00
Open 2:30pm-7pm. Closed Sun. No cards. M° Saint-Paul.

This is the kind of shop whose address gets handed around from family to family when the little one has broken an heirloom wineglass or the stopper to the ca-rafe has mysteriously vanished. L'Arlequin stocks hundreds of styles from every period (the house specialty is nineteenth century), and at a wide range of prices.

Belle de Jour

18th arr. - 7, rue Tardieu
46 06 15 28, fax 42 54 19 47
Open 10:30am-7pm. Closed Sun. V, AE, MC. M° Abbesses.

Inside this dark and mysterious shop is a treasure trove of old or rare perfume bottles and cosmetic flacons. Alongside atomizers from the turn of the century are crystal powder jars and cunning little cut-glass ring dishes. If one of your precious bottles is cracked, you can have it repaired here. Collectors from the world over know this address at the foot of the Butte Montmartre.

La Brocante de Marie-Jeanne

17th arr. - 14, rue Saussier-Leroy - 47 66 59 31
Open 11am-7pm. Closed Sun, Mon. No cards. M° Ternes.

Among all the glasses and crystal, sold in sets or individually, and the liqueur decanters and the toiletry accessories, it would be surprising if Marie-Jeanne Schuhmann couldn't find that out-of-the-ordinary miniature carafe you've been hunting for. But if she can't, you can still console yourself with a beautiful Art Deco vase, or perhaps a delicate water bottle for your bedside.

Galerie Altero

7th arr. - 21, quai Voltaire
42 61 19 90, fax 40 20 03 30
Open 10:30am-12:30pm & 2:30pm-7pm (Mon 2:30pm-7pm). Closed Sun. V. M° Palais-Royal.

This is another one of those places worth seeing even if you are not a collector of rare crystal. Seventeenth-century furniture and eighteenth-century vitrines function as the décor for the gallery's glittering display of crystal and glass from Venice, Spain, Bohemia, and even farther afield.

CURIOS & UNUSUAL OBJECTS

Air de Chasse

7th arr. - 8, rue des Saints-Pères - 42 60 25 98
Open 10:30am-1pm & 2pm-7pm (Mon 2pm-7pm). Closed Sun. V, AE. M° Saint-Germain-des-Prés.

Jeanine Gerhard has tracked down a spiffing array of antiques associated in some way or another with the hunt. Her fascinating shop displays prints, decorative objects, bronze animal statuettes, duck decoys, and terracotta birds. A recent acquisition: a curious set of silverware with handles of carved deer antlers, from the Austrian court.

Bleu Passé

17th arr. - 24 bis, bd de Courcelles - 42 67 57 40
Open 11am-7pm. Closed Sun. No cards. M° Villiers.

It's easy to fall under the spell of the pretty Provençal furniture, painted in soft tones of gray, white, and pale blue. But there are more manageably sized (and priced) pieces on sale as well, among them some superb embroidered bed linens, damask tablecloths, pictures, and English china (1,900 F for a tea service for six). The English silver on display is both covetable and affordable.

Galerie 13 rue Jacob

6th arr. - 13, rue Jacob
43 26 99 89
Open 2:30pm-7pm. Closed Sun. V, AE, MC. M° Saint-Germain-des-Prés.

A specialist in antique games (although she swears she never plays with them herself), Martine Jeannin supplies collectors with mint-condition dominoes, backgammon sets, chess pieces, card games, and mah-jongg tiles, all charmingly displayed in her inviting shop.

Nicole Kramer

1st arr. - 5, allée Desmalter, Louvre des Antiquaires
42 61 57 95
Open 11am-1pm & 2:30pm-7pm. Closed Mon. V, AE, DC. M° Palais-Royal.

Eighteenth-century French pill boxes and fans are her specialty, but Nicole Kraemer's tastes are quite catholic, extending even (for example) to antique surgical and instruments.

Marylis Lièvre

7th arr. - Antique gallery of Au Bon Marché department store (2), stand n°12, 38, rue de Sèvres - 45 48 63 25
Open 9:30am-7pm. Closed Sun. No cards. M° Sèvres-Babylone.

Button, button, who's got the button? Marylis Lièvre has hundreds of them! Admire her cache of pearl, silver, brass, glass, and enamel specimens, shown to advantage in a Second Empire baker's display case. Hat pins and belt buckles are on offer too, at prices that keep collectors and other fibulomaniacs coming back for more.

Les Rives d'Hippone

1st arr. - 8, rue de Valois
42 96 32 30, fax 42 96 10 97
Open 2pm-6pm Wed-Thu-Fri & by appt. Closed Sat-Tue. No cards. M° Palais-Royal.

In an immense, vaulted seventeenth-century crypt, Denise Orsini presents a wealth of charming, decorative objects—furniture, pictures, ceramics, faïence—from bygone days. Her tastes run to pieces which were considered avant-garde in their day, whether that day was the eighteenth century or the 1940s.

Emmanuel Thiriot Bernard Escher

16th arr. - 29, rue de la Tour
45 04 46 54
Open 2:30pm-7pm. Closed Sun. No cards. M° Passy.

Original accent pieces, most with interesting histories, collected with unfailing but highly eclectic taste. On our last visit we came upon a beautiful sideboard from the 1950s next to a lovely Chinese cabinet, and a ship model from the turn of the century set beneath a large lacquered panel signed by Jouve. Don't come looking for something practical; everything here is deliciously frivolous and delightfully decorative.

DRAWINGS & ENGRAVINGS

Galerie de Bayser

2nd arr. - 69, rue Sainte-Anne
47 03 49 87
Open 10am-6pm (Sat 11am-4pm). Closed Sun. No cards. M° Pyramides.

Since 1936 the Galerie de Bayser has stood as an authority on Old Master drawings from the Renaissance to the nineteenth century. Bruno de Bayser is a world-renowned collector, whose selection of drawings reflects a wide-ranging, unusually refined taste.

Maison Maurice Rousseau

9th arr. - 42, rue La Fayette
47 70 84 50
Open 9:30am-12:30pm & 2pm-6pm. Closed Sun. No cards. M° Le Peletier.

Four generations of Rousseaus have occupied the Rue Lafayette, where they deal in fine prints. Denise Rousseau, a certified expert, perpetuates the family tradition with architectural engravings, views of the Paris of yesteryear, and allegorical or mythological subjects.

FABRICS

Aux Fils du Temps

7th arr. - 33, rue de Grenelle
45 48 14 68, fax 42 22 44 79
Open 2pm-7pm & by appt. Closed Sat, Sun. V, AE, MC. M° Sèvres-Babylone.

In an early-nineteenth-century décor, Marie-Noëlle Sudre sits pretty amid her treasures: bolts and bolts of antique fabric from all over the planet. These printed, woven, or embroidered textiles, which date from antiquity to 1925, are truly a collector's dream. If you're looking for something specific, you should call ahead, and Sudre will have things ready when you arrive. She can also show you her impressive selection of rare antique clothing, which boasts pieces from as far back as the seventeenth century.

Les Indiennes

4th arr. - 10, rue Saint-Paul
42 72 35 34, fax 42 72 78 85
Open 2:30pm-7:30pm (mornings by appt). Closed Sun. V, AE, DC. M° Saint-Paul.

The Silk Road passes through the Rue Saint-Paul: here is a wonderland of shimmering brocades, damasks, and satins, many from the eighteenth century. Yards of exotic and colorful samples of silken fabrics from the East are on view here, fairly calling out to be crafted into cushions, curtains, or fashion accessories.

LE LOUVRE
des
ANTIQUAIRES
Enter into
this unique place,
the one and only antiques
centre in the world
where 250 antique dealers
display their diverse
and rare objets d'art.
A bar, restaurant,
and an exhibition room
are at your disposal
to help you enjoy discovering
the Louvre des Antiquaires.
THE LARGEST WINDOW
ON THE ANTIQUE WORLD.
2, PLACE DU PALAIS ROYAL 75001 PARIS, TÉL 42 97 27 00.
OPEN TUESDAY THROUGH SUNDAY 11 A.M TO 7 P.M. • PARKING.
FOREIGN EXCHANGE • EXPERT VALUATION ON REQUEST.
Evolution

FANS

Georges Antiquités

1st arr. - 26, rue de Richelieu
42 61 32 57
Open 12:30am-6:30pm (Sat by appt). Closed Sun. V, MC. M° Palais-Royal.

A most refined presentation of ivory objects and charming collectibles. Every period from Louis XIV to Louis-Philippe is represented in a ravishing display of fans made of tortoiseshell, lace, feathers, mother-of-pearl, tulle with sequins, finely worked bone, painted parchment, ostrich plumes, and more. Prices vary drastically.

FIREPLACES

Jean Lapierre

3rd arr. - 58, rue Vieille-du-Temple - 42 74 07 70
Open 11am-7pm. Closed Sun, Mon. No cards. M° St-Paul.

Oak doors, parquet floors, stairs, and other antique architectural elements are sold either "as is" or nicely restored. But the chief attraction here is the Burgundian stonework: fireplaces in their entirety or in separate pieces, mostly eighteenth century, as well as some interesting carved well copings. In short, this is the place to find antique stone objects or sculpture.

Andrée Macé

8th arr. - 266, rue du Faubourg-Saint-Honoré
42 27 43 03, fax 44 40 09 63
Open 9:30am-12:30pm & 2pm-6:30pm. Closed Sun. No cards. M° Ternes.

Andrée Macé has built her reputation on stone garden ornaments—busts, statues, fountains, garden seats—that add a classical note to the landscape. She also presides over an imposing inventory of stone or marble fireplaces dating from the Gothic age to the Directoire period.

FOLK ART

Georges Bernard

8th arr. - 1, rue d'Anjou
42 65 23 83
Open 10:30am-1pm & 1:30pm-6:30pm. Closed Sun. V, AE. M° Concorde.

Antique objects and documents relating to the history of crafts, tools, cooking, and wine are presented here by Marc Higonnet (the grandson of the shop's founder, Georges Bernard). While that description may sound dry as dust, the items on display are absolutely fascinating, and mostly beautiful to boot. The finely worked keys, nut crackers, corkscrews, and old-fashioned baking utensils are eminently collectible. Scientific and optical instruments and curious writing implements complete this eclectic inventory.

Le Cochelin-Madame Macary

1st arr. - 16, allée Jacob, Louvre des Antiquaires
42 61 50 96
Open 11am-7pm. Closed Mon (Sun & Mon in Jul & Aug). V, AE. M° Palais-Royal.

Food—in its raw or cooked state—is the link that connects the antiques collected here. On the menu: vintage coffee grinders, cake tins, etched glasses, provincial ceramic pitchers, corkscrews... A real feast of culinary collectibles!

L'Herminette

1st arr. - 4, allée Germain, Louvre des Antiquaires
42 61 57 81
Open 11am-7pm. Closed Mon (Sun & Mon in Jul & Aug). V, AE, DC. M° Palais-Royal.

An *herminette* is an adze, just one of the many antique iron tools offered here for sale by Christiane Leblic, a specialist in the field of eighteenth- and nineteenth-century folk art. She also displays small carved wooden objects, copper utensils, and butter molds. Prices range from a few hundred to several thousand francs.

Michel Sonkin

7th arr. - 10, rue de Beaune
42 61 27 87
Open 2:30pm-7pm & by appt. Closed Sat, Sun. V, AE. M° Rue du Bac.

Jeanne and Michel Sonkin's gallery, located on the site of the barracks of Dumas's Musketeers, provides a window into the daily life of their forebears. On display are beautiful examples of antique French country furniture, sturdy wrought-iron pieces, folk-art objects (butter molds, salt boxes, sheep collars..), and old-fashioned artisan's tools.

JEWELRY

Garland

2nd arr. - 13, rue de la Paix
42 61 17 95
Open 10am-1pm & 2pm-6:30pm. Closed Sun. V, AE, DC, MC. M° Opéra.

Minouche Messager never sells one of her rare and antique jewels without a twinge of regret. She is the queen of antique jewelry in Paris; some of the pieces that have passed through her shop are such treasures as the bracelet offered to Sarah Bernhardt by the czar, and a superb nineteenth-century necklace that belonged to King Farouk. Her husband, Bernard Messager, a former craftsman at Cartier, makes the fine contemporary jewelry sold here.

Gillet

4th arr. - 19, rue d'Arcole
43 54 00 83
Open 11am-1pm & 1:30pm-6pm. Closed Sun, Mon. V, AE, DC, MC. M° Cité.

Hidden away among the souvenir shops that surround Notre-Dame, this charming boutique stands out with its eighteenth-century décor and its covetable selection of romantic jewelry: you'll find authentic antique pieces as well as fashionable ornaments from the 1940s.

Gustave

8th arr. - 416, rue Saint-Honoré - 42 60 14 38
Open 10am-6:30pm & by appt. Closed Sat, Sun. V, AE, DC. M° Concorde.

Founded in 1874, this firm was the first in Europe to import cultured pearls. Here you'll find lovely antique ornaments set with stones of a quality one rarely sees nowadays, including pieces signed by Van Cleef and Boucheron.

Miller

1st arr. - 233, rue Saint-Honoré
42 61 63 13, fax 42 61 22 97
Open 11am-6:30pm. Closed Sun. V, AE, DC, MC. M° Tuileries.

Strategically situated near the Place Vendôme, the jeweler's mecca of Paris, Miller purchases preowned pieces, and sells them for half what these fine jewels would cost new. In addition to recently crafted ornaments, there is a tempting array of Art Nouveau, Art Deco, and 1940s jewelry. Watches are sold with a one-year guarantee.

LINENS

Ollivary

6th arr. - 1, rue Jacob
46 33 20 02
Open 10:30am-12:30pm & by appt. Closed Sun, Mon. No cards. M° St-Germain-des-Prés.

As she has done for the past 50 years, Madame Ollivary continues to reign over her microscopic shop, which features the Provençal *boutis* (intricately stitched quilts) that are currently so fashionable. Also on sale is an attractive range of vintage bedspreads and linens.

Vivement Jeudi

5th arr. - 52, rue Mouffetard
43 31 44 52
Open Thu only 10am-8pm. No cards. M° Place Monge.

The shop's name means "Can't wait 'til Thursday," for that is the only day of the week when you can visit Dominique and Pierre Bénard-Depalle's marvelous shop. In a setting conceived to resemble the most delightful apartment imaginable, the couple displays superb household linens from the seventeenth through nineteenth centuries, as well as a desirable collection of small furniture pieces, lamps, and decorative accessories. The scene changes each week, according to what the owners discover in the course of their visits to flea markets and provincial dealers.

MINERALS, GEMS & SHELLS

Claude Boullé

6th arr. - 28, rue Jacob
46 33 01 38
Open 10:30am-12:30pm & 2pm-7pm (Mon 10:30am-12:30pm). Closed Sun. No cards. M° Mabillon.

Boullé is a name to conjure with in the field of rare and unique minerals. Among the famous collectors of "pretty stones" who have frequented this shop are André Breton, Roger Caillois, and Vieira da Silva. The display features beautiful limestone bowls from Tuscany, marble from Bristol, jasper from Oregon, sandstone from Utah... all as beautiful as works of art.

Deyrolle

7th arr. - 46, rue du Bac
42 22 30 07, fax 42 22 32 02
Open 9am-12:30pm & 2pm-6pm (Sat until 5:30pm). Closed Sun. V. M° Rue du Bac.

A fabulous shop, this sumptuous mansion houses an astonishing array of minerals of every size and description. In addition, there are wondrous exhibits of shells, fossils, butterflies, botanical specimens, and stuffed animals—from partridges to polar bears. Kids love it!

Sciences, Art et Nature Boubée

5th arr. - 87, rue Monge
47 07 53 70
Open 10am-1pm & 2pm-7pm (Sat 10am-5:30pm).

Closed Sun. V, DC, MC. M° Place Monge.

Inheritor of the famous house of Boubée, founded in 1846, Françoise Morival deals in the treasures of the natural world: among her fascinating collections are minerals, fossils, shells, rare insects, and other taxidermic delights. Each piece is sold with an identification card that certifies its authenticity.

MIRRORS & FRAMES

Marguerite Fondeur

7th arr. - 24, rue de Beaune
42 61 25 78
Open 2pm-6pm. Closed Sun. No cards. M° Rue du Bac.

There is no risk of getting stuck with a tricked-up phony cherub from the Italian or Spanish trade here, in this fine old establishment founded by Marguerite Fondeur's parents. However, the acquisition of a lovely gilded-wood piece or a mirror from the eighteenth century, with full proof of authenticity, involves a significant investment. Handsome solid-wood furniture (not gilded) from the same period is also offered for sale.

Cadres Lebrun

8th arr. - 155, rue du Fg-St-Honoré - 45 61 14 66
Open 2:30pm-7pm. Closed Sat, Sun. No cards. M° Saint-Philippe-du-Roule.

Mirrors, consoles, barometers, and carved wood all can be found here in addition to some magnificent picture frames. With examples from the Renaissance to the nineteenth century, Lebrun's is one of the largest collections in Paris. Annick Lebrun is the fifth generation of her family to run this establishment, founded in 1847. The restoration work is top-notch.

Navarro

6th arr. - 15, rue Saint-Sulpice
46 33 61 51
Open 2:30pm-7pm. Closed Sun, Mon. V, AE, MC. M° Odéon.

Colette Navarro is mad for gilt and gold leaf. Her mirrors, barometers, and gilded wood from the seventeenth, eighteenth, and nineteenth centuries are graciously lent out for "home trial" before purchase. Certificates of authenticity are available upon request.

MUSICAL INSTRUMENTS

André Bissonnet

3rd arr. - 6, rue du Pas-de-la-Mule - 48 87 20 15
Open 2pm-7pm & by appt. Closed Sun. No cards. M° Bastille.

Brother of the noted Parisian butcher Jean Bissonnet, André—himself a butcher for years—one day turned in his cleaver and apron, exchanging them for the antique musical instruments he loves—and can play very well. He transformed his butcher shop (the décor is still virtually intact) into a shrine to the ancient muses of harmony and music; it is surely one of the city's more unusual shops.

> *Don't plan to do much shopping in Paris in August—a great many stores are closed for the entire vacation month.*

PORCELAIN & CHINA

Hélène Fournier-Guérin

6th arr. - 25, rue des Saints-Pères - 42 60 21 81
Open 11am-1pm & 3pm-7pm (Mon 3pm-7pm). Closed Sun. AE. M° Saint-Germain-des-Prés.

Here is an eminently tasteful selection of mostly eighteenth-century porcelain and faïence from the best sources: Moustiers, Marseille, Strasbourg, Rouen, and Nevers. This show is run by certified experts.

L'Imprévu

6th arr. - 21, rue Guénégaud
43 54 65 09
Open 2:30pm-6:30pm. Closed Sun. AE. M° Odéon.

Under the sign of the unexpected (*imprévu*), you'll discover barbotines, those brightly colored poured ceramics often fashioned in relief, which were so popular in the late nineteenth century: dessert plates, asparagus plates, oyster plates and the like, from Salins, Sarreguemines, and Longchamp. L'Imprévu is also a noted source for English majolica from Wedgwood, Minton, and George Jones, for nineteenth-century printed plates from such manufacturers as Creil-Montereau, Choisy-le-Roi, and *trompe-l'œil* platters adorned with fish or reptiles in the style known as "Bernard Palissy." Last but not least, L'Imprévu also deals in Second Empire objects and furniture.

Lefebvre et Fils
7th arr. - 24, rue du Bac
42 61 18 40
Open 10am-12:30pm & 2pm-7pm. Closed Sun. No cards. M° Rue du Bac.

Parisian society heads to Lefebvre to purchase their faïence, china, and porcelain figurines (Victor Hugo and Marcel Proust both shopped here in their day). This respected establishment, now well over 100 years old, is run by the city's leading expert in antique ceramic ware. The newly remodeled interior is handsome indeed, and the welcome as warm as ever.

Nicolier
7th arr. - 7, quai Voltaire
42 60 78 63
Open 10:30am-noon & 2:30pm-6pm. Closed Sun, Mon. No cards. M° Palais-Royal.

For three generations, Nicolier has presented an astounding collection of rigorously selected faïence, with examples excavated in Iran, majolica from Renaissance Italy, Chinese exportware, and Iznik ceramics. Pieces from all over Europe, including Delft, Sèvres, Saxony, Rouens, Moustiers, Nevers, and Chantilly are of the highest quality, and in perfect condition. All sales are accompanied by a certified guarantee.

La Table en Fête
17th arr. - 71-73, pl. du Dr. Félix-Lobligeois, Square des Batignolles
46 23 75 49, fax 46 27 49 19
Open 10am-noon & 2pm-7pm. Closed Sun, Mon. V. M° Rome.

In their two lovely shops, aglitter with silver, crystal, and fine china, Annick and Didier Marcouire present tableware with a history, dating from 1850 to about 1950. There are always some 30 china services in stock from quality manufacturers (Haviland, for example), as well as stemware from Baccarat, and flatware from Ercuis, Christofle, and Puiforcat: all priced at 50 percent less than they would cost new.

Trésors du Passé
8th arr. - 131, rue du Fg-St-Honoré & 2, rue Saint-Philippe-du-Roule - 42 25 05 39
Open 10am-1pm & 2:30pm-7pm. Closed Sun. No cards. M° Saint-Philippe-du-Roule.

The treasures in question include stunning pieces of antique faïence (seventeenth and eighteenth century), Sèvres porcelain, and Asian ceramics. But owner Jacqueline Pollès is particularly proud of her collection of Provençal faïence from Moustiers and Marseille. The shop's walls are adorned with drawings and prints inspired by Watteau and Boucher, which are also for sale.

Vandermeersch
7th arr. - 27, quai Voltaire
42 61 23 10
Open 10am-noon & 2pm-6:30pm. Closed Sun, Mon. AE. M° Palais-Royal.

One of the founders of the Paris Biennale, Pierre Vandermeersch was a major figure in the world of antiques. His son, Michel, carries on the business in a shop situated on the ground floor of the Villette mansion (where Voltaire died). The stock is small but very select: this is a prestigious address for china and faïence.

POSTCARDS

Octopus
13th arr. - 115 bis, rue Léon-Maurice-Nordmann
45 35 88 48
Open 11am-2pm & 4pm-7pm. Closed Sat, Sun. No cards. M° Gobelins.

Vintage postcards are the specialty of the house, with a particular emphasis on specimens from the French provinces. These nostalgic scenes make delightful (and relatively inexpensive) mementoes of a journey through France. Collectors should note this address.

RUGS & TAPESTRIES

Berdj Achdjian
8th arr. - 10, rue de Miromesnil - 42 65 89 48
Open 10am-12:30pm & 2pm-6:30pm (Sat 2pm-6pm). Closed Sun. No cards. M° Miromesnil.

Berdj Achdjian's name is a byword among collectors of fine rugs. This distinguished gallery is home to prize examples from every region and ethnic origin: Kazakh, Caucasian, Armenian, and Chinese rugs are displayed alongside sublime Savonnerie carpets, rare Coptic textiles, and contemporary designs created by such artists as André Lhote. Top museums number among Achdjian's most assiduous clients.

Boccara
8th arr. - 184, rue du Fg-St-Honoré - 43 59 84 63
Open 10:30am-1pm & 2:30pm-6:30pm. Closed

Sun. No cards. M° Saint-Philippe-du-Roule.

No need to look any further for that tapestry you have been wanting to hang in your *salon*. From the Middle Ages, the Renaissance, the Baroque era, or the Age of Enlightenment, Jacqueline Boccara has them all. She supplies tapestries to major European sales and auctions as well as to museums. If there is something she doesn't have, she will find it for you. And she also displays an array of collector's items and old drawings that she sells for reasonable (considering...) prices.

Galerie Chevalier

7th arr. - 17, quai Voltaire
42 60 72 68, fax 42 86 99 06
Open 10am-1pm & 2pm-7pm (Mon 2pm-6pm; Sat 11am-7pm). Closed Sun. AE. M° Palais-Royal.

Chevalier opened in 1917, and today the founder's twin grandsons carry on the family tradition of selling and restoring exquisite rugs and tapestries. Certified appraisers, Pierre and Dominique Chevalier offer pieces of the highest quality, such as a seventeenth-century Bruges tapestry with a mythological theme, a fifteenth-century Flemish tapestry depicting the wine harvest, or some splendid eighteenth-century examples from Europe's royal factories.

Lefortier

8th arr. - 54, rue du Fg-St-Honoré - 42 65 43 74
Open 10:30am-12:30pm & 2pm-6:30pm. Closed Sat, Sun. V, AE, DC, MC. M° Concorde.

When a firm of this quality turns 100, it may safely be regarded as an institution. Government officials come to Lefortier from all over the world to choose gifts of state; connoisseurs know that here they will receive a reliable appraisal of their antique rugs and tapestries. Madame Potignon-Lefortier, who runs the establishment, is an official expert for the Customs department and the Court of Appeals.

Robert Mikaeloff

8th arr. - 23, rue de La Boétie
42 65 24 55, fax 49 24 05 16
Open 9am-noon & 2pm-7pm. Closed Sun. V, AE. M° Miromesnil.

To fully appreciate Robert Mikaeloff and his passion for silk rugs from Tabriz or for the rare Keshans he collects, you must see him in action as he presents and comments on these superb pieces. For the convenience of his clients, he maintains a restoration service.

SCIENTIFIC & NAUTICAL INSTRUMENTS

Arts et Marine

8th arr. - 8, rue de Miromesnil
42 65 27 85, fax 42 65 30 59
Open 11am-7pm (Sat 2pm-6pm). Closed Sun. V. M° Miromesnil.

Jean-Noël Marchand-Saurel knows all there is to know about model ships, from shipbuilders' large-scale mock-ups to miniature vessels in ivory. All those afflicted with nostalgia for things marine come here to fish for dioramas, carved whales' teeth, eighteenth-century hourglasses, and antique ships in bottles (1,500 F and up). Restoration services are provided.

Balmès-Richelieu

3rd arr. - 21, pl. des Vosges
48 87 20 45
Open 10am-noon & 2pm-7pm (Mon 2pm-7pm). Closed Sun. No cards. M° Bastille.

Monsieur Balmès's great specialty is clocks and scientific instruments dating from the Renaissance through the nineteenth century, but his shop also holds some of the most beautiful marine articles in Paris.

Alain Brieux

6th arr. - 48, rue Jacob
42 60 21 98, fax 42 60 55 24
Open 10am-1pm & 2pm-6:30pm (Sat 2pm-6pm). Closed Sun. V, AE, DC, MC. M° Saint-Germain-des-Prés.

Alain Brieux has a bad case of "collectionitis." His array of medical antiquities is world-class: here you'll find wooden anatomy models, anatomical plates, surgical and optical instruments, and rare books on medicine. Brieux also offers accurate "diagnoses" of the origins and history of scientific antiques, making him one of the major figures in his field.

Galerie Atlantide des Cinq Sens

1st arr. - 3, rue Sauval
42 33 35 95
Open 11am-7pm (Sat 1pm-7:30pm). Closed Sun. V, AE, DC. M° Louvre.

Among the nautical treasures here are handsome ships in bottles, scale-model reproductions, porthole covers, sea chests, and evocative seascapes in watercolors or oils. Also provided is a restoration service for antique model ships and paintings.

SILVER & GOLD

Argenterie des Francs-Bourgeois

4th arr. - 17, rue des Francs-Bourgeois - 42 72 04 00
Open 10:30am-7pm (Mon 2pm-7pm; Sun 11am-1pm & 2pm-7pm). V, MC. M° St-Paul.

This is a treasure trove for silver-fanciers. The shop overflows with flatware and holloware for sale at eminently reasonable prices. The serving pieces—samovars, chafing dishes, platters—come largely from hotels, and a wide range of styles is represented: Victorian, Napoléon III, bistro, and classic. The silver-plated flatware sold by the kilo (400 F) is of decent quality; superior pieces are, naturally, sold singly or in sets.

Éléonore

8th arr. - 18, rue de Miromesnil - 42 65 17 81
Open 10am-noon & 2pm-6pm. Closed Sat, Sun. V, AE. M° Miromesnil.

Claude-Gérard Cassan and Sophie de Granzial are walking catalogs of French silver—from the Renaissance to the 1880s—and they offer a remarkable range of antique plate and curiosities. The pair regularly exhibit their best pieces at the Paris Biennale shows. They also offer a restoration service.

Kugel

8th arr. - 279, rue Saint-Honoré - 42 60 86 23
Open 10am-1pm & 2:30pm-6:30pm (Mon 2:30pm-6:30pm). Closed Sun. No cards. M° Concorde.

Nicolas and Alexis, sons of Russian émigré Jacques Kugel who founded the firm, proudly carry on the family tradition in their three-level shop, which brims over with a princely display of silver, antique carved ivory and gold *bibelots*, as well as seventeenth-century paintings, exquisite furniture, and all manner of rare and curious objects of great beauty. The Kugel name is a guarantee of high quality, recognized by connoisseurs and auctioneers worldwide.

Au Vieux Paris

2nd arr. - 4, rue de la Paix
42 61 00 89
Open 10am-12:30pm & 2pm-6:30pm. Closed Sun. V, AE, DC, MC. M° Opéra.

Founded in 1849, this is the oldest establishment of its kind in Paris. Michel Turisk has a reliable eye for old gold, and presents a selection of gold boxes from the Regency and Empire periods, timepieces, and precious curios from the seventeenth, eighteenth, and nineteenth centuries.

TOYS, GAMES & DOLLS

Sophie du Bac

7th arr. - 109, rue du Bac
45 48 49 01
Open 11am-6:30pm. Closed Sun. No cards. M° Sèvres-Babylone.

The ravishing creatures who populate this shop are rare, handmade dolls. Examples from the late nineteenth century sell for 50,000 to 150,000 F; if you prefer dolls from the early twentieth century, you can expect to pay a bit less (5,000 to 15,000 F). All sorts of desirable accessories are offered for sale as well: delicate china dresser sets, opaline dishes for dolly's tea parties, miniature ivory tableware, delicious doll furniture crafted around 1890, and every imaginable article of dainty clothing.

Robert Capia

1st arr. - 24-26, galerie Véro-Dodat - 42 36 25 94
Open 10am-7pm. Closed Sun. No cards. M° Palais-Royal.

Robert Capia, known far and wide by collectors, is the city's foremost specialist in antique dolls. He has set up shop in the picturesque Véro-Dodat gallery, which was opened in 1826. His dolls are all signed by the top names of yesteryear (Jumeau, Steiner, Bru, Rohmer, Gaultier, Schmitt). Prices are high, but justified by the quality. Also on display are other charming playthings: ivory dominoes, construction sets with engraved illustrations, and mechanical toys. Capia's workshop handles all after-sales service.

We're always happy to hear about your discoveries and receive your comments on ours. We want to give your letters the attention they deserve, so when you write to Gault Millau, please state clearly what you liked or disliked. Be concise but convincing, and take the time to argue your point.

Curiosités et Jouets Anciens

17th arr. - 65, rue Laugier
45 74 88 74
Open 11am-12:30pm & 2:30pm-7pm (Sat 10:30am-12:30pm; Mon 2:30pm-7pm). Closed Sun. V, AE, DC, MC. M° Pereire.

All aboard for an exciting trip to the land of toy trains! Laurent de Beauvais specializes in locomotives, passenger and freight cars, and all the paraphernalia that electric train buffs need to keep their railroads running smoothly. He'll also put your damaged equipment back on track in his repair shop.

Aux Soldats d'Antan

5th arr. - 67, quai de Tournelle
46 33 40 50, fax 44 07 33 45
Open 2pm-7pm. Closed Sun. V, AE. M° Maubert-Mutualité.

Jacques Stella boasts one of the best collections in the antique toy-soldier business. Average prices for these tiny lead warriors range around 400 to 800 F. Stella's sideline is chivalric medals and insignias, of which he is a noted connoisseur.

La Tortue Électrique

5th arr. - 5-7, rue Frédéric-Sauton - 43 29 37 08
Open 2pm-7pm. Closed Sun, Mon. No cards. M° Maubert-Mutualité.

The electric turtle referred to on the sign is actually a rare game from early in this century. Crammed into this shop opposite Notre-Dame are games of strategy and skill, chessmen, puzzles, tops, target games, and antique coin-activated toys. The cheerful owner is an authority on toys.

UMBRELLAS & WALKING STICKS

Antoine

1st arr. - 10, av. de l'Opéra
42 96 01 80
Open 10am-7pm. Closed Sun. V, AE. M° Palais-Royal.

In 1745 Monsieur and Madame Antoine moved to Paris from Auvergne and set themselves up at either end of the Pont-Neuf, where they rented umbrellas to bridge-crossing pedestrians. In 1760 they opened a shop in the galleries of the Palais-Royal, purveying canes, umbrellas, and parasols. Today the worthy descendant of this dynasty, Madame Lecarpentier-Purorge, still offers a choice collection of antique umbrellas, walking sticks, and riding crops.

Lydia Bical

92200 Neuilly - 31, rue de Chartres - 46 24 14 30
Open 3pm-7:30pm. Closed Sun, Mon. No cards. M° Porte-Maillot.

This remarkable spot features hundreds of canes produced in the years preceding 1930: canes by Dandy with gold knobs, canes carved by doughboys in the trenches, canes identifying the owner as a Dreyfus supporter, canes depicting Georges Clemenceau. Then, of course, there are the sword canes, rifle canes, cosh canes (a weighted weapon similar to a blackjack), and professional canes (undertakers and police, among others). And we must not forget the absinthe canes, blowgun canes, fire-starting canes, and the rather salacious model with a set of mirrors that permits the voyeur to peek beneath ladies' skirts.

Madeleine Gély

7th arr. - 218, bd Saint-Germain - 42 22 63 35
Open 9:30am-7pm. Closed Sun. No cards. M° Rue du Bac.

Madeleine Gély stocks hundreds of canes in astonishing shapes—from antique walking sticks and collector's items to utilitarian or ceremonial canes. Equally fascinating are the dual-function canes, such as watch-canes, pipe-canes, cigarette-holder canes, horse-measurer canes, and a whisky cane with the original flask, stopper, and glass intact. In addition, Madeleine Gély's selection of antique and new umbrellas is the most complete (and attractive) in town.

AT YOUR SERVICE

BABY-SITTERS

Ababa

15th arr. - 8, av. du Maine
45 49 46 46
Open daily 24 hours. No cards. M° Montparnasse.

Ababa leaves us agaga! This multiservice agency provides competent, friendly baby-sitters on just an hour's notice, 24 hours a day, 365 days a year. The cost? Most reasonable indeed: 29 F per hour, plus an agency fee of 60 F. English-speaking sitters are available, but they should be booked in advance.

Two reliable au pair services are:

L'Accueil Familial des Jeunes Étrangers, **23, rue du Cherche Midi, 6th arr., 42 22 50 34, open 10am-4pm (Sat until noon), closed Sun; and**
L'Amicale Culturelle Internationale, **27, rue Godot-de-Mauroy, 9th arr., 47 42 94 21, open 10am-12:30pm & 1:45pm-5:30pm, (Wed until 3pm, Thu until 1pm, Fri answering machine), closed Sat & Sun.**

BEAUTY & HEALTH

Beati Corpus & Ismery James Agency

9th arr. - 1, rue Moncey
48 74 33 16
Open daily 24 hours. V, AE, MC. M° Trinité.

Put your feet up at home and have them pampered by professionals. Pedicures and manicures are among the services provided by this dynamic agency, which also offers massage, body-waxing, and hair-styling, all in the comfort of your own home.

Some establishments change their closing times without warning. It is always wise to check in advance.

CLOTHING REPAIR

Mermoz Retouche-Couture

8th arr. - 21, rue Jean-Mermoz - 42 25 73 36
Open 9:30am-6pm. Closed Sun, Mon. No cards. M° Franklin-D.-Roosevelt.

This is an address to hold on to, since good alterations specialists are so rare. Nothing daunts Mermoz Retouches, whether it's a matter of lengthening, shortening, or repairing leather and suede. Reasonable prices.

COURIER

Bunny Courses

92150 Suresnes - 3-5, rue Curie - 45 06 45 06
Open 8am-6:30pm. Closed Sat, Sun. No cards.

These are the people to call for urgent transport and deliveries. Message delivery in Paris costs 60 F, with an express service priced at 240 F. Delivery with a driver and vehicle is also possible. All the firm's messengers are equipped with radio contacts to headquarters.

DRY CLEANERS & LAUNDRY

Delaporte

8th arr. - 62, rue François-Ier
43 59 82 11
Open 9am-7pm (Sat 9am-5pm). Closed Sun. No cards. M° George-V.

The Delaporte dry-cleaning shop is owned by Jean-Claude Lesèche, a famous name in Paris dry cleaning, specializing in garments that need individual attention (lace or sequined dresses, for instance). His mother taught him the secrets of the trade, and he learned his craft well. All the top tailors and dressmakers on Avenue Montaigne value his expert services.

Gallois

1st arr. - 215, rue Saint-Honoré - 42 60 44 00
Open 9am-12:30pm & 1:30pm-6pm. Closed Sat, Sun. No cards. M° Tuileries.

These cleaners will give your spots and stains the attention they deserve. They'll cope with the trickiest dry-cleaning problems, but this top-quality care doesn't come cheap... Pick-up and delivery, however, are free.

Huguet

16th arr. - 47, av. Marceau
47 20 23 02
Open 9am-7pm. Closed Sat, Sun. No cards. M° George-V.

Huguet's classy shop looks more like a Viennese tea room than a dry-cleaning establishment! Haute-couture neighbors and Paris celebrities depend on Huguet for superb cleaning at prices that include free delivery (120 F for a man's suit). And there's an extra attraction: shirts are lovingly hand-washed and ironed here the old-fashioned way.

Letourneur-Lesèche

17th arr. - 8, bd de Courcelles - 47 63 24 33
Open 8:30am-6pm. Closed Sat, Sun. No cards. M° Villiers.

Excellent, speedy work and some of the fairest prices around. This shop is happy to handle delicate fabrics, suede, leather, and lampshades—and delivery is free.

Vendôme

1st arr. - 24, rue du Mont-Thabor
42 60 74 38, fax 46 05 26 74
Open 8am-5pm (Sat 8am-4pm). Closed Sun. No cards. M° Concorde.

Just like in the old days, Christophe Meyrard, Vendôme's launderer, hand-washes delicate garments with soap flakes, then carefully irons the clothes by hand. Luxurious, and fearfully expensive: the hourly charge for ironing is 180 F. And when you consider that an heirloom christening gown or embroidered tablecloth can take up to five hours...!

GENERAL REPAIRS

Brico-Speed

9th arr. - 9, rue Alfred-Stevens - 48 78 34 09
Open 8am-8pm (Mon 10am-8pm; Fri 8am-3pm). Closed Sat, Sun. No cards. M° Pigalle.

A leaky faucet, a wiring problem, a piece of furniture that needs fixing: if you need a handyman, call Fernand Cuperman at Brico-Speed. Plumbing, electricity, and carpentry are all right up his alley. He'll be at your door the same or the next day, for a charge of 213 F per hour for labor, plus 190 F for the visit. Free estimates, if necessary.

The prices in this guide reflect what establishments were charging at press time.

HIRED HANDS

Les Grooms de Paris

16th arr. - 73, av. Paul-Doumer
45 04 45 05, fax 45 04 50 05
Open 9am-7pm. Closed Sun (Delivery 24 hours). V, AE, DC, MC. M° La Muette.

Liveried footmen from this elegant stable can give your parties a certain cachet: for 800 F, one will stand at the door for an entire evening! And while it may seem excessive to hire a uniformed deliveryman to present a bottle of Champagne, it would be more than appropriate if the gift in question were a precious piece of jewelry. Les Grooms de Paris deliver the goods within three hours of your call, every day until midnight. Within the city limits they charge 200 F, to which you must obviously add the cost of the gift. Catalog of services available on request.

Beati Corpus & Ismery James Agency

9th arr. - 1, rue Moncey
48 74 33 16
Open daily 24 hours. V, AE, MC. M° Trinité.

Originally a hairdresser's, this firm rapidly expanded into a multi-service agency. In addition to home hairdos, a team of stylists will perform manicures, make-up, leg-waxing, or massage. The delivery service will bring you flowers, Champagne, or cigarettes (even at 2am; 150 F); personnel will also baby-sit, walk the dog, organize children's tea parties, paint, do housework or gardening. You can call for a cook to concoct the exotic dish of your choice or a student to wait in for the meter reader (250 F

The mysterious shrinking tower

What would the Paris skyline be without this most Parisian of silhouettes? Yet the *Eiffel Tower*, a masterpiece of engineering conceived by the genius of Gustave Eiffel, had a close shave with the wreckers' ball in 1909. Luckily, the pioneers of radio and telephone saw the tower's potential use and came to the rescue. Interestingly, the tower's height can vary by as much as six inches depending on the temperature: the hotter, the higher. When completed in time for the World Exhibition in 1889 it was the tallest construction on earth, standing 300 meters (975 feet) high on its four steel feet. For the best view, tackle the 1,652 steps to the top (the short of stamina can take the elevator) an hour before sunset.

per half-day). Estimates and further details available on request.

Ludéric

92300 Levallois-Perret
3, rue du Dr-Dumont
47 59 04 04, fax 47 57 21 70
Open 9am-7pm. Closed Sat, Sun. No cards. M° Pont-de-Levallois.

The "Ludéricians" all look like their boss, Olivier Maurey: stylishly preppy and bursting with enthusiasm. Launched in 1975, this service agency is true to its motto: "Everything is possible." Everything? From baby-sitting, shopping, and chauffeuring to dog-sitting and more. Ludéric also organizes receptions and special events, caters, promotes new products, and provides theater tickets at the last minute. By the time you read this Ludéric will no doubt have created a new service to meet the ever-growing needs of its clients. A yearly membership fee (800 F for individuals, 2,000 F for corporate accounts) provides access to all services.

HOME DELIVERY

FOOD

L'Asie à Votre Table

48 40 50 30, fax 48 40 12 66
Open 9am-7pm. Closed Sun. No cards.

For a Chinese, Vietnamese, or Thai dinner, phone your order to Laurence Nguyen in the morning. Cost is around 120 F per person, plus 120 F for delivery.

Aux Délices de Scott

47 63 71 36, fax 44 15 90 06
Open 8:30am-7pm. Closed Sun. V, MC. M° Malesherbes.

For people who like to lunch in the office or don't have time to cook, this fine caterer offers a choice of twelve meals-on-a-tray. Prices range from 93 to 150 F per person and delivery is free in the eighth and seventeenth arrondissements when you order a minimum of four trays.

Fauchon Service Plus

47 42 60 11
Open 10:30am-6pm. Closed Sun. V, AE, DC, MC.

Seven choices of quality cold meals-on-a-tray, costing from 140 to 400 F. Free delivery within Paris for a minimum order of four trays.

Les Frères Layrac

46 34 21 40
Open daily 3pm-midnight. V, AE, DC, MC.

If you can't go round to the shop in the Rue de Buci, home delivery is only a phone call away. Festive and varied ideas for dinners organized at the last minute. The seafood platter at 350 F for two is a real treat. Delivery: 50-100 F, depending on location.

Jacques Hesse

40 93 05 05 - By Minitel, 3615 code Jacques Hesse.
Open 9am-11pm. Free delivery in Paris. V.

Hesse delivers to companies and individuals, changes his menu daily, and comes up with exciting specials, like the *bachelor platter* for lonely dads on their own in the vacation month of August. Service is fast and efficient.

FRUIT BASKETS & FLOWERS

Interfruits

17th arr. - 89, av. de Wagram
42 27 80 10
Open 10am-7pm. Closed Sun, Aug. 70 F delivery charge for Paris. M° Wagram.

Baskets of in-season or exotic fruit are nicely done up and delivered. Interfruit has swiftly become a classic in its field (about 350 to 3,500 F for a lovely basket).

Téléfleurs France

10th arr. - 15, rue Martel
48 01 24 24
Open 8:30am-7pm. Closed Sun. M° Château-d'Eau.

This chain of florists delivers anywhere in France, with 4,000 shops at your service.

IRONING

Paris Repassage

19th arr. - 167, rue de Crimée - 40 36 02 03
Open 8:30am-1pm & 3pm-7pm (delivery 9am-9pm). Closed Sat, Sun. No cards.

If you hate to iron but love that freshly pressed look, call on Paris Repassage. Your clean laundry will be picked up at your home, then returned 48 hours later, impeccably ironed. Prices? 12 F for a shirt, 18 F for pleated pants, 24 F for a pleated skirt. Free delivery if the bill comes to 120 F or more.

Monday, like Sunday, is a day of rest for many shopkeepers.

LOCKSMITHS

B.F.C.

10th arr. - 17, rue de Belzunce - 42 81 96 19
Open 8am-12:30pm & 2pm-7pm. Closed Sat, Sun. No cards. M° Poissonnière.

An honest, friendly locksmith who can copy just about any type of key. If you find yourself locked out of your home, he will get you back inside for 250 F. Incidentally, his shoe-repair service is excellent too.

MAID SERVICE

Maison Service

16th arr. - 10, rue Mesnil
45 53 62 30, fax 44 05 18 60
Open 9am-noon & 2pm-6pm. Closed Sat, Sun. No cards. M° Victor-Hugo.

You ought to know from the start that the personnel here is top-notch—and temporary. The woman who deigns to answer your call will inform you in no uncertain terms that Maison Services hires only French from France between 30 and 60 years old, possessing five years of certified experience and excellent references, and ready to serve "a privileged social class." If that sounds like it fills the bill, you will be charged about 150 F per hour for someone to do your ironing, your cleaning, your cooking, for a minimum of four hours. Ladies' companions and governesses can be hired on the same basis, for four or five months, but be advised that these grand ladies of household help have never heard of volume discounts. Rates go up on Sundays and holidays.

Sélection Suzanne Reinach

92100 Boulogne - 11, rue Thiers - 46 08 56 56
Open 9:30am-5pm. Closed Sat, Sun. No cards. M° Porte de Saint-Cloud.

This agency is proud of picking its butlers, domestics, cooks, drivers, secretaries, and so on out of the top drawer. New household employees are given a trial run before being offered a permanent contract. Agency fees vary from 5,200 to 12,000 F, depending on the type of staff you want to hire.

RENT-A- . . .

AIRPLANE

Euralair

93350 Le Bourget - Aéroport du Bourget - 49 34 62 00
Open daily 24 hours. V, AE, DC, MC. RER Le Bourget (B).

This is a wonderful service if you have the means, and we mean the means! A Mystère Falcon 20 is yours for 11,450 F per day, to which you add 21,600 F per hour of flying time, as well as lodgings for the two pilots and the stewardess if you travel for more than two days. Should a Mystère be too small, ask for one of the nine Boeing 737s.

BICYCLE

Paris Vélos-Rent a Bike

5th arr. - 2, rue du Fer-à-Moulin
43 37 59 22, fax 47 07 67 45
Open 10am-12:30pm & 2pm-7pm. Closed Sun. V, MC. M° Censier-Daubenton.

A wide range of town and mountain bikes, but nothing for children—unless they're small enough to sit in one of the kiddies' seats for hire. Daily rental rates range from 90 to 140 F, a weekend costs from 160 to 220 F, and a week from 495 F. A 2,000 F deposit is required.

BOAT

H.B.I. (House Boat International)

19th arr. - 12, quai de la Seine
40 38 95 35
Open daily 8am-7pm. No cards. M° Stalingrad.

Little house boats (8 berths) that are relatively easy to maneuver can be rented here for 1,300 to 1,800 F a day, or 3,200 to 4,200 F a weekend. If you prefer to leave the steering to someone else, the services of a skipper can be hired for an additional charge. A lovely way to discover the city's canals.

COMPUTER

LocaMac

11th arr. - 5, passage Turquetil - 43 73 51 51
Open 9:30am-1pm & 2pm-6:30pm. Closed Sat, Sun. No cards. M° Nation.

Various kinds of personal computer but especially Macs, famed for their user-friendliness. You can hire a Mac SE or Mac II for 48 hours, a week, a month, or a year, all at very reasonable sliding rates. The machine is delivered to your home, collected at the end of your contract, and exchanged immediately in the unlikely event that something should go wrong.

EIFFEL TOWER

Salle Gustave-Eiffel

7th arr. - Champ-de-Mars
44 11 23 33, fax 44 11 23 22
Open daily 9am-6pm. No cards. M° Bir-Hakeim.

For a really chic reception with a panoramic view, why not hire this room on the first floor of the Eiffel Tower, 185 feet up? You can even rent a private elevator. The soundproofed, air-conditioned room will accommodate 450 people for a cocktail party, 300 attending a meeting or show, and 150 for a seated dinner. Equipment includes movie and projection equipment, sophisticated lighting, stages, and podiums. And the price? 24,000 F per day.

EQUIPPED OFFICE

Agaphone

17th arr. - 68 bis, bd Péreire
44 01 50 00, fax 40 54 99 77
Open 8am-8pm (Sat 9am-noon). Closed Sun. No cards. M° Wagram.

No need to miss any phone calls when you go away. For 750 to 980 F a month plus VAT, you can have them transferred to Agaphone, who will take messages or orders and record appointments. When you return, the details are phoned or faxed to you, or sent by Minitel. Agaphone also offers typing and word-processing services.

Club Sari Affaires

La Défense - CNIT. 2, pl. de La Défense
46 92 24 24, fax 46 92 24 00
Open 8:30am-7:30pm (Sat 9am-1pm). Closed Sun. V, AE, DC, MC. RER Grande-Arche (A).

Fully equipped offices measuring between 145 and 600 square feet cost from 1,000 to 3,000 F a day. A private phone line and Minitel are already installed and a computer is provided on request, while a team of full-time secretaries will handle the mail, messages, and word processing. Those who need a year-round base in the Paris area might prefer the yearly rate, which includes additional services (36,500 F).

FORMAL OUTFIT

Eugénie Boiserie

9th arr. - 32, rue Vignon
47 42 43 71
Open 10am-noon & 1pm-6pm. Closed Sun, Mon. No cards. M° Madeleine.

In business for over 35 years, Eugénie Boiserie carries a stunning collection of haute-couture gowns for hire (from 800 F per weekend, plus deposit). The vast selection of dresses is hidden away in the back of the store (the front is given over to old-fashioned gift items), where they are shown to customers by appointment. No accessories are available, but alterations can be arranged.

Les Costumes de Paris

9th arr. - 21 bis, rue Victor-Massé - 48 78 41 02
Open 1pm-7pm (Sat 10am-7pm). Closed Sun, Mon. V, MC. M° Saint-Georges.

Among the charming, droll, and zany costumes fit for the fanciest fancy-dress ball is an enchanting collection of evening gowns by Loris Azzaro, Thierry Mugler, Diamant Noir, and others in sizes 36 to 44 (which roughly translates to American sizes 6 to 14). The gowns are in excellent condition, and rent for 600 to 1,200 F per weekend. Since the company started up in 1952 it has created more than 20,000 costumes for movies and TV, ranging from caveman outfits to hippie fashions. Costume rental costs between 400 and 600 F plus VAT for a week. It's best to book ahead in case alterations are needed. You can even have a costume made to measure—ask for an estimate.

Au Cor de Chasse

6th arr. - 40, rue de Buci
43 26 51 89
Open 9am-7pm (Mon 2pm-6pm). Closed Sun. V, AE, MC. M° Mabillon.

Famous since 1875 and doted on by several generations of Parisians, this stylish shop hires out morning clothes, top hats, tuxedos, and other formal apparel for men (rental fees range between 400 and 1,000 F). Shirts and accessories are offered for sale, and alterations are handled by expert tailors.

Top Boy

10th arr. - 35, bd de Strasbourg
47 70 40 78, fax 42 46 43 90
Open 10am-6:30pm. Closed Sun, Mon. V, MC. M° Château-d'Eau.

Sophie Glasman rents, sells, and designs evening clothes and mascarade costumes for men and women at reasonable prices (they start at 150 F). You can even rent a bridal gown, for a fee of 650 to 1,500 F. Sophie also supplies the French film industry with wigs, beards, and moustaches of her own making–if you like, she'll make a hairpiece to your specifications in record time!

FURNITURE

ABC Ruby

16th arr. - 11, rue Chanez
46 51 06 42
Open 9am-noon & 2pm-6pm. Closed Sat, Sun. No cards. M° Porte-d'Auteuil.

Furnish your apartment in 48 hours with this all-inclusive service that provides furniture, linens (except curtains), tableware, and appliances. Short or long-term hire. There's not much on display in the shop, so it's best to send details of what you require for an estimate.

HELICOPTER

Hélicap

15th arr. - Héliport de Paris, 4, av. de la Porte-de-Sèvres
45 57 75 51
Open 9am-7pm. Closed Sat, Sun. No cards. M° Balard.

See Paris and La Défense from the air, or Versailles and its surroundings, or take a trip to the Château d'Esclimont for dinner, touching down on the lawn out front. The possibilities are endless: the cliffs at Étretat on the Norman coast, Mont Saint-Michel, the castles on the Loire. By now you're probably wondering what the price for such trips could be... Figure on 6,200 F per hour, including one stop.

HOT-AIR BALLOON

Air Ballon Communication

6th arr. - 12, rue Bonaparte
43 29 14 13
Open 10am-12:30pm & 2pm-7pm (Mon 2pm-7pm). Closed Sun. No cards. M° Saint-Germain-des-Prés.

For your first view of France from a hot-air balloon. You take off near the Château de Maintenon, 50 minutes' drive from Paris, but there's no telling where you'll touch down. In any case, the flight lasts about an hour and a car takes balloonists back to Paris. Be sure to book several weeks ahead for an unforgettable flight over the Beauce countryside and the Eure Valley. The cost, including insurance, is 1,500 F for one person or 2,500 F for two, plus VAT.

LIMOUSINE

Alliance Autos

94160 Saint-Mandé
5 bis, av. Foch
43 28 20 20, fax 43 28 27 27
Open daily 24 hours. V, AE.

The leader in chauffeur-driven limousines, Alliance Autos has conquered a demanding clientele of CEOs, film stars, and media moguls. But you needn't be a celebrity to benefit from Alliance's personalized service. Harried business people and travelers touring the capital are all accorded the "star treatment." Instead of fighting for a taxi, why not arrive in Paris in a chauffeured Mercedes Class S (or a Renault Safrane)? A bilingual driver will be your guide, and facilitate your visit in any way he can. To give you an idea of the prices: transfer from Roissy-Charles de Gaulle to Paris, 800 F (Mercedes), 600 F (Safrane); a half-day (four hours), 2,100 F (Mercedes); a full day (nine hours), 3,000 F (Mercedes). Other types of vehicles (buses, trucks, vans) are also available.

RECREATIONAL VEHICLE

Le Monde du Camping-Car

91160 Ballainvilliers - 54, av. de la Division-Leclerc
64 49 01 87
Open 9am-noon & 2pm-7pm. Closed Sun. V, AE, DC, MC. RER Saint-Michel-sur-Orge (C).

Take to the wide open road in a spiffing new RV (the French call them "camping cars") from Autostar and Challenger. Choose from this firm's stock of more than 100 vehicles. Weekly rental rates are 3,990 F (September through March), 4,600 F (April through June), 6,050 F in July, and 7,100 F in August.

SAFE

Solon

11th arr. - 126, bd Richard-Lenoir - 48 05 08 34
Open 8:30am-noon & 1:30pm-6pm. Closed Sat, Sun. No cards. M° Oberkampf.

Protect your valuables in a safe or strongbox for 800 F a month. This fee doesn't include transport, however, which varies according to distance, the weight of the safe, and how many floors the delivery-man must walk up. Same-day opening service.

SKI & CLIMBING EQUIPMENT

La Haute Route

4th arr. - 33, bd Henri-IV
42 72 38 43
Open 9:30am-1pm & 2pm-7pm (Mon 2pm-7pm). Closed Sun. V, MC. M° Bastille.

This is the place to rent ski equipment in winter and climbing gear in summer, for two days, a week, a month, or longer. Sliding rates and reasonable deposits. Expect to pay 120 F per week to rent a pair of cross-country skis.

TELEVISION & STEREO

Locatel

92100 Boulogne - 31, rue de Solférino - 46 09 94 90
91000 Evry - 3, pl. de Vanoise - 60 78 57 58
93100 Montreuil - 13, av. Gabriel-Péri - 48 58 91 92
78306 Poissy - 2-10, rue Charles-Édouard-Jeanneret
30 65 59 59
Open 10am-7pm. Closed Sun. V, MC.

One of the oldest TV hire services, with ten branches in Paris and fifteen or so in the surrounding area. They'll deliver within 24 hours and lend you a set should yours require repair. The cheapest TV rents for 85 F a month (minimum 24 months), a VCR 100 F, and a hi-fi with CD player 190 F (minimum two years). Locatel also rents answering machines, car telephones, and satellite dishes.

TRAIN

SNCF

10th arr. - 162, rue du Fg-St-Martin - 40 18 84 56
Open 8:30am-12:30pm & 1:30pm-5:15pm (Fri until 3:30pm). Closed Sat, Sun. No cards. M° Gare de l'Est.

The French railroad company will rent you an 80-seat second-class car, a sleeping car, a restaurant car, a disco car, or even a whole train. Just phone two months ahead for a free estimate.

■ SHOE REPAIR

Central Crépins

3rd arr. - 48, rue de Turbigo
42 72 68 64
Open 8am-2:30pm & 3:30pm-7pm (Sat 8am-1pm). Closed Sun. No cards. M° Arts-et-Métiers.

Bags, suitcases, saddles, and clothes, Central Crépins repairs everything in leather. Discounts are available to regulars with a membership card.

La Cordonnerie Anglaise

4th arr. - 28, rue des Archives
48 87 11 43, fax 48 87 14 47
Open 9:30am-7pm (Mon noon-7pm). Closed Sun. V, AE, MC. M° Hôtel-de-Ville.

You can have your shoes waterproofed in this dependable, full-service shoe-repair shop. Excellent shoe-care products, small leather goods, and luggage are sold here.

Cordonnerie Vaneau

7th arr. - 44, rue Vaneau
42 22 06 94, fax 45 49 34 23
Open 9am-7pm. Closed Sun. V, AE, DC, MC. M° Saint-François Xavier.
17th arr. - 51, bd Gouvion-Saint-Cyr - 45 72 20 78
Open 9am-1pm & 2pm-7pm (Sat 9am-1pm; Mon 2pm-7pm). Closed Sun. Call 42 22 06 94 for information.

The best for the finest. Vaneau is where feet shod by Lobb, Weston, or Aubercy go to have repairs done. The impeccable workmanship can restore footwear that only looks fit for the dustbin. It will cost about 550 F to give a pair of men's shoes a new lease on life. A new service at the Cordonnerie Vaneau: custom-made footwear for women (from 4,500 F) and men (8,000 F).

Pulin

8th arr. - 5, rue Chauveau-Lagarde - 42 65 08 57
Open 9am-7pm. Closed Sun. V, AE, DC, MC. M° Madeleine.

Gérard Pulin's wide range of services includes changing the color of your shoes, raising and lowering heels, and mixing custom-made polish—all within 48 hours. Home pickup and delivery service available for an extra charge.

BEAUTY

■ BEAUTY SALONS

Institut Carita

8th arr. - 11, rue du Fg-St-Honoré - 44 94 11 00

Open 9am-7pm (Mon by appt only). Closed Sun. V, AE, DC, MC. M° Concorde.

Carita's famous name now belongs to Shiseido, the Japanese cosmetics company. Redesigned by the divine Andrée Putman, the salon's luxurious but restrained décor in tones of beige and brown is functional and simply stunning. The ground floor is occupied by a reception area and private rooms. The salon's corps of hair stylists, supervised by celebrity *coiffeur* Bruno Pittini, practice their art on the upper floor, where other beauty services are also dispensed (stars and other bigwigs are pampered in royally appointed private booths). Carita treatments fully deserve their excellent reputation; expert beauticians can impart a permanent curl to eyelashes, or shape eyebrows and lips with a special tattooing technique. They perform facials that will make your skin look fresh and firm (437 F for the Basic2 formula), or apply makeup for a glamorous soirée. A full-day top-to-toe luxury treatment costs 2,500 F. Men are welcome at Carita, too, and have a whole floor all to themselves.

Guerlain

6th arr. - 29, rue de Sèvres
42 22 46 60
Open 9:30am-6:45pm (Sat 9:45am-7pm). Closed Sun. V, AE, DC, MC. M° Sèvres-Babylone.
8th arr. - 68, av. des Champs-Élysées - 47 89 71 80
Open 9:45am-7pm. Closed Sun. V, AE, DC, MC. M° Franklin-D.-Roosevelt.
Scents & cosmetics only: *1st arr., 15th arr., 16th arr.*

Guerlain is tops in beauty care. Expert technicians dispense the very latest skin-care treatments—they'll even restructure your wrinkles—you can rest assured that your face is in the very best hands. So lie back and enjoy the luxurious surroundings while Guerlain's excellent Issima line of skin-care products is applied to your face for a relaxing hour and a quarter (about 550 F, including makeup). Manicure, pedicure, and depilatory services are available as well. Be sure to stop at the perfume counter to try some of the enchanting house fragrances.

Lancôme

8th arr. - 29, rue du Fg-St-Honoré - 42 65 30 74
Open 10am-7pm. Closed Sun. V, AE, DC, MC. M° Concorde.

Isabella Rossellini's haunting beauty projects Lancôme's public image, but director Béatrice Braun, who runs the Lancôme institute, is the woman behind the scenes who makes sure the products deliver what they promise. An exclusive "beauty computer" measures skin smoothness, elasticity, moisture level, and degree of dryness and/or oiliness, then produces a prescription for personalized skin care (210 F for the diagnosis). Services offered in the institute's handsome, comfortable salons include a Niosome treatment, a bioenergizing massage (900 F), and body sloughing followed by a lymphatic drainage massage.

Ingrid Millet

8th arr. - 54, rue du Faubourg-Saint-Honoré
42 66 66 20, fax 42 66 63 86
Open 9am-6pm. Closed Sun. V, AE, DC, MC. M° Madeleine.

Madame Millet doesn't devour the quantities of caviar she buys; no, she slathers it (in cream form) on her clients' faces! Her specialized skin-care services include a facial mask/tonic/rejuvenation treatment, an energizing facial (590 F), and an all-over body treatment with a particularly effective sloughing action (790 F). The salon's soothing green-and-white décor makes it an oasis of calm and relaxation on the busy Faubourg-Saint-Honoré.

Institut Yves Saint Laurent

8th arr. - 32, rue du Faubourg-Saint-Honoré
49 24 99 66, fax 49 24 97 10
Open 8:30am-8:30pm. Closed Sun. V, AE, DC, MC. M° Concorde.

Personalized beauty care is dispensed in glossy surroundings, designed by decorator Jacques Grange. Among the facial treatments, we can vouch for the Précurseur 3 option, which makes skin look radiant and blooming (880 F for a 100-minute session). The exfoliating body treatment (680 F), energizing massage, manicure, and pedicure leave one feeling pampered and beautifully groomed. Stylists also do minutely detailed makeup jobs, using cosmetics from the Saint Laurent range (gorgeous colors). They give advice and tips on how to reproduce a similar effect at home. The 90-minute lesson costs 950 F.

Anne Sémonin

2nd arr. - 2, rue des Petits-Champs - 42 60 94 66
Open 10:30am-7pm. Closed Sun. V, AE, MC. M° Bourse.

Anne Sémonin's beauty preparations are all based on natural ingredients—essential oils and trace elements—which she mixes right before your eyes. Her specialty is personalized skin creams, adapted to different types and textures of facial skin and their special problems. Prices are pretty reasonable (160 F for a basic moisturizing cream), and a full line of excellent treatments is available, notably a 90-minute facial (400 F).

Sothys

8th arr. - 128, rue du Fg-St-Honoré - 45 63 98 18
Open 9:30am-7pm (Sat 10am-5pm). Closed Sun. V, AE, DC, MC. M° Saint-Philippe-du-Roule.

How deluxe! How chic! Sothys provides fifteen private air-conditioned booths (all equipped with cellular phones), where a capable staff indulges clients with a wide variety of beauty treatments, ranging from deep facial cleansing to slimming techniques: our favorite involves a bath in highly carbonated water paired with hydro-massage (410 F). It's quite tickly and pleasant, take our word for it! The latest house innovation for improving.

DEPILATION

Ella Baché

2nd arr. - 8, rue de la Paix
42 61 67 14
Open 10am-6:30pm (Mon 11am-6:30pm; Sat 9:30am-5pm). Closed Sun. V, AE, MC. M° Opéra.

Cold wax is Ella Baché's secret weapon against unwanted hair. The treatment starts with a mentholated disinfecting lotion, then waxing and the application of a soothing moisturizing cream. Prices? Legs, 160 F; bikini line, 100 F; underarms, 75 F. Facials are performed here too (from 250 F). The latest innovation at Ella Baché is a fruit-acid serum treatment to smooth out wrinkles.

Institut George-V

8th arr. - 12, av. George-V
47 23 49 77
Open 9am-7pm. Closed Sat, Sun. No cards. M° George-V.

Nary an unwanted hair will survive once Antoinette gets through with you. For 25 years she has been removing unwanted hair from heavenly bodies: the Crazy Horse Saloon girls are loyal clients. The salon is unprepossessing (just two rooms on the fifth floor), but the service and products are first-rate. Antoinette swears by a special pale-pink bees' wax, made just for her by an unnamed skilled artisan; and her far-famed technique leaves legs smooth and silky for at least three weeks. By appointment only, from 200 F.

HAIR SALONS

Patrick Alès

8th arr. - 37, av. Franklin-Roosevelt - 43 59 33 96
Open 9am-7pm (Wed 10am-6pm). Closed Sun, Mon. V, MC. M° Franklin-D.-Roosevelt.

Patrick Alès is the mind behind the excellent "Phyto" line of hair treatments. Formerly a stylist with Carita, Alès developed the products in his spare time (in his garage, no less) with the help of his friend and collaborator, Olga. She tried each formula on herself, and numbered them according to how many times each had been tested (shampoo S88: 88 trials). Today, Alès continues to come up with new products, which you can try out for yourself at his Paris salon. Henna treatments, for example, to strengthen fine, lifeless hair, cost from 200 to 400 F. A haircut from the house star, Romain, currently commands 600 F.

Bruno

6th arr. - 15, rue des Saints-Pères - 42 61 45 15
Open 9:30am-6:30pm. Closed Sun, Mon. V, MC. M° Saint-Germain-des-Prés.

Considered to be one of the greatest *coiffeurs* on earth, Bruno boasts a star-studded list of clients. He is not frequently found in the salon that bears his name (he splits his time between New York and the Institut Carita in Paris, of which he is the "artistic director"), but never mind: all the stylists who work here were trained by the master himself—and it shows. A shampoo, superb cut, and styling are tariffed at 400 F.

Camille Darmont

16th arr. - 61, rue de la Tour
45 03 10 99
Open 10am-7pm (Thu 1pm-8pm; Sat 9am-1pm). Closed Sun, Mon. V, MC. M° Passy.

A former biologist, Camille Darmont is one of the most esteemed hair specialists in Paris. Her 100 percent natural, perfume-free treatments for problem hair are reputed for their effectiveness, particularly those aimed at thinning hair (400 F per treatment for women; 275 F for men). Also notable are her honey-milk shampoo (80 F) and herbal conditioner, which put vitality back into lifeless long locks.

Jean-Louis David International

8th arr. - 47, rue Pierre-Charron
43 59 82 08, fax 43 59 80 38
Open 10am-7pm (Wed 11am-7pm). Closed Sun. V, AE, DC, MC. M° Franklin-D.-Roosevelt.

Businessman/coiffeur Jean-Louis David's most ambitious venture, on the Rue Pierre-Charron, is always swarming with heads eager to wear the latest JLD style. We must say, he is a first-rate manager, and he knows how to keep his customers satisfied, notably with innovative ideas like Quick Service for women in a hurry (dry cut, mousse and gel, you're out in twenty minutes), or the Mistershop (same principle, for men). Jean-Louis David International, the top-of-the-line division, charges 515 F for a shampoo, cut, and style, while the "diffusion" sector, less exclusive, charges considerably less.

Desfossé

8th arr. - 19, av. Matignon
43 59 95 13
Open 9am-6:15pm. Closed Sun. V. M° Franklin-D.-Roosevelt.

For men only. Executives, politicians, socialites, and others who pay close attention to their image frequent Desfossé. In addition to hair care (260 F for a wash, cut, and style), skin care, massage, manicure, and pedicure services are offered. An old-fashioned shave, performed with a straight-edge razor, preceded by a hot-towel wrap and facial massage, costs 150 F. Pressed for time? You can grab a quick lunch right here, while having your nails buffed or your pores deep-cleansed!

Jacques Dessange International

8th arr. - 43, av. Franklin-Roosevelt - 43 59 31 31,
fax 42 56 24 90 (also: 3rd arr., 4th arr., 6th arr., 7th arr., 11th arr., 15th arr., 17th arr.)
Open 9:30am-6:30pm. Closed Sun, Mon. V, MC. M° Franklin-D.-Roosevelt.

Pretty, stylish cuts; expert coloring; and rigorous hygiene (a brand-new brush is used for each client) are the Dessange trademarks. A shampoo, cut, and style will cost 400 F if you're a woman, a bit less if you're a man. Good hair-treatment products are sold for use at home; and the stylists offer highly effective hair masks or split-end treatments if you wish.

Jean-Pierre Eudes

16th arr. - 81, av. Victor-Hugo - 45 01 55 04
Open 9am-7pm (Thu 9am-9pm). Closed Sun. V. M° Victor-Hugo.

Housed in a huge, luxuriously appointed Paris apartment, Jean-Pierre Eudes's hair-styling salon boasts custom-designed furniture and light fixtures. Eudes specializes in elegant coiffures for evening. He will coax your locks into a spectacular chignon for 450 F. Hair and beauty treatments are offered as well, based on natural ingredients and exclusive Chinese formulas. Dry-hair cutting is another specialty of the house.

Léonor Greyl

8th arr. - 15, rue Tronchet
42 65 32 26
Open 9:30am-6:30pm. Closed Sun, Mon. V, MC. M° Madeleine.

Aided and abetted by her husband, a chemist who formulates her products, Léonor Greyl works wonders on dull, lifeless hair with her various powders, freeze-dried roots, wheat-germ oil, and sundry other secret ingredients. But make no mistake: there's no hocus-pocus in Greyl's hair-care treatments (shampoo, manual and electric massage, scalp packs, and the list goes on), for they yield excellent results. A cut costs 150 F; a permanent 450 F.

Harlow

1st arr. - 24, rue Saint-Denis
42 33 61 36
Open 10am-8pm (Mon noon-8pm; Wed noon-9pm). Closed Sun. V. M° Châtelet.
9th arr. - 4, rue de Sèze
47 42 40 67
Open 10am-7pm (Thu noon-9pm). Closed Sun, Mon. V, MC. M° Madeleine.
16th arr. - 70, rue du Ranelagh - 45 24 04 54
Open 9:30am-6:30pm (Wed noon-9pm). Closed Sun, Mon. V. M° Ranelagh.

Many women want a good haircut that doesn't require elaborate upkeep. For them, Harlow and company have come up with wash-and-wear hair. The salon's atmosphere is relaxed, and service is fast. Coloring (especially in red and auburn tones) is a specialty (400 F).

Jean-François Lazartigue

8th arr. - 5, rue du Fg-St-Honoré - 42 65 29 24 (also: 6th arr., 9th arr., 15th arr.)
Open 9:30am-6:30pm. Closed Sun. V, AE, DC, MC. M° Concorde.

Decorated in tonic tones of green and white, the Lazartigue salon presents the highest standard of creature comforts. Each private booth boasts a telephone and an individual closet (including, of course, a lock for your fur). The staff is perfectly charming, too. An assessment of your hair and scalp, plus a styling, costs 400 F. For home treatments, customers are encouraged to purchase the salon's range of products made with natural ingredients.

Jean-Marc Maniatis

8th arr. - 18, rue Marbeuf
47 23 30 14 (also: 1st arr., 6th arr., 9th arr.)
Open 9:30am-6:30pm. Closed Sat, Sun. V. M° Franklin-D.-Roosevelt.

His first clients were photo stylists from the fashion press; they raved about the Maniatis technique of precision scissoring one tiny section of hair at a time for chic, superbly shaped cuts. His reputation grew, and now Maniatis is one of the city's best-known *coiffeurs*. The stylists who work with him are well trained and fast; they do a lot of work for celebrities, models, journalists, and so on. The salon is friendly, noisy, and always busy, so be prepared to wait. A shampoo, cut, and styling cost 478 F.

Jacques Moisant

6th arr. - 93, rue de Seine
46 33 51 21
Open 10:30am-7pm (Fri 10:30am-8pm). Closed Sun, Mon. V, MC. M° Odéon.

Want to know where Claudia Cardinale (and lots of other film celebrities) has her hair done? Right here in Saint-Germain-des-Prés. And we understand why: from the shampoo-cum-massage to the expert cuts and styling, this salon treats all its customers like movie stars! If you're set on having Moisant himself handle your hair, expect to pay 507 F for the shampoo, cut, and styling. The salon's other seven stylists charge 345 F for the same service.

■ MANICURE & PEDICURE

Institut Carita

8th arr. - 11, rue du Fg-St-Honoré - 44 94 11 00
Open 9am-7pm (Mon by appt only). Closed Sun. V, AE, DC, MC. M° Concorde.

Entrust your feet to Monsieur Ho, and he will work his brand of Oriental magic to make your tired tootsies feel like new again. Carita is also the place to come for an expert "French manicure": white polish is applied to the very end of the nail, resulting in an impeccably groomed finish (but don't even contemplate it unless your hands are in perfect condition).

Institut Laugier

17th arr. - 39 bis, rue Laugier
42 27 25 03
Open 9:30am-7pm (Sat & Mon 9:30am-6pm). Closed Sun. V, MC. M° Ternes.

Some of the best manicures and pedicures in Paris are performed at the Institut Laugier. Hands are cared for on the ground floor, where the exclusive Supernail treatment (160 F) is yours for the asking, as are vitamin baths and artificial nails for both sexes (400 F). Downstairs, feet are pampered with massage, vibrating baths, pumice stones, and a skin-sloughing treatment (280 F). Before they leave, clients are strongly encouraged to purchase a whole slew of (effective, but costly) products to prolong the benefits of the salon's treatments.

L'Onglerie

8th arr. - 78, av. des Champs-Élysées - 42 25 15 73
9th arr. - 26, rue Godot-de-Mauroy - 42 65 49 13
Open 10am-7pm. Closed Sun, Mon. M° Franklin-D.-Roosevelt, Madeleine.
16th arr. - 1, rue François-Ponsard - 42 15 05 14
Open 10am-7pm. Closed Sun. V, MC. M° La Muette.

The house specialty is American-style artificial nails, made of the same tough resins used in dentistry. These nails are absolutely "unchewable", besides having a revolting taste! Ten artificial nails, applied and polished, cost 330 F. Complete manicure and pedicure services are also offered. For information on other L'Onglerie locations in Paris, call 47 73 90 07.

Institut Revlon

16th arr. - 19, rue de Bassano
47 20 05 42
Open 9:30am-6:30pm (Sat 10:15am-5:30pm). Closed Sun. V, MC. M° George-V.

Revlon's reputation for nail care is worldwide and well deserved. The institute near the Champs-Élysées employs four medically certified pedicurists, as well as seven manicurists who will take your hands in hand and make them as lovely as they can possibly be. The house products are excellent and most effective. Manicures are tariffed at 175 F (195 F with a hot-cream treatment), pedicures at 280 F (nail polish included).

SCENT & COSMETICS

L'Artisan Parfumeur

7th arr. - 24, bd Raspail
42 22 23 32
9th arr. - 22, rue Vignon
42 66 32 66
Open 10:30am-2:30pm & 3:30pm-7pm (Mon 11:30am-7pm). Closed Sun. V, AE, DC, MC. M° Sèvres-Babylone, Madeleine.

This perfumer's shop looks like a stage set, rich with gilt and velvet drapery. The fragrances are equally voluptuous, based on musk, gardenia, rose, iris... not, we emphasize, the sort of scents worn by shrinking violets! We like the pungent Lavande Créole (280 F) and the sensual Mûre et Musc (320 F). Popular as well are the aromatic pomanders that diffuse these heady perfumes, and an exquisite selection of gift items: jewelry, fans, combs, and other decorative trifles.

Body Shop

6th arr. - 7, rue de l'Ancienne-Comédie - 44 07 14 00
Open 10:30am-7:30pm (Sun 2pm-7pm). V, MC. M° Odéon.

Anita Roddick's cruelty-free cosmetics sold in recyclable containers are featured here. Try the banana shampoo for dry hair, the menthol lotion to refresh your tired feet, or the unscented bath oil that won't clash with your favorite perfume. The lip balms come in several tasty flavors: rum-raisin, apricot, kiwi, and more!

Parfums Caron

8th arr. - 34, av. Montaigne
47 23 40 82
Open 10am-6:30pm. Closed Sun. V, AE, DC, MC. M° Franklin-D.-Roosevelt.

Caron's perfumes are fragrances in the grand French tradition. The house recently decided to relaunch some of its most successful scents, introduced between 1911 and 1954: N'Aimez Que Moi (rose, cypress, iris, violet), Or et Noir (spicy Oriental rose) have thus captured a new generation of elegant women, who line up to have delicate Art Deco scent bottles filled (or refilled) from perfume "fountains." Caron is also noted for its face powders and irresistibly soft swan's-down powder puffs.

Comptoir Sud-Pacifique

2nd arr. - 17, rue de la Paix
42 61 74 44
Open 9:30am-7:30pm. Closed Sun. V, AE, DC, MC. M° Opéra.

Josée Fournier has a passion for Polynesia. She was the first to market monoï oil in Paris some years ago, and followed up that initial success with a line of perfumes that recall her beloved Pacific islands. Their practical packaging (roll-on perfume, aluminum flasks) make her exotic scents even more attractive. Fragrances can be concocted to your specifications for 450 to 550 F, depending on the ingredients. You'll also want to try the ginseng shampoo, wild-berry exfoliating gel, and vanilla body oil. Pretty travel accessories, bath scents, and perfumed candles complete the Comptoir's range of divinely fragrant merchandise.

Diptyque

5th arr. - 34, bd Saint-Germain
43 26 45 27, fax 43 54 27 01
Open 10am-7pm. Closed Sun, Mon. V, MC. M° Maubert-Mutualité.

Diptyque is now over 30 years old, but the shop doesn't show its age. The marvelous, exclusive fragrances are as appealing as ever; the fresh L'Ombre dans l'Eau is a perennial bestseller; the latest addition to the line is Virgilio, a green scent with notes of basil and cedarwood. You'll find all the house scents available in candle form, and there is also a selection of cozy Shetland lap robes.

Fragonard

2nd arr. - 39, bd des Capucines - 42 60 37 14
Open 9am-6pm (Sun by appt only). V, AE, MC. M° Opéra.

Based in Grasse, the French perfume capital, since 1926, Fragonard recently opened a Paris showcase for its fragrances and cosmetics. Displayed here in an authentic Art Deco setting are the full range of sixteen house scents (150 F for 250 ml), and some deliciously light toilet waters for children, perfumed with lemon, vanilla, or lavender. Gift boxes of scent and makeup start at 60 F. Don't miss the interesting perfume museum located one floor above the shop.

Annick Goutal

1st arr. - 14, rue de Castiglione 42 60 52 82 (also: 7th arr., 17th arr.)
Open 10am-7pm. Closed Sun. V, AE, DC. M° Opéra.

Annick Goutal's unique fragrances are sold in elegant boutiques decorated in beige and gold tones. Our favorite scents are the deliciously citrusy Eau d'Hadrien, the romantic Heure Exquise, and the ultrafeminine Rose Absolue. The newest addition to the range is the intensely sensual Gardenia Passion. Goutal's soaps, bath oils, and scented pebbles (to scatter in lingerie drawers) make wonderful gifts.

Grain de Beauté

6th arr. - 9, rue du Cherche-Midi - 45 48 07 55
Open 10:30am-7pm (Mon 2:30pm-7pm). Closed Sun. V, MC. M° Sèvres-Babylone.

Traditional English furniture and chintzes make an appropriate setting for traditional English scents by such renowned perfumers as George F. Trumper, Penhaligon's, Floris, and Czech & Speake, whose toilet waters, soaps, potpourri, and other fragrant miscellanea are featured here.

Herboristerie du Palais-Royal

1st arr. - 11, rue des Petits-Champs - 42 97 54 68
Open 8:30am-7pm. Closed Sun. V, MC. M° Palais-Royal.

Natural cosmetics have been this shop's specialty since the 1930s. The herbal shampoos, face creams, massage gels, and cleansing lotions are of uniformly high quality. The best-selling product is a blend of wheat-germ oil, hazelnut oil, sesame oil, and wheat (75 F for 4 ounces): amazingly light and non-greasy feeling, it's a versatile moisturizer for face and body, particularly recommended for use after exposure to the sun.

Maître Parfumeur et Gantier

1st arr. - 5, rue des Capucines 42 96 35 13
Open 10:30am-6:30pm. Closed Sun. V, AE, DC, MC. M° Opéra.
7th arr. - 84 bis, rue de Grenelle - 45 44 61 57
Open 10am-2pm & 3pm-7pm. Closed Sun. V, AE, DC, MC. M° Rue du Bac.

Jean-François Laporte's extravagant scents are for those who like to leave a trail of lingering fragrance in their wake. Both men and women can find assertive toilet waters here, with evocative names like Rose Muskissime or Fleurs de Comores. Laporte's signature scents are also sold as pot-pourri or room fragrances. Don't miss his elegant, very dandified perfumed gloves.

Patricia de Nicolaï

7th arr. - 80, rue de Grenelle 45 44 59 59
Open 10am-2pm & 2:30pm-6:30pm. Closed Sun, Mon. V, AE, DC, MC. M° Rue du Bac.

Guerlain's granddaughter, Patricia de Nicolaï, perpetuates the family tradition of creating enchanting perfumes. To date, her collection comprises nine scents for women and four for men. We especially like Mimosaïque, Jardin Secret and the new Sacre Bleu, an Oriental-style floral fragrance (240 F for 50 ml). Alongside perfumed candles, room sprays, and pot-pourris, you'll find delicate carved crystal flacons, which can be engraved with your name.

Jean Patou

8th arr. - 7, rue Saint-Florentin - 44 77 33 00
Open 10am-1pm & 2pm-7pm. Closed Sun. V, AE, DC, MC. M° Concorde.

Normandie, L'Heure Attendue, Moment Suprême... The celebrated creator of Joy perfume has reissued a dozen of the house's top scents, launched between 1925 and 1964 (250 F for 50 ml). They are available once more in this attractive shop, where you can also obtain the famed Huile de Chaldée, an oil that ensures an even, golden tan.

Les Salons du Palais-Royal

1st arr. - 142, galerie de Valois, in Palais-Royal Gardens
49 27 09 09, fax 49 27 92 12
Open 9am-7pm. Closed Sun. V, AE, DC, MC. M° Palais-Royal.

Shiseido, the Japanese cosmetics firm, presides over this elegant, somehow mysterious shop tucked away in the arcades of the Palais-Royal. The fantastical décor perfectly sets off the eight exotic house fragrances, each constructed around a single, rare note: Ambre Sultan, Roses de Nuit, Iris Silver Mist, Bois et Musc and the rest are unforgettable scents, not available from any other store.

Sephora

16th arr. - 50, rue de Passy
45 20 03 15 (also: 1st arr., 9th arr., 13th arr., 14th arr.)
Open 10am-7pm (Sat 10am-7:30pm). Closed Sun. V, AE, DC, MC. M° Passy.

If you'd rather avoid dealing with salespeople, and prefer to read labels, look at bottles, and decide for yourself what makeup you need, then Sephora, the "beauty supermarket," is for you. Cosmetics and perfumes of every type are on offer: face creams, body-care products, cosmetics, and accessories (hairbrushes, barrettes, mirrors...) from major manufacturers are all neatly displayed.

Shu Uemura

6th arr. - 176, bd Saint-Germain - 45 48 02 55
Open 10am-7pm (Mon 11am-7pm). Closed Sun. V, AE, DC, MC. M° Saint-Germain-des-Prés.

As soon as they cross the threshold of this shop, even the most fresh-scrubbed women are suddenly possessed by the urge to try the lipsticks, powders (fluffed on with terrific bamboo and silk brushes), pencils, and shadows, which come in an extraordinary palette of colors. A Japanese-style décor of wood and glass is the handsome setting for these no-less-handsomely packaged cosmetics, many of which come in reusable containers. Courteous, knowledgeable staff.

THALASSOTHERAPY

Biocéane

19th arr. - 22, rue de Flandre
40 36 58 01
Open 10am-7:30pm. Closed Sun, Mon. V, MC. M° Stalingrad.

No kidding, you can actually enjoy the benefits of sun and sea in the far-flung nineteenth arrondissement! Sea-water whirlpool baths, seaweed wraps, and a wealth of beauty treatments based on elements taken from the sea will restore your skin tone and boost your morale. Traditional beauty treatments are available as well, from massage to "permanent" makeup for brows, eyelashes, and lips. An in-house boutique sells natural cosmetics, vitamins, sea-shell meal, and herbal teas.

Villa Thalgo

8th arr. - 218-220, rue du Fg-St-Honoré - 45 62 00 20
Open Mon 11am-7pm, Tue & Thu 9am-8:30pm, Wed 9am-7pm, Fri 10am-7pm, Sat 10am-6pm. Closed Sun. V, AE, DC, MC. M° Ternes.

Take a sea-cure right in the heart of Paris! Below the Golden Tulip Hotel is the city's first thalassotherapy center, with a (reconstituted) sea-water swimming pool. Seaweed-based body- and skin-care treatments are offered, as well as more traditional beauty care (manicure, massage, sauna, Turkish baths...). After a morning of pampering yourself, you can lounge by the pool and nibble at a nutritionally balanced lunch. Prices vary according to the type of treatment: hydrojet, 200 F; whirlpool bath, 250 F; seaweed wrap, 300 F; memberships are available.

BOOKS & STATIONERY

ART

Artcurial

8th arr. - 9, av. Matignon
42 99 16 19, fax 43 59 29 81
Open 10:30am-7:15pm. Closed Sun, Mon. V, AE, DC, MC. M° Champs-Élysées-Clemenceau.

One floor up from Artcurial's lively contemporary art gallery, this fabulous bookstore boasts some 8,000 works on fine arts, graphics, and crafts. Look here for the exquisite and erudite books on art, design, and fashion from the Éditions du Regard (e.g. Anne Bony's monumental series on twentieth-century design), as well as an interesting selection of works (primarily Japanese) on fashion and textiles.

Librairie Lecointre-Ozanne

6th arr. - 9, rue de Tournon
43 26 02 92, fax 46 33 11 40
Open 10am-7pm (Sat 10am-6pm). Closed Sun, Mon. V, MC. M° Odéon.

Books on all the avant-garde movements of the twentieth century, whether in architecture, applied arts, photography...

Typography buffs (we know you're out there!) will find a selection of reference books on that recondite subject.

Léonce Laget

6th arr. - 76, rue de Seine
43 29 90 04
Open 9am-noon & 2pm-6:30pm (Mon 2pm-6:30pm). Closed Sun. V, MC. M° Odéon.

The history of architecture will be an open book to you, after a visit to this impressive bookshop, which offers an unequalled selection of rare and important works on the subject. Catalog available.

Librairie Maeght

4th arr. - 12, rue Saint-Merri
42 78 27 64
Open 10am-7pm (Mon 10:30am-6:30pm). Closed Sun. V, AE, DC, MC. M° Rambuteau.

Vying for your attention with lithographs by the Galerie Maeght's stable of artists (more affordable, incidentally, than you might think) are all the most important books on every aspect of contemporary art. In many languages.

Librairie F. de Nobele

6th arr. - 35, rue Bonaparte
43 26 08 62, fax 40 46 85 96
Open 9am-noon & 2pm-7pm. Closed Sat, Sun. V, MC. M° Saint-Germain-des-Prés.

Belgian by birth and over 100 years old, Nobele is the bookshop of reference when it comes to the fine arts, decorative arts, works on collectible antiques, and on the history of books. An extraordinary stock of old or rare art books, at amazingly reasonable prices. Catalog upon request.

ENGLISH-LANGUAGE

Brentano's

2nd arr. - 37, av. de l'Opéra
42 61 52 50, fax 42 61 07 61
Open 10am-7pm. Closed Sun. V, MC. M° Pyramides.

Brentano's deservedly remains a favorite among Americans in Paris for its remarkable array of American, English, and French books, periodicals, records, and art books. Bestsellers of the week are always displayed at the entrance. And there are also large children's and business sections.

Galignani

1st arr. - 224, rue de Rivoli
42 60 76 07, fax 42 86 09 31
Open 10am-7pm. Closed Sun. V, MC. M° Tuileries.

Galignani, purported to be the oldest English bookshop on the continent, was established in 1805 on the Rue Vivienne by Giovanni Antonio Galignani, descendant of a famous twelfth-century publisher from Padua, Italy. In the mid-1800s Galignani moved to the Rue de Rivoli, near the terminus of the Calais-Paris train, and the shop has passed from father to son and so on down the line. Recently remodeled and enlarged, the shop offers an even broader selection of English, American, and French hardcovers and paperbacks, lots of children's literature, plus a fabulous international selection of art books.

Don't plan to shop on Sundays—the vast majority of Paris stores are closed.

La Librairie Internationale

6th arr. - 78, bd Saint-Michel
43 26 42 70, fax 40 51 74 09
Open 10am-7pm. Closed Sun. V, MC. M° Saint-Michel.

This bookshop lives up to its name, stocking a wide selection of English, American, Spanish, and German literature, plus dictionaries and paperbacks in English (over 10,000). Also lining the shelves are books on painting, design, architecture, photography, graphics, and music. An entire section is given over to books on teaching or learning English. The adjacent room is equipped so that you may listen to and watch audiotapes and videotapes before purchasing them. The computerized book-ordering service is fast and efficient, and special sales are held throughout the year. Catalogs available.

Shakespeare & Company

5th arr. - 37, rue de la Bûcherie - 43 26 96 50
Open daily noon-midnight. No cards. M° Saint-Michel.

Commune with the spirits of Joyce, Gertrude Stein, Alice B. Toklas, and many others who once haunted Shakespeare and Co. This landmark on the quay by Notre-Dame is a late-night favorite with buyers and browsers in search of new or second-hand English and American books.

W.H. Smith

1st arr. - 248, rue de Rivoli
44 77 88 99
Open 9:30am-6:30pm. Closed Sun. V, AE, DC, MC. M° Concorde.

This is the closest thing to the perfect self-service bookstore: it is easy to locate almost any item among the over 40,000 English and American titles, from current and classic fiction, biographies, cookbooks, and travel guides to children's books, language methods, history, and English-language videos... The magazine and newspaper section is huge and often very crowded. As for the staff, it's efficient and friendly... and very British.

Tea and Tattered Pages

6th arr. - 24, rue Mayet
40 65 94 35
Open daily 11am-7pm. No cards. M° Duroc.

A charming place to browse through a wide selection of English and American used books, and to enjoy a leisurely cup of tea (see *Tea rooms*).

Tonkam

11th arr. - 29, rue Keller
47 00 78 38
Open 10:30am-noon & 1pm-7pm (Mon 1pm-7pm). Closed Sun. M° Ledru-Rollin.

Sylvie Tonkam is the resident expert on *bandes dessinées*—comic books and albums. Her vast inventory includes an impressive collection of American comics, some old and collectible. T-shirts, too.

Village Voice

6th arr. - 6, rue Princesse
46 33 36 47, fax 46 33 27 48
Open 11am-8pm (Mon 2pm-8pm). Closed Sun. V, AE, DC, MC. M° Mabillon.

Nowadays the Village Voice controls the turf once so jealously guarded by Sylvia Beach's original Shakespeare and Co.—a mecca for Americans in Paris, especially writers, journalists, and literary types. The Village Voice hosts well-attended poetry readings and book-signing parties, and supplies voracious readers with an intelligently chosen selection of titles. Books special-ordered on request by the knowledgeable staff.

Tea in the Pagoda

The movies saved *La Pagode* ("the Pagoda") from the threat of demolition. Since 1931 it has been one of the city's most attractive film houses. The French architects responsible for La Pagode fell under the collective fin-de-siècle enchantment with all things Oriental; the structure's elegant décor delighted guests at high-society receptions in the 1890s. Later the Chinese Embassy dropped plans to buy La Pagode (the ambassador apparently objected to some wall paintings depicting Chinese warriors being soundly trounced by the Japanese). The Oriental flavor lingers on in the tea rooms and garden, additional reasons to visit this pagoda at 57bis rue de Babylone in the seventh arrondissement. Across the street at number 68, Ciné-images sells posters and other souvenirs of the world's greatest movies.

■ FILM & PHOTOGRAPHY

La Chambre Claire

6th arr. - 14, rue Saint-Sulpice
46 34 04 31, fax 43 29 89 22
Open 10am-7pm. Closed Sun. V, MC. M° Odéon.

This bookshop is given over entirely to photography—with some 4,000 different works, it is the official supplier to several of the world's greatest museums. A truly remarkable place, run by Monsieur Zahar; some discounted books are available.

Ciné-Doc

9th arr. - 45, passage Jouffroy
48 24 71 36
Open 10am-7pm. Closed Sun. V, MC. M° Rue Montmartre.

This flea market-style shop in the delightful Passage Jouffroy is piled high with a fascinating jumble of publications pertaining to the movies, plus posters, postcards, and photographs. The interesting displays in the shop windows change often and add to the already lively ambience.

■ FOOD & COOKING

Librairie Gourmande

5th arr. - 4, rue Dante
43 54 37 27, fax 43 54 31 16
Open daily 10am-7pm. V, MC. M° Saint-Michel.

At La Librairie Gourmande you will find a mouthwatering array of cookbooks, for amateurs and pros alike, as well as works on the history of French and foreign cooking (some volumes date from the sixteenth century). Wide-ranging collections treating traditional and nouvelle cuisine, recipes by Balzac and Dumas, plus a diverse range of works on oenology make this one of Paris' most appetizing bookshops, despite the high prices. You can bank on a warm welcome and excellent service from owner Geneviève Baudon.

Librairie des Gourmets

5th arr. - 98, rue Monge
43 31 16 42, fax 43 31 60 32
Open 10:30am-7pm. Closed Sun, Mon. V, MC. M° Censier-Daubenton.

A bright and tidy shop where gourmets, gourmands, and good cooks will feel right at home, thanks to the owner's cordial welcome. All the latest French cookbooks are on hand, as well as a wide selection of gastronomic classics.

Le Verre et l'Assiette

5th arr. - 1, rue du Val-de-Grâce
46 33 45 96, fax 46 33 56 80
Open 10am-12:30pm & 2pm-7pm (Mon 2pm-7pm). Closed Sun. V, AE, DC, MC. M° Port-Royal.

Too many chefs may spoil the broth, but they certainly don't spoil Le Verre et l'Assiette. Feast your eyes on the window display: a pot-pourri of books and accessories pertaining to gastronomy and oenology—from unique corkscrews to rare editions on Celtic cookery. This is the bookshop most frequented by famous chefs, gourmets, and wine buffs. In addition to the thousands of volumes on food and drink, there is an appealing selection of gift ideas (the wine taster's ideal traveling case, for example). *Bon appétit!*

GENERAL INTEREST

Delamain

1st arr. - 155, rue Saint-Honoré
42 61 48 78, fax 40 15 91 69
Open 10am-7:30pm. Closed Sun. V, AE, DC, MC. M° Palais-Royal.

Delamain is the oldest bookstore in France, founded in 1710 under the arcades of the Comédie-Française. About 100 years ago the original shop burned down, and Delamain moved to its current location on the Rue Saint-Honoré. Thousands of volumes on French literature, travel, history, and art (in French only) are available new or used. The first floor is given over to the graphic arts, photography, film, and theater.

Gibert Jeune

2nd arr. - 15, bd Saint-Denis
42 36 82 84
Open 10am-7pm. Closed Sun. V, MC. M° Strasbourg-Saint-Denis.
5th arr. - 23-27, quai Saint-Michel - 43 54 57 32
5th arr. - 4-6, pl. Saint-Michel
43 25 91 19
Open 9:30am-7:30pm. Closed Sun. V, MC. M°St-Michel.

This multistory book emporium is renowned among the city's student population for its broad inventory, special sales, and huge collection of secondhand hardcovers and paperbacks. There's a fine selection of English and American books (you might consider selling your own used or unwanted books here).

La Hune

6th arr. - 170, bd Saint-Germain
45 48 35 85, fax 45 44 49 87
Open 10am-11:45pm. Closed Sun. V, AE, MC. M° Saint-Germain-des-Prés.

La Hune is a favorite among Parisian intellectuals, bibliophiles, and inveterate browsers. It stays open late and stocks an impressive array of books on architecture, contemporary art and design, as well as classics and contemporary literature. The mezzanine houses works on the graphic arts, photography, theater, and film.

FNAC

1st arr. - Forum des Halles, Porte Lescot - 40 41 40 00, fax 40 41 40 86
6th arr. - 136, rue de Rennes
49 54 30 00, fax 49 54 30 03
17th arr. - 26-30, av. des Ternes
44 09 18 00, fax 44 09 18 01
La Défense - 2, pl. de La Défense
46 92 29 00, fax 46 92 29 04
Open 10am-7:30pm (Mon 1pm-7:30pm). Closed Sun. V, MC. M° Les Halles, Montparnasse, Ternes, RER La Défense (A).

FNAC is the biggest bookstore chain in Europe, with a low-price policy that means you can read more for less: French books sell for five percent under standard retail, while foreign editions are discounted even more. Miles of shelves are packed with a vast and varied stock of volumes ranging from do-it-yourself manuals, cookbooks, and guides to high-brow fiction, poetry, and philosophy. The stores are immense and densely packed with book-loving humanity, particularly on weekends. The salespeople are qualified and knowledgeable, though it often seems like they are rarer than first editions (which means, however, that one can browse here for hours undisturbed).

La Librairie des Femmes

6th arr. - 74, rue de Seine
43 29 50 75, fax 42 22 62 73
Open 10am-7pm. Closed Sun. V, AE, MC. M° Odéon.

This is not a feminist bookshop per se. It is a publisher/ bookseller's showcase that highlights books written by or about women (including many books by men). The first-floor sales area is one of the most attractive in Paris—sunny, spacious, and user-friendly. The Librairie des Femmes, which recently celebrated its twentieth anniversary, also organizes worthwhile photo and print exhibits.

Librairie René Thomas

5th arr. - 28, rue des Fossés-Saint-Bernard
46 34 11 30, fax 43 29 78 64
Open 9:30am-7pm (Mon 2pm-7pm). Closed Sun. V, MC. M° Maubert-Mutualité.

This charming little shop features more than 10,000 works on the natural sciences (in several languages). It was renovated not long ago, and is now managed by specialists affiliated with the natural history museum. You will find nature guides, works on gardening, ecology, history, and much more, plus a large children's-book section. A wealth of guidebooks is on hand as well.

La Maison du Dictionnaire

14th arr. - 98, bd du Montparnasse
43 22 12 93, fax 43 22 01 77
Open 9am-6:30pm. Closed Sat, Sun. V, AE, MC. M° Raspail.

This ever-expanding bookstore in the Montparnasse shopping center features more than 4,000 new and used dictionaries (general, technical, and special-interest) in 150 languages. Even more astounding is the Pivothèque reading room, open to the public, in which you may sit and browse through any book before buying it.

Virgin Megastore

1st arr. - Galerie du Carrousel du Louvre, 99, rue de Rivoli - 49 53 52 90
Open 10am-10pm (Sun noon-8pm). Closed Tue. V, AE, DC, MC. M° Palais-Royal.
8th arr. - 52, av. des Champs-Élysées - 49 53 50 00
Open 10am-midnight (Fri & Sat 10am-1am). V, AE, DC, MC. M° George-V.

Virgin's exhaustive stock of fiction and non-fiction can be perused until midnight (even later on weekends). Better still, the store posts prices that are five percent under normal retail. The new Virgin store in the Carroussel du Louvre specializes in art books.

MUSIC

La Flûte de Pan

8th arr. - 49 & 59, rue de Rome
42 93 65 05, fax 42 93 51 47
Open 10am-6:30pm. Closed Sun. V, MC. M° Europe.

The array of sheet music ranges from classical to jazz, with a significant section dedicated to folk melodies. There are books, too, both new and used, on music and musicians.

Paroles et Musique

5th arr. - 81, bd St-Michel
43 54 68 90, fax 43 54 59 70
Open 10am-7pm. Closed Sun. V, MC. M° Saint-Michel.

Pop, rock, and classical music are all well represented in the vast selection of sheet music for voice and instruments from French and foreign publishers.

RARE BOOKS

Librairie Pierre Bérès

8th arr. - 14, av. de Friedland
45 61 00 99,
fax 43 59 79 13
Open 9am-6pm (Sat 9am-12:30pm & 2pm-6pm). Closed Sun. No cards. M° George-V.

The grand old man of the city's rare-book trade possesses one of the world's most precious inventories, which includes illuminated manuscripts, incunabula (pre-sixteenth-century printed books), and works illustrated by contemporary artists. Even if, like most mortals, you lack the means to acquire one of these treasures, if you are a true bibliophile you owe it to yourself to visit this remarkable address.

Carnavalette

3rd arr. - 2, rue des Francs-Bourgeois - 42 72 91 92
Open daily 10:30am-6:30pm. V, MC. M° St-Paul.

A gold mine for collectors of first editions (Zola and Hugo, among others), antique prints of Paris and France, and hard-to-find journals published between 1850 and 1920. We recently spotted an issue of *Charivari* with an original lithograph by Daumier, selling for a little over 200 F.

Courant d'Art

6th arr. - 79, rue de Vaugirard
45 49 36 41, fax 45 49 21 16
Open 11am-7:30pm. Closed Sun. V, AE, DC. M° St-Placide.

Art is the passion of bookseller Marie-Josée Grandjean. Her Rue de Vaugirard shop is a showcase for books on art—from studies and monographs of painters, sculptors, and artisans, to sales catalogs from Christie's, Sotheby's, or Drouot. On display is an impressive collection of engravings, reproductions, auction and exhibition catalogs, back issues of art magazines, and all sorts of other unfindables. Not to mention a noteworthy collection of books on film and photography.

Librairie du Cygne

6th arr. - 17, rue Bonaparte
43 26 32 45, fax 43 26 92 68
Open 10am-noon & 2pm-7pm. Closed Sat, Sun. V, MC. M° Saint-Germain-des-Prés.

The Librairie du Cygne seems to have tumbled out of a Balzac novel. The ancient oak bookcases of this austere shop groan with signed first editions and illustrated works by the greats—Stendhal, Molière, Anatole France, Maupassant, Zola, and Hugo. A wide-ranging array of books on the decorative arts is another specialty of the house.

Librairie du Pont-Neuf

6th arr. - 1, rue Dauphine
43 26 42 40, fax 43 25 34 60
Open 9:30am-noon & 2pm-6:30pm. Closed Sun, Mon. V. M° Saint-Michel.

This charming shop run by Claude Coulet features a nineteenth-century reading room, with shelves packed with first editions, illustrated works, and reprints by Carteret, Vicaire, and Pia. The lovely setting, just across from the Pont-Neuf, and one of the best selections of antiquarian books in Paris, make the Librairie du Pont-Neuf a must-visit for bibliophiles and curious browsers alike.

TRAVEL BOOKS

Institut Géographique National

8th arr. - 107, rue de La Boétie
43 98 80 00, fax 43 98 85 05
Open 9:30am-7pm (Sat 10am-12:30pm & 2pm-5:30pm). Closed Sun. No cards. M° Franklin-D.-Roosevelt.

Need a map? Of course you need a map! Those published by the IGA are meticulously detailed, and will delight travelers, tourists, hikers, and bikers who want to know just where they are.

Le Tour du Monde

16th arr. - 9, rue de la Pompe
42 88 73 59, fax 42 88 40 57
Open 10am-1pm & 2pm-7pm. Closed Sun, Mon. No cards. M° La Muette.

Travel-book buffs take note: Jean-Étienne and Edmonde Huret have earned their reputation as the Sherlock Holmes(es) of the book world. Their shop is chockablock with hard-to-find, out-of-print, and rare works on the far-flung and the right-next-door. They also stock a colorful selection of children's books.

STATIONERY

Armorial

8th arr. - 98, rue du Fg-St-Honoré - 42 65 08 18 (also 16th arr., 17th arr.)
Open 9:30am-6:30pm. Closed Sun. V, AE, DC. M° Miromesnil.

The desk sets and other sophisticated accessories crafted by this prestigious firm can be found in the offices of many cabinet ministers and other top-level executives with refined (and expensive) tastes.

Cassegrain

8th arr. - 422, rue Saint-Honoré (also: 6th arr.)
42 60 20 08, fax 42 61 40 99
Open 10am-7pm. Closed Sun. V, AE, DC. M° Concorde.

A venerable institution on the Rue Saint-Honoré, founded in 1919, Cassegrain has updated its image (while preserving its reputation for fine engraving, of course). A line of "youthful" leather accessories includes brightly colored lizard date and address books, boxes covered with marbleized paper, more boxes and picture frames in burled elm, and amusing gadgets for children. Cassegrain is one of the rare sources in France for the legendary notebooks from Smythson of Bond Street (bible paper, sewn bindings, leather covers—they cost a fortune, but they're worth it). Another Cassegrain store is located at 81, rue des Saints-Pères, in the sixth arrondissement.

Les Crayons de Julie

16th arr. - 17, rue de Longchamp - 44 05 02 01
Open 10am-7pm (Mon noon-7pm; Sat 10:30am-1pm & 2:30pm-6pm). Closed Sun. V, AE, DC. M° Trocadéro.

Traditionalists who like to feel the heft of a fountain pen in their hands when they write letters and thank-you notes love to browse in Julie's charming shop for old-fashioned writing instruments and handsome stationery.

Dupré Octante

8th arr. - 141, rue du Fg-St-Honoré & 36, rue d'Artois
45 63 10 11
Open 9:15am-6:30pm (Sat 10am-6pm). Closed Sun. V, AE. M° St-Philippe-du-Roule.

Every illustrator and graphic designer in Paris can be found, at one time or another, in this huge stationery shop on the Faubourg-Saint-Honoré. A considerable assortment of letter papers in lovely, exclusive colors is on view, as well as a full range of art and office supplies. In the equally well-stocked shop on the nearby Rue d'Artois is a complete line of drawing materials—from pencils and special papers to computer software.

The Filofax Centre

3rd arr. - 32, rue des Francs-Bourgeois
42 78 67 87, fax 42 78 67 88
Open 11am-7pm. Closed Sun. V, AE, DC. M° Saint-Paul.

This is one of just three Filofax Centres in the entire world (the others, should you care to note, are in London and Stamford, Connecticut). The famed Filofax diaries are on hand, of course, as well as the complete line of refills, in all their infinite variety (there's even a magnetized chessboard). We also spied some superb sterling-silver pens by the British manufacturer, Yard-O-Led.

Honoris Causa

5th arr. - 15, rue Claude-Bernard - 45 35 62 70
Open 11:30am-7:30pm (Mon 2:30pm-7:30pm). Closed Sun. V, AE. M° Censier-Daubenton.

Recycled paper in a wealth of muted shades has pride of place in this attractive shop. Sold by the sheet or in pads, it is accompanied by pencils crafted of hazelwood or chestnut, superb Lépine fountain pens (369 to 850 F), personalized embossing presses, and jaunty English bookbags in untreated leather (385 to 450 F).

Lavrut

2nd arr. - 52, passage Choiseul
42 96 95 54, fax 40 20 94 89
Open 9:15am-6:30pm (Sat 9:30am-12:30pm & 2pm-6pm). Closed Sun. V, AE. M° Quatre-Septembre.

An old-fashioned stationery shop, quite different from today's trendy "paper boutiques." Lavrut's inventory is vast, encompassing school, office, and art supplies, all of high quality. Even better, the prices are just right and the service is exemplary. Note, however, that this is not a place for leisurely browsing: customers state what they're looking for, and the clerks guide them around the warren of little rooms that make up the shop.

Mélodies Graphiques

4th arr. - 10, rue du Pont-Louis-Philippe - 42 74 57 68
Open 11am-7pm (Mon 2:30pm-7pm). Closed Sun. V, AE. M° Pont-Marie.

This pretty boutique, done up in blond wood, showcases desk accessories covered in marbleized paper. The papers, ten styles in all, are made by the well-known Florentine firm, Il Papiro, according to a process unchanged since the Renaissance. Sumptuous writing papers and calligrapher's supplies (including fifteen different shades of ink) are offered as well.

Papier Plus

4th arr. - 9, rue du Pont-Louis-Philippe
42 77 70 49, fax 41 54 75 18
Open noon-7pm. Closed Sun, hols. V. M° Pont-Marie.

At Papier Plus, you'll find writing paper sold by the kilo, blank notebooks, photograph albums, and files, in a host of vivid and pastel shades. Graphic designers and artists come here for the special etching and drawing papers, and the deluxe Cumberland colored pencils from England.

Sennelier

7th arr. - 3, quai Voltaire
42 60 72 15, fax 42 61 00 69
Open 9am-6:30pm (Mon 9am-noon & 2pm-6:30pm). Closed Sun. V, AE, DC, MC. M° Palais-Royal.

Appropriately located next to the École des Beaux-Arts, Sennelier has, in the course of its 100-year history, sold tons of art supplies to many well-known and aspiring artists. Here they find the best brands of paints and pigments, all manner of papers and sketch pads of excellent quality, canvas, easels, and framing equipment.

Stern

2nd arr. - 47, passage des Panoramas
45 08 86 45, fax 42 36 94 48
Open 9:30am-12:30pm & 1:30pm-5:30pm. Closed Sat, Sun. No cards. M° Bourse.

Stern started out in 1830, when the *grands boulevards* were the epicenter of elegant Parisian life. Now known throughout the world as engraver to royalty, aristocrats, and people of taste, Stern carefully conserves its traditions of using the finest papers, all crafted and engraved by hand. The firm has models available for every type of visiting or business card, invitations, and announcements, but Stern's draftsmen can also produce designs to your specifications. Engraved bookplates are a house specialty.

Stylos Marbeuf

8th arr. - 40, rue Marbeuf
42 25 40 49, fax 42 89 52 93
Open 9:30am-7pm. Closed Sun. V, AE, DC. M° Franklin-D.-Roosevelt.

If it's a fountain pen you're seeking, this is the place: the selection of famous French and imported brands is amazing to behold. Repairs are also handled here (though no gimcrack pens will be considered). Stylos Marbeuf now carries a huge (and expanding) range of diaries and refills by Mulberry, Oberthur, Cassegrain, and Filofax. And don't forget that the solid-gold pens and luxurious desk accessories make sumptuous gifts.

CHILDREN

BOOKS

Chantelivre

6th arr. - 13, rue de Sèvres
45 48 87 90
Open 10am-6:50pm (Mon 1pm-6:50pm). Closed Sun. V, MC. M° Sèvres-Babylone.

Enter here, all you bibliophiles in short pants and smocked dresses. Among the some 10,000 titles in stock are illustrated story books, fairy and folk tales, and novels. Also on hand are records and educational games, and there is a small selection of books and games in English. In a back corner of the shop is an inviting play area where children can draw, look at books, or listen to a story (told in French, of course).

CLOTHING

Baby Dior

8th arr. - 28, av. Montaigne
40 73 54 14
Open 10am-6:30pm. Closed Sun. V, AE, DC, MC. M° Franklin-D.-Roosevelt.

If you can afford to buy an entire set of baby clothes, wonderful; if you can't... at least indulge in one teeny little shirt with a ruffled collar, a set of sheets for the cradle, or a dressing gown. The knitted booties make a darling baby present, and there are also some other adorable gift items—picture frames, silver cups (from about 1,450 F), and such. Abominably expensive smocked dresses are available in sizes up to eight years (680 to 4,000 F, for a one-year-old).

Bonpoint

7th arr. - 67, rue de l'Université - 45 55 63 70
7th arr. - 7, rue de Solférino
45 55 42 79
8th arr. - 15, rue Royale
47 42 52 63
16th arr. - 64, av. Raymond-Poincaré
47 27 60 81
17th arr. - 184, rue de Courcelles
47 63 87 49
Open 10am-7pm. Closed Sun. V, AE, DC, MC. M° Solférino, Concorde, Victor-Hugo, Pereire.

These classic styles are designed to suit well-bred French children. For the last few years, Bonpoint has been trying to keep prices within reason, yet maintain the shop's renowned high quality. Pants are lined so they won't itch, hems are huge, and fabrics are made to last. The boutique specializes in children's formal dress: white gloves, straw hats, and other such romantic attire... ravishing!

Budget busters

Some people, we realize, are not happy unless they've paid top dollar (or franc, or whatever) to expand their little ones' wardrobe. For that segment of the population, we list the following addresses, where the children's clothes are dependably *chic et chers*: *Miki House* **makes absolutely adorable trendy togs for toddlers, as well as the cutest sneakers on earth (1 place des Victoires, 1st arr. - 40 26 23 00);** *Claude Vell* **dresses kids from 0 to 18 in a rainbow of subtle colors (8 rue du Jour, 1st arr. - 40 26 76 70);** *Cyrillus* **provides outfits for well-bred little ladies and gentlemen—kilts, little blazers, flannel bermudas, gorgeous plaid bathrobes (11 av. Duquesne, 7th arr. - 47 05 99 19).**
N.B.: like other French retailers, these shops put on worthwhile sales in January and July.

Cacharel
9th arr. - 34, rue Tronchet
47 42 12 61
Open 10:15am-7pm (Sat 10:15am-7:30pm). Closed Sun. V, AE, DC, MC. M° Madeleine.

Cacharel carries parkas, jackets, and blazers, as well as pleated skirts, Bermuda shorts, and dresses for children ages 4 to 18 years old. Girls look fetching in Liberty-print dresses, and boys handsome in the striped shirts.

Caddie Montaigne
8th arr. - 38, rue François-Ier
47 20 79 79
Open 10am-7pm. Closed Sun. V, AE, DC. M° George-V.

From the cradle through junior high, kids can be clothed here in designer togs with the most fashionable labels: Armani, Dior, Kenzo, Moschino, Rykiel... If you're dead-set on spending 800 to 2,000 F for a little dress, rest assured that here it will be no problem at all!

La Châtelaine
16th arr. - 170, av. Victor-Hugo - 47 27 44 07
Open 9:30am-6:30pm (Sat 9:30am-12:30pm & 2:30pm-6:30pm). Closed Sun, Mon. V, AE. M° Victor-Hugo.

This is the most luxurious children's clothing shop imaginable. Every item—dresses, jackets, shirts—is perfectly finished, and the babywear is the most elegant in all of Paris. It is designed exclusively for La Châtelaine by Molli, a Swiss lingerie firm. Clothes for youngsters of any age can be custom-made and will be delivered free of charge; alterations, too, are done gratis. This isn't so surprising when you consider that a tiny Shetland wool coat is priced at 1,460 F.

Remember that if you spend 2,000 F or more in a store, you are entitled to a full refund of the value-added tax (VAT). See Basics for details.

Chevignon Kids
6th arr. - 4, rue des Ciseaux
43 26 06 37
Open 10:15am-7pm. Closed Sun. V, AE, MC. M° Saint-Germain-des-Prés.

This is the place to find hideously expensive children's gear, inspired by the clothes American teenagers wore in the 1950s. Practically every item is stamped with the firm's logo—they should pay their customers for the free advertising!

Gina Diwan
15th arr. - 20, av. du Maine
42 22 27 09 (also 16th arr.)
Open 10:30am-7pm. Closed Sun. V, AE, DC, MC. M° Montparnasse.

Adorable, dressy rompers for babies are featured (380 F for a three-month-old), as well as hand-smocked dresses, embroidered tops, and blouses with petal collars. Alongside these tiny togs you'll find irresistible clothes for children up to fourteen years.

Jacadi
17th arr. - 60, bd de Courcelles - 45 72 27 42 (also: 1st arr., 2nd arr., 4th arr., 5th arr., 6th arr., 7th arr., 8th arr., 9th arr., 13th arr., 14th arr., 15th arr., 16th arr., 18th arr., 19th arr., 20th arr.)
Open 10am-7pm (Mon 10am-2pm). Closed Sun. V. M° Monceau.

Given the prices French parents are usually obliged to pay to outfit their children, Jacadi's merchandise offers pretty good value. The styles are attractive, though rather sedate... how many little American boys would dare show up at school in wool Bermuda shorts and knee socks? At any rate, there are some beautiful shirts and blouses, sturdy outerwear, and lots of lovely accessories (headbands, socks, hats, mittens, and scarves). Sizes start at birth and go up to age fourteen.

Du Pareil au Même

12th arr. - 122, rue du Fg-St-Antoine - 43 44 67 46
Open 10am-7pm. Closed Sun. V, AE, MC. M° Ledru-Rollin.

These low-priced children's togs are unexpectedly sturdy, colorful, and stylish to boot. No wonder mothers crowd in to look over the merchandise (new arrivals weekly) and choose a little dress (from 79 F), shirt, or pair of bright-hued jeans (85 F). This popular, swiftly expanding chain operates some fifteen stores in and around Paris.

Petit Faune

6th arr. - 33, rue Jacob
42 60 80 72
Open 10:30am-7pm (Mon 2:30pm-7pm). Closed Sun. V, AE. M°St-Germain-des-Prés.

Floral-print dresses, hand-knitted baby clothes, and separates for children from birth to age twelve in traditional styles to which bold, bright colors give a fashion kick. But as for the prices... they really do defy good sense!

Tartine et Chocolat

8th arr. - 105, rue du Fg-St-Honoré - 45 62 44 04
Open 10am-7pm (Sat 10am-1:30pm & 2:30pm-7pm). Closed Sun. V. M° Saint-Philippe-du-Roule.
16th arr. - 60, av. Paul-Doumer - 45 04 08 94
Open 10am-7pm (Mon 11am-7pm). Closed Sun. M° Passy.

The famous blue-and-white stripes that first made the brand a success have survived, though these days they represent only three percent of the collection. Aside from clothes (up to eight years), Tartine et Chocolat also sells lots of appealing accessories, children's furniture, and baby equipment. Little girls love the firm's fresh, innocent eau de cologne (alcohol-free), "P'titsenbon," in its pretty frosted-glass bottle.

Sonia Rykiel Enfants

6th arr. - 4 rue de Grenelle
49 54 61 10
Open 10am-7pm. Closed Sun. V. M° Sèvres-Babylone.

Suddenly, upon becoming a grandmother, Sonia Rykiel realized she had nothing to dress up Lolita and Tatiana, her two darling granddaughters. So she convinced her own daughter, Natalie, to oversee a line of children's clothing. If your idea of fashions for tots runs to long black sweaters with miniskirts, velvet sweatsuits, outfits embroidered with gold teddies, or jersey separates in sharp red, violet, fuschia, and gray, then Rykiel Enfants is for you.

Souleïado Pitchoun

16th arr. - 71, av. Paul-Doumer
42 24 99 34, fax 42 24 88 85
Open 10am-7pm (Mon 2pm-7pm). Closed Sun. V, AE, DC, MC. M° La Muette.

Pitchoun" is Provençal for "little one," an appropriate name for a shop where children from birth to age twelve can be kitted out with adorable togs crafted in bright Souleiado prints. Mind, the merchandise is not cheap (skirts start at 500 F), but the look is irresistibly sunny and heartwarming.

SHOES

Bonpoint

7th arr. - 65, rue de l'Université - 47 05 09 09
Open 10am-7pm. Closed Sun. V, AE. M° Solférino.

Having outfitted your children at Bonpoint n° 67, what could be easier than

Tiny togs for less

Bonpoint, **in this tiny shop, discounts its end lots of charming children's clothing (82 rue de Grenelle, 7th arr. - 45 48 05 45). For more cut-rate kids' clothes, try** *Le Mouton à Cinq Pattes*—**it's a madhouse, but the prices are lowest (10 rue Saint-Placide, 6th arr. - 45 48 20 49);** *Magic Stock*, **on the same street, same price policy (60 rue Saint-Placide, 6th arr. - 45 44 01 89). For excellent prices on warm outdoor and ski wear by French manufacturers, head for** *Mi-Prix* **(27 boulevard Victor, 15th arr. - 48 28 42 48).**

to walk next door to find footwear for their little tootsies? There are black Paraboots (extremely difficult to find anywhere else) for macho minimen, pastel-colored ballet slippers, tennis shoes, low-rise boots, and classic styles for school.

Cendrine

6th arr. - 3, rue Vavin
43 54 81 20
Open 9:30am-12:30pm & 2pm-7pm. Closed Sun. No cards. M° Vavin.

Has your child got delicate or hard-to-fit feet? Well, if so, Cendrine is the place to go. Not that these shoes are orthopedic. On the contrary, the styles are classic, but Cendrine will fit your kid with a half-sole or advise you on the best model to buy. Anxious mothers emerge confident in the knowledge that their darlings are correctly, comfortably shod.

Froment Leroyer

16th arr. - 50, rue Vital
42 24 82 70 (also: 6th arr., 7th arr., 8th arr.)
Open 10am-7pm. Closed Sun. V. M° La Muette.

Froment Leroyer purveys sturdy Start-Rite shoes (at about twice the U.S. price), as well as patent-leather slippers, low laced boots, canvas sandals—all those enduring children's styles that parents find so reassuring.

Till

6th arr. - 51, rue de Sèvres
42 22 25 25
Open 9:30am-7pm (Mon noon-7pm). Closed Sun. V. M° Sèvres-Babylone.

You can be sure that your little ones' feet will be properly fitted here. Till hires only experienced salespeople and will not sell any shoes that haven't been impeccably finished. Kids' tennis shoes have spongy linings, babies' shoes are reinforced and finished in leather. There are 300 designs displayed—from loafers to dress shoes to sandals and slippers. Average price: 200 F.

JUNIORS & TEENS

Autour du Monde

3rd arr. - 10-12, rue des Francs-Bourgeois - 42 77 46 48
Open 10:30am-7pm (Sun 2pm-7pm). V, AE. M° St-Paul.

All the brands that French adolescents love—Bensimon, Cimarron, Chipie, Ninos de Lorca—are sure to appeal to their American counterparts. All kinds of jeanwear, naturally, in all sorts of colors, escorted by the indispensable accessories: bandanas, thick socks, hip sunglasses, and more.

Chipie

1st arr. - 31, rue de la Ferronnerie - 45 08 58 74
Open 10am-1pm & 2pm-7pm (Mon from 11am). Closed Sun. M° Châtelet.
6th arr. - 16, rue du Four
46 34 17 25
Open 10am-7pm (Mon 11am-7pm). Closed Sun. M° Saint-Germain-des-Prés.

The brand's motto: "Quality and fun since 1967." Well, if that's supposed to mean that the *fun* comes from the label being pasted all over the front of the clothing, and the *quality* is in the cloth (which has a tough time surviving from one season to the next)... But who cares? This is carefully coded fashion for kids who want to look like all their friends.

Détails

1st arr. - 15, rue du Jour
40 26 75 65
Open 10:30am-7:15pm (Mon noon-7:15pm). Closed Sun. V, AE, MC. M° Les Halles.

Adèle and Patricia are two fashion-wise sisters who present an eclectic panorama of up-to-the-minute clothes ranging from streetwise to sedate. Young style mavens will love the colorful collection, with offerings by such trendmeisters as Pablito, Xüly Bet, Prisma, and Witberg. Children's clothes by Cacharel and Grain de Lune are displayed as well.

Kenzo Enfants

1st arr. - 3, pl. des Victoires
40 39 72 87
Open 10am-7pm (Mon 11am-7pm). Closed Sun. V, AE, DC, MC. M° Palais-Royal.

Kenzo captivates the younger set with his signature prints, vivid colors, and splendid accessories, priced markedly lower than his first-tier line. The clothes are of good quality, and identifiably "Kenzo."

Naf-Naf

17th arr. - 10, av. des Ternes
42 67 30 30, fax 42 67 22 06
Open 10am-8pm. Closed Sun. V. M° Ternes.

The little pink pig that is Naf-Naf's mascot has a bright and tidy new home here, filled to bursting with relatively inexpensive, youthful clothes that exactly mirror current trends. Droll and cheerful prints cover leggings, T-shirts, bare little cotton dresses that look great on teenage girls; pretty too are the ribbed-silk T-shirts and peppy skirts and sweaters. Boys will love the baggy casual trousers and flashy print shirts. Kids willingly whip out their wallets and spend weeks' worth of pocket money on Naf-Naf accessories.

New Man

6th arr. - 12, rue de l'Ancienne-Comédie - 43 54 44 95
Open 10am-7:30pm. Closed Sun. V. M° Odéon.

Not just for men. These casual clothes with considerable cachet are crafted in denim, gabardine, cotton, or *cupro*, an attractive new fiber blend.

Yam de Bonpoint

7th arr. - 86, rue de l'Université - 45 51 17 65
Open 10am-7pm. Closed Sun. V, AE, DC, MC. M° Solférino.

Ever notice how girls over ten years of age rebel at the idea of wearing "babyish" clothing? What they want are trendy togs that prove that they've moved into the teenage sphere. Bonpoint's newest collection is aimed at kids from twelve to sixteen, with such grown-up offerings as a herringbone jacket with a nipped-in waist (1,150 F), and corduroy shorts teamed up with a skinny-ribbed sweater (370 F and 440 F).

SHOES

Free Lance

6th arr. - 30, rue du Four
45 48 14 78
Open 10am-7pm. Closed Sun. V, AE, DC, MC. M° Saint-Germain-des-Prés.

Rusted metal seems to be the dominant note in the décor, but never mind. Free Lance has the footwear that teenagers want: lace-ups with rubber or "tire" soles, towering wedgies, 1950s patent leathers, pretty ballet slippers, hobnail boots, and leather sandals. They may not be the most comfortable shoes, but that's not what's important here.

Jonak

6th arr. - 70, rue de Rennes
45 48 27 11
Open 10:15am-7pm (Mon 11am-7:15pm). Closed Sun. V, MC. M° Saint-Sulpice.

Fashionable footwear made in Italy, sold at factory prices (from 290 F). Young girls adore Jonak's canvas or leather lace-up boots and the feather-light ballerina slippers.

Marie Lalet

4th arr. - 16, rue du Bourg-Tibourg - 40 27 08 05
Open 11am-7pm. Closed Sun, Mon. V, MC. M° Hôtel-de-Ville.

Essentially a boutique for heavy-duty footwear from Doc Martens, this shop also presents some 45 other models (for men, women, and children) that offer just about anything one could wish for in the way of color and style. Many different leathers too (aged, oiled, patent, suede...). Check out the authentic hiking boots by Galibier, a top manufacturer.

Mosquitos

6th arr. - 25, rue du Four
43 25 25 16 & 99, rue de Rennes - 45 48 58 40
Open 10:30am-7:30pm. Closed Sun. V, AE, MC. M° Rennes.

The colorful, youthful styles, often adorned with embroidery or metal studs, are absolutely up to date. Today's favorite? The "Trust" booty, which sports a chunky heel and a thick lug sole.

■ TOYS

Le Ciel Est à Tout le Monde

5th arr. - 10, rue Gay-Lussac
46 33 21 50
Open 10am-7pm. Closed Sun, Mon. V. RER Luxembourg (B).

"The sky belongs to us all!" proclaims the sign of this store, a kingdom of kites. There are more than 100 different models to choose from, for beginners to veteran collectors. If, like Charlie Brown, you run into a "kite-eating tree," don't panic: this shop handles all manner of repairs.

Il Était Une Fois

6th arr. - 1, rue Cassette
45 48 21 10
Open 10am-7:30pm. Closed Sun. V, AE. M° Saint-Sulpice.

This traditional toy store located in a splendid vaulted cellar presents one of the city's prettiest selections of playthings. There are charming rattles and cuddly stuffed toys for the tiniest tots, model trains and puppets to amuse older kids. Free delivery within Paris.

Jouets & Cie

1st arr. - 11, bd de Sébastopol - 42 33 67 67
Open 10am-7pm. Closed Sun. V, AE, DC. M° Châtelet.

Rather alarming, the gigantic gold baby doll that serves as this company's mascot. He presides over a vast emporium of games, scale models, toys, puzzles, costumes, and, yes, dollies that sell for less than what they would cost in traditional toy shops or department stores. The latest electronic games and cassettes are on hand, as well as outdoor games, craft sets, robots, and baby toys. Shopping baskets are a welcome convenience; special promotional sales are held throughout the year.

Multicubes

4th arr. - 5, rue de Rivoli
42 77 10 77
Open 10am-7pm (Mon 2pm-7pm). Closed Sun. V, AE. M° Saint-Paul.
15th arr. - 110, rue Cambronne - 47 34 25 97
Open 10:30am-2pm & 2:30pm-7pm. Closed Sun, Mon. V, AE. M° Vaugirard.

Every year we look forward to the new collection from Erzgebirge, the land of wooden-toy makers. Some of the playthings are pure marvels and quite pricey, coveted by old and young alike. There are mobiles, yo-yos, model farms and animals, as well as dolls with real hair created by Käthe Kruse (a Bauhaus disciple). There are also Yuletide decorations from Germany and Scandinavia.

Au Nain Bleu

8th arr. - 406-410, rue Saint-Honoré - 42 60 39 01
Open 10am-6:30pm. Closed Sun. V, AE. M° Concorde.

A paradise for children since 1836, this world-famous toy shop carries a staggering stock of playthings to tempt you. On the lower level, visit old friends like Mickey Mouse and Babar; or hop a ride on a spirited rocking horse with real leather trappings. There's a great variety of enchanting dolls and doll clothes (accessory kits start at 500 F), plastic and china tea services, and for boys, lots of remote-control cars and motorcycles; all kids love the costume section, with masks and makeup for every occasion. Prices? Well, miniature French grocery shops start at 700 F; stuffed animals in every size and shape cost from 250 to 3,500 F. Le Nain Bleu sells many exclusive models you won't find elsewhere.

Pain d'Épices

9th arr. - 29, passage Jouffroy
47 70 82 65
Open 10am-7pm (Mon 1pm-7pm). Closed Sun. V. M° Rue Montmartre.

Tucked in the lovely Passage Jouffroy, just opposite the Musée Grevin (see below) this shop is surely one of the most delightful in town. Reproductions of old-fashioned toys—tops, hoops, gyroscopes, puppets, pretty cut-outs, and paper dollies—make charming presents for good little children. And the gift baskets for newborns (from 280 F) are irresistible.

La Pelucherie

6th arr. - 74, rue de Seine
46 33 60 21
Open 10:30am-7:30pm. Closed Sun. V. M° Odéon.
8th arr. - 84, av. des Champs-Élysées - 43 59 49 05
Open 10am-11pm (Sun 11:30am-11pm). V, AE, DC. M° George-V.

A boon for night owls, this stuffed-animal kingdom on the Champs-Élysées stays open late. From wee teddy bears to a gargantuan elephant, dogs of every breed, raccoons, bees, Bambis, and Dumbos coexist in exemplary harmony here. There's also a section for newborns that displays darling baby clothes. La Pelucherie delivers within Paris and all over the world, and every item carries a lifetime guarantee.

Si Tu Veux

2nd arr. - 68, galerie Vivienne
42 60 59 97
Open 10am-7pm. Closed Sun. Mail-order catalog. V. M° Bourse.

Nestled cozily in the heart of this neoclassic gallery is a gold mine of attractive, reasonably priced playthings for children. Many of the toys and crafts are educational, others are appealingly old-fashioned (note the dolly-sized kitchenware). Owner Madeleine Deny also presents a wealth of tiny toys (rings, jacks, marbles, miniature yo-yos) that make perfect party favors. Speaking of parties, you'll find all manner of supplies for your kid's next birthday bash; in fact, if you like, the store will organize the party for you! Next door is a space reserved for nostalgic grownups. Remember those teddy bears stuffed with straw that you loved as a child? Well, you can find them here, alongside painted tin toys, dainty china services, and romantic Victorian paper dolls.

Zig et Puce

7th arr. - 22 bis, rue Jean-Nicot - 47 05 30 58
Open 10am-7pm. Closed Sun, Mon. No cards. M° Latour-Maubourg.

The premises are small, but the stock is enormous and prices are right! Tricycles hang from the ceiling, boxes of Legos, dolls, games are piled high. While you browse, your kids can examine the trove of amusing gadgets and gimcracks displayed on the counter.

WHERE TO TAKE THE KIDS

MUSEUMS

The following is a list of museums of special interest to children.

Centre Georges-Pompidou

4th arr. - 120, rue St-Martin, entrance pl. Georges-Pompidou or "Piazza Beaubourg" - 44 78 49 17
Open 2pm-6pm. Closed Sun, Tue. No cards. M° Les Halles.

This Parisian cultural center hosts children's workshops (conducted in French) on Wednesday and Saturday afternoons. The themes are usually linked to the museum's current exhibitions. Keep in mind too that children are generally delighted by the colorful pop-art fountain by Nikki de Saint-Phalle just outside the Center on the Place Stravinsky.

Cité des Enfants

19th arr. - 30, av. Corentin-Cariou - 40 05 70 00 & 46 42 13 13
Open 9:30am-5pm (Sat 10am-6pm; Sun 10am-7pm). Closed Mon. No cards. M° Porte-de-la-Villette.

Part of the Cité des Sciences et de l'Industrie is dedicated exclusively to children: the new and exciting Cité des Enfants. Kids between the ages of three and twelve can participate in 90-minute "Discovery" programs held every day: these high-tech yet user-friendly experiments illustrate such themes as the world of animals, the human body, robots, the weather... Fascinating and lots of fun. Children delight too in the "Géode," a mirrored geodesic dome that houses a huge panoramic movie screen, and in the Argonaute, an authentic submarine. The Planetarium and Inventorium (main exhibition center) also offer plenty of entertainment and instruction, including video games for hands-on play.

Musée de l'Armée

7th arr. - Hôtel National des Invalides - 44 42 37 67
Open 10am-6pm (Oct 1-Mar 31: 10am-5pm). Admission: 32 F, reduced rate: 22 F, children under 7: free. No cards. M° Invalides.

This military museum exhibits arms, uniforms, and scale models of famous battle scenes, and screens films of World Wars I and II.

Musée National des Arts d'Afrique et d'Océanie

12th arr. - 293, av. Daumesnil - 44 74 84 80
Open 10am-noon & 1:30pm-5:30pm (Sat & Sun 12:30pm-6pm). Closed Tue. No cards. M° Porte-Dorée.

This museum located on the edge of the Bois de Vincennes (site of a terrific zoo) features the largest aquarium in Paris. Children adore the crocodile pit.

For more details on museums in Paris, consult the *Arts & Leisure* chapter.

Musée Grévin

9th arr. - 10, bd Montmartre
47 70 85 05
Open daily 1pm-7pm (School hols 10am-7pm, last admission 6pm). V. M° Rue Montmartre.

Founded in 1882, this wax museum features spookily convincing renditions of historic and other famous figures (including Barbie and Madonna, no less). As an extra added attraction, there are "fun house" mirrors to amuse children of all ages. The price of admission also entitles you to attend a magic show.

Musée de la Marine

16th arr. - Palais de Chaillot, pl. du Trocadéro
45 53 31 70
Open 10am-6pm. Closed Tue. No cards. M° Trocadéro.

Exhibits and scale models relating to naval history and marine archaeology are favorites with older children at the Musée de la Marine. The museum also displays maritime art, as well as artifacts of the technical, historical, and scientific evolution of navigation. In fact, the exhibits are far less dry and dusty than they may sound!

Palais de la Découverte

8th arr. - Av. Franklin-Roosevelt - 40 74 80 00
Open 9:30am-6pm (Sun 10am-7pm). Closed Mon. Restaurant. No cards. M° Franklin-D.-Roosevelt.

This old-fashioned, decidedly low-tech museum makes an interesting outing for scientifically inclined children over eight years old. Experiments are conducted by staff members every afternoon for the public. A list of daily activities is posted to the left of the museum's entrance.

Museum National d'Histoire Naturelle

5th arr. - Jardin des Plantes, 57, rue Cuvier - 40 79 30 00
Open 10am-5pm (Sat & Sun 11am-6pm). Closed Tue, hols. No cards. V. M° Jussieu.

The spectacular Evolution Gallery inaugurated in June 1994 presents the museum's zoological collections (which had not been displayed since 1965) in a soaring, glass-roofed hall. Kids are mesmerized by the exhibits, which range from butterflies, to stuffed giraffes, to the skeleton of an 81-foot-long rorqual. Entertaining and educational: a must-see.

PARKS & GARDENS

Here are some city parks with particular appeal for children.

Bois de Boulogne

16th arr.

Entrances are located at the Porte Maillot, Porte Dauphine, and Les Sablons. This enormous wooded park, which covers part of the sixteenth arrondissement and the suburb of Neuilly, features a lake, horseback-riding clubs, a lovely children's park and petting zoo (Jardin d'Acclimatation), a marvelous floral garden (Parc de Bagatelle), and innumerable hiking and biking paths that wind through trees and lawns. Bicycles for adults and children are available for rental.

For further details about parks and gardens in Paris, as well as for information on swimming pools and other sports, see the *Arts & Leisure* chapter.

Jardin du Luxembourg

6th arr. - Main entrance bd St-Michel, near pl. Edmond-Rostand - 40 79 37 00
Open daily dawn-dusk. M° Vavin. RER Luxembourg.

Within these attractive landscaped gardens, situated between Saint-Michel and Montparnasse, kids can expend their excess energy go-karts, pony rides, a puppet theater, sandboxes, jungle gyms, swings, a merry-go-round and more. For tiny tots, there is an enclosed play

Bonjour, Mickey!

Disneyland Paris, the European home of Mickey, Minnie, Donald, and their pals is situated some 20 miles east of Paris, accessible by car or by RER. Since the park opened in April 1992, 10 new attractions have been added for a total of 39, including *Les Mystères du Nautilus*. Based on Jules Verne's *20,000 Leagues Under the Sea*, it features a tour of Captain Nemo's infamous submarine and an attack by a giant squid! Admission to the theme park is 250 F (175 F for children 3 to 11), a bit less in off-season. Prices for food and lodging have come down since the resort first opened: inexpensive set meals and children's menus are now widely available, and hotel rates have been scaled back considerably. The inevitable Disney souvenirs, however, are still pretty pricey. To avoid spending much of your day waiting in line, your best bet is to visit Disneyland on a weekday—preferably in off-season. Please turn to Marne-la-Vallée in the "Suburbs" chapter, p. 96 for restaurants and p. 140 for hotels.

area reserved for toddlers five and under.

Jardin des Plantes

5th arr. - Main entrance 57, rue Cuvier - 40 79 30 00
Open daily 7:30am-5:45pm (summer 7:30am-7:45pm). M° Gare d'Austerlitz.

The Botanical Gardens (Jardin des Plantes) contain more than 10,000 classified plants. There is also a Winter Garden (Jardin d'Hiver), with many tropical specimens, and a rather amazing Alpine Garden (Jardin Alpin), which includes mountain- and polar-region plants. The Jardin's open-air zoo is always a big hit with youngsters.

Parc Floral de Paris

12th arr. - Esplanade du Château de Vincennes, Rond-Point de la Pyramide
43 74 60 49
Open Nov-Feb 9:30am-5pm; Mar & Oct 9:30am-6pm; Apr-Sep 9:30am-8pm. Entrance: 10 F; 6-12: 5 F; 0-6, 65 & over: free. M° Château-de-Vincennes.

A small fee admits kids to a playground full of delightful things to do and try. Amusement-park rides cost extra, and the miniature golf course (dotted with reproductions of famous Parisian landmarks) commands a fee of 30 F. Children also love the Butterfly Garden and the Nature Cabin.

Parc de la Villette

19th arr. - Main entrance av. Jean-Jaurès, near Porte de Pantin - 42 40 76 10
Hours vary, call for information. M° Porte-de-la-Villette.

Lots and lots of space, with seven themed gardens, broad lawns, and a fantastic "dragon" sliding board. After an educational tour of the Cité des Sciences, kids can unwind here.

CHEAP CHIC

Alaïa

4th arr. - 18, rue de la Verrerie - 40 27 85 58
Open 10am-7pm. Closed Sun. V, AE, DC. M° Hôtel-de-Ville.

Sexy knits and winsome accessories (shoes, gloves, hats, belts) all bearing the unmistakable stamp of the tiny Tunisian designer. The clothing comes from the previous year's collections, and sells at a 50 percent reduction from the original price (dresses from 2,000 to 3,000 F, skirts 1,000 to 1,500 F).

Don't plan to shop on Sundays—the vast majority of Paris stores are closed.

L'Annexe des Créateurs

9th arr. - 19, rue Godot-de-Mauroy - 42 65 46 40
Open 11am-7pm. Closed Sun. V. M° Havre-Caumartin.

Gaultier, Versace, Kenzo, Moschino, Escada... These are just some of the labels you'll find here. The clothes date from the previous season, and are marked down a hefty 30 to 40 percent. The evening clothes (for men and women) are particularly good value. New this year: a selection of bridal gowns. Lots of accessories, too.

L'Astucerie

15th arr. - 105, rue de Javel
45 57 94 74
Open noon-2pm & 3pm-7pm (Sat noon-6pm). Closed Sun, Mon. V. M° Félix-Faure.

Previously owned but hardly worn top-label clothing for women and children is the backbone of this boutique's inventory.

Bargain City

Manufacturers' outlets present unbeatable bargains in clothes, shoes, and accessories on the *Rue d'Alésia* **(14th arr., between the Place Victor-et-Hélène-Basch and the Rue des Plantes).**
Head to *Mac Douglas* **(n°120 - 43 95 68 03) for fashionable leather gear, to** *Stock 2* **(n°92- 45 41 65 67) for designs by Daniel Hechter for the entire family, to** *Cacharel* **at n°114 (something for everyone here, too) (45 42 53 04), to** *SR Store* **(n°64 - 43 95 06 13) for greatly reduced fashions by Sonia Rykiel, and to** *Blanc Bleu* **(n°72 - 40 44 56 65) for its famous sportwear. And discount houses stand cheek-by-jowl with the most prestigious names in tableware on the** *Rue de Paradis* **(10th arr.). Remember, though, that rooting out a good buy requires considerable time and patience!**

Insiders know that they can buy Hermès silk-twill scarves here for 700 F, as well as Kelly bags in box calf, Vuitton luggage, and the occasional Chanel accessory.

Dépôt-Vente de Passy

16th arr. - 14, rue de la Tour
45 20 95 21 (women)
16th arr. - 25, rue de la Tour
45 27 11 46 (men)
Open 10am-7pm (Mon 2pm-7pm). Closed Sun. V. M° Passy.

Catherine Baril, a pioneer of the consignment system in Paris, pampers her elegant clientele with barely used couture and designer cloth-ing and accessories at truly unbeatable prices. The shop at number 25 offers clothing for men: suits by Dior, Saint Laurent, Cerutti, Hugo Boss, priced from 1,200 F.

Chipie Stock

14th arr. - 82, rue d'Alésia
45 42 07 52
Open 10:15am-7pm (Mon 2pm-7pm & Sat 10am-7pm). Closed Sun. M° Alésia.

"Stock" is the way the French say "designer outlet." Chipie Stock sells seconds and previous-season models of the youthful, cheerful Chipie label: look for lots of stylish sweaters, jeans, jean jackets (285 F), and colorful sneakers, all of which look best on the under-30 set.

André Courrèges

1st arr. - 7, rue de Turbigo, 1st floor - 42 33 03 57
Open 10:15am-6pm. Closed Sun, Mon. V. M° Étienne-Marcel.

Prices are slashed by 50 to 90 percent on the preceding season's collection. This is the only shop where Courrèges's creative clothing is sold at discount.

Le Dépôt des Grandes Marques

2nd arr. - 15, rue de la Banque, 3rd floor - 42 96 99 04
Open 10am-7pm. Closed Sun. V, MC. M° Bourse.

Rack after rack of designer menswear is set out for your inspection at this third-floor shop near the stock exchange. All the best labels are represented: Renoma, Cerruti, Valentino, Jacques Fath, Dior, and more, priced at an average of 40 percent under normal retail. Look for top-name suits (Balmain, for example) priced from 1,650 to 3,500 F, as well as Cacharel silk ties, Harris tweed and pure cashmere jackets. Cotton shirts from Balmain or Guy Laroche are an excellent buy at 250 F. Lots of stockbrokers invest their clothing budgets here, but so do many executives and political types who recognize a good deal when they see one.

Les Deux Oursons

15th arr. - 106, bd de Grenelle - 45 75 10 77
Open 10am-7pm (Mon 2pm-7pm). Closed Sun. V, AE, DC, MC. M° La Motte-Picquet Grenelle.

Pre-worn furs, many with designer labels, all in excellent condition, keep women coming winter after winter to the sign of the "Two Teddy Bears." Blue fox or mink jackets start at 2,000 F; end lots from such prestigious designers as Ricci, Dior, and Revillon go for 30 percent less than elsewhere. Some shearling and leather

Marché Saint-Pierre

18th arr. - Pl. du Marché Saint-Pierre
"None priced lower!" "Sensational bargains!" "Special one-day sale!" Such are the slogans (which we've freely translated for you) that lure crowds of shoppers to the Marché Saint-Pierre, the foremost fabric discount market in Paris. On the ground floor of *Tissus Reine*, (open 9:15am-6:30pm, Mon 2pm-6:30pm & Sat until 6:45pm; closed Sun; 46 06 06 31), which carries the widest choice of fabrics, look for cottons priced as low as 15 F per meter (approximately three feet), silk, velvet, satin (29 F per meter), and felt (perfect for lining drawers and closets). The first floor is devoted to woolens, fake fur, notions, and patterns. On the second floor, upholstery and decorating fabric are grouped; all the fabrics designers are here. On the third floor, you will find curtain material. Before you leave, look out from the store and admire the fabulous unobstructed view of Sacré-Cœur.

coats are usually in stock as well. A full range of services includes repairs, expert cleaning, and installment-plan payment.

Diapositive Stock

14th arr. - 74, rue d'Alésia
45 39 97 27
Open 10:15am-7pm (Mon 2pm-7pm; Sat 10am-7pm). Closed Sun. V. M° Alésia.

At this outlet store prices are slashed on attractive print bodysuits, nicely tailored wool flannel suits, leggings with colorful floral or animal motifs, and much more. The clothes all date from the preceding season, but they are ticketed a full 50 percent below regular price.

Dorotennis Stock

14th arr. - 74, rue d'Alésia
45 42 40 68
Open 10:15am-7pm (Mon 2pm-7pm). Closed Sun. M° Alésia.

Even if these sporty clothes are two seasons old, their avant-garde design means they still look very fashionable when you buy them—at one-quarter their regular price! Summer collections arrive in mid-December, winter clothes at the end of July.

Fabienne

16th arr. - 77 bis, rue Boileau
45 25 64 26
Open 10am-1:30pm & 3pm-7pm. Closed Sun, Mon. V, MC. M° Exelmans.

Consignment shops for men's clothing are rare indeed, so here is a good one to keep in mind. The inventory changes regularly of course, but you can usually count on finding Cerutti suits, jackets by Armani and Versace (1,500 to 3,000 F), Burberry trench coats (850 to 1,500 F), and exclusive John Lobb shoes.

Fabrice Karel Stock

14th arr. - 105, rue d'Alésia
45 42 42 61
Open 10:15am-7pm (Mon 2pm-7pm). Closed Sun. M° Alésia.

Timeless, classic knitwear that never goes out of fashion is sold here for half its original price. From June to August, prices are slashed an additional 30 percent: that's 80 percent off, girls, what are you waiting for?

Anna Lowe

8th arr. - 35, av. Matignon
43 59 96 61
Open 10:30am-7pm. Closed Sun. V, AE, DC, MC. M° Miromesnil.

Discounted haute couture and deluxe ready-to-wear. Clothing from previous seasons and outfits worn on the runway designed by the top names in fashion—Ungaro, Valentino, Armani, Lacroix, and more—sell for far below their original prices. Superb evening gowns and cocktail dresses are marked down by 50 percent (2,500 F for a short frock; 5,000 F for a long, formal dress). City clothes, accessories, and extravagant costume jewelry are all attractively priced.

Mendès

1st arr. - 65, rue Montmartre
42 36 83 32
Open 10am-6pm (Fri & Sat 10am-5pm). Closed Sun. V. M° Sentier.

In this unassuming shop you'll discover ultrachic womenswear from Christian Lacroix and from Saint Laurent's Rive Gauche and Variations ready-to-wear lines ticketed at half the original price. The inventory is large and the sales staff is both courteous and competent but oddly, there are no fitting rooms.

Mi-Prix

15th arr. - 27, bd Victor
48 28 42 48
Open 9:30am-7pm. Closed Sun. No cards. M° Porte-de-Versailles.

Tog yourself out from head to toe at Mi-Prix, a long-established fashion outlet that features the top names in designer clothing and accessories. End lots from Missoni, Ferré, Lagerfeld, and Myrène de Prémonville are discounted by 50 to 70 percent. Also on sale is high-fashion footwear by Miss Maud, Maud Frizon, Chantal Thomass, and others. Complete your outfit with a chapeau from Marie Mercié or Philippe Model (200 to 300 F). Men will find silk ties from Valentino at the rock-bottom price of 69 F, and suits from name designers.

Réciproque

16th arr. - 89-123, rue de la Pompe - 47 04 30 28
Open 10:30am-7pm. Closed Sun, Mon. V, DC, MC. M° Rue de la Pompe.

Thrifty ladies of the jet-set, show-biz, and business worlds bring the clothes they no longer want (but can't bear to give away—how do you think they got so rich?) to Réciproque. Manager Nicole Morel displays only the finest designer clothing from recent collections (Chanel, Mugler, Alaïa, Lacroix...), all of it in excellent condition. These spacious, quiet stores are delightful places to browse; the ambience is anything but thrift shop. Men's clothing is featured at 101 rue de la Pompe.

Sangriff

9th arr. - 2, rue Charras
42 80 00 27
Open 9:30am-7pm (Mon 10am-7pm). Closed Sun. V, AE, DC, MC. M° Havre-Caumartin.

Sangriff sells distinctive leatherwear for women and men from prestigious manufacturers (Dior, Nina Ricci, Cerutti 1881, Saint Laurent...) at unbeatable discount prices. Alterations and after-sales service.

Solde Trois

8th arr. - 3, rue de Vienne
42 94 99 67
Open 10:30am-1:30pm & 2:30pm-6pm (Sat 10:30am-2:30pm). Closed Sun. V, MC. M° Saint-Augustin.

Two boutiques set side by side, where Lanvin's collections for men and women are sold for half (or less!) their original prices. Men's shirts are irresistible at 350 F, and we can't imagine that a woman would willingly leave the shop without at least a silk scarf (200 F) or a handbag. These already low prices are slashed by another 50 percent at the semiannual sales in mid-January and mid-June.

EYEWEAR

Hervé Domar Optic

6th arr. - 48, rue Dauphine
46 33 88 99
Open 10am-8pm (Mon 3pm-8pm). Closed Sun. V, AE, DC, MC. M° Odéon.

These eyeglasses are full-fledged fashion accessories. The frames, presented in a spacious shop lined with cherrywood display cases, come from Japan (Akussan), from Traction Productions in the Jura Mountains, and from California, U.S.A. (L.A. Eyeworks). Hervé Domar also makes glasses to your specifications, in gold or tortoiseshell: you choose the design, and he will craft the specs to fit your face.

Jean Lafont

8th arr. - 11, rue Vignon
47 42 25 93
Open 10am-6:30pm. Closed Sun, Mon. V, MC. M° Madeleine.

The star of the house creations is dubbed "Génie," a frame that looks good on nearly everyone, from 7 to 77! It comes in a wide palette of colors and materials. Lafont has also updated the "three-piece" frame (FDR wore it), available in a variety of shapes. And the firm's colored metal frames are also deservedly popular.

Latin Optique

5th arr. - 31, bd Saint-Michel
43 29 31 79
Open 10am-7:15pm (Mon 2pm-7pm). Closed Sun. V, MC. M° Saint-Michel.

Owner Samuel Raymond is a *visagiste*, which means that he specializes in suiting the glasses he makes to the specific contours and features of your beautiful face. He measures and studies your mug before proposing a frame that he can (if you wish) hand-craft for you in about 48 hours. Latin Optique also has a huge stock (some 20,000) of ready-made frames, and a workshop on the premises to assure quick service.

Alain Mikli

4th arr. - 1, rue des Rosiers
42 71 01 56
Open 11am-7pm (Mon 2pm-7pm). Closed Sun. V, AE, DC, MC. M° Saint-Paul.

Mikli is one of the hottest places in town to shop for eyeglasses. The latest creations incorporate technical innovations such as a combination of metal and plastic in matte or glossy colors. Allow a two- to ten-day turnaround for a pair of glasses, depending on how much work is involved. Expect to pay from 650 F for classic frames to 5,000 F for the most sophisticated specs.

Optic Bastille

11th arr. - 38, rue de la Roquette - 48 06 87 00
Open 10am-7:30pm (Mon 2pm-7:30pm). Closed Sun. V, AE, DC, MC. M° Bastille.

When Bastille trendies need glasses, this is where they come for funny or fashionable frames by Mikli, Claude Montana, Agnès B., and Alfred Paris. Don't miss the bat-wing frames by Eye-Wear; another pair mimics the Eiffel Tower—a perfect souvenir (for the near-sighted) of a Parisian holiday.

DEPARTMENT STORES

BHV

4th arr. - 52-56, rue de Rivoli
42 74 90 00
Open 9:30am-7pm (Wed 9:30am-10pm). Closed Sun. V, AE. M° Hôtel-de-Ville.

From Americans in search of converters for their electrical appliances, to do-it-yourselfers in need of a handful of nails, everyone in Paris eventually winds up in the BHV basement, a treasure trove of tools, hardware, and home-improvement items. What's more, you can count on competent advice from the sales staff on how to use or install your purchases. Savvy artists and sculptors appreciate the BHV's first floor, which is stocked with canvases, easels, brushes, and clay at unbeatable prices. Features and services include: in-house specialists to install goods and materials, from wallpaper to floor tiles to convertible-car roofs and more; a bridal registry with complimentary "house kit" and a five-percent discount on anything the couple buys in the store during their first year of wedded bliss; an engraving service for adorning china and glass with initials or the family coat of arms; repairs of all sorts, done on the premises (you can have your pearls restrung or your fishing reel adjusted). Purchases totaling over 1,500 F are delivered free of charge.

Le Bon Marché

7th arr. - 5, rue de Babylone
44 39 80 00, fax 44 39 80 50
Open 9:30am-7pm. Closed Sun. V, AE, DC. M° Sèvres-Babylone.

The good old Bon Marché is cultivating a chic, updated look with sharper advertising and a greater emphasis on fashion, home décor, and gourmet foods. This full-service store boasts worthwhile men's and women's clothing departments, made more tempting still by frequent sales that are not to be missed. Top features (in addition to an unusually courteous staff) include an eye-popping collection of Oriental carpets (store number 1, third floor), and an antique gallery (store number 2, upper floor). La Grande Épicerie, a huge, alluringly stocked food hall, is open every day but Sunday until 9pm. Among the items on offer are 150 types of tea, 240 kinds of cheese, and more than 200 different products "imported" from Fauchon. The grocery prices are competitive, and the wine department is impressive indeed (though we wish it were not so close to the fish and seafood stand...). The Bon Marché also provides a convenient in-house travel agency, a ticket agency, and a bank. Other services include custom-tailored clothing for men; fur storage and restoration, and a wonderful children's crafts department. Naturally, there are gift registries for brides and newborns.

Galeries Lafayette

9th arr. - 40, bd Haussmann
42 82 34 56 (also: 15th arr.)
Open 9:30am-7pm (Thu 9:30am-9pm). Closed Sun. V, AE, DC. M° Chaussée-d'Antin.

On an average day, 100,000 women between the ages of 20 and 40 stroll through Les Galeries Lafayette. What lures them is an enormous selection—three full floors—of clothing and accessories, ranging from avant-garde designers like Jean-Paul Gaultier, Yohji Yamamoto, and Azzedine Alaïa, to such classic labels as Cacharel, Dior, and Guy Laroche. The store labels (hip "Avant-Première," "Briefing" career clothes, and casual clothes signed "Jodhpur") combine fashion with good value. The "Mode Plus" service helps women put together a look that fits their personality and lifestyle. The dazzling table and kitchenware department on the basement level is a paradise for those who love to cook or entertain. Weary shoppers may pause for refreshment at Le Grill, Lina's Sandwiches, or at Angelina, an outpost of the famed Parisian tea room. For a beauty break, you can stop at the Jean-Marc Maniatis hair salon or the Carita beauty center. Lafayette 2, next door, houses the men's store (dubbed the Galfa Club), and a deluxe food emporium, Lafayette Gourmet. More than a supermarket (though it is a very good one), Lafayette Gourmet is a gastro-playground, with a multitude of stands for snacking and sampling: Petrossian's caviar and smoked salmon, Lenôtre's pastries and food-to-go, a Champagne bar, an oyster bar, a salad bar, and more.

Marks & Spencer

4th arr. - 88, rue de Rivoli
44 61 08 00
Open 9:30am-8:30pm (Mon & Tue 9:30am-8pm; Sat 9:30am-7:30pm). Closed Sun. V. M° Châtelet.
9th arr. - 35, bd Haussmann
47 42 42 91
Open 9:30am-7pm (Tue 10am-7pm). Closed Sun. V. M° Chaussée-d'Antin.

Ever faithful to its mission, Marks & Spencer brings a little bit of cozy old England to the hard-edged French capital. The stores are always busy, particularly at back-to-school time, when mothers stock up on the sturdy children's clothing (lambswool and cashmere sweaters, kilts, Oxford shirts...), and at Christmas, when shoppers crowd in for traditional holiday foods, decorations, and gaily packaged gifts. All year round, we visit Marks & Sparks to find fixings for an authentic English tea: tea, of course (loose and in bags), biscuits (cookies), marmalades, scones, crumpets, muffins, and the rest. Delicious, reasonably priced packaged smoked salmon is available whole, in slices, or marinated in dill. And we love the selection of chutneys, bottled sauces, and other typically English condiments. Note, however, that an ever-expanding array of exotic foodstuffs (including Indian, Mexican and U.S. goodies) is offered as well, and tastings are held regularly at the new Rue de Rivoli store. Marks & Spencer is also justly known for traditional, affordably priced woolens and tweeds; long-wearing lingerie and underwear for the entire family; and inexpensive, profusely scented toiletries. The storewide sales in January, July, and August offer particularly fine buys.

Monoprix

9th arr. - 97, rue de Provence
48 74 37 13 (also: 2nd arr., 3rd arr., 4th arr., 5th arr., 6th arr., 8th arr., 9th arr., 10th arr., 11th arr., 12th arr., 13th arr., 15th arr., 17th arr., 18th arr., 19th arr.)
Open 9am-8pm (Thu 9am-9pm). Closed Sun. V. M° Chaussée-d'Antin.

"The basics are what we do best." That's the Monoprix motto. A big factor in the stores' success is their strategic locations in the capital's busiest neighborhoods. Monoprix purveys in-house labels of clothing and toiletries of good quality at rock-bottom prices. Lately, successful efforts have been made to give added fashion oomph to the ready-to-wear, with lines designed by hip, young stylists. Monoprix regularly puts so-called luxury goods (caviar at Christmas, for example, or cashmere sweaters in the fall) within the reach of the average consumer. The supermarket selection continues to grow, with ready-to-eat dishes, catering services (at some stores), and the excellent Monoprix Gourmet line, which includes coffee, pasta, vacuum-packed ready-cooked entrées, low-calorie products, and a new line of quick-cooking dishes for hungry folks in a hurry.

Le Printemps

9th arr. - 64, bd Haussmann
42 82 50 00 (also: 13th arr., 20th arr.)
Open 9:35am-7pm (Thu 9:35am-10pm). Closed Sun. V, AE, DC. M° Havre-Caumartin.

Le Printemps cultivates an image of quintessentially Parisian chic and elegance. The store targets a slightly more mature clientele than its neighbor, Les Galeries Lafayette. The ideal Printemps customer is a woman of style and taste who appreciates refinement in both her dress and her surroundings. Le Printemps is housed in three separate Art Nouveau buildings: Le Printemps de la Mode, Le Printemps de la Maison, and the Brummell shop for men. The main Mode store features top-quality women's and children's wear; name designers are well represented, and the selection of accessories is immense. Here too you'll find a Jean-Louis David hair salon, an Yves Rocher beauty institute, and many convenient services including a fashion consultant (Mode Plus), travel and ticket agencies. After a marathon shopping session, it's a pleasure to relax in the Brasserie Flo on the sixth floor, under Le Printemps's gorgeous stained-glass dome. Next door, Le Printemps de la Maison is an entire store (eight floors) devoted to home décor, household linens, table and kitchenwares. The store's private-label "Primavera" collection ranges from handcrafted gift items to furniture designed by the likes of Andrée Putman and Philippe Starck. Here prospective spouses may present their wish list at La Boutique Blanche, the premier bridal registry in France. The ground floor of the Maison store was recently revamped in lavish style (marble and crystal everywhere!) to create Le Printemps de la Beauté, a showcase for perfumes, cosmetics, and beauty paraphernalia from major manufacturers. As for the Brummell shop, men will be delighted to find everything they need, from underwear and socks to cashmere top coats, under one roof. All the best designers are on hand, and there is a special wardrobe-consulting service to help men pull their look together.

Prisunic

8th arr. - 109, rue de La Boétie - 42 25 27 46
Open 9am-midnight. Closed Sun. V. M° St-Philippe-du-Roule.
also: 2nd arr., 11th arr., 12th arr., 13th arr., 15th arr., 16th arr., 17th arr., 18th arr., 19th arr., 20th arr.
Open 9am-8pm or 9pm depending on stores. Closed Sun.

Never content to rest on its marketing laurels, Prisunic has practiced the art of creative retailing ever since it opened up for business some 50 years ago. The newly renovated branch on the Champs-Élysées is open until 10pm (midnight in summer). Every couple of weeks, the chain's inventive merchandising team comes up with a new theme or sales promotion to spark shoppers' enthusiasm. Prisunic's strong points are its clever, colorful housewares at affordable prices—dishes, linens, lamps, and gadgets; a grocery section that offers fresh, fine-quality produce every day (Forza is the house brand of canned and packaged goods); a vast array of makeup and toiletries; and sturdy, adorable children's clothing, all at budget prices.

La Samaritaine

1st arr. - 19, rue du Pont-Neuf
40 41 20 20, fax 40 41 23 24
Open 9:30am-7pm (Thu 9:30am-10pm). Closed Sun. V, AE, DC. M° Pont-Neuf.

"You can find anything at the Samaritaine!" is the proud boast of this four-store complex, affectionately known as the "Samar." For our money, the Samaritaine's top feature (so to speak...) is a fabulous view of Paris, visible (April to October) from the rooftop terrace of the main store (number 2). Another panoramic view of the city and the Seine spreads out beyond the windows of the fifth-floor Toupary restaurant, exuberantly decorated by American Hilton McConnico. On to the merchandise: sporting goods and gear are a major draw; they occupy all of store number 3. What's more, on this store's second floor shoppers can practice their putt, scale a climbing wall, test a tennis racquet, or play a little table tennis. The sixth floor is home to a pet shop, a great treat for children. Children also adore store number 1, a multilevel wonderland of toys, dolls, and games. Store number 4 presents an exhaustive range of TVs, hi-fi equipment, and electronic goods. Homewares, fashion, and cosmetics fill the floors of store number 2. Just a sampling of the services available at La Samaritaine: golf lessons, courses in tailoring or in bicycle-repair and maintenance; a nursery where mothers shopping with small children can rediaper them and warm their bottles; picture-framing; silver-refinishing; an in-house astrologer; and so on and on...

Find the address you are looking for, quickly and easily, in the index.

Aux Trois Quartiers

1st arr. - 23, bd de la Madeleine - 42 97 80 12
Open 10am-7pm. Closed Sun. M° Madeleine.

If you haven't been near Aux Trois Quartiers for several years, you won't recognize the place! Though the name is the same, in 1991 the interior was gutted, expanded, and transformed into a deluxe, trilevel shopping mall. Formerly the preserve of tastefully dressed matrons and their prim daughters, Aux Trois Quartiers now draws crowds of customers—including a large percentage of tourists—with its critical mass of 75 chic shops. Madelios, a quality men's store, is here alongside the colorful clothing of Kenzo, Dorothée Bis, and Tehen for women, Bang & Olufsen audio, restaurants, take-out shops, and much more.

FASHION FOR HIM & HER

Agnès B.

1st arr. - 3-6-10-19, rue du Jour - 42 33 04 13
6th arr. - 13, rue Michelet (Women) - 46 33 70 20
6th arr. - 22, rue St-Sulpice (Men) - 40 51 70 69
16th arr. - 17, av. Pierre Ier de Serbie (Women)
47 20 22 44
16th arr. - 25, av. Pierre Ier de Serbie (Men) - 47 23 36 69
Open 10am-7pm. Closed Sun. V, AE, MC. M° Les Halles, Port-Royal, Odéon, Iéna.

Agnès B. designs an ageless collection of fashionable clothing that virtually anyone can live with. In fact, if these casual classics didn't wear out so quickly, one could keep them in one's closet for decades! However that may be, Agnès B. presents comfortable, easy styles for the entire family at relatively affordable prices: fleece cardigans, sweatshirts, and sweaters for a sporty look, lots of stripes and, for more dressy occasions, silk, linen, and leather outfits enhanced with ethnic accessories.

APC

6th arr. - 3, rue de Fleurus
42 22 12 77 (Women)
6th arr. - 4, rue de Fleurus
45 49 19 15 (Men)
Open 10:30am-7pm (Mon & Sat 11am-7pm). Closed Sun. V, DC, MC. M° Saint-Sulpice.

APC stands for *Atelier de Production et Création*, a label dreamed up by the creative Jean Touitou. Understated elegance is the key to his fashion vision: for women, slim pants, simple but beautifully crafted blouses, alluringly feminine suits; for men, tasteful sweaters (not so easy to find these days), and casual oiled-canvas pants—very rugged and masculine.

Giorgio Armani

1st arr. - 6, pl. Vendôme
42 61 55 09
1st arr. - 25, pl. Vendôme
42 61 02 34
Open 10am-7pm (Mon 11am-7pm). Closed Sun. V, AE, DC, MC. M° Tuileries.

Armani's Parisian outpost is a cathedral of mirrors, furnished with cubical seating crafted of glowing wood. Armani has a couple of thousand stores all over the planet, and hundreds of thousands of faithful customers: it's a marketing miracle, really, since the price of an off-the-rack Armani suit is about the same as a ticket on the Concorde from Paris to New York! But do go in for a look-see (the sales staff may not seem glad to see you, but never mind them), and bring plenty of money in case you find something irresistible. If you can't bear to leave the shop empty-handed, there's always the Armani cologne; it's far more reasonably priced than the clothes. A few doors away, at number 25, is the Emporio Armani shop, featuring more youthful, affordable looks (jeans from 500 F).

Céline

8th arr. - 38, avenue Montaigne - 49 52 08 79
8th arr. - 24, rue François-Ier
47 20 22 83
Open 10am-7pm. Closed Sun. V, AE, DC, MC. M° Franklin-D.-Roosevelt.

Best known as a bootmaker, Céline has expanded its production to include well-made, well-bred ready-to-wear for women and men. Jackets, coats, and suits come in rich-textured tweeds, and there are nicely cut trousers (with narrow or wide legs) in leather or buttery suède. Céline's famed loafers and bags adorned with brass bits are updated each season, with fresh colors and detailing. New and attractive are grained-leather rucksacks in pastel hues, and bucket bags in bright-colored suède.

Cerruti 1881

8th arr. - 27, rue Royale (Men) - 42 65 68 72
Open 10am-7pm. Closed Sun. V, AE, MC. M° Madeleine.
8th arr. - 15, pl. de la Madeleine (Women) - 47 42 10 78
Open 10:15am-7pm. Closed Sun. V, AE, DC, MC. M° Madeleine.

Elegant, urbane Nino Cerruti runs this fashionable clothing firm, established in 1881. His mission in life is to perpetuate the tradition of the Italian men's suit—as classy as a Ferrari, characterized by uncommon color combinations and top-quality fabrics: silk, linen, or soft wools. The distinctive Cerruti look has won over such sartorial paragons as Richard Gere and Michael Douglas. For women, Cerruti presents a collection of rather austere but elegantly cut "executive" suits and greatcoats, as well as sophisticated leather accessories: the shoulder bag in lamb (from 1,350 F) or iguana skin is a cult item among fashion insiders.

Charvet

1st arr. - 28, pl. Vendôme
42 60 30 70
Open 9:45am-6:30pm. Closed Sun. V, AE, DC, MC. M° Opéra.

Charvet is an institution. It has been serving the same clientele from generation to generation. Clients' measurements are kept on record for decades, so that the faithful can order their shirts and whatnot by telephone and have them delivered. Whether you're in the market for a dozen fine Egyptian cotton shirts or a simple pair of cuff links, you will receive the same welcome and courteous service.

Charvet's women's wear is classic, not to say severe (suits, blouses, and blazers). One especially covetable item is the firm's voluptuous paisley silk dressing gown, a gift for men that women love to wear. Prices are steep.

Les Copains

8th arr. - 4, rue du Fg-St-Honoré - 42 66 67 68
Open 10am-7:30pm (Sat 10am-7pm). Closed Sun. V, AE, DC, MC. M° Concorde.

Cabinets of pickled oak and floors of Verona marble set the stage for this upscale line of Italian ready-to-wear. The upper floor is reserved for menswear, designed in a sporty yet elegant spirit (note the suede sneakers, for instance). Women can choose from among five different collections of coordinated clothing fashioned in the most select fabrics: linen, silk, cashmere... We love the clever wool-crêpe suits that move effortlessly from office to evening thanks to removable organdy collars and cuffs.

L'Éclaireur

4th arr. - 3 ter, rue des Rosiers
48 87 10 22
Open 10:30am-7pm (Mon 2pm-7pm). Closed Sun. V, AE, DC. M° Saint-Paul.

For women: Dolce & Gabbana, Moschino Couture, Helmut Lang, Martine Sitbon, Ann Demeulemeester, Martin Margiela, John Galliano—all the hot, hip clothes you want right *now*. For men: Paul Smith, Juliano Fujiwara, Dries van Noten, Momento Due—togs with a definite downtown attitude. To create the proper environment in which to wear these clothes, L'Éclaireur's owners, Armand and Martine Hadida, present furniture and trendy *bibelots* by Borek Sipek, Hilton McConnico, André Dubreuil, and Fornasetti (whose eerie designs are now furiously fashionable).

Louis Féraud

8th arr. - 88, rue du Fg-St-Honoré - 42 65 27 29
Open 10am-7pm. Closed Sun. V, AE, DC. M° Champs-Élysées-Clemenceau.

Louis Féraud started his career in Cannes in the '50s, dressing such stars as Brigitte Bardot, Kim Novak, and Liz Taylor. Today his creations are still ultra-feminine, sporting vivid colors, luxuriant prints, and extravagant embroideries. Féraud's new men's shop, next door at number 90, promotes a bright, relaxed Mediterranean look. Suits start at 3,000 F.

Jean-Paul Gaultier

1st arr. - 7, rue du Jour
40 28 01 91
2nd arr. - 6, rue Vivienne
42 86 05 05
Open 10am-7pm (Sat 11am-7pm). Closed Sun (& Mon 1st arr.). V, AE, DC, MC. M° Les Halles, Bourse.

The staff is astonishingly courteous, the innovative clothes are presented in sparkling glass wardrobes, the cutting-edge accessories gleam... there is electricity in the air! Gaultier's clothes are impeccably cut and yet extremely provocative: cropped rubber sweaters, Cossack-style skirts, shoes with astrakhan trimmings; it's an inimitable mix of materials, and of weird, wonderful styles. The bronze-green décor with video screens built into the floor is whimsical and fun. The Junior Gaultier line (presented in the Rue du Jour shop) is a boon for Jean-Paul's less moneyed fans, of every age.

22h48 Un Soir Dominique Coubes

2nd arr. - 38, rue Étienne-Marcel - 42 33 54 69
Open 11am-7:30pm (Sat 10:30am-7:30pm). Closed Sun. V, AE. M° Étienne-Marcel.

Designer Dominique Coubes burst onto the scene with a line of clothing inspired by the countryfolk of central France. His appealing takes on French peasant blouses and farmer's work jackets jibe perfectly with fashion's current rustic-ecological mood.

Romeo Gigli

3rd arr. - 46, rue de Sévigné
48 04 57 05
Open 11am-7pm. Closed Sun, Mon. V, AE, MC. M° Saint-Paul.

Romeo Gigli turned a disused printing plant into a Venetian fairyland full of rich colors and sumptuous fabrics. The gorgeous overcoats (for men and women) are particularly tantalizing: we can just imagine pulling one on over a subtly hued cashmere sweater, a shimmering baroque shirt, and a pair of Gigli's beautifully cut trousers (1,400 F).

Daniel Hechter

8th arr. - 66, rue François-Ier
40 70 94 38
Open 10:30am-7:30pm. Closed Sun. V, AE, DC, MC. M° George-V.

This is Hechter's main showcase, decorated with

paintings by the designer himself. His easy-to-wear clothes for work or play are moderately priced (2,400 F for a woman's suit, 600 F for a man's shirt) and fashionable in a classic, understated way.

Kenzo

1st arr. - 3, pl. des Victoires
40 39 72 03
7th arr. - 16-17, bd Raspail
42 22 09 38
Open 10am-7pm (Mon 11am-7pm). Closed Sun. V, AE, DC, MC. M° Palais-Royal, Sèvres-Babylone.

Kenzo designs clothes and accessories for the whole family. Vivid colors, soft shapes, ethnic or floral prints, and billowing shirts remain his trademark. N.B.: the semiannual storewide sales in January and July lower prices by as much as 50 percent.

Loft Design By...

8th arr. - 12, rue du Fg-St-Honoré - 42 65 59 65
Open 10am-7pm. Closed Sun. V, AE, DC, MC. M° Concorde.

Everyday basics in comfortable fabrics: combed-cotton T-shirts sold in packs of three (295 F), cotton and linen pants, "miner" jackets (595 F), sweaters in merino wool, mercerized cotton shirts (395 F), and washed-silk jackets for women and men (895 F). Colors are low-key but definitely fashionable. Many garments are sold in cloth bags for easy storage.

Mettez

8th arr. - 12, bd Malesherbes
42 65 33 76
Open 10am-7pm. Closed Sun. V, AE. M° Madeleine.

This venerable establishment boasts a faithful clientele, most of whom come from the world of politics or the theater. Since 1847 Mettez has consistently found buyers for their linen hunting and hacking jacket (3,350 F), as well as Austrian jackets by Giesswein or Staff. Knickers, loden capes, and corduroy pants abound, as do cozy Gloverall duffle coats from England (1,600 F).

Missoni

7th arr. - 43, rue du Bac
45 48 38 02
Open 10am-7pm. Closed Sun. V, AE, DC, MC. M° Rue du Bac.

Missoni's conservative yet sumptuously crafted collections are aimed primarily at (rich) people who love muted contrasting colors, interesting textures, mossy mohair, and (for summer) glazed linen. Sweaters start at about 2,000 F.

Claude Montana

1st arr. - 3, rue des Petits-Champs - 40 20 02 14
Open 11am-7pm. Closed Sun. V, AE, DC, MC. M° Palais-Royal.
7th arr. - 31, rue de Grenelle
42 22 69 56
Open 10:15am-7pm. Closed Sun. V, AE, DC, MC. M° Sèvres-Babylone.

Though Claude Montana still goes in for structured silhouettes bedecked with accessories (metal belts, lots of zippers), a touch of softness has crept into the women's clothes of late, in the form of tulip sleeves and fluid pants. Lots of black remains the trademark of Montana's futuristic style. The leather clothing for men (check out those quilted jackets) is of the highest quality and superbly designed.

Thierry Mugler

2nd arr. - 10, pl. des Victoires
42 60 06 37
Open 10am-1pm & 2pm-7pm (Mon from 11am). Closed Sun. V, AE, DC, MC. M° Palais-Royal.
8th arr. - 49, av. Montaigne
47 23 37 62
Open 10am-7pm. Closed Sun. V, AE, DC, MC. M° Franklin-D.-Roosevelt.

Thierry Mugler's eye-catching premises, done up by Andrée Putman in blinding blue, look a bit like something from outer space. A master of such materials as whipcord, jersey, piqué, and gabardine, Mugler tailors clothes with strict lines and few frills. His high-tech designs are for glamorous women and exuberant men. You may well boggle at the prices—but just consider your purchase an investment; the Mugler style is beyond mere fashion. The second-tier Diffusion line is just a hair less expensive.

Old England

9th arr. - 12, bd des Capucines - 47 42 81 99
Open 9:30am-6:30pm (Mon 9:30am-12:30pm & 2pm-6:30pm). Closed Sun. V, MC. M° Opéra.

This 100 percent French firm, founded in 1867, embodies English elegance with blazers, jackets, suits, raincoats, sweaters, and myriad accessories from the British Isles. Traditional favorites here are the Derek Rose striped pajamas (why not buy a lovely dressing gown to go with them?), Turnbull and Asser shirts, Brigg umbrellas, Mason and Pearson brushes, and Floris or Atkinson eaux-de-toilette. Should your Chester Barrie suit need alterations, the advice of the in-house tailors is invaluable. Climb to the top of the store's monumental staircase to find the women's and children's departments.

Pastille

11th arr. - 19, rue de la Roquette - 48 06 61 73
Open 10:30am-7:30pm. Closed Sun. V, MC. M° Bastille.

Need a lacy, stretchy, sexy black dress for a night on the town? The selection on hand here is quite impressive, with offerings by Corinne Cobson, Bisous-Bisous, and Soap Studio. For the boys, there are sleek cigarette-leg pants with a definite 1950s feel.

Renoma

16th arr. - 129 bis, rue de la Pompe - 44 05 38 38
16th arr. - 118, rue de Longchamp - 44 05 38 25
Open 10am-7:15pm. Closed Sun. V, AE, DC, MC. M° Rue de la Pompe.

The menswear is pretty pricey (suits run from 3,000 to 6,000 F) but it is stylish and handsomely cut. The weather-proof Roméo outfit is perfect for golfing, biking, or flirting in the rain (1,800 F). Classic women's suits cost about 2,500 F. Renoma also manufactures a desirable line of luggage and small leather goods.

Scapa of Scotland

6th arr. - 71, rue des Saints-Pères - 45 44 18 50
Open 10am-7pm. Closed Sun. V, AE, MC. M° Sèvres-Babylone.

Displayed alongside beautiful Irish sweaters knitted of cotton or wool are sporty separates and wonderful coats (duffles and greatcoats) of classic cut, all crafted of first-rate fabrics. They cost a fortune, but are worth the investment: these clothes wear forever and are timelessly styled. Helpful but unobtrusive service.

David Shiff–Club des 10

8th arr. - 13, rue Royale
42 66 43 61
Open daily 10am-6pm. V, AE, MC. M° Concorde.

Chic, top-quality clothing from the finest makers is presented on three levels, decorated to look like a posh private club. Yet the prices are eminently reasonable. Men's suits in wool and cashmere or super 100 start at 1,500 F; half that sum buys three men's shirts. There is always a selection of sale merchandise from the previous season on hand, and an in-house tailor will take care of any alterations.

Bill Tornade

1st arr. - 1, rue de Turbigo
42 21 35 52
Open 11am-7:30pm. Closed Sun. M° Les Halles.

A former butcher's shop in Les Halles is the setting for Bill Tornade's inventive designs, inspired by the '60s and '70s. Some pieces feature clever juxtapositions of stripes and herringbone patterns, patchwork, and plaid. Others are crafted of vintage materials given a new lease on life. Ribbed Lycra jeans for women cost about 500 F; men's and women's suits are priced around 2,000 F.

Ventilo

2nd arr. - 27 bis, rue du Louvre - 42 33 18 67
Open 10:30am-7pm (Mon noon-7pm). Closed Sun. V, AE, MC. M° Louvre.

Earth and wood tones dominate both the shop and the comfortable, becoming clothes offered for sale. The house style is more than a little reminiscent of Ralph Lauren's designs, but with a Continental twist. The shop's lower level is reserved for the menfolk, the main and first floors for women. Lots of cotton shirts and jeans are proposed for both sexes. Up on the top floor, decorative objects for the home share space with a bright, pleasant tea room.

Gianni Versace

8th arr. - 62, rue du Fg-St-Honoré - 47 42 88 02
Open 10am-7pm. Closed Sun. V, AE, DC, MC. M° Concorde.

Versace's flagship boutique in Paris was designed by Pierluigi Pizzi (who creates the marvelous stage sets at La Scala opera house in Milan). This wildly extravagant décor is reason enough to wander over for a look, even if you don't want to pay thousands of francs for a gold lamé biker's jacket or a sequin-spangled micro-mini. In the equally ruinous new homewares department you can pick up a silk throw pillow for 1,600 F. To view Versace's less costly Istante line and a bravura collection of accessories, stroll down to 11, rue du Faubourg-Saint-Honoré.

Don't plan to shop on Sundays—the vast majority of Paris stores are closed.

Y'S Yohji Yamamoto

1st arr. - 25, rue du Louvre (Women) - 42 21 42 93
1st arr. - 47, rue Étienne-Marcel (Men) - 45 08 82 45
Open 10:30am-7pm (Mon 11:30am-7pm). Closed Sun. V, AE, DC, MC. M° Louvre.

"Minimalism forever" sums up the Japanese couturier's second-tier (but not inexpensive) collections of ready-to-wear for men and women. Sober lines, muted colors, a slim and finely worked silhouette characterize these clothes. Beautiful blouses for women start at about 1,000 F.

AND ALSO . . .

Aquascutum

1st arr. - 10, rue de Castiglione - 42 60 09 40
Open 10am-7pm. Closed Sun. V, AE, DC, MC. M° Tuileries.

Since 1850, quality and comfort: suits, sweaters and the famous Kingsway trench (Bogie wore it!).

Burberry's

8th arr. - 8, bd Malesherbes
42 66 13 01
Open 10am-7pm. Closed Sun. V, AE, DC, MC. M° Madeleine.
6th arr. - 55, rue de Rennes
45 48 52 71
16th arr. - 56, rue de Passy
42 88 88 24
Open 10am-7pm (Mon 2pm-7pm). Closed Sun. V, AE, DC, MC. M° Saint-Germain-des-Prés, Passy.

Great trench coats, rain hats, cashmere scarves and sweaters; unbearable sales clerks.

Ralph Lauren

8th arr. - 2, pl. de la Madeleine - 44 77 53 50
Open 10am-7pm. Closed Sun. V, AE, DC. M° Madeleine.

Hey, if you really want to pay twice the U.S. price for the Lauren look, who are we to hold you back? The display windows are beautifully done.

FLOWERS & PLANTS

FLOWER SHOPS

Franck Cordier

8th arr. - 6, rue de la Renaissance - 47 20 47 99
Open 9am-8:30pm (May-Sep 9am-10:30pm). Closed Sun. V, AE, DC. M° Alma-Marceau.

Noteworthy newcomer Franck Cordier composes subtle color groupings of "simple" flowers (forget-me-nots, daffodils...) for his charming and poetic bouquets. Come spring, look for baskets of fragrant roses, lilacs, and green apples; fall brings deep-hued arrangements of freesia, purple-beech leaves, chestnuts, and plump grapes; in winter, Cordier makes use of superb foliage and fruits from South Africa (450 F and up). His surprising moss sculptures and ivy topiaries (from 650 F) last and last.

Patrick Divert

16th arr. - 7, pl. de Mexico
45 53 69 35, fax 47 27 81 04
Open 9am-8pm (Sun 10am-1:30pm). V, AE. M° Trocadéro.

Subtle interplays of textures—barks, wood, moss, and braids of aromatic plants—mark the style of Divert's rustic yet extremely refined bouquets. Wildflowers and old-fashioned roses add their charm to these appealing compositions.

Élyfleurs

17th arr. - 82, av. de Wagram
47 66 87 19, fax 42 27 29 13
Open 24 hours. V. M° Wagram.

It's 2am and you're seized with the urge to send a sumptuous bouquet to a friend in Berlin. No problem: your thoughtful present will be delivered in France or in any major European city, in record time thanks to the efficient service provided around the clock by Élyfleurs.

Liliane François

7th arr. - 119, rue de Grenelle
45 51 73 18, fax 45 51 07 04
Open daily 8am-8:30pm (Sun 8am-7pm). V, AE, DC. M° Invalides.

Liliane creates amazing arrangements featuring fruits and vegetables, as well as only slightly less surprising mixes of berry-laden branches, uncommon foliage, and abundant bunches of fresh flowers. A true artist. Bouquets are priced from 350 F.

Guillet

7th arr. - 99, av. La Bourdonnais
45 51 32 98, fax 46 36 77 49
Open 9:30am-12:30pm & 2pm-7pm. Closed Sun, Mon. V, AE. M° École-Militaire.

This long-established florist specializes in floral decorating schemes and, in its own workshop, creates stunning silk flowers for centerpieces, corsages, and bridal headdresses. Faithful clients include the Opéra and the Comédie-Française, as well as some of the city's major department stores.

Lachaume

8th arr. - 10, rue Royale
42 60 57 26, fax 42 97 44 55
Open 9am-7pm (Sat 9am-6pm). Closed Sun. V, AE. M° Madeleine.

This is probably the most famous florist in Paris, and it's been here for over a hundred years. Marcel Proust stopped by every day to pick out the orchid he wore in his lapel (you can get the same kind today, for 150 F). The quality of the flowers is perfection itself. Short of buying a bouquet, you can admire the 150 varieties of flowers arranged in enormous vases in the shop window. Full bouquets start at about 450 francs.

Les Mille Feuilles

3rd arr. - 2, rue Rambuteau
42 78 32 93, fax 42 78 17 90
Open 10am-8pm. Closed Sun, Mon. V. M° Rambuteau.

Arguably the best florist in the Marais, bursting with blossoms in the most delicate hues. Come here for the freshest flowers, both rare and familiar, artfully disposed in antique or contemporary vases. Like us, you'll want to buy the whole store (but in view of the prices, you probably won't).

Moulié-Savart

7th arr. - 8, pl. du Palais-Bourbon
45 51 78 43, fax 45 50 45 54
Open daily 8am-8pm (Sun 9am-1pm). V, AE. M° Invalides.

Hidden behind a hedge of magnolias, camelias, and jasmine on the beautiful Place du Palais-Bourbon, this patrician florist presides over a most fragrant inventory of rare flowers and plants. Every bloom is dewy fresh, every arrangement is exquisitely tasteful.

Flowers, flowers everywhere

Some 1,800 varieties of flowers are raised in Paris's greenhouses, located in the Auteuil area, and from time to time marvelous flower exhibits are held. You can pick up exhibit schedules at the local city hall) or contact the Direction des Parcs et Jardins de la Ville de Paris, 3 av. de la Porte d'Auteuil, 16th arr., 40 71 74 00.

Au Nom de la Rose

6th arr. - 4, rue de Tournon
46 34 10 64, fax 44 07 15 72
Open 9am-9pm (Sun 10am-1pm & 2pm-6pm). V. M° Odéon.

Dani is the name of the rose who runs this divine shop; she's an ex-pop singer who now spends her time in the fragrant company of roses, nothing but roses! From ultrasophisticated blooms that look as if they were made of porcelain, to blowsy old-fashioned roses that bring back memories of grandmother's garden, all these flowers are sublime. You can purchase an armful for a dewy bouquet, or buy a single, perfectly graceful rose (from 20 F).

Au Pot de Fer Fleuri

5th arr. - 78, rue Monge
45 35 17 42
Open 11am-midnight (Mon 2pm-9pm). No cards. M° Monge.

The aptly named Violette lovingly composes beautiful, personalized bouquets. Note that her shop, a favorite with lovers, actors, and theater folk, is open until late at night.

Marianne Robic

7th arr. - 41, rue de Bourgogne
44 18 03 47, fax 45 55 28 68
Open 8am-8pm (Sat 8am-7pm). Closed Sun. V, AE. M° Varenne.

In Marianne's gorgeous garden, flowers are presented in handsome terracotta pots or in pretty baskets. Stone statues, wrought-iron furniture, and painted-wood consoles create a romantic atmosphere. We can't resist her pots of wild pansies, which at just 60 F are a relatively reasonable indulgence!

Christian Tortu

6th arr. - 6, carrefour de l'Odéon (also: 8th arr.)
43 26 02 56, fax 43 29 71 99
Open 9am-8pm. Closed Sun. V. M° Odéon.

The darling of the shelter mags, Christian Tortu is a gifted flower designer, probably the most talented of his generation. He has an inimitable knack (and Lord knows his imitators are legion!) for blending rare and delicate flowers with simple greenery or tropical plants. Tortu's bouquets are per-

Flower supermarkets

These establishments sell remarkably fresh flowers, and they'll deliver anywhere in Paris: *Monceau Fleurs,* **open 9am-8pm (Sun 9:30am-1:30pm) (delivery is 30-40 F), 4th arr., 2 quai des Célestins, 42 72 24 86; 6th arr., 84 bd Raspail, 45 48 70 10; 8th arr., 92 bd Malesherbes, 45 63 88 23; 16th arr., 60 av. Paul-Doumer, 40 72 79 27; 17th arr., 2 place du Général Koenig, 45 74 61 39.**
Armfuls of flowers can be found at *La Grange,* **6th arr., 7, rue de Buci, 43 26 19 34, open daily 9:30am-8:30pm (Sun until 7pm); delivery is 50 F, even in an emergency, and credit cards are accepted.**
Other addresses: *Lamartine Fleurs,* **16th arr., 188 av. Victor-Hugo, 45 04 29 50, open 9am-7:30pm (Mon 2pm-7:30pm), closed Sun.**
And *Primfleurs,* **17th arr., 80, av. de Villiers, 124, av. de Wagram, 42 27 13 06, open 8:30am-7:45pm (Sun until 6:45pm).**

fect and quite natural looking, yet they're also sophisticated and somehow wild... His prices have risen quite as rapidly as his popularity with the media.

René Veyrat
8th arr. - 168, bd Haussmann
45 62 37 86, fax 42 89 16 34
Open 8:30am-7pm (Mon 8am-7pm; Sat 8:30am-6pm). Closed Sun. V. M° Courcelles.

You'll be captivated by the window displays of this corner shop on the Boulevard Haussmann. The flowers and plants are of exemplary quality, the service is charming. Large bouquets start at about 450 F.

Vilmorin
1st arr. - 2 ter et 4, quai de la Mégisserie
42 33 61 62, fax 40 26 18 28
Open 9:30pm-7pm (Mar-Jun: Sun 9:30am-6:30pm). V. M° Châtelet.

Gardeners should plan to spend at least a few hours browsing among the shrubs, rosebushes, bedding plants, herbs, bulbs, and more on display at the biggest garden store in town. The seed department alone has been known to absorb the green of thumb for entire afternoons. Gardening equipment and house plants are on sale here as well.

We're always happy to hear about your discoveries and receive your comments on ours. We want to give your letters the attention they deserve, so when you write to Gault Millau, please state clearly what you liked or disliked. Be concise but convincing, and take the time to argue your point.

FLOWER MARKETS

Marché aux Fleurs de l'Ile de la Cité
4th arr. - Pl. Louis-Lépine (quai de Corse)
Open 8am-7:30pm. Closed Sun. M° Cité.

Marché de la Madeleine
8th arr. - Pl. de la Madeleine (east side)
Open 8am-7:30pm. Closed Sat, Sun, Mon (exc hols). M° Madeleine.

Marché des Ternes
17th arr. - Pl. des Ternes
Open 8am-7:30pm. Closed Mon. M° Ternes.

FOOD

A yen for the exotic and a return to French culinary roots are the two most prominent—and paradoxical—features of the current Paris food scene. Palates titillated by travels to far-off lands crave those same foreign flavors when they get back home: hence the proliferation of stores offering foodstuffs and prepared dishes from all over the world. It's an amazing development; less than a generation ago, the chauvinistic French were particularly insular in their eating habits. But their current flirtation with foreign cuisines doesn't mean they've forsaken their native gastronomy. *Au contraire,* demand is increasing for fine aged cheeses and bread with old-fashioned flavor. And sales of sweets—pastry, ice cream, chocolate—are booming: people are ready to lay out lots and lots of francs to buy the very best.

BAKERIES

Au Bon Pain d'Autrefois

11th arr. - 45, rue Popincourt
43 55 04 48
Open 6:30am-8pm. Closed Sat, Sun. No cards. M° Saint-Ambroise.

The delicious scent of sourdough wafts forth from this pretty bakery (designated an architectural landmark), which features superb pain de campagne (the classic country loaf), rustic rye breads, and delicious brioches. Jean-Pierre Leroy's special rotating oven also produces delectable pastries.

Daniel Dupuy

9th arr. - 13, rue Cadet
48 24 54 26
Open 7am-8pm. Closed Tue. No cards. M° Cadet.

Daniel's prize-winning pain de campagne, made of natural leavening agents and stone-ground flour, lives up to its vaunted reputation. Connoisseurs know that bread with this sort of authentic flavor is indeed worth seeking out. The same can be said of Dupuy's specialty, the Rochetour: he keeps the recipe a closely guarded secret

Espace Gourmand

4th arr. - 27, rue des Archives
42 72 93 94
Open 7:30am-8pm. Closed Sun. No cards. M° Hôtel-de-Ville.

Delicious breads, with special mention for the Provençal fougasse, stuffed with tomatoes and herbs, or with leeks and Roquefort cheese. The humble baguette, too, is extraordinary here. Don't overlook the sandwiches, which rise well above the average.

A la Flûte Gana

226, rue des Pyrénées
43 58 42 62
Open 7:30am-8pm. Closed Sun, Mon. No cards. M° Gambetta.

Elbow your way in, if you must, but don't leave Isabelle and Valérie's bakery without at least one "flûte Gana" tucked under your arm! Perfected by their father, Bernard Ganachaud, this crusty sourdough bread is justly famous. The wood-fired ovens also turn out wonderfully chewy organic bread, tantalizing nut loaves studded with the freshest filberts or walnuts, and raisin bread chockablock with plump fruit. There's also a wide variety of down-home apple pastries and buttery brioches.

Le Fournil de Pierre

4th arr. - 109, rue Saint-Antoine - 42 72 95 28 (also: 2nd arr., 6th arr., 7th arr., 8th arr., 9th arr., 12th arr., 14th arr., 15th arr., 17th arr.)
Open 7:30am-7:30pm. Closed Sun. No cards. M° Bastille.

The chain's many shops in the greater Paris area sell homestyle breads whose sole flaw is that they are not always as oven-fresh as we might wish. But the variety of loaves is astonishing (there are more than twenty), and we like the buns, cookies, and pastries for their simple homemade goodness.

Le Moulin de la Vierge

14th arr. - 105, rue Vercingetorix - 45 43 09 84 & 82, rue Daguerre
43 22 50 55
Open 8am-8pm. Closed Sun. No cards. M° Denfert-Rochereau.
15th arr. - 166, av. de Suffren
47 83 45 55
Open 7:30am-8pm. Closed Sun. No cards. M° Sèvres-Lecourbe.

Basile Kamir stands his ground against government authorities who frown on the use of wood-fired ovens for baking bread. He thus continues to turn out incomparably crusty loaves that fill his beautiful bakery with a heady, yeasty fragrance. All Kamir's breads are made from organic, stone-ground flour; the country flûtes, walnut bread, fougasses, and multigrain loaves are just a few of our favorites. The cakes and pastries are famously good as well.

Au Pain d'Antan

18th arr. - 2, rue Eugène-Sue
42 64 71 78
Open 8am-1pm & 3:30pm-7:45pm (Sat 8am-8pm; Mon 10am-1pm & 2pm-7:45pm). Closed Sun. No cards. M° Jules-Joffrin.

Jacques Sousa's handcrafted sourdough loaves bake to crisp, crusty perfection in his brick-lined oven. That same oven (it dates from 1920) also yields huge, round country breads and full-bodied ryes (the walnut-studded variety is excellent with cheese). For a sweet treat, try the sugar-sprinkled fouace aveyronnaise, a specialty of the house.

Au Panetier

2nd arr. - 10, place des Petits-Pères - 42 60 90 23
Open 8am-7:15pm. Closed Sat, Sun. No cards. M° Bourse.

Even if you don't want to buy one of the old-fashioned loaves of hazelnut bread, raisin bread, or the house specialty: pain de Saint-Fiacre (all baked in a wood-fired oven), this excellent bakery is worth a visit just for a look at the adorable etched-glass and tile décor.

Poilâne

6th arr. - 8, rue du Cherche-Midi - 45 48 42 59
Open 7:15am-8:15pm. Closed Sun. No cards. M° Sèvres-Babylone.
15th arr. - 49, bd de Grenelle
45 79 11 49
Open 7:15am-8:15pm. Closed Mon. No cards. M° Saint-Sulpice.

Lionel Poilâne is indubitably the best-known baker on the planet; he can be seen hawking his famous sourdough bread in magazines and on television screens throughout the world. And even though his products are sold all over Paris in charcuteries and cheese shops, goodly numbers of Poilâne fans think nothing of crossing town and standing in line to *personally* buy their favorite bread still warm from his ovens. Poilâne's walnut bread is, in a word, delicious, and we are also particularly fond of the shortbread cookies (sablés) and the rustic apple turnover (which makes a delicious and inexpensive dessert, accompanied by a bowl of thick crème fraîche).

Max Poilâne

14th arr. - 29, rue de l'Ouest
43 27 24 91
Open 8:30am-7:30pm. Closed Sun. No cards. M° Gaîté.
15th arr. - 87, rue Brancion
48 28 45 90
Open 7:15am-8pm. Closed Sun. No cards. M° Porte-de-Vanves.

Max Poilâne's bread bears a distinct resemblance to that produced by his brother, Lionel (see above). That's natural enough, since their father taught both of them the secrets of the trade. Max bakes big, hearty loaves with a sourdough tang, delicious rye bread studded with raisins, and buttery white bread that makes a first-class sandwich. For a teatime treat, try the luscious apple tarts. If you can't wait to try these goodies, just take a seat in the bakery's tea room.

Poujauran

7th arr. - 20, rue Jean-Nicot
47 05 80 88
Open 8:30am-8:30pm. Closed Sun. No cards. M° Latour-Maubourg.

He's a real darling, that Jean-Luc Poujauran! His bakery may be in a ritzy neighborhood, but he hasn't gone high-hat; food writers regularly wax lyrical over his talent, but his head hasn't swelled an inch. And though he bakes a wonderful country loaf with organically grown flour, he's not the type to think he's the greatest thing since sliced bread. Let's just hope he never changes. And let's hope that we will never have to give up his delicious little rolls (or his olive or his poppy seed or his walnut bread), his old-fashioned pound cake (quatre-quarts), his buttery Basque cakes, or the terrific frangipane-stuffed galettes that he bakes for the Epiphany (Three Kings' Day, January 6).

■ CATERERS

Dalloyau

15th arr. - 69, rue de la Convention
45 77 84 27, fax 45 75 27 99
Open 9:30am-7:30pm (Sun 9am-7pm). V, AE. M° Convention.

The oldest catering firm in Paris (founded in 1802), Dalloyau is also indubitably one of the best. The dishes on its appetizing menu are fit for a king (in case one is coming to your party). Choose from oysters gently stewed in Champagne, Bresse chicken with prawns, stuffed suckling pig, and a thrilling selection of desserts (the famous Dalloyau chocolate macaroons are our favorite!).

Exclusiv'

17th arr. - 35, rue Lantiez
42 26 09 29, fax 42 26 09 44
Open 9am-6pm. Closed Sat, Sun. No cards. M° Guy-Môquet.

The up-and-coming caterer, with lots of amusing and original ideas, like the "biodegradable" buffet Exclusiv' threw for the Ministry of the Environment! The food is equally clever and stylish: duck carpaccio with citrus accents, avocado-stuffed mushrooms, mini-crêpes Suzette, and sweet canapés on banana-bread bases. Each dish is so artistically presented (at one affair painters' palettes were used as plates...) that it's almost a shame to disturb the effect by eating it!

Potel et Chabot

16th arr. - 3, rue de Chaillot
47 20 22 00, fax 40 70 90 72
Open 8am-7pm. Closed Sun. No cards. M° Iéna.

Potel et Chabot is an old-established Parisian caterer—and perhaps the most successful. It handles cocktail parties, receptions, and other soigné soirées for the Opéra, the prime minister's office, and for the president himself! The food runs to well-wrought classic dishes (stuffed saddle of lamb, chicken stuffed with foie gras and truffles), but of late, we've noticed some innovative specialties on the menu: tiny potatoes stuffed with foie gras or smoked salmon, mini-cheese ravioli dressed with truffle vinaigrette, red mullet with eggplant fondue, and lemony nougat glacé.

CHARCUTERIE & TAKEOUT

Charcuterie Chédeville

1st arr. - 18, pl. du Marché-Saint-Honoré
42 61 04 62, fax 42 60 45 12
Open 8am-1:30pm & 2:30pm-6:30pm (Sat 8am-2pm). Closed Sun. V, AE, DC. M° Pyramides.

The Ritz, Crillon, George V and other classy hotels buy their traditional French charcuterie here. The quality is excellent, the choice is wide. Recommended are the York ham, the old-fashioned pork knuckle (great picnic food), the elaborate ballottines, and the pigs' trotters stuffed with foie gras.

Claude Charles

6th arr. - 10, rue Dauphine
43 54 25 19
Open 8am-2pm & 3:30pm-8pm. Closed Sat, Sun. No cards. M° Porte-Dauphine.
7th arr. - 135, rue Saint-Dominique - 47 05 53 66
Open 8:30am-8pm (Sat 8:30am-1:30pm & 4pm-8pm). Closed Sun. No cards. M° École-Militaire.

This prize-winning charcuterie, one of the finest in Paris, is the all-city champ when it comes to boudin blanc (white sausage). During the Christmas season, when boudin blanc is a traditional component of holiday meals, Charles Claude displays some twenty varieties, all with different flavorings (truffles, prunes, pistachios, and such). Andouillette (that's chitlin's, honey) is another specialty, and we are great fans of Claude's sumptuous terrines (sweetbreads, duck breast and foie gras, herbed ham), his tarts, and succulent hams.

Au Cochon d'Auvergne

5th arr. - 48, rue Monge
43 26 36 21
Open 9am-1pm & 4pm-7:30pm (Sun 9am-1pm). Closed Mon. No cards. M° Cardinal-Lemoine.

José Léon really knows how to cook a juicy ham—his is certainly one of the most toothsome in town. Equal praise is warranted for his head cheese, and for the rich rillettes and confits he fashions from Southwestern geese sent up to Paris just for him. Do make a point of sampling his excellent sugar-free compotes, made from prime, organically grown fruits.

Coesnon

6th arr. - 30, rue Dauphine
43 54 35 80
Open 8:30am-8pm. Closed Sun, Mon. V. M° Odéon.

Because true practitioners of the charcutier's art are becoming ever harder to find, and because Gérard Robert is one of its most eminent representatives, we recommend that you make a special point of visiting this wonderful pork emporium. Robert's boudin blanc and boudin noir are legendary (his chestnut-studded black pudding has won slews of awards); what's more, his salt- and smoke-cured pork specialties are top-notch—especially when accompanied by the crisp yet tender sauerkraut he pickles himself. So step up to counter with confidence, knowing that you will be competently and courteously served.

Flo Prestige

1st arr. - 42, pl. du Marché-Saint-Honoré - 42 61 45 46
16th arr. - 61, av. de la Grande-Armée - 45 00 12 10
16th arr. - 102, av. du Président-Kennedy - 42 88 38 00
Open daily 8am-11pm. Delivery. V, AE, DC, MC. M° Pyramides, Argentine, Passy.
7th arr. - 36, av. de La Motte-Picquet - 45 55 71 25
Open daily 9:30am-9:30pm. Delivery. V. M° La Motte-Picquet.

9th arr. - 64, bd Haussmann, Le Printemps - 42 82 58 82
Open 9:35am-7pm. Closed Sun. Delivery. V, AE, DC, MC. M° Havre-Caumartin.
12th arr. - 211, av. Daumesnil - 43 44 86 36
Open daily 8am-9:30pm. Delivery. V. M° Daumesnil.
12th arr. - 22, av. de la Porte de Vincennes - 43 74 54 32
Open daily 9:30am-11pm. Delivery. V. M° Saint-Mandé-Tourelle.
15th arr. - 352, rue Lecourbe 45 54 76 94
Open daily 10:30am-9:30pm. Delivery. V, AE, DC. M° Sèvres-Lecourbe.

Early or late, every day of the year, you have a sure source of delicious bread, fine wine, yummy desserts—in short, of wonderful meals with Flo Prestige. The selection of foodstuffs is varied and choice, and covers a wide range of prices, from the excellent house sauerkraut to prestigious Petrossian caviar.

Gargantua

1st arr. - 284, rue Saint-Honoré
42 60 52 54, fax 42 61 49 81
Open daily 8am-9pm (Sun 8am-8pm). V, AE, MC. M° Tuileries.

The opulent window displays of this well-known charcuterie could satisfy even the gigantically robust appetite of its Rabelaisian namesake. There are cured meats, foie gras, and terrines, of course, but Gargantua also carries an abundance of prepared dishes, breads, wines, pastries, and ice cream. It's a fine place to go to put together a picnic.

Jaouën

15th arr. - 79, rue Lecourbe
47 34 94 76
Open 9am-1pm & 4pm-7:30pm (Sun 9am-1pm). Closed Mon. V. M° Sèvres-Lecourbe.

This is one of the rare shops in the city where all the charcuterie is still made on the premises. Special mention goes to the game terrines, goose foie gras (perfectly trimmed, available year round), and succulent poached hams.

Boutique Layrac

6th arr. - 29, rue de Buci
43 25 17 72
Open daily 9:30am-2am. V, AE, DC. M° Mabillon.

What better place to compose an elegant late-night supper for two than this bright and inviting garden of gourmandise, which fairly overflows with delicacies both savory and sweet? Prepared dishes can be delivered to your door.

Pou

17th arr. - 16, av. des Ternes
43 80 19 24
Open 9:30am-7:15pm. Closed Sun, Mon. M° Ternes.

Pou is divine, an excellent charcuterie whose sober décor and rich displays resemble nothing so much as a palace of earthly delights. A look in the window is an irresistible invitation to buy and taste: black and white boudin sausages, duck pâté en croûte, glittering galantines, cervelas sausage studded with pale-green pistachios, and sumptuous pastries too. Since everything really is as good as it looks, making a choice is quite a task. And given the prices, paying isn't so easy, either.

Schmid

10th arr. - 76, bd de Strasbourg - 46 07 99 02
Open 9am-7pm (Sat 8:30am-6:45pm). Closed Sun. V. M° Gare-de-l'Est.
17th arr. - 36, rue de Lévis 47 63 07 08
Open 9am-7:30pm. Closed Sun. V. M° Villiers.

Naturally, with a name like Schmid, you would expect this shop to specialize in sauerkraut. And you wouldn't be wrong. It is excellent—fine, crisp, and tart. But don't overlook the tasty sausages, aged Munster, the light and airy Kugelhopf cake, and other Alsatian treats.

Vigneau-Desmaret

6th arr. - 105-107, rue de Sèvres
42 22 23 23, fax 42 22 74 64
Open 9am-8:30pm. Closed Sun. V, MC. M° Vaneau.

If ever you should lose your appetite, come over to this old-fashioned charcuterie... we guarantee you'll find it! Who wouldn't salivate at the sight of a rosy poached ham wrapped in a snowy linen cloth? Who wouldn't long for a bite of perfectly aged saucisson? Also on hand are light vegetable or fish terrines and an entire list of groceries, vegetables, cheeses, and fruits. And now, Vigneau-Desmaret boasts an admirable range of Italian delicacies.

Vignon

8th arr. - 14, rue Marbeuf
47 20 24 26
Open 8am-8:30pm (Sat 9am-7:30pm). Closed Sun. V, AE. M° Franklin-D.-Roosevelt.

A rather grand marble façade sets the luxurious tone for this respected

Parisian charcuterie. Monsieur Vignon turns out a superb terrine of foie gras, remarkable galantines of chicken and duck studded with truffles or pistachios, game pâtés, and hearty, old-fashioned head cheese. Fans of Parma ham should note that Vignon stocks the excellent La Slega brand from Langhirano.

CHEESE

Alléosse

17th arr. - 13, rue Poncelet
46 22 50 45
Open 8am-1pm & 4pm-7:30pm (Sun 9am-1pm). Closed Mon. V. M° Ternes.

Father and son Roger and Philippe Alléosse purvey some of the finest cheeses in Paris. With the obsessive zeal of perfectionists, they turn, rinse, brush, and otherwise groom their farmhouse fromages down in the ideally dank depths of their seven maturing cellars. If the shop's astounding stock leaves you at a loss, don't hesitate to seek advice from the staff: they'll introduce you to little-known cheeses from all over France. We understand why so many chefs choose to shop *chez* Alléosse.

Androuët

8th arr. - 41, rue d'Amsterdam - 48 74 26 90
Open 10am-1:30pm & 2:30pm-7:30pm. Closed Sun. V, AE, MC. M° St-Lazare.

Pierre Androuët, that most renowned *fromager*, having retired and sold this medieval-looking cheese shop near the Gare Saint-Lazare, nothing is quite the same. Quality varies: superbly aged cheeses sit side by side with far less worthy examples...the rule of thumb for purchasing cheese at Androuët is now "Let the buyer beware"!

Barthélémy

7th arr. - 51, rue de Grenelle
45 48 56 75
Open 8:30am-1pm & 3:30pm-7:30pm (Sat 8:30am-1:30pm & 3pm-7:30pm). Closed Sun, Mon. V. M° Rue du Bac.

Roland Barthélémy reigns over a treasure trove of cheeses that he selects from farms all over the French countryside, then coddles to perfect ripeness in his cellars. He is also the creator of several marvelous specialties that have the *Who's Who* of French officialdom beating a path to his door (he supplies the Élysée Palace, no less). The Boulamour (fresh cream cheese enriched with crème fraîche, currants, raisins, and Kirsch) was Barthélémy's invention, as was a delicious Camembert laced with Calvados. We also enjoy the amusing Brie Surprise. But not to worry, tradition is never neglected here, witness the rich-tasting Alpine Beaufort, French Vacherin, and other prime mountain cheeses which are a Barthélémy specialty. The luxuriously creamy Fontainebleau is made fresh on the premises. Take one of the appetizing cheese trays sold here as your contribution to a dinner party: your hostess will love it!

Marie-Anne Cantin

7th arr. - 12, rue du Champ-de-Mars - 45 50 43 94
Open 8:30am-7:30pm (Sun 8:30am-1pm). Closed Mon. V. M° École-Militaire.

Like father, like daughter: Marie-Anne Cantin is a worthy successor to the late Christian Cantin. The cheeses she selects and matures herself benefit from unstinting doses of tender loving care. She is

Seventh heaven for foodies

Ministries, embassies, and well-heeled residents of the posh seventh arrondissement are lucky to live amid some of the best food shops in Paris. Quality is the rule and you can fill your market basket as fast as you empty your pocketbook in the Rue du Bac, the Rue Saint-Dominique and the Rue Cler. On the way, give your eyes a feast too by peeking into some of the flowered courtyards tucked away behind wrought-iron gates. Try the bread from Jean-Luc Poujauran (20 rue Jean-Nicot), caviar from Petrossian (18 boulevard de Latour-Maubourg), cheese from Marie-Anne Cantin (12 rue du Champ-de-Mars), and chocolates from Debauve et Gallais (30 rue des Saints-Pères).

an ardent defender of real (read: unpasteurized) cheeses and is one of the few merchants in Paris to sell Saint-Marcellins as they are preferred on their home turf—in their creamy prime, not in their chalky youth. And so it is with the other cheeses she sells, all of which retain the authentic flavors of their rustic origins.

Alain Dubois

17th arr. - 80, rue de Tocqueville - 42 27 11 38
Open 8am-1pm & 4pm-7:30pm (Sun 8am-1pm). Closed Mon. V. M° Malesherbes.
17th arr. - 79, rue de Courcelles - 43 80 36 42
Open 8:30am-1pm & 4pm-7:30pm (Mon 4pm-7:30pm) Closed Sun. V. M° Courcelles.

Alain Dubois's Gruyère, aged for at least two years in his cellars, is a royal treat. And there's more: Dubois offers farmhouse goat cheeses, unpasteurized Camembert, and authentic Époisses (which he rinses religiously with marc de Bourgogne). The problem is, this expert cheese merchant offers so many enticements (some 200) that we don't know which way to turn. You will not be astonished to learn that Dubois supplies premium cheeses to such great restaurants as Lucas-Carton, Guy Savoy, Michel Rostang, Laurent, and more.

Ferme Poitevine

18th arr. - 64, rue Lamarck
46 06 54 40
Open 9am-1pm & 4pm-7:45pm (Sun 9am-12:30pm). Closed Mon. V, AE. M° Lamarck-Caulaincourt.

Jack Chapu, the cheese man, is a Montmartre personality. His many perfectly matured cheeses hail from all over the French countryside, but we particularly enjoy the flavorful Munsters, the rich Camemberts, and the tender little goat cheeses marinated in herbed olive oil. Country wines, regional charcuterie, and yummy desserts may also be purchased here.

Ferme Saint-Germain

9th arr. - 20, rue Cadet
47 70 62 38
Open 8am-1:30pm & 4pm-7:30pm (Sun 8am-1:30pm). Closed Mon. V, MC. M° Cadet.

Little Miss Muffet would love this tiny cheese store, whose specialties are pérail and galet-du-relevant—mild, creamy curd cheeses made from ewe's milk and goat's milk respectively. But that's not all: farmhouse yogurt, deliciously runny Saint-Félicien, and firm mountain cheeses are on offer as well, alongside some specimens from farther afield, like Cheddar, Provolone, and Spanish Manchego. And the *patronne* also whips up a mean tiramisù!

La Ferme Saint-Hubert

8th arr. - 21, rue Vignon
47 42 79 20
Open 8:30am-7:30pm (Mon noon-7:30pm). Closed Sun. V, AE, DC. M° Madeleine.

Cheese seller Henry Voy is so passionate about his vocation that he has no time for anything else. Morning and night you can find him tending to his Beauforts (aged for a minimum of two years), his farmhouse chèvres, Corsican sheep cheeses, or his exclusive Saint-Hubert. He travels all over France, seeking out the most flavorful specimens. For true aficionados, Voy unearths such rarities as unpasteurized butter churned with spring water, and delicate goat's-milk butter.

La Fromagerie Boursault

14th arr. - 71, av. du Général-Leclerc - 43 27 93 30
Open 8am-12:30pm & 4pm-7:30pm (Sun 8am-12:30pm). Closed Mon. V. M° Alésia.

It was here that Pierre Boursault created the triple-creme cheese that bears his name. And it is here, naturally enough, that you will find Boursault at its rich, golden best. Owner Jacques Vernier has made the shop one of the most pleasant in Paris, a showcase for the rare cheeses that he seeks out himself in the French hinterlands. Like incomparable Beauforts aged under his supervision in their native Alpine air; farmhouse goat cheeses (ah, those Picodons!); handcrafted Saint-Nectaire from Auvergne, which has nothing in common with the industrially produced variety; and flawless Camemberts. This is one of the few places on the planet where one may buy Bleu de Termignon, a blue-veined summer cheese from Savoie.

Remember that if you spend 2,000 F or more in a store, you are entitled to a full refund of the value-added tax (VAT). See Basics for details.

CHOCOLATE & CANDY

La Bonbonnière Saint-Honoré & La Bonbonnière de la Trinité

8th arr. - 28, rue de Miromesnil - 42 65 02 39
Open 10am-7pm. Closed Sat, Sun. V, MC. M° Miromesnil.
9th arr. - 4, rue Blanche
48 74 23 38
Open 9am-7pm (Sat 10am-7pm). Closed Sun. V. M° Trinité.

The charming little store on the Place d'Estienne-d'Orves dates from 1925. A real sweetshop, it stocks some 60 kinds of jam, 25 types of honey, 60 varieties of tea, and countless candies. The chocolate truffles are quite good, but for us, the irresistible attraction here is the range of bitter and super-bitter chocolates sold in great, thick slabs that are perfect for cooking or guilty nibbling.

Les Bonbons

6th arr. - 6, rue Bréa
43 26 21 15
Open 10am-1:30pm & 2pm-8pm (Mon 2pm-8pm). Closed Sun. V. M° Vavin.

Madame Lesieur's minuscule shop will bring out the child in even the most strait-laced adult: it's candyland come to life! We grant you that caramels (hard and soft), candied violets, nougats, and barley-sugar sticks are terrible for your teeth, but what a lift they give your spirits! All the traditional sweets of the French provinces are gathered here: cocons de Lyon, ardoises d'Angers, bêtises de Cambrai, and more, alongside divinely sticky gingerbread from Basel or Dijon, and satisfyingly substantial slabs of handmade chocolate.

Christian Constant

6th arr. - 37, rue d'Assas
45 48 45 51
Open daily 8am-9pm. V, AE. M° Rennes.
7th arr. - 26, rue du Bac
47 03 30 00
Open daily 8am-8pm. V. M° Rue du Bac.

Christian Constant, who chooses the best cocoa beans from the West Indies, Tahiti, Ecuador and elsewhere, is a genius with chocolate. His brilliant innovations include a line of flower-scented chocolates (try the ylang-ylang, vetiver, or the jasmine varieties...), chocolates filled with delicately spiced creams, others spiked with fruit brandies or cordials, still others incorporating nuts and dried fruit (the Conquistador is loaded with hazelnuts, honey, and cinnamon). Constant recommends that we buy his wares in small amounts, for optimum freshness and flavor. Well, given the prices (460 F per kilo), for most people quantity purchases are out of the question!

Debauve et Gallais

2nd arr. - 33, rue Vivienne
40 39 05 50
7th arr. - 30, rue des Saints-Pères - 45 48 54 67
Open 10am-7pm. Closed Sun. V, AE, DC. M° Bourse, Sèvres-Babylone.

With its picturesque shop-front designed by renowned nineteenth-century architects Percier and Fontaine (classified as a landmark by the Beaux-Arts) and its interior decorated with painted pillars, orange-wedge mirrors, and antique lamps, Debauve et Gallais has loads of charm. The filled chocolates, soft caramels, hazelnut pralines, and chocolate truffles, all prettily displayed in glass jars, are nearly as delectable as the setting.

Au Duc de Praslin

16th arr. - 125, av. Victor-Hugo - 44 05 18 08
Open 10am-7pm. Closed Sun. V, AE, DC, MC. M° Victor-Hugo.

Named for a seventeenth-century aristocrat whose cook invented the confection known as the praline, the Duc de Praslin specializes in crunchy caramel-coated almonds (about 230 F per kilo). You'll also want to sample some of the delicious variations on that basic theme: amandas (almonds, nougatine, and cocoa), mirabos (nougatine and orange, covered with milk chocolate), and passions (chocolate-coated caramelized almonds). An assortment composed of seven varieties sells for around 275 F.

A l'Étoile d'Or

9th arr. - 30, rue Fontaine
48 74 59 55
Open 10:30am-8pm. Closed Sun. V, AE, MC. M° Blanche.

Denise Acabo does not make her own chocolate; rather, she is a true connoisseur who selects the very best handcrafted chocolates made in France, and presents them, in a laudable spirit of impartiality, to her delighted customers (while explaining to interested parties the connection between chocolate and eroticism...). The famed Bernachon chocolates from Lyon are sold in this beautiful turn-of-the-century shop, as well as Dufoux's incomparable palets, and wonderful soft-centered bouchées from Voiron.

La Fontaine au Chocolat

1st arr. - 101, rue Saint-Honoré
42 33 09 09, fax 49 27 90 75
Open 10am-6:50pm (Mon 9:30am-6:30pm). Closed Sun. M° Palais-Royal.

Pervading Michel Cluizel's shop is a scent of chocolate so intense that your nose will flash an alert to your sweet tooth, and (we guarantee!) have you salivating within seconds. Whether you try one of the five varieties of palets au chocolat or the croquamandes (caramelized almonds coated with extra-dark chocolate), the mendiants studded with nuts and dried fruit, or the bold Noir Infini (99 percent cocoa, perfumed with vanilla and spices), you're in for an unforgettable treat.

Foucher

2nd arr. - 30, av. de l'Opéra
47 42 51 86
Open 10am-7pm. Closed Sun. V, AE, DC. M° Opéra.

Since 1918, Foucher has earned a solid reputation for its full-flavored dark chocolates. Of the 37 varieties proposed, we're partial to the Cognac-spiked truffles—a treat to be consumed in moderation, of course! Also worthy of note are Foucher's tender fruit jellies in an alluring range of thirteen flavors.

Jadis et Gourmande

4th arr. - 39, rue des Archives
48 04 08 03
Open 10am-7:30pm (Mon 1pm-7:30pm). Closed Sun. V. M° Hôtel-de-Ville.
8th arr. - 49 bis, av. Franklin-Roosevelt - 42 25 06 04
Open 9:30am-7:30pm (Mon 1pm-7pm, Tue 9:30am-7pm; Sat 10am-7pm). Closed Sun. V. M° Franklin-D.-Roosevelt.
5th arr. - 88, bd de Port-Royal
43 26 17 75
Open 9:30am-7pm (Thu, Fri, Sat 9:30am-7:30pm). Closed Sun. V. M° Port-Royal.
8th arr. - 27, rue Boissy-d'Anglas - 42 65 23 23
Open 9:30am-7pm (Sat 10:30am-1:30pm & 2:30pm-7pm; Mon 1pm-7pm). Closed Sun. V. M° Madeleine.

It is delightful indeed to browse around this sugarplum palace, where one is tempted in turn by delicious bonbons, hard candies, caramels, and chocolate in myriad forms. The thick slabs of cooking chocolate make one want to rush to the kitchen and whip up a rich devil's food cake! Our favorite confection here is a thick braid of dark chocolate studded with candied orange peel and hazelnuts. Prices range from about 210 to 350 F per kilo.

Lenôtre

7th arr. - 44, rue du Bac
42 22 39 39
Open daily 9am-8pm (Sun 9am-1pm). V. M° Rue du Bac.
15th arr. - 61, rue Lecourbe
42 73 20 97
16th arr. - 44, rue d'Auteuil
45 24 52 52, fax 42 30 79 45
& 49, av. Victor-Hugo
45 01 71 71
17th arr. - 121, av. de Wagram - 47 63 70 30
92200 Neuilly - 3, rue des Huissiers - 46 24 98 68
Open daily 9am-9pm. V, AE, DC. M° Sèvres-Lecourbe, Michel-Ange-Auteuil, Victor-Hugo, Wagram, Pont-de-Neuilly.
8th arr. - 15, bd de Courcelles - 45 63 87 63
Open daily 7:30am-9pm. V. M° Villiers.
16th arr. - 193, av. de Versailles - 45 25 55 88
Open daily 8am-9pm (Sun 8am-8pm). V. M° Exelmans.
8th arr. - 5, rue du Havre
45 22 22 59
Open 10am-7pm. Closed Sun. V. M° Havre-Caumartin.
9th arr. - 40, bd Haussmann, Lafayette Gourmet
42 80 45 75
Open daily 9am-7:45pm. Closed Sun. V. M° Chaussée-d'Antin.
92100 Boulogne - 79 bis, route de la Reine - 46 05 37 35
Open daily 9am-9pm (Sun 9am-1pm). V, AE. M° Jean-Jaurès.

Gaston Lenôtre's range of chocolates includes classic, intensely flavored truffles and remarkable palets d'or filled with rich, subtle buttercream. Brisk turnover ensures the freshness of all these marvelous confections. In addition to chocolates, Lenôtre produces creamy caramels, nougatines and, around Christmas, meltingly tender candied chestnuts. Everything on sale here is beautifully packaged.

La Maison du Chocolat

8th arr. - 52, rue François-Ier
47 23 38 25
9th arr. - 8, bd de la Madeleine - 47 42 86 52
Open 10am-7pm. Closed Sun. V. M° Franklin-D.-Roosevelt, Madeleine.
8th arr. - 225, rue du Fg-St-Honoré - 42 27 39 44
Open 9:30am-7pm. Closed Sun. V. M° Ternes.

There's something of the alchemist about Robert Linxe: never satisfied, he is ever experimenting, innovating, transforming mere cocoa beans into something very precious. His chocolates (450 F per kilo) are among the finest in Paris, maybe even in the world. His renowned buttercream fillings—lemon, caramel, tea, raspberry, and rum—will carry you away to gourmet heaven.

A la Mère de Famille

9th arr. - 35, rue du Fg-Montmartre - 47 70 83 69
Open 8:30am-1:30pm & 3pm-7pm. Closed Sun, Mon. V. M° Rue Montmartre.

Perhaps the oldest candy shop in Paris (it dates back to 1761), La Mère de Famille is certainly the handsomest, with a façade and interior from the nineteenth century (note the Second Empire-style cashier's booth). The shop's sweet inventory includes luscious jams, candied fruits, and bonbons from all over France. The chocolates are prepared by the current owner, Serge Neveu, and sell for 344 F per kilo. We love the Whiskadines (soft chestnut centers laced with whisky) and the Délices de la Mère with their suave almond and rum-raisin filling.

Peltier

7th arr. - 66, rue de Sèvres
47 83 66 12
Open 9:30am-8pm (Sun 8:30am-7pm). V. M° Duroc.
7th arr. - 6, rue Saint- Dominique - 47 05 50 02
Open 8:15am-7:45pm (Sun 8:15am-7pm). V. M° Solférino.

Peltier's palets d'or (dark chocolates filled with chocolate buttercream and topped with a daub of real gold leaf) are a treat: light, suave, and balanced. The legion of filled varieties, made with premium ingredients, are at least equally as luscious (try the licorice or ginger soft centers to see what we mean).

Puyricard

7th arr. - 27, av. Rapp
47 05 59 47
Open 8am-8pm. Closed Sun (exc hols). V. M° Alma-Marceau.

This shop is the exclusive Parisian source of the sweet (some might say, slightly too sweet) chocolate truffles produced by the Provençal firm, Puyricard. Like the chocolates, the delicious calissons d'Aix (almond candies: 196 F per kilo) are made by hand in small batches. A house specialty is the Clou de Cézanne (298 F per kilo), a chocolate with a light nougatine and pine-nut filling shaped like the paving nails used on the streets of Aix-en-Provence in Cézanne's time.

Richart

7th arr. - 258, bd Saint-Germain
45 55 66 00, fax 47 53 72 72
Open 10am-7pm (Mon & Sat 11am-7pm). Closed Sun. V. M° Solférino.

A top-notch *chocolatier* from Lyon has established a Parisian outpost near the House of Parliament. This elegant emporium sells superbly presented chocolates with smooth, scrumptious buttercream fillings, and addictive dark-chocolate bars made from Venezuelan cocoa beans. The Petits Richarts, mini-chocolates that weigh just one-sixth of an ounce, are perfect for nibbling with a clear conscience.

Christian Tholoniat

10th arr. - 47, rue du Château-d'Eau - 42 39 93 12
Open 8am-7:30pm (Sun 8:30am-6pm). Closed Wed. V. M° Château-d'Eau.

Within these walls, a master pastry chef spins, sculpts, blows, and shapes sugar and chocolate into tiny people, landscapes, fruit, flowers, and even wee houses (with furniture!). Incredibly enough, his creations taste as good as they look. Special applause goes to Tholoniat's delicious and unusual pear- and orange-flavored chocolates.

COFFEE & TEA

Betjeman and Barton

8th arr. - 23, bd Malesherbes
42 65 86 17
Open 9:30am-7pm. Closed Sun. V, MC. M° Madeleine.
11th arr. - 24, bd des Filles-du-Calvaire - 40 21 35 52
Open 10am-7pm. Closed Sun, Mon. V. M° Filles-du-Calvaire.

The name on the sign and the shop's décor are veddy, veddy British, but the firm itself is 100 percent French, directed nowadays by Didier Jumeau-Lafond. The range of premium teas on offer is quite extensive, comprising over 160 natural and flavored varieties. Indeed, B and B's teas are of such high quality that Harrod's of London (no less) deigns to market them. To help you choose your blend, the staff will offer you a cup of tea—a comforting and highly civilized custom. Vera Winterfeldt's excellent jams and a line of refreshing fruit "waters" intended to be consumed icy-cold in summer, are worth seeking out here.

Brûlerie des Ternes & Torréfaction de Passy

16th arr. - 28, rue de l'Annonciation - 42 88 99 90
Open 9am-7:30pm (Sun & hols 9am-1pm). Closed Mon. No cards. M° La Muette.
17th arr. - 10, rue Poncelet 46 22 52 79
Open 9am-1:30pm & 3:30pm-7:30pm (Sun & hols 9am-1pm). Closed Mon. V. M° Ternes.

Coffees from all over the globe are roasted and ground to perfection in this commendable shop, which draws a clientele made up, in part, of the chic and famous. Featured is the fabled Blue Mountain coffee from Jamaica, a rare and costly treat. Each customer's individual blend is automatically recorded on a computer, so the recipe need never be lost or forgotten. Flavored coffees (orange, chocolate, vanilla...) are justly popular, and there are 70 kinds of tea in stock as well.

Espace Café

11th arr. - 89, bd de Charonne - 43 70 28 92
Open 10am-7pm. Closed Sun, Mon. No cards. M° Avron.

Michel Toutain has a futuristic outlook on coffee. The shop's computer produces a sensorial analysis that allegedly matches the customer's personality with a particular bean or blend. But, of course, one may simply go in and ask for one's preferred brew: Javanese, Moka, Negus, Mexican, or any one of a number of house specialties. All beans sold are rigorously selected and roasted fresh each day.

Mariage Frères

4th arr. - 30-32, rue du Bourg-Tibourg - 42 72 28 11
6th arr. - 13, rue des Grands-Augustins - 40 51 82 50
Open 10:30am-7:30pm (Tea room noon-7pm). V, AE. M° Hôtel-de-Ville, St-Michel.

Founded by a family of explorers, one of whose ancestors participated in a delegation sent by Louis XIV to sign a trade agreement with the Shah of Persia, Mariage imports no fewer than 350 varieties of tea from 30 countries. This comprehensive selection, coupled with the firm's unceasing expansion and promotional efforts, makes Mariage Frères the high temple of tea in Paris. Top-of-the-line products include the exquisite Bloomfield Darjeeling, a splendid golden-tipped Grand Yunnan, and other rarities that may be sampled in the shop's tea room, accompanied by pastries or light snacks (see *Tea Rooms*).

Le Palais des Thés

6th arr. - 35, rue de l'Abbé-Grégoire - 45 48 85 81
14th arr. - 21, rue Raymond-Losserand - 43 21 97 97
Open 10:30am-7pm. Closed Sun, Mon. V. M° Rennes, Gaîté.
16th arr. - 21, rue de l'Annonciation - 45 25 51 52
Open 10:30am-7pm (Sun 10am-1pm). Closed Mon. V. M° Passy.

Founded in 1986 by a consortium of 45 tea lovers, this establishment has risen quickly in the ranks of Parisian tea merchants. More than 350 types of tea can be found here, and a helpful staff is on deck to guide your choice. Those fond of flavored teas (we see you purists out there frowning!) will appreciate the seven-citrus blend and the monks' tea made with ten aromatic plants. All the paraphernalia required by the tea ritual—from teapots to strainers to cups—is also in stock. True tea fanatics will go gaga over the jellies and candies perfumed with their favorite brew. Frequent customers should be sure to ask for the shop's *carte de fideli-thé*, good for a ten percent discount.

Torréfaction Valade

12th arr. - 21, bd de Reuilly 43 43 39 27
Open 8:45am-2:15pm & 3:15pm-7:30pm. Closed Sun, Mon. V, AE. M° Dugommier.

In his modern, clean-lined shop, Pascal Guiraud celebrates his passion for coffee, a passion that he shares with his equally enthusiastic customers. Beans from Cuba, Brazil, Kenya, Costa Rica, Haiti, and elsewhere release an irresistible aroma as they roast (and they are prepared only as needed, so the coffee is absolutely fresh). The house blends are marvelous as well: we like the Italian Roast, which is one of the most popular, the Turkish Special, and the spicy Orient Express. Don't overlook the shop's prestigious selection of jams, honey, and condiments, or the 110 kinds of tea.

Twinings

8th arr. - 76, bd Haussmann
43 87 39 84
Open 10am-7pm. Closed Sun, Mon. V. M° St-Augustin.

Twinings' utterly English boutique is, so they claim, the only place to procure genuine Earl Grey tea (15 F per 100 g), the kind still drunk in quantity by the Grey family. Another exceedingly rare variety, Darjeeling Ringtong, is also available, for a rather more hefty sum (60 F per 100 g). Regular customers have their names and favorite blends recorded in a large, bound ledger (very chic). Tea fanciers will be glad to learn that Twinings also sells tea in bricks, just as it was sold back in the fourteenth century.

Verlet

1st arr. - 256, rue Saint-Honoré - 42 60 67 39
Open 9am-7pm. Closed Sun. No cards. M° Palais-Royal.

The Verlet family has been roasting and selling coffee beans in their delightful turn-of-the-century shop since 1880. Pierre Verlet imports the finest coffees from Papua, Costa Rica, Colombia, Jamaica, Malabar, Ethiopia, and Brazil, and he also produces several subtle and delicious house blends. He will even create one specially for you, for he is a master at balancing different aromas, different degrees of acidity and bitterness to suit personal taste. If you prefer to sample before you buy, take a seat at one of the little tables and try, perhaps, the Petit Cheval blend, a marvelously balanced and smooth Moka. Verlet also stocks a selection of teas from all over the world and an appetizing array of dried fruits. At lunchtime, crowds pour into the shop for an excellent croque monsieur or a slice of cake and a cup of fragrant coffee.

■ ETHNIC FOODS

Aux Cinq Continents

11th arr. - 75, rue de la Roquette
43 56 79 69, fax 43 79 57 45
Open 9:30am-1pm & 4pm-8pm (Sun 9:30am-1pm). V, AE, DC. M° Bastille.

The Abramoff family reigns over one of the city's most comprehensive sources of grains, cereals, and imported delicacies. No fewer than fifteen kinds of rice are on stock here (including wild rice at 90 F per kilo), along with ten varieties of dried beans (the black beans complement any kind of smoked meat), and various grades of semolina. Exotica include a delicious dried mullet roe (called "poutargue," 350 F per kilo), Iranian pistachios, pastrami, corned beef, chewy Central European breads, and flavored vodkas. The store also boasts a fascinating supply of arcane kitchen utensils. Aux Cinq Continents is worth a visit for its nose-tickling scents alone.

Le Comptoir Irlandais

11th arr. - 153, bd Voltaire
43 71 25 81
Open 10am-8pm. Closed Sun. V, AE. M° Charonne.

Our Irish eyes smile at the array of foodstuffs imported from the auld sod: Kerrygold butter and orange marmalade spiked with whiskey for the top o' the morning; rich Irish shortbread and chocolates for tea; homegrown beers (Murphy's, Harp, Smithwick's) and whiskeys for later in the day. Also on hand are cozy woolens and tweed caps—as suitable for Paris as for Dublin—and Celtic music on CDs and cassettes.

Davoli-La Maison du Jambon

7th arr. - 34, rue Cler
45 51 23 41
Open 8am-1pm & 4pm-7:30pm (Sun & Wed 8:30am-1pm). Closed Mon. V. M° École-Militaire.

Fresh stuffed pasta headlines the offerings: cappelletti filled with meat, tortellini filled with spinach, and scallop-stuffed ravioli to name but a trio of exemplary offerings. The Parma ham is excellent, and the rosy, unctuous mortadella is imported direct from Bologna. A selection of fine Italian wines (as well as liqueurs and aperitivi) lets you wash all this good stuff down in proper style.

The General Store

7th arr. - 82, rue de Grenelle
45 48 63 16
16th arr. - 30, rue de Longchamp - 47 55 41 14
Open 10am-7:30pm. Closed Sun. V, AE, DC. M° Rue du Bac, Boissières.

Tacos, tortillas, and all the other traditional fixings for a Tex-Mex feast may be found in this spic-and-span little shop. But the inventory doesn't stop there: You'll find buttermilk-pancake mix, a selection of California wines (not just Paul Masson), familiar American packaged foods

(Karo syrup, cream cheese, canned pumpkin, chocolate chips, Hellmann's mayo), and even fresh cranberries at holiday time. If you crave a sweet snack, look for the delectable pecan squares and cookies whipped up fresh every day. As you would expect, English is spoken, and you can count on a warm welcome.

Jo Goldenberg

4th arr. - 7, rue des Rosiers
48 87 20 16
Open daily 8:30am-midnight (Sat 8:30am-2am). V, AE, DC. M° Saint-Paul.

For over 60 years, this far-famed little grocery-cum-restaurant has supplied the Ashkenazi community of Paris with stuffed carp, zesty herring with a procession of sauces, smoked salmon, corned beef, smoked tongue, and even caviar, which you can wash down with one of the many different vodkas.

Goldenberg

17th arr. - 69, av. de Wagram
42 27 34 79
Open daily 8:30am-midnight. V. M° Ternes.

Familiar deli fare, made measurably more exotic by the fact that it's served within sight of the Arc de Triomphe. There's herring, there's corned beef, there's gefilte fish (stuffed carp), there's pastrami, and that well-known Yiddish dessert, the brownie.

I Golosi

9th arr. - 6, rue de la Grange-Batelière - 48 24 18 63
Open 9:30am-midnight. Closed Sun. V. M° Richelieu-Drouot.

I Golosi stands out from the Italian food shops that in recent times have been springing up around Paris like *funghi*. Owner Marc Tonazzo, formerly with the estimable Enoteca wine bar (see *Wine Bars*), has gathered about him a choice selection of transalpine delicacies, including pink Sardinian saffron, olive oil from around Lake Garda, the sweet and spicy fruit condiment known as mostarda di Cremona, traditional balsamic vinegar at a most attractive price, and no fewer than 40 varieties of pasta. The wine section is uncommonly fine, with all the top labels from the Veneto, Piedmont, Tuscany, and Lombardy present and accounted for.

Heratchian Frères

9th arr. - 6, rue Lamartine
48 78 43 19
Open 8:30am-7:30pm. Closed Sun. V, MC. M° Cadet.

All the mellifluous idioms of the Near East and the Balkans are spoken (and understood) at this fascinating, fragrant bazaar. The sales staff will help you to fat, purple Kalamata olives, golden thyme-blossom honey, genuine sheep's-milk feta, Salonikan yogurt (made from a mix of cow's and sheep's milk), and savory kibbeh (bulghur and ground lamb, onions and pine nuts deep-fried or—for the daring—served raw). Nice prices.

Izraël

4th arr. - 30, rue François-Miron - 42 72 66 23
Open 9:30am-1pm & 2:30pm-7pm (Sat 9:30am-7pm). Closed Sun, Mon. V. M° Saint-Paul.

Solski and Françoise Izraël are the masters of this colorful, richly scented realm of spices, herbs, exotic foods and condiments. Burlap sacks overflow with basmati rice from Pakistan and Thailand; crates burst with fat dates and figs from Turkey; Greek olives soak in barrels of herbed, lemony marinades. Curries, chutneys, and pink lentils have journeyed from India to this Paris spot; from Mexico, tacos and several types of fiery chilis. Argentinian empanadas, Louisiana pecans, Chinese candied ginger, and no fewer than five types of coconut milk are just some of the other international representatives found in this fascinating food shop.

Kioko

2nd arr. - 46, rue des Petits-Champs - 42 61 33 66
Open 10am-7pm. Closed Sun. No cards. M° Pyramides.

All the hard-to-find ingredients that go into Japanese cuisine can be purchased at this unprepossessing little grocery. In addition to tofu, taro, Japanese-style rice, and wheat noodles, Kioko stocks ten types of sake and good native beers, like Kirin and Sapporo. Labels are translated from Japanese into French to ease (!) your shopping experience.

Marks & Spencer

4th arr. - 88, rue de Rivoli
44 61 08 00
Open 9:30am-8:30pm (Mon & Tue 9:30am-8pm; Sat

9:30am-7:30pm). Closed Sun. V. M° Châtelet.
9th arr. - 35, bd Haussmann
47 42 42 91
Open 9:30am-7pm (Tue 10am-7pm). Closed Sun. V. M° Chaussée-d'Antin.

The food section of this all-British emporium provides ample evidence that English gastronomy is not, as Parisians tend to think, a joking matter. The French are genetically incapable, for example, of producing good bacon. Marks & Spencer's is wonderful: meaty, smoky, with no nasty bits of bone, no inedible rind. The cheese counter features Stilton, Cheddar, Leicester, and other delicious English dairy products, and the grocery shelves are crowded with all sorts of piquant condiments and chutneys. Teas, biscuits, jams, and marmalades are legion, of course, and a special refrigerated case offers fresh sandwiches for a quick lunch on the run. Prices in the Paris branch are considerably higher than on Marks & Sparks' home turf.

Mourougane

10th arr. - 83, passage Brady
42 46 06 06
Open 9:30am-8:30pm. Closed Sun. V. M° Strasbourg-Saint-Denis.

Over the past decade, Indo-Pakistani cooking has conquered Paris with its sunny, fragrant, spicy dishes. Mourougane, set in the quiet Passage Brady, carries marvelous basmati rice, poppadums, chutneys, and all the colorful spices, chilis, and curries one might need to compose a full-course Indian or Pakistani feast.

Chinatown, My Chinatown

The developers who built the cluster of Manhattan-inspired skyscrapers around the Avenues d'Ivry and de Choisy (13th arrondissement) intended them for Parisian buyers; but local investors didn't care for all that concrete. Instead, immigrants from war-torn Southeast Asia who poured into the city in the mid 1970s took over the towers. Today, Chinatown's 40,000 residents have put a vivid Asian stamp on the area's culture, cuisine, and commerce. Sample them all at *Tang Frères*, a multifarious market-cum-restaurant at 44 av. d'Ivry.

Au Régal

16th arr. - 4, rue Nicolo
42 88 49 15
Open daily 9:30am-11pm. V, AE. M° La Muette.

Delicacies from all the Russias are spotlighted here: caviar, vodkas of every description, coulibiac (salmon baked in a pastry crust), and pirozhki (more pastry-wrapped nibbles), marinated herring and blinis, vatrouchka (cheesecake) and walnut tart.

Spécialités Antillaises

20th arr. - 14-16, bd de Belleville - 43 58 31 30
Open 10am-7:15pm (Sat & Sun 9am-7:15pm). Closed Mon. V. M° Belleville.

Here's a one-stop shop for Creole fixings and takeout foods. Among the latter, we recommend the scrumptious stuffed crabs, the crispy accras (salt-cod fritters), the Creole sausage, and a spicy avocado dish called féroce d'avocat. The grocery section offers tropical fruits flown in fresh from the West Indies, as well as a selection of exotic frozen fish (shark, gilthead...), and an intoxicating array of rums and punches.

Tang Frères

13th arr. - 48, av. d'Ivry
45 70 80 00
Open 9am-7:30pm. Closed Mon. No cards. M° Porte-d'Ivry.

Three times a week a cargo plane flies into Paris bearing a shipment earmarked for the Tang brothers. This gastronomic dynasty runs the biggest Asian supermarket in town, stocked with all manner of mysterious (to the uninitiated) roots, powders, dried mushrooms, canned bamboo shoots, rice and noodles, birds' nests, sharks' fins, and so on... and on—there are literally thousands of items to choose from. Don't miss the great ready-to-eat Peking duck.

Than Binh

5th arr. - 18, rue Lagrange
43 54 66 11
Open 9:30am-7:30pm. Closed Mon. No cards. M° Maubert-Mutualité.

From perfumed rice to instant soups, from fresh tropical fruit and vegetables to dried fish, sweet bean cakes, and a selection of prepared foods (terrific fresh dim-sum), Than Binh stocks a staggering assortment of Chinese, Japanese, and Vietnamese food products. Throngs of Asian shoppers come here regularly to purchase their culinary supplies, but the crowds don't seem to faze the calm and amiable staff.

Au Village Italien

11th arr. - 50, bd du Temple
47 00 81 52
Open 8:30am-1pm & 4pm-8pm. Closed Sun. V, AE. M° République.

Silvia and Rita Calvi offer the usual range of Italian products—fresh pasta, homemade pesto, delicious charcuterie—but their wine section is truly special. Priced from 26 to 176 F, these top-flight bottles come from all over the Boot. We're particularly fond of the Vinsanto di San Felice, a delectable dessert wine. Speaking of dessert, the Calvi sisters were the first in Paris to sell homemade tiramisù, still a specialty of the house. Home delivery for orders over 400 F.

FRUITS & VEGETABLES

Le Fruitier d'Auteuil

16th arr. - 5, rue Bastien-Lepage - 45 27 51 08
Open 7am-1pm & 3:30pm-7:45pm. Closed Sun. No cards. M° Michel-Ange-Auteuil.

Bernard Rapine, president of the Fruit Retailers' Union, has a personal and professional interest in displaying the best produce he can find. He claims — and we have seen it to be true—that any store posting the union label (the word *fruitier* printed over a basket of fruit) is honor-bound to provide top-quality merchandise and service. Rapine's shop is a fine example.

Halles Trottemant

1st arr. - 36, rue Coquillière
42 33 79 66
Open 8am-1pm & 4:30pm-7:30pm (Sat 8am-1pm). Closed Sun. V. M° Les Halles.

Rare varieties of lettuce and greens (including arugula and genuine mesclun), fresh herbs, wild mushrooms, and jewel-like berries compose this eminent greengrocer's high-class stock. To dress your salad, choose one of the fine oils offered here—we favor the unusual pistachio oil from the Berry region in central France.

Palais du Fruit

2nd arr. - 74, rue Montorgueil - 42 33 22 15
Open 8am-7:30pm (Sun & hols 8am-1pm). Closed Mon. No cards. M° Les Halles.

Superb fruits and vegetables from all over the globe, beautifully presented. Even when skies are gray in France, in Chile or the Antilles gorgeous produce ripens in the sun, then is picked and packed off to this cheerful store. Wide choice, remarkable quality.

Some establishments change their closing times without warning. It is always wise to check in advance.

GOURMET SPECIALTIES

Caves Augé

8th arr. - 116, bd Haussmann
45 22 16 97, fax 44 70 08 80
Open 9am-7:30pm (Mon 1pm-7:30pm). Closed Sun. V, AE, DC. M° Saint-Philippe-du-Roule.

Augé was one of the first shops in town (maybe the only?) where eccentric gourmets could purchase such rare delicacies as bear steaks, reindeer roasts, and elephant trunks. Nowadays this luxurious little shop specializes in fine wines and brandies. There is still a small grocery section, which includes excellent tinned foods (always handy to have in the cupboard) and an enticing assortment of boxed cookies. But the pride of the house is its wine cellar (the oldest in Paris) which features an exceptional choice of "minor" Bordeaux, great Burgundies, Cognacs, and Calvados.

Detou

2nd arr. - 58, rue de Tiquetonne - 42 33 96 43
Open 8am-6pm (Sat 8am-noon). Closed Sun. No cards. M° Les Halles.

Home bakers browse happily among the pastry supplies that comprise Detou's principal stock-in-trade: baking chocolate, powdered almonds, candied fruit, and the like. But there are also rare and delicious jams here, as well as unusual cookies and quality canned goods (the mushrooms are particularly fine). Next door, the younger Detou oversees a tempting stock of smoked salmon, foie gras, caviar, wines, and spirits. First-rate merchandise at surprisingly moderate prices.

Faguais

8th arr. - 30, rue de La Trémoille - 47 20 80 91
Open 9:15am-7pm. Closed Sun. V. M° Franklin-D.-Roosevelt.

Yes, Grandmother would feel quite at home in this charming gourmet shop. A dizzying variety of temptations is set out neatly on the shelves. Old-fashioned jams, oils, honeys, cookies, spices, vinegars, and condiments fairly cry out to be bought and sampled. As the shop's pervasive fragrance implies, fresh coffee beans are roasted on the premises daily.

Fauchon

8th arr. - 26, pl. de la Madeleine - 47 42 60 11
Open 9:40am-7pm. Closed Sun. V, AE, DC. M° Madeleine.

In 1886, at the age of 30, Auguste Fauchon opened his *épicerie fine* on the Place de la Madeleine, specializing in quality French foodstuffs. The rest is history. After more than a century, Fauchon is the uncontested paragon of what a luxury gourmet emporium should be. The entire staff of 300 employees is committed to the task of tasting, testing, and selling the very finest, the rarest, the most unusual foods in the world. The number of spices alone—4,500—is enough to make your head spin. And you'll find such delicacies as black-fig or watermelon preserves, lavender or buckwheat honey, Mim tea from India or Kee-yu tea from China, lavish displays of prime vegetables and fruits, and a world-renowned collection of vintage wines and brandies. As for the pastries, well... you should know that Pierre Hermé is one of the finest *chef-pâtissiers* in the business.

Fouquet

8th arr. - 22, rue François-Ier
47 23 30 36
Open 9:30am-7:30pm. Closed Sun. V, AE, DC, MC. M° Champs-Élysées-Clemenceau.
9th arr. - 36, rue Laffitte
47 70 85 00
Open 9:30am-6:30pm. Closed Sat, Sun. V, AE. M° Peletier.

Christophe Fouquet is the most recent representative of the illustrious family of grocers who have been selling choice foodstuffs at this address since 1852. Fine chocolates are a long-standing specialty at this pretty, old-fashioned shop, but don't overlook the rare mustards (flavored with blackcurrants, oranges, or raspberries), appetizing bottled sauces, vinegars distilled according to a secret house recipe, liqueur-laced jams, fruity olive oils, imported cakes and cookies, and excellent eaux-de-vie. All the items are attractively packaged and make appreciated gifts.

Hédiard

7th arr. - 126, rue du Bac
45 44 01 98
8th arr. - 21, pl. de la Madeleine - 43 12 88 77
Open 9:30am-9pm. Closed Sun. V, AE, DC. M° Sèvres-Babylone, Madeleine.
16th arr. - 70, av. Paul-Doumer - 45 04 51 92
17th arr. - 106, bd de Courcelles - 47 63 32 14
Open 9:30am-10pm. Closed Sun. V, AE, DC. M° La Muette, Courcelles.

A home for the Nation

The *Triumph of the Nation* is the theme of the bronze group sculpted by Jules Dalou that now stands on the Place de la Nation. The work was originally planned for the *Place de la République*, but an official jury decided otherwise. For a closer look at the figures, take the underground walkway to the gardens in the center of the sea of traffic that surrounds the square. Exhaust fumes were less of a problem in 1880, when the first national holiday was celebrated here on July 14. A short walk away in the *Rue de Picpus*, eminent members of the French nobility executed during the Revolution (the guillotine stood for a time on the Place de la Nation) are buried in the *Picpus Cemetery*. Today, this green and placid resting place is exclusively reserved for descendants of those same noble families.

92200 Neuilly-sur-Seine
135, rue de Longchamp
47 22 90 82
Open 9am-1pm & 3pm-7pm. Closed Sun. V. M° Pont-de-Neuilly.

Only the most select foodstuffs are deemed worthy of entry into this shrine of epicureanism, founded in 1854. Distinguished smoked salmon from the best "schools," sophisticated sugars and syrups, pedigreed Ports, vintage wines and brandies, and over 4,500 carefully chosen grocery items attract virtually every cultivated palate in town. Even the ordinary is extraordinary here: mustard spiked with Cognac; vinegar flavored with seaweed; opulent fruits and vegetables, always perfect, that hail from the ends of the earth. Many of the items are as costly as they are exotic, but the wines consistently offer excellent value for the money. Hédiard's flagship store on the Place de la Madeleine was recently remodeled and expanded. It now houses the famous Créplet-Brussol cheese shop and a tasting bar in the wine department. And, not to be outdone by its rival across the *place*, Hédiard, like Fauchon, has opened a classy new restaurant above the store.

CAVIAR & SALMON

Boutique Flora Danica

8th arr. - 142, av. des Champs-Élysées - 44 13 86 25
Open 9am-10pm (Sun 10am-8pm). V, AE. M° George-V.

Does the phrase "Danish gastronomy" sound fishy to you? So it should, for salmon in myriad forms is its very foundation. Delicate pink specimens from the Baltic Sea are sold here, both smoked and marinated with dill. We suggest that you sample the delicious Danish herring—along with the entire array of sweet-and-sour sauces that go with it—then wash it all down with an icy, pale Carlsberg beer.

Caviar Kaspia

8th arr. - 17, pl. de la Madeleine - 42 65 33 52
Open 9am-midnight. Closed Sun. V, AE. M° Madeleine.

Caviar, it would seem, is best savored in a setting of serene austerity. Such is the impression made by the stark interior of Caviar Kaspia, where the choicest Russian and Iranian roes are sold, along with an assortment of superb smoked fish. The tender, buttery salmon is flawless, but we come for the fine smoked eel, trout, or sturgeon, all of which are models of their kind. Should a hunger pang occur at the sight of these delights (how could it not?), just step upstairs to the first-floor restaurant, where all the house specialties may be ordered à la carte.

Comptoir du Saumon

4th arr. - 60, rue François-Miron - 42 77 23 08
8th arr. - 61, rue Pierre-Charron - 45 61 25 14
15th arr. - 116, rue de la Convention - 45 54 31 16
17th arr. - 3, av. de Villiers
40 53 89 00
Open 10am-10pm. Closed Sun. V. M° Saint-Paul, Franklin-D.-Roosevelt, Boucicaut, Villiers.

The French are crazy about smoked salmon. And it is this untempered enthusiasm that's behind the success of the Comptoir du Saumon, where Irish, Swedish, Norwegian, and Scottish fish are sold at attractive prices. Also stocked are smoked trout and eel, Dutch herring, Danish marinated herring, and Iranian caviar. The premium vodkas and aquavits are perfect partners for the fish, and if you really can't wait for a taste, grab a table at the snack bar.

Dominique

6th arr. - 19, rue Bréa
43 27 08 80
Open daily 12:15pm-2:30pm & 7:15pm-10:30pm. V. M° Vavin.

Dominique has been a fixture on the Montparnasse circuit since time immemorial, and will probably remain so, despite occasional lapses in food and service. The take-out shop remains an excellent source of caviar, Danish smoked salmon and herring, as well as tender blinis, zakuski (traditional Russian hors d'œuvres), and vodka, of course.

Petrossian

7th arr. - 18, bd de Latour-Maubourg - 45 51 70 64
Open 9am-8pm. Closed Sun. V, AE. M° Latour-Maubourg.

The Petrossian family introduced sturgeon eggs to France in the 1920s, a commercial coup that won them the undying gratitude of the newly born Soviet Union. Today the Petrossians still enjoy the privilege of choosing the very best roes on site at

Caspian fishing ports. In addition to sublime oscetra, sevruga, beluga, and pressed caviar, there are remarkably rich and unctuous Norwegian smoked salmon, smoked eel and sturgeon, Russian salmon roe, and a multitude of excellent vodkas. Splendiferous gift baskets can be composed according to your tastes and budget.

ESCARGOTS

L'Escargot de la Butte

18th arr. - 48, rue Joseph-de-Maistre - 46 27 38 27
Open 8:30am-7:30pm. Closed Sun, Mon. V. M° Guy-Môquet.

"It's really a shame, but there are no more escargots de Bourgogne left in France," laments Monsieur Marchal. He imports them, therefore, from Germany. But his petits-gris come straight from the Provençal countryside, and arrive still frisky at his little shop located at the foot of the Butte Montmartre. He stuffs them with a deliciously fragrant blend of pure butter, garlic, and parsley and they are a remarkable treat!

La Maison de l'Escargot

15th arr. - 79, rue Fondary
45 75 31 09
Open 8:30am-8pm (Sun & hols 9am-1pm). Closed Mon. V. M° Émile-Zola.

Snail fanciers from surrounding neighborhoods think nothing of making the trek to this commendable shop. Live petits-gris and escargots de Bourgogne of all sizes are prepared with a delicious snail butter—which is not too strong, not too bland—that is made according to the specifications of a secret recipe developed here in 1894. The butter may also be purchased separately. If you want to sample the wares on the spot, cross the street to the little stand opposite the shop.

FOIE GRAS

Le Comptoir Corrézien

15th arr. - 8, rue des Volontaires - 47 83 52 97
Open 9am-1pm & 3pm-8pm (Mon 3:30pm-8pm). Closed Sun. V. M° Volontaires.

Chantal Larnaudie is an energetic young woman who comes from a long line of foie-gras specialists. The specimens she offers in her shop, whole poached fatted goose liver, preserved in a terrine, are fine indeed, and attractively priced to boot. Don't miss her wide selection of fra-grant wild mushrooms, sold fresh in season, or dried.

Comptoir du Foie Gras

1st arr. - 6, rue des Prouvaires
42 36 26 27, fax 40 26 32 16
Open 8am-7pm. Closed Sun, Mon. V. M° Les Halles.

This shop is the Parisian outpost of Bizac, a renowned foie-gras processing firm from Brive, in southwestern France. Foie gras in tins and jars comes fully cooked or, if you prefer, lightly cooked (heated just to 90 degrees). If you wish to try your hand at preparing your own terrine de foie gras, raw duck and goose livers are available.

Divay

10th arr. - 50, rue du Fg-St-Denis - 47 70 06 86
Open 7am-1:30pm & 4pm-7:45pm (Sun & Wed 7am-1:30pm). Closed Mon. V. M° Château-d'Eau.
17th arr. - 4, rue Bayen
43 80 16 97
Open 8am-1:30pm & 3:30pm-7:15pm (Sat 8am-7:15pm; Sun 8am-1pm). Closed Mon. V. M° Ternes.

Priced at 650 F per kilo, Divay sells the least expensive fattened goose liver to be found in the city. What's more, it's delicious. You'll find great traditional charcuterie here, too.

Dubernet

1st arr. - Forum des Halles, Porte Lescot, level -2, 42 33 88 46
Open 10:30am-7:15pm. Closed Sun. V. M° Châtelet.
7th arr. - 2, rue Augereau
45 55 50 71
Open 9am-1:30pm & 3:30pm-7:30pm. Closed Sun, Mon. V. M° École-Militaire.
92800 Puteaux - Centre commercial Les Quatre Temps, level 2 - 47 73 70 02
Open 10am-8pm. Closed Sun. V. RER La Défense (A).

These foies gras come from Saint-Sever, in the Landes region of southwestern France. Whole fatted goose and duck livers are sold fully cooked in tins or lightly cooked (just pasteurized) in hermetically sealed jars. Prices are moderate.

Aux Ducs de Gascogne

1st arr. - 4, rue du Marché-St-Honoré - 42 60 45 31
Open 10am-7pm. Closed Sun. V. M° Pyramides.
4th arr. - 111, rue Saint-Antoine - 42 71 17 72

Open 9:30am-2pm & 3pm-8pm (Mon 3pm-8pm). Closed Sun. V. M° Saint-Paul.
8th arr. - 112, bd Haussmann
45 22 54 04
Open 10am-7:15pm (Mon noon-7:15pm). Closed Sun. V. M° Saint-Augustin.
15th arr. - 221, rue de la Convention - 48 28 32 09
Open 9:30am-1pm & 4pm-8pm (Sat 9:30am-1pm & 5pm-8pm; Sun 9:30am-1pm). Closed Mon. V. M° Convention.
20th arr. - 41, rue des Gatines - 43 66 99 99
Open 9am-12:45pm & 3pm-7:45m (Mon 3pm-8pm). Closed Sun. V. M° Gambetta.

This multistore chain specializes in tinned and lightly cooked foie gras, as well as other Southwestern favorites (the thick peasant soup—garbure—sold in jars is excellent indeed). Steep prices, but owner Claude Soria is a real charmer.

Foie Gras Luxe

1st arr. - 26, rue Montmartre
42 36 14 73, fax 40 26 45 50
Open 6am-12:15pm & 2:30pm-5pm (Mon 8am-noon & 2:30pm-5pm). Closed Sat, Sun. V, AE. M° Les Halles.

This reliable, long-established shop sells raw foie gras year-round, as well as lightly cooked fatted goose and duck livers. More luxury: Iranian caviar and marvelous cured hams from Parma, San Daniele, and the Ardennes are also for sale.

Jean Legrand

8th arr. - 58, rue des Mathurins - 42 65 50 46
Open 10am-2pm & 3pm-6:30pm. Closed Sat, Sun. V, AE, DC, MC. M° Havre-Caumartin.
17th arr. - 11, rue Pierre-Demours - 40 55 92 20
Open 8am-2pm & 4:30pm-7:30pm (Sun 8am-1:30pm). Closed Mon. V. M° Charles-de-Gaulle-Étoile.

This reputable processing concern turns out a fine terrine of fresh fatted goose liver, an equally tasty poached version (priced at a hefty 960 F per kilo), duck foie gras in a terrine, and some interesting canned entrées: daube of boar with cranberries, beef goulash, and lotte in mustard sauce.

HONEY, JAMS & SYRUP

Les Abeilles

13th arr. - 21, rue de la Butte-aux-Cailles - 45 81 43 48
Open 11am-8pm. Closed Sun, Mon. V. M° Corvisart.

Buzz over here to taste (free!) rare honeys from all over the world. Examples? How about coffee-blossom honey from Guatemala, or mimosa honey from Mexico, or bramble-blossom honey from the French countryside? If you bring your own container, you can purchase honey made by Parisian bees in the Bois de Vincennes. Other enticements include honey-spiked mustards, chutneys, cookies, cosmetics, and pure beeswax polish for your prized antiques.

Daire

8th arr. - 71, rue du Rocher
45 22 23 13
Open 9:30am-2pm & 2:30pm-7pm (Sat 9:30am-1pm & 2:30pm-7pm). Closed Sun. V. M° Villiers.

Renée Daire stocks a dozen of the most select French honeys: pine, oak, chestnut, heather, lavender, rosemary, thyme, acacia, and more. Pollen and royal jelly are also on sale, as well as a richly honey-flavored gingerbread studded with walnuts and filberts. For a change of pace from wine or beer, try the honeyed hydromel—mead—that the ancient Druids favored. The delicious homemade jams that glitter invitingly on the shelves are prepared by none other than Madame Daire herself.

Le Furet-Tanrade

10th arr. - 63, rue de Chabrol
47 70 48 34
Open 8:30am-8pm. Closed Sun (exc hols). V, AE. M° Gare-du-Nord.

Alain Furet is a *chocolatier* first and foremost, but he also makes fabulous jams from recipes developed by Monsieur Tanrade, long the top name in French preserves. Furet took over the Tanrade plant, and now turns out succulent jams (raspberry, strawberry, apricot, blackcurrant...); he also has put the finishing touches on a recipe of his own, for *confiture au chocolat*—a landmark!

La Maison du Miel

9th arr. - 24, rue Vignon
47 42 26 70
Open 9:30am-7pm (Mon 9am-6pm). Closed Sun. V. M° Madeleine.

Make a beeline to this "House of Honey" to try varieties from the various regions of France. There's Corsican honey, luscious pine honey from the Vosges mountains (which comes highly recommended for bronchial irritations), Provençal lavender honey, as well as choice varieties from the Alps and Auvergne, all rigorously tested by a busy hive of honey tasters. In addition, you'll find honey "by-products," such as beeswax, candles, pollen, and royal jelly, as well as a wide range of honey-based cosmetics.

A la Mère de Famille

9th arr. - 35, rue du Fg-Montmartre - 47 70 83 69
Open 8:30am-1:30pm & 3pm-7pm. Closed Sun, Mon. V. M° Rue Montmartre.

Founded in 1761, this adorable emporium is the dean of Paris sweetshops. Today it is still a showcase for the very best sugarplums that the French provinces produce. You'll find specialties from every region, including exquisite jams and honeys and delicious dried fruits.

OILS

A l'Olivier

4th arr. - 23, rue de Rivoli
48 04 86 59
Open 9:30am-1pm & 2pm-7pm. Closed Sun, Mon. V. M° Saint-Paul.

Connoisseurs know that this shop is an excellent source for several fine varieties of olive oil, as well as walnut oil, grilled-almond oil, pumpkin-seed oil, and hazelnut oil. The main attraction, however, is an exclusive, top-secret blend of virgin olive oils. We applaud the store policy of selling exceptionally expensive and perishable oils in quarter-liter bottles. Fine vinegars and mustards are presented too—everything you need to mix up a world-class vinaigrette!

C.E.P.O.

11th arr. - 88, av. Parmentier
43 55 26 56
Open daily 8:30am-12:30pm & 2:30pm-8pm (Sun 8:30am-12:30pm). No cards. M° Parmentier.

Tuscan native Gianpaolo Grazzini presides over a cache of top-quality olive oils that hail mostly from Italy, but also from the best oil mills of Corsica and Haute-Provence. The pick of the crop, in our estimation, is the sublimely fruity, extra-virgin oil produced by the Moulin des Pénitents in southern France.

Jean-Claude Cornu

9th arr. - 82, rue de Clichy
48 74 60 86
Open 9am-1:30pm & 3pm-8:30pm (Sat 9am-1pm). Closed Sun. V, MC. M° Place-de-Clichy.

Inside this adorable little shop is a veritable treasure trove of top-quality oils. First pressings of all sorts are featured—from peanut, sunflower, and nettle to poppy, walnut, and hazelnut. Fragrant, fruity olive oil from Tunisia comes highly recommended, but conspicuous consumers may prefer the horrendously expensive variety from Provence.

PASTA

Cipolli

13th arr. - 81, rue Bobillot
45 88 26 06
Open 7am-1pm & 3:30pm-7:30pm. Closed Sun. No cards. M° Place-d'Italie.

Signor Cipolli kneads and stretches his golden dough into an appetizing array of pasta specialties. The tagliatelle and ravioli have an authentic, old-fashioned flavor, while his lasagne is nothing short of sublime. The stuffed pastas (cappelletti filled with minced beef and ham, or mushrooms, or spinach and ricotta; "priests' hats" stuffed with salmon or ricotta and ham) are tender and savory. Prices range from 43 to 75 F per kilo.

Mille-Pâtes

1st arr. - 5, rue des Petits-Champs - 42 96 03 04
Open 9am-8pm. Closed Sun. V, AE. M° Bourse.

The Pronzato family sells hand-wrought dried pasta from Pisa as well as 40 varieties of fresh pasta (made twice daily). Don't overlook the fabulous cured venison and boar from Piedmont, nor the dazzling selection of Italian wines.

TRUFFLES

Maison de la Truffe

8th arr. - 19, pl. de la Madeleine - 42 65 53 22
Open 9am-9pm (Mon 9am-8pm). Closed Sun. V, AE, DC. M° Madeleine.

Alongside extraordinary charcuterie, foie gras, smoked salmon, and take-out foods, this luxurious gourmet shop offers truffles (freshly dug or sterilized and bottled) at prices that are emphatically not of the bargain-basement variety. The season for fresh black truffles runs from October to late March; fresh white truffles are imported from Italy in November and December. Owner Guy Monier recently set aside a corner of his shop for tasting: customers may order from a brief menu featuring dishes made with the sublime fungus (truffes en salade, truffes en feuilleté, truffles with fresh pasta, in risotto...). Look too for the range of oils, vinegars, and mustards all perfumed with—you guessed it!

HEALTH FOODS

Le Bol en Bois

13th arr. - 40, rue Pascal
47 07 07 01
Open 9:30am-9:30pm. Closed Sun. V. M° Gobelins.

Specialists in macrobiotic fruits and vegetables, the "Wooden Bowl" also imports health foods from Europe and Japan. Wholegrain breads and rice, tofu-based foods, fresh dairy products and vegetables are selected and sold by Mr. Sakaguchi, who also cooks up tasty vegetarian dishes in his restaurant annex.

Épicerie Biologique

10th arr. - Marché Saint-Martin, 31-33, rue du Château-d'Eau - 42 02 86 25
Open 8:30am-1pm & 3:30pm-7:30pm (Sun 8:30am-1pm). Closed Mon. V. M° Jacques-Bonsergent.

This stand is an excellent reason to visit the Marché Saint-Martin, a picturesque covered market off the beaten tourist track. Organic fruits and vegetables arrive fresh every day, there is a tempting stock of wholesome jams and honeys, good whole-grain breads, and fine dairy products. If your natural lifestyle does not exclude the pleasures of wine, why not try an organic Bordeaux or Côtes-de-Provence (20 to 30 F the bottle)?

Grand Appétit

4th arr. - 9, rue de la Cerisaie
40 27 04 95, fax 44 59 81 75
Open 10am-8pm (Fri & Sun 10am-4pm). Closed Sat. V. M° Bastille.

Madame David is committed to healthy living and a healthy environment. Her range of macrobiotic and natural foods is supplemented by a selection of "earth-friendly" household products. The supply of organically grown fruits and vegetables is renewed three times a week for freshness. The shop's annex restaurant (vegetarian, of course) is very popular—even more so since Elton John was spotted there!

Herboristerie du Palais-Royal

1st arr. - 11, rue des Petits-Champs - 42 97 54 68
Open 10am-7pm. Closed Sun. V. M° Pyramides.

A venerable herbalist's shop that presents a vast and fragrant inventory of dried medicinal plants and herb teas. The 600 varieties are stocked in a cool, dark cellar to preserve their beneficial properties. Also on hand are plant-based health, beauty, and hygiene products.

Au Jardin des Plantes

14th arr. - 50, rue des Plantes
45 42 96 98
Open 9am-12:30pm & 3:30pm-7:30pm (Sun 9am-12:30pm). Closed Mon. No cards. M° Alésia.

Fresh organic produce, including fruits, vegetables, yogurt, butter, cream, cheese, and bread (the latter from the excellent Moulin de la Vierge, see *Bakeries*) arrives each and every day to Marc Savier's shop. Every day but Sunday, that is, when Marc can be found hawking his wholesome wares at the open-air health-food market on the Boulevard Raspail (M° Notre-Dame-des-Champs or Sèvres-Babylone).

ICE CREAM & SORBET

Le Bac à Glaces

7th arr. - 109, rue du Bac
45 48 87 65
Open 11am-7:30pm. Closed Sun. No cards. M° Sèvres-Babylone.

These guaranteed handmade ice creams and sorbets are crafted of top-quality ingredients, with no artificial additives. Doubting Thomases are encouraged to watch the *glaciers* busily at work in their glassed-in kitchen. Alongside the standards, you'll find some delicious liqueur-flavored ices and other uncommon concoctions, like gingerbread ice cream and carrot or tomato sorbets. We always find it difficult to decide between the scrumptious nougat ice cream and the honey-and-pine-nut combo. All these icy delights may be taken home in cartons or enjoyed on the spot in the tiny ice-cream parlor.

Baggi

9th arr. - 33, rue Chaptal
48 74 01 39
Open 10:30am-7:15pm. Closed Sun, Mon. V, MC. M° Blanche.

The Baggis are not newcomers to the ice cream trade. Since 1850 their shop has been a mecca for lovers of frozen desserts.

Today, many aficionados consider Guy Baggi, the firm's current creative force, to be the ice prince of Paris! Guy is forever dreaming up new flavor combinations—and winning prizes for them. Who wouldn't want to pin an award on the Princesse (wild strawberry and white-peach ice creams) or on the Chocolatine (a symphony in chocolate, orange, and caramel), or the justly celebrated Biscuit Rothschild? The flavors and dessert creations on hand on any given day vary in accordance with the seasons and Baggi's mood.

Baskin-Robbins

6th arr. - 1, rue du Four
43 25 10 63
Open daily noon-midnight (Sun 2pm-midnight). No cards. M° Mabillon.

The French tend to find Baskin-Robbins ice creams too sugary-sweet and unnecessarily rich; but they are genuinely intrigued by the flavors: maple-walnut, banana-chocolate swirl, peanut-butter and chocolate. On summer nights, French ice-cream fans come out of the woodwork to join the tourists of every other nationality to sip good ol' American milkshakes, a Baskin-Robbins specialty.

Battistelli

4th arr. - 61, rue Quincampoix - 42 71 10 45
Open daily 11am-midnight. V. M° Rambuteau.

Battistelli, the Corsican ice-cream man, is a recent arrival on the scene. He's bound for major-league status, we decided, after tasting his luscious licorice, date, honey, and coffee ice creams and his incredibly true-tasting fruit sorbets (the crab-apple variety is especially memorable). For a delicious overview, try a *palette*, a sampling of several flavors presented so that each remains distinct and delectable. Excellent coffee, too.

Berthillon

4th arr. - 31, rue St-Louis-en-l'Ile - 43 54 31 61
Open 10am-8pm. Closed Mon, Tue. V. M° Pont-Marie.

Berthillon is the most famous name in French ice cream. The firm's many faithful fans think nothing of waiting in line for *hours* just to treat their taste buds to a cone or dish of chocolate-nougat or glazed-chestnut ice cream. Berthillon's sorbets are our particular weakness: pink grapefruit, fig, wild strawberry... The entire repertoire comes to some 70 flavors, including many seasonal specialties.

Häagen-Dazs

8th arr. - 49, av. des Champs-Élysées - 45 63 43 44 (also: 1st arr., 5th arr., 6th arr., 8th arr., 14th arr., 16th arr.)
Open daily noon-1:30am. V, MC. M° Franklin-D.-Roosevelt.

America's ice-cream specialist has captured the palates of Parisian gourmands with their range of "exotic" flavors ("Macadamia nut? *Qu'est-ce que c'est?*"). Cones and sundaes are further enhanced by your choice of yummy toppings: walnuts, almonds, hot fudge... There's definitely something to be said for enjoying a dish of Caramel Explosion ice cream at a sidewalk terrace on the Champs-Élysées!

Pascal Le Glacier

16th arr. - 17, rue Bois-le-Vent - 45 27 61 84
Open 10:30am-7pm. Closed Sun, Mon. V. M° La Muette.

Pascal Combette, formerly of Deauville, has come to town determined to give Berthillon a run for its money! He is indeed winning lots of converts with his exceptionally delicate, flavorful sorbets, among the best we've tasted anywhere: blood-orange, rhubarb, passionfruit, and mango are all tops. But the ice creams are pretty darn good, too: we recommend the Tahitian vanilla, bitter-chocolate and cinnamon, the Kirsch and candied-fruit combo, and the fabulous chocolate ice cream studded with bits of orange peel.

Raimo

12th arr. - 59-61, bd de Reuilly - 43 43 70 17
Open 9am-midnight. Closed Mon. M° Reuilly-Diderot.

Sorbets and ice creams produced according to time-honored methods, with strictly fresh ingredients. Raimo's strong suit is concocting seductive flavor combinations; some of the most successful are pear-filbert, ginger-honey, and cinnamon-mandarin orange.

Gilles Vilfeu

1st arr. - 3, rue de la Cossonnerie - 40 26 36 40
Open daily Oct-Apr: noon-7pm (Fri & Sat noon-1am); mid Apr-mid Sep: noon-1am. No cards. M° Les Halles.

Vilfeu's imaginative productions include surprising and sophisticated novelty flavors—tea, lavender, and foie-gras sorbets—an ice based on Beaujolais nouveau, and ice creams flavored with licorice, cinnamon, and ginger. We also strongly encourage you to sample the sumptuous frozen desserts, notably the molded cream-cheese sorbet served with a vivid raspberry coulis.

■ MEAT, GAME & FOWL

Au Bell Viandier

6th arr. - Marché Saint-Germain, 4, rue Lobineau
40 46 82 82
Open 8am-1pm & 4pm-8pm (Sun 8am-1:30pm). Closed Mon. M° Mabillon.

Serge Caillaud is the reigning king of Parisian butchers. Rigorous selection and skillful preparation are the hallmarks of these meats, which hail from the best French producers. There's milk-fed veal and fine beef from the Limousin region, farm-bred pork, poultry from Bresse and Challans (including superb capons for the year-end holidays), and premium game in season. Caillaud's specialties include a truffled roast of beef, veal stuffed with apricots or studded with prunes and pistachios, any of which would garner applause as the centerpiece of a dinner party.

Boucherie Coquillière

1st arr. - 32, rue Coquillière
42 33 22 22, fax 42 33 39 24
Open 6am-1pm & 4pm-7:30pm (Sat 8am-1pm). Closed Sun. No cards. M° Louvre.

Jean-François Boyer is a passionate pro, a man who wouldn't sell a piece of meat he hadn't personally inspected and selected. His meat is élite: the veal comes from the Corrèze region, the beef from Aberdeen (and is it ever tasty!), the lamb from the high meadows of Sisteron. The poultry is exclusively of the free-range variety. Not surprising, then, that Boyer supplies such noted restaurants as the Grande Cascade and Chez Pauline.

Boucherie Lamartine

16th arr. - 172, av. Victor-Hugo - 47 27 82 29
Open 6am-7:30pm. Closed Sun. V. M° Victor-Hugo.

Christian Prosper and son sell some of the best meat in France in this pretty, old-fashioned butcher shop. It's not cheap, mind, but then you can't put a price on perfection, can you? The expertly aged beef is sublime. And the milky-pink veal always cooks up to juicy perfection, unlike the more commonly available varieties, which have an annoying tendency to shrink in the pan. House specialties include a leg of lamb stuffed with lamb kidneys, filet mignon studded with foie gras, and lamb noisettes with a mint stuffing à la Troigros. There is an exciting selection of charcuterie as well (we're partial to the terrine au vouvray).

Le Coq Saint-Honoré

1st arr. - 3, rue Gomboust
42 61 52 04, fax 42 61 44 64
Open 8:30am-1pm & 4pm-7pm (Sat 8:30am-1pm). Closed Sun. V, AE. M° Pyramides.

We might as well make it clear right away: For our money, Le Coq Saint-Honoré is one of Paris's top poulterers. It's no coincidence that the list of its customers boasts such culinary notables as Robuchon, Savoy, Senderens, and Claude Terrail of La Tour d'Argent. The refrigerated cases display choice Bresse chickens and guinea hens (fast becoming prohibitively expensive), as well as laudable Loué pullets, Challans ducks, and plump rabbits from the Gâtinais region south of Paris. In season, look for the fine selection of game, including authentic Scottish grouse—a rare and wonderful treat.

Rôtisserie Cambronne

15th arr. - 90, rue Cambronne - 47 34 36 55
Open 7:30am-12:30pm & 4pm-7:30pm (Sun 7:30am-1pm). Closed Mon. V. M° Vaugirard.

What are the hallmarks of premium fowl? Freshness, first and foremost, because the fresher the chicken, the better it tastes. But lineage counts as well, and the birds here are pedigreed—from Loué, Périgord, and other renowned regions—along with ducks from Challans and, in season, one of the city's finest selections of furred and feathered game from Sologne.

Patureau

9th arr. - 1, rue Saint-Lazare
45 26 44 06
Open 8am-1pm & 3:30pm-8pm (Sun 8am-1:30pm). Closed Mon. V. M° Notre-Dame-de-Lorette.

Oh, it's an appetizing sight indeed: an array of golden-brown birds turning slowly on spits, smelling ever so deliciously of herbs and spices. If, for example, you're exhausted after a day in the nearby *grands magasins*, Philippe Patureau's rotisserie can supply you with a ready-made dinner, in the form of an organically raised, perfectly roasted chicken, duck, guinea fowl, or quail.

PASTRY

Bourdaloue

9th arr. - 7, rue Bourdaloue
48 78 32 35
Open 7am-7:30pm (Sun 7am-6:30pm). Closed Mon. V, MC. M° Notre-Dame-de-Lorette.

L'amour, toujours l'amour is what we feel for Bourdaloue's Puits d'Amour, a jam-and-puff-pastry concoction that was created here in the 1800s. We also have an enduring affection for the excellent apple turnovers (among the best we've ever tasted in Paris), the hazelnut delights, and Bourdaloue's own ice creams and delectable chocolate truffles. Tea room.

Paul Bugat

4th arr. - 5, bd Beaumarchais
48 87 89 88, fax 48 87 73 70
Open 8:30am-8pm. Closed Mon. V. M° Bastille.

Paul Bugat is a passionate esthete who orchestrates sweet pastry, chocolate, sugar, and cream into exquisite gâteaux. The specialties of the house are delicious, jewel-like petits-fours, along with the Clichy (chocolate buttercream and mocha cream on an almond-sponge base), the Pavé de Bourgogne (almond sponge cake and blackcurrant mousse), and the Almaviva (chocolate-mousse cake). Tea room.

Noël Clément

17th arr. - 120, av. de Villiers
47 63 40 90
Open 7:15am-8pm (Sat 7:15am-1:30pm & 4pm-8pm; Sun 7:30am-1:30pm & 4pm-8pm). Closed Wed. No cards. M° Pereire.

Noël Clément is a young *pâtissier* with a bright future ahead. His pastries are nothing short of sublime: the millefeuille is a textbook example of what that often botched sweet should be; his mousses are light and full-flavored. Best of all, Clément keeps the sugar content down in all of his cakes. He bakes excellent bread as well. Prices are eminently reasonable.

Christian Constant

6th arr. - 37, rue d'Assas
45 48 45 51
Open daily 8am-9pm. V, AE. M° Rennes.
7th arr. - 26, rue du Bac
47 03 30 00
Open daily 8am-8pm. V. M° Rue du Bac.

After a stroll in the Luxembourg Gardens, why not indulge in a treat from Christian Constant's shop on the Rue d'Assas? And one needn't feel too guilt-ridden, because these cakes are low in sugar, additive-free, all-natural, and incredibly light. Try a millefeuille, or one of Constant's deep, dark, and exotic chocolate cakes: the Caracas, the Macao, or the poetically named Orfeu Negro. Constant's sorbets (100 F per liter) and frozen desserts are well worth the money. Tea room.

Coquelin Aîné

16th arr. - 67, rue de Passy
45 24 44 00, fax 40 50 12 91
Open 9am-7:30pm (Sun 9am-1pm). Closed Mon. V. M° Passy.

Coquelin enjoys a solidly established reputation with its solidly establishment clientele. Joining the traditional pastries created for holidays (the King's Cake for the feast of the Epiphany is a neighborhood favorite) are the shop's tempting, original desserts, such as the Hérisson d'Automne ("Autumn Hedgehog"), a frozen coffee- and chestnut-flavored sweet. Excellent ice creams and chocolates may be purchased here too. Tea room.

Michel Couderc

11th arr. - 6, bd Voltaire
47 00 58 20
Open 8:30am-1:30pm & 3pm-8pm. Closed Mon. V, MC. M° République.

Michel Couderc takes pride in his toothsome candies, pastries, ice creams, and chocolates, all on display in this picturesque shop just off the bustling Place de la République. We suggest that you at least sample the rustic "peasant" and apricot tarts, and the more sophisticated Turquois (macaroons with chocolate mousse), the Délice (sponge cake, caramelized almonds, and whipped cream with vanilla and chocolate), or the Ambre (praline and chocolate mousselines with crushed nougat and walnuts). Good chocolates (350 F per kilo), authentic Kirsch-soaked cherries, and a wonderful bitter-cocoa sorbet are additional reasons to note this fine address.

Dalloyau

2nd arr. - 25, bd des Capucines
47 03 47 00
Open 8:30am-7:30pm (Sat 9am-7:30pm). Closed Sun. V. M° Opéra.
6th arr. - 2, pl. Edmond-Rostand - 43 29 31 10
Open daily 8:30am-7:30pm (Sun 8:30am-8pm). M° Cluny-La Sorbonne, RER Luxembourg (B).
8th arr. - 99-101, rue du Fg-St-Honoré
42 99 90 00, fax 45 63 82 92
Open daily 8:30am-9pm. No cards. M° St-Philippe-du-Roule.
15th arr. - 69, rue de la Convention
45 77 84 27, fax 45 75 27 99
Open daily 9am-8pm (Sun 8:30am-8pm). V, AE. M° Boucicaut.

Deservedly famous, Dalloyau is a temple of *gourmandise* revered by every discerning sweet tooth in town. Among the most renowned specialties are the memorably good macaroons, the chocolate-and-mocha Opéra cake (created in 1955 and still a bestseller), and the Mogador (chocolate sponge cake and mousse napped in raspberry sauce; 30 to 40 F per portion). Christmas brings succulent glazed chestnuts and gluttonously rich Yule logs; Easter calls for chocolate hens and bunnies romping among praline eggs and bells in the adorable window displays.

Gallet

16th arr. - 10, rue Mignard
45 04 21 71
Open 7am-1:15pm & 3pm-7:45pm. Closed Sun, Mon. No cards. M° Rue de La Pompe.

A reliable source of English treats for both the breakfast and the tea tables: buns, muffins, scones, and pancakes, always fresh and always delicious. Special orders are gladly accepted for holiday cakes and pies.

Jean-Paul Hévin

7th arr. - 16, av. de La Motte-Picquet
45 51 77 48, fax 45 51 92 73
Open 10am-7:30pm. Closed Sun. M° La Motte-Picquet-Grenelle.

Jean-Paul Hévin is an artist whose preferred medium is chocolate. His chocolate cakes are inspired symphonies, whose deep, dark intensity is tempered by fruit, spices, nuts, and caramel. Recent compositions include a mille-feuille au chocolate, a chocolate-mousse ice cream, and (in another register entirely) a liltingly fresh gâteau of pears and caramel on an almond-sponge base.

Lenôtre

Information: see Lenôtre page 249, Chocolate & Candy.

Normandy native Gaston Lenôtre opened his first shop in Paris in 1957. His pastries and elaborate desserts are now internationally recognized as classics: the Casino, the Plaisir, the Carrousel... perhaps his most memorable creation is the Fantasme, a voluptuous fantasy in chocolate (chocolate sponge cake and bitter-chocolate mousse).

A. Lerch

5th arr. - 4, rue du Cardinal Lemoine - 43 26 15 80
Open 7:30am-1:30pm & 3:15pm-7pm. Closed Mon, Tue. No cards. M° Cardinal-Lemoine.

Traditional Alsatian pastries hold the place of honor here, from Kugelhopf (a spongy dome-shaped yeast cake, with or without raisins) to the region's justly famed fruit tarts, featuring bilberries, blue plums, or rhubarb topped with meringue. Friendly prices.

Pierre Mauduit

10th arr. - 54, rue du Fg-St-Denis - 42 46 43 64
Open daily 8am-8pm. V. M° Château-d'Eau.
10th arr. - 12, bd de Denain
48 78 05 30
Open daily 7am-8pm. V. M° Gare-du-Nord.

Mauduit's windows, with their glittering displays of flawless little cakes and confections, attract quite an audience. In summer, fruit mousses garnished with fresh fruit or fruit purées sparkle invitingly, while winter brings the delicious Cointreau-flavored Tambourin, or the Mont-Blanc with caramelized almonds; the refreshing Pacifique dessert (raspberry and lime bavarian creams) is available year-round. Prices are modest for this level of quality.

Millet

7th arr. - 103, rue Saint-Dominique - 45 51 49 80
Open 9am-7pm (Sun 9am-1pm). Closed Mon. V. M° Invalides.

Jean Millet, whose shop is virtually an institution in this chic neighborhood, ranks among the foremost practitioners of the art of French pastry. He turns out superb cakes and desserts that often give starring roles to seasonal fruit. Among Millet's bestsellers are his exceptional pear charlotte, his divine Sully (Sauternes mousseline, wild strawberries, white peaches, and pineapple), and the silken almond-milk Royal with raspberries, pears, oranges, and a fresh-tasting raspberry purée.

Le Moule à Gâteaux

14th arr. - 17, rue Daguerre
43 22 61 25 (also: 5th arr., 15th arr., 17th arr., 20th arr.)
Open 8am-7:30pm (Sun 8am-1:30pm). Closed Mon. V. M° Denfert-Rochereau.

This prospering chain specializes in traditional, homestyle cakes fashioned by young pastry cooks who care about their craft. They use time-tested recipes that we wish we still had the leisure (and know-how) to prepare in our own kitchens. We love the apricot feuilleté covered with a golden short crust; the Mamita, a poem in chocolate and crème fraîche; and the Carotin filled with almonds, filberts, and carrots. Reasonable prices.

Gérard Mulot

6th arr. - 76, rue de Seine
43 26 85 77
Open 7am-8pm. Closed Wed. No cards. M° Mabillon.

Mulot is an endlessly inventive personality, never happier than when he is working out a new idea to complete his line of delectable pastries. The poetically named Nuée d'Or ("Golden Cloud") is a dreamy combination of honey mousseline and candied fruit; Été Indien ("Indian Summer") combines tea-flavored and orange-flavored mousselines. In a more down-to-earth vein, Mulot also fashions wonderfully flaky, buttery croissants.

Péché Mignon

18th arr. - 12, rue du Ruisseau - 42 54 06 41
Open 7:30am-1:30pm & 3:30pm-8pm (Sat 7:30am-8pm; Sun 7:30am-2pm). Closed Mon. No cards. M° Jules-Joffrin.

Genius at work: Michel Lebreton is an innovative, creative pastry chef on the cusp of culinary fame. His versions of classic cakes are irreproachable, but we are fondest of the surprises he concocts in accordance with the season and his mood. Recommendations? We have several: the rhubarb tart, the green-apple tart, and the chocolate fantasies flavored with violets or roses—they're all as sweetly sinful as the name of the shop implies!

Stohrer

2nd arr. - 51, rue Montorgueil - 42 33 38 20
Open daily 7:30am-8:30pm. V. M° Les Halles.

The shop is decorated with rosy, corpulent allegories of Fame painted by Paul Baudry (he also decorated the Paris Opéra) in 1860; these charming murals are pleasant to contemplate while scarfing down a few of Stohrer's butter-rich pastries: the dark-chocolate Criollo, the refreshing Royal Menthe, the Black Forest cake, almond-filled Pithiviers, and flaky croissants all come highly recommended.

Find the address you are looking for, quickly and easily, in the index.

REGIONAL FRENCH SPECIALTIES

La Campagne

14th arr. - 21, rue Daguerre
43 20 02 72
Open 8am-1pm & 4pm-7:30pm (Sat 3:30pm-7:30pm; Sun 8am-12:30pm). Closed Mon. M° Denfert-Rochereau.

Michel Caillot's network of suppliers stretches to the regions of Cantal, Aveyron, Corrèze, and Brittany, bringing him a choice catch of provincial charcuterie, cheeses, and breads. We especially like the chestnut-studded boudin, the chunky pâtés, and rustic sausages, as well as the Breton buckwheat cakes and fougace (flat bread) from Laguiole.

La Campagne

15th arr. - 111, bd de Grenelle - 47 34 77 05
Open 7am-9pm. Closed Sun. No cards. M° La Motte-Picquet-Grenelle.

Michel Christy is a passionate defender of the French *terroir*, particularly the Southwest and the Basque country. Genuine farmhouse flavor distinguishes his foie gras, charcuterie from Ibaïona and Bayonne, and lusty (prize-winning!) house cassoulet.

Charcuterie Lyonnaise Terrier

9th arr. - 58, rue des Martyrs
48 78 96 45
Open 8:30am-1pm & 4pm-7:30pm (Sun 8:30am-12:30pm). Closed Mon. No

cards. M° Notre-Dame-de-Lorette.

For generous Lyonnais charcuterie, Terrier is *the* outpost in Paris. Among the typical treats on hand are sausage studded with truffles and pistachios, golden-brown pâtés en croûte, pike and salmon quenelles, Burgundy ham, head cheese, and genuine rosette sausage, the pride of Lyon.

A la Cigogne

8th arr. - 61, rue de l'Arcade
47 38 73 91
Open 8am-7pm (Sat 9am-6:30pm). Closed Sun. V. M° Saint-Lazare.

This firm turns out innovative food products rooted in the culinary traditions of Alsace: sweet pretzels, Kugelhopf (a sweet yeast cake) thickly dusted with cinnamon, and an unctuous cream-cheese tart. The region's classic dishes are not neglected, however—witness La Cigogne's wonderful strudel, quiche Lorraine, cherry, blueberry, and damson-plum tarts and, in the sausage category, cervelas, weisswurst, beerwurst, and bratwurst.

Comtesse du Barry

17th arr. - 23, av. de Wagram
46 22 17 38
Open 9am-8pm. Closed Sun. V. M° Charles-de-Gaulle-Étoile.
4th arr. - 93, rue Saint- Antoine - 40 29 07 14
Open 10am-7pm. Closed Sun, Mon. V. M° Saint-Paul.
15th arr. - 317, rue de Vaugirard - 42 50 90 13
Open 9:30am-7:30pm (Mon 2:30pm-7pm). Closed Sun. V. M° Vaugirard.
6th arr. - 1, rue de Sèvres
45 48 32 04
Open 9:30am-7:30pm. Closed Sun. V. M° Sèvres-Babylone.
9th arr. - 13, rue Taitbout
47 70 21 01
Open 10am-7:30pm. Closed Sun. V. M° Chaussée-d'Antin.
16th arr. - 88 bis, av. Mozart
45 27 74 49
Open 10am-1pm & 2pm-7pm (Mon 2pm-7pm). Closed Sun. V. M° Jasmin.

From the Gers in southwestern France comes an extensive line of regional food products: duck and goose confits, foie gras, fatted duck breasts (available fresh, vacuum-packed), as well as galantines, rillettes, excellent little pâtés, good prepared foods (in tins or jars), and frozen entrées.

L'Espace Gard

8th arr. - 53, av. Franklin-D.-Roosevelt - 40 76 07 14
Open 9am-6pm. Closed Sat, Sun. No cards. M° Franklin-D.-Roosevelt.

Look beyond the brochures and posters vaunting the charms of the Gard region, and you'll discover a selection of traditional foods and wines produced by local artisans. Taste the sunny South in such specialties as buffalo pâté, puréed salt cod from Nîmes, Collorgues's fragrant olive oil, walnut wine from Saint-Roman, and delicious unfiltered apple juice made in Vigan.

La Ferme du Hameau

15th arr. - 223, rue de la Croix-Nivert - 45 32 88 70
Open 8:30am-1pm & 3:30pm-7:30pm. Closed Sun, Mon. No cards. M° Porte-de-Versailles.

Two regions of France share top billing in this tantalizing shop: Jean Bouttier is a Normandy native, while his wife hails from Sancerre. From Monsieur's home turf come prime Camembert, farmhouse Pont-L'Évêque, lusty Livarot made with unpasteurized milk, rustic boudin noir from Mortagne, and lipsmacking hard apple cider. Madame's birthplace contributes tangy goat cheeses, notably a creamy farmer's cheese (faisselle de chèvre de Sancerre) and crottins de Chavignol, and a frisky white wine that partners them perfectly.

Jean-Claude et Nanou

17th arr. - 46, rue Legendre
42 27 15 08
Open 8am-1pm & 4:30pm-8pm (Sun 8:30am-1pm). Closed Mon. No cards. M° Rome.

Here's the sort of country food we can never get enough of. Jean-Claude and Nanou sell flavorful sausages dried under the ashes of a smoldering fire, aromatic mountain sausage, and fresh Tomme (an unmatured cheese with a distinctive "barnyard" taste).

Chez Teil– Produits d'Auvergne

11th arr. - 6, rue de Lappe
47 00 41 28
Open 9am-1pm & 3:30pm-7:30pm. Closed Sun, Mon. No cards. M° Bastille.

This turn-of-the-century shop is home to a mouthwatering selection of authentic Auvergnat charcuterie, processed by Patrick Teil himself at his family's meat-curing plant in Cayrols. By eliminating the middle man, Teil can market his hams, sausages, spreads, pigs' trotters, and pâtés at attractive prices.

Try his cheeses too, along with the fine crusty flat bread (fouace) and countrified sweets on display.

Terroirs et Traditions

12th arr. - 18, rue Jaucourt
40 02 06 16
Open 9am-1pm & 3pm-8:30pm. Closed Mon. No cards. M° Nation.

Very good regional specialties from Auvergne and the Basque country make this shop worth a visit. Try the Basque ham spiced with fiery Espelette peppers, the expertly matured sheep cheeses, and authentically flavored terrines. If you're fond of andouillette (tripe sausage), you really should sample the one sold here.

A la Ville de Rodez

4th arr. - 22, rue Vieille-du-Temple - 48 87 79 36
Open 8am-1pm & 3pm-7:30pm. Closed Sun, Mon. No cards. M° Hôtel-de-Ville.

Guy and Alice Boillot import earthy foodstuffs from Aveyron and Cantal for Parisians in need of some good country cooking. Fresh sausage studded with chunks of pork (not ground up, but cut with a knife, hence the name: saucisse au couteau) competes for your attention with mutton tripe (tripoux), minced pork (fritots), stuffed pig's ears and trotters, and more. Sharp Laguiole lords over the cheese section, accompanied by buttery blue Fourme d'Ambert, and farmhouse Saint-Nectaire. Country sweets, jams, and sturdy vin de Marcillac complete this rustic picture. Note that La Ville de Rodez is the place to find all the classic cuts of pork that simmer together with vegetables for a classic potée auvergnate.

■ SEAFOOD

Le Bar à Huîtres

14th arr. - 112, bd Montparnasse - 43 20 71 01
Open daily noon-2am. V, AE. M° Vavin.

At the outdoor oyster bar, you can purchase dozens of succulent oysters, opened for you free of charge by the nimble-fingered *écaillers* and neatly arranged on disposable trays (no deposit, no return). Just remember to place your order in advance.

Poissonnerie du Dôme

14th arr. - 4, rue Delambre
43 35 23 95
Open 7am-1pm & 4pm-7:30pm (Wed 7am-1pm). Closed Sun, Mon. V. M° Vavin.

The lucky residents of Montparnasse can satisfy their urge for seafood at this marvelous fish store, perhaps the best in Paris. Manager Jean-Pierre Lopez admits only "noble" fish (sole, turbot, lotte, sea bass, and the like) to his classy emporium. The merchandise, from French (particularly Breton) and foreign waters, is snapped up by such eminent restaurants as L'Ambroisie and La Tour d'Argent. Need we mention that these rare and succulent denizens of the deep command regally high prices?

Don't plan to shop on Sundays—the vast majority of Paris stores are closed.

■ WINE & SPIRITS

L'Arbre à Vins

12th arr. - 2-4, rue du Rendez-Vous
43 46 81 10, fax 43 44 67 07
Open 9:30am-12:30pm & 4pm-7:30pm. Closed Mon. V. M° Picpus.

This fascinating wine shop dates back to 1893. The superb vaulted cellars house Bordeaux both great and modest and a comprehensive range of Burgundies. Rounding out the selection are tasty, inexpensive country wines.

Le Bourguignon du Marais

4th arr. - 52, rue François-Miron - 48 87 15 40
Open 11am-midnight. Closed Sun. M° Saint-Paul.

Burgundy, of course, cops top billing at this excellent wine shop. The owner obligingly unearths fine bottles from his cellar to match your menu, and what's more, his prices are quite attractive. The adjoining wine bar and restaurant also feature Burgundian specialties.

The British Corner

7th arr. - 153, rue de Grenelle - 47 53 88 01
Open 10:30am-1:30pm & 2:30pm-7pm. Closed Sun. V. M° Latour-Maubourg.

Attention whisky lovers: the British Corner stocks 65 different kinds of single-malt Scotch whiskies. Some of them (though not the cheaper ones, of course) have reached the venerable ages of 15, 21, or 30 years.

La Cave à Millésimes

15th arr. - 180, rue Lecourbe
48 28 22 62, fax 48 28 34 82
Open 9am-1pm & 3:30pm-7:30pm (Sun 9am-noon). Closed Mon. V, DC. M° Vaugirard.

Older vintages, mostly of Bordeaux, but also of Burgundy are cached in the cool, seventeenth-century cellars of this worthwhile wine shop. You'll be pleasantly surprised by the generally affordable prices.

> ## Clos Montmartre
>
> **Once upon a time, Montmartre was covered with windmills and vineyards. Today, the sole remaining *vignoble* covers a hillside opposite the celebrated Lapin Agile cabaret, at the corner of Rue Saint-Vincent and Rue des Saules. The wine produced by these Gamay and Pinot Noir grapes is a modest tipple indeed, but the harvest is celebrated with a colorful parade and lots of bacchic bonhomie on the first Saturday of October.**

Cave de l'École Polytechnique

5th arr. - 42, rue de la Montagne-Ste-Geneviève
43 25 35 80
Open 1:30pm-8:30pm. Closed Sun, Mon. No cards. M° Cardinal-Lemoine.

In the wine business for more than half a century, Jean-Baptiste Besse must be credited with having converted many a Parisian to the cult of Bacchus. Though the shop may look like a colossal shambles, Besse will infallibly locate just the bottle you desire, from a modest red Cheverny to a majestic Château Cheval-Blanc. His choice of dessert wines (Sauternes, Banyuls, Beaumes-de-Venise) always flabbergasts us, as does his judicious selection of Cognac and Port.

Cave Estève

4th arr. - 10, rue de la Cerisaie
42 72 33 05, fax 42 72 47 04
Open 9:30am-12:30pm & 2:30pm-7:30pm. Closed Sun, Mon. V. M° Nationale.
5th arr. - 292, rue Saint-Jacques - 46 34 69 78
Open 10am-1pm & 3pm-8pm. Closed Sun, Mon (exc in Dec). V. M° Port-Royal.

For Jean-Christophe Estève, wine isn't just a business; it's more like a sacred vocation. Endowed with a formidable palate, this Gascon native declares that every region of France produces good wines—it's just a question of tracking them down. Given his pedagogic bent (he used to be a Spanish teacher), he'll be happy to help you choose from among 250 Bordeaux, and his expanding range of Burgundies and growers' Champagnes.

Les Caves du Savour Club

14th arr. - 120 or 125, bd Montparnasse - 43 27 12 06
Open 10am-8pm (Sun 10am-12:30pm). Closed Mon. M° Vavin.

The Savour Club is a wine warehouse that has managed to rise above the grayness of its underground premises (a Montparnasse parking garage) with a bright, light décor. Inside, you'll find bottlings appropriate for every occasion, each with a card bearing an informative description and comments. There are wines for everyday drinking (country wines for under twenty francs), as well as special treats for connoisseurs (Château Haut-Brion, Richebourg, etc.). Of particular interest are the (often inexpensive) wines personally selected by such mega-chefs as Robuchon, Loiseau, Troisgros, and Bocuse.

Jean Danflou

1st arr. - 36, rue du Mont-Thabor
42 61 51 09, fax 42 61 31 62
Open 9am-1pm & 2pm-6pm. Closed Sat (exc in Dec), Sun. V, AE. M° Tuileries.

Pierre Danflou-Glotin, the third generation of Danflous to run this shop, sells absolutely exquisite, fragrant, heady eaux-de-vie (clear fruit brandies) distilled especially for him in Alsace. You must sample his extraordinary aged Kirsch, his Poire Williams, his perfumed Framboise. A line of elegant Cognacs, Armagnacs, and Calvados is also proposed, along with a small selection of wines from Burgundy and Bordeaux. Prices start at around 200 F and soar straight up from there.

Georges Dubœuf

8th arr. - 9, rue Marbeuf
47 20 71 23, fax 47 20 11 16
Open 9am-1pm & 3pm-7pm. Closed Sun, Mon. M° Franklin-D.-Roosevelt.

What Lionel Poilâne is to bread, Georges Dubœuf is to Beaujolais: an assurance of quality. His Paris shop stocks excellent representatives from all the villages of Beaujolais, but Dubœuf is not parochial by any means. His numerous wine-making chums all over France supply him with (for example) fine Burgundies from de Montille, de Vogüé, Rousseau, and Trapet, Métaireau's Muscadets, Guigal's Côtes-du-Rhône, and Alsatian vintages from Trimbach.

Legrand Filles et Fils

2nd arr. - 1, rue de la Banque
42 60 07 12, fax 42 61 25 51
Open 8:30am-7:30pm (Sat 8:30am-1pm & 3pm-7pm). Closed Sun, Mon. V, AE, MC. M° Bourse.

Even if the wines were not half so interesting as they are, Legrand's wine shop would be worth a visit for its old-fashioned charm and warm atmosphere. Francine Legrand offers a fascinating selection of carefully chosen, inexpensive country wines from up-and-coming growers in the South and the Val de Loire, along with a far-ranging inventory of prestigious Burgundies and Bordeaux (note the many wines from average vintage years, affordably priced). Also, a few uncommon bottlings: luscious Muscat de Beaumes-de-Venise, Vin de Paille du Jura, and some excellent vintage Ports. Legrand's impressive stock of eaux-de-vie is now one of the finest in town.

Nicolas

8th arr. - 31, pl. de Madeleine
42 68 00 16. 250 stores in Paris.
Open 9am-8pm. Closed Sun. V, AE. M° Madeleine.

Looking better than ever with a spruce gold-and-bordeaux décor, Nicolas's innumerable stores in the Paris area continue to present a wide, diverse, and appealing range of wines for every budget. The chain's monthly promotions are well worth following: featured are (for example) French wines from unfamiliar or underrated appellations—the Ardèche, Corbières, or Savoie—, imports (Spanish, Italian, and even Lebanese bottlings), and the occasional oenological curiosity, all offered at attractive prices. The multilevel flagship store on the Place de la Madeleine has a huge inventory of more than 1,000 different wines, including rare, old Bordeaux. Nicolas is also an excellent source of fine distilled spirits (check out the selection of single-malt whiskies). The Avenue Wagram shop stays open until 10pm, the Ancienne-Comédie store until 9. Home delivery service available.

Le Repaire de Bacchus

17th arr. - 39, rue des Acacias
43 80 09 68 (also: 2nd arr., 6th arr., 7th arr., 9th arr., 15th arr., 16th arr., 18th arr.)
Open 10:30am-1:30pm & 3:30pm-8pm. Closings on Sun & Mon vary in the different stores. M° Argentine.

Dominique Fenouil continues, despite the economic *crise*, to inaugurate new branches of the Repaire de Bacchus with admirable frequency. Smart marketing isn't everything, of course: this sleek, dynamic chain owes its success to a judicious choice of wines and, especially, to the excellent advice dispensed by the sales staffs (several of whom, in our experience, speak English). From the reliable house-label wines to fine growers' Burgundies, from little-known "village" appellations to Bordeaux's *grands crus*, the wines are selected with an eye to quality and value. Several branches sponsor clubs (membership fee: 200 F) where each month members may enjoy a small taste of (say) a vintage Latour, a Burgundy from the Comtes de Lafon, or perhaps a prestigious single-malt whisky.

Au Verger de la Madeleine

8th arr. - 4, bd Malesherbes
42 65 51 99, fax 49 24 05 22
Open 10am-1:15pm & 3pm-8pm (Sat until 7:30pm). Closed Sun. V. M° Malesherbes.

Jean-Pierre Legras's staggering collection encompasses such unique and extravagant bottles as a Cognac Impérial Tiffon 1810, a Porto Barros dated 1833 (once the property of the French ambassador to Lisbon), a Solera Sercial Madeira from 1835, and a Clos-Peyraguey 1893. Such treasures are not for everyday drinking, but they make impressive, indeed unforgettable, gifts. All the first growths of Bordeaux (Cheval-Blanc, Pétrus...) are on hand as well, along with superb Burgundies from Montrachet and Meursault, and hard-to-find wines like Château-Grillet and Jasnières. For the faint of wallet, there are inexpensive offerings from the Côtes-d'Auvergne, Saint-Pourçain, and Saumur.

Vins Rares Peter Thustrup

2nd arr. - 30, av. de l'Opéra
46 33 83 53, fax 45 48 68 43
Open 10am-7pm. Closed Mon. V, AE, DC. M° Opéra.

Peter Thustrup, now associated with the Foucher specialty food shop, harbors an unquenchable passion for old, rare vintages. It leads him to auction rooms all over the world, in pursuit of such treasures as antique Yquem, ancient Pétrus, and Mouton-Rothschild from another age (which sell, incidentally, for about 18,000 F—just to give you an idea). Bordeaux, obviously, is well represented, but Thustrup can also show you some exceptional Vendanges Tardives from Alsace, mature Burgundies, and collectible Côtes-du-Rhônes. He recently added an expanded (and quite attractive) range of younger, lower-priced bottles (45 to 100 F) from the world's wine-growing regions.

GIFTS

Un Air de Giverny

7th arr. - 10, rue de Bellechasse - 45 55 83 69
Open 11am-6:30pm. Closed Sun, Mon. V, AE, MC. M° Solférino.

You have a passion for the Impressionists? Then this charming boutique is a "must" stop on your itinerary. Monet's famous blue-and-yellow china is on sale here, of course, but you'll also discover a selection of decorative objects in those colors, and others that date from the Impressionists' heyday, among them household linen from Quimper, handcrafted faïence, watercolors, and pretty antique curios.

Axis

11th arr. - 13, rue de Charonne - 48 06 79 10
Open 10:30am-7:30pm. Closed Sun. V, MC. M° Bastille.

Witty, imaginative, and amusing gift ideas are the Axis trademark. But this policy does not exclude the useful: the Alessi coffeepot and the Dualite toaster are trendy as all get-out, but they do help you get breakfast on the table efficiently! Axis also produces its own collection of vases, picture frames, tableware, and rugs, all sporting droll or unusual designs.

La Boîte à Musique

1st arr. - 9, rue de Beaujolais
42 96 55 13
Open 10am-7pm (Aug 2:30pm-7pm). Closed Sun. V, MC. M° Palais-Royal.

Music boxes tinkle merrily away in this delicious little shop under the Palais-Royal arcades. The mechanisms are Swiss, dependable, and made to last, while the boxes themselves have a pleasingly old-fashioned look. Prices vary according to the complexity of the design and the number of tunes and notes the box plays. The simplest, an ideal gift for a newborn (whose name and birthdate can be engraved on the box), costs about 200 F. The finest music box in the store, made of rare wood with a sophisticated mechanism that plays four tunes and well over a hundred notes, will set you back over 30,000 F.

Chaumette

7th arr. - 45, av. Duquesne
42 73 18 54, fax 42 73 12 45
Open 10am-6:30pm. Closed Sat, Sun. M° St-François-Xavier.

Gérard Danton is no ordinary dealer in knickknacks and *bibelots*. He has a genuine passion for faïence and for glass objects that reproduce and reinterpret nature. On our last visit to his enchanting shop, we found an extraordinary lamp base adorned with mauve-tinged irises; glazed ceramic cachepots displaying bunches of grapes or vegetable still lifes; and stunning reproductions of ancient Roman glass. Prices for these small marvels range from a couple hundred to several thousand francs.

Les Comptoirs de la Tour d'Argent

5th arr. - 2, rue du Cardinal-Lemoine - 46 33 45 58, fax 43 26 39 23
Open 10am-midnight (Sun noon-midnight). Closed Mon. V, AE, DC. M° Maubert-Mutualité.

Dinner at the Tour d'Argent may be out of reach, but you can always scrape up a few francs to purchase a small souvenir bearing the restaurant's logo! There is a wealth of classic tableware (crystal, silver, china, embroidered napery) and lots of determinedly tasteful accessories (how about a Tour d'Argent silk tie?). The good tinned foie gras, duck confit, lobster bisque, and the Brut Champagne also sport the house colors, and like the rest are high-priced.

L'Entrepôt

16th arr. - 50, rue de Passy
45 25 64 17
Open 10:30am-7pm (Fri & Sat 10:30am-7:30pm). Closed Sun. V. M° Passy.

Here's a treasure trove of clever gift items and household gadgets that will charm even the most blasé shopper. You'll find an impressively diverse array of stationery, tableware, clothing—even jams and jellies! A delightful bazaar, improbably located in the classy Passy neighborhood.

Homme Sweet Homme

4th arr. - 43, rue Vieille-du-Temple - 48 04 94 99
Open 11am-7pm. Closed Sun. V. M° Saint-Paul.

Despite the cutesy-pie name, this shop stocks an interesting variety of (primarily masculine) gifts in a grand range of prices (25 to 2,000 F). Wallets in all sizes, attractive fountain pens, geometric photo holders from the 1940s, and tiny tools are just a few of the clever and useful items on sale. For the man who has everything (including a sense of humor), there's even a little fan in the form of a robot.

Itinéraire Forestier

16th arr. - 35, rue Duret
45 00 08 61
Open 10:30am-7:30pm (Mon noon-7:30pm). Closed Sun. V. M° Argentine.

In the 1930s, this was a cheese and dairy shop, but an ex-landscape gardener has transformed the place into an original boutique that follows the rhythms of the seasons and holidays. Itinéraire Forestier carries all the tableware and decorative touches one would need to create a festive atmosphere for Halloween, Christmas, Valentine's Day, April Fool's, and so on, as well as an attractive selection of handcrafted pottery and garden accessories for year-round use.

Rita Kim

10th arr. - 79, quai de Valmy
42 39 82 49
Open 1pm-7pm. Closed Sun, Mon. No cards. M° République.

We love Rita's collection of plastic stuff from the '60s. There's tableware, campy knickknacks to accent your "day-core" and irresistibly kitsch costume jewelry—don't miss the "Jesus" watch with the name of an apostle at each hour; it's the height of taste! Or how about an inflatable tie? Lots of other hilarious items are on sale for under 100 F.

La Maison des Artisans

12th arr. - 14, cours de Vincennes - 43 41 61 63
Open 10:30am-1:30pm & 2:30pm-7pm. Closed Sun, Mon. V, MC. M° Nation.

For the best in French handcrafts: the Maison des Artisans presents creative, beautifully wrought objects made according to traditional methods. Come here to admire useful and decorative objects in faïence, pewter, and glass (perfume bottles from 160 F), jewelry crafted in precious wood and silver, or in Altuglas and gilded bronze (brooches from 200 F).

Florent Monestier

7th arr. - 47 bis, av. Bosquet
45 55 03 01
Open 10:30am-7:30pm (Mon noon-7:30pm). Closed Mon. V, MC. M° École-Militaire.

Here's a charming boutique crammed with highly presentable gifts for young and old. Decorative accents for the table—napkins, candles, glassware—and old-fashioned toys for children are well represented. Lots of whimsical holiday-themed items at Christmas and Easter.

Nature et Découvertes

1st arr. - Forum des Halles, level -3, 10 bis, rue de l'Arc-en-Ciel - 40 28 42 16
Open 10:30am-7:30pm. Closed Sun. V, AE, DC, MC. M° Châtelet.
1st arr. - Galerie du Carrousel du Louvre, 99, rue de Rivoli - 47 03 47 43
Open 10am-8pm (Mon & Wed 10am-10pm). Closed Tue. V, AE, DC, MC. M° Palais-Royal.

Bringing people and nature together (albeit for a profit) is the laudable aim of Nature et Découvertes. Fascinating, ecologically correct gift items abound, including games, crafts, and gadgets that make science child's play for kids of all ages. And there is a host of uncommon decorative and useful objects that emphasize conservation.

Don't plan to shop on Sundays—the vast majority of Paris stores are closed.

Pain d'Épices Maison

9th arr. - 35-37, passage Jouffroy - 47 70 51 12
Open 10am-7pm (Mon 12:30pm-7pm). Closed Sun. V, MC. M° Rue Montmartre.

The windows of this delightful shop, situated in the picturesque Passage Jouffroy, are a feast for the eyes. Accessories and decorative items that make a home feel inviting and cozy are found here (potpourri, table decorations, lampshades...), alongside old-fashioned color prints, picture frames, and cookie tins—everything is beautifully displayed.

Robin des Bois

4th arr. - 15, rue Ferdinand Duval
48 04 09 36, fax 48 04 56 41
Open daily 10:30am-7:30pm (Sun 2pm-7:30pm). V, MC. M° Saint-Paul.

The headquarters of the Association for the Protection of Humanity and the Environment is also a source of ecologically sound gifts for yourself or the folks back home. Vegetable ivory is carved into pretty ornaments and buttons; jojoba oil replaces whale oil in the body-care products on display, and (naturally) all the stationery is made of recycled paper. Recycled clothing is now sold here too.

Tant qu'il y aura des Hommes

6th arr. - 23, rue du Cherche-Midi - 45 48 48 17
Open 10:30am-1:30pm & 2:30pm-7pm (Sat 10:30pm-7pm). Closed Sun. V, AE. M° Sèvres-Babylone.

Among the handsome and practical gifts for men on sale here, we particularly liked the silk boxer shorts, the luggage (with lots of detachable pockets), and leather goods that look as if they could withstand hard wear, classic Irish crewneck sweaters, and a good-looking leather-trimmed jacket for rough-and-tumble types. The beautiful coordinated shirts and ties, we've been assured, make highly acceptable gifts.

Territoire

8th arr. - 30, rue Boissy-d'Anglas
42 66 22 13, fax 40 07 05 27
Open 10:30am-7pm. Closed Sun. V, AE, MC. M° Madeleine.

What was once a hardware store is now a bright and spacious shop brimming with ideas for leisure activities. The stock changes with the seasons; in spring, the gardening section burgeons with Wilkinson tools and terracotta pots. In summer, sporting goods take over a greater share of shelf space (we saw an impressive foldable black canvas boat), and in winter, fireside games feature more prominently. There are plenty of amusing gifts for children, including reproductions of old-fashioned board games and some spectacular kites. Prices range from about 50 to 5,000 F.

La Tuile à Loup

5th arr. - 35, rue Daubenton
47 07 28 90
Open 10:30am-7pm (Sun 10am-1pm). Closed Mon. V, AE. M° Censier-Daubenton.

As peaceful as a village square, this exceptional shop carries traditional handcrafts from all over France. You'll find beautiful glazed pottery from Savoie, Provence, Burgundy, and Alsace, and stoneware from Puisaye and Le Maine. There are handmade wooden objects, rustic tableware, wrought-iron weather vanes, and decorative tiles for the kitchen, bath, or fireplace. Fascinating, too, are the many books documenting popular art forms and regional history.

Michèle Wilson

14th arr. - 116, rue du Château - 43 22 28 73,
fax (16) 85 32 17 27
Open 8:30am-8pm (Sat 2pm-8pm). Closed Sun. V, MC. M° Pernety.

Puzzle buffs and art lovers alike adore Michèle Wilson's handcrafted wooden puzzles, which depict paintings or prints from the Louvre, the Musée d'Orsay, the Institut du Monde Arabe, and other well-known museums. Some of the puzzles are easy to put together (60 pieces), while others are considerably more mind-bending (5,500 pieces). Subjects run the gamut from Persian miniatures to Impressionist paintings or maps—talk about educational! At the workshop next door, you can look on and learn how a puzzle is made.

We're always happy to hear about your discoveries and receive your comments on ours. We want to give your letters the attention they deserve, so when you write to Gault Millau, please state clearly what you liked or disliked. Be concise but convincing, and take the time to argue your point.

Thank God, the architect doesn't sing

Good intentions don't always work. The *Bastille opera house* was conceived as a way of bringing opera to the masses, but as a side effect its construction has inexorably turned a traditional working-class neighborhood into a magnet for the trendy and fashionable. Art galleries and nightspots are ousting carpenters, craftsmen, and cabinetmakers, while many venerable buildings are being demolished to clear the way for up-market apartment blocks. The good news is that this opera house is cheaper and more accessible than its grander counterpart, the Opéra Garnier: you don't even have to dress up. An impressive array of technical devices makes the Opéra Bastille a director's dream—and at least from the inside you can't see the grim gray exterior!

HOME

BATH & KITCHENWARE

BATH

Beauté Divine

6th arr. - 40, rue Saint-Sulpice - 43 26 25 31
Open 10am-1pm & 2pm-7pm (Mon 2pm-7pm). Closed Sun. V, AE, DC. M° Saint-Sulpice.

Régine de Robien has amassed a treasure trove of antique and modern accessories for the bath. The Italian-made linen guest towels are especially attractive, but it would be hard to find anything in this shop that isn't divinely beautiful! Your purchase, however small, will be swathed in scented tissue paper and sprinkled with tiny perfumed beads.

Saponifère

6th arr. - 59, rue Bonaparte
46 33 98 43
Open 10:15am-7pm. Closed Sun. V, AE, MC. M° St-Sulpice.

Sweetly scented and neatly arranged, this shop offers a wealth of charming accessories for the bath, from pretty pots and jars to snuggly towels (from 100 F), powder puffs, natural sponges, and perfumed toiletries.

CUTLERY

Isler–La Coutellerie Suisse

1st arr. - 44, rue Coquillière
42 33 20 92
Open 9am-noon & 2pm-6pm. Closed Sat, Sun. No cards. M° Les Halles.

Not a single element of the shop's décor has altered in 50 years, but then neither has the excellent quality of Isler's Swiss knives (including the world-famous Tour Eiffel brand). All the great French chefs select their kitchen knives from among the 100 models in stock; and there are 40 types of pocketknives as well. The firm's bestseller is a survival pocketknife with (at least) 29 functions (multiuse pliers, ballpoint pen, screwdriver—you get the idea) which comes in a leather case equipped with a compass, sharpening stone, mirror... The trusty old penknife seems awfully ordinary in comparison!

Kindal

2nd arr. - 33, av. de l'Opéra
42 61 70 78
Open 10am-6:30pm (Mon 11am-6:30pm). Closed Sun. V, AE, DC. M° Opéra.

Faithful to its family tradition, Kindal has preserved its handsome mahogany paneling that dates back to the shop's opening in 1905. Knives of every sort are on view: table, hunting, and pocket representatives with wooden or precious horn handles. Prices start at about 50 F and rise to 12,000 F for certain collectors' items. Knives are repaired and sharpened on the premises.

KITCHENWARE

La Carpe

8th arr. - 14, rue Tronchet
47 42 73 25
Open 9:30am-7pm (Mon 1:30pm-7pm). Closed Sun. V, AE, DC, MC. M° Madeleine.

For some 70 years the Loiseau family has furnished chefs and knowledgeable home cooks with utensils at the cutting edge of kitchen technology. All the wares are intelligently displayed by type, so that you can find what you want quickly. The sales staff is friendly and generous with its good advice. Another store in the neighborhood, A la Petite Carpe (13, rue Vignon), carries a selection of gadgets and gizmos for the table. Catalog available.

Culinarion

17th arr. - 83 bis, rue de Courcelles - 42 27 63 32
Open 10:15am-7pm (Mon 11:15am-7pm). Closed Sun. V, AE. M° Courcelles.

Culinarion is a dependable source of kitchen classics (cast-iron pots, charlotte molds, tart pans) at reasonable prices. But adventurous cooks will love the selection of arcana and novelties, like the combination mills that let you salt and pepper with one hand, or the shopping bag specially designed for frozen foods. We also admire the shop's handsome selection of bar and tableware.

Dehillerin

1st arr. - 18-20, rue Coquillière - 42 36 53 13
Open 8am-6pm (Mon 8am-12:30pm & 2pm-6pm). Closed Sun. V. M° Louvre.

Since 1820, the cream of the French food establishment has purchased their *batteries de cuisine* at Dehillerin. More recently, they have been joined by large numbers of American and Japanese culinary enthusiasts. Dehillerin stocks a truly amazing range of cookware, superb knives, copper pots, and every imaginable baking utensil. We suggest you come early in the day to shop here, and above all, don't be in a hurry. Some of the sales clerks speak English and are quite helpful.

L'Esprit et le Vin

17th arr. - 81, av. des Ternes
45 74 45 79
Open 10am-7pm (Mon 2pm-7pm). Closed Sun. V, AE, DC. M° Argentine.

From special stemware to thermometers, decanters to cellar logs, wine-country maps to eccentric corkscrews, all the paraphernalia that wine buffs require can be purchased in this bright little shop.

Kitchen Bazaar

1st arr. - Galerie des Trois Quartiers, 23, bd de la Madeleine - 42 60 50 30
15th arr. - 11, av. du Maine
42 22 91 17
Open 10am-7pm. Closed Sun. V, AE. M° Madeleine, Montparnasse.

Kitchenware from Kitchen Bazaar is always both high-style and high-performance. The latest small appliances are always available here, with a preference for those with the sleekest designs. There's an interesting selection of cookbooks.

Geneviève Lethu

1st arr. - 91, rue de Rivoli
42 60 14 90
Open 10am-7pm (Mon 1pm-7pm). Closed Sun. V. M° Louvre.
6th arr. - 95, rue de Rennes
45 44 40 35
14th arr. - 25, av. du Général-Leclerc - 45 38 71 30
Open 10:15am-7pm (Mon 2pm-7pm). Closed Sun. V. M° Saint-Sulpice, Mouton-Duvernet.
17th arr. - 1, av. Niel
45 72 03 47
Open 10am-7pm (Mon 2pm-7pm). Closed Sun. V. M° Ternes.

There are Geneviève Lethu shops all over Paris, presenting vast selections of bright, practical, cheerful kitchen furniture, utensils, tableware, and linen. The ever-growing collections of affordably priced dishes in lots of pretty colors and patterns are coordinated with fabric or wipe-clean tablecloths. We also particularly like the attractive, inexpensive glassware in myriad shapes and sizes.

Mora

1st arr. - 13, rue Montmartre
45 08 19 24, fax 45 08 49 05
Open 8:30am-5:45pm (Sat 8:30am-noon). Closed Sun. V, MC. M° Les Halles.

The shopfront is modern, but Mora is an old established firm that dates back to 1814. The most esoteric items of culinary equipment can be found among the astonishing collection of knives, pots and pans in stainless steel, cast iron, or copper, and the very best cake and tart pans coated with new-age anti-adhesives (there are 6,000 items in stock). Amateur cooks benefit from the same low prices as restaurant and catering pros, and they are greeted with the same amiability. The cookbook section boasts over 200 titles; if you think a picture is worth a thousand words, inquire about the cooking-demonstration videos.

> *Don't plan to do much shopping in Paris in August—a great many stores are closed for the entire vacation month.*

Simon

2nd arr. - 36, rue Étienne-Marcel & 48, rue Montmartre - 42 33 71 65
Open 8:30am-6:30pm. Closed Sun. V, AE. M° Étienne-Marcel.

Simon supplies kitchen and tableware to the likes of the Hôtel Méridien, the Café de la Paix, and the École de Cuisine in Osaka, Japan. But it also sells its vast range of dishes, glasses, and utensils at the same prices to any customer who walks in off the street. For typically French tableware (the sort you see in traditional brasseries), the prices can't be beat. You'll also find wine pitchers, carafes, and ice cream *coupes* that will add an agreeable Gallic touch to your table. The Rue Montmartre store specializes in kitchen supplies, while the store around the corner on Rue Étienne-Marcel (same phone) deals chiefly in tableware.

Taïr Mercier

5th arr. - 7, bd Saint-Germain
43 54 19 97
Open 11am-7pm (Sat 11am-1pm & 2:30pm-7pm). Closed Sun, Mon. V. M° Maubert-Mutualité.

Place mats in appealing shapes (fruits, animals, city skylines) cut out of brightly colored pieces of plastic are big sellers here (25 to 65 F). But we also discovered attractive two-tone plastic shopping bags, melamine fish platters, clear plastic knife rests, and absolutely stainproof plastic-coated aprons, all of which convinced us that *plastique, c'est chic!*

FURNISHINGS

CONTEMPORARY FURNITURE

Academy

6th arr. - 5, pl. de l'Odéon
43 29 07 18
12th arr. - 68, rue du Fg-St-Antoine - 43 42 19 19
Open 9:30am-1pm & 2:30pm-7pm. Closed Sun, Mon. No cards. M° Odéon, Bastille.

Jean-Michel Wilmotte was the designer selected to decorate the space beneath the Louvre's glass pyramid, and to create the furnishings placed throughout the Grand Louvre. The shop that showcases his collection is austere, like the materials Wilmotte prefers: perforated sheet metal, glass slabs, chipboard. Prices for these singular pieces vary widely.

Arredamento

4th arr. - 18, quai des Célestins
42 74 33 14, fax 42 74 38 15
Open 10am-12:30pm & 2pm-7pm. Closed Sun, Mon. V, AE. M° Sully-Morland.

In a spacious and handsome two-level shop, Valentine Boitel and Bernard Renaudin present a wide-ranging selection of top Italian furniture and lighting designs. Connoisseurs with well-lined wallets and a taste for contemporary Italian design will applaud the modular storage units by Capellini, the sofas by Zanotta, coffee tables from Fontana Arte, and lamps by Flos. Fine French design is represented as well, though on a smaller scale—there are some marvelous lamps by Gilles Derain.

Avant-Scène

6th arr. - 4, pl. de l'Odéon
46 33 12 40, fax 46 33 92 78
Open 10am-7pm (Mon 2pm-7pm). Closed Sun. V, MC. M° Odéon.

An eclectic choice of limited-edition furniture and objets d'art by young designers is on display at this impressive shop on the Place de l'Odéon. Élisabeth Delacarte presents hauntingly beautiful furniture by Mark Brazier-Jones, delicately finished pieces by Frank Évennou, fabrics and beds by Jean-Michel Cornu, and more. Prices start at around 200 F (for a small gilt dish) and soar up to 45,000 F and beyond for, say, a table by Dubreuil.

Collectania

1st arr. - 168, rue de Rivoli
44 50 55 00, fax 42 96 16 01
Open 9:30am-7pm. Closed Sun. V, AE, DC. M° Palais-Royal.

Just opposite the Louvre, Collectania is itself virtually a museum of twentieth-century architect-designed furniture. Artistically presented in this vast space are reissues of designs by Le Corbusier, Frank Lloyd Wright, Gerrit Rietveld, Andrea Branzi, and Shiro Kuramata. These exclusive pieces obviously command high prices, but the quality of the furniture and the expert advice dispensed by the staff (all professional interior designers) more than justify the cost.

Monday, like Sunday, is a day of rest for many shopkeepers.

Écart International

4th arr. - 111, rue Saint-Antoine - 42 78 79 11
Open 10am-6:30pm. Closed Sun. No cards. M° Saint-Paul.

The headquarters of Écart International occupies a town house in the Marais. A bright, spacious, strikingly handsome showroom displays reissues of pieces by the great designers of the early twentieth century, including Mallet-Stevens, Eileen Gray, Pierre Chareau, and Le Corbusier. Écart also shows work by talented French style-setters (Sacha Ketoff, Sylvain Dubuisson, Patrick Naggar, Olivier Gagnère), as well as designs by its own star, Andrée Putman. Obviously, prices are high.

Édifice

7th arr. - 27 bis, bd Raspail
45 48 53 60, fax 45 48 25 81
Open 10am-7pm. Closed Sun. V. M° Sèvres-Babylone.

Each month, Sarah Nathan, owner of Édifice dreams up a splendid setting to highlight a piece or ensemble of pieces by a favorite designer. She is particularly keen on avant-garde furniture, like Mario Botta's armchair, Guillaume Saalburg's screen, Ingo Maurer's splendid lamp... The store presents almost all of Philippe Starck's creations for the home (his Costes chair and the self-supporting bookcase among them), alongside designs by Ettore Sottsass, Gae Aulenti, and Borek Sipek.

> *Don't plan to do much shopping in Paris in August—a great many stores are closed for the entire vacation month.*

En Attendant Les Barbares

2nd arr. - 50, rue Étienne-Marcel - 42 33 37 87
Open 10:30am-7pm (Sat 11am-6:30pm). Closed Sun. V, AE. M° Étienne-Marcel.

The vogue for metal furniture bristling with sharp points started here, with designers Garouste and Bonetti. A comprehensive collection of their "Barbarian Baroque" pieces is on view, abetted by the work of young designers like Marie-Thérèse Migeon (colorful candlesticks and ashtrays), Agnès Pottier, Éric Schmitt, and Jacques Jarrige.

État de Siège

6th arr. - 1, quai de Conti
43 29 31 60
7th arr. - 94, rue du Bac
45 49 10 20
Open 11am-7pm (Mon 2pm-7pm). Closed Sun. V, AE. M° Pont-Neuf, Rue du Bac.
8th arr. - 21, av. de Friedland
42 56 64 75
Open 10:30am-7pm (Mon 2pm-7pm). Closed Sun. No cards. M° George-V.
12th arr. - 45, rue de Lyon
43 43 25 97
Open 11am-1pm & 2pm-7pm (Mon by appt). Closed Sun. V. M° Bastille.

You are certain to find a seat to suit you among the staggering assortment stocked here. From Louis XIII *fauteuils* to the most avant-garde chair/sculpture, État de Siège displays some 150 different designs, many available in a variety of colors and finishes. Prices vary according to the quality of the wood or metal in question, the workmanship (hand- or factory-finished), and the style.

Galerie Neotu

4th arr. - 25, rue du Renard
42 78 96 97
Open 11am-7pm. Closed Sun. V, AE, DC, MC. M° Hôtel-de-Ville.

Furniture collectors with a taste for the "neo" find this multifaceted gallery a sure source of esthetic thrills. Some say the furniture and objects displayed here are the rare and precious antiques of the future. Whether or not that will prove to be the case, owner Pierre Staudenmeyer spotlights works by young artists, painters, sculptors, and architects, particularly those pieces that straddle the border of art and design. Most are one-off or limited editions, and are thus quite expensive; but the gallery also exhibits some reasonably priced objets d'art.

Meubles et Fonction

6th arr. - 135, bd Raspail
45 48 55 74
Open 9:30am-12:30pm & 2pm-7pm. Closed Mon. V, MC. M° Notre-Dame-des-Champs.

For 35 years this upscale gallery has championed the cause of French and international design, showing work by such luminaries as Arne Jacobsen and Pierre Paulin. The furniture, lighting fixtures, and fabrics on display are reliably the cream of the crop.

Nestor Perkal

3rd arr. - 8, rue des Quatre-Fils - 42 77 46 80
Open 2pm-7pm. Closed Sun, Mon. V, AE. M° Saint-Paul.

Nestor Perkal, interior architect and designer, has a thing for bright, primary colors. So for his marvelous shop, Perkal has selected pieces from Memphis, that wild and crazy bunch of designing Italians, and from the Spanish firm Ediciones. Well before Spain and the *movida* were trendy, Perkal was showing avant-garde designs from Madrid, Seville, and, of course, Barcelona.

Protis

8th arr. - 153, rue du Fg-St-Honoré - 45 62 22 40
Open 9:15am-7pm (Sat 10am-1pm & 2:30pm-6:30pm). Closed Sun. M° Saint-Philippe-du-Roule.

White walls and a gray-tile floor set the glass-and-steel furniture off to advantage. Protis presents its own designs (coffee tables in glass and black lacquered metal), Italian pieces by Cattelan, Bieffeplast, Tonon, and Technolinea (with an outstanding line of office furniture in walnut or rosewood), and a host of creations by noted architects. We recently admired Bernard Dequet's handsome line of pearwood and molded aluminum furniture.

VIA

6th arr. - 4-6-8, cour du Commerce Saint-André
43 29 39 36
Open 10am-1pm & 2pm-6pm. Closed Sun. M° Odéon.

VIA stands for *Valorisation de l'Innovation dans l'Ameublement*; in other words, an association for promoting innovative furniture design. Housed in spacious quarters on the Left Bank, this gallery/shop/showroom gives young designers a boost. VIA alumni include such luminaries as Jean-Michel Wilmotte, Philippe Starck, and Pascal Mourgue.

OUTDOOR FURNITURE

Le Cèdre Rouge

1st arr. - 22, av. Victoria
42 33 71 05
Open 10am-7pm (Mar-Jul: Mon 11am-7pm). Closed Sun, Mon (winter). V. M° Châtelet.

Furniture for the patio and garden, in Burmese teak or colonial-style wicker, is the specialty of Le Cèdre Rouge. But you will also find handsome little volcanic-stone tables in a score of colors, and copies of eighteenth-century furniture executed in steel and canvas. We could browse for hours among the many elegant pieces of handcrafted pottery (over 2,000 in stock) from Biot, Aubagne, and Tuscany. A section devoted to decorative objects for indoors includes lamps, Florentine ceramics, and lovely rustic baskets.

Jardins Imaginaires

6th arr. - 9 bis, rue d'Assas
42 22 90 03, fax 45 49 01 53
Open 10:30am-1pm & 2pm-7pm (Mon 2pm-7pm). Closed Sun. V, AE. M° Rennes.

A medley of handsome antique furnishings full of grace and wit; a selection of modern furniture and objets d'art for sophisticated gardens and conservatories; an original selection of statuary, pottery, urns, and basins... the "imaginary gardens" evoked in this wonderful shop brim over with charm, humor, and taste.

SOFAS & CHAIRS

Un Fauteuil Pour Deux

6th arr. - 9, rue Corneille
43 29 74 32
Open 10:30am-7pm (Mon 2pm-7pm). Closed Sun. V. M° Odéon.

Bernard Maxime updates classic French chairs and sofas by splashing them with brilliant color or upholstering them with unusual fabrics. A browse around this shop will yield scores of decorating ideas, even if you don't fancy lugging (or shipping) furniture back home. Ornamental objects and accessories are also on view, at prices ranging from 400 to 100,000 F.

First Time

6th arr. - 27, rue Mazarine
43 25 55 00, fax 43 25 03 84
Open 10am-6:45pm (Mon 2pm-6:45pm). Closed Sun. V, MC. M° Odéon.

Noted designer Didier Gomez heads this interior decorating firm, which manufactures chairs (7,000 to 10,000 F) and sofas (17,000 to 20,000 F) signed by Gomez himself, or by his equally well-known colleagues, Christian Duc and Andrée Putman.

HARDWARE

Garnier

12th arr. - 30 bis, bd de la Bastille - 43 43 84 85
Open 9am-12:30pm & 1:30pm-6pm (Fri until 5pm). Closed Sat, Sun. No cards. M° Bastille.

Established in 1832, Garnier is a specialist in ornamental hardware and locks. Reproductions of

Louis XV, Louis XVI, Directoire, Empire, and English locks and plaques are still manufactured and displayed—though not sold—here. A friendly and informative staff can provide a list of dealers who handle any model you might be interested in acquiring.

Quincaillerie Leclercq

11th arr. - 151, rue du Fg-St-Antoine - 43 43 06 41
Open 8:30am-6pm (Sat & Mon 8:30am-noon & 2pm-6pm). Closed Sun. V, AE, MC. M° Ledru-Rollin.

This is undoubtedly the most delightful hardware store on the Faubourg-Saint-Antoine (the cabinetmaker's and woodworker's quarter). Arlette, one of France's few female locksmiths, welcomes you into her domain, where she and her colleagues fashion handmade copies of locks and other hardware, working from antique originals. Some of the hard-to-find items available here are handcut crystal knobs for banisters and brass plaques for 1930s armoires.

■ INTERIOR DECORATION

HOME DÉCOR

La Chaise Longue

1st arr. - 30, rue Croix des Petits-Champs - 42 96 08 81
Open 11am-7pm. Closed Sun. V, AE, MC. M° Palais-Royal.
3rd arr. - 20, rue des Francs-Bourgeois - 48 04 36 37
Open 11am-7pm (Sun 2pm-7pm). V. M° Saint-Paul.
6th arr. - 8, rue Princesse
43 29 62 39
Open noon-8pm. Closed Sun. V. M° Mabillon.

A gay and colorful shop chock-full of amusing items to add a touch of whimsy to the house. For the kitchen, there is enameled metalware (plates, pots, pitchers, and so on), multicolored glasses, special barbecue grills, and piles of gadgets; for the office or *salon*, there are hammered metal picture frames, trendy wire baskets by Filo di Ferro, pot-pourri, and papier-mâché vases. Browsing here is lots of fun.

The Conran Shop

7th arr. - 117, rue du Bac
42 84 10 01, fax 42 84 29 75
Open 10am-7pm (Mon noon-7pm). Closed Sun. V. M° Sèvres-Babylone.

Terence Conran's huge home decoration shop occupies a former warehouse that boasts a metal structure designed by Gustave Eiffel. Opened in late 1992, the shop caused quite a stir, and continues to draw crowds of hip home-lovers with a broad, eclectic inventory of furniture (many exclusive pieces), imported linens, designer kitchen and tableware, clever lamps, exotic garden tools and furniture, trendy gift items, and upscale foodstuffs. It takes hours to examine the entire store, but the time goes quickly—and so will your money, if you give in to temptation!

Elle

6th arr. - 30, rue Saint-Sulpice
43 26 46 10
Open 10:30am-7pm. Closed Sun. V, AE, MC. M° St-Sulpice.

Chosen by the style-conscious editors of *Elle Décoration*, the tableware, lamps, lap rugs, and many other decorative and useful objects on display are both lovely to look at and a pleasure to use.

Étamine

7th arr. - 63, rue du Bac
42 22 03 16, fax 42 84 12 47
Open 10am-7:30pm (Mon 1pm-7:30pm). Closed Sun. V, AE. M° Rue du Bac.

Étamine's new bilevel boutique numbers among the trendiest home-décor shops in Paris, with a superb collection of fabrics from all over the globe: neoclassic prints and cut velvets from Timney and Fowler, a horsehair look-alike made with a vegetable fiber from the Philippines, and a plethora of attractive wallpaper designs. Also on hand is a selection of sofas, lamps, objets d'art, and a few choice antique pieces.

Galerie du Bac

7th arr. - 116, rue du Bac
40 49 03 03, fax 40 49 00 96
Open 10am-1pm & 2pm-6:30pm. Closed Sun. V, AE. M° Rue du Bac.

Galerie du Bac is a handsome, spacious showcase for the latest creations for the home by Missoni—linens and upholstery fabrics, sheets, and towels. Don't miss the gorgeous Italian wallpapers (crinkled, waxed, "pre-worn"...), or the Woodnotes woven-paper rugs.

David Hicks

6th arr. - 12, rue de Tournon
43 26 00 67
Open 10:30am-6:30pm. Closed Sun, Mon. V. M° Odéon.

A warm, urbane atmosphere reigns in this pretty shop, a source for marvelous fabrics, rugs, and accent pieces. The rugs—dhurries, English wool carpeting in 70 different patterns, and tinted palm-fiber matting—can be made up in the colors of your choice. Also on view are gorgeous fabrics inspired by eighteenth-century designs; the patterns come in bright, slightly acidic colors printed on cotton or silk. The splendid decorative objects are not the sort one sees everywhere; we were enchanted by some etched Austrian wine glasses, copied from an eighteenth-century model. Decorating service available.

A pungent pilgrimage

Paris had a *sewer system* **as early as 1370, but the waste emptied straight into the River Seine. Epidemics followed plagues, and public hygiene made little further progress until 1854, when a series of drains and aqueducts channeled the worst of the city's sewage twelve miles downstream. A vast program to eliminate and purify the last outflows from the capital was launched in 1984. Although we now take the benefits of modern waste-treatment plants for granted, it is interesting to see how a city sewer plant works—and how nasty it smells! Visit the city's** *Sewer Museum* **at the Left Bank side of the Pont de l'Alma. Open Sat-Wed from 11am to 5pm. Admission: 25 F. Guided tours are offered as well. M° Alma-Marceau.**

Juste Mauve

16th arr. - 29, rue Greuze
47 27 82 31
Open 10am-7pm (Mon 11pm-7pm; Oct-May: Sat 11am-7pm). Closed Sun. V. M° Trocadéro.

Anne-Marie de Ganay's shop has all the charm of a cozy English home, with its mix of mahogany (coffee tables from 6,000 F) and flowered chintz, low stools and Chinese cachepots (900 F), picture frames in burled elm and marquetry (650 F). Piles of lacy cushions and a selection of ravishing lingerie lend a frothy, feminine note.

Miller et Bertaux

4th arr. - 27, rue du Bourg-Tibourg - 42 77 25 31
Open 11am-1:30pm & 2pm-7pm. Closed Sun, Mon. V, AE, DC. M° Saint-Paul.

A world that is at once both fragile and rough-hewn, exotic and natural—in any case, brimming with charm and fantasy. The tree-branch lamps, palm-leaf chairs, wrought-iron tables, and tulip-printed fabrics perfectly sum up the "ecology-chic" that is the dominant trend in French interior decoration today.

Les Olivades

17th arr. - 21, av. Niel
42 12 01 31
Open 10am-7pm (Mon 2pm-7pm). Closed Sun. V. M° Ternes.

The wonderful warmth and charm of Provence is infused into this sunny shop. Redolent of olive oil and lavender, bright with the colors of the Midi, Les Olivades displays, among other treasures, traditional Provençal print fabrics. If you're not handy with a needle, there are many small items already made up: bags, eyeglass cases, makeup cases, skirts, shawls, and even the sunniest umbrellas imaginable.

Souleïado

6th arr. - 78, rue de Seine
43 54 62 25, fax 46 34 25 98
Open 10am-7pm. Closed Sun. V, AE, DC, MC. M° Odéon.
16th arr. - 83-85, av. Paul-Doumer - 42 24 99 34
Open 10am-7pm (Mon 2pm-7pm). Closed Sun. V, AE, DC. M° La Muette.

Thanks to Charles Demery, Provençal fabrics are known and sought after the world over. Souleïado's original designs, many dating from the eighteenth century, are available in a riot of cheerful colors. Coordinated wallpaper and oilcloth (30 patterns) are on hand too, and the home-décor department also offers quilted bedspreads with matching sheets, tablecloths, fabric-covered boxes, shopping bags, picture frames and—the firm's best-seller—place mat and napkin sets. The space devoted to fashion continues to grow: wool shawls sell for around

1,000 F, and there are very trendy men's shirts as well.

Vivement Jeudi

5th arr. - 52, rue Mouffetard
43 31 44 52
Open Thu 10am-8pm. No cards. M° Monge.

Open only on Thursdays, this absolutely charming house-within-a-house presents antiques and humbler second-hand (but first-quality) furniture, linens, and decorative objects for the home. All the merchandise has been lovingly collected by the shop's two owners, assiduous frequenters of flea markets all over France.

MISCELLANY

Au Chêne-Liège

14th arr. - 74, bd du Montparnasse - 43 22 02 15
Open 9:30am-6:30pm. Closed Sun. V. M° Montparnasse.

A *chêne-liège* is a cork-oak, and cork is the specialty of this well-known Montparnasse emporium. And we've seen the most amazing range of articles, all in cork—accessories for the wine cellar, for the desk and office, luggage and handbags, and even women's clothing (believe us, nothing could be less kinky!).

Passementeries de l'Ile de France

11th arr. - 11, rue Trousseau
48 05 44 33
Open 9am-5:30pm (Fri 9am-5pm). Closed Sat, Sun. M° Ledru-Rollin.

One of the last surviving specialists in silk braid and fringe (to trim curtains, chairs, and lampshades, for example), who will design to the customer's specifications. The firm also manufactures reproductions of period trims, as well as a line of contemporary designs.

Passementerie Nouvelle

1st arr. - 15, rue Étienne-Marcel - 44 76 90 70
Open 9am-6pm. Closed Sat, Sun. No cards. M° Étienne-Marcel.

When France needs new trimmings for the draperies at Versailles or Fontainebleau, it's La Passementerie Nouvelle to the rescue! In addition to reproductions of historic pieces, the company works with period-style braids, trims, and fringe specially adapted for contemporary fabrics.

S.M.H.

11th arr. - 76, bd Richard-Lenoir
43 57 47 25, fax 43 55 09 95
Open 9am-12:30pm & 2pm-6pm. Closed Sun. V. M° Richard-Lenoir.

Single- and double-curved moldings, cornices, carved door frames, baseboards, and rosettes (in pine, oak, tropical wood, polyurethane, or Styrofoam) will dress up even the plainest prefab bungalow. SMH will cut all these elements to measure, then you take them home, paint them, put them up... and presto! Good-bye suburbia, hello Versailles! SMH also sells all sorts of supplies for do-it-yourself picture-framers.

Some establishments change their closing times without warning. It is always wise to check in advance.

RUGS & NEEDLEPOINT

Brocard

4th arr. - 1, rue Jacques-Cœur
42 72 16 38, fax 42 72 04 77
Open 9am-noon & 2pm-5pm. Closed Sat, Sun. No cards. M° Bastille.

If needlework is your favorite pastime, do make time to stop in here. Brocard manufactures all manner of canvases in many sizes. Vintage embroideries and needlepoint receive careful restoration here.

Casa Lopez

6th arr. - 27, bd Raspail
45 48 30 97 (also: 2nd arr., 16th arr.)
Open 10:15am-12:45pm & 2:15pm-6:30pm. Closed Sun. V. M° Sèvres-Babylone.

Casa Lopez presents handsome jacquard rugs in geometric patterns, many of which are reversible. Most designs are available in ten different sizes, in a range of 90 colors, for reasonable prices (8,500 F for a two by three meter rug). Palm-fiber rugs in checkerboard, herringbone, or houndstooth patterns have loads of casual charm, and we love the wool carpets with raised lozenge, diagonal, or ribbon motifs. Certain designs are also available on canvas, to make coordinating petit-point chair backs and seats.

Toulemonde-Bochart

2nd arr. - 10, rue du Mail
40 26 68 83
Open 10am-6:45pm. Closed Sun. V. M° Sentier.

This award-winning firm's claim to fame is its collection of contemporary rugs designed by the top names: Andrée Putman, Hilton McConnico, Christian Duc, Jean-Michel Wilmotte. Decorative dhurries, sisal, and palm fiber matting are pretty too, and considerably less expensive.

WALLPAPER & FABRICS

Besson

6th arr. - 32, rue Bonaparte
40 51 89 64
Open 9:30am-6:30pm. Closed Sun, Mon. V, AE, MC. M° Saint-Germain-des-Prés.

The choicest English and French decorator fabrics and wallpapers have been featured at Besson for some 30 years. The range of nostalgic, romantic, exotic, and rustic patterns is considerable, and the sales staff, bursting with good advice, is also gratifyingly generous with samples.

Manuel Canovas

6th arr. - 5, rue de Furstenberg - 43 26 89 31
Open 10am-6:30pm (Mon 11am-6:30pm). Closed Sun. V, AE, MC. M° Saint-Germain-des-Prés.

Textile designer and manufacturer Manuel Canovas came up with a style that revolutionized interior decorating in the 1960s. This master colorist drew his inspiration from extensive travels in India, Japan, and California, as well as from imagined botanical gardens. Canovas's extraordinary chintzes are done in slightly acid tones, while muted shades are preferred on such sophisticated fabrics as moiré. Coordinated wall coverings are available as well, and in the shop next door, fashion and home accessories are made up in Canovas fabrics.

Casal

7th arr. - 40, rue des Saints-Pères
45 44 78 70, fax 40 49 19 54
Open 9:30am-6pm. Closed Sat, Sun. No cards. M° Saint-Germain-des-Prés.

Casal's signature jacquard prints, inspired by traditional paisley patterns and kilim rug designs, look terrific on sofas. But in this spacious, skylit showroom (formerly an artist's studio) you will also find fabrics by Brunschwig, Jean-Michel Wilmotte, and Decortex.

Pierre Frey

6th arr. - 5, rue Jacob
46 33 73 00 (also: 1st arr.)
Open 10am-6:30pm. Closed Sun. V. M° St-Germain-des-Prés.

This firm is a family affair with an international reputation. Although the designers draw a good deal of their inspiration from traditional eighteenth- and nineteenth-century French patterns, Pierre Frey is also known for its vast—and ever-growing—line of contemporary fabrics and wall coverings. In the *Patrick* Frey home-décor shops, you'll find a selection of handsome bed linens, cushions, shawls, fabric-covered boxes, and laminated trays, all in the Frey signature prints.

Nobilis Fontan

6th arr. - 40, rue Bonaparte
43 29 21 50
Open 9:30am-6:30pm. Closed Sun. M° Saint-Germain-des-Prés.

Since it opened in 1928, this decorating firm has enjoyed a reputation for the high quality and sophisticated taste of its designs. Refined, but not conservative, Nobilis Fontan has always managed to evolve intelligently, keeping pace with contemporary trends (recent additions to the Nobilis stable: Robert Le Héros, Ravage, and Miller et Bertaux). The wallpapers on display here are relatively expensive, but they are beautifully made. The fabric patterns are inspired by classic English, Japanese, and Chinese models, and coordinate perfectly with the wall coverings. Nobilis has extended its line of merchandise to include architect-designed furniture and, in a recent development, shoes and chapeaux.

Tissus Reine

18th arr. - Place du Marché Saint-Pierre - 46 06 02 31
Open 9:15am-6:30pm (Mon 2pm-6:45pm; Sat 9:15am-6:45pm). Closed Sun. V, MC. M° Anvers.

A decorator will help guide your choice among all the fabric designers represented here. Large upholstery department.

Zuber

3rd arr. - 5, bd des Filles-du-Calvaire - 42 77 95 91
Open 10am-6pm. Closed Sun. M° Filles-du-Calvaire.

The dynamic owner has revitalized the venerable firm of Zuber, boosting its level of creativity to new heights. Using time-honored printing methods and working from a library of more than 100,000 antique patterns, Zuber's is an eye-popping collection of wallpapers: *trompe-*

l'œil, panoramas, marbled, and damask papers, as well as sublime friezes, cornices, and borders of roses and other flowers in the sub-tlest of tints. Orders (excluding special orders) can be filled in 48 hours.

LIGHTING

Artémide
11th arr. - 6-8, rue Basfroi
43 67 17 17
Open 9:30am-12:30pm & 1:30pm-6pm. Closed Sat, Sun. No cards. M° Charonne.

If you are curious to see what sort of lamps and light fixtures the best European designers have come up with lately, come to Artémide. Mario Botta, Vico Magistretti, Ettore Sottsass, and Richard Sapper are just some of the famous names represented in this huge loft showroom.

Capeline
16th arr. - 144, av. de Versailles - 45 20 22 65
Open 10am-7pm. Closed Sun, Mon. No cards. M° Exelmans.

In this vast workshop, known to all the best Parisian decorators, craftspeople still turn out pleated, gathered, and skirted lampshades in paper, silk, or cotton, just like in the good old days.

Ready Made
6th arr. - 38-40, rue Jacob
42 60 28 01, fax 49 27 07 78
Open 10am-12:30pm & 1:30pm-7pm. Closed Sun, Mon. V. M° Saint-Germain-des-Prés.

Italian halogens are the specialty of this sleek and trendy shop near Saint-Germain. Flos, Artémide, and Arteluce are a few of the manufacturers on hand; we particularly admire the floor lamps designed by Jean-François Crochet in metal and Murano glass. The sister store next door exhibits furniture that is equally select, with an accent on reissues of 1930s classics by Eileen Gray, Breuer, Macintosh, and Chareau.

Veronèse
8th arr. - 184, bd Haussmann
45 62 67 67
Open 9am-12:30pm & 2pm-6pm (Sat 10am-6pm). Closed Sun. AE. M° St-Philippe-du-Roule.

From the simplest wall sconce to the most monumental chandelier, all of Veronèse's glorious glass lighting fixtures are mouth-blown and hand-finished by master craftsmen from Murano. The firm also handles special orders and custom pieces.

LINENS

La Châtelaine
16th arr. - 170, av. Victor-Hugo - 47 27 44 07
Open 9:30am-6:30pm (Sat 9:30am-12:30pm & 2:30pm-6:30pm). Closed Sun, Mon. V, AE. M° Rue de la Pompe.

For superb linens for your bed, bath, and table, in satiny cotton, cotton muslin, organdy, or linen, this shop comes highly recommended. All these items can be embroidered at your request, or you can have pieces specially tailored to your needs (extra-large bath sheets, odd-size tablecloths...).

Find the address you are looking for, quickly and easily, in the index.

Agnès Comar
8th arr. - 7, av. George-V
49 52 01 89
Open 10:30am-1pm & 2pm-7pm. Closed Sun. V, AE. M° Alma-Marceau.

Always bubbling with fresh, elegant ideas for the home, international decorator Agnès Comar has come up with a line of gorgeous, satiny cotton or linen bed sheets. Available in white, ecru, and a subtle water-blue tint, they can be embroidered if you like, or edged with pleats or lace (look for the coordinating travel and makeup bags). Comar also makes table skirts with luxurious quilted borders, and appliquéd bedspreads that coordinate with curtains and cushions. Expect to pay top prices for these opulent linens (4,000 F for a set of sheets and pillowcases).

Fanette
15th arr. - 1, rue d'Alençon
42 22 21 73
Open 1pm-7pm. Closed Sun. M° Montparnasse.

Fanette's specialty is vintage household linen: embroidered pillowcases, damask tablecloths, and Provençal *boutis* (quilted bedspreads). All the pieces are in excellent condition, sold in a charming country-style shop decorated with pretty antiques, curios, and baskets (all of which are for sale).

Peau d'Ange
16th arr. - 1, rue Mesnil
45 53 78 11
Open 10:30am-noon & 2pm-6:30pm. Closed Sun. No cards. M° Victor-Hugo.

A delightfully refined little boutique, Peau d'Ange is awash in frothy vintage linens (embroidered sheets

Bohemian booksellers

The *bouquinistes* of Paris are a unique and colorful clan of used-book sellers who hawk their wares from quayside stands in the first, fourth, fifth, and sixth arrondissements. Because *bouquinistes* are a rather bohemian bunch, they don't keep regular hours, though most open for business on weekend afternoons. As you stroll along the Seine, take some time to sift through the piles of magazines, books, and papers—who knows? You may unearth a first edition! At the very least, you'll find a map or vintage print to hang in your study, a charming souvenir of a Parisian sojourn.

embellished with openwork cost 250 F; a sheet plus two pillowcases go for 600 F). Hand-embroidered tablecloths range between 300 and 6,000 F, depending on size and quality. Another specialty: old-fashioned bridal gowns, which are altered to the bride's size, then laundered, starched, and ironed just before the big day!

Porthault

8th arr. - 18, av. Montaigne
47 20 75 25
Open 9:30am-6:30pm (Sat & Mon 9:30am-1pm & 2pm-6pm). Closed Sun. V, AE, DC. M° Alma-Marceau.

Everyone who loves luxurious linens knows Porthault. Even if you can't afford these signature prints and exquisite embroideries (they are, of course, direly expensive—a tablecloth can cost up to 50,000 F), you can browse, finger (discreetly!), and admire them in this tony shop on the Avenue Montaigne. A lower-priced line, Porthault Studio, was recently introduced—but even lower-than-regular prices here aren't cheap. A pair of sheets and two pillowcases in embroidered cotton start at 2,500 F and quickly climb to 35,000 F.

■ TABLEWARE

CANDLES

Cir

6th arr. - 22, rue Saint-Sulpice
43 26 46 50, fax 43 54 61 77
Open 10am-7pm (Mon 11am-7pm). Closed Sun. V, MC. M° Odéon.

In the wax-processing business since 1643, Cir offers a considerable choice of candles in a variety of classic and imaginative shapes. Current bestsellers are "cake," "caviar," and "sandwich" candles. These, like any candle in the shop, may be personalized with your name or initials for a modest fee.

Point à la Ligne

7th arr. - 25, rue de Varenne
42 84 14 45
16th arr. - 67, av. Victor-Hugo - 45 00 96 80
Open 10am-7pm. Closed Sun. V, AE, DC. M° Rue du Bac, Victor-Hugo.

You are certain to find candles to match your centerpiece or tablecloth (or your eyes, for that matter) in this pretty boutique. There are dozens of shades available, each one coordinated with paper napkins, plates, and tablecloths. Candle holders are available as well, in clear or colored glass, along with hurricane lamps and a line of candles in imaginative shapes that echo the seasons or holidays. If you wish, Point à la Ligne will custom-illuminate your house or garden for a special party.

CRYSTAL, CHINA & SILVER

Baccarat

8th arr. - 11, pl. de la Madeleine - 42 65 36 26
Open 9:30am-6:30pm (Sat & Mon 10am-6:30pm). Closed Sun. V, AE, DC. M° Madeleine.

Baccarat's flagship store on the Place de la Madeleine boasts a bright, harmonious décor that highlights the extraordinary brilliance of the firm's superbly wrought crystal stemware, decorative accents, and objets d'art. New additions to the collection include a stunning line of chandeliers ("Saphir") by Patrice Butler and bold crystal jewelry by talented young designers.

Au Bain Marie
8th arr. - 10, rue Boissy-d'Anglas - 42 66 59 74
Open 10am-7pm. Closed Sun. V, AE, DC. M° Concorde.

In a setting that recalls the lobby of a palatial hotel, Aude Clément presents a glittering assortment of eminently desirable tableware, kitchenware, and accessories. Even the items that aren't expensive antiques look as if they ought to be: embroidered table linens, genuine crystal, or just-glass glasses (initialed or not, as you wish), real and faux pearl-handled cutlery... Pieces by contemporary designers (watch for Frank Évennou's Champagne bucket) and by talented artisans (the hand-decorated faïences are superb) are exhibited alongside witty, inexpensive treasures for the table. Don't miss the huge accumulation of cookbooks and magazines on food and wine.

Bernardaud
8th arr. - 11, rue Royale
47 42 82 66
Open 9:30am-6:30pm. Closed Sun. V, AE. M° Concorde.

Since 1863, the Limoges-based Bernardaud has been a standard-bearer for French china manufacturers. Following the lead of other prestigious tableware manufacturers, Bernardaud opened a showcase on the Rue Royale to display the entire array of its collections. New and noteworthy is the reissue of a service owned by Queen Marie-Antoinette; in a more modern vein, look for Olivier Gagnère's spectacular Ithaque and Lipari cups.

Cristalleries de Saint-Louis
8th arr. - 13, rue Royale
40 17 01 74
Open 9:30am-6:30pm. Closed Sun. M° Concorde.

This venerable firm (founded in 1586) which long crafted crystal for the kings of France, continues to maintain the highest standards of quality. A visit to Saint-Louis's dazzling showplace on the Rue Royale will have you too longing to adorn your table with mouth-blown, hand-cut crystal stemware, decanters encrusted with gold, and filigreed or opaline vases...

Daum
2nd arr. - 4, rue de la Paix
42 61 25 25
Open 10am-7pm (Mon 11am-7pm). Closed Sun. V. M° Opéra.

Daum's elegant dual-level showrooms are situated in premises formerly occupied by the great couturier, Worth. Slate-gray walls and green-glazed bronze furniture form an ideal setting for the firm's latest creations. On the ground floor are the limited-edition (200 or 300 copies) glass pieces, in luminous colors: Fassianos's cobalt-blue head, carafes with cactus stoppers by Hilton McConnico, and baroque designs by Garouste and Bonetti. The lower level is devoted to Daum's lovely crystal table services.

Devine Qui Vient Dîner
15th arr. - 83, av. Émile-Zola
40 59 41 14
Open 10:30am-7:30pm. Closed Sun, Mon. V. M° Charles-Michels.

This red-and-gray shop is known for its noteworthy assortment of late-nineteenth- and early-twentieth-century tableware, and its many finely crafted reproductions. Prices are amazingly reasonable for the antique ceramic ware, colored glasses, silver-plated table accessories, and such.

Dîners en Ville
7th arr. - 27, rue de Varenne
42 22 78 33, fax 45 44 87 25
Open 11am-7pm. Closed Sun. V. M° Sèvres-Babylone.

It's hard not to notice this shop, with its multiple display windows that wrap around the corner of the Rue du Bac and the Rue de Varenne. It's even harder not to stop and gape at the lavish tables draped in old-fashioned paisley tablecloths and set (by owner Blandine de Grancey) with turn-of-the-century French or English dishes, colorful Bohemian crystal, and antique table decorations. Inside, there are glasses in an enchanting array of tints and, on the upper floor, a section devoted to the ritual of tea, with teapots, tea services, vintage cookie jars, and silver accessories.

La Faïence Anglaise
6th arr. - 11, rue du Dragon
42 22 42 72
Open 11:30am-7pm (Mon 2pm-7pm). Closed Sun. V, AE, MC. M° St-Germain-des-Prés.

Anglophiles and other tea fanciers will love the selection of small Victorian antiques, figurines, and 1930s lamps available here. But dishes and table and tea accessories are the principal specialty of the house. Teapots, cake plates, and tea caddies range in price from about 300 to 500 F. Fifteen different models of Wedgwood china are displayed (plates run from 56 to 152 F each).

Gien

8th arr. - 18, rue de l'Arcade
49 24 07 77
Open 10am-7pm. Closed Sun, Mon. V, AE. M° Madeleine.

The Gien faïence factory, founded in 1821, has been granted a new lease on life. Noted designers have been commissioned to create new patterns that are now on view in Gien's Paris showroom: Paco Rabanne came up with a service of square plates with delicate ridges, while Jean-Pierre Caillères designed triangular plates edged with black speckles. In a more traditional vein, Dominique Lalande painted his plates with fruit motifs and added a black-and-white border. People who prefer the Gien services that their grandmothers owned will be happy to see that they are still available.

Muriel Grateau

1st arr. - 132, galerie de Valois - 40 20 90 30
Open 11am-7pm (Mon 2pm-7pm). Closed Sun. V, AE. M° Palais-Royal.

A talented designer and woman of taste, Muriel Grateau has amassed a highly sophisticated collection of old and new Murano glasses, Limoges china, and linen napery in a superb palette of muted earth and mineral tones (sublime blues, grays, purples, and greens). The mix of antique and contemporary pieces on a single table creates a ravishing effect that you will surely want to reproduce at home.

Lalique

1st arr. - Galerie du Carrousel du Louvre, 99, rue de Rivoli - 42 86 01 51
Open 10:30am-7:30pm. Closed Tue. M° Palais-Royal.
8th arr. - 11, rue Royale
42 66 52 40
Open 9:30am-6:30pm. Closed Sun. M° Concorde.

Three generations of creative Laliques have earned an international following with their enchanting crystal designs. Marie-Claude Lalique, who succeeded her father, Marc, at the head of the company in 1977, creates marvelous contemporary pieces in the true Lalique spirit—like her Atossa vase, decorated with a circlet of amber crystal-and-opaline flowers. In the courtyard of the Rue Royale shop, Lalique has opened another boutique, devoted to "the art of the table." Accompanying the Lalique crystal glasses and plates are linens, silver flatware, and china by prestigious manufacturers.

La Maison du Week-End

6th arr. - 26, rue Vavin
43 54 15 52, fax 40 51 72 07
Open 10am-7:30pm. Closed Sun. V, AE. M° Vavin.

If your idea of a weekend treat is a shopping spree for linens and dishes to fill up your cupboards, we've got just the address for you. Old-fashioned damask tablecloths, in a range of seven pastel shades, are made to order here (from about 300 F); damask towels sell for 278 F with fringe, 178 F without. You'll also find table services in earthenware or china; the most recent addition to the line is a china tea service decorated with tiny old-fashioned blossoms. Do you feel that what is lacking in your life is a gilded garden chair? Look no further.

Manufacture de Sèvres

1st arr. - 4, pl. André-Malraux
47 03 40 20, fax 42 61 40 54
Open 11am-6pm. Closed Sat, Sun. V. M° Palais-Royal.

In a sleek, contemporary setting, with glass-and-brushed-steel shelves, La Manufacture de Sèvres presents its superb collections of hand-painted, gold-trimmed china. Each piece is a work of art; some are designed by noted artists—Lalanne, Mathieu, Van Lith, and Coloretti, among others. Also on display are reproductions of such extraordinary objets d'art as the dancers sculpted by Léonard and Carpeaux. Prices for plates range from 500 to 10,000 F, and the most expensive vase commands some 200,000 F. Special orders are completed in one to three months.

Odiot

8th arr. - 7, pl. de la Madeleine - 42 65 00 95
Open 9:30am-6:30pm (Sat 10am-1pm & 2:15pm-6:30pm). Closed Sun. V, AE. M° Madeleine.

Silversmiths in Paris since 1690, this traditional firm continues to reissue pieces cast in eighteenth- and nineteenth-century molds. For shoppers of more modest means, there are some fine items in silverplate, china, and crystal.

The adorable baby cups and rattles make appreciated christening gifts.

Pavillon Christofle

2nd arr. - 24, rue de la Paix
42 65 62 43
Open 9:30am-6:30pm. Closed Sun. V, AE. M° Opéra.
6th arr. - 17, rue de Sèvres
45 48 16 17
Open 9:30am-7:30pm. Closed Sun. V, AE, DC, MC. M° Sèvres-Babylone.
8th arr. - 9, rue Royale
49 33 43 00
Open 9:45am-6:30pm. Closed Sun. M° Concorde.
16th arr. - 95, rue de Passy
46 47 51 27
Open 9:45am-6:45pm (Mon 1pm-6:45pm). Closed Sun. V, AE. M° La Muette.

Christofle was founded in 1833, and began to produce the plated silverware that was to make the firm its fortune. Since then, Christofle has become the world's premier exporter of table silver. A current bestseller is the clean-lined, contemporary Aria setting. Another recent creation, the Talisman line of Chinese-lacquered settings, owes its beauty and durability to a jealously guarded secret process. Christofle has also enjoyed notable success with reproductions of its designs from the 1920s (like the coveted tea service in silver plate with briarwood handles), and a handsome line of classic china.

Peter

8th arr. - 191, rue du Fg-St-Honoré - 45 63 88 00
Open 10am-6:30pm (Mon 1:30pm-6:30pm; Sat 10am-1pm & 2pm-6:30pm). Closed Sun. V, AE. M° Ternes.

For a couple of centuries, Peter's exclusive silverware patterns have adorned the dinner tables of the rich and refined (the Aga Khan and the Agnellis appear on the clients list, just to give you an idea). The most sumptuous setting in the shop, fashioned of lapis lazuli and vermeil, is priced just shy of 15,000 F. But Peter accommodates less opulent tastes as well, with beautifully designed contemporary silver, china services, crystal, and jewelry.

Puiforcat

8th arr. - 2, av. Matignon
45 63 10 10
Open 9:30am-6:30pm (Sat & Mon 9:30am-1pm & 2:15pm-6:30pm). Closed Sun. V, AE, DC. M° Franklin-D.-Roosevelt.

A few years ago, Éliane Scali, director of this world-renowned silversmithing firm, had the bright idea to reissue Jean Puiforcat's stunning 1930s designs (for example, the table settings for the oceanliner *Normandie*). More recently Puiforcat added a gift and jewelry department that stocks merchandise for nearly every budget. A silver-plated centerpiece sells for 1,400 F, a pretty silver bangle bracelet commands 1,050 F. Puiforcat also commissions modern pieces from well-known designers such as Andrée Putman and Manuel Canovas.

Quartz Diffusion

6th arr. - 12, rue des Quatre-Vents
43 54 03 00, fax 40 05 16 29
Open 10:30am-7pm (Mon 2:30pm-7pm). Closed Sun. V, MC. M° Odéon.

There's lots of space in this shop, all of it devoted to the delicate art of the glassmaker. The objects on display are signed by such talented artists as Baldwin, Guggisberg, Bouchard, Hinz, Gilbert... Not everything is terrifyingly fragile or expensive, witness the "laboratory" glass carafe and salad bowl (150 F and 180 F, respectively). Glass dinner plates and wine glasses are available as well as glass tabletops, screens, and shelves. Quartz is the exclusive source of a layered colored glass called Décor A IV.

Quatre Saisons

14th arr. - 88, av. du Maine
43 21 28 99 (also: 16th arr.)
Open 10:30am-7pm (Mon noon-7pm). Closed Sun. V. M° Gaîté.

Here's a terrific collection of high-quality wooden table and kitchenware: carving boards, salad bowls, cheese boards (from 100 F) and more. Appealing, inexpensive glassware (8 to 80 F) is also on hand, along with rustic baskets and an assortment of fabric and plastic tablecloths in attractive colors.

IMAGE & SOUND

PHOTO & FILM

Cipière

11th arr. - 26, bd Beaumarchais - 47 00 37 25
Open 9:30am-6:30pm. Closed Sun. M° Bastille.

Michel Cipière, a certified appraiser of photographic equipment from every era, sells new and second-hand cameras (the latter in prime condition, of course). Every imaginable brand is in stock; some of the older cameras are rarities that will fascinate collectors. Expect a warm welcome and professional advice.

FNAC

1st arr. - Forum des Halles, 1, rue Pierre-Lescot, level -3, 40 41 40 00
6th arr. - 136, rue de Rennes 49 54 30 00
Open 10am-7:30pm. Closed Sun. V. M° Les Halles, Saint-Placide.
17th arr. - 26, av. des Ternes 44 09 18 00
Open 10am-7:20pm. Closed Sun. V. M° Ternes.

The FNAC conscientiously carries major brands of cameras and electronics at prices that (for France) are most competitive. All the equipment you could want for developing and printing film is in stock, and the customer service is excellent. There are over 28 FNAC outlets dotted around Paris, where you can buy rolls of film, spools of super-8 film, and blank video cassettes, as well as have your holidays snaps developed.

Immo-Photo-Video-Son

9th arr. - 73, bd de Clichy 42 82 02 80
Open 11am-7:30pm. Closed Sun. V. M° Place-de-Clichy.

You can buy or sell (good) used cameras here, or leave your photography equipment to be sold on consignment. Professionals and hobbyists alike will find a large selection to suit specific needs. The helpful staff is often willing to bargain over prices.

La Maison du Leica

11th arr. - 52, bd Beaumarchais - 48 05 77 67
Open 9:30am-1pm & 2pm-7pm. Closed Sun, Mon. M° Chemin-Vert.

For the many fans of this manufacturer, the Maison du Leica sells new and used equipment, and repairs all Leica models. Prices are competitive with those of the big discount store, FNAC, and the service is above reproach.

■ RECORDED MUSIC & STEREO GEAR

Crocodisc

5th arr. - 42, rue des Écoles 43 54 47 95
Open 11am-7pm. Closed Sun, Mon. V. M° Maubert-Mutualité.

In this discount record paradise, you can find reasonably priced imports, used records, compact discs, and cassettes. Every genre is represented: rock, reggae, funk, blues, country, film scores, etc. In addition, you can listen to the records, and you can also have them set aside and pay several days later.

Crocojazz

5th arr. - 64, rue de la Montagne-Sainte-Geneviève 46 34 78 38
Open 11am-1pm & 2:15pm-7pm. Closed Sun, Mon. M° Maubert-Mutualité.

This is a branch of the aforementioned Crocodisc, and it specializes in jazz, country, and blues. Lots of interesting imports.

Disco Revue

1st arr. - 55, rue des Petits-Champs - 42 61 21 30
Open 11am-7pm. Closed Sun. V. M° Pyramides.

You may have to hunt a bit to locate this shop, tucked away in the back of a courtyard, but rock 'n' roll record collectors will find the effort well worth it. Vintage 45s and 33s are bought and sold here, and although the management's preferences run to discs from the '50s and '60s, there are examples from all eras in stock, including many rare and collectible recordings. CDs and laserdiscs imported from Japan are also on hand.

FNAC Musique

9th arr. - 24, bd des Italiens 48 01 02 03
Open 10am-midnight. Closed Sun. V. M° Richelieu-Drouot.
12th arr. - 4, pl. de la Bastille 43 42 04 04
Open 10am-8pm (Wed & Fri 10am-10pm). Closed Sun. V. M° Bastille.

The store on the Boulevard des Italiens carries all types of music on cassettes, CDs, video and laserdiscs, but rock, jazz and French pop predominate. Appropriately for a store that adjoins the Opéra, the Bastille FNAC is more oriented toward classical music and opera. Plus, at both locations, you'll find a music bookshop, sheet music, and a ticket agency for concerts and musical events.

Oldies but Goodies

4th arr. - 16, rue du Bourg-Tibourg - 48 87 14 37
Open noon-1:30pm & 2pm-7:30pm. Closed Sun. V, AE. M° Hôtel-de-Ville.

This shop specializes in used records, including jazz, blues, and rock'n'roll in French and American versions (check out the hysterical French "covers" of U.S. pop songs from the 1960s—the lyrics are even worse!). There are all sorts of goodies to be found here, be they old or rare or cheap.

Virgin Mégastore

8th arr. - 56, av. des Champs-Élysées - 49 53 50 00
Open 10am-midnight (Fri & Sat 10am-1am). V. M° Franklin- D.-Roosevelt.

The FNAC's British rival scored a big one, when it carried off this prime location on the Champs-Élysées. "Mega" only begins to describe Virgin's vast inventory of books, records, stereo gear, video paraphernalia, and computer equipment. The staff is young and often only minimally competent (that's why we go elsewhere for pricey electronic merchandise), but the record department is strictly fab. The newest, the oldest, the best, and the weirdest recordings can be found here; new releases are regularly hooked up to earphones, so that you can give a listen before you buy. You can gloat over your new acquisitions over refreshments at the Virgin Café, at the top of the store's monumental marble staircase.

VIDEO

Playtime

7th arr. - 44, av. Bosquet
45 55 43 36
Open daily noon-9pm (Sat 10am-9pm; Sun 11:30am-4:30pm). V. M° École-Militaire.
16th arr. - 36, av. d'Eylau
47 27 56 22
Open daily noon-midnight (Sat 10am-midnight; Sun 11:30am-4:30pm). V. M° Trocadéro.

This is the place for movie buffs, where they can rent video cassettes from the collection of more than 3,000 titles, including a good selection of films in English. The help is very friendly, and cassette tapes are also available. Nonmembers pay 45 F per cassette per day.

Stéréorama

17th arr. - 67, rue Legendre
46 27 32 22
Open 11am-1:30pm & 3pm-8pm. Closed Sun. V. M° Place-de-Clichy.

A worthwhile selection of art films and Hollywood classics is offered here in VO (*version originale*). Members who pay a 400 F annual fee can rent movies for 30 F a pop; nonmembers pay 45 F per film.

JEWELRY

ANTIQUE JEWELRY

See Antiques *section page 193.*

PRESTIGE JEWELRY

René Boivin

8th arr. - 49, av. Montaigne
47 20 82 64 (also: 2nd arr.)
Open 10am-1pm & 2:30pm-6:30pm. Closed Sun. V, AE. M° Franklin-D.-Roosevelt.

Boivin specializes in jewels with a secret (the Chrysalis watch that changes before your eyes) and cleverly assembled "living" ornaments that actually move: animals, flowers, fruit... The shop is a gem, too, designed in marble and bleached oak by decorating biggie Alain Demachy.

Boucheron

1st arr. - 26, pl. Vendôme
42 61 58 16
Open 10am-6:30pm (Sat 10am-1pm & 2pm-6:30pm). Closed Sun. V, AE, DC, MC. M° Opéra.

Alain Boucheron, the current—dynamic!—bearer of the Boucheron family torch and president of the Comité Vendôme, has led his firm into new areas, including fragrances. But Boucheron's backbone remains prestige jewelry and watches. Beautiful gems are brought forth for inspection on plush trays, in an opulent environment of wood paneling and friezes...such is the luxury for which Boucheron has stood for generations. The more accessible "Boutique" collections feature (for example) a handsome steel watch with an interchangeable bracelet (8,900 F) and the Parfum ring, in gold and semiprecious stones (from 8,800 F), inspired by the distinctive Boucheron perfume flacon.

Bulgari

8th arr. - 27, av. Montaigne
47 23 89 89
Open 10am-1pm & 2:30pm-7pm. Closed Sun. M° Alma-Marceau.

The house of Bulgari got its start in Rome in 1881 when Sotirio Bulgari began selling jewelry (which he

The hole in Les Halles

Many Parisians still regret that the city's famous food market, installed here since the twelfth century, was not preserved when the merchants moved out to Rungis in 1969. The *trou* **("hole")** *des Halles,* **dug after the market was destroyed, became a tourist attraction in its own right during the 1970s, while developers argued with the city over what should be done with it. One idea was simply to fill it in again; another was to flood it to make a lake linked up to the Seine. A dozen or so architects had their projects rejected before the present Forum shopping center was approved and built. While indistinguishable from similar emporia worldwide, the Forum at least has the merit of carrying on the centuries-old tradition of trade. Above ground, the site has been attractively landscaped and the surrounding streets are full of echoes of the past for those who care to listen.**

made at night) from a pushcart in the streets. Today Bulgari jewels are among the most imitated in the world. The house style is typified by massive pieces, such as carved stones mounted on gold rings or necklaces. Although certain jewels are stratospherically priced, other pieces are more affordable: a handsome steel watch sells for 8,800 F. If that is still too rich for your blood, note that Bulgari's unisex fragrance, Eau Parfumée (based on green tea) is priced to sell at 1,200 F per flacon!

Cartier

1st arr. - 7 & 23, pl. Vendôme
40 15 03 51
Open 10am-6:30pm. Closed Sun. V, AE, DC, MC. M° Opéra.
2nd arr. - 13, rue de la Paix
49 26 16 50
Open 10am-7pm (winter 10am-6:30pm). Closed Sun. V, AE, DC, MC. M° Opéra.
8th arr. - 51, rue François-ler
40 74 61 85
Open 10am-6:30pm (Mon 11am-6:30pm; Sat 10:30am-6:30pm). Closed Sun. V, AE, DC, MC. M° Franklin-D.-Roosevelt.

"It is better to have authentic junk than fake Cartier," exclaims Dominique Perrin, chief executive of Cartier, the most copied name on earth. Founded in 1847, the firm still produces enviable jeweled ornaments for the rich and royal: many are on display, at the Cartier showcase on the Rue de la Paix. Not to mention fine timepieces like the celebrated Santos watch (9,800 F for the ladies' version, 10,200 F for the men's) and such nearly affordable trinkets as the famous three-gold rolling ring (3,700 F).

Chaumet

1st arr. - 12, pl. Vendôme
44 77 24 00, fax 42 60 41 44
Open 10am-6:30pm. Closed Sun. V, AE, DC, MC. M° Opéra.

Jeweler in Paris since 1780, Chaumet belongs to the highly select association of *Haute Joaillerie de France,* a group that fosters traditional French design and craftsmanship in fine jewelry. Though Chaumet's creations have beguiled such connoisseurs as Napoléon, Queen Victoria, and countless maharajahs, the firm also produces elegant timepieces, gold jewelry, leather goods, and writing instruments that are perfectly appropriate for fast-paced modern life. Prices for the "Boutique" line start at 4,200 F, watches at 8,000 F, and leather accessories at 600 F.

Mauboussin

1st arr. - 20, pl. Vendôme
44 55 10 00
Open 10am-6:30pm. Closed Sun. V, AE, DC, MC. M° Opéra.

Established in 1827, the house of Mauboussin exudes the aura of security and comfort one associates with old families, for whom the purchase of fine jewelry is the natural way to celebrate life's big moments. With a multicolored Arlequin brooch, for instance, which combines brilliant enamel and gem stones, or a Nadia ring: a glowing pearl-and-gold band set with a diamond or colored gemstone.

Don't plan to shop on Sundays—the vast majority of Paris stores are closed.

Mellerio dits Meller

1st arr. - 9, rue de la Paix
42 61 57 53
Open 10am-1pm & 2pm-6:30pm. Closed Sun (& Sat in Jul, Aug, Sep). V, AE, DC, MC. M° Opéra.

When Queen Marie de Medicis awarded her loyal Lombard chimney sweeps licenses as peddlers, later as street vendors, and finally as jewelers (their reward for having overheard and reported a plot against the Crown), she probably had no idea that she was founding a dynasty. Now, some fourteen generations later, the great house of Mellerio is by no means resting on its ancient laurels. The dean of fine jewelers in France, the Mellerio family combs the worldwide gem markets for outstanding stones that measure up to their noble standards.

Poiray

2nd arr. - 1, rue de la Paix
42 61 70 58
Open 10am-6:30pm (Mon & Sat 11am-1pm & 2pm-6:30pm). Closed Sun. V, AE, DC. M° Opéra.
8th arr. - 46 av. George-V
47 23 07 41
Open 11am-7pm. Closed Sun. V, AE, DC. M° George-V.

Poiray is the youngest of the great French jewelry firms. Designer Nathalie Hocq presents two collections annually, but favorite pieces are retained over the seasons. A current hit is the Symbole ring (14,500 F) which can be engraved with a few tender words. Poiray is also renowned for fine watches. The ladies' version (6,800 F) can be fitted onto any one of 400 interchangeable bracelets!

Alexandre Reza

1st arr. - 23, pl. Vendôme
42 96 64 00
Open 10am-1pm & 2pm-6:30pm. Closed Sun. M° Opéra.

Alexandre Reza is a major dealer in precious stones. The jewels on display in his shop always seems to glow with the most beautiful gems around. An expert appraiser and collector, Reza transformed the boutique's lower level into a gallery, which presents reproductions fashioned according to traditional techniques. Admire, for example, the necklace of pear-shaped "diamonds" (actually paste stones by Flowliss): a stunning and—were it real—priceless piece.

Van Cleef et Arpels

1st arr. - 22, pl. Vendôme
42 61 58 58
Open 10am-6:30pm. Closed Sat, Sun. V, AE, MC. M° Opéra.

The most innovative of the Place Vendôme's jewelers, and originator of the gold evening bag set with precious gems, this firm boasts an exclusive mounting technique: the setting fades into the background, thus emphasizing the quality of the stones. Prices reflect this high level of workmanship and creativity, but even relatively modest budgets can find happiness with the Van Cleef "Boutique" line: rings, earrings, and butterfly pendants start at about 4,000 F.

Harry Winston

8th arr. - 29, av. Montaigne
47 20 03 09
Open 9:30am-1pm & 2:30pm-6:30pm. Closed Sat, Sun. V, AE, DC, MC. M° Alma-Marceau.

American jeweler Harry Winston is one of the world's most prestigious diamond dealers. He sells uncut diamonds from his own mines to other dealers and retailers, or displays them in his own showrooms. Many of the best-known diamonds on earth have passed through Winston's hands, including the famous Taylor-Burton diamond. The entrance to the establishment is discreet and most intimidating; clients must have an appointment and consent to be virtually frisked at the door. In the two second-floor rooms, decorated in period style, showcases present diamond jewelry and ornaments crafted in a traditional, fairly sober style. How much, you ask? In the millions of dollars... these jewels are destined for an international clientele seeking a recession-proof investment.

FINE JEWELRY

A & A Turner

8th arr. - 16, av. George-V
47 23 88 28
Open 10:30am-1pm & 2pm-6:30pm. Closed Sun. V, AE. M° Alma-Marceau.

Decorated with carved wood and antique red floor tiles, this gallery is nothing if not luxurious. Françoise Turner designs striking jewels: "major" rings (some are hand-carved) from 5,000 F, and necklaces of rock crystal tipped in gold (40,000 F and up). On our last visit we admired large beads of malachite, slate, horn, gold, or faceted gems, which can be added to a pearl necklace, hung on a chain, or simply strung on a leather thong (from 25,000 F). More affordable is Turner's new line of solid-gold jewelry, with prices hovering around the 5,000 F mark.

Arthus Bertrand

6th arr. - 6, pl. St-Germain-des-Prés - 42 22 19 20
Open 10am-6:30pm (Sat 10am-12:30pm & 2pm-6:30pm). Closed Sun, Mon. V. M° St-Germain-des-Prés.

Opposite the church of Saint-Germain-des-Prés, next door to the Deux Magots, stands Arthus Bertrand, a venerable maker of religious medals and Academicians' swords. Families with a sense of tradition come here for engagement rings wrought in an utterly classic style. No one, however, comes to Arthus Bertrand for the warm welcome, which is about as friendly as a court martial. The firm also specializes in reproductions of antique jewelry displayed at the Louvre. Small, elegant pieces start at around 600 F.

Chanel Horlogerie

1st arr. - 7, pl. Vendôme
42 86 28 00
Open 10am-1pm & 2pm-6:30pm (Mon & Sat from 10:30am). Closed Sun. V, AE, DC, MC. M° Tuileries.

The décor of Chanel's newest boutique for timepieces on the Place Vendôme is reminiscent of Mademoiselle's private apartment. Coromandel screens, luscious suede sofas, and lacquered furniture invite you into the boutique to take a look. Inside, you will find the complete line of Chanel's fine watches, designed by artistic director Jacques Helleu. The Chanel staff will help you discover this beautiful collection ranging from the signature leather and chain watch to the ultimate luxury: the diamond pavé link-bracelet watch.

Ebel

1st arr. - 2, pl. Vendôme
42 60 82 08
Open 10am-1pm & 2:30pm-6pm. Closed Sun, Mon. V, AE. M° Tuileries.

Since 1911 Ebel's "architects of time" have been striving to make the perfect watch. They succeeded at last, and you can see the results at the Ebel gallery on the Place Vendôme (decorated by Andrée Putman): splendid, accurate timepieces set with diamonds and sapphires (from 8,000 F). Ebel also offers a line of jewelry by Italian designer Alexandra Gradi: necklaces and rings fashioned from rounded, tightly linked gold chain, and ravishing rings composed of colored gems on wide gold bands (ring prices range from 2,300 to 12,000 F). An impeccably courteous reception is the house rule.

Fred

8th arr. - 6, rue Royale
42 60 30 65
Open 9:30am-6pm (Mon & Sat 9:30am-12:30pm & 2pm-6pm). Closed Sun. V, AE, DC, MC. M° Concorde.
8th arr. - 74, av. des Champs-Élysées - 43 59 68 10
Open 10:30am-7pm (Mon & Sat 10:30am-1pm & 2pm-7pm). Closed Sun. V, AE, MC. M° Franklin-D.-Roosevelt.

Fred's jewelry and watches have a resolutely sportive spin, witness the Force 10 (in gold and rigging) and Force Douce (gold and rubber) lines. Notable too are the watches that combine steel and leather (from 4,000 F), and the evening bags in mother-of-pearl set with exotically carved gems. The popular Concerto ring in gold and pearls sells for 6,500 F. Fred Joaillier also has a boutique in the Galerie du Claridge (a shopping arcade off the Champs-Élysées).

Ilias Lalaounis

1st arr. - 364, rue Saint-Honoré - 42 61 55 65
Open 10am-6:30pm. Closed Sun. V, AE, DC, MC. M° Concorde.

Lalaounis crafts jewels of 20- and 22-carat gold in keeping with ancient traditions. The precious metal is hammered by hand in the firm's Greek workshops, situated at the foot of the Acropolis. While most of the ornaments sold here are costly indeed, we spotted a lovely little ring for 850 F, and a cup bearing the image of Alexander the Great for 350 F.

Jar's

1st arr. - 7, place Vendôme
42 96 33 66
Open 9am-1pm & 2:30pm-6pm. Closed Sun. No cards. M° Opéra.

Overrun with business, this jeweler prefers to maintain a peerless standard of quality by limiting orders. Specializing in resetting the jewels that you already own, the magic worked by Jar's turns your old, tired baubles into contemporary gems.

Jean Dinh Van

2nd arr. - 7, rue de la Paix
42 61 74 49
Open 9:30am-6:30pm (Sat 10:30am-6:30pm). Closed Sun. V, AE, DC, MC. M° Opéra.

Jean Dinh Van crafts avant-garde jewelry for everyday wear. His clasps are world famous: "handcuff" clasps give chains and pearl necklaces a fresh look, while the "lock" clasp adorns soberly styled gold bangle bracelets. Dinh Van's steel watches are the height of fashion, and his new PI pendant (a 24-carat hammered gold disk on a leather thong) is huge hit with those who can afford the 12,000 F price tag.

La Perle

16th arr. - 85, av. Raymond-Poincaré - 45 53 07 62
Open 10am-12:45pm & 1:45pm-6:15pm. Closed Sat (exc in Nov & Dec), Sun. V. M° Victor-Hugo.

If you care to present your daughter with her first string of pearls or have your old string reset with precious stones, La Perle offers a variety of cultured pearls custom-strung to your liking as bracelets (5,500 F and up), earrings, ropes, or single strands. The firm also designs an exclusive line of pearl jewelry.

O.J. Perrin

16th arr. - 33, av. Victor-Hugo - 45 01 88 88
Open 10am-1pm & 2pm-6pm. Closed Sun. V, AE, DC, MC. M° Victor-Hugo.

Elegant, easy-to-wear jewelry featuring clever combinations of gold, leather, silver, and satin. The ladies' watch, for example, comes with interchangeable bracelets of leather or cultured pearls. We also love Perrin's gold Liberty clip, the silver-and-gold Venetian ring (3,200 F), and the Méridienne ring.

Pomellato

8th arr. - 66, rue du Fg-St-Honoré - 42 65 62 07
Open 10am-7pm. Closed Sun. V, AE, DC, MC. M° Champs-Élysées-Clemenceau.

The Paris headquarters of Pomellato, the famed Milanese jeweler, is elegantly decked out in gray marble with large display windows. Pomellato's clever, original collections showcase creative pieces, such as the animal pendants that can be enriched with precious stones, or the Teardrop hoop earrings that flatter the face, or the impressive rings in brushed or polished gold set with semiprecious stones (under 10,000 F).

COSTUME JEWELRY

Artcurial

8th arr. - 9, av. de Matignon
42 99 16 16
Open 10:30am-7:15pm. Closed Sun, Mon. V, AE, MC. M° Franklin-D.-Roosevelt.

For limited-edition jewels designed by modern artists, crafted in bronze, vermeil, silver, and gold, plan a visit to the fascinating gift shop of the Artcurial gallery. You'll find "violin" pendants by Arman, Paul Bury's spherical jewels, Piero Dorazio's enameled-gold ornaments, and Claude Lalanne's juicy-looking clusters of glass currants and grapes.

Cap d'Ambre

1st - 21, rue des Petits-Champs - 42 97 43 16
Open 11am-7pm. Closed Sun. V, AE, MC. M° Bourse.

A stable of young designers produces the fascinating ornaments displayed here. Delphine Nardin and Aline Gui present chunky acrylic rings set with colored cabochons (440 F); MX Design shows brushed Plexiglas pieces in a rainbow of hues. And there are clever contemporary watches (from 440 F) and reproductions of antique jewels in vermeil and gems. Prices range from 395 to 895 F.

Césarée

6th arr. - 43, rue Madame
45 48 86 86
Open 9am-7pm. Closed Sun. V, DC, MC. M° Saint-Sulpice.

Laurence Coupelon takes coral, horn, jade, malachite, terracotta, bronze, and glass and transforms these disparate elements into uncommonly alluring *bijoux*. Exotic and indefinably ethnic, they don't look like run-of-the-mill costume pieces; what's more, they are not exorbitantly priced.

Cipango

6th arr. - 14, rue de l'Échaudé
43 26 08 92
Open 2pm-7pm (Sat 11am-1pm & 2pm-7pm). Closed Sun, Mon. V, AE, MC. M° Saint-Germain-des-Prés.

The most desirable costume jewelry in this fashion-conscious corner of

Paris is crafted here at Cipango. Shells, semiprecious stones, antique ivory, jade, and coral are transformed into ornaments that attract plenty of notice. Cipango's artisans have a special talent for blending old and new elements, mixing different materials, and harmonizing colors.

Isadora

7th arr. - 10, rue du Pré-aux-Clercs - 42 22 89 63
Open 11am-7pm (Mon 2pm-7pm). Closed Sun. V, AE, MC. M° Rue du Bac.

The ornaments on view here will not leave you indifferent: you either love Isadora's jewelry, or you hate it! Colorful, structured with architectural precision, and highly decorative—the necklaces have a faintly African flavor.

Alexis Lahellec

1st arr. - 14-16, rue Jean-Jacques-Rousseau
42 33 40 33
Open 11am-7pm (Sat noon-7pm). Closed Sun. V, AE, DC, MC. M° Louvre.

Fabulous fake stones, glass beads, bogus gold, and even papier-mâché go into the glorious "gadget" jewelry dreamed up by Alexis Lahellec. A very '70s look, and prices that range from reasonable to... deranged.

Les Montres

6th arr. - 58, rue Bonaparte
46 34 71 38
Open 10am-7:30pm. Closed Sun. V, AE, DC, MC. M° Saint-Germain-des-Prés.

Do you collect watches? Then this shop is a must. You'll discover vintage timepieces from the '30s and '40s by Jaeger Le Coultre, Breitling, Longines, Omega and others, as well as a top-notch repair workshop. Watches purchased here are guaranteed for a year.

Othello

6th arr. - 21, rue des Saints-Pères - 42 60 26 24
Open 10:30am-7:15pm. Closed Sun. V, AE, MC. M° Saint-Germain-des-Prés.

Sheherazade would have loved the jewelry on display at Othello. Terracotta, pink ivorywood, coral, jade beads, and even yew-tree roots are used in the creation of these exotic ornaments straight out of a fairy tale. Prices begin at 300 F.

LEATHER & LUGGAGE

Aïcha

4th arr - 19, rue Pavée
42 77 62 65
Open 11am-7pm (Mon 2:30pm-7pm). Closed Sun. V, AE, DC. M° Saint-Paul.

Vivid colors—lipstick red, ultraviolet, cobalt blue—amusing shapes, and strong, wear-resistant leathers make the hand and shoulder bags sold here an excellent fashion investment.

La Bagagerie

6th arr - 41, rue du Four
45 48 85 88 (also: 8th arr., 14th arr., 15th arr., 16th arr.)
Open 10:15am-7pm (Sat 10am-7pm). Closed Sun. V, AE, DC, MC. M° Saint-Germain-des-Prés.

Prices are rising here, we note, but La Bagagerie's colorful bags, belts, luggage, and leather accessories are reliably in tune with the season's fashions. Designs run from classic to pure fantasy; we especially like the combinations of timeless shapes (envelopes, bucket bags...) and vivid shades that are the shop's specialty.

Bottega Veneta

6th arr. - 6, rue du Cherche-Midi - 42 22 17 09
Open 10am-7pm. Closed Sun. M° Sèvres-Babylone.

The well-known, high-quality Venetian leather goods are all on display, including the unparalleled braided lambskin bags lined in leather. And there are at least 40 models of classic, versatile handbags in eleven colors, including bright red and green. The lizard pocketbooks are expensive but always in fashion. And check out the handsome line of leather and vinyl luggage, which includes both soft and hard suitcases. An urbane staff proffers advice on how to clean or repair old leather.

William Aimard Camus

6th arr. - 25, rue du Dragon
45 48 32 16
Open 10:30am-7pm (Mon 2pm-7pm). Closed Sun. V, AE, MC. M°St-Germain-des-Prés.

Handsome leather backpacks that grow softer and more supple with age are sold here at eminently reasonable prices (800 to 1,500 F), alongside sturdy suitcases especially designed for air travel.

Carpenter

2nd arr. - 43, rue du Sentier
42 33 49 35
Open 8:30am-6:30pm (Sat 8:30am-1pm). Closed Sun. No cards. M° Bonne-Nouvelle.

Leather clothing for men and women, crafted in the finest skins and shearling, from the same manufacturer who works for the top couturiers of the Avenue Montaigne. These high-class designs turn up (a season or two later) at this address, marked down by a whopping 40 percent.

Groom

6th arr. - 13, rue du Cherche-Midi - 45 48 49 36
Open 10am-1pm & 2pm-7pm. Closed Sun. V, AE, MC. M° Saint-Sulpice.
16th arr. - 17, rue Gustave-Courbet - 47 27 02 77
Open 10am-12:45pm & 1:30pm-7pm (Mon noon-7pm). Closed Sun. V, AE, MC. M° Victor-Hugo.

A chic designer showcase presents these highly original handbags to best advantage. We're partial to the triangular clutch purses in vivid shades of red and yellow, but others prefer the funny little bag that looks like a gift-wrapped *cadeau*. Less expensive and most practical is the nylon bucket-bag priced at 530 F.

Gucci

1st arr. - 350, rue Saint-Honoré - 42 96 83 27
8th arr. - 2, rue du Fg-St-Honoré - 42 96 83 27
Open 9:30am-6:30pm (Wed 10:30am-6:30pm). Closed Sun. V, AE, DC, MC. M° Concorde.

Vast showrooms sumptuously decorated in pale marble and lemon-wood display leather goods manufactured in Florence by the third generation of the Gucci family. Current bestsellers include a calfskin backpack with Gucci's signature bamboo-style handle (5,600 F) and silk-twill scarves in classy floral prints (1,200 F). In addition to the firm's famed luggage in leather and vinyl or in canvas with distinctive red and green stripes, you'll find handsome small leather goods (numerous gift possibilities), costume jewelry, and shoes (note the new version of Gucci's classic lady's loafer, perched on a high column heel!). The store at 2, rue du Faubourg-Saint-Honoré is reserved exclusively for ready-to-wear fashions: well-bred blazers, silk blouses, and lots of supple leather jackets and pants.

Henell's

10th arr. - 14, av. Claude-Vellefaux - 42 06 85 94
Open 9am-noon & 1:30pm-7pm (Sat 10am-noon & 2:30pm-7pm). Closed Sun. V, AE, MC. M° Colonel-Fabien.

For classy leather goods, from shoulder bags to shoes, in ostrich, lizard, buffalo, and other rare skins, have a look in here. No, the address is not the most fashionable in town, but the service can't be beat: any item can be custom-ordered in your choice of color and size (most articles are ready in a month's time).

Hermès

8th arr. - 24, rue du Fg-St-Honoré - 40 17 47 17
8th arr. - 42, av. George-V
47 20 48 51
Open 10am-6:30pm (Sat & Mon 10am-1pm & 2:15pm-6:30pm). Closed Sun. V, AE, DC, MC. M° Concorde, George-V.

Hermès has purveyed fine leather goods long enough to reign supreme as the undisputed leader of the pack when it comes to saddles, handbags, luggage, and all the accompanying accoutrements of fine living and traveling. But what about the prices? Are they reasonable? Well, take a look at the workmanship. Check the finish on the leather goods: the Kelly (1956) or Constance (1969) or (the latest) Bugatti bag, all of which come in a dozen different leathers. Think of the meticulous hand-crafting that went into the cutting, sewing, and fitting of these bags, or into the voluptuous sets of matched luggage. Now are you ready to whip out your credit card? What's more, if you want something special, such as a leather cover for your bicycle seat or for the cockpit of your private jet, the Hermès custom-craftsmen will gladly oblige.

Jean-Louis Imbert

2nd arr. - 44, rue Étienne-Marcel - 42 33 36 04
Open 10am-7pm. Closed Sun. V, AE, MC. M° Louvre.

As handsome as they are practical, these leather or fabric bags (priced from 800 to 1,300 F) make a definite fashion statement. To go with, there is a host of accessories, including hats, shoes, and shawls.

Lancel

9th arr. - 8, pl. de l'Opéra
47 42 37 29 (also: 6th arr., 8th arr., 17th arr.)
Open 10am-7pm. Closed Sun. V, AE, MC. M° Opéra.

Chic and typically Parisian leather accessories (belts, bags, wallets, key tags...) and fashionable—though never flashy—luggage. Complete lines of the latter are available in canvas as well as leather. On the whole, the craftsmanship is remarkable, and prices are in line with the quality.

Loewe

8th arr. - 57, av. Montaigne
45 63 73 38
Open 10am-7pm. Closed Sun. V, AE, DC, MC. M° Franklin-D.-Roosevelt.

Loewe (say: Lou-AY-vay), a patrician Spanish firm, is absolutely the last word in leather and suede clothing, handbags, luggage, and accessories. Belts start at 600 F; superb cuffed gloves sell for 900 F. But we really swoon over the gorgeous bags (from 2,000 F) with clasps and buckles inspired by eighteenth-century Spanish jewels.

Longchamp

1st arr. - 390, rue Saint-Honoré - 42 60 00 00
Open 10am-7pm. Closed Sun. V, AE, DC, MC. M° Concorde.

A huge selection of supple, sturdy handbags, luggage, and accessories in leather, nylon, or canvas with leather trim. Attractive detailing sets these bags apart; and in addition to being fashionable, they are crafted to take a lot of heavy wear. From 700 F.

Didier Ludot

1st arr. - 23-24, galerie Montpensier - 42 96 06 56
Open 10:30am-7pm. Closed Sun. V, AE, DC, MC. M° Palais-Royal.

Didier Ludot's shop is located under the arcades of the Palais-Royal, which, in and of itself, is a good enough reason to come and see how he lovingly reconditions previously owned bags from Morabito and Hermès. He also carries a line of "surgical" bags used by doctors at the turn of the century and some superb 1920s-to-'30s suitcases lined with suede in box calf.

Mac Douglas

8th arr. - 155, rue du Fg-St-Honoré - 45 61 19 71
Open 10am-6:15pm. Closed Sun. V, AE, DC, MC. M° Saint-Philippe-du-Roule.

Are you a leather lover? If the answer is yes, then you'll want to head straight for Mac Douglas. You'll discover an infinite variety of well-cut clothes in glossy or dyed lambskin, goatskin, calfskin, suede, and shearling. There are snuggly jackets in crinkled sheepskin, luxurious calfskin coats, and dyed lambskin skirts. Prices are on the high side, but the designs are consistent in quality, conscientiously crafted, and available in lots of fashion colors. Good sales in January and July.

La Maroquinerie Parisienne

9th arr. - 30, rue Tronchet
47 42 83 40
Open 9:30am-7pm (Mon 1pm-7pm). Closed Sun. V, MC. M° Madeleine.

A huge trilevel shop filled with an enormous selection of leather goods, ranging from coin purses and suitcases (Delsey, Samsonite, Longchamp), to canvas bags and fine box-calf handbags. Belts, gloves, and umbrellas are also featured, and everything is sold at fifteen percent under regular retail. At sale time in mid-January to mid-February, prices are even lower.

Morabito

1st arr. - 1, pl. Vendôme
42 60 30 76
Open 9:45am-6:45pm. Closed Sun. V, AE, DC. M° Tuileries.

Choose between custom-made luggage and handbags in the skin you fancy (box calf, ostrich, etc.) and the color you prefer, or a sportier line of ready-made bags in textured calf (1,000 to 6,000 F). The made-to-measure bags are generally ready in two to three days, and prices start at about 6,000 F. Perfect service, of course, from this long-established firm reputed for quality. Custom-made leather-bound desk diaries are a recent addition to Morabito's elegant inventory.

Muriel

8th arr. - 4, rue des Saussaies
42 65 95 34
Open 10am-6:30pm. Closed Sun. V. M° Champs-Élysées-Clemenceau.

A wall lined with neatly organized drawers, a well-polished wooden counter: what a pleasure to buy gloves at this traditional *gantier*'s shop! For dress or sport, you'll find a wonderful selection of gloves for men and women, crafted in kid, ostrich, antelope, or lamb trimmed with mink or lined with silk (from 350 F). Pigskin gloves are available in an amazing range of nineteen colors (700 F).

Prada

6th arr. - 5, rue de Grenelle
45 48 53 14
Open 10:30am-7pm. Closed Sun. V, AE, MC. M° Sèvres-Babylone.

Versatile bags whose simple, classic shapes in

nylon or nylon and leather move effortlessly from office to opera house, are the strong suit of this renowned Italian firm. Prices, however, are very high.

Terre de Bruyère

17th arr - 112, bd de Courcelles - 42 27 86 87
Open 10:30am-7:30pm. Closed Sun. V. M° Ternes.

Canvas, leather, or both together are the materials of choice for a handsome range of handcrafted bags, backpacks, and attaché cases. They come in subdued, countrified shades of green, beige, and gray-black. Considering the workmanship, they are quite reasonably priced.

Louis Vuitton

8th arr. - 54, av. Montaigne
45 62 47 00
8th arr. - 78 bis, av. Marceau
47 20 47 00
Open 9:30am-6:30pm. Closed Sun. V, AE, DC, MC. M° Franklin-D.-Roosevelt, Charles-de-Gaulle-Étoile.

Vuitton lovers, here's a test. Put your bag down at the airline counter of an airport. Watch it disappear into a crowd of other Vuittons... now try and identify it! Yet for many, the monogrammed Vuitton bag is a cult object. It consists of printed linen coated with vinyl, reinforced with lozine ribs (which look like leather; Vuitton jealously guards the formula), with untreated leather for handles and straps, copper for rivets and hard corners. Don't like monograms? Then look to Vuitton's Tassili line: the yellow épi leather is winning many fans; and you may be taken with the Alma bag, designed in the '30s for Coco Chanel and recently reissued (1,950 F). And the computer carrying case in green épi leather (7,900 F) is the last word in executive chic.

MENSWEAR

Arnys

7th arr. - 14, rue de Sèvres
45 48 76 99
Open 10am-7:30pm. Closed Sun. V, AE, DC, MC. M° Sèvres-Babylone.

Always lots of window-shoppers in front of Arny's boutique, admiring the display of beautifully coordinated ready-to-wear. Inside, you'll find a huge selection of lush double-ply cashmere sweaters in some twenty different shades (3,200 F), an equally vast array of nubbly Irish tweed sport jackets, smart silk (1,200 F) or cotton (850 F) shirts, and a dizzying collection of limited-edition ties. Upstairs is the ultimate in luxury: the custom-tailoring department.

Pierre Balmain

8th arr. - 44, rue François-Ier
47 20 98 79
8th arr. - 25, rue du Fg-St-Honoré - 42 66 45 70
Open 10am-7pm (Sat 11am-7pm). Closed Sun. V, AE, MC. M°Franklin-D.-Roosevelt, Concorde.

Bernard Sanz, the new designer of Balmain's menswear, formerly exercised his considerable talents for Hermès and Saint Laurent. Neither staid nor extravagant, his style displays a dashing touch of color. His winter outerwear is inspired by the Tyrol, with loden capes and car coats; there are also chalk-striped suits with British flair, and elegant tuxedos with tapered pants. To give you an idea of the prices: shirts cost about 600 F, suits start at 4,500 F.

Berteil

8th arr. - 3, pl. Saint-Augustin
42 65 28 52
Open 10am-7pm (Mon 2pm-7pm). Closed Sun. V, AE, DC. M° Saint-Augustin.

Berteil clothes the upper-middle-class male in garments conceived for the active life: fishing, riding, hunting, and the rest. But the handsome tweed jackets, well-cut trousers, oiled-canvas coats, and nubbly sweaters are more often worn in restaurants, at the movies, to gallery openings, or for a stroll in the Luxembourg Gardens.

Hugo Boss

1st arr. - 2, place des Victoires - 40 28 91 64
Open 10am-7pm (Mon 11am-7pm). Closed Sun. V, AE, DC, MC. M° Palais-Royal.

Philippe Starck designed this monumental trilevel boutique, with an atmosphere reminiscent of an English tailor's shop (writ *very* large). Customers come here for the immense choice offered of every item of masculine clothing, from suits to socks. Clothes and accessories are stylish, colorful, and reasonably priced for the quality. We admired the good-looking leather parkas that start at 3,000 F.

Marcel Bur

8th arr. - 138, rue du Fg-St-Honoré - 43 59 45 68
Open 9:30am-12:30pm & 1:30pm-7pm (Mon 2pm-

7pm). Closed Sun. V, AE, DC, MC. M° St-Philippe-du-Roule.

Marcel Bur's suits are the stuff dreams are made of. Bur's Saxbury "miracle fabric," made of combed, carded, blended, 100 percent pure wool, is guaranteed uncreasable. We are pleased to note that Bur's formerly conservative colors have brightened up a bit. A custom two-piece suit runs upward of 10,000 F, but semicustom models go for about half that sum. On the main level you'll find lots of lush cashmere items, as well as the firm's attractive house cologne, Marcel Bur pour Homme.

Cifonelli

8th arr. - 31 & 33, rue Marbeuf - 43 59 39 13

Open 10am-7pm. Closed Sun. V, AE, DC. M° Franklin-D.-Roosevelt.

When Arturo Cifonelli opened for business in the '30s, he introduced a timeless, Anglo-Italian style that immediately captured a distinguished clientele. Cifonelli's son, Adriano, perfected his father's design. The shoulder, back, and sleeve fittings are all impeccably precise. So providing the 15,000 F tab suits your pocketbook, you, too, can have people ask for the address of your tailor. These are noble threads indeed. The ready-to-wear (sold at number 33) is no less classy, and not much less expensive.

Costardo

2nd arr. - 69, rue de Richelieu 49 27 03 79

Open 10am-7pm. Closed Sun. V, AE, MC. M° Bourse.

A man could easily assemble a complete, reasonably priced, and utterly fashionable wardrobe at Costardo. Suits (1,000 F) are offered in relaxed or fitted cuts, in a wide array of fabrics. Alterations are handled in-house, quickly, and at no extra charge. Shirts come in three sleeve lengths with a choice of two collar styles. For the quality, the prices here would be hard to beat.

Henry Cotton's

2nd arr. - 52, rue Étienne-Marcel - 42 36 01 22

Open 11am-7pm. Closed Sun. V, AE, DC, MC. M° Louvre.

An Italian take on American-style sportswear, sold in a typically trendy Parisian boutique. The clothes are well designed, but rather expensive (the look is not very different from, say, J. Crew). The rainwear in particular has a dash of Italian panache.

Christian Dior Boutique Monsieur

8th arr. - 11, rue François-Ier 40 73 54 44

Open 9:30am-6:30pm (Mon & Sat 10am-6:30pm). Closed Sun. V, AE, DC, MC. M° Franklin-D.-Roosevelt.

Patrick Lavoix, the artistic director of Christian Dior Monsieur, brings a fresh, personal style to what had become a rather staid house, mired in the fashion no man's land of "good taste." Lavoix's suits are admirable; their soft-shouldered silhouette is quite Continental—nipped in at the waist and narrow at the hips. Recent collections feature city suits of sheared combed wool, in subtle patterns that look almost like solids (from 5,200 F); and there's an over-sized velvet-collared topcoat with a 1950s feel. For casual wear, Lavoix favors tweeds, tweeded corduroy, and handsomely detailed shetland sweaters. Dior's new signature accessory is the vest: it comes in silk toile de Jouy for a dandified look, or in Fortuny-print crushed velvet for evening.

Façonnable

6th arr. - 174, bd Saint-Germain - 40 49 02 47

Open 10am-7pm (Mon 2pm-7pm). Closed Sun. V, AE, DC. M° Saint-Germain-des-Prés.

For work or for play (polo, cricket, golf...), these clothes create an elegant yet easy image. Typically French style distinguishes the casual wear: cable sweaters, rugby shirts, twill or canvas trousers show by their cut and color that they were not made in the U.S.A. The suits (about 4,000 F) are of fine quality, but there again, the cut is definitely "Continental." The accessories (socks, ties, underwear, etc.) are attractive, well made, and coordinated to within an inch of their lives!

Gianfranco Ferré

8th arr. - 44, av. George-V 49 52 02 74

Open 10am-7:30pm. Closed Sun. V, AE, DC, MC. M° George-V.

Though his major focus is the haute-couture line he designs for Dior, Gianfranco Ferré creates a line of men's clothing as well, characterized by a flawless cut, irreproachable collars, light and supple fabrics. Every detail is attentively crafted, as his elegant customers doubtless demand. If you are looking for something in a less stodgy vein, ask to see Ferré's embroidered leather jackets (15,000 F), just the thing to wear backstage at a rock concert.

Gruno et Chardin

2nd arr. - 8, rue du Mail
42 96 22 48
Open 10am-7pm. Closed Sun. V, AE, MC. M° Sentier.

In an inviting décor of warm wood, tall mirrors, and leather armchairs, this Belgian manufacturer displays a remarkable collection of highly desirable leather coats and jackets. All the finishing touches on the bikers' jackets, parkas (3,000 to 6,000 F), and warmly lined car coats are sewn by hand. Most models are in suede, buttery-soft lamb, or textured goatskin, in an enticing range of colors.

Givenchy Gentleman

8th arr. - 56, rue François-Ier
40 76 00 21
Open 10am-7pm. Closed Sun. V, AE, DC, MC. M° Franklin-D.-Roosevelt.

Blond wood and lots of light create an ambience conducive to browsing through Givenchy's refined, impeccably finished ready-to-wear for men. If your taste runs to classic, elegant clothes for office or casual occasions, you will appreciate the superb poplin shirts, the lean-lined suits (from 4,250 F), and the distinguished accessories (pigskin gloves, suspenders, wristwatches, eau de cologne), all in Givenchy's timeless, never trendy, signature style.

Eternal rest

Père-Lachaise is the largest—and "busiest"—cemetery in Paris. Currently its most notorious denizen is rock star Jim Morrison, but Abelard and Heloise, Molière, Chopin, Delacroix, Marcel Proust, Oscar Wilde, and Édith Piaf all repose here as well. The beautiful trees and grounds, the fascinating tombstones and monuments make Père-Lachaise an ideal spot for a meditative stroll.

Green Some

16th arr. - 40, rue Vital
45 04 69 63
Open 9:30am-12:30pm & 2pm-7pm (Mon from 10:30am). Closed Sun. V. M° La Muette.

Though the premises are small, this likeable shop offers a broad range of classic men's suits, in virtually wrinkle-free super 100 wool, at most attractive prices (under 3,000 F). Cotton shirts go for the single price of 320 F, and silk ties in a vast choice of patterns sell for 225 F. Lots of politicians and men-about-town shop here.

Island

2nd arr. - 4, rue Vide-Gousset
42 61 77 77
Open 10am-7pm. Closed Sun. V, AE, DC, MC. M° Bourse.

If you've been invited to a house party in Provence and need a few things to fill out your weekend wardrobe, head over to Island. You'll find the same sort of chic casual gear—from polo shirts, sweaters, soft trousers, and sporty parkas—that all the French guests will be wearing. Dockstep and Bass are the footwear brands of choice, but if you're smart, you'll have bought them in the U.S. for less than half the price charged here.

Lanvin Homme

8th arr. - 15, rue du Fg-St-Honoré - 44 71 31 33
Open 10am-6:45pm. Closed Sun. V, AE, DC, MC. M° Concorde.

The venerable Lanvin label has tailor-made itself a place at the forefront of the French menswear world. This shop, which appears on the registry of historic monuments, is a charming product of the Roaring Twenties, and was recently redecorated by Terence Conran. In addition to five floors filled with tempting merchandise, the shop houses Le Café Bleu (wonderful coffees and teas) and a gift shop featuring contemporary creations by Hilton McConnico and others. As for the clothing, every piece is worthy of the Lanvin label. Behind the array of suits, shirts, and accessories stands a small army of craftsmen who draw on 50 years of Lanvin experience. Dozens of hours of work are dedicated to the fabrication of each custom suit. Lanvin's ready-to-wear line is designed by Dominique Morlotti; his flannel suits with embroidered quilted-silk vests are things of beauty, and far less flashy than they sound.

Lapidus
8th arr. - 35, rue François-Ier
47 20 69 33
Open 10am-6:45pm. Closed Sun. V, AE, DC, MC. M° Franklin-D.-Roosevelt.

Classic men's clothing with a dash of French chic that makes them interesting—but never eccentric! The accessories are of fine quality, and sufficiently timeless so that you can be sure of wearing them season after season.

Marcel Lassance
6th arr. - 17, rue du Vieux-Colombier - 45 48 29 28
Open 10am-7pm. Closed Sun. V, AE, DC, MC. M° Saint-Sulpice.

For over a decade now the Left Bank's upper crust has been donning Monsieur Lassance's fashionable men's clothes. He will perhaps go down in social history as the man who helped transform President Mitterrand's sartorial habits. The attractive pants, jackets, suits, shirts, and sweaters are designed for intellectuals—real or pseudo—who like a comfortable, elegant look.

Pape
7th arr. - 4 av. Rapp
47 53 04 05
Open 10:30am-7:30pm (Mon 2pm-7:30pm). Closed Sun. V, AE, DC, MC. M° Alma-Marceau.

Pape is a traditional English haberdasher, ensconced in a two-level wood-paneled shop in the heart of Parisian preppy-land. In addition to the made-to-measure clothing, Pape proposes a handsome and unmistakably British selection of ready-to-wear: classic suits, nicely cut overcoats, and classic sweaters in lambswool or cashmere. Among the accessories, look for the wonderful (expensive!) socks.

Rykiel Homme
7th arr. - 194, bd Saint-Germain - 45 44 83 19
Open 10am-7pm. Closed Sun. V, AE, DC, MC. M° Saint-Germain-des-Prés.

Larger, airier premises now show Sonia Rykiel's menswear to greater advantage. The Rykiel man has a sporty attitude toward life: he prefers terry track suits, polo shirts, quilted vests, and smart microfiber parkas to traditional three-piece suits. In fact, Rykiel does design men's suits, but traditional they are not: they are crafted in touchable washed silk, and in linen for summer (about 5,000 F).

Yves Saint Laurent Rive Gauche
6th arr. - 12, pl. Saint-Sulpice
43 26 84 40
Open 10am-7pm. Closed Sun. V, AE, DC, MC. M° Saint-Sulpice.

Saint Laurent's signature style for men. Ready-to-wear suits start at 6,000 F, others made partly to measure sell for 10,000 F. You can add a touch of the inimitable Saint Laurent chic with a brightly colored suede vest (red, green, cobalt blue...) or a dashing silk tie in one of 400 exclusive designs.

Francesco Smalto
8th - 44, rue François-Ier
47 20 70 63
16th - 5, pl. Victor-Hugo
45 00 48 64
Open 10am-7pm. Closed Sun. V, AE, DC, MC. M° Franklin-D.-Roosevelt, Victor-Hugo.

Inventor of extravagant fabrics based on sable or orchids (that's right!), Francesco Smalto was trained at the renowned École Camps. He continues to uphold his title of master tailor, serving a clientele of celebrities and millionaires. Smalto's innovations include the world's lightest suit: made of super 100 wool, it weighs just over twenty ounces! Custom suits (with the signature Smalto nipped-in waist) command 25,000 F and more. But take heart: Smalto also manufactures less cripplingly expensive ready-to-wear (suits from 5,500 F), and the new Ambassadeur line for younger, less wealthy customers.

Paul Smith
7th arr. - 22, bd Raspail
42 84 15 30
Open 10am-7pm (Mon 11am-7pm). Closed Sun. V, AE, DC, MC. M° Rue du Bac.

English designer Paul Smith made his début in Paris with three lines of menswear: chic and classic (suits from 4,000 to 6,000 F), smart and casual, and a young, funky collection based on jeans. The huge and attractive shop also offers all the paraphernalia a man could want, from shoes and socks to cuff links and toothbrushes.

Olivier Strelli
7th arr. - 7, bd Raspail
45 44 77 17
Open 11am-7pm (Mon 2pm-7pm). Closed Sun. V, AE, MC. M° Rue du Bac.

Strelli likes to give a man a choice: each suit he designs is offered in no fewer than 25 nuances between beige and dark brown! Strelli's style is relaxed, his jackets (3,000 F) are supple and unstructured.

Torregiani
8th arr. - 38, rue François-Ier
47 23 76 17
Open 10am-7pm. Closed Sun. V, AE, DC. M° Franklin-D.-Roosevelt.

Torregiani is an authorized dealer for Brioni suits, but you will also find a wide array of other beautiful, hand-sewn suits in the finest wool (priced from 9,500 to 12,000 F). Brioni ties are somewhat less expensive, though no less exclusive; also in stock are men's shirts in luxurious printed silk.

Victoire Homme
1st arr. - 10-12, rue du Colonel-Driant
42 97 44 87
Open 10am-7pm. Closed Sun. V, AE, DC, MC. M° Palais-Royal.

Fussy about your shirts? Then take a look at the exclusive Hartford line available here: there are fifteen different shades of blue! They can be coordinated with any of a number of hip designer trousers and jackets for a smart, sporty look that is quintessentially Parisian.

Ermenegildo Zegna
2nd arr. - 10, rue de la Paix
42 61 67 61
Open 10am-7pm (Mon 11am-7pm). Closed Sun. V, AE, DC, MC. M° Opéra.

Renowned the world over, Ermenegildo Zegna is one of the giants of Italian fashion. He invented the pure-wool, no-wrinkle "high-performance" fabric that he uses so skillfully in his custom or ready-to-wear suits, priced from 5,600 to 8,750 F (custom suits start at 8,000 and soar to 12,000 F). Zegna's progressive approach to classic clothes embraces lively touches of color and an extended range of accessories. A sophisticated and charming welcome awaits you in this must-browse shop, a favorite with Parisian fashion plates.

ACCESSORIES

BELTS

Losco
4th arr. - 20, rue de Sévigné
48 04 39 93
Open 11am-1pm & 1:30pm-7pm. Closed Sun, Mon. V, AE, MC. M° Saint-Paul.

The specialist for belts. Leather, lizard, colored, braided—you name it, all the styles are right here. Pick your belt and your buckle, or choose one of the ready-made models. Attractive prices.

HATS

Motsch pour Hermès
8th arr. - 42, av. George-V
47 23 79 22
Open 10am-6:30pm (Sat & Mon 10am-1pm & 2:15pm-6:30pm). Closed Sun. V, AE, DC, MC. M° George-V.

Mad about hats? Motsch has been making and repairing top-notch toppers for over a century. Now part of the Hermès empire, the firm still turns out the smartest panamas, Borsalinos, fedoras, and derbies, handcrafted according to traditional methods. All hats are custom-blocked for a perfect fit.

Anthony Peto
1st arr. - 12, rue Jean-Jacques-Rousseau - 42 21 47 15
Open 11am-7pm. Closed Sun. V, AE, DC, MC. M° Louvre.

Husband of hat-designer Marie Mercié, Anthony Peto creates chic chapeaux for men (650 to 1,100 F), which he presents in this shop along with models imported from all over the world (England, Australia, Russia, Mexico...). From French bérets to handsome top hats, you'll find an unparalleled selection of headgear here. There are lots of dashing accessories too: canes, ties, tie pins, and cuff links to complete an elegant masculine look.

SHIRTS

Equipment
2nd arr. - 46, rue Étienne-Marcel - 40 26 17 84
Open 10:30am-7pm (Mon 11am-7pm). Closed Sun. V, AE, DC, MC. M° Louvre.

Basic white poplin shirts with *trompe-l'œil* buttons, China-blue embroidered shirts, denims with folksy scenes stitched on, ruffled-front specials, and so forth—Equipment sets the classics on their ear! Equipment shirts are always exotic and comfortable. Prices for poplin: under 700 F; silk shirts sell for around 1,000 F. Sunny décor, and accommodating service.

Hilditch & Key

1st arr. - 252, rue de Rivoli
42 60 36 09
Open 9:30am-6:30pm (Sat 9:30am-6pm). Closed Sun. V, AE, DC, MC. M° Concorde.

Hilditch & Key shirtmakers, established nearly a century ago, is the last bastion of menswear shops in which refinement borders on the sublime. British poplins, fine cottons from France, and heavy Japanese silk are among the 500 select fabrics to choose from. Cuffs and collars are made to measure, with extraordinary accuracy (from 1,850 F). Ready-to-wear shirts are also available. And it's impossible not to mention the celebrated Hilditch & Key sweaters: gorgeous double-ply cashmere V-necks come in 30 colors and cost 2,450 F. There are also divine silk dressing gowns and handmade silk ties.

Sulka

1st arr. - 2, rue de Castiglione
42 60 38 08
Open 9:30am-6:30pm (Mon & Sat 10am-6:30pm). Closed Sun. V, AE, DC, MC. M° Tuileries.

Sulka is a paragon of refinement. The shop's discriminating clientele arrives from far-flung nations and provinces for made-to-measure shirts in poplin, silk, flannel, or wool. First-time orders of custom shirts must be for six or more (at 2,400 F each). Before filling the order, a pilot shirt is made, which you take home, wear, wash, then bring back for inspection. If that seems like too much trouble, you can purchase Sulka's fine ready-to-wear shirts instead (1,200 F). Also available are double-ply cashmere sweaters, five-ply cashmere jackets, polo shirts, ties, umbrellas, socks... And Sulka recently opened a new custom-tailoring department (suits from 18,000 F).

SHOES

Carvil

8th arr. - 67, rue Pierre Charron - 42 25 54 38
Open 10am-1pm & 2pm-7pm (Mon 2pm-7pm). Closed Sun. V, AE, DC, MC. M° Franklin-D.-Roosevelt.
8th arr. - 4, rue Tronchet
42 88 20 97
Open 10am-7pm (Mon 11am-7pm). Closed Sun. V, AE, DC, MC. M° Madeleine.

The only place a Carvil shoe pinches is the pocketbook. This footwear is known as the playboys' favorite, and it's a good thing that most playboys have large bankrolls. But you do get what you pay for: excellent quality and high style, whether yours is conservative or eccentric.

Church's

2nd arr. - 42, rue Vivienne
42 36 22 92
Open 10am-2pm & 3pm-6:30pm. Closed Sat, Sun. V, AE, DC, MC. M° Bourse.
8th arr. - 23, rue des Mathurins - 42 65 25 85
Open 10am-6:15pm. Closed Sun. V, AE, DC, MC. M° Havre-Caumartin.

Church's shoes are reputed to be indestructible. But that's not why they're perennial favorites with French and Italian dandies. No, what they like is the ineffable English chic of the Grafton wingtip and the buckled Westbury model. They shoes don't come cheap (you may want to wait for the semi-annual sales), but Church's shoes may be relied upon to last forever.

Michel Delauney

1st arr. - 6, rue de l'Oratoire
42 60 20 85
Open 10am-12:30pm & 2pm-6:30pm. Closed Sun, Mon. V, AE, DC, MC. M° Louvre.

Delauney's are elegant, marvelously comfortable, solidly built shoes. Models ranging from loafers to riding boots can be purchased ready-to-wear (from 1,850 F) or custom-made in your choice of leather (2,200 F and up). Or Michel Delauney can design an exclusive model for you alone: that will cost from 7,500 F, and require two months of work. Sale periods in January and June are understandably popular.

Fenestrier

6th arr. - 23, rue du Cherche-Midi - 42 22 66 02
Open 10am-1pm & 2pm-7pm (Sat 10am-7pm). Closed Sun. V, AE, MC. M° Sèvres-Babylone.

Sturdy, classic, good-looking: Fenestrier's leather shoes are all Goodyear welted; there are canvas and nubuck styles too, in a jolly array of colors. And the ankle boots are of top quality, comparable to the better-known Weston brand. Prices? From 1,380 to 3,850 F.

John Lobb

8th arr. - 51, rue François-Ier
45 61 02 55
Open 10am-7pm. Closed Sun. V, AE, DC, MC. M° George-V.

Sublimely comfortable, perfectly proportioned shoes finished to fit the most demanding feet. Such are the masterpieces John Lobb cobbles together for his privileged customers (who include England's royal family, don't you know). There are hand-decorated, custom-made house slippers (1,200 F), as well as classic lace-up oxfords, crafted according to traditional methods. Prices for custom shoes start at 14,000 F per pair and require a six-month wait. The ready-to-wear line includes loafers and low boots as well as classic wingtips (from 2,200 F).

Fratelli Rossetti

8th arr. - 54, rue du Fg-St-Honoré - 42 65 26 60
Open 10am-6:50pm. Closed Sun. M° Concorde.

In the beginning were casual shoes... The Rossetti family then launched into the loafer and dress shoe markets. Success followed their every step. Nowadays Fratelli Rossetti's men's lines feature a host of smart designs, including white or two-tone Derbys in textured pigskin, rough-cut boat shoe-style loafers, and riding boots in kangaroo, zebu, or calfskin. All these models are uncommonly light on the foot, the summum of understated elegance (for about 1,500 F).

Weston

1st arr. - 3, bd de la Madeleine - 42 61 11 87
6th arr. - 49, rue de Rennes
45 49 38 50
16th arr. - 97, av. Victor-Hugo - 47 04 23 75
17th arr. - 98, rue de Courcelles - 47 63 18 13
Open 10am-7pm. Closed Sun. V, AE, MC. M° Madeleine, Saint-Germain-des-Prés, Victor-Hugo, Courcelles.
8th arr. - 114, av. des Champs-Élysées - 45 62 26 47
Open 9:30am-7pm. Closed Sun. V, AE, MC. M° George-V.

Westons are expensive, handsome, and superbly finished shoes; as their name does not imply, they are designed and manufactured in France. Styles are on the conservative side, but the shoes do last for a long, long time. All models come in a choice of three widths; prices start at around 1,500 F.

UNDERWEAR

Amatchi

4th arr. - 13, rue du Roi-de-Sicile - 40 29 97 14
Open 11:30am-7:30pm (Sun 2:30pm-7:30pm). Closed Tue. V, AE, MC. M° St-Paul.

Not for women only! Amatchi features nifty underwear for men by Nikos, Calvin Klein, Dolce & Gabbana, and l'Homme Invisible in lots of seductive styles.

We're always happy to hear about your discoveries and receive your comments on ours. We want to give your letters the attention they deserve, so when you write to Gault Millau, please state clearly what you liked or disliked. Be concise but convincing, and take the time to argue your point.

VESTS

L'Escalier d'Argent

1st arr. - 42, galerie Montpensier, jardin du Palais-Royal - 40 20 05 33
Open 1pm-7pm (Sat 2:30pm-7pm). Closed Sun, Mon. V, AE, DC, MC. M° Palais-Royal.

Ravishing handmade vests in shimmering hues, decorated with garden-inspired motifs (from 1,000 F). You'll be looking for excuses to remove your jacket when you wear one of these dashing creations. So why not just slip it on over a shirt?

OPEN LATE

BOOKSTORES

La Hune

6th arr. - 170, bd Saint-Germain
45 48 35 85, fax 45 44 49 87
Open 10am-11:45pm. Closed Sun. V, AE, MC. M° Saint-Germain-des-Prés.

If you get an urge to reread some Breton or Baudelaire late at night, head over here. Beautiful art books, too.

Shakespeare & Company

5th arr. - 37, rue de la Bûcherie - 43 26 96 50
Open daily noon-midnight. No cards. M° Saint-Michel.

Not to be confused with the legendary Shakespeare and Company of Sylvia Beach (though owner George Whitman claims that he is carrying on her tradition). Shelves are filled to the bursting point in this modern Prospero's cell, with books new and old covering every subject imaginable.

DRUGSTORES

Be it premium bubbly or Alka-Seltzer, a little night music or earplugs for a noiseless morning after... the Drugstores of Paris have got it all—at all hours!

Newsstands

For all you newshounds, kiosks are open 24 hours a day at the following addresses: 33 & 52, av. des Champs-Élysées, 8th arr. - 45 61 48 01; 16, bd de la Madeleine, 8th arr. - 42 65 29 19; 2, bd Montmartre, 9th; Place Charles-de-Gaulle, av. de Wagram, 17th; 16, bd de Clichy, 18th arr.; as well as in train stations and Drugstores until 2 am.

Drugstore Publicis

6th arr. - Drugstore Saint-Germain, 149, bd Saint-Germain - 42 22 92 50
Open daily 10am-2am. V, AE, DC. M° Saint-Germain-des-Prés.
8th arr. - Drugstore Champs-Élysées - 133, av. des Champs-Élysées - 44 43 79 00
8th arr. - Drugstore Matignon, 1, av. Matigon
43 59 38 70
Open daily 9am-2am. V, AE, DC. M° Charles-de-Gaulle-Étoile, Franklin-D.- Roosevelt.

Multistore Opéra

9th arr. - 6, bd des Capucines
42 65 83 52
Open daily 10am-11pm (Sat & Sun 10am-midnight). V. M° Opéra.

FLOWERS

Élyfleurs

17th arr. - 82, av. de Wagram
47 66 87 19, fax 42 27 29 13
Open daily 24 hours. V. M° Wagram.

See *Flowers* section, page 239.

FOOD & DRINK

L'Alsace

8th arr. - 39, av. des Champs-Élysées - 43 59 44 24, fax 42 89 06 62
Open daily 24 hours. V, AE, DC, MC. M° Franklin-D.-Roosevelt.

Beyond the main restaurant is a catering service-cum-boutique where you can purchase essentially Alsatian specialties—sauerkraut, charcuteries, foie gras, etc. There is a carry-out service should you be tempted to take home a dish for a midnight snack.

A l'An 2000

17th arr. - 82, bd des Batignolles - 43 87 24 67
Open daily 5pm-midnight (Sun 11am-midnight). V, AE. M° Rome.

After an evening at the Théâtre des Arts-Hébertot, you can put together a nice post-theater supper with provisions from L'An 2000. All sorts of appetizing dishes are on display at this spacious emporium. From caviar to charcuterie, from bread and fresh-vegetable terrines to wine, cheese, and fresh fruit, you'll find all the makings of a charming midnight feast. Free delivery in Paris for orders over 300 F.

Flo Prestige

1st arr. - 42, pl. du Marché-St-Honoré - 42 61 45 46
Open daily 8am-11pm. Delivery. V, AE, DC. M° Pyramides.
See the other branches in Food *section page 244.*

Flo boutiques are cropping up all over town. They are perfect places for late-night food shopping. Temptations include foie gras from Strasbourg, Norwegian smoked salmon, beautiful cheeses, and irresistible pastries, plus Champagne or a lusty country wine to wash it all down.

Les Frères Layrac

6th arr. - 29, rue de Buci
43 25 17 72
Open daily 9:30am-2am. V, AE, DC. M° Mabillon.

There is a wide selection of prepared dishes, but the pride of Les Frères Layrac is its seafood platter (just under 400 F for two). Free delivery.

Nocto

8th arr. - 23, bd des Batignolles - 43 87 64 79
Open daily 11am-midnight (Sun 4pm-11pm). V. M° Clichy.

A pleasant little supermarket for late-night shopping. The merchandise is of distinctly higher quality than most such establishments offer. Good choice of prepared salads; a take-home meal-on-a-tray costs about 60 F.

PHARMACIES

Grande Pharmacie Daumesnil

12th arr. - 6, pl. Félix-Eboué
43 43 19 03, fax 46 28 82 22
Open daily 24 hours. M° Daumesnil.

Grande Pharmacie de la Place

9th arr. - 5, pl. Pigalle
48 78 38 12
Open daily 9am-1am (Sun 3pm-1am). M° Pigalle.

Pharmacie Les Champs

8th arr. - 84, av. des Champs-Élysées - 45 62 02 41
Open daily 24 hours. M° George-V.

Note the convenient, *all-day-all-night* hours of this drugstore.

24-HOUR POST OFFICE

Poste du Louvre

1st arr. - 52, rue du Louvre
40 28 20 00
Open daily 24 hours. M° Louvre.

The central post office is open 24 hours a day. Long-distance telephone calls can be made from the first floor, ordinary postal transactions on the ground floor.

RECORD STORES

Champs-Disques

8th arr. - 84, av. des Champs-Élysées - 45 62 65 46
Open daily 10am-midnight (Sun noon-8pm). V. M° George-V.

Let there be music! Here in this shop on the world's most beautiful avenue is a broad selection of popular and classical recordings.

Virgin Mégastore

8th arr. - 56, av. des Champs-Élysées - 40 74 06 48
Open daily 10am-midnight (Fri & Sat 10am-1am). V. M° Franklin-D.-Roosevelt.

Jazz, classical, pop, and rock, on records, CDs, and cassettes—but that's not all: there are books (on the lower level) too, video and audio gear, computer equipment, and a terrific restaurant/bar upstairs where a piano player holds forth at night (a great place to people-watch).

SPORTING GOODS

CLOTHING & EQUIPMENT (GENERAL)

L'Aigle

6th arr. - 141, bd Saint-Germain - 46 33 26 23
Open 10am-7pm. Closed Sun, Mon. V, AE, MC. M° Saint-Germain-des-Prés.

Kit yourself out with all the necessary gear for fishing, riding, boating, and hiking at L'Aigle. Great boots (the black rubber riding boots are the last word in cheap country chic) and basic sportswear for real outdoors types—and for those of us who just like the rugged look.

Chattanooga

7th arr. - 53, av. Bosquet
45 51 76 65, fax 47 53 01 50
Open 10:30am-1:30pm & 2:30pm-7:30pm (Sat 10:30am-7:30pm). Closed Sun. V, DC, MC. M° École-Militaire.

Skateboards, roller skates, surfboards, bodyboards, frisbees, kites, and boomerangs: every bit of equipment that today's speed-crazy kids covet can be found here, alongside all the trendy togs that go with (athletic shoes—wait till you see the prices!—tank tops, bicycling shorts, and the rest). Some good-quality second-hand equipment is available as well.

Go Sport

1st arr. - Porte Pierre-Lescot, Forum des Halles, level -3, 45 08 02 77
Open 10:30am-7:30pm (Sat 10am-7:30pm). Closed Sun. V, AE, DC, MC. M° Châtelet.
12th arr. - 110, bd Diderot
43 47 31 17
13th arr. - 30, av. d'Italie
45 80 30 05
15th arr. - 16, rue Linois, Centre Beaugrenelle
45 75 70 82
Open 10am-7:30pm. Closed Sun. V, AE, DC, MC. M° Reuilly-Diderot, Place-d'Italie, Charles-Michels.
14th arr. - 68, av. du Maine
43 27 50 50
Open 10am-7:30pm. Closed Sun. V, AE, MC. M° Gaîté.

Cinema without Borders

Want to see a forgotten or rare movie from New York, New Delhi, or New South Wales? Join the film buffs who haunt a host of tiny art cinemas in the area bounded by the Quai Saint-Michel, Boulevard Saint-Michel, Rue Saint-Jacques, and Rue Soufflot. These theaters often feature avant-garde and foreign flicks in their original languages. Action Christine in the Rue Christine is devoted mainly to Hollywood classics. The projectionist takes special pride in his work, and you can ask when buying your tickets whether the copy is of good quality. Also worth a visit: Cinoche in the Rue de Condé, Saint André des Arts, in the street of the same name, and Les 3 Luxembourg, Rue Monsieur-le-Prince.

16th arr. - 12, av. Porte de Saint-Cloud - 40 71 95 19
Open 10:30am-7:30pm. Closed Sun. V, AE, DC, MC. M° Porte-de-Saint-Cloud.
17th arr. - 2, pl. de la Porte-Maillot - 40 68 22 46
Open 10:15am-7:15pm. Closed Sun. V, AE, DC, MC. M° Porte-Maillot.

The stores in this fast-growing international chain vary drastically in size and style from one to another, but all conduct business according to the same successful formula: friendly help, professional advice, and quality equipment. Some of the stores specialize in equestrian equipage (the Les Halles and Montparnasse branches). Tennis and fitness gear are featured at every branch.

K-Way

1st arr. - 3, av. de l'Opéra
42 60 88 20, fax 49 27 04 07
Open 10am-7pm. Closed Sun. V, AE, DC, MC. M° Pyramides.

K-Way waterproof parkas and anoraks are lightweight, colorful, and attractively fashioned, but best of all, they fold up into tiny packages that can be stowed away with ease. The entire family can be fitted out here from head to toe with foul-weather gear or ski togs.

Lacoste

1st arr. - 372, rue Saint-Honoré
(also: 2nd arr., 6th arr., 8th arr., 15th arr., 16th arr., 17th arr.)
42 61 55 56, fax 42 61 61 39
Open 10am-7pm. Closed Sun. V, AE, DC, MC. M° Concorde.

There's lots more here besides the famous polo shirts (which come in a dizzying array of 60 colors). The Lacoste flagship store also carries well-made clothing for all sorts of sports, as well as a full line of excellent tennis equipment.

Au Petit Matelot

16th arr. - 27, av. de la Grande-Armée - 45 00 15 51
Open 10am-7pm (Mon 2pm-7pm). Closed Sun. V, MC. M° Argentine.

Now over 200 years old, Au Petit Matelot is aging quite gracefully. This purveyor of traditional Breton fisherman's shirts (you know, with the blue and white stripes) carries top-of-the-line foul-weather gear, snug pea coats, and rugged oiled-canvas outerwear. Both ladies and gentlemen are outfitted here for the hunt, the saddle, or the tiller. Be advised that only sporting *clothes* are found at the Petit Matelot—you'll need to go elsewhere for your equipment.

■ DANCE

Flashdance

8th arr. - 17, rue de la Pépinière - 42 93 05 71
Open 10am-7pm. Closed Sun. V, MC. M° St-Lazare.

Flashy, stretchy gear for dancing and exercising (brands include Vicard leotards and Freddy tights and slippers), as well as beautiful swimwear by Livia. A friendly, professional staff helps clients choose the most flattering fit.

Repetto

2nd arr. - 22, rue de la Paix
44 71 83 00
Open 10am-7pm. Closed Sun. V, AE, DC, MC. M° Opéra.

Repetto has served the dance community since 1947, providing baby ballerinas and professional primas with dainty practice slippers, toe shoes, and tutus. Jazz dancers will find the soft footwear they need, and the leotards, tights, and warm-up gear (available in a rainbow of colors) are just as suitable for exercise class as for a session at the *barre*. High prices.

FISHING

Au Martin-Pêcheur

1st arr. - 28, quai du Louvre
42 36 25 63, fax 42 36 50 25
Open 9:30am-7pm. Closed Sun, Mon. V, AE, DC, MC. M° Pont-Neuf.

This respected establishment has changed little over the years—it is still one of the most picturesque shops in Paris. In addition to a full array of deep-sea and fly-fishing equipment, there's a section for diving accessories, including underwater-photography gear by Ikelite.

Motillon

15th arr. - 83 bis, rue de l'Abbé-Groult - 48 28 58 94
Open 9am-7pm (Mon 10:30am-7pm). Closed Sun. V, AE, DC, MC. M° Convention.

Professional advice is lavished on customers at this venerable institution, which sells the necessities, the accessories, and the luxuries for every sort of fishing. What's more, any item can be mail-ordered from the wonderful catalog.

GOLF

Le Comptoir du Golf

17th arr. - 22, av. de la Grande-Armée
43 80 15 00, fax 47 63 89 91
Open 9:30am-7pm (Mon 2pm-7pm). Closed Sun. V, AE, MC. M° Argentine.

A very British sort of place, right down to the coolly reserved reception. Shoes, clubs, and carts abound; there is a house line of golf togs in addition to clothing by well-known makers.

Golf-Plus

17th arr. - 212, bd Pereire
45 74 08 17, fax 45 74 78 24
Open 10am-7pm (Mon 2pm-7pm; Thu 10am-8pm). Closed Sun. V. M° Porte-Maillot.

Owner Laurence Schmidlin, a former French golf champion, offers friendly assistance to his customers. Good-quality clothes and equipment are sold at competitive prices, and if you find the same item elsewhere for less, you can come back and receive a store credit, plus ten percent. Mighty sporting of him, we say! Dependable service and advice; equipment rental.

HUNTING & SHOOTING

Alex

8th arr. - 63, bd de Courcelles - 42 27 66 39
Open 9am-7pm. Closed Sun, Mon (exc during hunting season: 4pm-6pm). V, MC. M° Courcelles.

Alex features the finest brands of rifles, as well as good selections of sights and binoculars, hunting knives, and cartridges. As for hunting-related clothing, you won't find a collection like this anywhere else: the storm coats are especially good-looking and practical. There is also an interesting hunting-themed gift department, which includes clever little knives in the form of ducks and cuckoos.

Gastinne Renette

8th arr. - 39, av. Franklin-Roosevelt - 43 59 77 74
Open 10am-7pm. Closed Sun, Mon. V, AE, DC, MC. M° Franklin-D.-Roosevelt.

Gastinne Renette markets its own renowned make of rifles. The prices these firearms command is not of the giveaway variety: they start at 20,000 F. But there are also used guns at attractive prices. An added feature is the shooting range in the shop's basement, where customers can test the merchandise. Extremely diversified, Gastinne Renette carries books, archery equipment, and even security systems, as well as a first-rate selection of clothes for hunting and riding—just look at the gorgeous leather jodhpurs and the beautifully crafted bags!

Saillard

1st arr. - 8, rue de Richelieu
42 96 07 78, fax 42 86 87 71
Open 9:30am-7pm. Closed Sun, Mon. V, AE, DC, MC. M° Palais-Royal.

A specialist in firearms since 1815, Saillard just bought out the even more venerable firm of Fauré Le Page. The magnificently restored shop displays high-precision, hand-decorated rifles, as well as handcrafted knives, carbines for target shooting and competition, sights, and other such accessories. Every item of equipment for riding to hounds is on hand (the saddles are extraordinary), and there is an admirable array of superbly elegant outdoor clothing.

Tir 1000

13th arr. - 90, rue Jeanne-d'Arc - 45 83 34 41
Open 10am-7pm (Sat 10am-6:30pm). Closed Sun. V. M° Nationale.

Tir 1000 stocks a broad selection of revolvers, knives, sights, and offers repair services too. Meanwhile, on the basement level, there's a shooting range for handguns, which is open to members (2,000 F for an annual membership); beginners can sign up for lessons in target shooting.

■ RIDING

Duprey

17th arr. - 5, rue Troyon
43 80 29 37
Open 9:30am-12:30pm & 1:30pm-6:30pm. Closed Sun. V. M° Charles-de-Gaulle-Étoile.

Hidden away on a little street near the Arc de Triomphe since 1902, this reputable shop is a family affair upheld by three generations. Duprey riding equipment is preferred in the classiest horsey circles. The excellent and comfortable saddles, virtually custom-made, display superb workmanship (from 9,000 F). Stirrups, bridles, girths are on hand as well; there is no apparel for the rider, but everything in leather for your mount.

Hermès

8th arr. - 24, rue du Fg-St-Honoré - 40 17 47 17
8th arr. - 42, av. George-V
47 20 48 51
Open 10am-6:30pm (Sat & Mon 10am-1pm & 2:15pm-6:30pm). Closed Sun. V, AE, DC, MC. M° Concorde, George-V.

Luxurious equipment for horse and rider. Hermès turns out roughly 60 saddles a month, all handmade in the firm's workshops to the customer's specifications, in a wide choice of fine leathers. Hermès riding boots are sublime. Should you wish to organize your own racing team, Hermès can kit out your jockeys with their famous colored silks.

Padd

15th arr. - 14, rue de la Cavalerie - 43 06 56 50
Open 10am-7pm (Mon 10am-6pm). Closed Sun. V, AE, MC. M° Cambronne.

Saddle up! Here's an excellent address for every kind of saddle at every sort of price. They come from all over: Spain, England, the United States. The clothing department is well stocked with hacking jackets, helmets, boots, crops, and jodhpurs. The store may not be chic (go to Duprey for that), but the inventory is extensive.

■ SKIING

La Haute Route

4th arr. - 33, bd Henri-IV
42 72 38 43
Open 9:30am-1pm & 2pm-7pm (Mon 2pm-7pm). Closed Sun. V, MC. M° Bastille.

You can rent everything here but the mountain: complete ski equipment in the winter, rock-climbing gear in the summer. Camping equipment is also available for rent at utterly reasonable prices.

Passe Montagne

11th arr. - 39, rue du Chemin-Vert
43 57 08 47, fax 43 22 24 24
Open 11am-7pm (Sat 10am-7pm; Tue 11am-9pm). Closed Sun, Mon. V. M° Saint-Ambroise.
14th arr. - 102, av. Denfert-Rochereau - 43 22 24 24
Open 11am-7pm (Sat 10am-7pm; Wed 11am-8pm). Closed Sun, Mon. V. M° Denfert-Rochereau.

Passe-Montagne can outfit you with all the gear you need for virtually any mountain sport, be it climbing, hiking, alpine or cross-country skiing. Both stores are open Wednesday until 9pm. Equipment rental is available at the Chemin-Vert store only.

Au Vieux Campeur

5th arr. - 48, rue des Écoles
43 29 12 32
Open 10:30am-7:30pm. Closed Sun. V. M° Cardinal-Lemoine.

Housed in sixteen shops all clustered around the main address, the Vieux Campeur is definitely the place to go for all manner of sporting equipment. The latest innovations and variations on a theme arrive here first. Climbing and mountaineering remain the specialty of the house (a climbing wall lets you try out shoes—and your technique!—before you confront the real thing). But the Vieux's reputation for quality extends to the entire stock, from running shoes to tennis racquets, all sold with professional advice. We suggest that you avoid shopping here on a Saturday, as the crowds are horrendous.

Don't plan to shop on Sundays—the vast majority of Paris stores are closed.

WIND-SURFING

Mistral

16th arr. - 24, rue Mirabeau
45 24 38 55, fax 40 50 15 44
Open 10am-1pm & 2:15pm-7pm. Closed Sun, Mon. V. M° Mirabeau.

This windsurfing shop reflects the polish of its tony neighborhood: the boards are the finest made, the swimsuits are *très chic*, and the staff consists primarily of handsome beach boys. A number of designs are available but only one level of quality—the best. These are serious boards for the committed windsurfer.

Surf and Shop

13th arr. - 105, rue Bobillot
45 81 52 63, fax 45 81 53 56
Open 10am-1pm & 2pm-7pm. Closed Sun, Mon. V, MC. M° Place-d'Italie.

A well-stocked source for boards and accessories: wet suits, helmets, sails, and more. The top brands in all this equipment are available, and the staff offers sound advice to guide your choice. Repairs are also handled here.

TOBACCONISTS

CIGARS & TOBACCO

NO BARGAINS HERE

In Paris, you will note, cigars cost an arm and a leg. Why? The state considers them a "drug" and taxes heavily. But take heart: at the shops we have listed in this section you are sure to find a fresh, high-quality cigar and not, as too often happens, a once-choice cheroot that has turned into a roll of stale, bitter-tasting compost.

Boutique 22

16th arr. - 22, av. Victor-Hugo
45 01 81 41, fax 45 01 75 20
Open 10am-7pm (Mon 2pm-7pm). Closed Sun. V, AE, DC. M° Charles-de-Gaulle-Étoile.

A mecca for cigar lovers. Here you'll find not only Davidoff's "1000" but every other brand of Havana cigar imported in France, including slim Joyitas and thick Hoyo des Dios and Carousoas. Boutique 22 is big on lesser-knowns as well and has the exclusive distributorship for the Compagnie des Caraïbes. Discover such Caribbean delights as sweet and aromatic Cerdeaus, robust Juan Clementes, and claro claro/50 Don Miguels, from Cabo Verde. Also featured are humidors and vaults (including some refurbished antique models). For the haute-couture crowd, custom vaults can be made to measure and monogrammed on request (they come equipped with a patented climate-control system that keeps cigars fresh for a month). Accessories? Of course: deluxe lighters and fountain pens (Dupont, Cartier, Dunhill, Mont-Blanc), plus crystal wares by Lalique, Daum, and Baccarat.

La Cave à Cigares

10th arr. - 4, bd de Denain
42 81 05 51
Open 8am-7pm. Closed Sat, Sun. V. M° Gare-du-Nord.

Owner Gérard Courtial is the inventor of the much-imitated vertical humidifier/display case. Although he is by profession a member of the *confrérie des maîtres pipiers* (brotherhood of master pipemakers), he is nevertheless a cigar connoisseur and an excellent source of information and advice. Do not miss his collection of pipes, including such brands as Chacom, Dunhill, and Butz-Choquin. Also, a wide range of smokers' accessories, for experts and novices.

A la Civette

1st arr. - 157, rue Saint-Honoré
42 96 04 99, fax 42 60 44 78
Open 8:30am-7pm (Sat 9:30am-6:30pm). Closed Sun. V, AE. M° Palais-Royal.

Habitués refer to this venerable establishment as the Civette du Palais-Royal. Founded in 1716, it was the first tobacconist in Paris, for many years *the* place of pilgrimage for cigar and tobacco lovers. Casanova even mentions it in his memoirs. Tobacco goods featured run the gamut from everyday chewing weed to the very best Havanas, including the Hoyo de Monterrey, imported directly from Cuba. La Civette boasts an inventory of 20,000 cigars stored in a climate-controlled vault. Also available is a wide range of accessories: deluxe lighters and pipes (Chacom, Butz-Choquin, Dunhill), humidors in all shapes and sizes, pens, and leather goods.

Some establishments change their closing times without warning. It is always wise to check in advance.

Drugstore Publicis

6th arr. - 149, bd Saint-Germain - 42 22 92 50
Open daily 10am-2am. V, AE, DC. M° St-Germain-des-Prés.
8th arr. - 133, av. des Champs-Élysées - 44 43 79 00
8th arr. - 1, av. Matignon
43 59 38 70
Open daily 9am-2am. V, AE, DC. M° Charles-de-Gaulle-Étoile, Franklin-D.-Roosevelt.

A large selection of good-quality humidified cigars is available at each of the three Drugstore Publicis shops year-round and late into the night.

Lemaire

16th arr. - 59, av. Victor-Hugo
45 00 75 63, fax 45 01 70 65
Open 8:30am-7:45pm (Sat 9am-7:45pm). Closed Sun. V, AE, DC. M° Victor-Hugo.

Bernard Lecrocq presides over one of France's most prestigious tobacconists. Here you will find the cigar of your dreams perfectly preserved and presented with rare flair. Havanas and San Domingos—Zinos, Don Miguels, and Juan Clementes—top the list. Lecrocq's astonishing vaults accommodate thousands of cases of cigars in ideal conditions. Cigar boxes and humidors sold here are guaranteed for workmanship and reliability (the gamut runs from a solid cedarwood three-cigar pocket humidor to a vault the size of a writing desk). Pipe smokers will discover the entire range of tobaccos available in France, plus a large selection of pipes (all major brands, with a particularly good collection of meerschaums). Lemaire's vast stock of accessories embraces the finest lighters, cases, and pouches.

PIPES

Au Caïd

6th arr. - 24, bd Saint-Michel
43 26 04 01
Open 10am-7pm. Closed Sun. V, AE, DC. M° Odéon.

The charming *mesdames* Schmitt still reign over this pipe-smokers' paradise. Featured is a top selection of pipes in clay, china, cherry, and briar, as well as meerschaum and corncob pipes. Accessories include tobacco pouches and cigar cases, cigar holders, and pipe racks, which the Duke of Windsor and Jean-Paul Sartre appreciated in their day. The service is renowned.

Dunhill

2nd arr. - 15, rue de la Paix
42 61 57 58, fax 42 60 63 67
Open 9:30am-6:30pm (Mon & Sat 10am-6:30pm). Closed Sun. V, AE, DC. M° Opéra.

The Alfred Dunhill shop remains the domain of men—and women—who have about them the expensive aroma of Havana cigars and fine leather. Foremost among the luxurious items presented in this mahogany-paneled, turn-of-the-century shop are, of course, the famed Dunhill pipes, among the world's best...and priciest. Collectors will not want to miss the mini-museum of clay, briar, and meerschaum pipes. Dunhill is also a gift shop, with a large selection of sunglasses, wristwatches, leather goods, and pens (after all, Dunhill owns Mont-Blanc). But the lion's share of the shop is given over to smokers' accessories: expensive lighters, cigarette holders, cigar boxes, and humidors in rare woods.

H G

17th arr. - 7, av. de Clichy
43 87 70 88
Open 10am-7pm. Closed Sun. V. M° Place-de-Clichy.

Gilbert Guyot is one of the three remaining master pipemakers in France. When we visit his shop, we generally find Guyot crafting, repairing, restoring, or smoking a pipe and sizing up his clients. Before selling a customer his wares, Guyot personally interviews him, because, as Guyot puts it, "The pipe is the man." All kinds of pipes in every imaginable material and in a wide range of prices are sold in an atmosphere of quality and time-honored tradition.

WOMEN'S WEAR

DESIGNERS

Azzedine Alaïa

4th arr. - 7, rue de Moussy
42 72 19 19
Open 10am-7pm. Closed Sun. V, AE, DC, MC. M° Hôtel-de-Ville.

More women dream of pouring themselves into an Azzedine Alaïa creation than can actually—decently—do so. The tiny Tunisian's artful cutting, stretch fabrics, and suggestive seaming do wonders for svelte silhouettes. What they do to less-than-heavenly bodies we will leave to your imagination. Still, if Tina Turner dares to wear Alaïa, why shouldn't we? Alaïa's huge boutique is a must-see on the fashion circuit. While you're there, check out his newest innovation: a fabric said to ward off the evil effects of magnetic fields—so you can dress for less stress!

Anvers

7th arr. - 7 & 16, rue du Pré-aux-Clercs - 42 86 84 40
Open 10:30am-7pm. Closed Sun. V, AE, DC, MC. M° Saint-Germain-des-Prés.

In recent years the Rue du Pré-aux-Clercs has become one of the most fashionable streets in Paris. The Belgian city of Anvers (Antwerp, to us) is the home of this young design firm's guiding spirits, Martine Hillen and Anne Kegels. Their beautiful boutique presents clothes for women and men crafted in fine natural fabrics—wool, cotton, linen, silk. Muted shades like beige, silvery green, sand, rust, or chocolate are used for their collection of knit pieces that can be combined to create interesting layered effects. A line of less costly clothing for juniors is a recent—welcome—addition.

Jun Ashida

8th arr. - 34, rue du Fg-St-Honoré - 42 65 09 30
Open 9:45am-6:45pm. Closed Sun. V, AE, DC, MC. M° Concorde.

When Ashida is not designing clothes for the Empress of Japan, he creates a line of luxurious and sophisticated ready-to-wear for elegant, fortyish women. His supremely feminine suits move effortlessly from office to opera (about 6,000 F), and his cocktail dresses are visions in silk, silk mousseline, and printed crêpe de chine. The Miss Ashida line, also on sale here, offers a more youthful look.

Loris Azzaro

8th arr. - 65, rue du Fg-St-Honoré - 42 66 92 06
Open 10am-7pm. Closed Sun. V, AE, DC. M° Champs-Élysées-Clemenceau.

The ground floor of the shop does nothing to prepare customers for the luxury that awaits them in the gray-marble showroom upstairs. There the imperturbable Loris supervises, while his gauzy, glittery gowns are fitted on jet-set celebrities. Though he may be scoffed at by more classic couturiers, his customers adore the way Azzaro plunges a neckline, slits a sheath, and flatters the figure with a sequined bustier. Predictably, his prices are far from negligible, though the ready-to-wear (dresses: 4,000 to 7,000 F) is more attainable than the couture (15,000 F and up).

Balenciaga

8th arr. - 10, av. George-V
47 20 21 11
Open 10am-7pm (Sat 10am-12:30pm & 2pm-7pm). Closed Sun. V, AE, DC, MC. M° Alma-Marceau.

With the real Balenciaga long gone, the name is more a label than a creative design philosophy. The strong points of the clothes (designed by Josephus Melchior Thimester) are their clear colors, structured lines, and sophistication. Most successful are the shapely, beautifully cut "power suits" in cashmere and soft wools (just under 10,000 F) and the fluid, diaphanous cocktail and evening dresses (from 7,500 F).

Pierre Balmain

8th arr. - 44, rue François-Ier
47 20 98 79
8th arr. - 25, rue du Fg-St-Honoré - 42 66 45 70
Open 10am-7pm (Sat 11am-7pm). Closed Sun. V, AE. M° Franklin-D.-Roosevelt, Concorde.

The fashion world was thrown into a tizzy when Oscar de la Renta was named couturier for the venerable House of Balmain. In fact, de la Renta's balanced, well-proportioned clothes with their fluttery, feminine lines are a faithful, though updated, reflection of the Balenciaga spirit. The ready-to-wear range sports a more youthful image, with lots of knits, dashing suits patterned on riding habits, long great-coats in subtle shades, and for evening, a bouquet of delicate frocks fashioned of silk, mousseline, and velvet.

Étienne Brunel

7th arr. - 70, rue des Saints-Pères - 45 44 41 14
Open 10am-7pm. Closed Sun. V, AE, MC. M° Sèvres-Babylone.

Lyon-native Mireille Étienne designs strikingly original clothes which are also perfectly wearable. Her most recent collections have featured shimmering fabrics (satin, raw silk, wool, or velvet mixed with a little Lycra), most effective for bustier tops and interestingly cut dresses. Suits have the polish and meticulous detailing that well-dressed women require. For those with a sense of daring (and humor!) there are some crazy little numbers made of straw, plastic, foam, terrycloth (not bad, those!), feathers, and patchworks of leather or lace. Reasonable prices.

Barbara Bui

1st arr. - 23, rue Étienne-Marcel - 40 26 43 65
Open 10:30am-7pm. Closed Sun. V, AE, DC. M° Étienne-Marcel.

For women, designer Barbara Bui blends European style and Oriental silhouettes, using delicate, fragile fabrics (silk, velvet, airy organza). Check out her beautiful skin-colored blouses, typical of her timeless, ultrafeminine style.

Cardin

8th arr. - 27, av. de Marigny
42 66 92 25
Open 10am-7pm. Closed Sun. V, AE, DC, MC. M° Champs-Élysées-Clemenceau.

Energetic middle-aged ladies (who remember Pierre's glory days back in the 1960s) go for Cardin's city suits (8,000 F), cocktail dresses, and firmly tailored seven-eighths-length coats. Cardin's ready-to-wear collections and "licensed" accessories lack the whimsical spirit and forward-looking attitude that continue to inspire his haute-couture designs.

Jean-Charles de Castelbajac

1st arr. - 5, rue des Petits-Champs - 42 60 37 33 & 31, pl. du Marché-Saint-Honoré
42 60 78 40
6th arr. - 6, pl. Saint- Sulpice
46 33 87 32
Open 10am-7pm. Closed Sun. V, AE, DC, MC. M° Bourse, Saint-Sulpice.

The world of Castelbajac is one of vibrant primary colors, playful patterns, and ethnic prints splashed across relaxed, casual clothing. Knitwear, crafted along rustic lines, is the house specialty. Ever more space is devoted in these bright, appealing shops to Castelbajac's furniture and home accents, which also sport whimsical motifs in crayon-box hues.

Chanel

1st arr. - 31, rue Cambon
42 86 28 00
8th arr. - 42, av. Montaigne
47 23 74 12
Open 9:30am-6:30pm (Sat 10am-6:30pm). Closed Sun. V, AE, DC, MC. M° Concorde, Franklin-D.-Roosevelt.

The most famous fashion house on the face of the earth, Chanel is also the most copied. To be sure that your good money is going for the *real* house logo (and not just any old interlocked Cs), spend it here, at the mother of all Chanel stores. Yes, you'll find the authentic tweed *tailleurs*, the pearls, the bracelets, the chain-link belts, the quilted bags that the world adores. Designer Karl Lagerfeld continues to redefine the house image. Each season he invents an outrageous new take on the Chanel suit jazzed up with some startling accessories—a micromini version, for example, with a short, cropped jacket, enhanced by over-the-knee athletic-striped hose, platform pumps, and a huge, fuzzy hat...

Chloé

7th arr. - 3, rue de Gribeauval
45 44 02 04
Open 10am-6:30pm. Closed Sun. V, AE, DC, MC. M° Rue du Bac.
8th arr. - 54, rue du Fg-St-Honoré - 44 94 33 00
Open 10am-7pm. Closed Sun. V, AE, DC, MC. M° Concorde.

The ubiquitous Karl Lagerfeld is back in the designer's seat at Chloé. The latest collections have been totally unstructured, featuring roomy felt or cashmere overcoats, wide and fluid suède skirts, lacy "mermaid" dresses, and layered floats of pastel mousseline for evening.

Comme des Garçons

2nd arr. - 42, rue Étienne-Marcel - 42 33 05 21
Open 11am-7pm. Closed Sun. V, AE, DC, MC. M° Louvre.

The *vendeurs* size you up as you walk in, and if they don't like your "look," you can expect a pretty frosty reception. Indeed, the store itself exudes precious little warmth. Interestingly, designer Rei Kawakubo is now moving away from the "wretched" look, with its droopy knits, frayed seams, and depressing colors. A recent collection offered several surprising variations on the theme of a man's suit. A new departure? Seems so, yet some things never change: Kawakubo's styles are still subversive, still androgynous, and still very expensive.

> *Remember that if you spend 2,000 F or more in a store, you are entitled to a full refund of the value-added tax (VAT).* *See* Basics *for details.*

Courrèges

8th arr. - 40, rue François-Ier
47 20 70 44
Open 9:45am-6:45pm. Closed Sun. V, AE, DC, MC. M° Franklin-D.-Roosevelt.

André Courrèges typified fashion in the late '60s and early '70s. Now that the styles of that era are back in vogue, Courrèges's multicolored knit A-line dresses with squared or asymmetric necklines, his geometric silhouettes, his stark white accessories are enjoying renewed popularity. Expect to pay from 4,000 F for a suit, 3,000 F for a dress, and about 4,500 F for a candy-colored parka.

Christian Dior

8th arr. - 30, av. Montaigne
40 73 54 44
Open 9:30am-6:30pm (Sat & Mon 10am-6:30pm). Closed Sun. V, AE, DC, MC. M° Franklin-D.-Roosevelt.

Once you enter Dior's gray-and-white flagship store, you can spend the entire day choosing everything you need to be impeccably (and expensively) attired at all times. From lace-lavished lingerie to chic city suits (from 7,000 F), sportswear to organza ball gowns designed by Gianfranco Ferré (the current Monsieur Dior), chic chapeaux to mink-cuffed kid gloves in a rainbow of hues, no detail is neglected. You can also dress your home and your children here in the same obviously opulent style.

Dorothée Bis

2nd arr. - 46, rue Étienne-Marcel - 42 21 04 40
Open 10am-7pm (Mon 11am-7pm). Closed Sun. V, AE, DC, MC. M° Louvre.

After a stint in fashion purgatory, the Jacobsons are back with a vibrant, youthful collection of vampy stretch, Lycra, and viscose knits (lots of openwork), shimmering Lurex sweaters and pants, and iridescent leather pea coats. In a (slightly) more conservative vein is a gray linen suit—but even that is shot through with shiny silver threads!

Jacques Fath

8th arr. - 32, av. Pierre-Ier-de-Serbie - 47 23 09 38
Open 10am-7pm (Sat 10:30am-6:30pm). Closed Sun. V, AE, DC, MC. M° George-V.

Jacques Fath's flamboyance marked fashion in the 1950s. His knock-'em-dead style lives on in sumptuous evening gowns inspired by his designs, and in dashing seven-eighths jackets enriched with jeweled buttons and elaborate appliqués. Among the elegant accessories are the famous house fragrances, practically unfindable elsewhere: Green Water and Fath de Fath.

Hélène Gainville

8th arr. - Arcades du Lido, 78, av. des Champs-Élysées
43 59 32 18
Open 10:30am-7pm. Closed Sun. V, AE. M° George-V.

Hélène Gainville custom-designs smart city suits (for your power lunches), frothy cocktails frocks (for your romantic dinners), and gowns for your most extravagant evenings at prices close to what you'd pay for deluxe ready-to-wear. What's more, in her lovely trilevel boutique done in soothing pastel tones and warm wood, she will provide just the right accessories to complete your look, from hats to bags to shoes. And when Prince Charming finally shows up and sweeps you off your feet, Hélène will create a magical gown for the occasion (see *Wedding Gowns*, page 323).

Boutiques Givenchy

8th arr. - 8 & 3, av. George-V
47 20 81 31 & 44 31 50 23
& 28, rue du Fb-St-Honoré
42 65 54 54
Open 9:30am-6:30pm. Closed Sun. V, AE, DC. M° Alma-Marceau, Concorde.

Audrey Hepburn long represented the quintessential Givenchy style: inaccessible, regal, and ethereal. Givenchy's daytime look features city sportswear in tweeds, plaids, corduroy, and heathered wools, complemented with classy accessories. For evening, there are enchanting little satin-backed crêpe cocktail dresses paired with metallic-toned parkas. Upscale ready-to-wear is displayed across the street, at number 3, where suits start at 6,000 F and cocktail dresses at 7,500 F.

Irena Gregori

7th arr. - 130, rue du Bac
42 22 79 73
Open 10:30am-7:30pm. Closed Sun. V, AE, DC, MC. M° Sèvres-Babylone.

Designer Irena Gregori creates fresh, vivid, uncomplicated styles that can be worn from morning to night. Her preferences run to fluid fabrics, comfortable knits, and stretchy synthetics that flatter a wide range of figures. Women on the go are buying up her new crushed silk skirts, which are ever so practical for travel. Prices are attractive, winter and summer, but at sale time they are downright irresistible.

Irié

7th arr. - 8, rue du Pré-aux-Clercs - 42 61 18 28
Open 10:15am-7pm. Closed Sun. V, MC. M° Rue du Bac.

A sober yet surrealistic black-and-white setting shows off Irié's collection of hip, sophisticated clothes. Silk, angora, wool gabardine, and never-wrinkle polyester crêpe are the major components of this designer's sexy, close-to-the-body creations. Irié is one of the darlings of the Left Bank set, who adore his boutique's courteous staff ("Madame, may I say that I think you've made an excellent choice...") and the relatively reasonable prices. Highlights of recent collections are wonderfully gay, colorful prints (fish, planets, alphabets, penguins...), oversized transparent shirts in fabulous colors, stretch minis, and soft panne-velvet tops.

Paule Ka

7th arr. - 192, bd Saint-Germain - 45 44 92 60
Open 10:30am-7pm. Closed Sun. V, AE, DC. M° Saint-Germain-des-Prés.

Serge Coifinger's ideal of feminine beauty runs to the Grace Kelly or Jackie Kennedy type. His swingy A-line dress under a cropped spencer jacket adorned with bows harks back charmingly to the 1960s. Worth a look too are the smart little hats and bags, and other enticing accessories.

Emmanuelle Khanh

6th arr. - 2, rue de Tournon
46 33 41 03
Open 10:15am-7pm. Closed Sun. V, AE, DC. M° Odéon.

For the woman over 35 who wants to dress in a chic but unostentatious style, Emmanuelle Khanh designs feminine suits (pretty embroideries) and long, swirling dresses in warm hues for winter and unusual pastel shades for summer. The coordinated separates are just right for a fashionable working woman's wardrobe.

Michel Klein

7th arr. - 6, rue du Pré-aux-Clercs - 42 60 37 11
Open 10am-7pm. Closed Sun. V, AE, DC, MC. M° Saint-Germain-des-Prés.

Klein's designs have simple yet strong lines and an appealing, timeless style. Easy to wear, versatile, and comfortable, his clothes are excellent investments. Lately we've admired his satin Chinese jackets in bright blue, ecru, or black, and his remarkably well cut pants and leatherwear. The Klein d'Œil line, about 30 percent less expensive than the top of the range, offers similarly attractive clothes in a narrower choice of models and colors.

Christian Lacroix

8th arr. - 73, rue du Fg-St-Honoré - 42 65 79 08
8th arr. - 26, av. Montaigne
47 20 68 95
Open 10am-7pm. Closed Sun. V, AE, DC. M° Concorde, Alma-Marceau.

Christian Lacroix's vivid, scintillating creations marry Provençal folklore with fantasy prints in a sun-drenched, theatrical style. His most recent shows sent out Lurex or sequined jackets with pagoda shoulders, slinky slip dresses, and soft pants in bold bayadère stripes. Lacroix's ready-to-wear is dreadfully expensive, but the accessories—especially the fake-gem-studded jewelry of Byzantine inspiration—are accessible (if not exactly affordable), and give lots of fashion "juice" for the money. Walk up to the shop's second floor to check out sale items from the previous season, marked down by 50 percent. New this year: the Bazar line, a less expensive collection of colorful, young-at-heart pieces.

Karl Lagerfeld

8th arr. - 19, rue du Fg-St-Honoré - 42 66 64 64
Open 10am-7pm. Closed Sun. V, AE, DC, MC. M° Concorde.

Versatile, prolific Karl Lagerfeld, who infused brilliant new life into the house of Chanel, continues to design clothes and accessories for his personal label. Mix-and-match is the season's watchword: tweed jackets top floaty chiffon skirts, both for day and evening. But this year's "Most Coveted" award goes to Lagerfeld's superb poplin blouses (2,500 F).

Lanvin

8th arr. - 22, rue du Fg-St-Honoré - 44 71 31 83
Open 10am-7pm (Mon & Sat 10am-1pm & 2pm-7pm). Closed Sun. V, AE, DC, MC. M° Concorde.

Lanvin promotes a modern approach to dressing. The classically elegant pieces can be be coordinated at will, to create outfits that move gracefully from day to evening. Plenty of accessories are on hand to personalize the look, such as scarves and jewelry (from 400 F) with Art Deco motifs created for Jeanne Lanvin in the '20s.

Guy Laroche

6th arr. - 47, rue de Rennes
45 48 18 50
16th arr. - 9, av. Victor-Hugo
45 01 82 75
Open 10am-7pm. Closed Sun. V, AE, DC, MC. M° Saint-Germain-des-Prés, Victor-Hugo.
8th arr. - 29, av. Montaigne
40 69 69 50
8th arr. - 30, rue du Fg-St-Honoré - 40 06 01 70
Open 9:30am-6:30pm (Sat 10am-7pm). Closed Sun. V, AE, DC, MC. M° Alma-Marceau, Concorde.

True to the principles of the late Guy Laroche, designer Jean-Pierre Marty creates three distinct ready-to-wear lines for women who like a well-bred, finished look. The Boutique collection presents conservatively chic clothes for day; the Montaigne line features cocktail and evening dresses; and the more youthful (and less expensive) Alternance line offers suits from 2,900 F. Also on view is a collection of young-at-heart sportswear—bermudas, car coats, blazers, and embroidered Perfecto-style jackets—in denim and similar casual fabrics. Lots of accessories, too.

Lolita Lempicka

4th arr. - 13 bis, rue Pavée
42 74 50 48
Open 10:30am-7pm. Closed Sun. V, AE, DC. M° Saint-Paul.
16th arr. - 46, av. Victor-Hugo - 45 02 14 46
Open 10am-7pm. Closed Sun. V, AE, DC. M° Victor-Hugo.

Lolita Lempicka has plunged headlong into a romantic, dandified look that one might call *"Les Liaisons Dangereuses* Meets Mata Hari." On view are ruffled blouses, close-fitting velvet jackets, and short skirts in pin-striped gabardine with bits of lace peeking out below the hem. Lolita Bis is the designer's second-tier line, more youthful, less costly, and easier to wear.

Max Mara

6th arr. - 37, rue du Four
43 29 91 10
Open 10:30am-7pm. Closed Sun. V, AE, DC, MC. M° Saint-Germain-des-Prés.

Max Mara's flagship store displays the full range of this Italian maker's labels, from the urbane Max Mara line (wonderful coats) to the sportier Weekend collection, the very "couture" Élégante label, the creative Sportmax line, etc. The staff is courteous and genuinely helpful.

Mariot Chanet

8th arr. - 7, rue de Surène
48 24 37 37
Open 10:30am-6:30pm. Closed Sun. V. M° Madeleine.

Olivier Chatenet and Michèle Meunier, alias Mariot Chanet, show their supple, fluid designs for men and women in a "salon"-style setting reminiscent of the old couture houses. Chatenet has worked with Alaïa and Mugler, while Meunier's creden-tials include Comme des Garçons and Girbaud. Lots of novel details make their clothes noticeable and new without being flashy. Figure on spending 7,000 to 8,000 F for an elegant *tailleur.*

Issey Miyake

4th arr. - 3, pl. des Vosges
48 87 01 86
Open 10am-7pm. Closed Sun. V, AE, MC. M° St-Paul.

In a deliberately theatrical setting, Issey Miyake's extravagant, extraordinary designs seem even more dramatic. While they look rather disconcertingly like rags on their hangers, when worn these soft, draped, pleated, sculpted, and cleverly knotted clothes prove to be impressive, even stately: Miyake's long duster coat, for example, makes even an unassuming individual look like a high priest! The prices these pieces command is terrifying—the merest T-shirt costs about 1,000 F. Miyake's second-tier line, Plantation (boutique at 17, boulevard Raspail), is slightly more affordable.

Robert Merloz

7th arr. - 32, rue de Grenelle
40 49 08 16
Open 10am-7pm. Closed Sun. V, AE, DC, MC. M° Sèvres-Babylone.

Long the right arm of Yves Saint Laurent, Merloz struck out on his own in 1993 opening a gorgeous store on the fashionable Rue de Grenelle. His high-waisted, vibrantly colored dresses have a romantic Renaissance air, while his supple knit jersey suits and trousers have a trendy '70s feel.

Monday, like Sunday, is a day of rest for many shopkeepers.

Claude Montana

7th arr. - 31, rue de Grenelle
45 49 13 02
Open 10:15am-7pm. Closed Sun. V, AE, DC. M° Sèvres-Babylone.

Short or long, Montana's skirts and dresses show a lot of leg. Zippered sheaths, undulating asymmetrical hems, molded shoulders, and sculpted sleeves compose a wardrobe for a high-tech vamp who isn't afraid to attract a little attention. The clothes are beautifully tailored (Montana's vivid leather pants and jackets are the definitive statement on the subject). The designer's second line, State of Claude Montana, is a less expensive version of his evening and weekend wear, complete with coordinated accessories. You'll find it at 3, rue des Petits-Champs in the first arrondissement (40 20 02 14).

Popy Moreni

4th arr. - 13, pl. des Vosges
42 77 09 96
Open 10am-7pm (Mon 11am-7pm). Closed Sun. V, AE, DC, MC. M° Saint-Paul.

Popy Moreni is one of the "grandes dames" of fashion design; her multifaceted talent extends to clothes, accessories, furniture, and housewares. This versatile Italian often looks to the Commedia dell'Arte for inspiration: note the oversized Pierrot collars on tulle dresses, shantung blouses, and "venetian blind" skirt, complete with a pull cord to adjust the length. Charming and expensive.

Hanae Mori

8th arr. - 17-19, av. Montaigne - 47 23 52 03
8th arr. - 5, pl. de l'Alma
40 70 05 73
Open 10am-7pm. Closed Sun. V, AE, DC, MC. M° Alma-Marceau.

Hanae Mori has replaced her flowery prints with sumptuous cashmere, occasionally combined with silk, often patterned with checks, stripes, or her signature butterflies. Don't miss the good-looking accessories: Mori's scarves and stoles are particularly covetable.

Thierry Mugler

2nd arr. - 10, pl. des Victoires
42 60 06 37
Open 10am-1pm & 2pm-7pm (Mon from 11am). Closed Sun. V, AE, DC, MC. M° Palais-Royal.

The boutique, designed by Andrée Putman, puts one in mind of a futuristic comic strip. As for the clothes, they are designed for heroines: strong women, sex bombs, and glamorous sirens who want structured suits that underline feminine curves. Slit skirts, geometric cutouts, and brilliantly colored leather are the highlights of Mugler's latest collections.

Claudie Pierlot

1st arr. - 4, rue du Jour
42 21 38 38
Open 10:30am-7pm (Mon 1pm-7pm). Closed Sun. V, AE, MC. M° Les Halles.

Light-hearted suits, sweaters, shirts, and accessories for a fresh, youthful look. These are practical, pretty designs that can form the basis of a pulled-together wardrobe for work and play.

Myrène de Prémonville

8th arr. - 32, av. George-V
47 20 02 35
Open 10am-7pm (Mon 2pm-7pm). Closed Sun. V, AE, DC, MC. M° George-V.

Young, modern women—including Kathleen Turner, Jane Fonda, and Isabelle Adjani—love Prémonville's sophisticated clothes: dressy suits, crêpe pants, curvy riding jackets in alluring colors (lilac, raspberry...). This designer has a great sense of graphic style, evident in her strong accessories—we noticed some wonderful grosgrain bucket bags and a host of boldly emphatic earrings.

Paco Rabanne

6th arr. - 7, rue du Cherche-Midi - 40 49 08 53
Open 10am-7pm. Closed Sun, Mon. V, AE, MC. M° Sèvres-Babylone.

Paco Rabanne lives to defy convention. Remember his metal dresses, his plastic and paper skirts? Well, these days he favors structured suits and feminine frocks, displayed in his "new age" boutique, designed by Éric Raffy.

Georges Rech

8th arr. - 273, rue Saint-Honoré - 42 61 41 14
Open 10am-7pm (Mon 11am-7pm). Closed Sun. V, AE, DC, MC. M° Concorde.
16th arr. - 23, av. Victor-Hugo - 45 00 83 19
Open 10am-7pm (Mon 1pm-7pm). Closed Sun. V, AE, DC, MC. M° Victor-Hugo.

Rech makes clothes for active women with lots of personality, as vivacious as they are beautiful. House designer Danièle Jagot has adopted a more fluid, unstructured line lately, proposing comfortable tweed vests worn with jodhpurs for day, and flowing satin or velvet cocktail dresses with jeweled buttons for evening. The detailing on every item is impeccable, and the Rech sales staff is very nearly perfect, too.

Nina Ricci

8th arr. - 17, rue François-Ier
49 52 56 00
Open 10am-6:30pm (Sat 10am-1pm & 2:15pm-6:30pm). Closed Sun. V, AE, DC, MC. M° Franklin-D.-Roosevelt.

Quintessentially feminine clothes for romantic women with lots of money: cashmere capes (30 different shades), polka-dotted chiffon dresses, and embroidered velvet bustiers are typical of the soft-edged Ricci look. The store also presents a full range of gift items, voluptuous household linens, and the house line of makeup in pastel packages designed by Garouste and Bonetti. At 19, rue François-Ier you'll find sale merchandise marked down by 50 percent.

Rochas

8th arr. - 33, rue François-Ier
47 23 54 56
Open 10am-7pm (Sat 10am-6:30pm). Closed Sun. V, AE, DC, MC. M° Franklin-D.-Roosevelt.

Rochas's recently launched line of luxurious women's wear is designed with plenty of panache by Peter O'Brien. These are classic clothes given an extra spark of chic by an original approach to fabric: tweed and silk are juxtaposed, wool shows up for evening alongside mousseline and lace, organza comes out in the daylight escorted by jersey and bouclé knits. A wealth of elegant accessories—bags, jewelry, sunglasses, scarves—complete a modern, feminine yet unfussy look. The Rochas woman can also decorate her house and set a sophisticated table with the firm's line of deluxe linens and tableware.

Sonia Rykiel

6th arr. - 175, bd Saint-Germain - 49 54 60 60
Open 10am-7pm. Closed Sun. V, AE, DC, MC. M° Saint-Germain-des-Prés.

Her signature black velours separates shot through with gold threads, her wide trousers, long tunics, striped sweaters, and body-skimming silhouette are as popular as ever. The clothes are discreetly updated from season to season to keep up with trends, but what women like about Sonia Rykiel's designs is their comforting familiarity and flattering, uncomplicated lines.

Yves Saint Laurent

6th arr. - 6, pl. Saint-Sulpice
43 29 43 00
8th arr. - 38, rue du Fg-St-Honoré - 42 65 74 59
16th arr. - 19, av. Victor-Hugo - 45 00 64 64
Open 10am-7pm. Closed Sun. V, AE, MC. M° St-Sulpice, Concorde, Victor-Hugo.

Saint Laurent is a byword for French fashion. For more than 30 years, Dior's successor has been the standard-bearer of Parisian elegance, with his rigorously conceived, luxuriously detailed collections. His recently redesigned showcase on the Faubourg Saint-Honoré is now twice its former size, the better to display the full range of the Saint Laurent genius: superb furs, opulent evening clothes, incomparably elegant city attire and sportswear, jewelry, and accessories. Also on hand are YSL's acclaimed fragrances, cosmetics, and the skincare line represented by the eternally divine Catherine Deneuve.

Jil Sander

8th arr. - 52, av. Montaigne
44 95 06 70
Open 10am-6:30pm. Closed Sun. V, AE, DC, MC. M° Franklin-D.-Roosevelt.

German designer Jil Sander is now making her mark(s) in Paris as well as in New York, London, and Milan. Her superbly finished clothes have a timeless elegance that extends to the smallest detail. Sander's fashion basics offer top value for the money: impeccable lines characterize her raincoats, cashmere knits, and suits crafted of wrinkle-resistant menswear fabrics (6,000 to 11,000 F). Beautifully cut trousers, available in a dozen styles, start at 2,300 F.

Jean-Louis Scherrer

8th arr. - 51, av. Montaigne
42 99 05 83
Open 9:30am-6:30pm (Sat 10am-6:30pm). Closed Sun. V, AE, DC, MC. M° Franklin-D.-Roosevelt.

The firm that bears his name is no longer run by Jean-Louis Scherrer, who got squeezed out by his one-time backers. Éric Mortensen is at the haute-couture designing desk now, while Scherrer's former assistant, Emmanuel Chaussade, handles the ready-to-wear lines. The house continues to produce attractive draped cocktail dresses, ladylike suits, embroidered blazers and such. Ravishing handbags and jewelry.

Junko Shimada

2nd arr. - 54, rue Étienne-Marcel - 42 36 36 97
Open 10am-7pm (Mon 2pm-7pm; Sat 11am-7pm). Closed Sun. V, AE, MC. M° Louvre.

A playful spirit and sexy silhouette are Shimada's trademarks. She gives classic clothes an alluring spin by cutting them close to the body, witness the sophisticated gray suit that she presents in a fresh, updated version in every collection (6,000 F).

Angelo Tarlazzi

7th arr. - 74, rue des Saints-Pères - 45 44 12 32
Open 10am-7pm. Closed Sun. V, AE, DC, MC. M° Sèvres-Babylone.

Tarlazzi creates sensual, unabashed designs, splashed with bright colors and crafted in elaborately worked fabrics. Prices are stiff, but, thankfully, there is the Tarlazzi 2 line to temper the whole. These clothes are hot stuff, not for the flabby or the faint of heart. Still, if you've got the requisite figure, try slipping into one of Tarlazzi's draped skirts, laced-up cocktail dresses, or his long stretch-jersey T-dress with bias-sewn satin ruffles (4,900 F), and you can bet you'll steal the scene at any party.

Find the address you are looking for, quickly and easily, in the index.

Chantal Thomass

1st arr. - 1 rue Vivienne
40 15 02 36
Open 10am-7pm (Mon 11am-7pm). Closed Sun. V, AE, MC. M° Bourse.

The queen of wasp-waists, form-fitting dresses, provocative suits, and sexy stockings reigns over this huge emporium housed in an eighteenth-century mansion. Here, just a stone's throw away from the trendy Place des Victoires, spread out over three levels, all of Chantal's multifarious creations are on view. If you don't feel like shopping, just wander around and admire the décor: there's a *fumoir*, salon, library, and (naturally!) a boudoir.

Yuki Torii

2nd arr. - 38-40, galerie Vivienne - 42 96 64 66
Open 10am-7pm. Closed Sun. V, AE, MC. M° Bourse.

Don't be misled by the austerity of the boutique; unlike her designing compatriots, this Japanese stylist does not go in for dramatic, ascetic "draperies." Yuki Torii likes bright colors, exuberant floral prints, and clever detailing. Don't miss the exclusive embroidered patchwork shawls. These clothes are supple, wearable, and highly original. Pricey, too, of course.

Emanuel Ungaro

8th arr. - 2, av. Montaigne
47 23 61 94
Open 10am-7pm. Closed Sun. V, AE, DC, MC. M° Alma-Marceau.

Rousing colors and mad mixes of prints are Emanuel Ungaro's signatures: flowers, leopards, and geometrical motifs run riot along his draped dresses, curvy skirts and jackets. His Ungaro Solo Donna and Ungaro Parallèles lines are slightly more affordable than the top-tier ready-to-wear. Marvelous accessories, if you can only afford a "taste" of Ungaro.

Valentino

8th arr. - 17-19, av. Montaigne - 47 23 64 61
Open 10am-7pm. Closed Sun. V, AE, MC. M° Alma-Marceau.

The Roman designer Valentino came, saw, and conquered the world of French fashion. Celebrities and commoners alike flock to his boutique in search of elegant styles in everything from socks to spectacles. His superbly cut flannel suits, tweed jackets, sweaters, and shawls are chic, comfortable, and easy to wear. Valentino goes all out for evening, with frothy silk mousseline frocks, and dreamy gowns sprinkled with sequins or jet embroidery—we understand why Liz Taylor wanted him to make her umpteenth wedding dress! Oliver is Valentino's more youthful, affordable line (sweaters from 800 F, women's suits around 3,000 F).

Irène van Ryb

6th arr. - 53, rue du Four
42 22 77 17
Open 10:30am-7:30pm (Mon 2pm-7:30pm). Closed Sun. V, AE, DC, MC. M° Sèvres-Babylone.

Lots of imagination and fine tailoring go into Irène van Ryb's collections. The trousers, in particular, are handsomely cut. A contemporary look for women of every age, at reasonable prices.

READY-TO-WEAR & SPECIALTY SHOPS

Absinthe

1st arr. - 74, rue Jean- Jacques-Rousseau - 42 33 54 44
Open 11am-7:30pm (Mon 2pm-7:30pm). Closed Sun. V, MC. M° Louvre.

Marthe Desmoulins tracks down designers of the new generation—Dries Van Noten, Christophe Lemaire, Yoneda Kasuko, Costume Nazionale, Charlotte Nilson, among others—and brings their creations together in her hip, hot boutique. If you want to know what's news in fashion, this is a good place to start. Just in: a small selection of handmade shoes by Andreas (from 3,000 F).

Elle

6th arr. - 30, rue Saint-Sulpice
43 26 46 10
Open 10:30am-7pm. Closed Sun. V, AE, MC. M° St-Sulpice.

The famed fashion weekly of the same name is the marketing force behind this bright, pink-hued store set in the heart of Saint-Germain. The ground floor overflows with spiffy, affordable clothes and accessories for today's women. Climb the monumental staircase, and you'll discover a wonderland of home furnishings and décor.

Franck & Fils

16th arr. - 80, rue de Passy
46 47 86 00
Open 9:45am-6:45pm (Mon 1:30pm-6:45pm). Closed Sun. V, AE, DC, MC. M° La Muette.

A huge department-style store devoted exclusively to women, Franck & Fils has just been fully refurbished from stem to stern. The selection of merchandise is nothing short of colossal: from lingerie (a whole floor full!) to designer ready-to-wear, from the store's own-label clothing to luxurious furs and leatherwear, from custom-designed wedding gowns to every imaginable accessory—hats, jewelry, shoes, bags, scarves—all the top names in fashion are gathered together here. When you've shopped till you're ready to drop, stop for refreshments at the Lenôtre tea room.

Inès de La Fressange

8th arr. - 14, av. Montaigne
47 23 08 94
Open 10am-6:30pm. Closed Sun. V, AE, DC, MC. M° Alma-Marceau.

Inès, once the "face" of Chanel (until she fell out of favor with Kaiser Karl) launched her own boutique a while back, amid much media brouhaha. Set on the swank Avenue Montaigne, the shop is a roaring success. You'll find impeccably cut wardrobe basics (the best-selling stretchy dress goes for 1,800 F) and smart, expensive accessories (a rainbow of suede loafers, jewelry, hats), all produced, designed, or selected by Inès herself. A line of opulent household linens and decorative objects is on hand as well.

Joseph

8th arr. - 14, av. Montaigne
47 20 39 55
Open 10am-7pm. Closed Sun. V, AE, MC. M° Alma-Marceau.

A tone less hip than the London store, Joseph in Paris is nonetheless a magnet for fashion trendies. They come to browse among the designer togs (Prada, Alaïa, Dolce & Gabbana), purchase a genuine Joseph sweater—they're so nice and roomy—, or try on a pair of Manolo Blahnik shoes. The in-store café is a perfect place to relax with a cup of tea while eyeing the merchandise.

Kashiyama

6th arr. - 147, bd Saint-Germain - 46 34 11 50
Open 10am-7pm (Mon 11am-7pm). Closed Sun. V, AE, DC, MC. M° Saint-Germain-des-Prés.

The windows that wrap around an entire corner of the Boulevard Saint-Germain offer a tantalizing glimpse of what's inside: beauteous garments by the hottest designers—Dolce & Gabbana, Jean Colonna, Ann Demeulemeester, Sybilla, Alberta Ferretti, and others, all the cream of the current fashion crop. Downstairs, a lavish array of lascivious, lacy lingerie awaits. We cringe at the prices (the semiannual sales are worth your close attention), but we have nothing but praise for the helpful staff.

Irina Kate

7th arr. - 4, rue de la Chaise
45 49 31 19
Open 11am-7pm. Closed Sun. V, AE, DC, MC. M° Sèvres-Babylone.

With a sharp eye for fashion and a keen sense of value, Irina Kate presents a judicious selection of labels and styles (Marella, Max Mara, Irène Van

Ryb...). Her sizeable stock includes dresses (from 1,000 F), suits (we saw a lovely linen summer suit by Marella for 1,500 F), and good-looking separates that she will help you pull together for an individual look. Reasonable prices (considering the neighborhood...).

Maria Luisa

1st arr. - 2, rue Cambon
47 03 96 15
Open 10:30am-7pm. Closed Sun. V, AE, DC, MC. M° Concorde.

In this buttoned-up neighborhood you're unlikely to find a more avant-garde fashion boutique than this one. Maria Luisa is Venezuelan, and she is blessed with an infallible sense of style. Her stable of designing stars includes Martine Sitbon, Helmut Lang, John Galliano, and Martin Margiela. Accessories too are at the cutting edge of fashion, with bags by 31 Février, hats by Le Corre, and glorious jewelry by Berao and Valluet.

Plein Sud

2nd arr. - 2, rue Vide-Gousset
42 36 75 02
Open 10am-7pm. Closed Sun. V, AE, MC. M° Palais-Royal.

Models and actresses (including Julia Roberts) favor this trendy boutique, which features the sun-kissed creations of designer Fayçal Amor. The cotton waistcoats are absolutely adorable, and the long dresses are fluttery and flattering. Each season brings a new crop of exciting discoveries.

Don't plan to shop on Sundays—the vast majority of Paris stores are closed.

Victoire

2nd arr. - 12 & 10, pl. des Victoires - 42 61 09 02
Open 9:30am-7pm. Closed Sun. V, AE, MC. M° Bourse.

For a comprehensive view of what's happening in fashion, have a look-in at Victoire. Young and veteran designers alike make up the eclectic mix of clothing and accessories that reflects owner Françoise Chassagnac's unerring taste: Romeo Gigli, Donna Karan, Callaghan, and a handful of newcomers who change each season. The merchandise at number 10 is on the whole more youthful, sporty, and affordable.

Emiliano Zapata

6th arr. - 50, rue de Sèvres
43 06 37 79
Open 10am-7:30pm. Closed Sun. V, AE, DC, MC. M° Duroc.

Gisèle Guy chooses only a few pieces from her favorites designers' collections each season, so that her boutique offers an expertly edited, very personal version of the top fashion trends. With Gisèle's style sense to guide you, you'll find that putting together an outfit can indeed be a pleasure rather than a chore. The range of prices is wide: there are suits by Thierry Mugler and dresses by Moschino, as well as creations by lesser-known designers with far smaller price tags.

Zenta

8th arr. - 6, rue de Marignan
42 25 72 47
Open 10am-7pm (Sat 11am-7pm). Closed Sun. V, AE, DC. M° Franklin-D.-Roosevelt.

Some fifteen designers are represented in this spacious boutique. In addition to confirmed talents like Popy Moreni, Chantal Thomass, Martine Sitbon, Karl Lagerfeld, and Lolita Lempicka, you'll discover the creations of the up-and-coming generation—which you can be first on your block to wear!

FURS

Behar

10th arr. - 45, bd de Strasbourg - 47 70 12 33
Open 9:30am-12:30pm & 2pm-6:30pm. Closed Sun. V, AE, DC, MC. M° Château-d'Eau.

Luxuriously full seven-eighths-length coats in dark, lustrous mink are the stars of Behar's collection, but there are beautiful silver-fox coats as well, and blue-fox jackets for 4,000 F.

Sprung Frères

16th arr. - 5, av. Victor-Hugo
45 01 70 61
Open 10am-7pm (Mon 2pm-7pm). Closed Sun. V, AE, DC, MC. M° Charles-de-Gaulle-Étoile.

Definitely not for dowagers, these superbly cut furs (some designed by Chloé Bruneton) have loads of youthful style and chic.

Révillon

6th arr. - 44, rue du Dragon
42 22 38 91
Open 10:30am-6:45pm (Mon 11am-6:45pm). Closed Sun. V, AE, DC. M° Sèvres-Babylone.
8th arr. - 17-19, rue du Fg-St-Honoré - 40 17 98 98
Open 10am-7pm. Closed Sun. V, AE, DC. M° Concorde.

Révillon has been the symbol of luxurious furs since 1723. And they are still the most beautiful in the world. Here style goes hand in hand with quality. Of the fur-lined coats, muskrat suits, reversible jackets in blue mink or astrakhan displayed upstairs, none is priced lower than 50,000 F—in fact, they're generally four times that if you're into sable or chinchilla. Prices on the ground floor are somewhat less fearsome. Fur coats and jackets for men are housed on the lower level, and there is an enticing collection of colorful leatherwear as well.

KNITS

Crimson

8th arr. - 8, rue Marbeuf
47 20 44 24
Open 10am-7pm. Closed Sun. V, AE. M° Franklin-D.-Roosevelt.

Cashmere or lambswool sweaters in a rainbow of shades, plus sweaters you'd swear are as soft as cashmere, made of wool from the first shearing of a lamb's belly (700 F). Roll necks, V-necks, and Irish knitwear in unusual colors are also on display at prices from 1,400 to 1,650 F.

Fac-Bazaar

6th arr. - 38, rue des Saints-Pères - 45 48 46 15
Open 11am-7pm. Closed Sun, Mon. M° St-Germain-des-Prés.

Fac-Bazaar's knits sport creative designs in subtle, low-key colors. A typically Left Bank look.

Christa Fiedler

16th arr. - 87, av. Paul-Doumer - 40 50 84 08
Open 10:30am-1pm & 1:30pm-7pm (Mon 2:30pm-7pm). Closed Sun. V. M° La Muette

Onetime model turned knitwear designer, Christa Fiedler marries comfort and elegance in her upbeat, elegant collections. She uses strong reds, blues, and blacks in her lambswool sweaters for the winter months; soft pastel colors and cotton lisle for summer. And she stocks plenty of accessories: turbans, scarves, and gloves. Every item is lovingly detailed and finished.

Richard Grand

1st arr. - 229, rue Saint-Honoré - 42 60 58 73
Open 10am-7pm. Closed Sun. V, AE, MC. M° Tuileries.

This cashmere specialist has been in business now for over a quarter of a century. His spectacular range of 70 colors in 100 styles for ladies and men is pretty nigh unbeatable. Richard Grand also manufactures feather-light cashmere-and-silk sweaters in a magnificent array of hues. Because the firm controls its own manufacturing, it can offer top-of-the-line chic at prices that start around 1,350 F.

Aux Laines Écossaises

7th arr. - 181, bd Saint-Germain - 45 48 53 41
Open 10am-1pm & 2pm-7pm (Mon 2pm-7pm). Closed Sun. V. M° Rue du Bac.

Owner Paul-Émile Clarisse greets his customers warmly and guides them around the shop "to feel the wares": snuggly lambswool pullovers, Shetland sweaters, double-ply cashmeres, Fair Isle knits in tender, heathered tones (around 700 F), and rugged fisherman's sweaters (from 500 F). Kilts from Glasgow in a dozen different tartans are sold in a conservative mid-calf length. But if you prefer yours fashionably short, the extra can be cut off and made into a jaunty plaid scarf!

LARGE SIZES

Marina Rinaldi

6th arr. - 56, rue du Four
45 48 61 57
Open 10:30am-7pm. Closed Sun. V, AE, DC, MC. M° Sèvres-Babylone.

Generous curves are well served by these attractive fashions by an Italian maker. Rather than mask the fuller figure, they underscore its roundness in a most feminine way. Pretty prints, fluid fabrics, and three different lines: Marina Rinaldi, the most expensive (and elegant); Marina Sport; and Persona, the least costly collection.

Rondissimo

9th arr. - 42, rue Vignon
42 66 54 77
Open 10am-7pm. Closed Sun. V, AE. M° Havre-Caumartin.

In French, women with fuller figures are called *rondes*, hence the name of this chain (with several stores in and around Paris). The good-looking clothes are made chiefly of knits and silky fabrics that flow over the body and flatter the silhouette.

LINGERIE

La Boîte à Bas

16th arr. - 77, rue de Longchamp - 47 55 11 55
16th arr. - 16, av. Mozart
42 24 89 98
Open 10:30am-7pm (Mon 2pm-7pm). Closed Sun. V, MC. M° La Muette.

It's all stockings and tights here, and all the major brands are represented: Gerbe, Dior, La Perla, Osé (the up-and-comer), Wolford, and so forth. There are at least 8,000 pairs in stock and range from the coolest to the warmest (prices range from 40 to 500 F).

Alice Cadolle

1st arr. - 14, rue Cambon
42 60 94 94
Open 9:30am-1pm & 2pm-6:30pm. Closed Sun. V, AE, MC. M° Concorde.

Alice Cadolle invented the brassiere in 1889. Sales have been holding up well ever since; here you can find custom-made, partly custom-made, and ready-to-wear bras, lingerie, and swimsuits (the latter are housed on the shop's third floor).

Les Folies d'Élodie

16th arr. - 56, av. Paul-Doumer - 45 04 93 57
Open 10am-7pm (Mon 11am-7pm). Closed Sun. V, AE, DC, MC. M° Trocadéro.

Two sisters, Catherine and Nanou, reign over the two Folies boutiques. Their collections are aimed at millionairesses who will settle for nothing less than silk and lace dressing gowns and underwear. Frothy bed linen and lavish wedding dresses are also presented. If you need a tulle skirt, a satin bustier, or a transparent organza coat, this is the place to look.

Natori

1st arr. - 7, pl. Vendôme
42 96 22 94
Open 10am-7pm. Closed Sat, Sun. V, AE. M° Tuileries.

Seductive lingerie is the specialty here: your eyes will pop (so just think what *his* will do!) when you get a load of Natori's silk negligees, beaded body suits, slinky nightgowns, robes, and undies.

Les Nuits d'Élodie

17th arr. - 1 bis, av. Mac-Mahon - 42 67 68 95
M° Charles-de-Gaulle Étoile.

See *Les Folies d'Élodie* above.

Nulle Part Ailleurs

1st arr. - 15, rue de Turbigo
42 21 95 64
Open 10:30am-7pm. Closed Sun. V, AE, DC, MC. M° Étienne-Marcel.

A gigantic inventory of stockings, tights, and patterned pantyhose—the choice of sizes, shades, and motifs will leave you reeling! Clingy bodysuits and leggings in Lycra or cotton will show off the shape you're in—or out of!

Capucine Puerari

6th arr. - 63, rue des Saints-Pères - 42 22 14 09
Open 11am-7pm. Closed Sun. V, AE, DC, MC. M° Saint-Germain-des-Prés.

A spacious new boutique gives Capucine Puerari lots of room to display all her designing talents: there's youthful, sexy underwear and lingerie; smoothing, flattering bodysuits; and satiny, beautifully detailed swimsuits. The choice is wide, the staff is helpful, the prices (for Paris, mind!) are reasonable.

Sabbia Rosa

6th arr. - 73, rue des Saints-Pères - 45 48 88 37
Open 10am-7pm. Closed Sun. V, AE, MC. M° Sèvres-Babylone.

This boutique is happy to receive couples in search of a few grams of satin or an ounce of crêpe de chine with which to spice up an evening...

Chantal Thomass

6th arr. - 11, rue Madame
45 44 07 52
Open 10am-7pm (Mon 11am-7pm). Closed Sun. V, AE, DC, MC. M° St-Sulpice.

This lingerie is in a class of its own: garter belts, brassieres, panties, and negligees are musts for collectors.

SWIMSUITS

A la Plage

7th arr. - 6, rue de Solférino
47 05 18 94
Open 10:30am-6:30pm. Closed Sun. V, DC, MC. M° Assemblée-Nationale.
16th arr. - 17, rue de la Pompe - 45 03 08 51
Open 10am-7pm (winter 10am-1pm & 2pm-7pm). Closed Sun. V, DC, MC. M° La Muette.

The most beautiful swimsuits and cover-ups by Hunza, Dior, Scherrer, and other top labels are available here year-round. There's a children's collection, too.

Erès

8th arr. - 2, rue Tronchet
47 42 24 55
Open 9:30am-7pm. Closed Sun. V, AE, DC. M° Madeleine.

6th arr. - 4 bis, rue du Cherche-Midi - 45 44 95 54
16th arr. - 6, rue Guichard
46 47 45 21
Open 10am-7pm. Closed Sun. V, AE, DC. M° Sèvres-Babylone, La Muette.

Erès, the swimwear specialist, sells two-piece suits separately—a brilliant idea! There is an incredible choice of adjustable tops and bottoms to flatter just about any figure. What's more, they're beautifully made and as chic as can be (from 750 F). The Beachwear collection includes coordinates for before and after *la plage.* Upstairs: a lingerie department and a newly expanded section of all-season separates in cotton, Lycra, and viscose.

WEDDING GOWNS

Hélène Gainville

8th arr. - Arcades du Lido, 78, av. des Champs-Élysées, 43 59 32 18
Open 10:30am-7pm. Closed Sun. V, AE. M° George-V.

Hélène Gainville and her fairy-fingered seamstresses will create the wedding gown you've dreamed about since you were small. Made to your measurements, hand-beaded and embroidered, in silk, satin, organza, or lace, these classic, timeless dresses are truly fit for a princess. Naturally, Hélène will be happy to make your veil, headpiece, and other accessories too. Chic traveling clothes and ensembles for the mother of the bride can be custom-made here as well.

Monday, like Sunday, is a day of rest for many shopkeepers.

Monique Germain

6th arr. - 59, bd Raspail
45 48 22 63
Open 12:30pm-7pm (Sat 1pm-6pm). Closed Sun, Mon. V, MC. M° Sèvres-Babylone.

The display window is classic and conventional—anything but exciting. But inside—surprise!—you'll see sculpted bustiers for bare-shouldered brides, sheath dresses with tulle overskirts, and gowns that can be transformed into cocktail frocks after the big day. Alongside is a wealth of stylish accessories, including hats, wreaths, and other pretty headgear.

SHOES & ACCESSORIES

Bally

2nd arr. - 35, bd des Capucines - 42 61 67 34
Open 9:30am-6:30pm. Closed Sun. V, AE, DC, MC. M° Opéra.

Bally is best known for shoes, of course, but the firm's many Parisian branches also propose a splendid selection of fine luggage, handbags, silk scarves, and fashion accessories. Special orders welcome.

Casa Costanza

7th arr. - 34, rue de Grenelle
42 84 18 10
Open 10:30am-noon & 12:30pm-7pm. Closed Sun. V, AE, MC. M° Sèvres-Babylone.

Hand-sewn Italian shoes crafted of supple or exotic leathers are the specialty of the *casa.* The designs are always in tune with current fashions, witness the recent collections featuring cycling shoes, low boots, buckled loafers (600 F), and strappy sandals.

Chéri-Bibi

11th arr. - 82, rue de Charonne - 43 70 51 72
Open 11am-1pm & 2pm-7pm. Closed Sun, Mon. V, AE, MC. M° Charonne.

All manner of adorable little hats (*bibis*) hang on the walls of this trendy shop, where celebrities and anonymous followers of fashion choose their bérets, caps (we love the one with a "target" design), beanies, veiled cocktail hats, and turbans. From 350 to 1,500 F.

Robert Clergerie

1st arr. - 46, rue Croix-des-Petits-Champs - 42 61 49 24
Open 10am-7pm. Closed Sun. V, AE, DC, MC. M° Palais-Royal.
6th arr. - 5, rue du Cherche-Midi - 45 48 75 47
Open 9:30am-7pm. Closed Sun. V, AE, DC, MC. M° Sèvres-Babylone.

Clergerie's much-copied wedgies, metallic faux-croco loafers, and tall-girl pumps with column heels are adored by fashionable *Parisiennes.* Basic shapes vary little from season to season: the designer just changes a detail or two. But the color schemes are always inventive and up-to-the-minute, with warm, muted shades in winter, pastels and flashy brights in summer.

Un Dimanche à Venise

6th arr. - 50, rue du Four
42 22 52 38
Open 10am-7:30pm. Closed Sun. V, AE, DC, MC. M° Sèvres-Babylone.

A newcomer to the footwear scene. What makes this shop worthwhile is the selection of more-or-less obvious copies of shoes by more upscale manufacturers. The quality is perfectly respectable, the styles are always right in fashion, and the prices are A-OK.

Salvatore Ferragamo

6th arr. - 68-70, rue des Saints-Pères - 45 44 01 24
Open 10am-7pm. Closed Sun. V, AE, DC, MC. M° Sèvres-Babylone.

Shoemaker to the stars, inventor of the stiletto heel, Ferragamo creates extravagant footwear dressed up with beads, embroideries, and shimmering bits of mirror or mica. But there are many classic models to choose from as well, and every pair, whether plain or fancy, is miraculously light and comfortable. What's more, with a range of fourteen sizes and seven widths, Ferragamo's shoes rival custom-made shoes for fit. The Florentine firm's Parisian boutiques are paragons of elegance; in addition to footwear, they present tony leather accessories (change purses: 475 F) and deluxe ready-to-wear.

Maud Frizon

6th arr. - 83, rue des Saints-Pères - 42 22 06 93
Open 10:30am-7pm. Closed Sun. V, AE, MC. M° Sèvres-Babylone.

Characters in Judith Krantz novels covet Maud Frizons as much as they do Cartier baubles. Styles are audacious and always feminine, with a subtle use of canvas and lizard, suede and leather. There are heels for all seasons and heights, as well as a plethora of ballet slippers, beach and evening sandals, pumps, and dreamy boots. Prices, 1,450 to 2,700 F.

Harel

8th arr. - 64, rue François-Ier
47 23 96 57
8th arr. - 8, av. Montaigne
47 20 75 00
Open 10am-6:45pm. Closed Sun. V, AE, DC. M° Franklin-D.-Roosevelt, Alma-Marceau.

If you pride yourself on your elegance, you can't afford to ignore Harel. In fact, you owe it to yourself to own at least one pair of these marvelous shoes. Choose from three different arches, three widths, and five heel heights: it all adds up to sheer luxury in footwear. Pumps, sandals, and walking shoes come in a choice of satin, lizard, ostrich, snakeskin, and kid. Colors? There are more than 30. Prices start at 1,800 F and soar skyward from there. Harel shoes are crafted to last a lifetime; if they don't, they'll be sent back to the factory for repairs.

K-Jacques

4th arr. - 16, rue Pavée
40 27 03 57
Open 10:30am-7pm. Closed Sun. V, AE, MC. M° St-Paul.

Colette, the famous French author, launched the K-Jacques sandal in Saint-Tropez, some 60 years ago. Reminiscent of the footwear that Spartans sport in B-movies, the sandal comes in every shade from natural brown to metallic turquoise. Lots of other Provençal accessories are on display: great boots like the ones Camargue cowboys wear, straw bags, ceramics, and Biot glassware (the kind with the tiny bubbles trapped inside).

Charles Kammer

7th arr. - 14, rue de Grenelle
42 22 91 19
Open 10am-7pm. Closed Sun. V, AE, DC, MC. M° Sèvres-Babylone.

Shoes as comfortable as bedroom slippers, for trotting about the city in style. In summer, look for lovely sandals and strappy numbers; in winter, you'll find high-rising vamps and thigh boots in softest leather. Kammer gives you lots of fashion for what is, in fact, a reasonable amount of money.

Stéphane Kélian

1st arr. - Les Trois Quartiers, 23, bd de la Madeleine, 42 96 01 84
2nd arr. - 6, pl. des Victoires
42 61 60 74
7th arr. - 13 bis, rue de Grenelle - 42 22 93 03
8th arr. - 26, av. des Champs-Élysées - 42 56 42 26
Open 10am-7pm. Closed Sun. V, AE. M° Madeleine, Bourse, Sèvres-Babylone, Franklin-D.-Roosevelt.
3rd arr. - 36, rue de Sévigné
42 77 87 91
Open 10am-1pm & 2pm-7pm. Closed Sun. V, AE. M° Saint-Paul.
8th arr. - Galerie Point-Show, 66, av. des Champs-Élysées, 42 25 56 96
Open 10:30am-7:30pm. Closed Sun. V, AE. M° Franklin-D.-Roosevelt.
16th arr. - 20, av. Victor-Hugo - 46 24 67 81
Open 10:30am-7pm. Closed Sun. V, AE. M° Pont-de-Neuilly.

King of the braided-leather shoe, Stéphane Kélian has based his reputation on this technique. He also adds jazzy touches to classic styles. Sculptural heels, fine details, fashionable shapes in shoes for women and men are found in all of the city's Kélian stores.

Lario 1898

6th arr. - 56, rue du Four
45 48 44 65
Open 10am-7pm (Mon noon-7pm). Closed Sun. V, AE, MC. M° Sèvres-Babylone.

Sleek lines and simple, dainty features distinguish Lario's elegant footwear. Women with feet on the small side are best served by the elastic-backed suède loafers in gold, red, cream, or black, or by the smart pumps, dashing sneakers, and delicate lace-up ankle boots that Lario presents in its enticing window display.

Sidonie Larizzi

8th arr. - 8, rue de Marignan
43 59 38 87
Open 10am-7pm. Closed Sun. V, AE, MC. M° Franklin-D.-Roosevelt.

Sidonie Larizzi designs for couturiers, and also produces a collection with her own label. Her boutique creations blend classicism with originality. Alongside the dressy pumps (from 1,800 F) you'll discover delicious boudoir mules with swan's-down pompoms, and some to-drool-over handbags. Studio Larizzi is a lower-priced (but still very stylish) second-tier line priced between 900 and 1,500 F (28, rue de La Trémoille, 47 23 35 08. Closed Sat & Sun).

The prices in this guide reflect what establishments were charging at press time.

John Lobb

8th arr. - 51, rue François-Ier
45 61 02 55
Open 10am-7pm. Closed Sun. V, AE, MC. M° George-V.

Outrageously expensive shoes for demanding feet whose owners have money to spend. You must place your order six months in advance for a pair of sumptuous, custom-made walking shoes, golf shoes, or riding boots. Remarkable footwear from every point of view. Prices are staggering (even for the new ready-to-wear line).

Christian Louboutin

1st arr. - 19, rue Jean-Jacques-Rousseau - 42 36 05 31
Open 11am-7:30pm. Closed Sun. V, AE, MC. M° Louvre.

You don't have to have a shoe fetish to find Louboutin's footwear irresistibly sensual and alluring. A student of the great Roger Vivier, he creates jewels for the feet—just look at the gold leaf, passementerie, and velvet that adorn some of the towering heels! Prices, predictably, are high: from about 1,400 F a pair.

Mancini

16th arr. - 72, av. Victor-Hugo - 45 00 48 81
Open 10am-1:30pm & 2pm-6:30pm (Mon 2pm-6:30pm; Sat 10am-1pm & 2:30pm-6:30pm). Closed Sun. V, AE, DC, MC. M° Victor-Hugo.

René Mancini first made the black-tip shoe for Chanel, and in 1964 he introduced square toes. His daughter, Claire, carries on the family tradition. A portion of the collection is handmade, and it is possible to match your shoes to your dress for a mere 3,000 F and a ten-day wait. Mancini's ready-to-wear shoes are made in Italy and are more affordable, with loafers priced at 1,200 F.

Laurent Mercadal

6th arr. - 56, rue de Rennes
45 48 43 87
Open 10:15am-7pm. Closed Sun. V, AE, DC, MC. M° Saint-Germain-des-Prés.

Laurent Mercadal cobbles classic but stylish women's shoes that are always tuned into current fashion trends. A limited number of basic models is offered in a vast assortment of skins and combinations, in beautiful colors. Reasonable prices (from 695 F).

Marie Mercié

2nd arr. - 56, rue Tiquetonne
40 26 60 68
6th arr. - 23, rue Saint-Sulpice
43 26 45 83
Open 11am-7pm. Closed Sun. V, AE, DC, MC. M° Étienne-Marcel, Odéon.

The Queen of Hats. Her boutiques are stuffed with chic and shocking chapeaux that are guaranteed to grab lots of attention. Marie Mercié designs fantastical headgear that is featured in the fashion shows of many top couturiers.

Philippe Model

6th arr. - 25, rue de Varenne
45 44 76 79
Open 10am-7pm (Mon noon-7pm; Sat 11am-7pm). Closed Sun. V, AE. M° Rue du Bac.

Rare is the woman who would not look fetching in a hat by Philippe Model. His shop overflows with colorful toppers: picture hats, fedoras, feathered and beribboned models, airy straw hats, and jaunty panamas. Model is currently one of the brightest stars in the fashion-accessory firmament.

Palais Cardinal

2nd arr. - 145, galerie de Valois - 42 60 54 13
Open 11:30am-7pm (Mon 2pm-7pm). Closed Sun. V. M° Palais-Royal.

A tiny palace indeed, crammed with delicious hair ornaments (headbands from 115 F), tasteful handbags, and unusual costume jewelry. Owner Dominique Laborde (ex-Carita) will even make up personalized hair accessories just for you (you supply the fabric).

Peinture

7th arr. - 18, rue du Pré-aux-Clercs - 45 48 18 52
Open 10am-7pm. Closed Sun, Mon. V. M° Rue du Bac.

Liberty's celebrated floral and paisley shawls are gathered together here: in cotton or wool for 200 F, or in light yet warm wool challis (450 F). Liberty fabrics are also sold here by the meter, in a choice of patterns even wider than at the firm's London headquarters.

Michel Perry

1st arr. - 13, rue de Turbigo
42 36 44 34
Open 11am-7pm. Closed Sun. V, AE, DC, MC. M° Étienne-Marcel.

Fashionable to the utmost degree, Michel Perry designs fresh, unusual, always glamorous footwear that flatters the feet. The heels of his mules and pumps are particularly inventive.

Andréa Pfister

1st arr. - 4, rue Cambon
42 96 55 28
Open 10am-7pm (Mon 2pm-7pm). Closed Sun. V, AE, DC, MC. M° Concorde.

Pfister makes fine, delicate shoes to suit the comely foot and well-turned ankle. This is Parisian elegance *par excellence*. Embroidered or sequined evening shoes sell for around 2,000 F. The price for a pair of elegant snakeskin shoes can slither up considerably higher.

Rassay & Jean Barthet

8th arr. - 5, rue de Surène
42 65 35 87
Open 11am-6:30pm. Closed Sat, Sun. V, AE, DC. M° Madeleine.

Most of the planet's celebrities have stuck their heads through the door of this institution—and with good reason. Jean Barthet makes hats that are refined and spectacular in their elegance. This is high fashion at over-the-top-hat prices!

Fausto Santini

6th arr. - 4 ter, rue du Cherche-Midi - 45 44 39 40
Open 10am-7pm (Mon 11pm-7pm). Closed Sun. V, AE, MC. M° Sèvres-Babylone.

The Rue du Cherche-Midi was already chockablock with shoe stores, but Santini moved in anyway; and he lost no time in winning an enviable reputation. His handbags and shoes are outstanding for their glowing leathers in myriad hues, delicate curved lines, and fashionable finishing touches.

Walter Steiger

6th arr. - 5, rue de Tournon
46 33 01 45
Open 10am-7pm (Mon 2pm-7pm). Closed Sun. V, AE, DC. M° Odéon.
8th arr. - 83, rue du Fg-St-Honoré - 42 66 65 08
Open 10am-7pm. Closed Sun. V, AE, DC. M° Franklin-D.-Roosevelt.

Steiger's sophisticated shoes come in several heel heights: we love the pleated satin model on towering spikes! For sport and casual wear, the firm produces ineffably chic leather sneakers with molded soles, soft loafers, and spiffy lace-ups. Evening shoes are lined in gold; the pretty ballerina slippers boast heels studded with faux gems. Note also that Steiger's fake-lizard skin (printed on leather) is utterly convincing and much less pricey than the genuine article. Pumps start at about 1,300 F.

François Villon

6th arr. - 58, rue Bonaparte
43 25 98 36
Open 10am-7pm (Mon 10am-1pm & 2pm-7pm). Closed Sun. V, AE. M° Saint-Germain-des-Prés.

François Villon's high-quality footwear is beyond fashion, as Lauren Bacall, Faye Dunaway, Mia Farrow, and Liz Taylor will all confirm. Villon boots are incomparable (around 2,500 F), and the shop also presents attractive dress pumps and casual flats, including the Balletine, a ballerina-style shoe on a one-and-a-quarter-inch heel, available in a host of colors and skins (900 to 1,300 F, guaranteed one year).

ARTS & LEISURE

ART GALLERIES

GEOGRAPHY

A gallery's address is a fairly reliable indicator of its artistic allegiance. The Right Bank, from Avenue Matignon to Avenue de Messine, is the place to view established contemporary artists; the Left Bank, from Rue Guénégaud to Rue des Beaux-Arts, is home to slightly more "advanced" art. The turf of the real avant-garde extends from Beaubourg and Les Halles to the Bastille.

FINE ART

Aréa

3rd arr. - 10, rue de Picardie
42 72 68 66, fax 42 72 53 49
Open 2pm-7:30pm (Thu 2pm-9pm; Sun 3pm-7pm). Closed Mon, Tue. V, MC. M° République.

For a look at what's new, visit Aréa, a gallery devoted to discovering young talents. Among the interesting artists on view recently, we noted Gilles Marrey and Zwy Milshtein. Eight exhibitions each year present artists whose works have never been shown.

Artcurial

8th arr. - 9, av. Matignon
42 99 16 16
Open 10:30am-7:15pm. Closed Sun, Mon. V, AE, DC, MC. M° Champs-Élysées-Clemenceau.

Artcurial is a multi-faceted gallery that boasts one of the finest art bookshops in all of Europe, in addition to collections of contemporary furniture, carpets, and ceramics designed by noted artists, signed lithographs and stunning limited-edition jewelry. Works by de Chirico, Sonia Delauney, Arman, Arp, Laurens, Masson, Miró, and Zadkine may be admired—and purchased—here.

Bernheim Jeune

8th arr. - 83, rue du Fb-St-Honoré - 42 66 60 31 & 27, av. Matignon - 42 66 65 03
Open 10:30am-12:30pm & 2:30pm-6:30pm. Closed Sun, Mon, hols. V, AE, DC, MC. M° Champs-Élysées-Clemenceau.

A respected elder of the art world. Bernheim Jeune specializes in paintings and sculpture from the Impressionists to the present day. That means works by Monet and Pissarro, or Belloni and Fulerand, Lhoste, Pugliese, Polles, or Monreal. The gallery has also published *catalogues raisonnés* of the complete works of Renoir and Bonnard.

Gilbert Brownstone

3rd arr. - 26, rue Saint-Gilles
42 78 43 21, fax 42 74 04 00
Open 11am-7pm. Closed Sun, Mon. No cards. M° Chemin-Vert.

American picture dealer Gilbert Brownstone presents works by recognized contemporary artists who mine the post-Minimalist and Abstractionist veins. Always worth a visit.

Durand-Dessert

11th arr. - 28, rue de Lappe
48 06 92 23, fax 48 06 92 24
Open 2pm-7pm (Sat 11am-7pm). Closed Sun, Mon. V, MC. M° Bastille.

In a gallery space that was once a factory, Liliane and Michel Durand-Dessert display European avant-garde at its loftiest level. You'll find such international high-flyers as Richter, Beuys, Merz, Kounelis, Morellet, Garouste, Lavier, and Tosani. The gallery's bookstore is a wonderful place to linger and browse through the latest art publications.

Espace Photographique de Paris

1st arr. - Nouveau Forum des Halles, place Carrée, Grande-Galerie
40 26 87 12, fax 42 25 42 05
Open 1pm-6pm (Sat & Sun 1pm-7pm). Closed Mon. V, MC. M° Les Halles.

The most comprehensive photographic gallery in town. Jacques Lowe, Ralph Gibson, Bill Brandt, Emmet, Gowin, and other major figures have shown here; retrospectives and *hommages* bring works of the masters to this fascinating gallery.

Galerie Apomixie

6th arr. - 19, rue Guénégaud (in the courtyard)
46 33 03 02, fax 43 29 76 15
Open 11am-1pm & 2pm-7pm. Closed Sun, Mon. V, AE, MC. M° Odéon.

Housed in a seventeenth-century space that is tucked in a historic courtyard, the Galerie Apomixie presents an impressive roster of artists. Several contemporary tendencies are represented: the New Realism (Villeglé), the École de Nice (Ben), Conceptualism (Poivret, Patrick Raynaud), Abstraction (Tony Soulié, Ballester), and more.

King Louis sees the light

It's hardly surprising that Louis XIV, the Sun King, preferred light to shadow—it was he who first had the bright idea to illuminate Paris at night (notably to discourage thieves, murderers, and other criminals who operate under cover of darkness). Squads of torch-bearers were therefore hired to light up the night. Centuries later, in the 1960s, it occurred to the powers-that-be that they could show off the city's monuments (and discourage unwanted visitors) by floodlighting them after dark. New forms of street lighting are illuminating the nocturnal cityscape; color has recently added another dimension, bathing the renovated neighborhood of La Villette with splashes of red and blue.

Galerie Barbier-Beltz
4th arr. - 7, rue Pecquay
40 27 84 14, fax 40 27 81 15
Open 2pm-7pm. Closed Sun, Mon. No cards. M° Rambuteau.

A discreet, elegant little gallery run by a man who has never hesitated to pursue such "difficult" artists as Barré, Dufour, Kallos, Messagier, and Pincemin. They have lately been joined by such estimable painters as Barbara Thaden and Tom Wesselmann.

Galerie Berggruen
7th arr. - 70, rue de l'Université
42 22 02 12, fax 42 22 57 43
Open 10am-1pm & 2:30pm-7pm. Closed Sun, Mon. V, MC. M° Solférino.

H. Berggruen retired and now Madame Audouard oversees the gallery's collection of modern classics (Dali, Klee, Masson, Matisse, Miró, Picasso). She has developed the stake in Surrealism, and has given the gallery a new, more contemporary direction with works by Raysse, Erro, and Kowalski.

Galerie Claude Bernard
6th arr. - 5-7, rue des Beaux-Arts
43 26 97 07, fax 46 33 04 25
Open 9:30am-12:30pm & 2:30pm-6:30pm. Closed Sun, Mon. No cards. M° Saint-Germain-des-Prés.

In a district where fine galleries abound, this is surely one of the very best. Works by Bacon and Bonnard have graced these walls, alongside unforgettable images by Balthus, Botero, Giacometti, Hockney, and Nevelson. Today, you can view works by Peter Blake, Truphemuss, and Csernus.

Galerie Alain Blondel
4th arr. - 4, rue Aubry-le-Boucher - 42 78 66 67
Open 11am-1pm & 2pm-7pm (Sat 2pm-7pm). Closed Sun, Mon. V, AE, MC. M° Les Halles.

Alain Blondel's gallery deals in works by realist, figurative, and representational artists. A recent show featured Francine Van Hove, who paints as Vermeer did, from live models in her studio. Technically amazing.

Galerie Jeanne Bucher
6th arr. - 53, rue de Seine
43 26 22 32, fax 43 29 47 04
Open 9am-1pm & 2pm-6:30pm (Sat 10am-noon & 2:30pm-6:30pm). Closed Sun, Mon. No cards. M° Saint-Germain-des-Prés.

Faithful to the École de Paris of the 1960s, and to a particularly sensitive vision of painting, typified by Dubuffet, Bissière, De Staël, Viera da Silva, and Jean-Pierre Raynaud.

Galerie Claire Burrus
11th arr. - 16, rue de Lappe
43 55 36 90, fax 47 00 26 03
Open 2pm-7pm (Sat 11am-7pm). Closed Sun, Mon. No cards. M° Bastille.

Claire Burrus, a pioneer in this now-hip gallery district, champions post-Conceptual artists like Finlay, Thomas, Nils-Udo, and Felice Varini. A few of the old-guard from her former gallery, Le Dessin, are also present: look for works by Agid, Baruchello, Degottex, and Voss.

Galerie Farideh Cadot
3rd arr. - 77, rue des Archives
42 78 08 36, fax 42 78 63 61
Open 11am-7pm. Closed Sun, Mon. No cards. M° St-Paul.

Farideh Cadot owns one of the most important galleries in Paris, thanks to his provocative, perspicacious choice of artists. No sectarianism here: painting, sculpture, and photography are all (well) represented, with such artists as Boisrond, Favier, Laget, Oppenheim, Raetz, Rousse, and Tremblay. And Cadot is always on the prowl for new, exciting work.

Galerie Callu-Mérite

6th arr. - 17, rue des Beaux-Arts
46 33 04 18, fax 40 51 82 21
Open 1pm-7pm (Sat 10am-7pm; & by appt). Closed Sun, Mon. No cards. M° Saint-Germain-des-Prés.

In addition to established artists like Chaissac, Lacasse, and Bryen, François Callu-Mérite promotes such young up-and-comers as Ramon, Carole Rayes, Dananaï, Bruetchy, and Petrus de Man. The gallery displays paintings, drawings, and sculpture.

Galerie Louis Carré et Cie

8th arr. - 10, av. de Messine
45 62 57 07, fax 42 25 63 89
Open 10am-12:30pm & 2pm-6:30pm (Mon by appt). Closed Sun. No cards. M° Miromesnil.

Patrick Bongers, Louis Carré's grandson, carries on the family tradition by keeping alive the great names of this gallery's past, names like Delaunay, Dufy, Hartung, Léger, Poliakoff, and Soulages. He also exhibits more contemporary work by the likes of Estève and Hervé Télémaque, and even had Di Rosa paint his car!

Galerie Philippe Casini

3rd arr. - 13, rue Chapon
48 04 00 34, fax 48 04 06 08
Open 2:30pm-7pm. Closed Sun, Mon. No cards. M° Arts-et-Métiers.

Since 1985 Philippe Casini has championed artists who were virtually unknown in France, but who later went on to wide recognition: Helmut Dorner, Katsuhito Nishikawa, and Abraham David Christian are but a few examples.

Galerie de France

4th arr. - 52, rue de la Verrerie - 42 74 38 00
Open 10am-7pm (Mon 10am-6pm). Closed Sun. M° Hôtel-de-Ville.

Huge, museum-like premises that span three floors makes the Galerie de France an ideal venue for sculpture exhibits and art festivals. Artists represented here include Aillaud, Antoniucci, Brancusi, Degottex, Gonzales, Kantor, Manessier, Matta, Pincemin, Raynaud, Soulages, and Zao Wou-Ki. Recent exhibitions have showcased works by Cy Twombly, Martial Raysse, and Tom Wesselmann.

Galerie Di Méo

6th arr. - 9, rue des Beaux-Arts - 43 54 10 98
Open 10am-1pm & 2:30pm-7pm. Closed Sun, Mon. No cards. M° St-Germain-des-Prés.

Major artists whose work appears here include Cy Twombly, Michel Haas, Fautrier, Michaux, and Dubuffet. Less well known but most worthwhile are the paintings by contemporary Italian artists.

Galerie Maurice Garnier

8th arr. - 6, av. Matignon
42 25 61 65, fax 45 61 12 33
Open 10am-1pm & 2:30pm-7pm. Closed Sun, Mon. No cards. M° Champs-Élysées-Clemenceau.

Since 1978 Maurice Garnier has represented a single artist: Bernard Buffet, whom Picasso believed was the most talented painter of his generation (even geniuses can have an occasional lapse). Each year, in February and March, Garnier mounts a thematic exhibition of Buffet's work.

Galerie Daniel Gervis

7th arr. - 14, rue de Grenelle
45 44 41 90, fax 45 49 18 98
By appt only. Closed Sun. No cards. M° Sèvres-Babylone.

Daniel Gervis, co-producer of the FIAC, Paris's annual International Fair of Contemporary Art, also produces limited editions of engravings and lithographs. His taste runs toward the abstract, exemplified by such artists as Benrath, Olivier Debré, Dubuffet, Hartung, and Malaval.

Galerie Marwan Hoss

1st arr. - 12, rue d'Alger
42 96 37 96, fax 49 27 04 99
Open 10am-12:30pm & 2pm-6pm. Closed Sun. No cards. M° Tuileries.

Apart from a few great moderns, such as Matisse, Bonnard, and Calder, this gallery pipes a contemporary tune from Giacometti to Garcia, with some stopovers for Manolo Valdes, Hayden, and Zao Wou-Ki.

Galerie Yvon Lambert

3rd arr. - 108, rue Vieille-du-Temple - 42 71 09 33
Open 10am-1pm & 2:30pm-7pm (Sat 10am-7pm). Closed Sun, Mon. No cards. M° Filles-du-Calvaire.

Aloof and reserved, Yvon Lambert is an energetic promoter of the avant-garde. A onetime aficionado of Minimalist and Conceptual art, Lambert now aims in another direction. His enormous gallery is home to works by Lewitt, Oppenheim, Twombly, and Serrano, as well as Christo, Favier, Barcelo, and Anselm Kiefer.

Galerie Lelong

8th arr. - 13, rue de Téhéran
45 63 13 19, fax 42 89 34 33
Open 10:30am-6pm (Sat 2pm-6:30pm). Closed Sun, Mon. V, MC. M° Franklin-D.-Roosevelt.

Known as the "spiritual son" of Aimé Maeght, Daniel Lelong's prestigious gal-lery is one of the most important in Paris. In addition to his branches in Zurich and New York, he also runs a sideline publishing venture (you'll find the books, catalogs, and lithos on the gallery's lower level). Lelong's exhibits encompass works by great twentieth-century artists: Bacon, Calder, Chagall, Lindner, Moore, Bram Van Velde, as well as Adami, James Brown, Kienholz, Tàpies, and Donald Judd.

Galerie Louise Leiris

8th arr. - 47, rue de Monceau
45 63 20 56, fax 45 63 76 13
Open 10am-noon & 2:30pm-6pm. Closed Sun, Mon. No cards. M° Monceau.

Founded by D. H. Kahnweiler, this "picture dealer of the century" (Picasso, Léger, Gris, Braque, and others) is indeed a venerable and historically important gallery that should not be missed. The collections are tops in terms of quality and prestige, with works by Masson, Laurens, Beaudin, and, more recently, Élie Lascaux and Y. Rouvre.

Galerie J.-G. M.

6th arr. - 8 bis, rue Jacques-Callot
43 26 12 05, fax 46 33 44 83
Open 10am-1pm & 2:30pm-7pm (Sat 11am-7pm). Closed Sun, Mon (exc appt). No cards. M° Odéon.

Contemporary sculpture, a much-neglected discipline, occupies center stage at Jean-Gabriel Mitterrand's gallery. Artists shown here regularly include Igor Mittoraj, Nikki de Saint-Phalle, François Lalanne, and Takis.

Galerie Adrien Maeght

7th arr. - 42 & 46, rue du Bac
45 48 45 15, fax 42 22 22 83
Open 9:30am-1pm & 2pm-7pm. Closed Sun, Mon. V, AE, DC, MC. M° Rue du Bac.

A gallery that bears the name of Maeght is obviously going to have a prestigious catalog of the highest quality. And indeed this double space displays a varied menu of top twentieth-century artists, with works by Matisse, Chagall, Calder, and Bram Van Velde. A recent show featured paintings by Gérard Gasiorowski. The gallery also represents important designers (Olivier Gagnère...), publishes excellent art books, and offers limited editions of prints and engravings.

Galerie Daniel Malingue

8th arr. - 26, av. Matignon
42 66 60 33, fax 42 66 03 80
Open 10:30am-12:30pm & 2:30pm-6:30pm. Closed Sun. No cards. M° Franklin-D.-Roosevelt.

Twice a year, Daniel Malingue mounts well-publicized exhibitions of Impressionist masters and important twentieth-century artists; recent shows have focused on Dufy, Léger, Matisse, and Vlaminck, as well as César, Lobo, Matta, and Moore.

Galerie Nikki Diana Marquardt

4th arr. - 9, pl. des Vosges
42 78 21 00
Open 1pm-7pm. Closed Sun, Mon. M° Saint-Paul.

American gallery owner Nikki Marquardt displays a bold approach to contemporary art: she's willing to take a risk, and usually comes up a winner. She claims that one "doesn't need direction, just vision, to know about art." David Mach has done his special brand of sculpture installation here; sculpture by Vlugt, Flavin, and works by Dunoyer, Stefan Szczesny, and Kumrov have also been shown, to considerable critical acclaim.

Galerie 1900-2000

6th arr. - 8, rue Bonaparte
43 25 84 20, fax 46 34 74 52
Open 10am-12:30pm & 2pm-7pm (Mon 2pm-7pm). Closed Sun. AE. M° Saint-Germain-des-Prés.

This gallery is best known for its eye-popping exhibitions on such movements as Surrealism, Hyperrealism, and Pop Art. Represented are Max Ernst, Hérold, Marcel Jean, Matta, Picabia, Man Ray, Gaston Louis Roux, and Takis. Young artists with fresh viewpoints are also energetically promoted.

Paradise behind the walls

You'll have a better grasp of the original meaning of paradise—"walled garden"—when you visit the flower- and fountain-filled courtyards nestled within the white walls of the *Paris Mosque*. Built in 1922 in a predominantly Moroccan style, it also houses a library, Turkish baths, restaurant, and tea rooms. The interior is sumptuous, with stucco, carved wood, mosaics, and carpets reminiscent of a more leisurely age. Another view of Islam is afforded by the *Institute of the Arab World* on the nearby Quai Saint-Bernard, a futuristic nine-story structure of glass, concrete, and aluminum that includes a museum, art gallery, and documentation center.

Galerie Montenay

6th arr. - 31, rue Mazarine
43 54 85 30, fax 43 29 42 21
Open 11am-1pm & 2:30pm-7pm. Closed Sun, Mon. No cards. M° Odéon.

Marie-Hélène Montenay is the proud possessor of one of the most beautiful spaces in her part of town. From conceptual work to figurative painting, her choices are wide-ranging and always challenging. Ange Leccia and Bruce Marden have their niche here, and so does Malcolm Morley.

Galerie Odermatt-Cazeau

8th arr. - 71, rue du Fg-St-Honoré - 42 66 92 58
Open 10am-6:30pm. Closed Sun. M° Concorde.

This gallery specializes in works by nineteenth- and twentieth-century masters, Impressionists, and post-Impressionists. The sculpture exhibitions are particularly fine (Germaine Richier, Gonzales, Zadkine).

Galerie Gerald Piltzer

8th arr. - 78, av. des Champs-Élysées
43 59 90 07, fax 43 59 90 08
Open 10am-7pm. Closed Sun. V, MC. M° Franklin-D.-Roosevelt.

Gerald Piltzer's handsome space presents major American painters—Motherwell, Sam Francis—alongside rising younger artists (Adrienne Farb, Peter Briggs, Olivier Seguin...). You will also see representatives of the Russian school here: Malevitch, Filonov, Chagall; and a few French Abstractionists, notably Olivier Debré.

Galerie Denise René

7th arr. - 196, bd Saint-Germain
42 22 77 57, fax 45 44 89 18
Open 10am-1pm & 2pm-7pm (Sat from 11am). Closed Sun, Mon. No cards. M° Saint-Germain-des-Prés.

In 1945 Denise René's pioneering gallery became the rallying center for geometrical abstraction. Since then she has sung its praises the world over and adopted the offshoots of Constructivism, promoting the works of Agam, Albers, Claisse, Dewasne, Herbin, Naraha, Soto, and Vasarely. René's Right Bank outpost is located at 22, rue Charlot in the third arrondissement.

Galerie Schmit

1st arr. - 396, rue Saint-Honoré
42 60 36 36, fax 49 27 97 16
Open 9am-12:30pm & 2pm-6:30pm. Closed Sat, Sun. No cards. M° Palais-Royal.

Robert Schmit and his son, Manuel, present the greatest masters of the nineteenth and twentieth centuries in a gallery one visits as one would a museum. Ingres, Delacroix, Courbet, Corot, Boudin, Chagall, Dufy, Soutine, Utrillo, Vuillard... the amazing list goes on and on. The Schmits have also published *catalogues raisonnés* of the complete works of Boudin, Derain, and Stanislas Lépine.

Galerie Zabriskie

4th arr. - 37, rue Quincampoix
42 72 35 47, fax 40 27 99 66
Open 2pm-7pm. Closed Sun, Mon. No cards. M° Les Halles.

A mainly photographic gallery with a downtown (Manhattan) attitude, where photos are presented as if they were sculpture. Weegee, Klein, Friedlander, Peter Briggs, and Poivret: the gang's all here, with pictures full of vibrant temperament.

Don't plan to shop on Sundays—the vast majority of Paris stores are closed.

Didier Imbert Fine Art

8th arr. - 19, av. Matignon
45 62 10 40, fax 42 25 86 03
Open 10am-1pm & 2:30pm-7pm. Closed Sun. No cards. M° Champs-Élysées-Clemenceau.

Didier Imbert has transformed his gallery into a veritable museum. Exhibits of works by Brauner, Brancusi and the acclaimed *Henry Moore Intime* show, which were as intellectually stimulating as they were thrilling to view, have placed Imbert in the forefront of the Parisian art scene. Botero is the gallery's current darling.

Lavignes-Bastille

11th arr. - 27, rue de Charonne
47 00 88 18, fax 43 55 91 32
Open 11am-7pm. Closed Sun, Mon. V, AE, MC. M° Bastille.

Since 1985 Jean-Pierre Lavignes has filled his multilevel gallery with fascinating, sometimes violent work by contemporary artists working in the Realist and Expressionist veins: Calum Fraser, Grataloup, Hahn, Lukaschewsky, Rotella, Sandorfi, and, on occasion, Andy Warhol (his last Parisian show was held right here).

Baudoin Lebon

4th arr. - 38, rue Sainte-Croix-de-la-Bretonnerie
42 72 09 10, fax 42 72 02 20
Open 2:30pm-7pm. Closed Sun, Mon. No cards. M° Hôtel-de-Ville.

Allow us to forewarn you: this gallery is a little offbeat. Expect, for example, to see an exhibition of aboriginal art and works by Ben, Bissier, Dado, Dine, Michaux, Pagès, Rauschenberg, Titus-Carmel, and Viallat. Photography is another major focus at this eccentric gallery, established in a fabulous space.

HOBBIES & SPORTS

ART SUPPLIES

Adam Montparnasse

14th arr. - 11, bd Edgar-Quinet
43 20 68 53, fax 43 21 23 72
Open 9:30am-7pm (Mon 9:30am-12:30pm & 1:30pm-7pm). Closed Sun. V, MC. M° Edgar-Quinet.

For three generations, the Adam family has supplied artists and graphics designers with all the canvas, paper, paint, and ink they need, in every possible color and size. You want references? How about Braque, Soutine, and Modigliani? They all shopped here, and appreciated the sage advice dispensed by the competent staff. Sculptors, too, will find all their needs met here, and there is a new line of makeup and "special effects" supplies for filmmakers.

Sennelier

7th arr. - 3, quai Voltaire
42 60 72 15, fax 42 61 00 69
Open 9am-6:30pm (Mon 9am-noon & 2pm-6:30pm). Closed Sun. V, AE, DC, MC. M° Palais-Royal.

Appropriately situated next to the Beaux-Arts school, Sennelier has, in its century of existence, sold tons of art supplies to innumerable established and aspiring artists. Here they find the best brands of paints and pigments, paper and sketch pads of excellent quality, canvas, easels, and framing equipment. Sculptors too can purchase all of their special supplies right here.

ASTRONOMY

La Maison de l'Astronomie

4th arr. - 33, rue de Rivoli
42 77 99 55, fax 48 87 40 87
Open 9:45am-6:45pm. Closed Sun, Mon. V, MC. M° Hôtel-de-Ville.

Stargazers gather here for books, posters, and sky maps pertaining to astronomy, as well as instruments for searching the heavens: telescopes, photo equipment, binoculars, and specialized software. Introductory courses in astronomy are offered, as well as a course in astronomic photography.

BICYCLING

Paris By Cycle

14th arr. - 78, rue de l'Ouest
40 47 08 04, fax 43 35 28 83
Open daily 9:30am-1:30pm & 2pm-7:30pm. V, MC. M° Pernety.

Rent a city bike or a mountain bike by the hour (28 F) or by the week (300 F) from this competent, friendly team of specialists. A wide selection of bicycles is available for purchase, and there is a repair shop on the premises. Outings are organized, for gregarious bikers.

Paris Vélo-Rent a bike
5th arr. - 2, rue du Fer-à-Moulin
43 37 59 22, fax 47 07 67 45
Open 10am-12:30pm & 2pm-7pm. Closed Sun. V, MC. M° Censier-Daubenton.

Bicycle rental by the hour, day, or weekend. No racing bikes here, but you'll find plenty of city bikes and mountain bikes—the most practical varieties for the local terrain. Guided bicycle tours of the city are offered as well.

BOWLING

Bowling Mouffetard
5th arr. - 13, rue Gracieuse
43 31 09 35
Open daily 11am-2am. V, AE, MC. M° Place Monge.

One of this bowling alley's eight lanes can be yours for 20 F plus 8 F for shoe-rental (afternoon rate); or 25 F plus shoes (evening rate). On weekends and holidays, the tariff rises to 32 F. While you await your turn, you can play pool or pinball, or grab a sandwich at the snack bar.

COOKING

Le Cordon Bleu
15th arr. - 8, rue Léon-Delhomme
48 56 06 06, fax 48 56 03 96
Open 8:45am-7pm (Sat 8:45am-5pm). Closed Sun. V, MC. M° Vaugirard.

Cooking buffs may attend daily demonstrations given by master chefs (English-language translation available; 150 F for two and a half hours). If you are more interested in hands-on experience, week-long courses are held in regional cuisines, pastry-making, bistro cooking, and so on (3,000 to 4,000 F). Professional training leading to a Cordon Bleu diploma is also dispensed (from 22,000 to 36,000 F per trimester, depending on the level).

Ritz-Escoffier École de Gastronomie Française
1st arr. - 38, rue Cambon
42 60 38 30, fax 40 15 07 65
Open 9am-6pm. Closed Sat, Sun. V, AE, MC. M° Madeleine.

The school's facilities are set up opposite the very kitchens where nineteenth-century chef Auguste Escoffier exercised his incomparable art. Aspiring cooks can learn every aspect of the trade here, with professional-level courses; amateurs may register for the César-Ritz cycle, which lasts from one to six weeks. Each week, students attend four hands-on cooking and pastry-making courses (5,500 F per week), watch four demonstrations, and take one theory course (cheese, wine, etc.). For 230 F, anyone can attend a demonstration performed by a master chef. English-language courses are offered.

Princess Ère 2001
7th arr. - 18, av. de La Motte-Picquet
45 51 36 34, fax 45 51 90 19
Open 10:30am-5pm. Closed Sat, Sun. Prices: 580 F / course or 3,000 F for 6 courses, lunch incl; 650 F / course or 3,400 F for 6 courses directed by G. Sallé, lunch incl. No cards. M° École-Militaire.

Regional cooking, market cooking, cuisine nouvelle, low-calorie cooking, and the art of hospitality form the curriculum here. Courses (580 F per session) are taught by Marie-Blanche de Broglie and Gérard Sallé, chef of the Régence restaurant in the Hôtel Plaza-Athénée. In addition to French, the lessons are dispensed in English and Spanish.

DANCE

Centre de Danse du Marais
4th arr. - 41, rue du Temple
42 77 58 19
Open daily 9am-10pm. V. M° Hôtel-de-Ville.

Dance courses run the gamut from Argentinian tango and contemporary Japanese *buto* dancing to African dance, flamenco, or Brazilian and Asian dances. There are 32 disciplines in all, taught in somewhat tumbledown surroundings but in a friendly, non-threatening atmosphere.

Studio Paris-Centre
9th arr. - 54a, rue de Clichy
42 81 26 33, fax 42 81 26 33
Open daily 9:30am-8:30pm (Sat 9:30am-6pm; Sun 2pm-7pm). V, AE, MC. M° Liège.

This is the largest dance center in Europe; all the great names have shown up to practice here, at one time or another. Forty teachers are on hand to dispense courses in ballet, jazz, rock, and flamenco, or to lead you through a grueling barre au sol session (Kiniasef method). On Friday and Saturday evenings, you can learn to mambo, waltz, or cha-cha-cha. The membership fee is 200 F per year; courses cost 65 F per lesson or 1,100 F for twenty lessons.

GAMES

Boutique du Bridgeur

1st arr. - 28, rue de Richelieu
42 96 25 50, fax 40 20 92 34
Open 10am-6:30pm (Sat 10am-6pm). Closed Sun. V, AE, MC. M° Palais-Royal.

The boutique carries an immense range of playing cards, of course, but you will also find electronic partners, and magnetic card-and-board kits that allow you to play on the deck of a boat in gale-force winds! English-language books and magazines on bridge are offered for sale, as well as paraphernalia for scrabble, backgammon, and chess.

Game's

1st arr. - Forum des Halles, porte Lescot, level -2,
40 26 46 06, fax 40 26 55 91
Open 10am-7:30pm. Closed Sun. V, MC. M° Les Halles.

This is a grown-up's game shop featuring chess sets carved in precious woods or onyx, electronic games, brain-teaser puzzles, billiards, roulette wheels, slot machines, and more. Also, role-playing games complete with instruction books (in French and English) and the necessary figurines.

Games Work Shop

14th arr. - 13, rue Poirier-de-Narçay - 45 45 45 87
Open 10:30am-7pm. Closed Sun, Mon. V, MC. M° Porte-d'Orléans.

All the necessary equipment for strategy, simulated battle, and role-playing games is sold in this unobtrusive little shop.

Jeux Descartes

5th arr. - 52, rue des Écoles
43 26 79 83, fax 43 26 98 61
(also: 17th arr.)
Open 10am-7pm (Mon 11am-7pm). Closed Sun. V, MC. M° Cluny-La-Sorbonne.

American games of strategy and intelligence (in English!) may be purchased here, as well as juggling equipment (said to combat stress...), collectible figurines, and old-fashioned board games.

Rouge et Noir

6th arr. - 26, rue de Fleurus
43 26 05 77, fax 43 26 05 77
Open 10:30am-7pm (Mon 2:30pm-7pm). Closed Sun. V, AE, DC, MC. M° Vavin.

Games old and new, perfect for rainy weekends: checkers, mah-jongg, go, backgammon, and chess. There are puzzles, too, and tarot cards—even crystal balls!

Le Train Bleu

6th arr. - 55, rue Saint-Placide
45 48 33 78
16th arr. - 2-6, av. Mozart
42 88 34 70
Open 10am-7pm. Closed Sun. V, AE. M° Saint-Placide, La Muette.

This is a luxury supermarket for toys and games. The basement level is reserved for adult games, but all ages are amused by the fun stuff for kids sold on the other three floors.

GARDENING & FLOWER ARRANGING

Centre d'Art Floral Ikebana

17th arr. - 26, rue d'Armaillé
45 74 21 28, fax 45 74 21 46
Open 9am-noon & 2pm-6pm. Closed Sat, Sun. No cards. M° Charles-de-Gaulle-Étoile.

The Japanese tradition of flower arranging was originally a religious practice developed by Buddhist monks. There are several different schools of Ikebana in Japan. At this address you will be taught the pure and simple Ohara style. Greenery is included in the price of the lessons, but bring your own shears.

École d'Horticulture du Jardin du Luxembourg

6th arr. - 64, bd Saint-Michel
45 48 55 55, fax 42 34 35 19
Open 8am-noon & 2pm-6pm. Closed Sun. No cards. M° Notre-Dame-des-Champs.

Register in May for courses held from September to June on decorative gardens, or on the proper cultivation of fruit trees. The courses are free, but enrollment is limited.

Société Nationale d'Horticulture de France

7th arr. - 84, rue de Grenelle
45 48 81 00, fax 45 44 96 57
Open 9am-5:45pm. Closed Sat, Sun. Membership fee: 150 F / year. No cards. M° Rue du Bac.

Only association members are admitted to SNHF courses (the membership fee is 150 F). Nine different courses are given, including an introduction to gardening, the cultivation of roses, house plants, flower arranging, and so on. This is where you can learn to graft trees or create a garden on your balcony.

GOLF

Golf Club de l'Étoile

17th arr. - 10, av. de la Grande-Armée
43 80 30 79, fax 47 64 10 26
Open daily 8am-10pm. Membership: 2,600 F / year; 140 F / 30 mn. Entrance fee: 60 F. V. M° Charles-de-Gaulle-Étoile.

Polish your putting at this unusual practice range situated in a rooftop greenhouse; you can also loosen up your drive at one of the seven practice tees, or use a video simulation to help improve your swing. Six highly qualified pros are on hand to teach beginners the basics, as well as to give veteran players advice on how to achieve a better game.

HEALTH CLUBS

Club Jean de Beauvais

5th arr. - 5, rue Jean-de-Beauvais - 46 33 16 80
Open daily 7am-10pm (Sat 8:30am-7pm; Sun 9:30am-5pm). V, AE, DC, MC. M° Maubert-Mutualité.

A doctor supervises your progress, a chiropractor advises you, a gym instructor personally takes charge of your training, and a nutritionist supervises your diet. For those who have decided, finally, to take themselves in hand, it's a complete overhaul. For sporting types just looking for a tune-up, there's ski readiness in the fall and windsurfing prep in the spring. Annual membership rates range from 4,500 F to 6,700 F.

Espace Vit'Halles

3rd arr. - Place Beaubourg, 48, rue Rambuteau
42 77 21 71, fax 42 77 56 25
Open daily 8am-10pm (Sat 10am-7pm; Sun 11am-3pm). V. M° Rambuteau.

Nearly 120 classes per week are given by the center's twenty instructors in cardio-vascular fitness, body-building, and strengthening. Hi-lo, cardio-funky and funky-step, body sculpting, stretching, and localized workouts (abs and buns) are just some of the options available. For relaxing after a workout, there are saunas, a Turkish bath, Jacuzzi, and massage services. Personal trainers are on hand to design individualized fitness programs. The facilities are well-kept and clean, pleasant to use but unpretentious. Annual fee: 3,900 F per year (2,900 F for students). Short-term rates available.

Gymnase Club

1st arr. - 147 bis, rue Saint-Honoré - 40 20 03 03 (also: 1st arr., 8th arr., 9th arr., 11th arr., 12th arr., 13th arr., 14th arr., 15th arr., 16th arr., 17th arr., La Défense, Neuilly, Montigny-le-Bretonneux)
Open daily 7:30am-10pm (Sat 9am-7pm; Sun & hols 9am-5pm). Membership fee: 3,520-3,970 F / year. M° Palais-Royal.

This chain of fitness clubs operates centers all over Paris. Several have swimming pools and offer classes in aqua-gym. The menu of activities also comprises cardio-training, strengthening, body-building, and modern jazz dance. Among the post-workout attractions are a whirlpool bath, a sauna, and a Turkish bath. The competent staff can design a fitness program that meets individual needs, and for short-term visitors, books of tickets for a limited number of entries may be obtained at the clubs.

Vitatop-Club Plein Ciel

15th arr. - 8, rue Louis-Armand
45 54 79 00, fax 45 54 20 32
Open daily 7am-9pm (Sat 9am-7pm; Sun 9am-5pm). V, AE, MC. M° Balard.

The membership fees are high (5,450 F a year) but the variety of services is wide. Vitatop's state-of-the-art fitness equipment includes Stairmasters, electronic stationary bikes, rowing machines, a Gravitron, and more. Each club offers a pool (also used for popular aqua-gym classes), Jacuzzi, comfortable dressing rooms and showers, a sauna, and so forth. Courses are offered all day long in fitness and related disciplines (jogging, personal health/nutrition supervision) at no extra charge.

ICE SKATING

Patinoire des Buttes-Chaumont

19th arr. - 30, rue Édouard-Pailleron - 42 08 72 26
Open Wed 10am-9pm; Thu & Fri 4pm-11pm; Sat 10am-midnight; Sun 11am-7pm. Closed mid Jun-mid Sep. Prices: adults: 27 F; under 16: 21 F; skate rental: 18 F. M° Bolivar.

The one and only permanent ice-skating rink in Paris. Ice dancers and speed-skaters are given run of the rink for fifteen minutes each hour.

MUSIC

François Guidon
9th arr. - 16, rue Victor-Massé - 48 78 91 05
Open 2pm-7pm. Closed Sat, Sun. No cards. M° Pigalle.

François Guidon buys, restores, and sells jazz guitars. Molded instruments command 12,000 F, while handmade guitars (constructed like cellos) start at 16,000 F.

Hamm
6th arr. - 135-139, rue de Rennes - 44 39 35 35
Open 10am-7pm (Mon 2pm-7pm). Closed Sun. V, AE, MC. M° Saint-Placide.

Hamm is assuredly one of the city's best sources for all types of musical instruments. Six floors display pianos and synthesizers, percussion and wind instruments, guitars, and even a selection of antiques. Small studios are also rented here, for rehearsals or lessons.

Le Projet Musical
10th arr. - 23, rue du Fg-St-Denis
42 46 27 26, fax 48 24 58 53
Open 2pm-6pm. Closed Sat, Sun. No cards. M° Strasbourg-Saint-Denis.

Accordion, clarinet, guitar, flute: these instruments are taught by top-notch instructors. Solfège and voice lessons are also offered at this school, which is subsidized by the City of Paris. A yearly fee of 5,000 F entitles you to two hours of lessons per week.

NEEDLEWORK

L'Atelier de la Dentellière
13th arr. - 9, rue de Patay
45 86 14 78
Open Thu 2pm-5pm, Fri 1:30pm-7:30pm, Sat 2:30pm-5:30pm. Closed Sun-Wed. No cards. M° Porte-d'Ivry.

Under the tutelage of Lysianne Brulet, professor of lace-making, you'll learn how to use linen, cotton, or silk thread with finesse to make lace trim for curtains, blouses, and napkins. This painstaking work teaches the lovely rewards of patience. The fee for twelve courses is 1,700 F.

La Droguerie
1st arr. - 9, rue du Jour
45 08 93 27
Open 10:30am-6:45pm (Mon 2pm-6:45pm). Closed Sun. No cards. M° Les Halles.

Here is a gold mine for knitting fanatics. Not only will you find the needles and wool you seek, you can also count on the sales staff to help you get the hang of an unusually difficult stitch. And that's not all: the shop stocks a dazzling selection of trims—multicolored beads, feathers, sequins, and such are stored in antique candy jars and sold by the ladleful!

R. Malbranche
9th arr. - 17, rue Drouot
47 70 03 77
Open 9am-noon & 2pm-6pm. Closed Sat, Sun. No cards. M° Richelieu-Drouot.

For sale here are linen sheets, muslin napkins, linen handkerchiefs, and cambric placemats all delicately embroidered by hand—in short, it's the household linen of your dreams (at prices that leave you dreaming!). You can also learn how to make these masterpieces of patience yourself. Courses are taught by an award-winning needlewoman on Thursday afternoons (eight two-hour classes cost 700 F). You'll be taught all the basic stitches plus some of the more complicated ones that require considerable skill.

RACETRACKS

Hippodrome d'Auteuil
16th arr. - Bois de Boulogne
45 27 12 25
Openings vary. M° Porte d'Auteuil

The *Prix du Président de la République*, a hurdle race for French steeplechasers, is run here each year.

Hippodrome de Longchamp
16th arr. - Bois de Boulogne, route des Tribunes
44 30 75 00
Openings vary.

Home to the prestigious *Prix de l'Arc de Triomphe*, a highlight of the year's racing calendar.

Hippodrome de Vincennes
12th arr. - Bois de Vincennes, 2, route de la Ferme
49 77 17 17
Openings vary.

The big event at this track is the yearly *Prix d'Amérique*.

Remember that if you spend 2,000 F or more in a store, you are entitled to a full refund of the value-added tax (VAT). See Basics *for details.*

RIDING

Centre Équestre de la Cartoucherie de Vincennes

12th arr. - Route Champ-des-Manœuvres - 43 74 61 25
Open 9am-11pm (Sun morning). Membership fee: 150 F (lifetime). Membership: 400 F / year. Courses: 1,030 F / trimester (1 course / wk). No cards. M° Château-de-Vincennes.

Indoor and outdoor riding lessons are dispensed here, in the middle of the Bois de Vincennes. Riders who have proved their steadiness in the saddle are permitted to join groups for all-day outings in the forest. Small children may be introduced to equestrian pleasures at the Centre's pony club.

Centre Équestre de la Villette

19th arr. - 55, bd Mac-Donald - 40 34 33 33
9am-noon & 1:30pm-9:30pm (Sun 9am-noon; Mon 1:30pm-9:30pm). No cards. M° Porte-de-la-Villette.

On the plus side, this club offers modern facilities, well-cared-for horses reputed for their gentleness, and a spacious indoor ring. Unfortunately, with no woods in the vicinity, students have no opportunities for excursions.

ROCK CLIMBING

La Samaritaine

1st arr. - Magasin 3, 75, rue de Rivoli
40 41 20 20, fax 40 41 23 24
Open 9:30am-7pm (Thu 9:30am-10pm). Closed Sun. V, AE, MC. M° Pont-Neuf.

Before tackling the Alps or the Pyrenees (or the fascinating rock formations in the Fontainebleau Forest), perfect your rock-climbing technique on this five-meter-high wall. Beginners and seasoned climbers alike will be challenged by the wall's hollows, toe-holds, bumps, and projections. Equipment for a mountain holiday is also sold down here in the basement of La Samar's store number three.

SWIMMING

Aquaboulevard

15th arr. - 4, rue Louis-Armand
40 60 10 00, fax 40 60 18 39
Open daily 8am-11pm (Sat & Sun 8am-midnight). V. M° Balard.

Aquaboulevard made quite a splash when it opened its doors in 1989. The centerpiece of this gigantic sports, fitness, and leisure complex is an "aquatic park": the biggest pool in Paris, replete with water slides, rapids, toboggans, and other fun stuff that drives kids wild with joy. But water sports are only part of the action. Other possibilities include tennis, squash, bowling, billiards, bridge, ping-pong, and video games. You can work out at the gym, spruce up at the beauty salons, or chow down at one of several restaurants. You'll be shelling out too, to the tune of 75 F for an adult admission on weekends (children: 55 F), plus 200 F per hour for tennis, 60 F per half-hour for squash...

Piscine les Amiraux

18th arr. - 6, rue Hermann-la-Chapelle - 46 06 46 47
Hours vary. Admission: 13 F (under 16: 6.50 F). No cards. M° Simplon.

This beautiful pool, vintage 1930, is an architectural landmark. Open until 7:30pm on Mondays, for people who like a quick dip after work.

Piscine de la Butte-aux-Cailles

13th arr. - 5, pl. Paul-Verlaine
45 89 60 05
Hours vary. Admission: 13 F (under 16: 6.50 F). No cards. M° Place-d'Italie.

Set in a picturesque neighborhood, this lovely Art Deco establishment offers three pools. The larg-

Splash!

Clean, attractive municipal swimming pools can be found all over Paris; locating one that is open to you at a given hour is less easy, since schedules vary greatly. A *free booklet,* **available from the attendants at any of the city's 28 public pools, will give you specific addresses, opening hours, and pool sizes, along with a color picture of each facility. Admission to city pools is currently 13 francs. Regular swimmers can purchase a three-month pass for 189 francs. Listed below is a selection of some of the prettier pools in town.**

est is an indoor facility, but the two others are outdoor pools, fed by an artesian well.

Piscine Champerret-Yser

17th arr. - 36, bd de Reims
47 66 49 98
Hours vary. Admission: 20 F (under 16: 17 F). No cards. M° Pereire.

Bright, new, and modern, with a spiral sliding board that youngsters adore, this pool is enclosed by tall glass walls. There are tennis courts on the premises.

Piscine Henry-de-Montherlant

16th arr. - 32, bd Lannes
45 03 03 28
Hours vary. Admission: 13 F (under 16: 6.50 F). No cards. M° Porte-Dau-phine.

In a chic *quartier* not far from the Bois de Boulogne, this municipal pool is part of a sports complex that includes tennis courts and a gymnasium.

Piscine Jean-Taris

5th arr. - 16, rue Thouin
43 25 54 03
Hours vary. Admission: 13 F (under 16: 6.50 F). No cards. M° Place-Monge.

Students favor this splendid pool, which boasts a view of the Panthéon and the gardens of the Lycée Henri-IV. A special system makes it accessible to disabled.

Piscine Suzanne-Berlioux

1st arr. - Forum des Halles, 10, pl. de la Rotonde
42 36 98 44
Hours vary. Admission: 22 F (under 16: 17 F). No cards. M° Châtelet.

This new, 50 by 20 meter pool in the Forum des Halles is open several evenings a week.

Allô-Sports

If you're visiting Paris and wish to play tennis without spending huge sums on private clubs, contact *Allô-Sports* (Mon-Fri 10:30am-5pm - 42 76 54 54), a municipal sports hotline, for information on public and municipal courts. If your French is not up to that sort of project, check the addresses listed below.

TENNIS & SQUASH

Squash Montmartre

18th arr. - 14, rue Achille-Martinet - 42 55 38 30
Open 10am-11pm (Sat & Sun 10am-8pm). M° Lamarck-Caulaincourt.

If you schedule your game in off-peak hours (10am to 5:30pm) you can play at reduced rates on these fine, well-lit courts, then relax in the sauna, on the terrace, or in the billiard room. Several different rate structures are offered, and trial memberships are available too.

Tennis du Luxembourg

6th arr. - Jardins du Luxembourg, Pavillon Raynal
43 25 79 18
Open 8am-4:30pm. Price: 30 F / hour. No cards. M° Saint-Sulpice.

The six open courts are usually reserved well in advance by clubs and associations, but there is no reason not to try your luck...

MUSEUMS

MAJOR MUSEUMS

Cité des Sciences et de l'Industrie

19th arr. - 30, av. Corentin-Cariou - 36 68 29 30
Open 10am-6pm. Closed Mon. Admission: 45 F, reduced rate: 35 F. Cafeterias. Access for disabled. V, MC. M° Corentin-Cariou.

The gigantic steel, glass, and concrete Cité casts a formidable shadow across the wacky Parc de la Villette, with its geodome and moats, set in an enormous green swath along the Ourcq Canal. It is the world's largest science and industry museum, conceived for the 21st century. Yet you'll find that the Cité is, paradoxically, made to human measure. Floors are divided into modular cells, which are shuffled around to create scenic effects. Visitors are challenged to penetrate the mysteries of science. And we've found that it is best to be curious—and daring. Get the most out of the Cité by examining and playing with the exhibits. Scores of computer terminals beckon, ready to measure your knowledge, to lead you through experiments of weightlessness or the speed of sound, to activate robots, take you on a trip through outer space, heighten your senses, or put you in touch with experts in myriad fields of knowledge. Of particular interest to youngsters is the *Cité des Enfants*, filled with fascinating exhibits that make science "friendly" and fun. Kids also love the Géode movie theater, housed in a stainless-steel sphere: viewing a film projected by the Omnimax system (enhanced with holograms and lasers) is an experience no child will soon forget.

Galerie Nationale du Jeu de Paume

1st arr. - Jardin des Tuileries, corner pl. de la Concorde/ rue de Rivoli - 47 03 12 50
Open noon-7pm (Tue noon-9:30pm; Sat & Sun 10am-7pm). Closed Mon. Admission: 35 F, reduced rate: 25 F. V, AE. M° Concorde.

When its treasure trove of Impressionist masterpieces was ferried across the river to the new Musée d'Orsay, the Jeu de Paume lost its *raison d'être*. Then, a few years ago, it was decided that the space could be most advantageously used as a showcase for contemporary art. Magnificently restructured by architect Antoine Stinco, the museum was relaunched in 1991 by a dynamic team of art professionals. The inaugural exhibit, dedicated to Jean Dubuffet, was a resounding success. Subsequent shows featuring Ellsworth Kelly, Martial Raysse, Antoni Tàpies, and the photographers Tunga and Jana Sterbak, among others, also won great acclaim. The new Jeu de Paume combines the prestige of a national art institution with the excitement of an avant-garde gallery, plugged in to the way artists work today.

Musée d'Art Moderne de la Ville de Paris

16th arr. - 11, av. du Président-Wilson - 47 23 61 27
Open 10am-5:30pm (Sat & Sun 10am-7pm). Closed Mon. Admission: 14 F, exhibitions: 45 F, reduced rate: 35 F. Temporary exhibitions. Cafeteria. Access for disabled. V, AE, DC. M° Iéna.

The MAM has always been a vector of change. But while collections may waltz in and out, the various "isms" of modern art are always represented: from Fauvism (Vlaminck and Derain) to Cubism (Picasso and Braque) to Kinetism (Vasarely, Agam). And, of course, still on view is the celebrated *Electricity Fairy* by Raoul Dufy and Matisse's rapturous triptych, *Dance*. The fourth-level ARC (*Animation, Recherche, Confrontation*) is the liveliest section of the museum, used primarily to showcase contemporary art forms (plastic arts, photography, poetry, contemporary music and jazz). Often, several shows and events run simultaneously, with an accent on new talent.

Musée des Arts Décoratifs

1st arr. - Palais du Louvre, 107, rue de Rivoli
44 55 57 50
Open 12:30pm-6pm (Sun noon-6pm). Closed Mon, Tue. Admission: 25 F, reduced rate: 16 F. Temporary exhibitions. Access for disabled. No cards. M° Palais-Royal.

The Gallic penchant for living in beauty and comfort comes vividly alive in the 100-odd rooms and galleries of the Musée des Arts Décoratifs, which traces the history of French homes from the Middle Ages to the present. One-of-a-kind and mass-produced tapestries, ceramics, tableware, and furniture demonstrate how tastes and style have evolved. The exquisite suite of 1920s Art Deco rooms was crafted for fashion designer Jeanne Lanvin. Avant-garde furnishings by Breuer, Perriand, and others flank creations by Eames, Tallon, and Paulin in a sweeping panorama of the last 50 years of French and international design. Also on view is a delightful display of eighteenth- to twentieth-century toys—it is the largest collection of its kind in France. Housed at the same address are the Musée de la Mode (Fashion), which stages temporary exhibitions based on a huge inventory of clothing that dates back to the Renaissance; and the Musée de la Publicité (Advertising) which mounts thematic shows drawn from its vast archives. The museum library (109, rue de Rivoli) holds a treasure trove of documentation on arts and crafts, and the boutique carries an alluring array of books and gifts.

Crowds in the Louvre

Watch out, the crowds in the Musée du Louvre are heavy in the early morning, especially in summer. To have a quiet look at the *Venus de Milo*, **the** *Victory of Samothrace*, **the** *Mona Lisa*, **or other masterpieces of the collections, visit the Louvre after 3pm. And if you dream of being alone—or almost alone—in the galleries, plan to come on a Monday or a Wednesday at the end of the day: the museum is then open until 10pm.**

Musée de l'Homme

16th arr. - Palais de Chaillot, pl. du Trocadéro
44 05 72 72
Open 9:45am-5:15pm. Closed Tue. Admission: 25 F, reduced rate: 15 F. V, MC. M° Trocadéro.

The history of humanity on all five continents is the fascinating story that the Musée de l'Homme relates. It's a tale we understand better, now that the museum is no longer a daunting jumble! The remodeled entrance hall, as well as the anthropology, America, and Africa galleries are all new and improved (the rest of the collections are awaiting renovation). Descriptions and displays are now easy for the layman to understand. From the permanent collections, be sure to see the Chinese theater costumes, African masks, Indian jewelry, and Eskimo sculptures. Then stop at Le Totem, a restaurant-cum-tea room, for a restorative snack.

Musée du Louvre

1st arr. - Rue de Rivoli, Main entrance: Cour Napoléon - 40 20 51 51 (answering machine in English)
Open 9am-6pm (9am-10pm: Mon: Aile Richelieu only; Wed: the entire museum), temporary exhibitions: 10am-10pm. Closed Tue. Admission: 40 F before 3pm, 20 F after 3pm & Sun, under 18: free. V, AE, MC. M° Palais-Royal.

The Musée du Louvre is now the cleaned up, modernized, and much expanded Grand Louvre, symbolized by architect I.M. Pei's glittering glass pyramid. Although work will continue into 1997, most of the spectacular billion-dollar overhaul begun in 1983 is now complete. As visitors descend beneath the pyramid (in essence a high-tech skylight and entrance), they discover a huge underground complex with reception and ticket areas, shops, and restaurants. It is from this point, in the Cour Napoléon, that the 5 million people who now visit the Louvre each year set off to view the collections—preferably armed with one of the museum's color-coded maps.

If you've been put off by the Louvre in the past, we urge you to give it another go. You're sure to be impressed with the improvements that now make it possible to view 3,000 years worth of world art in a coherent, convenient way (though not, of course, in a single day!).

For an overview of the museum's holdings, as well as a look at the "New Louvre" that everyone's buzzing about, plan to visit the splendid new Richelieu Wing, inaugurated in November 1993 on the Louvre's 200th birthday. The Aile Richelieu, which runs along the Rue de Rivoli, adds nearly 237,000 square feet to the museum's total area; the increase of air, light, and viewing space is incalculable. On the ground floor you can view the Louvre's sculpture collection. Monumental works of classical French sculpture, such as the famed *Steeds of Marly*, are admirably displayed in covered courtyards. Here too you'll find the awesome winged bulls and bas-reliefs from the Assyrian palace of Khorsabad. Furniture and art objects, including Renaissance tapestries and the royal Treasure of Saint-Denis—don't miss those crown jewels!—have found a suitably sumptuous home on the Wing's first floor, amid Emperor Napoléon III's palatial salons. And on the second floor, bathed in natural light, are French paintings from the fifteenth to seventeenth century (including splendid pictures by Poussin, Claude Lorrain, and Le Sueur), as well as sublime paintings from the *École du Nord*, with works by Vermeer, Rembrandt, Cranach, Ruysdael... Rubens's suite of 24 scenes from the life of Marie de Médicis (mother of Louis XIII) are superbly presented in a room of their own.

Continue your visit in the adjoining Sully Wing, where 39 newly installed rooms present a spectacular panorama of French painting from the eighteenth and nineteenth centuries. The Ingres, Corot, and Delacroix rooms are not to be missed!

Commerce has also been given its due at the Grand Louvre, in the form of Le Carrousel du Louvre, an underground concourse lined with deluxe shops (note the inverted glass pyramid, also designed by I.M. Pei), and the furiously fashionable Café Marly, located on the first floor of the Richelieu wing.

Musée de la Marine

16th arr. - Palais de Chaillot, place du Trocadéro
45 53 31 70
Open 10am-6pm. Closed Tue. Admission: 31 F, reduced rate: 16 F. Guided tours, conferences, temporary exhibitions. Access for disabled. No cards. M° Trocadéro.

Ships ahoy! The world's largest maritime collection is solidly moored at Trocadéro, where waves of enthusiastic youngsters regularly inundate the Musée de la Marine. They may sail right by the magnificent Joseph Vernet paintings, but they always go overboard for the antique and modern naviga-tion-al instruments, the sidearms and cannons, and the colorful figureheads. Countless scale-model ships represent five centuries of maritime history, from caravels to atomic submarines.

Musée Marmottan

16th arr. - 2, rue Louis-Boilly
42 24 07 02
Open 10am-5:30pm. Closed Mon. Admission: 35 F. No cards. M° La Muette.

This Sleeping Beauty's Castle of a museum has just emerged from two years of renovations: the Empire furniture and paintings, the admirable medieval tapestries look better than ever in their refurbished surroundings. But the Marmottan is best known as a premier Impressionist showcase, with major works by Claude Monet, Renoir, Pissarro, Sisley, Morisot. Monet's *Impression, Soleil Levant*, stolen from the museum in 1985, again occupies a place of honor. The Marmottan is also home to the Wildenstein illuminated medieval manuscripts—a truly extraordinary collection.

Musée National d'Art Moderne Centre Georges Pompidou

4th arr. - 19, rue Beaubourg
44 78 12 33
Open noon-10pm (Sat & Sun 10am-10pm). Closed Tue. Admission: 30 F, reduced rate: 20 F. Restaurant, bar, cafeteria. Access for disabled. No cards. M° Hôtel-de-Ville.

When it opened on January 31, 1977, the Centre Georges Pompidou was called a hideous oil refinery, destined to rust away before the very eyes of a disgusted public. Today, it is recognized as an architectural landmark, the embodiment of a certain "romantic" vision of high-tech. Some 100 million visitors have passed through its modern art galleries, museum, cinemas, concert hall, library (with many books in English), industrial design center, and record archives (with extensive listening facilities).

Since exhibition space is limited, the Centre regularly reshuffles the paintings on view with others from its rich holdings. Picasso, Bonnard, Matisse, and Kandinsky are particulary well represented in a permanent collection that traces the history of modern art from Cubism to the present. One of the two screening rooms of the Cinémathèque (National Film Archives) is located in the building. And the sloping plaza in front teems with jugglers, mimes, caricaturists, fire-eaters, and other exotic fauna. Take note that the Centre's *Librairie* is one of Paris's best-stocked art bookstores, carrying deluxe editions published by the Centre (architecture, film, music, and so forth), plus temporary-exhibit catalogs, many of which have become collector's items. A $1 million overhaul of the museum is scheduled to begin in 1997; designated sections of the Centre will remain open to the public.

Note that national museums are generally closed on Tuesdays.

Musée d'Orsay

7th arr. - 1, rue de Bellechasse - 40 49 48 14
Open 10am-6pm (Thu 10am-9:45pm; Sun 9am-6pm). Closed Mon. Admission: 35 F, reduced rate: 24 F. V, AE, MC. M° Solférino.

To think that the former train station that is now the acclaimed Musée d'Orsay was slated for demolition, condemned as a horrid example of *fin de siècle* taste (it was designed in 1900 by architect Victor Laloux)! Saved in the nick of time, the derelict station's exterior and frame were restored and strengthened, then Italian architect Gae Aulenti worked her peculiar magic on the monumental interior, with impressive results. Now the Grand Central Terminal of nineteenth-century art, the Musée d'Orsay's collections trace the jagged path of painting, sculpture, photography, decorative and industrial art from 1848 to 1914. The museum's exhibitions are always major cultural events. Recent blockbusters have included shows on Van Gogh, Cézanne, Sisley, Degas, and Toulouse-Lautrec. Among the Orsay's treasures are Honoré Daumier's classic 36-bust series *Les Parlementaires* (1832); Claude Monet's *Rue Montorgueil* (1878), bursting with noisy life; Georges Seurat's pointillistic *Poseuse de Dos*, seemingly composed of little more than air and light; and Giovanni Boldini's Proustian *Portrait de Madame Max* (1896). The museum bookshop is large and well stocked; the gift shop displays many lovely and culturally correct trinkets.

Musée du Petit Palais

8th arr. - 1, av. Winston-Churchill - 42 65 12 73
Open 10am-5:40pm. Closed Mon. Admission: 26 F, reduced rate: 14 F. No cards. M° Champs-Élysées-Clemenceau.

Built in 1900 F or the *Exposition Universelle*, the Petit Palais houses an eccentric permanent collection that is largely neglected. In other words, you'll be able to enjoy an unobscured view of the exquisite Dutuit donation, featuring rare examples of Egyptian and Greek art, and the sumptuous Rembrandt self-portrait in Oriental garb. The Tuck Collection, comprising eighteenth-century furniture and tapestries, is also at home here. The municipal collections boast several gems: magnificent paintings by Courbet, Delacroix, Bonnard, Vuillard, and Cézanne, plus Impressionist works that have escaped the Musée d'Orsay dragnet. An entire hall is given over to a sublime series by Odilon Redon. Elsewhere you'll find sculptures by Auguste Rodin. Temporary exhibits held here are are of reliably high quality.

Musée National Picasso

3rd arr. - Hôtel Salé, 5, rue de Thorigny - 42 71 25 21
Open 9:30am-5:30pm. Closed Tue. Admission: 26 F, reduced rate: 17 F, under 18: free. V, MC. M° Saint-Paul.

This is indeed art in an artful architectural frame.

The magnificent seventeenth-century Hôtel Salé, one of the Marais's most spectacular private mansions, was painstakingly restored to house the paintings and artworks donated to the state by Picasso's heirs in lieu of death duties. Here you can rediscover one of this century's greatest artists through a complete panorama of his favorite works—"Picasso's Picassos." Proof of his precocity is offered by several astonishingly polished paintings done when the artist was fourteen years old—*The Barefoot Girl* and *Man with a Cap* among them. Picasso's private collection of works by his contemporaries—Cézanne, Braque, Matisse, Derain, and others—is also on view.

Museum tours

La Réunion des Musées Nationaux, which organizes most of the exhibitions at the national museums in Paris, offers guided tours of the Louvre and other museums and art galleries. For details phone 40 20 51 77 for the Louvre and 40 13 49 12 or 40 13 49 13 for the other

Muséum d'Histoire Naturelle

5th arr. - Jardin des Plantes, 57, rue Cuvier - 40 79 30 00

Open 10am-5pm (Sat & Sun 11am-6pm). Closed Tue, hols. V. M° Jussieu.

This magical, many-faceted museum-cum-garden is truly a marvel—best encountered bit by bit! In the verdant Jardin des Plantes (Botanical Garden) that surrounds the Muséum, sycamore-lined gravel lanes link carefully labeled flower beds and herb gardens to a charming zoo and an exotic tropical hothouse. Inside the Muséum itself, the big news is the opening of the spectacular Evolution Gallery. It provides a fascinating look at the unity and diversity of all Earth's creatures, through a dramatically presented parade of (eerily lifelike) stuffed specimens: rhinoceroses, giraffes, hippos, elephants... Lights and music, in addition to educational exhibits and videos, make the Gallery as entertaining as it is instructive. Parents visiting Paris with children should not miss it.

Equally impressive, in a more low-key way, are the Anatomy and Paleontology Gallery, filled with skeletons and prehistoric monsters; and the Paleobotany Hall, with plant specimens from two billion to 250 million years ago. The cavernous Mineralogy Hall is home to thousands of meteorites, giant crystals, and precious gems (the Salle du Trésor, or treasure hall, reveals an astounding wealth of emeralds, sapphires, rubies, turquoise, platinum, and gold nuggets from the Bank of France's safes). A flight of fancy awaits butterfly enthusiasts in the Entomology Hall's collections (45, rue Buffon), which also include about a billion beetles and other bugs!

OFF THE BEATEN TRACK

Cabinet des Médailles et Monnaies Antiques de la Bibliotèque Nationale

2nd arr. - 58, rue de Richelieu 47 03 83 30

Open daily 1pm-5pm (Sun noon-6pm). Admission: 20 F, reduced rate: 12 F. V. M° Bourse.

Even blasé numismatists are floored by this awesome collection of 400,000 coins and medals, including the world's largest collection of cameos and intaglios, precious works from antiquity—note the remarkable Hellenistic torso of Aphrodite—,the Middle Ages, and the Renaissance, plus Persian silverwork, and even some paintings by Boucher and Van Loo. Housed in the Bibliothèque Nationale building, it is one of the most venerable Paris museums.

Cristallerie de Baccarat

10th arr. - 30 bis, rue de Paradis - 47 70 64 30

Open 9am-6pm (Sat 10am-noon & 2pm-5pm). Closed

Museum pass

The *Carte Musée et Monuments* or Museum Pass, available at museums, monuments, and main Métro stations, allows you to wander at will through every one of the 62 museums and monuments in Paris and the greater metropolitan area, without waiting in line. The single-day pass sells for 70 F, the three-day pass for 140 F, and the five-day pass for 200 F.

Sun. V, AE, DC. M° Château-d'Eau.

After stocking up on china, silver, and crystal on the Rue de Paradis, where the foremost manufacturers of French tableware cluster in confraternal companionability, do make time to visit the Musée du Cristal. You'll gasp in amaze at Baccarat's most impressive creations, from stemware and perfume bottles to opaline objets d'art and sumptuous chandeliers.

Grévin–Forum des Halles

1st arr. - Forum des Halles, level -1, porte Lescot, Grand Balcon
40 26 28 50, fax 42 33 35 61
Open 10:30am-6:45pm (Sun & hols 1pm-6:30pm). Admission: 42 F, reduced rate: 36 F. No cards. M° Les Halles.

The Forum des Halles branch features Paris in the Belle Époque, a series of animated tableaux, and Reynaud's Optical Theater—the praxinoscope, predecessor of the Lumière brothers' cinematograph—which Reynaud operated in Montmartre from 1892 to 1900.

Maison de Balzac

16th arr. - 47, rue Raynouard
42 24 56 38
Open 10am-5:40pm. Closed Mon. Admission: 17 F, reduced rate: 9 F. Temporary exhibitions. No cards. M° Passy.

The rustic charm of Honoré de Balzac's modest house and verdant garden—*la cabane de Passy*, where he lived from 1840 to 1847—was only one reason the penurious novelist holed up here. The other is a discreet back entrance and escape route down the Rue Berton—because when Balzac wasn't penning *The Human Comedy*, he was keeping his eye out for debt collectors. The flavor of his checkered life comes through in his austere study stuffed with letters, documents, and everyday objects—an inkwell shaped like a padlock and primed for sixteen hours of work—and decorated with portraits of the women he loved and admired.

Maison de Victor Hugo

4th arr. - Hôtel de Rohan-Guéménée, 6, pl. des Vosges - 42 72 10 16
Open 10am-5:40pm. Closed Mon, hols. Admission: 17 F, reduced rate: 9 F. No cards. M° Bastille.

Victor Hugo lived from 1832 to 1848 in this seventeenth-century house on the Place des Vosges. In these seven rooms, he wrote several chapters of *Les Misérables* as well as scores of plays and poems. Family portraits, yellowed souvenirs, and piously preserved memorabilia rather blandly trace Hugo's tormented life. But the rooms do provide an excellent idea of how Hugo amused himself when he was not writing: drawing somber pen-and-ink sketches (executed in a state of "almost unconscious reverie," according to the artist), or cobbling together eccentric wooden cabinets. The haunting initials V. H. seem to appear everywhere.

Musée de l'Armée

7th arr. - Hôtel National des Invalides, 51, bd de Latour-Maubourg - 44 42 37 67
Open 10am-5pm (Apr 1-Sep 30: 10am-6pm). Admission: 32 F, reduced rate: 22 F. Concerts in Saint-Louis des Invalides church; cafeteria. No cards. M° Invalides.

Arm yourself for the onslaught of countless weapons and machines of war designed to slash, club, explode, flatten, puncture, and otherwise exterminate your neighbor. Every imaginable type of weaponry is on display in this extremely popular museum (right up there with the Eiffel Tower and the Château de Versailles in terms of tourist visits). The collections of military uniforms, arms and armor, maps, and paraphernalia are the richest in the world. They are housed in several buildings that surround the grand courtyard of Les Invalides, built as a veterans hospital at the behest of

Louis XIV, by architects Libéral Bruant and Jules Hardouin. Mansart erected the towering Dôme church, whose gilded cupola is visible from all over Paris. True to type, Napoléon appropriated the church as a monument to his own glory, and he is entombed in the elaborate carved-porphyry Emperor's Tomb under the dome. (Napoléon-trivia fans take note: the museum also boasts the bizarre stuffed white charger he rode on Saint Helena and the dog that kept him company during his exile on the island of Elba.) Among the exhibits are an amazing Renaissance sword engraved by Benvenuto Cellini, some magnificent East Asian weapons, and a moving display devoted to the Great War. A newly refurbished gallery relates the history of World War II and the Liberation of Paris. Coming soon: a demonstration room, where children can get their hands on actual weapons...!

Musée d'Art et d'Histoire de Saint-Denis

93200 Saint-Denis - 22 bis, rue Gabriel-Péri
42 43 05 10
Open 10am-5:30pm (Sun 2pm-6:30pm). Closed Tue. Admission: 15 F, reduced rate: 10 F. No cards. M° St-Denis-Porte-de-Paris.

Winner of the coveted Prix Européen du Musée, this marvelous former Carmelite convent (seventeenth and eighteenth centuries), superbly restored in 1981, makes the trip to dingy Saint-Denis worthwhile. On display is a fine collection of religious art and archaeological finds pertaining to the city and the Carmelite order. Easy to reach (the RER express subway takes you there from central Paris in just a few minutes), it is located next door to the phenomenal Cathedral of Saint-Denis, resting place of the French kings.

Musée d'Art Juif

18th arr. - 42, rue des Saules
42 57 84 15
Open Sun-Thu 3pm-6pm. Closed Fri, Sat, Jewish hols. Admission: 30 F, reduced rate: 20 F. No cards. M° Lamarck-Caulaincourt.

Objects used at temple services, popular art, scale models of synagogues from the thirteenth through the nineteenth century, rare books, contemporary paintings and drawings (Marc Chagall, among them) are on display at this fascinating museum housed in the Montmartre Jewish Center.

Musée d'Art Naïf Max Fourny-Musée en Herbe

18th arr. - Halle Saint-Pierre, 2, rue Ronsard -42 58 72 89
Open daily 10am-10pm (Sun & Mon 10am-6pm). Admission: 22 F, reduced rate: 16 F. Tea room. No cards. M° Anvers.

This two-in-one museum, housed in the sunny nineteenth-century Halle Saint-Pierre, is a charming place to spend an afternoon. A vast second-floor loggia houses Max Fourny's renowned collection of naïf and folk art. The ground floor features thematic exhibits for children that cover an almost infinite range of subjects. The museum also hosts a number of workshops for kids, spin-offs of the temporary shows.

Musée des Arts Asiatiques-Guimet

16th arr. - 6, place d'Iéna
47 23 61 65
Open 9:45am-6pm. Closed Tue. Admission: 27 F, reduced rate: 18 F. Audiovisual & conference rooms. No cards. M° Iéna.

A visit to this venerable temple of Asian art will whisk you across the vast territory of Oriental art: Khmer statues from ninth- through eleventh-century Cambodia; smiling gods and eyeless kings that well up in a halo of light. There is also a huge collection of Buddha paintings (from Nepal and Tibet), a Cubist-like head of Kasyapa sculpted in gray chalkstone (sixth-century China) and, from the monasteries of Hadda in Afghanistan, delicate, fragile stucco and dried-earth figurines. Chinese ceramics and porcelain fill several halls. N.B.: The museum is scheduled to close for a two-year period in late 1995, for a renovation that will make Guimet the world's foremost repository of Asian art.

Musée Bouchard

16th arr. - 25, rue de l'Yvette
46 47 63 46, fax 46 47 70 50
Open Wed & Sat 2pm-7pm. Closed Mon, Tue, Thu, Fri, Sun. Admission: 25 F, reduced rate: 15 F. Access for disabled. No cards. M° Jasmin.

Chisels and chips of stone, sketches and photos thumbtacked to the wall in delightful disarray—the liveliest sculptor's studio in town is the Musée Henri Bouchard (1875–1960). The masterful academic's work may leave some cool, but the guided tours and lectures on the sculptor's trade, won't.

Musée Bourdelle

15th arr. - 16, rue Antoine-Bourdelle - 45 48 67 27
Open 10am-5:40pm. Closed Mon. Admission: 17 F, reduced rate: 9 F. Access for disabled. No cards. M° Montparnasse.

Riotous green gardens strewn with Antoine Bourdelle's bronzes are hidden in the heart of old Montparnasse. We like to visit in the spring when the trees are bursting with blossoms. This house/museum has been suspended in time since the sculptor's death in 1929. Bourdelle's brawny art represents a powerful reaction to the sculpture of its time (he was, when young, Rodin's assistant). Giant original plasters are featured in the exhibit hall: *The Dying Centaur*, *The Polish Saga*, and the equestrian statue of Alvéar. The Beethoven series of bronze heads overflows with pathos. Don't miss the new galleries, designed by top architect Christian de Porzamparc.

Musée Carnavalet

3rd arr. - 23, rue de Sévigné
42 72 21 13
Open 10am-5:40pm. Closed Mon, hols. Admission: 27 F, reduced rate: 19 F. V, AE, DC. M° Saint-Paul.

A vivid panorama of Parisian history is presented here—from the city's ancient origins to the present day. The sound and fury of years gone by, the restitching of the urban fabric, the beautification and destruction of the metropolis are captured in topographical models of neighborhoods, scale models of monuments, paintings, prints and, for the modern era, photographs. The mansion that houses the museum is itself a prime exhibit: it is one of the most harmonious architectural ensembles in the Marais, with a lovely inner-court garden. From 1777 to 1796 the mansion was inhabited by Madame de Sévigné, famed in French letters for her epistolary excellence. French Revolution devotees will not want to miss the blood-stained letter Robespierre was writing when the Terror turned upon him. The temporary exhibitions mounted by the museum are always worthwhile.

Musée de la Chasse et de la Nature

3rd arr. - 60, rue des Archives
42 72 86 43
Open 10am-12:30pm & 1:30pm-5:30pm. Closed Tue. Access for disabled. V, MC. M° Hôtel-de-Ville.

Don't be put off by the gory theme—the history of the hunt—for this is a charming museum housed in a magnificent 1654 Marais mansion built by François Mansart. Always a hit with youngsters of all ages are the fine collections of weapons—from flint arrow-heads to precision firearms, carved powder horns, gold-encrusted carbines, ancient elephant guns... Impressive trophies from three continents and a superb collection of paintings by Rembrandt, Cranach, Dürer, and Monet, among others, round out the picture.

Musée Cognacq-Jay

3rd arr. - Hôtel de Donon, 8, rue Elzevir - 40 27 07 21
Open 10am-5:40pm. Closed Mon. No cards. M° St-Paul.

The ravishing Renaissance Hôtel de Donon holds a collection of eighteenth-century art and objets assembled by Ernest Cognacq, founder of La Samaritaine department store. He was a savvy connoisseur indeed, to judge by his acquisitions. Pictures signed by Fragonard, Greuze, and Watteau, exquisite furniture, and delicate porcelains compose a veritable feast for the eye. The museum's intimate atmosphere contributes to the delicious sensation of traveling back to a more graceful age.

Musée Eugène Delacroix

6th arr. - 6, rue de Furstenberg - 43 54 04 87
Open 9:45am-5:15pm. Closed Tue. Admission: 12 F, reduced rate: 8 F. No cards. M° Saint-Germain-des-Prés.

Anyone with a 100 F note in his pocket already owns a valuable Delacroix (1798–1863). In a secret garden off the Place Furstenberg, romantic as can be, the Eugène Delacroix home/museum (the painter's apartment and sunny studio are linked by a curious footbridge) is one of Paris's great little-knowns. There are no masterworks here, but rather a fine series of drawings, watercolors, and pastels (plus studies for such famous paintings as *The Death of Sarda-*

napalus), an astonishing self-portrait, the palette and easel this Romantic artist used to paint his early works, pages from his journal and various other oddities of the artist.

Musée du Grand Orient de France

9th arr. - 16, rue Cadet
45 23 20 92
Open 2pm-6pm. Closed Sun. Admission: free. V. M° Cadet.

This is no ill-lit hideaway for regicides and fearful free-thinkers, but a modern, rather stark museum of French Freemasonry. Displayed in glass cases in a somber hall are paintings, sculptures, engravings, and medals, pertaining primarily to political figures, intellectuals and military leaders. You will discover scores of illustrious names on the roster: Philippe-Égalité (a royal revolutionary who was guillotined during the Reign of Terror), Voltaire, Montesquieu, Marshal Joffre, the Comte de Bourbon-Condé, and, surprise, even a Roosevelt.

Musée Grévin

9th arr. - 10, bd Montmartre
47 70 85 05
Open daily 1pm-7pm (school hols: 10am-7pm). Admission: 48 F, reduced rate: 34 F. No cards. M° Rue Montmartre.

You and the other 650,000 annual visitors to the Musée Grévin will either chuckle at or pale among the petrified personages assembled here. The delirious décor of this monumental waxworks (the fourth most frequently visited museum in Paris) ranges from the Cabinet Fantastique, a charming little theater done up by Bourdelle and Chéret, to a madcap mob that includes Barbie (the doll), and other current celebrities. The basement galleries present scenes from France's eventful history.

Musée Gustave Moreau

9th arr. - 14, rue La Rochefoucauld - 48 74 38 50
Open 10am-12:45pm & 2pm-5:15pm (Mon & Wed 11am-5:15pm). Closed Tue. Admission: 17 F, reduced rate: 11 F. No cards. M° St-Georges.

"If you want to get a job done right, do it yourself," thought Symbolist painter Gustave Moreau (1826–1898). So he erected this Renaissance Revival building on the lovely Place Saint-Georges, a temple to his own posterity. It is worth a visit just to see the spectacularly baroque spiral staircase that links the third and fourth floors, where an enormous workshop and grand gallery house Moreau's works. Surrealist writer André Breton was for decades the sole defender of Moreau's prodigious talents, but the admiration of Matisse (his pupil) brought Moreau wider acclaim. We've spent hours rummaging through the nearly 6,000 drawings, studies and watercolors that verify Moreau's fertile creativity.

Musée de l'Histoire de France

3rd arr. - 60, rue des Francs-Bourgeois - 40 27 61 78
Open 1:45pm-5:45pm. Closed Tue. Admission: 15 F, reduced rate: 10 F. No cards. M° Hôtel-de-Ville.

What could be more precious than the history of a nation? Which explains the choice for the National Archives: the magnificent Hôtel de Soubise, considered by many to be the finest eighteenth-century town house in Paris. These exquisite apartments, decorated by Boucher, Natoire, Van Loo, and Adam, hold medieval manuscripts covering the period from the Merovingians (a Frankish dynasty that flourished from the fifth century to 751) to the Hundred Years' War, as well as an impressive collection of documents pertaining to the French Revolution (the *Declaration of the Rights of Man*). Long-running exhibits generally feature some sort of written document, so a working knowledge of French is helpful. Regardless of language, a stroll through the town house and gardens are worth the visit.

Musée Jean-Jacques Rousseau

95160 Montmorency - 5, rue Jean-Jacques-Rousseau
39 64 80 13
Open 2pm-6pm. Closed Mon. Admission: 20 F. No cards.

The wandering philosopher and scribe Jean-Jacques Rousseau settled down from 1757 to 1772 in this modest abode and penned *La Nouvelle Héloïse*, *L'Émile*, and the *Lettre à d'Alembert*. Rousseau's furniture, various letters and manuscripts are among the memorabilia. The charming garden's path of ancient lime trees—tradition has it that Rousseau planted two of them—leads to a tiny pavilion that houses the philosopher's workroom.

Musée Lambinet

78000 Versailles - 54, bd de la Reine - 39 50 30 32
Open 2pm-6pm. Closed Mon. Admission: 19 F, reduced rate: 13 F. No cards. RER Versailles-Rive Gauche (C).

No pomp and circumstance, as in the neighboring Château de Versailles. Here you will find a delightful eighteenth-century town house lost in a restful green garden, collections of Sèvres and Saint-Cloud porcelain, sculptures by Houdon, eighteenth-century paintings, period furniture plus nineteenth-century statuettes, and works by painters Dunoyer de Segonzac and André Suréda, all charmingly displayed.

Musée Tourgueniev

78380 Bougival - 16, rue Ivan-Tourgueniev - 45 77 87 12
Open Mar 22-Dec 22: Sun 10am-6pm & weekdays by appt. Admission: 25 F, reduced rate: 20 F. No cards.

This delightful *dacha* was the great Russian writer's slice of home (so what if it looks more like a Swiss chalet!). The author of *A Month in the Country* lived here happily, near friends Louis and Pauline Viardot (his cottage actually stands in their garden; pretty Pauline was his secret lover). Ivan Sergeyevich died here in 1883. A pleasant pilgrimage for Turgenev devotees.

Musée de la Mode et du Costume

16th arr. - Palais Galliera, 10, av. Pierre-Ier-de-Serbie
47 20 85 23
Temporary exhibitions only. Open during exhibitions: 10am-5:40pm. Closed Mon. Annual closings depending on exhibitions. Admission: 35 F, reduced rate: 25 F. Access for disabled. V. M° Iéna.

Housed here is one of the world's richest wardrobes: 100,000 costumes for men, women, and children of all social classes—from the eighteenth century to the present. Popular recent exhibits have focused on the designs of Givenchy, Jacques Fath, and the history of jeans.

Musée de la Monnaie

6th arr. - 11, quai de Conti
40 46 55 33
Open 1pm-6pm (Wed 1pm-9pm). Closed Mon. V. M° Pont-Neuf.

The end of the rainbow for numismatists: a staggering array of precious coins and medals housed in the gorgeous Hôtel des Monnaies. A mere 200 years or so after its creation (1768 by Louis XV), the Mint has been reborn as a museum. On display are coins from ancient times to the present. The mansion's court of honor and the many superb salons are alone worth the visit.

Musée de Montmartre

18th arr. - 12, rue Cortot
46 06 61 11
Open 11am-6pm. Closed Mon. Admission: 30 F, reduced rate: 20 F. Temporary exhibitions. No cards. M° Lamarck-Caulaincourt.

Relive the notorious Montmartre bohemia of politicians and artists (which include the likes of Picasso, Utrillo, Renoir, and Modigliani) in this sunny, charming museum that overlooks the hillside Clos Montmartre, one of the city's last remaining vineyards. Watch for the excellent temporary exhibitions.

Musée National des Arts d'Afrique et d'Océanie

12th arr. - 293, av. Daumesnil - 44 74 84 80
Open 10am-noon & 1:30pm-5:30pm (Sat & Sun 12:30pm-6pm); Aquarium: 10am-6pm. Closed Tue. Admission: 27 F, reduced rate: 18 F. Access for disabled. No cards. M° Porte-Dorée.

Kids love this place, with its crocodile pits and an immense aquarium swimming with piranhas. On the edge of the Bois de Vincennes at the Porte Dorée, the massive 1931 former Musée des Colonies is a remarkable example of the architecture of its age. Outside is a gigantic bas-relief depicting the flora and fauna of some riotously rich colonial kingdom. Inside are eye-popping collections of African masks, statues in wood and bronze, jewelry, and finery from Africa and Melanesia.

Musée National des Arts Traditions Populaires

16th arr. - 6, av. du Mahatma-Gandhi, Bois de Boulogne
44 17 60 00
Open 9:45am-5:15pm. Closed Tue. Admission: 17 F, reduced rate: 11 F. Access for disabled. No cards. M° Sablons.

This is the sort of museum that captivates some and loses others right off. Collections of handcrafts and folk art trace the development of customs and traditions in rural France. Arranged with startling precision and displayed in huge Plexiglas cases are a blacksmith's forge, a cooper's shop, the interior of a Breton peasant's house, a wheelwright's and carpenter's workshop, a trawler with sail spread, and numerous other life-size models, along with colorful regional costumes, farm implements, and decorative items.

Musée National de la Coopération Franco-Américaine

02300 Blérancourt, Château
(16) 23 39 60 16
Open 10am-12:30pm & 2pm-5pm (in winter 2pm-5pm). Closed Tue. Pkg. Admission: 15 F, 10 F on Sun, free for children under 18, ages 18-25 & over 60: 10 F.

This museum of Franco-American friendship is located in the seventeenth-century Château de Blérancourt, designed by Salomon de Brosse, architect of the Luxembourg Palace in Paris. Although it has undergone many changes over the centuries, Brosse's ornamented portals, pavilions, and portions of the *corps de logis* (the main part of the building) have survived. In 1915 Ann Morgan, daughter of American financier J. P. Morgan, set up a Red Cross infirmary in the château. After World War I she began the painstaking restorations that have only recently been completed. Blérancourt's permanent collection comprises some 50 paintings from the United States and France, formerly displayed at the Musée d'Orsay and the Centre Pompidou, plus a sculpture garden and landscaped grounds.

Musée National des Monuments Français

16th arr. - Palais de Chaillot, 1, pl. du Trocadéro
44 05 39 10
Open 10am-6pm. Closed Tue. Admission: 21 F, reduced rate: 14 F. Temporary exhibitions. Access for disabled. V, MC. M° Trocadéro.

This cathedral-size museum is chockablock with monumental yet scrupulously accurate phonies—plaster casts of French sculptures and architectural elements, from pre-Roman times to the nineteenth century. Spending a few hours here is a good way to become familiar with the typical features of the nation's architecture. The museum's lobby has just been refurbished in a pleasing 1930s style, and there is an attractive terrace restaurant (Les Monuments) and a well-stocked bookshop.

Musée National du Moyen-Âge, Thermes de Cluny

5th arr. - 6, pl. Paul-Painlevé
43 25 62 00
Open 9:15am-5:45pm. Closed Tue. Admission: 27 F, reduced rate: 13.50 F. V, MC. M° Saint-Michel.

All you need to know about the Middle Ages, from religious relics to everyday objects, is on display in the superb fifteenth-century Hôtel des Abbés de Cluny. The undisputed star of the collections is the famed series of tapestries, *The Lady and the Unicorn,* now displayed in a renovated gallery. But the museum's rich holdings also include paintings, stained glass, medieval furniture, jewelry, and sculpture. Most imposing are the 24 heads representing the Kings of Juda, removed from the façade of Notre-Dame. Recent acquisitions are a display of Hispano-Moorish ceramics and a collection of Coptic and Byzantine textiles. In the Gallo-Roman baths next door are the barrel-vaulted frigidarium ("cold bath") and other impressive halls, all beautifully restored.

Musée National de l'Orangerie des Tuileries

1st arr. - Jardin des Tuileries, corner quai des Tuileries/ place de la Concorde
42 97 48 16
Open 9:45am-5:15pm. Closed Tue. Admission: 27 F, reduced rate: 18 F. V, MC. M° Concorde.

Claude Monet's dazzling *Water Lilies,* painted in Giverny between 1890 and his death in 1926, hang here in the two oval basement rooms, custom-designed according to the wishes of the artist. Upstairs, the Walter-Guillaume collection contains just one Monet, but several undisputed masterpieces from the late nineteenth and the early twentieth century (by Modigliani, Renoir, Cézanne, Matisse, Picasso, Soutine, Derain...).

Musée Nissim de Camondo

8th arr. - 63, rue de Monceau
45 63 26 32
Open 10am-noon & 2pm-5pm. Closed Mon, Tue. Admission: 20 F, reduced rate: 14 F. No cards. M° Villiers.

This grand 1914 town house is a nearly exact replica of the Petit Trianon at Versailles. Count Moïse de Camondo built it on the edge of the Parc Monceau and filled it with his priceless collection of eighteenth-century furniture (designed by such master craftsmen as the Jacob brothers, Riesener, and Leleu), paintings (by Vigée-Lebrun and Hubert Robert), and sculptures (by Houdon and Pigalle). Sèvres porcelains, Beauvais tapestries, and rare Savonnerie carpets round out the exquisitely harmonious ensemble, perfectly restored and presented as the count knew it. A true labor of love.

Musée Pasteur

15th arr. - 25, rue du Docteur-Roux - 45 68 82 82

Open 2pm-5:30pm. Closed Sat, Sun. No cards. M° Pasteur.

The apartment where the great scientist and inventor Louis Pasteur lived is movingly simple, quite a contrast to the Byzantine chapel in which he is buried.

Musée de la Poste

15th arr. - 34, bd de Vaugirard - 42 79 23 45

Open 10am-6pm. Closed Sun. V, MC. M° Montparnasse.

A first-class museum, recently rejuvenated, for philatelists and anyone interested in the history of the postal service. Displays range from Roman wax tablets to featherweight airmail paper, from mailboxes to high-tech video encoders. On our last visit, our favorite piece was a rural mailman's bicycle from the nineteenth century. A word to the wise: bring a magnifying glass for a proper view of the stamp collections. Excellent gift shop.

Musée Auguste Rodin

7th arr. - Hôtel Biron, 77, rue de Varenne - 47 05 01 34

Open 10am-5:45pm (winter 10am-5pm). Closed Mon. Admission: 27 F, reduced rate: 18 F. Cafeteria in the park. V, AE, DC. M° Varenne.

Come when the roses in the courtyard bloom around Auguste Rodin's *The Thinker*, then wander through the eighteenth-century garden. Along the lanes stand the sculptor's monumental bronzes *The Burghers of Calais, The Hell Gate*, and the imposing *Balzac*, to name just a few. The 1728 Rococo town house belonged to the Duchesse du Maine and the Maréchal de Biron before it was divided into apartments where the likes of Matisse, Cocteau, and Rilke once lodged. Rodin moved in at the peak of his career, and his presence saved the house from demolition. Also on display is an impressive array of sketches and studies. Don't miss the excellent jade carving *Les Bavardes*, by Rodin's lover and fellow-sculptor, Camille Claudel. (See the following entry for the Rodin museum annex.)

Maison d'Auguste Rodin

92190 Meudon - Villa des Brillants, 19, av. Auguste-Rodin - 45 34 13 09

Open Jul 1-Sep 25: Fri, Sat & Sun 1:30pm-6:30pm. Closed Mon-Thu. Admission: 9 F, reduced rate: 5 F. No cards. RER Meudon-Val-Fleury (C).

The suburban annex to the Paris Musée Rodin is housed in the red-brick Louis XIII Villa des Brillants. The pastoral setting on a hill is one of the most enchanting sites in the Paris area. Studies for Rodin's masterworks are displayed here, and the sculptor's final resting place is here, too.

Musée de la Vie Romantique Maison Renan-Scheffer

9th arr. - 16, rue Chaptal 48 74 95 38

Open 10am-5:40pm. Closed Mon. Admission: 17.50 F, reduced rate: 9 F. Temporary exhibitions. No cards. M° Saint-Georges.

Ary Scheffer (1795-1858) was Louis-Philippe's court painter. Ernest Renan (1823-1892), the renowned writer, was Scheffer's nephew. But, surprise, this museum is given over to yet a third celebrity: George Sand. There are a few Scheffer paintings, nothing at all by Renan, and an interesting collection of Sand memorabilia that includes furniture and portraits, plus plaster casts of Sand's and Chopin's hands. The real attraction is the house—a handsome Restoration-period mansion with a charming garden at the end of an ivy-draped lane—where time stands still.

Musée Zadkine

6th arr. - 100 bis, rue d'Assas 43 26 91 90

Open 10am-5:40pm. Closed Mon. Admission: 17 F, reduced rate: 9 F. No cards. M° Vavin.

The Russian sculptor Zadkine (1911-1967), creator of the celebrated *La Femme à l'Éventail*, lived and worked here most of his life. Today, a forest of sculptures stands in the tiny garden, an idyllic enclave on the edge of Montparnasse. We like it best in the spring when the daffodils are in bloom.

PARKS & GARDENS

Generally speaking, Paris parks open their gates when the city's street lights go off, and close for the night when lights go on. For more precise information, call the Public Relations Service of the municipal Department of Parks and Gardens (Tel.: 40 71 74 00). A very pleasant lady will supply you with details (in French, *bien sûr*)!

Computerized Trees

Despite the ravages of pollution, dogs, and Dutch elm disease, Paris still has more trees than any other European capital. Nearly 200,000 trees line its streets and grace its parks and gardens, not to mention another 300,000 in the Bois de Vincennes and Bois de Boulogne. Plane trees are the most common, making up 43 percent of the total, and one of their number is the city's tallest tree, standing 136 feet high in the Avenue Foch. Chestnuts, sophoras, and lime trees are also well represented. But if we look on the shady side, the figures also show that 25 percent of Parisian trees will have disappeared by the year 2000. In an attempt to stop the rot, the city government is keeping a close watch on its woody heritage: every single tree now has a computer file detailing its surroundings, vital statistics, and state of health. An experimental greenhouse has been set up to study the effects of traffic pollution on different species, and 4,200 new trees are being planted every year.

Bois de Boulogne

16th arr. - M° Porte-Dauphine, Porte-d'Auteuil.

This immense park, which spreads over more than 2,000 acres in the city's western reaches, is a vestige of the primeval forests that once surrounded Paris. Long a royal domain, the Bois was presented to the capital with imperial munificence by Napoléon III, who stipulated that it be landscaped and maintained with municipal funds. Today the Bois is a paradise for runners, bikers, equestrians, and strollers. Dogs and kids alike love to come to the Bois for a romp along the many miles of hiking trails and lawns. Among the myriad attractions are a children's park with a little zoo (Le Jardin d'Acclimatation), a sumptuous rose garden (Le Jardin de Bagatelle), and a lake (le Lac Inférieur) for boating. Also situated within the park's ample precincts are two racetracks (Longchamp and Auteuil), the Roland-Garros tennis stadium where the French Open is held each spring, riding clubs, and a couple of first-rate restaurants: Le Pré Catelan and La Grande Cascade (see *Restaurants*).

Bois de Vincennes

12th arr. - M° Château-de-Vincennes, Porte-Dorée.

Even larger than the Bois de Boulogne, the Bois de Vincennes is similarly endowed with bike and bridle trails, nature paths, and sporting facilities. But it is also home to the city's sole Buddhist temple (complete with a 30-foot statue of Buddha), a world-class zoo where 1,100 animals frolic in naturalistic surroundings, an arboretum, and a fascinating museum of African and Oceanic arts. Our favorite features, though, are the Ferme Georges-Ville, a working farm open to the public on weekends and holidays, where city kids can get up close and personal with barnyard animals; and the Parc Floral, with its bouquet of thematic gardens (herbs, perennials, azaleas, aquatic plants...), its incredible "Valley of Flowers" rich with 100,000 plants, and its superb sculpture garden.

Espace Albert-Kahn

92100 Boulogne - 14, rue du Port - 46 04 52 80

Open Oct-Apr 11am-6pm (May-Sep 11am-7pm).

PARIS VISITE

THE KEY TO ALL YOUR TRANSPORT NEEDS IN PARIS.

La solution transport à tous vos déplacements dans la capitale.

Paris Visite is for 2, 3 or 5 days. This ticket allows you to travel anywhere in Paris and its region by metro, bus or RER, as well as SNCF lines, to Disneyland Paris-Resort, Versailles, Roissy-Charles-de-Gaulle and Orly airports. Paris Visite brings further advantages like 10% to 35% reductions on many of the Capital's touristic attractions. Available at main metro and RER stations.

Paris Visite, c'est un forfait transport de 2, 3 ou 5 jours pour découvrir Paris et sa région en bus, métro, RER et trains SNCF d'Ile-de-France, jusqu'au parc Disneyland Paris, Versailles et aux aéroports Roissy-Charles-de-Gaulle et Orly. Paris Visite vous permet également de bénéficier de réductions de 10% à 35% sur l'entrée de nombreux sites touristiques de la capitale. Paris Visite est en vente dans les principales stations de métro et gares RER, dans les gares SNCF d'Ile-de-France, dans les aéroports internationaux parisiens et dans les bureaux de l'office de tourisme de Paris. La RATP vous souhaite un agréable séjour.

RATP

l'esprit libre

Closed Mon. Admission: 20 F. M° Pont-de-St-Cloud.

This landscape garden on the banks of the Seine is one of Paris's prettiest, created in the early twentieth century by wealthy banker and philanthropist Albert Kahn, who dreamed of bringing together all his favorite scenes of nature in a single park. You may wander through a freshly renovated Japanese garden, a Vosges forest, a formal French garden, a placid lake bordered by trees, or a romantic English garden, as well as a coniferous and a deciduous wood. We particularly like to visit here from March to June, when the daffodils, hyacinths, azaleas, rhododendrons, and roses are in bloom.

Jardin du Luxembourg

6th arr. - 55 bis, rue d'Assas. Main entrance bd St-Michel, near place Edmond-Rostand
Open daily dawn-dusk. M° Vavin. RER Luxembourg.

Head for the Luxembourg Gardens when you need to entertain a couple of energetic kids; when you yearn to sit or stroll in leafy solitude; when you decide to take the pulse of Parisian life on a sunny Sunday afternoon. The Luxembourg offers activities galore for youngsters, from swings and sandboxes to pony rides and go-karts, not to mention a pool for launching little sailboats (the sort one pushes with a stick), or puppet shows that manage to amuse even children who don't speak French. Elsewhere, quiet paths wind through lawns and flower beds ornamented with statues honoring French artists and statesmen (many of these allegorical tributes are unintentionally hilarious). Inveterate people-watchers should note that the area of the garden closest to the Boulevard Saint-Michel is a veritable vivarium of vaguely arty or intellectual Left Bank types—it's an ideal place to observe Parisians in their natural habitat.

Jardin du Palais-Royal

1st arr. - Main entrances top rue Montpensier & after 1, rue de Valois
M° Palais-Royal.

For all its serene beauty, this garden maintains an almost secret air; never crowded, it is protected from urban noise by the noble houses that enfold it with their sculpted façades. In summer, it's an enchanting place to sit and watch pigeons bathe in the fountains along with little black swifts just flown back from Africa; or to listen to tiny French toddlers twitter in the sandboxes. The architecture embraces the seventeenth, eighteenth, nineteenth, and twentieth centuries: Richelieu lived in what was known as the Palais-Cardinal, later promoted to royal rank when Anne of Austria and the future Louis XIV moved there from the Louvre. The elegant arcades that run around three sides of the garden date from just before the Revolution, but the buildings behind them, now occupied by the Ministry of Culture and the Constitutional Council, were not completed until the Restoration. The current era is represented by the controversial black-and-white columns designed by Daniel Buren, and the polished steel fountains by Pol Bury.

Jardin des Plantes

5th arr. - Main entrance 57, rue Cuvier - 40 79 30 00
Open daily 7:30am-5:45pm (summer 7:30am-7:45pm). M° Gare-d'Austerlitz.

Louis XIII founded the Botanical Gardens in 1635, to encourage the study and cultivation of herbs and medicinal plants to treat royal ailments. In 1641 Louis XIV graciously opened the gardens to the public. Ever since, Parisians have enjoyed the shaded walks of the maze that surrounds the Belvedere, the park's sole surviving pre-Revolutionary edifice. The garden's senior tree, a stupendous cedar of Lebanon, also predates that war: it was planted in 1734. Here you will discover rare species of trees, flowering shrubs, and countless other plants from cold climes (in the delightful Alpine Garden) or warm (in the huge hothouse, a jungle of tropical flora and cacti). Reptiles, deer, bears, apes, and birds of prey populate quaint Second Empire buildings, which have been recently renovated. (See *Museums,* Muséum d'Histoire Naturelle.)

Jardin des Tuileries

1st arr. - Main entrances place de la Concorde & place du Carrousel
M° Tuileries.

When work is completed in 1996, the Jardin des Tuileries and adjoining

Jardin du Carrousel will link the Louvre and the Place de la Concorde with an uninterrupted avenue of lawns, walks, flowers, fountains, and statuary. For now, this historic area is still in a state of disarray. Excavations around the Louvre yielded an unexpected bonanza in the form of a large section of Philippe-Auguste's defensive wall, along with innumerable medieval artifacts. Preserving that archaeological bounty caused considerable delay in the reconstruction of the Tuileries Gardens. But soon, authorities assure us, the Tuileries will be a revitalized, coherently landscaped space worth of its central place in the capital's geography and the nation's history.

Parc André-Citroën

15th arr. - Main entrances rue Montagne-de-la-Fage & rue Balard
M° Balard.

With the Parc de la Villette (see below), the 35-acre Parc André-Citroën is the most ambitious project of its kind since the Second Empire, the "Golden Age of Parisian Parks." From the spectacular view of the Seine to the multitude of fountains, the canal, and ornamental ponds, water is a dominant theme in this imaginative landscape. Don't look for your garden-variety herbaceous borders here: the visionary architects who designed the park have composed thousands of trees, shrubs, and flowers into fantastic themed gardens of extraordinary botanical richness. The dark foliage of the Black Garden sets off the fragrant perennials of the White Garden. The *Jardin des Métamorphoses* changes with the seasons to reflect the alchemical transmutation of lead into gold. Then there are the Moss and the Rock Gardens, as well as a series of six gardens, each linked to a different color, metal, and sense (the Blue Garden, associated with mercury, is redolent of mint; fruit trees bloom in the Red Garden; a spring bubbles up in the Japanese-inspired Green Garden...). The rarest plants are housed in two tall glass-and-wood conservatories which close the perspective from the Seine. Officially opened late in 1992, the park is still a work in progress. Future plans include the landscaping of the river banks that abut the park, and the construction of a footbridge linking the gardens to the sixteenth arrondissement.

Parc de Belleville

20th arr. - Main entrance rue Piat, in front of rue des Envierges
Open year-round. Hours vary. M° Pyrénées.

This brand-new park in far-flung Belleville boasts an impressive pergola, an orangery, an open-air theater, and hills landscaped with waterfalls. Topping it all is a panoramic point—the highest in Paris—with a knock-your-socks-off view of the city. A new addition to the park is the poetically named Maison de l'Air, a weather museum open every afternoon but Monday, with lots of interactive exhibits that children particularly enjoy (27, rue Piat; admission: 22 F, reduced rate 11 F).

Parc des Buttes-Chaumont

19th arr. - Main entrance pl. Armand-Carrel
M° Buttes-Chaumont.

This wildly romantic hilltop park is crosscut by creeks and roaring waterfalls fed by the nearby Ourcq Canal. A tiny Greek Revival temple perches on a peak in the middle of a swan-filled lake. The temple and panoramic point are reached from below, via a suspension bridge, or from above, by crossing a narrow walkway 100 feet above the lake. The park's main cascade tumbles into a stylized grotto, recently renovated and opened to the public. This former quarry and dump was, in the late nineteenth century, transformed into one of Paris' most fashionable public gardens. The mark of the park's designer, Alphand, is

Nature walks

Paris isn't made only of asphalt and stone; nature thrives in parks, squares, and odd corners of each arrondissement. For guides to the city's flora and fauna, and some *suggested itineraries* that will allow you to discover them, pick up a *Sentiers Nature* guide at the local mairie (town hall of each arrondissement).

evident in the cast-concrete railings and benches sculpted to resemble tree branches. Millions of francs have been spent to restore the Buttes-Chaumont to its original splendor. A job well done!

Parc Georges-Brassens

15th arr. - Main entrance at corner of rue des Morillons & rue de Cronstadt
M° Convention.

The twin bulls who guard the entrance to this spacious park are survivors, so to speak, of the slaughterhouse that stood on the site until 1975. Other elements from the abattoir were also integrated into the landscape, such as the bell tower that dominates the center of the park, and the Grande Halle, once a horse's last stop before the glue factory, now the scene of a weekly used-book market. Other opportunities for peaceable pursuits are provided by the park's fragrance garden, a collection of 80 aromatic and medicinal herbs, a vineyard planted with Pinot Noir (memento of the now-vanished Clos Morillon, a famed Parisian *cru*), and a honey-producing beehive. Children are not forgotten: there are several playgrounds, a puppet theater, and a special wall on which kids (and adults, too) may hone their rock-climbing skills.

Parc Monceau

8th arr. - Main entrance bd de Courcelles, in front of place de la République-Dominicaine
M° Monceau.

The verdant *allées* of this picturesque park attract large crowds on weekends. But since most of the Sunday strollers are well-mannered inhabitants of the surrounding *beaux quartiers,* no untoward jostling ever seems to occur. Late in the eighteenth century, the artist and stage designer Carmontelle was hired by a princely patron to create "an extraordinary garden" on this site. Taking his mission to heart, he erected bogus Greek and Egyptian ruins, a Gothic castle, a Dutch windmill, and a minaret. Today only a pyramid and an ornamental lake with a colonnade remain of those imaginative edifices. The city of Paris acquired the Parc Monceau in 1860, and is now responsible for its maintenance. We hope that the current replanting and releveling of the park's grounds will not disturb the stately great maple or the Oriental plane tree (note its 22-foot girth), which have spread their branches here for 130 and 170 years respectively.

Parc Montsouris

14th arr. - Main entrance at the corner of av. Reille & rue Gazan
Open 9am-noon & 2pm-6pm. M° Porte-d'Orléans.

That energetic architect and engineer, Charles-Adolphe Alphand, whose legacy includes the Bois de Boulogne, the Bois de Vincennes, the Buttes-Chaumont, the Parc Monceau, and the Square des Batignolles, also supervised the construction of the Parc Montsouris. The lovely English-style gardens were created at the behest of Napoléon III, but were completed only after the fall of the Second Empire, in 1878. On opening day, the artificial lake which was the park's principal attraction, suddenly and inexplicably drained dry. The engineer responsible did the only proper thing under the circumstances: he committed suicide. But why let that tragic occurrence spoil your enjoyment? Concentrate instead on the charmingly serpentine paths shaded by Virginia tulip trees, an immense cedar of Lebanon, an American redwood, and Siberian elms.

Parc de la Villette

19th arr. - Main entrance av. Jean-Jaurès, near Porte de Pantin - 42 40 76 10
Hours vary, call for information. M° Porte-de-la-Villette.

Water, light, and greenery guided Bernard Tschumi's design for the Parc de la Villette. The result is an enchanting, indeed poetic "urban park for the 21st century." A long, winding avenue leads visitors through a succession of themed gardens: a bamboo grove signals the Energy Garden, ornamented with sculpture and Bernhard Leitner's *Sound Cylinder*; the Trellis Garden, with its grapevines, hops, and perennials, is dotted with seven sculptures by Jean-Max Albert; and the Water Garden is made even dreamier by F. Nakaya's *Cloud Sculptures.* Along the way are scattered a score of blood-red "follies" (the color recalls that La Villette was once the city's abattoir), which house, variously, a snack bar, a restaurant, a gazebo... Philippe Starck is responsible for the benches, lights, and other fixtures that strikingly combine function with elegant form. Though the park is difficult to reach from central Paris, your kids will thank you for herding them out here, where lawns may be walked and picnicked upon, and where imaginative playground activities abound. Do not under any circumstances miss the *Jardin du Dragon* with its wonderfully scary sliding board.

Square des Batignolles

17th arr. - Place Charles-Fillion
M° Brochant.

Another example of the ubiquitous Alphand's art (see above), the Square des Batignolles delights visitors with its winding paths, running stream, and its waterfall edged by weeping willows and ash trees. Hundreds of comically obese ducks paddle on a little lake, where equally gluttonous carp and gold-fish also dwell. The only jar-ring note in this otherwise harmonious ensemble is the incongruous statuary group called *Vultures* that rises up, black and forbid-ding, from the middle of the water. On weekends a carrousel often opens for business, creating a "village fair" atmosphere that is utterly charming. Before you leave, do walk around to the Place Charles-Fillion for a look at Sainte-Marie-des-Batignolles. With its triangular pediment and Tuscan columns, the church resembles a small Greek temple mysteriously set down in a Parisian square.

OUT OF PARIS

INTRODUCTION

Those lucky Parisians! Not only do they have the rare good fortune to live in a glorious city; that city is ringed with equally glorious woodlands and accessible countryside. Day-trippers from Paris can simply hop on a train and, an hour or so later, alight near one of half a dozen splendid forests complete with magnificent châteaux.

The forests are a legacy of the French monarchy. Avid hunters all, the kings of France naturally took a keen interest in their *chasses royales*, or private hunting grounds close to Paris, the capital of the realm. Thus the woodlands of the Ile de France, with their ancient stands of oak, beech, and hornbeam, have been exceptionally well preserved and responsibly managed over the centuries.

Senlis, for example, where Hugues Capet was elected king of France in 987, was a thickly forested royal estate favored for its excellent hunting. It is still hunting country today, as is neighboring ***Chantilly***, long celebrated for densely wooded forests, alive with game. Likewise, the châteaux at ***Fontainebleau***, ***Rambouillet***, and ***Saint-Germain-en-Laye*** are still surrounded by vast stretches of woodland, where scions of the royal Valois and Bourbon dynasties once galloped in pursuit of boars and stags. Even ***Versailles***, that epitome of regal grandeur, began life as a relatively humble hunting lodge lost amid swamps and trees.

Not everyone, of course, fancies the forest primeval. If more manicured landscapes are what your prefer, then why not visit the gorgeous castle gardens at ***Écouen*** and Rambouillet, or Le Nôtre's baroque *jardins à la française* at ***Vaux-le-Vicomte***, Chantilly, Saint-Germain-en-Laye, or Versailles?

For a rural antidote to urban stress, we recommend that you head for the farmlands of the Beauce region, southwest of Paris. The soothing sameness of these wheat-bearing plains is broken only by grain-gorged silos (this is the bread basket of France) and by the dramatic spires of ***Chartres*** cathedral. Or you could travel northwest from Paris, along the meanders of the Seine to where the Ile de France meets Normandy: here lies the Vexin, a region of farmlands and river valleys overflowing with bucolic charm. This is where Claude Monet spent the last years of his life, painting in his garden at ***Giverny***.

Thus, by venturing just 20, 30, or 50 miles beyond the Paris city limits and the bleaker *banlieues*, one discovers a bounty of gently beautiful scenery, bathed in the unique light that inspired not only Monet and the Impressionists, but also Corot, the Barbizon painters, Van Gogh, Derain, and the Fauvists. Punctuating these luminous landscapes are fascinating historic monuments and landmarks, as well as masterpieces of religious, civil, and domestic architecture—any of which would make an ideal destination for a fair-weather excursion.

Here, then, are our suggestions for ten easy day trips in the Ile de France, all calculated to combine fresh air and greenery with an equally healthy dose of culture. And naturally Gault Millau wouldn't dream of taking you anywhere without first scouting out the best places to dine and spend the night!

CHANTILLY

Reflected in the shimmering waters of its moat, the Château de Chantilly looks like a fairy-tale castle, almost too perfect to be true. And in a way, it is: the Renaissance-style Grand Château isn't much more than 100 years old (although the adjoining Petit Château dates from the sixteenth century). The castle that previously stood on this site was razed during the Revolution by angry citizens for whom Chantilly, fief of two ancient warrior families, the Montmorencys and the Condés, symbolized aristocratic privilege and military might.

The Grand Château houses the Musée Condé, a jewel of a collection which ranges from the curious—a wax head of King Henri IV, the pink Condé diamond—to the sublime: Piero di Cosimo's *Portrait of Simonetta Vespucci*, Raphael's *Virgin of Loreto*, works by Botticelli, several pictures by Poussin, two masterpieces by Watteau, a splendid series of Renaissance portraits by the Clouet brothers (including the famous *Catherine de Medicis* and *Henri III*), and an admirable collection of illuminated manuscripts. Arranged just as the Duc d'Aumale, the last owner of Chantilly, left it (with orders that it never be changed), the museum has the personal and agreeably eccentric style of a private collection.

Connoisseurs of fine horseflesh know Chantilly as the site of a famous racetrack and Thoroughbred training center. A fascinating "living museum" devoted to horses occupies the colossal eighteenth-century stables. From an architectural viewpoint, these Grandes Écuries are more imposing than the château itself. But then that is not so surprising when one considers that the Prince of Condé, who built the stables, was convinced that he would be reincarnated as a horse!

The château's majestic park, complete with a canal, gardens, and pools planned by seventeenth-century landscape artist André Le Nôtre, is crisscrossed by shady walks and velvety lawns. But the immense (nearly 16,000-acre) Chantilly forest, with its hiking paths and ponds (the étangs de Commelles), is by far the best choice for a long woodland ramble. Take care, though: between 9am and noon some 3,000 Thoroughbreds thunder into the forest for their morning workout!

The world's biggest hot-air balloon takes 30 visitors at a time up to an altitude of 150 meters for a bird's-eye view of Chantilly.

The ***Château de Chantilly*** *(about 50 kilometers north of Paris by Autoroute du Nord A1, exit at Survilliers) is open daily, except Tuesday, from March 1 through October 31, 10am to 6pm; from November 1 through February 28, 10:30am to 12:45pm and 2pm to 5pm. Reservations: (16) 44 57 08 00, Monday to Friday from 9am to noon, fax (16) 44 57 70 31. Admission: Château and park 37 F, children under 12: 10 F, groups: 32 F, students: 32 F; park 17 F, children under 12: 10 F.*

The ***Musée Vivant du Cheval*** *is open daily, except Tue; April 1 to Oct 31: 10:30am to 6:30pm (except in May and June: open Tue from 10:30am to 6:30pm; in July and Aug: open Tue from 2pm to 6:30pm); Nov 1 to March 31: 2pm to 5:30pm weekdays, and from 10:30am to 6:30pm on weekends. Call (16) 44 57 40 40 for information, fax (16) 44 57 29 92. Admission: 45 F, children under 16: 35 F , students & over 60: 40 F.*

RESTAURANTS & HOTELS

Campanile

60270 Gouvieux, 3 km N on N 16, route de Creil - (16) 44 57 39 24, fax (16) 44 58 10 05

Open year-round. 47 rms 270 F. Restaurant. Conf. Pkg. V, AE, DC, MC.

At the edge of the Chantilly forest, the Campanile is quiet and modern but not always well maintained. Restaurant.

Château de Montvillargenne

60270 Gouvieux, 3 km W on D 909, av. F.-Mathet - (16) 44 57 05 14, fax (16) 44 57 28 97

Open year-round. 10 stes 780-980 F. 138 rms 240-500 F. Rms for disabled. Restaurant. Heated pool. Tennis. Golf. Pkg. V, AE, DC, MC.

Set in extensive grounds, this magnificent nineteenth-century castle boasts warm wood paneling and elegant lounges. Renovated, well-equipped, smallish rooms and various leisure facilities.

12/20 Les Étangs

8 km SE, 60580 Coye-la-Forêt, 1, rue Clos-des-Vignes (16) 44 58 60 15, fax (16) 44 58 75 95

Closed Mon dinner, Tue, Jan 15-Feb 15. Open until 9:30pm. Priv rm: 65. Garden dining. Pkg. V, AE, DC, MC.

Summer visitors should slip under the bower that leads to an adorable garden to enjoy the slightly conventional but well executed cuisine. This year, try the foie gras sautéed with apples and honey, mushrooms in puff pastry with garlic cream, and braised snails. **C** 270-320 F. **M** 200 F (Sun, wine incl), 150 F, 270 F.

Hostellerie du Lys

60260 Lamorlaye, 7 km S on N 16, Lys-Chantilly, 63, 7e avenue (16) 44 21 26 19, fax (16) 44 21 28 19

Open year-round. 35 rms 195-500 F. Restaurant. Golf. Pkg. V, AE, DC, MC.

Situated in a large park, this opulent country inn provides comfortable rooms in a friendly, restful atmosphere. Tennis courts, golf course, and swimming pool are all within easy reach.

13 Le Relais Condé

42, av. du Maréchal-Joffre (16) 44 57 05 75

Closed Mon dinner, Tue (exc hols). Open until 10pm. Garden dining. V, AE, MC.

The somber interior of this nineteenth-century former Anglican chapel could use some livening up, but Jacques Legrand's well-crafted cooking is a sure value, although he goes a bit overboard with cream: warm duck sausage with a hazelnut-sprinkled salad, turbot with allspice, and pear tourte. Charming welcome. **C** 300-370 F. **M** 155 F, 280 F.

COMPIÈGNE

15 La Part des Anges

18, rue Bouvines (16) 44 86 00 00, fax (16) 44 86 09 00

Closed 1st wk of Feb school hols, Jul 31-Aug 21. Open until 10pm. Priv rm: 30. Terrace dining. Pkg. V, AE, MC.

When Cognac ages in the cask, the vapors that escape are called *la part des anges*. There's nothing vapory or vague about the clean, concentrated flavors of Francis Carpentier's cuisine, crafted from excellent ingredients: cauliflower cream with tiny shrimp, roast pork filet mignon with Chinese artichokes, fine cheeses, and a crispy pineapple turnover. Modest prices for both food and wine, warm welcome, and a sunny setting with a seductive, Latin feel. **C** 250-350 F. **M** 130 F, 280 F.

Château de Bellinglise

14 km N on D 142, Route de Lassigny, 60157 Elincourt-Ste-Marguerite - (16) 44 96 00 33, fax (16) 44 96 03 00

Open year-round. 2 stes 1,380-1,560 F. 33 rms 715-1,380 F. Restaurant. Tennis. Golf. Valet pkg. Helipad. V, AE, DC, MC.

This immense Louis XIII–era castle on a 600-acre estate has been remarkably preserved and restored; guests can stay in one of the attractive rooms in the hunting lodge. Pond, tennis, horseback-riding, rides in a hot-air balloon, skeet shooting, archery, helicopter rides, and conference facilities.

See also "Senlis" below.

CHARTRES

Long before Christianity had penetrated the Ile de France, before Caesar marched into Gaul—even then, Chartres was a holy place. Legend has it that every year Celtic druids assembled in Chartres to celebrate their mysteries around a sacred wellspring now immured in the cathedral crypt.

What is certain is that from the fourth century on, a sanctuary consecrated to the Virgin Mary brought the faithful to Chartres. When, in 876, Charles the Bald endowed the church with a precious relic (said to be the Virgin's tunic or veil), it gained even greater importance as a shrine, drawing pilgrims from all over Christendom in a steady stream that neither invasions, fires, nor revolutions have stanched. Even today, Catholic students organize a pilgrimage to Chartres each May in honor of the Virgin.

The ancestor of the current cathedral, a Romanesque structure built in the eleventh and twelfth centuries, was ravaged by fire in 1194. The flames spared only the crypt, two towers, and the lower portion of the western façade, with its majestic Portail Royal. But the people of Chartres very quickly set about rebuilding their cathedral, with so mighty a collective will—and generous contributions from rich lords and wealthy townspeople—that it was completed in the impressively short span of just 30 years. It is to the builders' speed that the cathedral owes its exceptional stylistic unity. And it is to their skill in applying new architectural advances—notably the flying buttress—that Chartres owes its soaring height and rare luminosity. Since the buttresses shouldered weight that would otherwise have fallen on the walls, the builders could make the walls higher, with taller windows.

It would be impossible for us to do justice here to the esthetic and spiritual riches of Chartres. A visitor with plenty of time, patience, curiosity, and an observant eye will find innumerable sources of pleasure and interest. Here, however, are a couple of features worth noting, one outside and one inside the cathedral.

The Portail Royal, unscathed by the fire of 1194, is one of the oldest examples of Gothic sculpture in existence. While the emphasis of the ensemble is on the figure of Christ, depicted in infancy and in majesty above each of the three doors, viewers often feel irresistibly drawn to the nineteen elongated figures, a combination of statue and column, that stand aligned on either side of the doors. Interestingly, these Old Testament figures belong to two different eras, the Romanesque and the Gothic; they are the survivors of the old cathedral and, at the same time, heralds of the new sculptural style that first emerged at Chartres. In their extraordinarily sensitive faces, in the contrast between their expressive features and their rigid, stylized bodies, a visitor can trace the mysterious passage from one age—one way of viewing and representing human reality—to another.

Inside the cathedral, among the ravishing, jewel-like shadows and colors of stained glass, there are three windows and a portion of another which, like the Portail Royal, predate the great fire. They are the windows inserted into the western façade, which depict the genealogy, life, and resurrection of Christ, and to the left, the fragment known as Notre Dame de la Belle Verrière (*The Madonna of the Window*), one of Chartres's most venerated images. They merit your special attention because they are the sole remaining examples of the miraculous *bleu de Chartres*, a blue tint rich (as we now know) in cobalt and copper, but which for centuries no glassmaker managed to reproduce.

In medieval times, Chartres was a flourishing town, its wealth based on cloth and farming. It was also an intellectual center, with a renowned philosophy school. Investigating the many ancient houses and churches in the Old Quarter (the fifteenth-century Maison Saumon and the Hôtel de la Caige; the medieval church of Saint-Pierre, with its striking stained glass) can be an extremely rewarding way to spend an afternoon.

Agriculture still thrives hereabouts, and the prosperous Beaucerons are fond of the table. Between a tour of the cathedral and a stroll through the town, hungry visitors will find any number of excellent eating places where they may relax and restore themselves.

*The **cathedral** (90 kilometers southwest of Paris by Autoroute A10) is open daily from 7:30am to 7:30pm from April 1 to September 30; and until 7pm from October 1 to March 31. For additional information, contact the Office du Tourisme, Place de la Cathédrale, (16) 37 21 50 00.*

RESTAURANTS & HOTELS

13 Le Buisson Ardent

10, rue du Lait - (16) 37 34 04 66

Closed Sun dinner. Open until 9:30pm. V, MC.

To judge by this restaurant's location in the shadow of the cathedral, one is likely to expect yet another tourist eatery with stratospheric prices. Not at all. The menu features nicely crafted dishes made from fresh market produce: sautéed langoustines with broccoli, warm foie gras with raspberries, veal kidney with shallot cream, and a crispy apple dessert with Calvados-enhanced butter. Courteous, lively service, reasonable selection of wines. **C** 280-320 F. **M** 108 F (exc Sat dinner), 158 F, 188 F, 245 F.

Le Manoir des Près du Roy

28300 Saint-Prest, 10 km NE on N 154 & D 6 - (16) 37 22 27 27, fax (16) 37 22 24 92

Open year-round. 20 rms 350-550 F. Restaurant. Half-board 400-575 F. Conf. Tennis. Golf. Pkg. Helipad. V, MC.

A fine weekend escape from Paris, for relaxing or for conferences. The 40-acre estate provides golf and tennis facilities, and the spacious, quiet, inviting rooms offer fresh flowers, beams, and fine views of the landscape. Even the older guest rooms have considerable charm.

Mercure

6, av. Jehan-de-Beauce

(16) 37 21 78 00, fax (16) 37 36 23 01

Open year-round. 48 rms 380-480 F. Rms for disabled. Conf. Garage pkg. V, AE, DC, MC.

Situated next to the railway station, some 300 meters from the cathedral, this hotel offers comfortable rooms, most of which look onto an indoor garden.

12/20 Relais de la Tour

28630 Nogent-le-Phaye, 8 km E on D 4, N 10, Le Bois-Paris - (16) 37 31 69 79

Closed Tue dinner, Wed. Open until 10pm. Air cond. Garage pkg. V.

The pleasant service helps customers forget the noisy highway and boring décor, and concentrate on the generous portions of duck foie gras, salmon tartare, Alsatian-style snails, and fish choucroute, all well prepared and served by a friendly staff. **C** 200-280 F. **M** 250 F (exc Sun dinner, wine incl), 86 F, 136 F, 188 F, 195 F (exc Sun dinner), 250 F.

Gault Millau's ratings are based solely on the restaurants' cuisine. We do not take into account the atmosphere, décor, service and so on; these are commented upon within the review.

La Sellerie

28630 Thivars, 7 km S on N 10,
48, rue Nationale - (16) 37 26 41 59

Closed Mon dinner, Tue, Aug 4-24. Open until 9:30pm.Terrace dining. Pkg. V.

Imagination is not Martial Heitz's strong point, but his traditional cuisine is elegant and well prepared. The smiling welcome and excellent Bordeaux add to the enjoyment of rabbit rillettes and carrot confit, sole fillet with asparagus tips, and chocolate soufflé. The décor mixes refinement with rustic charm, and there's a pleasant garden for summer lunches. C 280-400 F. **M** 98 F (exc Sun), 135 F, 280 F.

ST-SYMPHORIEN-LE-CHÂTEAU

Château d'Esclimont

(16) 37 31 15 15, fax (16) 37 31 57 91

Open daily until 9:30pm. Pool. Pkg. V, AE.

"It is my pleasure" is the motto that La Rochefoucauld had sculpted above the entrance to this radiant sixteenth-century jewel. Our pleasure, under the high ceilings of the four comfortable dining rooms, is Didier Macouin's harmonious (but sometimes overly complicated) cuisine: duck sweetbreads and foie gras in cannelloni, sea bream roasted with ginger and lemongrass, perfect gentian parfait. Superb wine list that will not be easy on your wallet. **C** 350-500 F. **M** 260 F (lunch exc Sun, wine incl), 320 F, 495 F.

Château d'Esclimont

(See restaurant above)

Open year-round. 6 stes 2,800 F. 47 rms 600-1,850 F. Conf. Heated pool. Tennis. Golf. Valet pkg. Helipad. V, AE.

The 47 rooms and 6 suites of this château are classic, comfortable, and handsomely situated amid 60 hectares of completely walled-in grounds. The site is at the bottom of a valley traversed by a river, near the road that connects Rambouillet and Chartres. Guests can play tennis, swim in the heated pool, and attend wintertime musical evenings. Perfect for a luxurious, romantic weekend, and only 45 minutes from Paris by car. Relais et Châteaux, of course.

ECOUEN

One needn't travel all the way to the Loire Valley to view a superb French Renaissance château. Just 20 or so kilometers north of Paris, stands Écouen, an admirably preserved castle built between 1538 and 1555 for King François Ier's closest comrade-in-arms, Constable Anne de Montmorency (the same man who commissioned the first château at Chantilly).

As befitted a great feudal lord and powerful military chief, the constable made Écouen a formidable fortress. Situated on a hill overlooking the broad plain below, surrounded by moats and fortified by steeply sloping walls, Écouen was designed to withstand even artillery fire—a wise precaution on the eve of the Wars of Religion, which ravaged the region in the later sixteenth century.

Yet the constable and his wife, Madeleine de Savoie, were also humanists and patrons of the arts, who engaged the best architects and sculptors of the day to embellish their home. Framed in the portico that leads to the grand courtyard, an equestrian statue of Anne de Montmorency in Roman warrior garb proclaims the constable's taste for antiquity. That taste is reflected in the château's architecture. Niches in the monumental colonnade of the southern (left) wing once housed Michelangelo's *Slaves* (now in the Louvre), presented to the constable by King Henri II.

In 1632, the constable's grandson, Henri II de Montmorency, was accused of conspiracy against the Cardinal de Richelieu, and beheaded. Écouen then reverted to the Condé family, but they spent little time there, preferring their estate at Chantilly. During the Revolution, the contents of the castle were confiscated by the state, and eventually dispersed.

Since 1962, Écouen has housed the Musée de la Renaissance, a unique collection of period French, Italian, and Flemish furniture and decorative arts. The most dazzling exhibit is surely the 246-foot-long tapestry displayed in the Galerie de Psyché. Woven in Brussels in the early sixteenth century, this masterpiece of silk, wool, and silver thread relates the story of David and Bathsheba.

What makes all the objects on view particularly interesting is their setting in the château's authentic, beautifully restored Renaissance interior. Do take the time to examine and admire the immense fireplaces, decorated with biblical scenes, for which Écouen was famous in its heyday. And nothing gives a better idea of the grandeur of a Renaissance lord's castle than the Grande Salle, where the Montmorencys received their vassals. A visitor cannot help but be impressed by the monumental fireplace of porphyry and polychrome marble; or with the magnificent gold-and-cerulean tile floor displaying the entwined initials of Anne de Montmorency and Madeleine de Savoie.

We like to wind up a tour of Écouen with a stroll in the garden; the park affords an impressive, sweeping view of the plain below. Hardier souls may prefer to explore the forest that borders the château.

*The **Château d'Écouen**, (Autoroute du Nord A1, exit n°3), is open daily from 9:45am to 12:30pm and 2pm to 5:15pm, except Tues and some holidays. Call 39 90 04 04 for information. Admission: 21 F, children under 18: free, students & over 60: 15 F, Sun: 15 F.*

FONTAINEBLEAU

Just as Versailles was created at the whim of young Louis XIV, Fontainebleau owes its splendor to the sudden caprice of Renaissance monarch François Ier, who in 1528 decided to transform a neglected royal manor near the forest of Bière into a personal residence fit for a king. After a humiliating two-year captivity in Madrid, the Roi Chevalier wanted to prove to Emperor Charles V and King Henry VIII of England (who were then erecting spectacular palaces at Grenada and Hampton Court, respectively) that he could equal, indeed surpass, them in magnificence.

Every aspect of the new château in Fontainebleau was calculated to glorify France's first absolute ruler. François Ier was the first French king, for example, to be addressed as "Majesty," a title previously reserved for the emperor. Today, his spirit is still tangibly present at Fontainebleau.

Over the centuries the actual architecture of the palace has undergone considerable alteration. The Galerie François Ier, the most celebrated decorative ensemble of the French Renaissance, was constructed between 1528 and 1530 and embellished with marvelous stuccowork and frescoes by the Florentine artist Il Rosso, a pupil of Michelangelo. The recently restored frescoes illustrate a complicated and fairly obscure symbolic scheme. One remarkable figure is an elephant emblazoned with fleur-de-lis and sporting a salamander (François Ier's emblem) on its forehead, which signifies the royal virtue of wisdom. Other scenes commemorate the king's Italian campaigns or his role as a patron of art and literature.

The Salle de Bal (ballroom) is another impressive Renaissance creation. Commissioned by François Ier, it was completed under the supervision of his son, Henri II, by architect Philibert Delorme, who also worked on the Louvre. Here the frescoes—superbly restored—were designed by Il Primatice and executed by Niccolo dell'Abbate, two of the foremost Italian artists of what came to be known as the first Fontainebleau school. The ballroom created such a sensation in its day that painters and engravers came from all over to record its sumptuous decoration. Even now, the room provides a fairly accurate idea of the opulence of the Valois court.

Though Fontainebleau was relatively neglected during the second half of the sixteenth century, it flourished once again under Henri IV. Dated from this era are the Cabinet de Théagène (marvelously preserved, it was the birthplace of Louis XIII) and the Chapelle de la Trinité, decorated with biblical frescoes by Mathieu Fréminet, a French master of the baroque.

The Bourbons made a habit of spending the autumn at Fontainebleau, and continued to embellish and enlarge the palace even after the court officially took up residence at Versailles. Marie-Antoinette, who loved Fontainebleau, completely redecorated several rooms, including the Salon du Jeu (Gaming Room) and the charming Boudoir de la Reine, which was designed by Mique, her favorite architect.

Napoléon, too, was fond of Fontainebleau, and refurnished the palace entirely. Today it boasts Europe's finest collection of Empire furniture, as well as extensive holdings of Napoleonic relics and memorabilia culled from various national museums.

The palace is surrounded by what is surely one of the most beautiful forests in France. In autumn and winter, hunters still gallop through the russet groves of oak, riding to hounds just as French kings did centuries before them. Less bloodthirsty nature enthusiasts prefer to explore the innumerable bridle and hiking paths, or scramble around the spectacular rock formations, cliffs, and gorges that make the Forêt de Fontainebleau an excellent and highly popular training ground for aspiring alpinists.

The ***Château de Fontainebleau*** *(65 kilometers south of Paris by Autoroute du Sud A6) is open daily (except Tuesday) from 9:30am to 12:30pm and 2pm to 5pm; the park and gardens are open from dawn to dusk. Call 60 71 50 70 for further information. Admission: 31 F, reduced rate: 20 F, children under 18: free.*

The ***Musée Napoléonien*** *is open from 2pm to 5pm (closed Sunday, Monday, and holidays). Call 64 22 49 80 for further information. Admission: 12 F, children under 12: free; groups by appointment.*

RESTAURANTS & HOTELS

14 Le Beauharnais

27, pl. Napoléon-Bonaparte
64 22 32 65, fax 64 22 17 33

Closed Dec 23-30. Open until 10:15pm. Priv rm: 90. Garden dining. Air cond. Heated pool. Valet pkg. V, AE, DC, MC.

The formerly slapdash service is now friendly and efficient, and the chef, Rémy Bidron, presents well prepared, inventive dishes: original beef jowls parmentière, pleasant marinated tuna fillet grilled with Provençal herbs, and curious sea scallops with avocado and Chinese truffles. Excellent choice of white Bordeaux. Refined yet relaxed dining room. The point lost last year comes back. **C** 300-450 F. **M** 180 F, 290 F.

L'Aigle Noir

(See restaurant above)

Closed Dec 24-30. 6 stes 1,500-2,000 F. 51 rms 950-1,200 F. Rms for disabled. Air cond. Conf. Heated pool. Golf. Valet pkg. V, AE, DC, MC.

Facing the garden or the château, the luxurious rooms are individually decorated in Louis XVI, Empire, or Restoration style. Modern comforts include satellite TV, books in English, a gym, and a sauna; horseback-riding and an indoor driving range, too. Courteous service.

Legris et Parc

36, rue Paul Seramy

64 22 24 24, fax 64 22 22 05

Open year-round. 5 stes 590 F. 26 rms 390-450 F. Restaurant. Half-board 480-570 F. Conf. V, AE, MC.

This pleasantly renovated building stands opposite the entrance to the château's grounds. The best of the extremely comfortable rooms (some with canopy beds) look out on the flowers of an indoor garden.

BARBIZON

Le Bas-Bréau

(16)

22, rue Grande

60 66 40 05, fax 60 69 22 89

Open daily until 9:30pm. Priv rm: 40. Garden dining. Heated pool. Valet pkg. V, AE, MC.

The likes of Robert Louis Stevenson and George Sand have tarried in this elegant auberge on the edge of the Fontainebleau forest, and one look at the garden will show you why. Jean-Pierre Tava takes good care of his guests in the newly redecorated dining room, while chef Alain Tavernier produces subtle and refined cuisine based on excellent products: fricassée of frogs' legs with shallot confit, fillet of bar with sea-urchin coral and fennel compote, puff pastry with caramelized mangoes. Excellent house breads. **C** 500-800 F. **M** 330 F, 390 F (weekday lunch, wine incl), 380 F.

Le Bas-Bréau

(See restaurant above)

Open year-round. 8 stes 1,700-2,800 F. 12 rms 950-1,500 F. Conf. Heated pool. Tennis. Golf. Valet pkg. Helipad. V, AE, MC.

Surely the most refined and luxurious inn of the Paris region, set amid sumptuous rose gardens and extensive grounds. Rooms are decorated with delightful simplicity; the salon was redecorated this year. Superb breakfasts. Relais et Châteaux.

Hostellerie Les Pléiades

(13)

21, rue Grande

60 66 40 25, fax 60 66 41 68

Open daily until 9:30pm. Priv rm: 40. Garden dining. Pkg. V, AE, DC, MC.

Whether to the sounds of birds singing in the garden or of a fire crackling in the fireplace, a dinner here is sure to make you feel cozy, and the classic cooking is sure to please. Try, on the first set menu, the fried whiting (a tad stingy), pollack in beurre blanc with excellent vegetables, Brie (the pasteurized variety), and a generous serving of warm tart. Charming service. **C** 260-380 F. **M** 145 F, 180 F, 280 F.

Hostellerie Les Pléiades

(See restaurant above)

Open year-round. 1 ste 650 F. 23 rms 320-550 F. Half-board 490-520 F. Conf. Pkg. V, AE, DC, MC.

A charming establishment with inviting, comfortable rooms, some of them on the small side. Professional reception and service.

See also Melun in "Vaux-le-Vicomte" below.

The **C** (A la carte) *restaurant prices given are for a complete three-course meal for one, including a half-bottle of modest wine and service.* ***M*** (Menu) *prices are for a complete fixed-price meal for one, excluding wine (unless otherwise noted).*

GIVERNY

It isn't a palace or royal legend that brings travelers to this tiny village 75 kilometers northwest of Paris, on the border of the Ile de France and Normandy regions; what draws crowds to Giverny is the artistic legacy of Claude Monet. From 1883 until his death in 1926, Monet lived and worked in these sublime surroundings, a setting he created largely by and for himself. Giverny provided the light, the multifaceted landscape, and the meandering Seine that the painter so loved. But Monet himself supplied the grand design, as well as 40 years of unrelenting efforts to make his ravishing garden a reality. It soon became the central motif of his pictures, and in the end, his garden was the only subject that Monet chose to paint.

Shortly before his death, assailed with doubts about the value of his pictures despite public acclaim for them, Monet came to regard the garden at Giverny as his ultimate creation. He employed six full-time gardeners to tend it, day in and day out. Sadly, Monet's beloved garden slowly went to seed after the painter died. Then in 1977 the American Versailles-Giverny Foundation undertook to restore it, along with Monet's house and studio. Well before Europe recognized his genius, America had embraced Monet at his first New York show in 1889. Now, owing in large part to American generosity, Monet's admirers may visit the house where he worked and entertained fellow artist Mary Cassatt, the poet Mallarmé, and many more.

Nothing less resembles a formal French garden than Giverny's glorious, painterly composition of flowers, water, and greenery. Ordinary fruit trees were banished from the orchard where the flower garden now blooms; Monet replaced them with exotic Japanese strains of ornamental cherry and apple. With the arrival of spring, perennial beds lose their disciplined, linear look under an exuberance of bright blossoms. Interestingly, except for the roses and peonies, all the flowers at Giverny are humble varieties: iris, foxglove, poppies, and lupine. Yet they are planted so artfully and their colors, textures,

Le Corbusier's design for living

Architect and urban planner *Le Corbusier* is probably best remembered for his rather joyless efforts to rationalize living space into modular units. However, at an earlier stage in his career he made a living by designing houses for the rich. One, the Villa Laroche, (10 impasse du Docteur-Blanche in the sixteenth arrondissement), is open to the public and affords a glimpse of an architect more concerned with space and light than with political correctness. The house was designed in 1923 for a banker and art collector, its pure lines intended as a backdrop to the works of Braque, Picasso, and Ozenfant. You can still see examples of Le Corbusier's furniture there, along with a few Cubist paintings and some striking sculptures.

and shapes are arrayed to such advantage that an observer's eye roams over the banks and borders of the garden with as much pleasure as it does over Monet's *Water Lilies*, which hangs in the Orangerie in Paris.

At the far end of the winding central path—take care not to trample the nasturtiums, which grow pretty much wherever they please—is the famous pond that Monet always insisted on showing off to his guests after lunch (he had paid a not-so-small fortune to have it installed). In spring, a curtain of languid wisteria nearly hides the "Japanese bridge," which looks out over a hypnotizing profusion of water lilies. Massed on the surface of the pond, they seem to form a huge artist's palette of delicate tints: white, yellow, pink, blue, and mauve.

The house and three studios at Giverny—including one Monet had built specially to paint *Les Nymphéas*—give the haunting impression of being actually inhabited; it's as if the people who lived and worked there have only just stepped out for a moment. Everything is exactly as it was on an ordinary day at the turn of the century, from the pots and pans set out in the kitchen (Monet loved rich, complicated cooking), to the master's fascinating collection of Japanese prints. To borrow a phrase from Marcel Proust, Monet's contemporary and admirer, the evocative atmosphere of Giverny rewards the pilgrims who journey there with a sense of time recaptured.

*The **Musée Claude Monet** (55 km on Autoroute A 13, 10 km on N 13BIS and 5 km on D 5) and the gardens are open every day (exc Monday) from April 1 through October 31: 10am to 6pm. Admission: 35 F for the house and gardens; 25 F for the gardens. Call (16) 32 51 28 21 for further information, fax (16) 32 51 54 18. Groups by appointment only.*

*Visit also the **Musée d'Art Américain**, 99, rue Claude-Monet. The museum, funded by Chicago art patrons Daniel and Judith Terra, is open every day (exc Monday) from April 1 through October 31: 10am to 6pm. Call (16) 32 51 94 65 for further information, fax (16) 32 51 94 67. Admission: 35 F, students & over 60: 20 F, children age 7 to 12: 15 F, children under 7: free; groups: by appointment: 20 F.*

RESTAURANTS & HOTELS

PACY-SUR-EURE

(13) Château de Brécourt

27120 Douains, by D 181
(16) 32 52 40 50, fax (16) 32 52 69 65

Open daily until 9:30pm. Priv rm: 350. Terrace dining. Pool. Pkg. V, AE, DC, MC.

Refinement and elegance are watchwords at this Louis XIII château with an elegant dining room overlooking a splendid park. The smiling staff keep the atmosphere warm. And the cuisine is scrupulously fresh and skillfully prepared. Why not indulge in perfectly cooked fillet of fresh hake with tiny clams, savory and tender beef fillet, and an unctuous crème brûlée with an orange tuile? The cellars are well stocked with fabulous bottles. **C** 300-400 F. **M** 210 F (weekday lunch, wine incl), 180 F (weekday lunch), 350 F (Fri dinner), 225 F, 340 F.

Château de Brécourt

(See restaurant above)

Open year-round. 5 stes 1,100-1,600 F. 25 rms 390-990 F. Half-board 650-1,100 F. Heated pool. Tennis. Pkg. Helipad. V, AE, MC.

The château provides mainly huge, comfortable, stylishly furnished rooms. Most have a splendid view over the grounds of this pretty Louis XIII château.

VERNON

12/20 Les Fleurs

71, rue Carnot - 32 51 16 80

Closed Sun dinner, Mon, Feb school hols, Jul 30-Aug 20. Open until 9:30pm. No pets. V.

Flowers brighten up the walls, the chair covers, and fill vases too in the pretty and cheerful dining room. The owner-chef offers an interesting menu of well prepared dishes like escargots à la normande, lamb fillet with truffles, snail-stuffed crêpes, and parfait au chocolat. **C** 210-340 F. **M** 100 F, 140 F, 150 F, 190 F, 220 F.

14 **La Gueulardière**
78270 Port-Villez, 5 km SE on N 15, Lieu dit Le Village - 34 76 22 12
Closed Sun dinner, Mon (exc hols). Annual closings not available. Open until 9:30pm. Garden dining. Air cond. Pkg. V, MC.

This picturesque site on the Seine, just across from Monet's house and gardens at Giverny, provides a perfect setting for Claude Marguerite's attractive dishes: chunks of lobster and artichokes with basil, duck fricassée, John Dory with creamed morels, and game in season. Excellent wines; wonderful welcome. **C** 350-400 F. **M** 150 F (exc Sun).

12/20 **Les Jardins de Giverny**
27620 Giverny, 6 km E on D 5, chemin du Roy - 32 21 60 80
Closed Sun dinner, Mon, Feb, Nov 2-16. Open until 9pm. Terrace dining. Pkg. V, AE.

A stone's throw from Claude Monet's house, this fine Norman residence is surrounded by roses and rare trees. This year, owner-chef Serge Pirault's cuisine seemed less concerned with product quality and less generously served than in the past. Confusing lobster salad with walnut vinaigrette and bland grilled red mullet with ratatouille lost the establishment its toque, in spite of the luscious chocolate and cherry ganache. Ups and downs in the cellar, too, but there's a great choice of Loire Valley whites. It's too bad, because the place itself is lovely. **C** 240-350 F. **M** 130 F (exc Sun), 190 F, 250 F.

Normandy
1, av. P.-Mendès-France
32 51 97 97, fax 32 21 01 66
Open year-round. 45 rms 295-350 F. Half-board 430 F. Air cond. Golf. Pkg. V, AE, MC.

This modern, convenient hotel has just opened in the town center. The rooms at the back are the quietest; all are comfortable, though somewhat lacking in originality. Breakfasts are generous and the welcome courteous.

RAMBOUILLET

Although it is now the peaceful summer retreat of the president of France, the château at Rambouillet has witnessed some of the more dramatic moments in the nation's history. In 1547 François Ier, who enjoyed hunting in the nearby forest, died in a tower of the castle, which then belonged to the captain of his guards. Forty years later, Henri III, driven out of Paris by the League, took refuge at Rambouillet. In 1815, before his departure for exile, Napoléon spent a last night of melancholy reflection at Rambouillet. It was there, too, that Charles X learned of the Revolution of 1830 and announced his abdication. And it was from Rambouillet, in August 1944, that General Charles de Gaulle gave the order for Leclerc's armored division to liberate Paris.

Yet Rambouillet has seen more tranquil times as well. Today, little remains of the sixteenth-century château, save the cool red-and-gray Salle des Marbres (Marble Hall). The eighteenth century and Empire are the periods now best represented at Rambouillet. The Count of Toulouse, a legitimized son of Louis XIV, purchased the château in 1705. He enlarged the existing structures and had the new west wing decorated with enchanting Rococo woodwork.For the garden, he commissioned a system of canals and artificial islands on which magnificent *fêtes* were held throughout the century. The count's son, the Duke of Penthièvre, completed the canals and, in the English garden, had an incredibly kitsch cottage constructed of seashells and slivers of mother-of-pearl.

In 1783, Louis XVI purchased Rambouillet for the exceptional hunting the nearby forest afforded. Marie-Antoinette was less than enthusiastic. She called the place "the toad hole" and longed for her Trianon at Versailles. To appease her, in 1785 Louis had the Neoclassic *laiterie* constructed, where ladies of the aristocracy came to sip new milk and sample fresh cheese. Today the dairy is no longer in operation, but the *bergerie*, built the following year, is still home to some 800 sheep, including 120 merinos descended from a flock presented to Louis XVI by the king of Spain (and those *moutons* of course refuse to mix with the other 680 "commoners").

Rambouillet was virtually abandoned during the Revolution, and its furniture removed and sold, but Napoléon took a fancy to the château and decided to restore it. Today, visitors may admire the emperor's study, his private apartments ornamented with "Pompeiian" frescoes, and the grand dining room—still used for state dinners—with its enormous, 550-pound bronze chandelier.

The densely treed forest of Rambouillet, a great favorite with hunters, hikers, and mushroom gatherers, covers close to half a million acres, and begins virtually at the door of the château.

*The **Château de Rambouillet** (located about 50 kilometers from Paris by Autoroute Chartres-Orléans A10) is open daily, except on Tuesday and when the president is in residence, from 10am to 11:30am and 2pm to 5:30pm (until 4:30pm from Oct 1 through Mar 31).*

*La **Laiterie de la Reine Marie-Antoinette** is open daily, except Tuesday, April 1 through September 30: from 10am to 11:30am and 2pm to 5:30pm, October 1 through March 31: from 10am to 11:30am and 2pm to 3:30pm. Call 34 83 00 25 for further information.*

RESTAURANTS & HOTELS

12/20 Le Cheval Rouge

78, rue du Général-de-Gaulle
30 88 80 61, fax 34 83 91 60

Closed Sun dinner, Jul 21-Aug 17. Open until 9:30pm. Priv rm: 50. Air cond. V, AE, DC, MC.

The flower-filled garden of this pleasant inn is just the place to enjoy traditional dishes prepared from the freshest ingredients: lobster crêpes, duck breast with raspberry-vinegar sauce. The dining room has a glassed-in garden and a terrace for summer dining. **C** 250-360 F. **M** 125 F (exc hols), 185 F.

Resthôtel Primevère

ZA du Bel-Air, rue J.-Jacquard
34 85 51 02, fax 30 59 25 66

Open year-round. 42 rms 260 F. Restaurant. Half-board 315-330 F. Pkg. V, AE, DC, MC.

Set back from the main road, this brand-new hotel offers bright, pleasant rooms and buffet breakfasts. The forest is nearby.

MONTFORT-L'AMAURY

La Toque Blanche

78490 Les Mesnuls, 4 km SE
12, Grande-Rue - 34 86 05 55

Closed Sun dinner, Mon, Dec 24-30, Aug 10-28. Open until 10pm. Garden dining. V, AE, DC, MC.

Jean-Pierre Philippe, a sturdy Breton, favors lighter versions of classic cuisine. He imports excellent seafood from his native province but doesn't neglect dishes to please landlubbers, and all his offerings are meticulously prepared: langoustine croustillant, fillet of John Dory with fried parsley. Attentive welcome. **C** 380-480 F. **M** 360 F.

See also Saint-Symphorien-le-Château in "Chartres" above.

ST-GERMAIN-EN-LAYE

In 1862 Emperor Napoléon III, an ardent archaeology buff (his great boast was that he had discovered the site of the Battle of Alésia, where Caesar defeated Vercingetorix, leader of the Gauls, in 52 B.C.), established the Musée des Antiquités Nationales at Saint-Germain-en-Laye. The oldest artifacts unearthed on French soil are housed in this fascinating museum, which follows the course of French history up to the time of the Merovingians, the first Frankish dynasty. Today, nothing could be simpler than to take this journey back in time, for the RER links Saint-Germain to the center of Paris in a matter of minutes.

On the museum's vast mezzanine, exhibits illustrate the millennia that preceded Rome's occupation of Gaul. It is strangely moving to contemplate these age-old vestiges of human artistry. Most of the pieces are quite small, like the *Dame de Brassempouy*, the oldest known representation of a human face, which is thought to predate Christ's birth by about 20,000 years; or the famous bone carving of a *Bison Licking Its Fur*, from Dordogne (16,000 B.C.); or the many images that remind us that in France too the buffalo roamed and the deer (and antelope) played—at least until the end of the Ice Age.

Even visitors with only a mild interest in archaeology will be riveted by artifacts discovered in the tombs of Celtic princes of the first Iron Age (Hallstatt period), particularly the funeral chariots, which indicate that the entombed were of noble rank, the iron swords, carved daggers, and personal ornaments. Other finds verify that Gaulish tribes traded with Greece and Etruria, thus invalidating the theory that Gaul lived in isolation before the Romans burst onto the scene. The very existence of coins minted by the principal Gallic tribes, of amphoras and other luxury goods, bears witness to the wealth of Gaul's aristocracy, and to their links with the Mediterranean world.

Exhibits on the upper floor document the period of Roman colonization and include a model of the Battle of Alésia, which marked the end of Gaul's independence. The number of statues representing Gaulish divinities underscores Rome's generally tolerant attitude toward foreign religions, while an abundance of manufactured goods—ceramics, glass objects—give us a picture of France's earliest industries. The barbarian invasions that followed this period of prosperity are evoked by jewels and impressively worked weapons excavated at Frankish tomb sites.

Though Saint-Germain-en-Laye is now synonymous with prehistory, it holds a significant place in the history of France. A prestigious royal château, it was the birthplace of Kings Henri II, Charles IX, and Louis XIV (who preferred it to all his other palaces until he built Versailles). From the twelfth century through the nineteenth, extensive building and remodeling altered the château's appearance many times over. What the visitor sees today is the Vieux Château, rebuilt under François Ier. This first important example of brick-and-stone architecture in the Ile de France was heavily restored in the nineteenth century.

The former splendor of Saint-Germain is perhaps best translated by Le Nôtre's magnificent gardens, and the Grande Terrasse bordered with linden trees. Moreover, with its 8,500 acres of flat, sandy paths, picturesque hunting pavilions, and majestic stands of oak, the Forest of Saint-Germain offers ideal hiking terrain within easy reach of Paris.

*The **Musée des Antiquités Nationales** in Saint-Germain-en-Laye (about 20 kilometers west of Paris by Autoroute de Normandie A13) is open daily, except Tuesday, from 9am to 5:15pm. Call 34 51 53 65 for further information.*

See also "The Suburbs" in the Restaurants (page 102) and Hotels (page 143) chapters.

SENLIS

When you walk through the narrow medieval streets of Senlis, don't be surprised if you suddenly recognize the set from your favorite French costume drama. This compact, well-preserved town on the border of the Ile de France and Picardy offers a fascinating glimpse into the history of pre-Revolutionary France. Understandably, it is a popular location with film-production companies.

North of the town, the Jardin du Roy (King's Garden) lies in what was once the moat surrounding a Gallo-Roman defensive wall. The garden affords a marvelous overall view of Senlis, and of one of the best-preserved Roman fortifications in France. About 13 feet thick and 23 feet high, the wall dates back to the barbarian invasions of the third century. It once linked together 28 watch towers, 16 of which have survived.

The nearby Château Royal, despite its grandiose name, is now nothing more than a park scattered with romantic ruins that date from antiquity to the Renaissance. Built on the site of a first-century Roman fortress, the château was a royal residence from the time of Clovis, in the fifth century, until the reign of Henri IV, early in the seventeenth century. It was there, in 987, that the Capetian line of monarchs was established, with the election of Hugues Capet, Duke of the Franks, to the throne of France.

If you cross the pretty square in front of the Cathedral of Notre-Dame, you can best admire the monumental portal with its celebrated Gothic sculpture. Begun in 1153, ten years before Notre-Dame de Paris, the cathedral at Senlis served as a model for those at Chartres, Amiens, and Reims. Yet by the sixteenth century, recurrent fires had made it necessary to rebuild the northern and southern façades practically from scratch. The work was directed by Pierre Chambiges, who created one of the finest (and last) examples of flamboyant Gothic architecture. Crowning the northern portal are the initial and emblematic salamander of François Ier.

After visiting the cathedral, we always take the time to wander through the winding, ancient streets of Senlis: Rue de la Tonnellerie, Rue du Châtel, Rue de la Treille, and Rue de Beauvais all boast sixteenth-century houses and mansions with splendid carved entrances (many of which are open to visitors in odd-numbered years, during the month of September for the Rendez-vous de Senlis).

You'll end up at the thirteenth-century church of Saint Frambourg, restored through the efforts of pianist and composer George Cziffra, and now used as a concert hall.

If you have time and a car, drive a few kilometers north to the Italianate Château de Raray, built in the seventeenth century, where Jean Cocteau filmed his magical *Beauty and the Beast*.

Who knows? Perhaps, as you stand admiring the fantastic hunting scenes sculpted on Diana's Gate, your own Beauty—or Prince Charming—will suddenly appear!

*The **Château Royal** and **Musée de la Vénerie** in Senlis (50 kilometers north of Paris by Autoroute du Nord A1) are open daily, except Tuesday and Wednesday morning, Feb 2-Oct 31: from 10am to noon and 2pm to 6pm (Nov 1-Jan 31: until 5pm).*
*The **Jardin du Roy** is open at all times.*
*The **cathedral** is open from 7am to 7pm. Call (16) 44 53 00 80 for information.*

RESTAURANTS & HOTELS

14 Le Vieux Logis

60700 Fleurines, 6.5 km N on N 17,
105, rue de Paris - (16) 44 54 10 13

Closed Sat lunch (Nov 1-Easter), Sun dinner, Mon, Aug 1-15. Open until 9:30pm. Priv rm: 40. Terrace dining. No pets. Pkg. V, AE, DC, MC.

The Vieux Logis's pretty terrace complements a comfortable dining room brightened by floral bouquets and smiling staff. Yann Nivet's classic cuisine shows polish and a dash of personality. Sample the herbed red mullet croutons, veal sweetbreads en cocotte, and warm stawberries with gingerbread ice cream. For around 200 F, you can have a very nice meal, in spite of the high-priced wine list. **C** 280-480 F. **M** 200 F (and up).

11/20 Auberge de Fontaine

60300 Fontaine-Chaalis,
8 km SE by D 330, 22, Grande-Rue
(16) 44 54 20 22, fax (16) 44 60 28 33

Closed Tue dinner, Wed. Open until 9:15pm. Garden dining. Pkg. V, MC.

Come here for a pleasant dinner in an attractive village auberge. We enjoyed the simple but carefully prepared seafood platter with lemon butter, veal kidney with shallots, and a fancifully named "Chalice of the Chaalis Monks" for dessert. **C** 250-320 F. **M** 115 F, 185 F.

Auberge de Fontaine

(See restaurant above)

Closed Tue, Wed. 8 rms 280-305 F. Half-board 325-410 F. Golf. Pkg. V, MC.

A hotel with lovely, quiet rooms in a deliciously attractive village.

See also Chantilly and Compiègne in "Chantilly," above.

VAUX-LE-VICOMTE

As we stand in the unfinished Grand Salon of Vaux-le-Vicomte, looking out over the intricate gardens designed by Le Nôtre, we can almost picture the scene... The dog days of August 1661: Nicolas Fouquet, France's brilliant finance minister, is entertaining his young sovereign, Louis XIV, at an indescribably lavish reception. A thousand fountains play in the magnificent *jardins à la française*, while Molière's troupe performs the comic ballet *Les Fâcheux*. Courtiers applaud the water jousts, the concerts, the fireworks... At dinner—prepared by Vatel, the foremost chef of his day—the king and his retinue are served on solid-gold plates. According to legend, the dinner did not sit well with Louis, whose suspicions—and envy—were aroused by such luxury. Historians claim that Colbert, Fouquet's rival for control of the royal treasury, had slandered Fouquet, insinuating that he was raiding the king's coffers. Or it may have been that the king set Fouquet up himself: wangling an invitation to Vaux, then watching the vainglorious minister flaunt his riches, and thus be hoist by his own petard!

Whoever laid it, the trap was sprung that August day at Vaux-le-Vicomte. A few weeks later, Louis sent d'Artagnan, the captain of his musketeers, to arrest Fouquet at Nantes. He then sent workmen to pack up the finest tapestries, furnishings, and paintings from Vaux and carry them straight into the royal collection. Louis summoned Fouquet's architect, Le Vau, his decorator, Le Brun, and his landscape designer, Le Nôtre, and ordered them all to begin work on the royal showplace at Versailles.

After a trial that dragged out over three years, the courts handed down a sentence of banishment for Fouquet. Louis, implacable, overruled them, and condemned his former minister to life imprisonment. Fouquet was, in all probability, a rascal. Yet the story of his fall and miserable end (after nineteen years in prison) still colors our view of Vaux's splendors with a tinge of melancholy.

It is largely thanks to Alfred Sommier, a sugar-refining magnate who purchased a dilapidated Vaux-le-Vicomte in 1875, that we can now see the château and gardens much as they were on that fateful day in 1661. Sommier spent prodigious amounts of money and energy to rebuild sagging roofs and walls, to furnish the nearly empty house with seventeenth-century antiques, and to restore the gardens to their former beauty. That last task alone took a good half-century. Using Le Nôtre's plans and contemporary engravings, Sommier was able to reconstruct the terraces, pools, and the complex system of pipes that feed the fountains. He planted acres of trees and bushes, and acquired antique statuary for the garden. Pieces were also commissioned from modern sculptors to replace the statues confiscated by Louis XIV.

In addition to the gardens, three levels of the château are now open to the public. On the upper floor are the Fouquets' private living quarters—studies, boudoirs, and bedrooms—handsomely fitted out with period furniture and hung with tapestries and reproductions of paintings from the minister's (confiscated) collection. Above the fireplace in Madame Fouquet's study is Le Brun's famous portrait of a smiling Nicolas Fouquet.

For us, the most appealing aspect of the reception rooms downstairs (the Grands Appartements) is Le Brun's decoration. Actually, the term *decoration* is not adequate to describe this virtuoso performance with paint, stucco, carving, and gilt. The scores of rosy nymphs, cherubs, squirrels (Fouquet's emblem), and other allegorical figures that populate the ceilings and woodwork of the Salon des Muses and Cabinet des Jeux (Gaming Room) fill these formal rooms with a rapturous charm. Le Brun's stucco-and-fresco décor in the Chambre du Roi (Royal Chamber) is the model for what later became known throughout Europe as the "French style," which reached its apotheosis at Versailles.

Bereft of its intended decoration, the Grand Salon demonstrates the measure of architect Le Vau's genius; the eye, unsolicited by bright allegories and visions, is naturally drawn outside, to the harmonious perspectives of the gardens, Le Nôtre's masterpiece. In their more modest way, the workrooms and staff quarters on the lower level are also quite interesting. The kitchens (in use until 1956) display a dazzling collection of copper pots and pans scoured to a high polish.

Those in search of rare sensations and exquisite atmospheres will surely want to visit Vaux-le-Vicomte by candlelight on a Saturday evening in summer. The scene is unforgettable—indeed, it is enough to rouse the envy of a king!

The ***Château de Vaux-le-Vicomte*** *(about 60 kilometers south of Paris by Autoroute du Sud A6) is open daily February 18 through October 31 and November 1 through November 12: from 11am to 5pm; April 1 through October 31: from 10am to 6pm. Admission: from 30 to 56 F.* ***Candlelight tours*** *are held Saturday and holidays evenings from May 1 through October 14: 8:30pm to 11pm. Admission: 45 to 75 F.* ***Fountain displays*** *are scheduled the second and final Saturday of each month from April through October: 3pm to 6pm. Call 64 14 41 90 for further information.*

RESTAURANTS & HOTELS

MELUN

Ibis

81, av. de Meaux
60 68 42 45, fax 64 09 62 00

Open year-round. 73 rms 270 F. Restaurant. Conf. Pkg. V, AE, DC, MC.

A comfortable hotel with reasonably priced rooms.

14

Auberge Briarde

77820 Les Ecrennes, 15 km E on N 105 & D 213 - 60 69 47 32, fax 60 66 60 11

Closed dinner Sun & Wed, Mon, Feb school hols, Aug 1-20. Open until 9:30pm. Priv rm: 16. V, AE, DC, MC.

Settle down by the fireplace in this comfortable dining room with rustic décor, and enjoy Jean Guichard's tasty and interesting cooking: scrambled eggs with fresh morels, John Dory with a sauce made from three kinds of pepper, and boned squab with a split-pea purée. Game in season. Complete but expensive wine list. Warm welcome by the *patronneD.* **C** 320-520 F. **M** 125 F, 150 F (weekdays, Sat lunch), 275 F, 355 F, 430 F.

Le Flamboyant

77127 Lieusaint, 13 km N on N 6, 98, rue de Paris
60 60 05 60, fax 60 60 05 32

Open year-round. 72 rms 290-330 F. Rms for disabled. Restaurant. Air cond. Conf. Pool. Tennis. Pkg. V, AE, DC, MC.

A modern hotel with attractive contemporary décor, right at the edge of the Sénart forest. Comfortable, soundproof, well equipped rooms.

Bleu Marine Grand Monarque

Melun-la-Rochette,
av. de Fontainebleau
64 39 04 40, fax 64 39 94 10

Open year-round. 5 stes 580 F. 45 rms 390-480 F. Conf. Restaurant. Heated pool. Tennis. Sauna.

The small but perfectly equipped rooms open onto the verdant grounds that lead into the forest. Excellent service.

14

La Mare au Diable

77550 Moissy-Cramayel, 8 km NW on N 6, 5 km N on N 6 - 64 10 20 90, fax 64 10 20 91

Closed Sun dinner, Mon (exc hols). Open until 10pm. Priv rm: 150. Garden dining. Pool. Pkg. V, AE, DC, MC.

The cooking is getting better all the time, so we're awarding this charming manor house, formerly owned by George Sand, an extra point. The rustic dining room overlooks romantic grounds where meals are served in summer. Well worth ordering are seafood parfait with a flavorful shellfish broth, juicy roast duck, or meats grilled over an open fire. The overall effect is much improved, with more experienced service yet the same warm and smiling welcome. **C** 350-400 F. **M** 200 F (lunch, wine & coffee incl), 150 F, 235 F, 330 F.

This symbol signifies hotels that offer an exceptional degree of peace and quiet.

VERSAILLES

Versailles, undoubtedly the world's most famous palace, has been a favorite destination for day-tripping Parisians since 1833, when King Louis-Philippe turned the château, which had been abandoned since the Revolution, into a "museum of the glories of France." Today, Versailles offers pleasures at every season, in every kind of weather. Visitors can amble through parks dotted with romantic statuary, admire a wealth of art, furniture, and architecture—comparing Louis this with Louis that—or simply spread out a blanket and picnic beside the Grand Canal.

It took Louis XIV just 40 years to build the palace and its park around a hunting lodge erected by his father, Louis XIII. And though his successors made many changes, Versailles still bears the unmistakable stamp of the Sun King, who from 1682 on made it the official residence of the court, the sole seat of royal power, and the political capital of France. The court's permanent presence explains the colossal proportions of the palace, which housed the royal family, the princes of the blood, the courtiers, the king's councilors, everyone's servants... it's little wonder, then, that the western façade of the palace stretches out to a width of nearly 2,000 feet.

Lodging his considerable household and entourage was not all that Louis had in mind when he built Versailles. He also saw the palace as a powerful propaganda tool, a monument to the glory of the French monarchy, and a showcase for masterworks by French artists and craftsmen. Versailles was open to all. The humblest subjects of the realm could wander freely through the Grands Appartements to gape at the cream of the royal collections. Classical statues and busts stood in marble-lined halls; paintings from the French and Venetian schools hung on walls covered in velvet, damask, and brocade. Today's tourists are the descendants of those visitors who, at the end of the seventeenth century, marveled at the dazzling Galerie des Glaces (Gallery of Mirrors) or the Salon d'Apollon before attending the king's supper or submitting a petition to Louis XIV as he made his way to Mass at the royal chapel.

But we have the advantage over those tourists of long ago, for we can visit parts of Versailles that were then off-limits to the public, even to courtiers. Among the most beautiful of the private quarters is the Petit Appartement, fitted out for Louis XV just above his official suite, a place where he could relax alone—or with friends (like Madame du Barry, who had her own room there).

A similarly intimate mood and scale are evident in the two Trianons, situated about half a mile from the main palace. The Grand Trianon was built in 1687 for Louis XIV, who spent many a quiet summer evening there surrounded by his family. Today it houses heads of state on official visits. The Petit Trianon is an exquisite Neoclassic structure designed by Gabriel in 1764 for Louis XV, who wished to live closer to his beloved botanical garden. It was also the preferred residence of Marie-Antoinette, whose spirit still pervades the place. There, on October 5, 1789, she learned of the Parisians' march on Versailles.

In fine weather, the gardens of Versailles are an irresistible invitation to wander. They cover over 200 acres with an enchanting variety of landscapes. The classical French *parterres* (flower beds), with their broad perspectives, pools, and lawns, were designed by Le Nôtre at the height of his powers; his is also the genius behind the marvelous *bosquets* (coppices) that combine thickly massed greenery and spectacular waterworks. Scattered throughout are hundreds of marble and bronze statues, many inspired by the myths of Apollo, with whom the Sun King strongly identified. If you happen to be in Versailles between May and September, make a point of touring the gardens when the Grandes Eaux are scheduled: all over the gardens, in every bed and *bosquet*, the fountains put on a magical display.

And in summer, it is well worth the effort to obtain tickets for a performance at the Opéra Royal, an architectural masterpiece by Gabriel, inaugurated in 1770 for the marriage of the future Louis XVI and the Archduchess Marie-Antoinette. The elegance of its proportions, its superb acoustics, and the splendor of its decoration make it perhaps the most beautiful theater in the world.

*The **Château de Versailles** (about 25 kilometers west of Paris by Autoroute de Normandie A13) is open daily, except Monday and some holidays, May 3 through September 30: from 9am to 6pm (until 5pm from October 1 to April 31). The **park and gardens** are open daily from dawn to dusk. Fountain displays are scheduled on Sundays from May 8 through end September: 3:30pm to 5pm. Call 30 84 74 00 for further information.*

RESTAURANTS & HOTELS

See "The Suburbs" in the Restaurants (page 104) and Hotels (page 143) chapters.

SIGHTS

Following is a highly condensed list of Versailles's most noteworthy sights.

The **Château de Versailles** with more than four million visitors per year (from May to September its parks host the Grandes Eaux and the Fêtes de Nuit); the **Trianon Palaces**; the **Salle du Jeu de Paume**; **Notre-Dame** church (designed by Hardouin-Mansart); the **king's vegetable garden** (school of horticulture); the **Carrés Saint-Louis** (modest lodgings during the time of the Old Régime); the **antiques** and **secondhand market** (passage de la Geôle, next to the colorful market at Notre-Dame); the **Hôtel des Ventes** (former home of the Light Cavalry); the delightful **Musée Lambinet** (with beautiful eighteenth-century paintings, see *Museums* section page 349); the **Couvent des Récollets**.

BASICS

GETTING AROUND

Paris is a rationally designed city divided into twenty *arrondissements*, or districts. Essential to getting around Paris is a knowledge of the excellent transportation system and a pocket-size street index called *Paris par Arrondissement*. Available in most bookstores and at major newspaper stands, it includes comprehensive maps of Paris, the subway system (Métro and RER), and bus routes.

BUSES

Riding the bus is a great—and cheap—way to tour the city. The n°20, 21, 24, 27, 47, 63, 69, 73, and 82 buses pass by many historical monuments. Buses take you almost everywhere within the metropolitan area for one or two tickets, depending on the length of your journey. You can purchase tickets (7 F) on the bus or a block (*carnet*) of ten tickets (41 F—an economical investment) at Métro stations or in *café-tabacs* that display the blue-green Métro ticket sign.

Most bus routes operate from 6:30am to 8:30pm, Monday through Saturday. Others (indicated at bus stops by a colored number inside a white disc) run until 12:30am, and operate every day including Sundays and holidays. *Noctambus* is the reliable skeleton service that runs late at night: buses leave Châtelet from special stops marked with the night owl-logo every hour on the half hour from 1:30am to 5:30am.

Every bus stop in Paris posts fares, times, routes, and bus numbers. When you enter the bus, punch your ticket(s) in the machine next to the driver. Do not punch travel passes or Carte Orange coupons: simply hold them up for the driver to see. When you wish to get off, signal the driver by pressing the red button near your seat. Getting around by bus is a good deal easier than it may sound; and listening to an irate Parisian bus driver caught in rush-hour traffic is also an excellent way to learn some interesting French words that you won't find in the dictionary!

Special three- (95 F) or five-day (150 F) tourist passes (*Paris Visite*), which allow unlimited travel on buses, the Métro, the RER express line, and the SNCF Ile-de-France lines, are sold at major Métro and RER stations. These passes also entitle holders to reduced rates at certain tourist attractions.

AIRPORT TRANSPORTATION

Roissybus ferries passengers to Charles-de-Gaulle airport from the Place de l'Opéra (Rue Scribe, in front of the American Express office), with departures every 15 minutes from 5:45am to 8pm, then every 20 minutes until 11pm. The journey to or from the airport takes about 45 minutes if traffic is moving well. The one-way fare is 35 F.

Another convenient way to reach the city's airports is to take the *Air France Bus*. It leaves every 15 minutes depending on the destination, from 3 different points in the capital: the Aérogare des Invalides to Paris-Orly (32 F), Esplanade des Invalides, 7th arr., 43 23 84 49; Le Palais des Congrès to Roissy-Charles-de-Gaulle (48 F), Place de la Porte Maillot, near the Air France agency, 16th arr., 44 09 51 52/3/5; and near the Arc de Triomphe to Roissy-Charles-de-Gaulle (48 F), at the top of Avenue Carnot, 17th arr. The bus makes the same stops on the return journey from the airports.

LIMOUSINES

See *Alliance Autos*, page 205.

MÉTRO

Getting the knack of the Métro system is a cinch. You'll find a Métro map posted at each station, outside on the street and inside as well. Let's imagine you want to go from the Gare du Nord to Saint-Germain-des-Prés. Locate the two stations on your map and check whether they are on the same line (each line is indicated by a different color). In this case they are, so follow the line from your station of departure to your station of arrival, then note the name of the station at the end of the line (in this instance it's the Porte d'Orléans). That means that Porte d'Orléans is the name of the direction you will be taking. Inside the station, look for signs indicating "direction Porte d'Orléans," and when you reach the platform, check again on the sign located in the middle of the platform. If you must change lines to reach your destination, consult a Métro map to ascertain which stop offers the relevant *correspondance*, or interchange.

Hours: first departure from the terminal: 5:30am; last departure from the terminal: 12:30am.

A single ticket is good for any one-way journey on the Métro system and within zones 1 and 2 of the RER system (see RER, below). Don't forget to keep your ticket until you leave the bus or Métro, for you may be asked to produce it by an R.A.T.P. official. Tourist or not, if you don't have it, you will have to pay an on-the-spot fine if you're caught.

The *R.A.T.P.* runs the Métro, the buses, and the RER. Information line: 43 46 14 14 from 6am to 9pm.

RER

The *Réseau Express Régional* is a network of fast commuter services linking the center of Paris to destinations all over the Greater Paris Region. Quite a number of interesting places to visit are accessible by RER, and you can pick up brochures listing these from any Métro information kiosk.

There is also a very good bicycle-hire service (*Roue Libre*) run by the RER that allows you to explore some beautiful woodlands around Paris (the Chevreuse Valley, the Forest of Saint-Germain-en-Laye...). The flat-rate system on the regular Métro does not apply to the RER unless you are traveling within the city, so you must consult the fee schedules posted on the automatic ticket machines to determine the cost of your journey.

AIRPORT TRANSPORTATION

The Orlyval system is a quick and carefree way to travel to or from Paris-Orly airport. To reach the airport, take the RER B line from, say, Châtelet, then change at Antony for the driverless elevated car that drops passengers off at both Orly terminals. The service operates from 6:30am to 9:15pm Monday through Saturday, 7am to 10:57pm on Sundays. The fare is currently 50 F (25 F for children under 11).

TAXIS

There are some 14,900 taxis available in Paris (until you really need one!). There are three ways of getting yourself a taxi: the first is simply to flag one down (it is available if its roof light is fully illuminated); the second is to go to a taxi stand (*Tête de Station*); the third is to phone a radio taxi that will arrive 5 to 10 minutes later at your address (the meter will already be running, but don't get in if it's more than 30 F). Normally, you pay 12 F to get in the cab and about 3.23 F per kilometer during daytime hours (7am-7pm) and 5.10 F at night (7pm-7am). Rates are higher to the suburbs, on expressways (i.e. to the airports), and on Sundays. Supplements are charged if the taxi leaves from a train station (5 F), if a fourth person is aboard (5 F), for each item of luggage (6 F), and for pets (3 F). Though not obligatory, a tip of 10 to 15 percent is customary. If you wish to report a problem or lodge a complaint, call 45 31 14 80, or write to Service des Taxis, 36, rue des Morillons, 75732 Paris cedex 15, indicating the taxi's license number as well as the date and time you were picked up.

Alpha-Taxis
45 85 85 85

Artaxi
42 41 50 50

G7 Radio
47 39 47 39

Taxis-Radio "Étoile"
42 70 41 41

TOURS

BY BUS

Cityrama

1st arr. - 4, pl. des Pyramides
44 55 61 00
Open daily Apr 1-Oct 31: 6:30am-10pm; Nov 1-Mar 31: 7:30am-8:30pm. V, AE, DC, MC. M° Palais-Royal.

Cityrama's double-decker, ultracomfortable tour buses whisk visitors all around Paris morning, noon, and night (for schedules and fares, call or pick up a brochure). A recorded commentary describes monuments, landmarks, and points of interest in the language of your choice. Cityrama will also show you around Versailles, Chartres, Disneyland Paris, and many other places of interest.

Walking tours

Discover the city on foot during a three-hour stroll with a theme. You can choose from luxury fashion, avant-garde fashion, Left Bank fashion, designer fashion, antiques and art galleries, or gift ideas. Cost for a pre-programmed tour (list available at the Office de Tourisme, 127 avenue des Champs-Élysées) is 180 F per person, which includes the services of a bilingual guide and a tea or coffee break. Personalized tours may be arranged by request: call *Shopping Plus* **at 47 53 91 17 for further details, fax 44 18 96 68.**

Paris et son Histoire

9th arr. - 82, rue Taitbout
45 26 26 77
Open 10am-noon & 2pm-6:30pm. Closed Sun & hols. Fee: 350 F, 500 F per couple. No cards. M° Trinité.

As the name indicates, this association specializes in the history of Paris (and the surrounding Ile-de-France region). Members attend lecture tours throughout the year; and from March to October, bus trips are organized to points of interest in the Paris area. Annual membership fees are 350 F (500 F for couples) and include a monthly bulletin of events. Meeting times and other information are provided by phone, or at tourist offices.

Paris Passion

18th arr. - 69, rue Damrémont
42 59 31 36, fax 42 59 48 55
Open 9am-1pm & 2pm-6pm. Closed Sun. Prices vary. M° Lamarck-Caulaincourt.

If you like the idea of an informed guided tour but don't care for buses, give Emanuelle Daras a call. This smart young woman has created a series of small, first-class, personalized tours. In a luxurious minivan (stocked with Champagne, no less), a maximum of five people at a time are taken to such places as artists' ateliers, foie-gras makers, the Cartier workshops, and much more.

France Tourisme Paris-Vision

1st arr. - 214, rue de Rivoli
42 60 31 25
Open daily Nov 1-Mar 31: 7am-9pm (Mon, Wed, Fri 8am-9pm); Apr 1-Oct 31: 7am-10pm (Mon 8am-10pm). V, AE, DC, MC. M° Tuileries.

Paris-Vision conducts guided tours of the city in just about any language you can think of. Trips to Versailles, Fontainebleau, Chartres, and more are scheduled as well. For details, consult the firm's brochure, available at the address above or at tourist offices.

R.A.T.P.

8th arr. - Pl. de la Madeleine (beside the flower market) - 40 06 71 45
Open 8:30am-7pm (Sat, Sun & hols in summer 6:30am-7pm); winter: 9:30am-12:30pm & 1:15pm-5:15pm. Closed Sat, Sun. V, MC.

Guided bus tours conducted in every imaginable language. Half- and full-day excursions to fascinating sites in the Ile-de-France and even further afield are also offered. For a free brochure listing destinations and prices, drop by the R.A.T.P. tourist office at the Madeleine, or at 53 bis, quai des Grands-Augustins in the sixth arrondissement (M° St-Michel).

T.A.S. Voyages

40 12 88 08, fax 40 10 89 02
Open daily 7:30am-midnight. Call for information. V, AE, DC, MC. M° Garibaldi.

T.A.S.: a new way to travel. Specialized in tours of Paris and the surrounding area, T.A.S. will pick you up at your hotel in a minibus holding 8 to 15 passengers and escort you on a guided tour conducted in your own language, for a day or half-day, morning, noon, or night.

■ BY BOAT

Bateaux Parisiens

7th arr. - Port de la Bourdonnais, Maurice Chevalier landing stage - 44 11 33 55
One hour tour. May-Oct.: 10am-10:30pm, departures every half-hour; Nov-Apr: 10am-6pm (w-e 10am-10pm), departures every hour. Lunch cruises by reservation only at 12:30pm (2 hours). Dinner cruises at 8pm (2:30 hours). Free pkg. V, MC. M° Champ-de-Mars.

Hop aboard one of Bateaux Parisiens' glass-sided river cruisers for a memorable guided tour of quayside Paris. A trilingual hostess gives the tour commentary, written by a certified professor of history. An illustrated guidebook is provided, free of extra charge. Lunch and dinner cruises are offered, featuring unlimited wine, waiter service, and even a dance band! Theme cruises can also be arranged; in fact, just tell Bateaux Parisiens what sort of tour you'd like, and they'll custom-design a cruise just for you.

Les Bateaux-Mouches

8th arr. - Port de la Conférence, Pont de l'Alma, Right Bank
40 76 99 99
Call for information. V, AE, DC, MC. M° Alma-Marceau.

These whales of river cruisers go nosing down the Seine packed with thousands of tourists, often eliciting a sarcastic smirk from Parisians. But the laugh is on the cynics. These fast, smooth boats provide one of the few ways to see Paris from a new angle. Take an early-morning or dusk cruise, when the light is at its loveliest. On night cruises, the Bateaux-Mouches' floodlights unveil a phantasmagoric cityscape that fascinates tourists and seen-it-all Parisians alike. Lunch and formal dinners are available on board at reasonable prices, considering the incomparable view that accompanies your meal.

Canauxrama

19th arr. - 13, quai de la Loire
42 39 15 00, fax 42 39 11 24
1-day cruise Apr-Oct: 8:30am-6pm; 3-hour cruise: 9:45am & 2:45pm. Closed Dec 25, Jan 1. Admission: 75-195 F, reduced rate for children (exc for 1-day cruise). No cards. M° Jaurès, Bastille.

Did you know that the Saint-Martin and the Ourcq Canals flow from the Seine in central Paris as far (upstream) as Meaux? Well, now you do. So why go by bus or subway when you can take a boat back from La Villette's Cité des Sciences? Canauxrama's cruises are one of the city's most pleasant, unhurried, uncrowded excursions. The view of Paris and the Ile-de-France from a comfortable canal boat (sunroof, on-board bar, guided tours) has a special charm. Canauxrama offers a day-long trip on the Canal de l'Ourcq through the lovely countryside between Paris and Meaux, with a stopover at Claye-Souilly for a picnic or bistro lunch. Also featured is a tour of the exciting La Villette neighborhood, which includes passage through the deepest lock in the Paris region. Departures take place at the pier opposite 5 bis, quai de la Loire (nineteenth arrondissement) and from the Paris-Arsenal canal port opposite 50, boulevard de la Bastille (twelfth arrondissement), just down from the new Opera house.

Paris-Canal

9th arr. - 19, quai de la Loire
42 40 96 97, fax 42 40 77 30
Departures 9:30am & 2:30pm (w-e also at 10am & 2:25pm); 1-day cruise on Sun in Jul & Aug only 190 F (Seine and Marne). Admission: 95 F, reduced rate for children. No cards. M° Solférino, Porte de Pantin.

Paris-Canal offers Canal Saint-Martin and Seine cruises from April 1 to November 13 on board the *Patache* and the *Canotier*, two comfortable riverboats that carry between 20 and 110 passengers. The ambience is particularly fine in the off-season. Personalized cruises are arranged on request. Reservations recommended.

Quiztour Continentale

9th arr. - 19, quai de la Loire
42 01 11 11, fax 42 01 00 09
Open 9am-6:30pm. Closed Sat, Sun. Reservation advisable. No cards.

Quiztour offers boats for private parties (quai de Grenelle) or personalized cruises (Dijon, Toulouse...). If you want to rent a houseboat or canal boat/hotel, this is the place to call.

Les Vedettes de Paris-Ile-de-France
7th arr. - Port de Suffren
47 05 71 29, fax 47 05 74 53
Open daily Apr 1-Sep 30: 10am-11pm; Oct 1-Mar 31: 10am-6pm (Sat & Sun 10am-10pm). V, AE, DC, MC. M° Bir-Hakeim.

A nostalgic dance-hall atmosphere reigns on these tea-dance cruises with such themes as historic Paris or the Val-de-Marne.

Les Vedettes du Pont-Neuf
1st arr. - Square du Vert-Galant, Pont-Neuf landing stage
46 33 98 38, fax 43 29 86 19
Open daily Apr-Oct: 10am-11pm; Nov-Mar: 10:30am-10:30pm (Fri, Sat & Sun 10:30am-11pm). M° Pont-Neuf.

The Vedettes du Pont-Neuf are medium-size boats that take passengers on one-hour pleasure cruises up and down the Seine. Cruises depart every 30 minutes from 10am to noon and from 1:30pm to 6:30pm in spring and summer, and every 45 minutes from 10:30am to noon and from 2pm to 6:30pm from late fall through the winter. Evening cruises along the illuminated banks of the Seine are conducted from 9pm to 10:30pm (departures every half hour; weekends only in the off-season). Group tours and parties are handled too.

AT YOUR SERVICE

TOURIST INFORMATION

For all the brochures and other "literature" that the sage sightseer might need:

Eiffel Tower Office
7th arr. - 45 51 22 15
Open May 1-Sep 30: 11am-6pm.

Bureau Gare d'Austerlitz
13th arr. - 7, bd de l'Hôpital
45 84 91 70
Open 8am-3pm. Closed Sun.

Located in the international arrivals area.

Bureau Gare de l'Est
10th arr. - pl. du 11 Novembre 1918
46 07 17 73
Open 8am-9pm (off-seas 8am-8pm). Closed Sun.

Located opposite track 25.

City lights

Admire Paris in all its splendor during a nighttime visit. Hundreds of the city's buildings and monuments are cloaked in illuminations when the sun goes down to show them at their best. Sparkling fountains, shining façades, glowing towers—you'll see the city in a new light. Monuments: Sun-Fri from dusk to midnight; Sat & eves of holidays until 1am. Fountains: Daytime Apr 1-Dec 31 from 10am to dusk; Nighttime Apr 1-Dec 31 Sun-Fri from dusk to midnight; Sat & eves of holidays until 1am.

Bureau Gare de Lyon
12th arr. - 20 bd Diderot
43 43 33 24
Open 8am-9pm (off-seas 8am-8pm). Closed Sun.

Located opposite track L/N.

Bureau Gare Montparnasse
14th arr. - 17, bd de Vaugirard
43 22 19 19
Open 8am-9pm (off-seas 8am-8pm). Closed Sun.

Located opposite track 18.

Bureau Gare du Nord
10th arr. - 18, rue de Dunkerque
45 26 94 82
Open 8am-9pm (off-seas 8am-8pm). Closed Sun.

Located opposite track 19.

Office de Tourisme de Paris
8th arr. - 127, av. des Champs-Élysées
49 52 53 54, fax 49 52 53 00
Open 9am-8pm. Closed May 1.

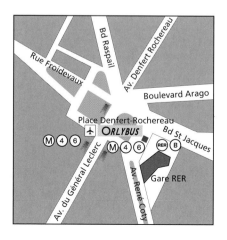

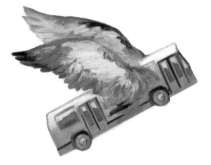

24-Hour Information Line
49 52 53 56

In English, of course.

ORIENTATION

Here are a few facts of French life for foreign visitors:

Remember that in France, the ground floor (*rez-de-chaussée*) is what Americans call the first floor; the French first floor (*premier étage*) corresponds to the American second floor, and so on.

When dining out, the **service charge** (15 percent) is always included in the bill. An additional tip can be left if you are satisfied with the service. Hairdressers are generally given a 10 to 15 percent tip. Porters, doormen, and room service are tipped a few francs. A hotel concierge makes all sorts of reservations for you (theater, restaurant, plane, train, and so on) and can offer advice about getting around in Paris; don't forget to tip the concierge afterward for his or her considerable services. Ushers at most movie houses, sporting events, ballets, and concerts expect a tip, and can be vengeful if you fail to shell out a couple of francs.

French and American **voltages** differ, so your electrical appliances (shavers, hairdryers) will require a transformer. You will doubtless also need an adapter for the round prongs of French plugs. These items can be obtained in the basement of the Samaritaine or the BHV department stores. (See *Department Stores* in the Shops chapter.)

Hallway lighting systems are often manually operated. Just to one side of the entrance, in a conspicuous place on each landing or near the elevator, you'll find a luminous switch that is automatically timed to give you one to three minutes of light. To enter many buildings, you must press a buzzer or a numerical code usually located at the side of the front door.

The French telecommunications services (FRANCE TELECOM) have created plastic **telephone cards** to be used instead of coins in public phone booths. They sell for 96 F or 40 F and may be purchased at the post office, cafés, and some bookstores. Their microchip technology gives you a certain number of units, which are gradually used up as you make your calls. Don't count too heavily on using telephones in cafés and restaurants unless you have a drink or meal there.

Most modern pay phones have instructions in English printed on them. A local call costs 1 F. You can **phone abroad** from most pay phones using either your plastic card or a large reserve of 5 F coins. Collect calls can be made from pay phones by dialing 19, then 33 after the tone, and then the code for the country you want (Australia, 61; Britain, 44; Canada and the United States, 11).

The Louvre **post office** (52, rue du Louvre, 1st arr., 40 28 20 00) has a 24-hour international telephone/telegraph/fax service. Also note that Paris telephone numbers have eight figures. If you should come upon an old-style Parisian number with only seven digits, you must dial 4 or 5 before the number.

USEFUL ADDRESSES

Here are some addresses and phone numbers of particular interest to English-speaking travelers:

CHURCHES

American Cathedral in Paris
8th arr. - 23, av. George-V
47 20 17 92, fax 47 23 95 30

American Church
7th arr. - 65, quai d'Orsay
47 05 07 99, fax 45 50 36 96

Christian Science
14th arr. - 36, bd Saint-Jacques
47 07 26 60

Church of Scotland
8th arr. - 17, rue Bayard
47 20 90 49

Great Synagogue
9th arr. - 44, rue de la Victoire
45 26 95 36

Liberal Synagogue
16th arr. - 24, rue Copernic
47 04 37 27, fax 47 27 81 02

St. George's (Anglican)
16th arr. - 7, rue Auguste-Vacquerie
47 20 22 51

St. Joseph's (Catholic)
8th arr. - 50, av. Hoche
42 27 28 56, fax 42 27 86 49

St. Michael's English Church
8th arr. - 5, rue d'Aguesseau
47 42 70 88, fax 47 42 70 11

EMBASSIES

American Embassy
8th arr. - 2, av. Gabriel
42 96 12 02, fax 42 66 97 83

Australian Embassy
15th arr. - 4, rue Jean-Rey
40 59 33 00, fax 40 59 33 10

British Embassy
8th arr. - 35, rue du Faubourg-Saint-Honoré
42 66 91 42, fax 42 66 95 90

Canadian Embassy
8th arr. - 35, av. Montaigne
44 43 29 00, fax 44 43 34 99

New Zealand Embassy
16th arr. - 7 ter, rue Léonard-de-Vinci
45 00 24 11, fax 45 01 26 39

ENGLISH-SPEAKING ORGANIZATIONS

American Center
12th arr. - 51, rue de Bercy
44 73 77 77, fax 44 73 77 66
Open 10am-7pm (Sat 9:30am-5pm). Closed Sun.

The Center's sensational new home, designed by architect Frank Gehry, opened to the public in 1994. The Center sponsors exciting theater and dance performances, prestigious art exhibitions, and offers courses in English, yoga, dance, theater, and exercise.

American Chamber of Commerce
8th arr. - 21, av. George-V
47 23 80 26, fax 47 20 18 62
Open 9am-5pm. Closed Sat, Sun.

American Express
9th arr. - 11, rue Scribe
47 77 70 00
Open daily 24 hours.

Here you'll find traveler's cheques and American Express card and travel services. You can also arrange to pick up mail and wire money or have money wired to you.

American Library
7th arr. - 10, rue Général-Camou
45 51 46 82
Open 10am-7pm. Closed Sun, Mon, French hols.

This privately run establishment houses the largest English-language library on the continent. There is also a selection of records and cassettes. You must, however, be an official resident of France (with a *carte de séjour*) to take books out of the library. An annual membership fee is charged.

British Council
7th arr. - 9, rue Constantine
49 55 73 23
Open 11am-6pm (Wed 7pm). Closed Sat, Sun.

The council sponsors a wide-ranging library of English books and records.

Canadian Cultural Center
8th arr. - 5, rue Constantine
45 51 35 73, fax 47 05 43 55
Open 9am-5:30pm (library from 1:30pm; art galleries until 7pm). Closed Sat, Sun.

The Canadian cultural center hosts dance, theater, and musical performances, and offers the services of a library and student-exchange program office.

HOSPITALS (ENGLISH-SPEAKING)

Hôpital Américain American Hospital of Paris
92200 Neuilly-sur-Seine - 63, bd Victor-Hugo
46 41 25 25, fax 46 24 49 38

More than 40 specialized services are offered. Dental services are also provided, and there is a 24-hour English-speaking emergency service (tel. 47 47 70 15). A consultation here can be paid for in dollars or francs. Many insurance plans honored.

Hôpital Franco-Britannique (British Hospital)

92300 Levallois-Perret - 3 rue Barbès
46 39 22 22

This hospital provides complete medical services.

PHARMACY

Swann Rocher Pharmacy

1st arr. - 6, rue Castiglione
42 60 72 96, fax 42 60 44 12
Open 9am-7:30pm. Closed Sun.

This is the only pharmacy in Paris where your English-language prescription will be translated and an equivalent medicine made up by a pharmacist.

PHONE DIRECTORY

Police/Help

17

Fire Department

18

SAMU (Ambulance)

45 67 50 50

S.O.S. Médecins

43 37 77 77 or 47 07 77 77,
fax 45 87 13 47

These doctors make house calls at any hour of the day or night, for about 200-300 F.

S.O.S. Crisis Line (in English)

47 23 80 80
Open 3pm-11pm.

S.O.S. Psychiatrie

47 07 24 24

Emergency psychiatric care.

S.O.S. Dentaire

43 37 51 00

An operator will direct you to a dentist offering emergency care in your neighborhood.

Centre Anti-Poisons

40 37 04 04

Poison Control Center.

DUTY-FREE SHOPPING

The bad news is that just about everything in France is subject to Value Added Tax (VAT). The charge is 18.6 percent on most items. The good news is that people living outside Europe can get a 100 percent VAT rebate on items they export from France. To qualify for a rebate, you must be at least 15 years of age, and spend more than 2,000 F *in one shop*.

To get reimbursed, have the store fill in the Détaxe Légale form (make sure the shop carries it before you make the purchase). Bring your passport, because you'll be required to show it. Along with the form, the store will supply you with an envelope bearing its address.

When you leave France, show the forms at the Bureau de Détaxe or at Customs and have the Customs officer stamp them. Then seal the forms in the envelope supplied by the shop and mail it back. Keep your receipt.

The rebate can be credited directly to your credit card. Some stores charge a commission for this service, while others (especially the duty-free shops on the Champs-Élysées and the Avenue de l'Opéra) charge no commission.

For further information, call 47 57 26 48.

GOINGS-ON

As an international city, Paris hosts many artistic festivals, trade fairs, and sporting events. Exact dates vary from year to year, so we've simply listed the month in which they occur.

French national holidays are January 1, May 1, May 8, July 14, and November 11; religious holidays fall on Easter, Easter Monday, Ascension Thursday, Pentecost Sunday and the following Monday, Assumption Day (August 15), All Saint's Day (November 1), and Christmas. A word of warning: banks and some shops will close early the day before a public holiday, and often a three-day weekend will become a four-day weekend when holidays fall on a Tuesday or a Thursday.

JANUARY

Prix d'Amérique
12th arr. - Hippodrome de Vincennes
49 77 17 17
Last Sun of Jan.
One of the most prestigious prizes in horse racing.

FEBRUARY

Foire à la Ferraille de Paris
12th arr. - Parc Floral de Paris, Bois de Vincennes
End Feb-beg Mar. Open 11am-7pm.
An amusing collection of taste treats and "junque."

MARCH

Jumping International de Paris
12th arr. - Palais Omnisports de Paris Bercy, 8, bd de Bercy - 44 68 44 68
End Mar-beg Apr.
International horse-jumping trials.

Salon International de l'Agriculture
15th arr. - Parc des Expositions, Porte de Versailles
Beg Mar. Open 10am-7pm.
Bring the kids to this international agricultural show.

Salon du Livre
15th arr. - Parc des Expositions, Porte de Versailles
End Mar. Open 10am-7pm (Sat 10am-10:30pm).
A mammoth book fair.

Salon de Mars
7th arr.- Espace Tour Eiffel, Quai Branly
End Mar-beg Apr. Open noon-9pm (Thu noon-11pm; Sat & Sun 10am-9pm).
Top-of-the-line antiques.

Salon Mondial du Tourisme et des Voyages
15th arr. - Parc des Expositions, Porte de Versailles
End Mar. Open 10am-7pm.
World tourism and travel.

Super Fundoor
12th arr. - Palais Omnisports de Paris Bercy, 8, bd de Bercy - 44 68 44 68
End Mar.
Indoor windsurfing competition.

APRIL

Foire de Paris
15th arr. - Parc des Expositions, Porte de Versailles
End Apr-beg May. Open 10am-7pm.
Food, wine, household equipment, and gadgetry.

Marathon International de Paris
Departure Avenue des Champs-Élysées, 8th arr; arrival Avenue Foch, 16th arr.
42 77 17 84
Beg Apr. Departure 9am.
26 miles or 42 kilometers, it's all the same to the runners.

Paris vous Invite au Théâtre
In all Paris theaters - 42 74 27 07
Throughout the month.
Two theater tickets for the price of one.

MAY

Championnats Internationaux de France de Tennis (French Open)
16th arr. - Stade Roland Garros, 2, av. Gordon-Bennett - 47 43 48 00
End May-beg Jun.
Top international tennis championship.

Les Cinq Jours de l'Objet Extraordinaire (Carré des Antiquaires Rive Gauche)
7th arr. - Rues de Beaune, de Lille, des Saints-Pères, de l'Université & quai Voltaire
Mid May. Open 11am-9pm (Tue 7pm-11pm).
Paris's top antique shops hold open house: rare and unusual objects.

Kiosques en Fête
7th arr. - Champ-de-Mars
12th arr. - Parc Floral
14th arr. - Parc Montsouris
16th arr. - Jardin du Ranelagh

19th arr. - Parc des Buttes Chaumont
40 71 76 47
May-Sep.
Free concerts in the parks.

JUNE

Course des Garçons de Café
1st arr. - Departure & arrival
at l'Hôtel de Ville - 42 96 60 75
Beg Jun.
Waiters race in the Paris streets holding a tray with a full bottle and a full glass of beer.

Fête de la Musique
Streets of Paris - 40 03 94 70
Jun 21. All day, all night.
Anyone who wants to can blow his horn on Music Day.

Prix de Diane Hermès
60500 Chantilly - Hippodrome de Chantilly
49 10 20 30
Mid Jun: 2pm.
Wear your classiest chapeau to this elegant day at the races, attended by the cream of Parisian society.

Salon International de l'Aéronautique et de l'Espace
93350 Le Bourget - Parc des Expositions du Bourget - 48 35 91 61
Only in odd-numbered years. Mid Jun. Open 9:30am-6pm.
Air shows by daredevil pilots; aircraft displays.

JULY

Arrivée du Tour de France Cycliste
8th arr. - Av. des Champs-Élysées
End Jul. Around 5pm.
The Tour de France cyclists triumphantly cross the finish line.

Bastille Day Eve
Jul 13: 9pm-2am.
A jolly evening: dance to rock, tango, and accordion bands in public squares and at neighborhood firehouses. The largest *bal* is the one on the Place de la Bastille, 12th arr.

Bastille Day
8th arr. - Av. des Champs-Élysées
Jul 14.
In the morning, a military parade on the Champs-Élysées celebrates the French national holiday (10am). Fireworks display in the evening in the Jardins du Trocadéro, 16th arr. at 10:30pm.

AUGUST

Virtually everything is closed in August, but true Paris-lovers regard this as the best month of the year to be in their favorite city.

SEPTEMBER

La Biennale des Antiquaires
1st arr. - Carrousel du Louvre, 99, rue de Rivoli
Mid Nov: noon-9pm.
Major antique show.

Journée du Patrimoine
44 61 20 00
One w-e mid Sep.
A celebration of France's architectural heritage: 300 monuments, ministries, town houses, and public buildings open to visitors.

OCTOBER

Fête des Vendanges
18th arr. - Butte Montmartre, corner of Rue des Saules & Rue Saint-Vincent - 42 52 42 00
First Sat in Oct.
A grape harvest at the only working vineyard within the city limits.

Foire Internationale d'Art Contemporain (FIAC)
7th arr. - Espace Tour Eiffel, Quai Branly
Beg Oct. Open noon-8pm (Thu noon-11pm; Sat & Sun 10am-8pm).
An international contemporary-art show.

Mondial de l'Automobile
15th arr. - Parc des Expositions, Porte de Versailles
Only in even-numbered years. Beg Oct. Open 10am-10pm.
The world's second-largest international automobile show.

Prix de l'Arc de Triomphe

16th arr. - Hippodrome de Longchamp
Beg Oct - 49 10 20 30

A day at the races and a chance to win a lot of money.

Salon d'Automne

7th arr. - Espace Tour Eiffel, Quai Branly - 49 52 53 54
End Oct. Open 11am-7pm (Wed 11am-10pm).

New artwork by budding talents.

Salon International de l'Alimentation (S.I.A.L.)

93420 Villepinte - Parc des Expositions, Paris-Nord
48 63 30 30, fax 48 63 31 36
Only in even-numbered years. Mid Oct.

An international food-products exhibit.

NOVEMBER

Maisons d'Automne

15th arr. - Parc des Expositions, Porte de Versailles
Mid Nov. Open 10am-7pm.

A trade show highlighting the latest innovations in home furnishings and décor.

Open de la Ville de Paris

12th arr. - Palais Omnisports de Paris Bercy, 8, bd de Bercy - 44 68 44 68
Nov 1-7.

The City of Paris Open Tennis Championships.

Trophée Lalique de Patinage Artistique

12th arr. - Palais Omnisports de Paris Bercy, 8, bd de Bercy - 44 68 44 68
Mid Nov.

A major figure-skating competition.

DECEMBER

Concours Hippique International de Paris

15th arr. - Parc des Expositions, Porte de Versailles
Mid Dec.

A major equestrian competition.

La Crèche

4th arr.- Place de l'Hôtel de Ville
Dec 6-Jan 8. Open 10am-10pm.

A giant nativity scene, with moving figures and music, set up on the esplanade outside City Hall.

Illumination des Quartiers

1st arr. - Faubourg St-Honoré; 8th arr. - Avenue Montaigne, Rue Royale, Champs-Élysées; 9th arr. - Grands Boulevards, Opéra

Christmas lights atwinkle in the city's main shopping districts.

Nocturne des Boutiques du Comité Vendôme

1st arr. - Place Vendôme
Dec 7. Open 7pm-midnight.

Luxury shops stay open late to celebrate the season.

Salon du Cheval et du Poney

15th arr. - Parc des Expositions, Porte de Versailles
Beg Dec. Open 10am-7pm (Tue 10am-10pm).

Horses and ponies galore, and all the accompanying trappings.

Salon Nautique International

15th arr. - Parc des Expositions, Porte de Versailles
Beg Dec. Open 10am-7pm (Fri 10am-11pm).

International boat show.

2,000 years of history

The past comes to life in Paristoric, a spectacular show in which Paris displays its history and monuments on a giant screen. Open 365 days a year at 78 bis, boulevard des Batignolles, 17th arr., tel. 42 93 93 46, fax 42 93 93 48. Shows start every hour, on the hour, from 9am to 6pm (9pm Fri, Sat, and in summer). Adults, 70 F, children and students, 40 F. M° Villiers.

INDEX

A

C

F

G

H

L

M

N

Q

R

S

W

Y

Z

RECEIVE A FREE SUBSCRIPTION TO "TASTES"

(A $40 VALUE)

BY FILLING OUT THIS QUESTIONNAIRE YOU'LL RECEIVE A COMPLIMENTARY ONE YEAR SUBSCRIPTION TO **"TASTES,"** OUR INTERNATIONAL NEWSLETTER.

NAME ______________________________

ADDRESS ______________________________

CITY ____________________ STATE ____________

ZIP ______________ COUNTRY ____________________

PHONE (   )   -

The AGP/Gault Millau series of guidebooks reflects your demand for insightful, incisive reporting on the best that the world's most exciting destinations have to offer. To help us make our books even better, please take a moment to fill out this anonymous (if you wish) questionnaire, and return it to:

Gault Millau Inc., P.O. Box 361144, Los Angeles, CA 90036
Fax: (213) 936-2883.

1. How did you hear about the AGP guides? Please specify: bookstore, newspaper, magazine, radio, friends or other.

2. Please list in order of preference the cities or countries which you would like to see AGP cover.

3. Do you refer to the AGP guides for your own city, or only when traveling?

A. (Travels) .... B. (Own city) .... C. (Both) ....

Please turn over

4. Please list, starting with the most preferred, the three features you like best about the Gault Millau guides.

A. .... B. ....

C. ....

5. What are the features, if any, you dislike about the Gault Millau guides?

6. Please list any features you would like to see added to the Gault Millau guides.

7. If you use other guides besides Gault Millau, please list below.

8. Please list the features you like best about your favorite guidebook series, if it is not Gault Millau.

A. .... B. ....

C. ....

9. How many trips do you make per year, for either business or pleasure?

Business: International: .... Domestic: ....

Pleasure: International: .... Domestic: ....

10. Please check the category that reflects your annual household income.

$20,000-$39,000 .... $40,000-$59,000 ....
$60,000-$79,000 .... $80,000-$99,000 ....
$100,000-$120,000 .... Other (please specify) ....

11. If you have any comments on the Gault Millau guides in general, please list them in the space below.

12. If you would like to recommend specific establishments, please don't hesitate to list them:

Name ***City*** ***Phone***

We thank you for your interest in the Gault Millau guides, and we welcome your remarks and recommendations about restaurants, hotels, nightlife, shops, services and so on.

307/95